THE GOAT SONG

A STORY OF ATHENIAN LIVES

IN THE ERA OF SOCRATES

By

Tom Young

For:
Donna and Don Summers
For long winter nights —
take a trip 2500 years
ago to sunny Greece.
   Tom Young

a representation of the sacrificial god in the form of a goat offered up on the eve of the ancient Athenian theatric festival of the City Dionysia at the altar of the temple of Dionysos Eleuthereus. It was here that the first tragedies were performed. The religious origins of the theatre (and especially the tragedy) are preserved in a literal translation of the Greek word, 'tragodia'- 'song on the occasion of the he-goat'. The cover image is an original design by Carla W. Young and Dana Rose.

Text Copyright © 2013 Tom Young
All rights reserved.
ISBN-10: 1481855662
EAN-13: 9781481855662
CreateSpace Independent Publishing Platform
North Charleston, South Carolina

For:

Carla Welsh Young

Jesse Young

Sienna Landoll

CONTENTS

List of Illustrations ix

List of Maps and Diagrams xv

List of Historical Persons xvii

Prologue xxxiii

A Note to the Reader xxxv

PART ONE | 1
Heroic Fathers, Scenes from the Days of The Miracle of Eleusis

1. In the Waters of the Euripis 3
2. The Servants' Errand Through Haunted Woods 17
3. Sacrifice to Poseidon 29
4. Gyges' First Fight 45

PART ONE | 2
Religion New and Old in Democratic Athens, Scenes of City Life

5. Anthesteria: Festival of Ghosts and
   Ever Renewing Life 63
6. Anthesteria: A Father's Satyrology 85

CONTENTS

PART ONE | 2
Religion New and Old in Democratic Athens, Scenes of City Life

7. Communion 97

8. Symposium 117

9. A Final Farewell for Old Friends 145

PART ONE | 3
Troubled Freedom, Scenes from the Golden Age of the Athenian Empire

10. Children of Strife 163

11. Demeter's Work 203

12. Ares' Work: Lust and Strife 245

13. Ares' Work: The Killing Zone 265

14. The School Yard King of the Hill 303

15. In the Household of the Olympian 337

16. Becoming a Man 359

17. Alcibiades and the Philosopher 371

18. Duty Calls: Alcibiades and Socrates at Potidaea 397

PART ONE | 4

ATHENIAN TRAGEDY, SCENES FROM THE CITY DIONYSIA AND THE TIME OF PLAGUE

19. Defending the Empire: Athens Declares War 425

20. Magnificent Alcibiades 451

21. Farewell to Artemis 475

CONTENTS

PART ONE | 4

ATHENIAN TRAGEDY, SCENES FROM THE CITY DIONYSIA AND THE TIME OF PLAGUE

22. Pomp and Circumstance 487

23. Medea's Man 541

24. Athenian Tartaros: The Plague 589

25. The Death of the Olympian 629

Glossary 649

ANNOTATED LIST OF ILLUSTRATIONS

Cover Design – Dionysos, the Goat Victim: a representation of the sacrificial god in the form of a goat offered up on the eve of the theatric festival of the City Dionysia at the altar of the temple of Dionysos Eleuthereus. It was here that the first tragedies were performed. The religious origins of the theater (and especially the tragedy) are preserved in a literal translation of the Greek word, 'tragodia'- 'song on the occasion of the he-goat'. The cover image is an original design by Carla W. Young and Dana Rose.

Figure 1 (Ch. 3) – POSEIDON: reproduced photograph of inside bottom of red figure kylix (wine cup) painted by Oltos, late 6th century B.C. The figure of Poseidon carrying his trident and fish as attributes of his domain of the seas has been painted on the actual bowl of the wine cup so that Poseidon would have been seen as running though a sea of wine. Around the perimeter of the figure can be seen in Greek letters the signature of the potter (translated as 'Kachrylion made this'). The color photograph appears in *An Introduction to Greek Mythology* by David Bellingham, Seacaucus, New Jersey, 1989. This wine cup is on display in the Acropolis Museum of Athens.

Figure 2 (Ch. 4) - ATHENIAN TRIREME: reproduced from original diagram found in book on history of ancient Athenian navy (John R. Hale, *Lords of the Sea*, New York, 2009, p.16).

Figure 3 (Ch. 5) - CHILDREN ENACTING THE *BASILINNA'S* MARRIAGE PROCESSION TO HER RITUAL WEDDING WITH DIONYSOS: the image is reproduced from a photograph of a small pitcher more than likely used by a child as part of the celebrations during Anthesteria. The *Basilinna's* (the Queen's) role was undertaken by the actual wife of the *Archon Basileus*, the official charged with supervision of the state religious festivals. There were no kings in Athens by the 5th century B.C., but the Archon administering the religious festivals retains the traditional title of 'Basilcus' since he, like the Athenian kings who first governed Athens, presides as high priest for many of the city's most ancient sacred ceremonies. During this ceremony, the ceremonial Archon Basileus' wife, the 'Basilinna', stands in for Persephone, the Queen of the underworld who with Dionysos in spring time will ascend from the realm of the dead to initiate the return of new life. The photograph is found on plate 44 in H. W. Parke, *Festivals of* *the Athenians*, London, 1977. The small wine pitcher is part of the Greek antiquities collection at the Metropolitan Museum of New York City.

Figure 4 (Ch. 6) – RAVING MAENADS: the image is reproduced from a photograph of a 5th century B.C. kylix, painted in the red-figure style by Makron and signed by the potter, Heiron. Maenads in ancient Athens were always associated with Dionysian celebrations and rites. The divine madness or raving of the Maenads comes from Dionysos' presence and thus one of the epithets of the god is 'Dionysos Mainomenos' (Dionysos who makes ecstatic - out of one's mind). The original photo is found in Ernst Buschor, *Greek Vase Painting.*, New York, 1978, Plate LXXIV. This kylix may be viewed at the Berlin Museum's collection of Greek antiquities.

Figure 5 (Ch. 6) – RITUAL DANCE OF SATYRS AND WOMEN: pictorial and literary evidence from this era implies that the men and women who dressed as companions of Dionysos during his festivals regarded the holidays of Dionysos as offering license for sexual play – not unlike Mardi gras in today's New Orleans or Rio de Janeiro. Amphorae were used to store oil and wine and often were the containers used in shipping these commodities to Athens' many overseas markets. The amphorae, filled with costly oil, also were often awarded as commemorative prizes for victors in contests such as the PanAthenaic games. The amphora here photographed dates from the 6th century B. C. and came from Attica, the region surrounding Athens that became part of the Athenian state during this century. The image is a reproduction of a photo taken of an amphora now in the Greek antiquities collection in the Basel Museum. The photography may be found in Eva C. Keuls., *The Reign of the Phallus, Sexual Politics in Ancient Athens*, Los Angeles, 1985, fig. 301.

Figure 6 (Ch. 6) – SATYRS AT PLAY: satyrs are always associated with the company of Dionysos. The men of Athens frequently donned the ithyphallic costume of the satyr, both as celebrants in the revelries of the komos associated with the festivals of Dionysos and as actors in the theatric productions of satyr plays and the comedies. The image is a reproduction of a photograph of a painted black-figured style kylix (drinking cup) from the Athenian workshop of Nikosthenes (545 -510 B.C.). Scholars propose that the workshop of Nikoshenes may have employed 40 to 50 workers. Most of the pottery was shipped to Italy and sold to Etruscans and Greek colonists who had founded towns on the Italian peninsula. By the middle of the fifth century, Athenian wares were shipped all around the eastern rim of the Mediterranean Sea. The rise of a commercial class in Athens whose wealth did not rest on land ownership certainly was one of the major drivers of both the Athenian democracy and her commercial empire. This kylix is now housed in the West Berlin Museum. The photograph may be found in Keuls, op. cit., fig. 262.

Figure 7 (Ch. 7) – HETAERAI AT SYMPOSIUM IN THE MEN'S QUARTERS: the image is a scene painted on a psykter (a wine jar used for cooling wine) by the 5th century Athenian red-figure style painter, Euphronios. The original photograph of the image may be found in Buschor, op. cit. fig. 112. The psykter is now housed in the Hermitage at St. Petersburg.

Figure 8 (Ch. 7) – *PITHOIGIA*: this image depicts Hermes evoking souls of the dead from their funeral *pithos* (burial urn) on the first day of the three day festival of Anthesteria, the 'Day of the Jars'. The sketch is taken from a photograph of an Attic lekythos (an oil jar with a particularly long and narrow neck) now housed at Jena University. The photograph may be found in Karl Kerenyi, *Dionysos Archetypal Image of Indestructible Life*, Princeton, 1976, fig. 91.

Figure 9 (Ch. 8) – ODYSSEUS EVOKING THE GHOST OF TEIRESIAS FROM THE UNDERWORLD: the design of this scene is taken from a red-figured krater, a two-handled mixing bowl used to mix wine and water. The ancient Athenians considered it barbarous to ever drink wine unmixed with water. The pure essence of the grape was stored in large amphorae so as ferment and then, when properly aged, it would be poured and mixed in a krater at a prescribed ratio of water to wine which could vary from 3:1 to 5:3 or 3:2 depending on the desired strength of the mixture. Sophisticated Athenians thought of these proportions as harmonic balances which would strike the 'golden mean' needed for drinking wine without excess drunkenness. Unmixed wine was called 'akratos' and there are many iconic scenes painted on kraters, amphorae, and kylikes that portray a beastly satyr drinking unmixed wine directly out of a large amphora. The krater painted with this Homeric scene of Odysseus' meeting with Teiresias is now in the collection at the Bibiotheque Nationale in Paris. The design is a reproduction of one found in Jane Harrison, *Prolegomena to the Study of Greek Religion*, Princeton University Press, 1991, fig. 9 on page 74.

Figure 10 (Ch. 8) – FLUTE GIRL AND HETAERAI IN *KOMOS* WITH MEN: a reproduction of a photograph (fig. 152) found in Keuls, op. cit., fig 152. The 5th century red-figured wine cup is painted by the Athenian 'Brygos' painter and is now on display in a collection housed in Wurzburg, Germany.

Figure 11 (Ch. 9) – THE JUDGEMENT OF PARIS: a reproduction of a photograph of a 6th century B. C. black-figure amphora. The photograph may be found in Buschor, op. cit., fig. 83.

Figure 12 (Ch. 16) – ZEUS PURSUING GANYMEDE: both scenes depicted in Figures 12 and 13 are often referenced in Ancient Greek tragedies and comedies as etiological accounts of the origin of the homoerotic relationship between an older man and a beardless youth. The relationship under certain conventional and carefully prescribed conditions was considered legitimate and pedagogically beneficial to the youth and as such was especially practiced by men of aristocratic families. The relationship, no doubt, for the ancient Athenians could go very wrong for the youth (the beloved) and the lover (the older man). Adolescent youths were often escorted and carefully watched by a slave-pedagogue so as assure that any interest of an older man in friendship with the youth did not devolve into a nonconsensual and merely lascivious practice of pederasty. The complex relationship between Alcibiades as a youth and Socrates as the older man described by Alcibiades in Plato's dialogue, *Symposium*, is almost inaccessible to modern readers who have no knowledge of this aristocratic tradition in ancient Greece. The most thorough and scholarly account of 5th century B. C. Greek homosexuality in its distinctive cultural context may be found in Kenneth J. Dover's book, *Greek Homosexuality*, Cambridge, Mass., 1978. This image of Zeus and Ganymede is a reproduction of a photograph of the inside bottom of a red-figured kylix. The photograph may be found in Keuls, op. cit., fig. 200. Keuls catalogues the location of this amphora as 'Ferrara 9351, cup, ARV 880, 12.

Figure 13 (Ch. 17) – LAIUS' ABDUCTION OF PELOPS' SON, CHRYSIPPUS: reproduction of photograph of 4th century Apulian (Greek workshop in Italy) krater. The photograph is found in Keuls, op. cit., fig. 260.

Figure 14 (Ch. 18) – PROMETHEUS AND ATLAS: reproduction of photograph of the inside bottom of 6th century B. C. Laconian kylix which now can be viewed in the Gregorian Etruscan Museum in Rome. The original photograph may be found in Carl Kerenyi, *Prometheus*, Princeton University Press, 1991, Plate VI.

Figure 15 (Ch. 22) – PROCESSION LED BY A SALPINX: reproduction of a photograph of a 6th century B. C. Attic lekythos, now housed in the British Museum, London. The original photograph may be found in Kerenyi, *Dionysos Archetypal Image of Indestructible Life*, ill. 61a.

Figure 16 (Ch. 22) – DIONYSOS ON A SHIP CART: the most ancient stories describing Dionysos' first appearance in Attica, all depict the god's arrival by ship at one of the coastal villages of Attica. These same stories almost always note that it is women who first meet Dionysos and then introduce him to the men who receive his gift of the grape vine. When the 6th century B. C. tyrant Pisistratus confederates the outlying villages and towns of Attica to Athens, he solidifies the bond by introducing state public festivals (such as the City Dionysia and Anthesteria, also a Dionysian festival), which in their symbols and liturgies conflate the various local traditions found in the towns and villages of Attica. The scene depicted in this image is a reproduction of a photograph of painting on an Attic skyphos (a two-handled cup characterized by a deep bowl). The cup is now housed in the Museo Cvico Archeologico, Bolonga. The original photograph may be found in Kerenyi, *op. cit.,* ill. 56.

Figure 17 (Ch. 22) – SILENUS TREADING OUT GRAPES: although this vase depicts the grape treader, Silenus, as working in a large bowl, the most ancient treading of the grapes occurred on the orchestra, a natural outcropping of stone that provided a floor for pressing out the juice of the grape. When the temples of Dionysos were constructed they always included in front of the porch of the temple, the sacred orchestra on which the first of the harvested grapes were to be blessed by being treaded at the god's sanctuary. Later, it is then the orchestra which serves as the dancing floor of the chorus in the ancient Greek theatrical performances. This image is a reproduction of a photograph on a Archaic vase decorated by the Amasis painter. The vase is housed in the Martin v. Wagner-Museum der Universitat of Wurzburg. The original photograph may be found in Kerenyi, op. cit., ill. 23.

Figure 18 (Ch. 22) – MAENAD DEFENDING AGAINST ADVANCES OF A SATYR: reproduction of photograph of 5th century B. C. red-figured style vase painted by Makron and signed by the potter, Hieron. The original photograph is found in Keuls, op. cit., fig. 310. The vase is catalogued by Keuls: Munich 2654, ABV 593, 41.

Figure 19 (Ch. 22) – MOTLEY BULL IN PROCESSION: reproduction of photograph of a 6th century Attic lekythos now housed in the British Museum, London. The original photograph may be found in Kerenyi, op. cit., fig. 61a.

Figure 20 (Ch. 22) – ORPHEUS AMONG THE THRACIANS: reproduction of photograph of a red-figured krater, now housed at 50 Berliner Winckelmannsprogramm (1890). The original photograph is found in Buschor, op. cit., Fig. 140.

Figure 21 (Ch. 22) – DIONYSOS SECOND BIRTH OUT OF THE THIGH OF ZEUS: the scene here depicted is the painter's illustration of a story which credited Athena with finding the slain remains of Dionysos after he has been murdered by the Titans in the Underworld. The goddess, according to the story, takes up Dionysos' heart and brings this to Zeus at Olympus. The heart is then sewn into Zues' thigh and then some time later Dionysos is born a second time from out of the thigh of Zeus, with Athena standing by to assist in his birth. Orphic religion speaks of yet a third birth of Dionysos in which Dionysos will assume the throne of heaven and usher in the third and final age of eternal live and blessedness for those who, like him, have been thrice born (once from an earthly mother, once spiritually at the sacred rites of Eleusis, and then finally at the resurrection from the dead in the third age ushered in by the Son of God, Dionysos). In our own era, one cannot but conclude that Paul of Tarsus was very familiar with the Orphic-Hellenic mystery religion, and he, more than likely, Hellenized the Messianic Savior of Judaism in his missionary zeal to explain the unknown God to Athenians and other Greeks. Figure 21 is a reproduction of a photograph of an amphora now housed in the Bibliotheque Nationale, Paris. The original photograph may be found in Kerenyi, op. cit., ill. 73.

Figure 22 (Ch. 22) – A COMIC SCENE OF *PHALLOPHORIAI* IN CITY DIONYSIA PROCESSION: photograph of a black-figure Attic kylix now housed in Museo Archeologica, Florence. The original photograph may be found in Kerenyi, op. cit., fig. 87.

Figure 23 (Ch. 23) – CHORUS PERFOMING IN TRAGEDY: reproduction of photograph of 5th century krater now housed in Basel, Antikenmuseum BS 415. The original photograph may be found in Erika Simon, *Festivals of Attica, An Archaeological Commentary*, The University of Wisconsin Press, 1963, Plate 32.

LIST OF MAPS AND DIAGRAMS

1. Artemision, Euboea 7
2. Attica and Boeotia 275
3. The Athenian Empire (450 B.C.) 350
4. Athens' *Agora* (440 B.C.) 433
5. Athens' Walls 439
6. Athens' Sacred Theater District 458

LIST OF HISTORICAL PERSONS

The following index is intended to assist the reader who wishes to explore the literary sources which I have, in part, relied upon to reconstruct the lived experience of the various historical characters that appear in the episodes of the novel. Each entry lists the chapters (Ch.) in which the historical character appears and then an ancient literary source which documents his or her historical existence. Finally, unless otherwise obvious, there is a brief statement of the role each person plays in the story of fifth century Athens.

ADEIMANTUS: Ch. 1, 3, 18 & 24, (Herodotus. *The Histories*, Bk. VIII: 4), the Corinthian Commander of the triremes Corinth sent to join the Greek naval fleet to oppose the Persian invasion of 480 B. C.

AEGEUS: Ch. 8 & 23, (*Schol. Vatic. Ad Euripid. Hippol.* 11, fragment of the lost beginning of Aristotle's *Constitution of Athens*), the father of Theseus (see 'Theseus') and the ancient Athenian King for whom the 'Aegean' Sea is named.

AESCHYLUS: Ch. 1, 2, 4,7,8,10,18,20,23,24 & 25, (*Persians*, written by Aeschylus is the oldest extant Greek play. The play was first performed at the City Dionysia in 472 B. C. with Pericles serving as the *choregus* who paid for the expenses of Aeschylus' trilogy of tragedies, among which was the prize winning *Persians*.).

AGARISTE: Ch. 8, (Plutarch. *Life of Pericles*, 3), the mother of Pericles and granddaughter of Cleisthenes, the Alcmaeonid who introduced radical democratic redistricting of political *demes* (districts of Attica and Athens) in 508 B.C.

AGATHON: Ch. 20, (Plato. *Symposium*, 173a), a contemporary of Socrates and a prize winning author of a lost and unknown tragedy.

ALCIBIADES: Ch. 12 & 14-25, (Thucydides. *History of the Peloponnesian War*, Bk. V: 43), Alcibiades, son of Clinias, is also a cousin of Pericles and a companion of Socrates. Plutarch's *Life of Alcibiades* describes Alcibiades as the notorious darling of the common people of Athens, a rich and handsome seducer of both men and women, an Olympic prize winner in the chariot competitions, and a general accused of treason during the Peloponnesian War.

AMYCLA: Ch. 11, (Plutarch. *Life of Alcibiades*, 1), Alcibiades' childhood Spartan nurse maid.

AMPHICTYON: Ch. 22, (Pausanias. *Pausanias' Description of Greece*, translated by James George Frazer, 1898, Vol. 1: 2-5), the perhaps pseudo-historical third king of Athens whose likeness is inscribed on an ancient clay tablet mounted on a wall in Kerameikos, the potters' district of Athens. The tablet shows Amphictyon welcoming Dionysos as he arrives in Athens, in the company of other gods.

ANAXAGORAS: Ch. 7, 8, 15 & 23, (Plato. *Phaedrus*, 270a), one of the pre-Socratic metic philosophers who mentored Pericles.

ANAXIMENES: Ch. 7, (Aristotle. *Metaphysics*, A3, 984a5), a 6th century B. C. philosopher of Nature from the city of Miletus in Ionia, the ancient name for the region on the northeastern coast of the Aegean Sea colonized by Ionian Greeks.

ARCHELAUS: Ch. 7 & 15, (Diogenes Laertius II, 16), The philosopher, Archelaus of Athens, was a pupil of Anaxagoras and the teacher of Socrates. According to the ancient sources, he is credited with transferring physical speculation to Athens, the kind of philosophy which Socrates, in Plato's *Apology*, contrasts with his inquiry concerning human excellence and political virtue.

ARCHIDAMUS: Ch. 19, 20 & 24, (Thucydides. *History of the Peloponnesian War*, Bk. II, 71) The King of Sparta who between 431 and 421 B.C. leads Peloponnesian allies and Spartan hoplite forces against Attica, but is unable to defeat the walled city of Athens.

ARIPHON: Ch. 14, (Plutarch. *Life of Alcibiades*, 1) Ariphon and his brother Pericles are appointed guardians of the three year old Alcibiades when his father Clinias dies in battle. Alcibiades mother, Dinomache, is Pericles' cousin since her father, Megacles, and Pericles' mother, Agariste, are brother and sister.

ARISTEUS: Ch. 18, 19 & 24, (Thucydides. *History of the Peloponnesian War*, Bk..I: 60), son of Adeimantus who leads the Corinthian forces and citizens of Potidaea in 432 B. C. in rebellion against the pro-Athenian governing party in Potidaea.

ARISTIDES: Ch. 7, 8 & 11, (Aristotle. *Constitution of Athens*, 23:5), Athenian General who led Athens during the decade after the defeat of the Persians in 480 B. C. Aristotle states that it is Aristides who first assessed the contributions to be paid by the allied cities so as to support the Athenian navy's capability to meet any future Persian threat to the Greek city states.

ARISTODICUS OF TANAGRA: Ch. 10, (Aristotle. *Constitution of Athens*, 25:4), one of the men charged with the assassination (461 B.C.) of Ephialtes who was the democratic reformer and colleague of Pericles.

ASPASIA: Ch. 7, 8, 15 & 22-25, (Plutarch. *Life of Pericles*, 32) The hetaera, who Pericles' takes as his second wife, is described by the ancient sources as being highly educated and a friend of the philosophers, Protagoras, Anaxagoras, and Socrates.

CALLAESCHRUS: Ch. 19 & 24, (Plato. *Charmides*, 153c & 169b), the father of Critias, one of Socrates' students.

CALLIAS: Ch. 10, 11 & 17, (Plato. *Protagoras*, 337d), one of the richest men in mid 5th century B. C. Athens.

CALLIAS (b): Ch. 18, (Thucydides. *History of the Peloponnesian War*, Bk. I: 61), General who led Athens' siege of Potidaea in 431 B.C.

CIMON: Ch. 5, 7, 8, 10, 15, 19, 22 & 23, (Thucydides. *History of the Peloponnesian War*, Bk. I: 98), General and leader of the aristocratic party in Athens during the three decades following the defeat of the Persians in 480 B.C.

CLEISTHENES: Ch. 2, 18 & 19, (Aristotle. *Constitution of Athens*, chapters 20-21), Cleisthenes, an Alcmaeonid great grandfather of Alcibiades and Pericles on their mothers' side, led a major democratic reform in 508 B. C. of Athens' governance.

CLEON: Ch. 18, 19 & 24, (Thucydides. *History of the Peloponnesian War*, 36-40), leader of the democratic party after the death of Pericles in 429 B. C.

CLINIAS: Ch. 1-15, 17, 19, 21-22 & 24, (Plutarch. *Life of Alcibiades*, 1), father of Alcibiades and Athenian hero at Artemisium naval battle with Persian fleet in 480 B. C.

CRITIAS: Ch. 19 & 24, (Xenophon. *Hellenika*, Bk. II: 11-56) A pupil of Socrates' who in his adult years leads the oligarchic 'Thirty' installed under Spartan auspices after Athens capitulates to Sparta in 404 B.C.

CRITO: Ch. 9, 10 & 24, (Plato. *Crito*), Socrates' life-long friend after whom Plato names one of the dialogues set during Socrates final days as he awaits his execution in Athens' prison.

CYLON: Ch. 8, 14, 15, 17 & 19, (Thucydides. *History of the Peloponnesian War*, Bk. I: 126), an Athenian aristocrat and Olympic Games champion who attempted to become a tyrant the first decade of the 6th century B. C.

DEMARATOS: Ch. 14, (Herodotus. *The Histories*, Bk. VII: 101-105), a Spartan in the camp of Xerxes during the Persian invasion of 480 B. C.

DEMOCRATES: Ch. 16, (Plutarch. *Life of Alcibiades*, 3), an admirer of Alcibiades with whom Alcibiades, while still quite young, runs away from home.

DICAEUS: Ch. 14, (Herodotus. *The Histories*, Bk. VII: 62-66), the Athenian who told the story concerning the miracle of Eleusis which portended the defeat of the Persian navy at Salamis, 480 B.C.

DINOMACHE: Ch. 8-12, 14, 16, 17 & 21-24, (Plutarch. *Life of Alcibiades*, 1),, mother of Alcibiades.

DIOGENES: Ch. 24, (Theophastus, *Opinions of the Physicists*, fr. 2 *ap*.), Diogenes of Apollonia, philosopher and physician who flourished around 446-430 B. C.

DIOPEITHES: Ch. 15, 16, 19 & 24, (Plutarch. *Life of Pericles*, 32), author of decree against atheism passed by Athenian Assembly sometime in the decade between 442 and 432 B.C.

ELPINICE: Ch. 5, 10, 11 & 15, (Plutarch. *Life of Cimon*, 4), sister of Cimon and the wife of Callias, one of the richest men in Athens.

EMPEDOCLES: Ch. 7, 10 & 24, (Aristotle. *Metaphysics*, Bk. Alpha 3, 984a), philosopher in first half of fifth century B.C., extant fragments remain from three of these treatises: (1) *On Nature*, (2) *Purifications*, (3) *Discourse on Medicine*.

EPHIALTES: Ch. 5, 8, 10-13, 15, 19 & 23, (Aristotle. *Constitution of Athens,* chapter 25), leader of the people who led democratic reforms that ended the governance of the aristocratic Areopagus Council in 462/61 B. C.

EURIPIDES: Ch. 5, 6 & 20-25, (Plato. *Phaedrus*, 268d), along with Sophocles and Aeschylus, the most honored of the 5th century B. C. Athenian tragic poets.

EURYBIADES: Ch. 1-4, (Herodotus, *The Histories*, Bk. VIII: 3), Spartan Commander of allied Greek fleet at Artemisium during Persian invasion of 480 B. C.

GORGIAS: Ch. 17 & 24, (Plato. *Gorgias*, 449a-460e), pupil of Empedocles and contemporary of Socrates, Gorgias is portrayed by Plato as a master of rhetoric, the art of persuasive speech.

HAGNON: Ch. 14 & 23-24, (Thucydides. *History of the Peloponnesian War*, Bk. II: 58), son of Nicias and general sent to end rebellion at Potidaea in 430 B. C.

HERODOTUS: Ch. 14, 22 & 23, (Aristotle. *Constitution of Athens*, chapter 14:3), author of *The Histories*, an account of the conflict between the Greeks and the Persian Empire in the late 6th and early 5th centuries B.C.

HESIOD: Ch. 4, 6, 9, 11, 13, 15 & 24, (Plato. *Timaeus*, 21: d), the poetry of Homer and Hesiod are central to the religious and heroic tradition of 5th century Greeks.

HIPPARCHUS: Ch. 1, 12 & 16, (Thucydides. *History of the Peloponnesian War*, Bk. VI: 53-59), son of Peisistratos killed by

Aristogiton and Harmodius as a result of Hipparchus' unwanted sexual advances towards Aristogiton's beloved Harmodius - Athenians believed this episode triggered the overthrow of the tyranny of Peisistratid family.

HIPPARETE: Ch. 22, (Plutarch. *Life of Alcibiades*, 8), first wife of Alcibiades.

HIPPIAS: Ch. 2, 5, 8, 13 & 14, (Thucydides. *History of the Peloponnesian War*, Bk. VI: 53-59), son of Peisistratos forced to flee Athens as the Athenians end the tyranny of Peisistratos and his sons - Hippias later joined forces with the Persian expedition in 490 B. C, but the Athenians defeated the Persians at Marathon and prevented the Persians from reinstalling Hippias as a regent of the Persian empire.

HIPPONICUS: Ch. 22, (Plutarch. *Life of Alcibiades*, 8), father of Hipparete, the wife of Alcibiades.

HOMER: Ch. 1, 3, 6, 8-11, 14, 15 & 22-24, (Plato. *Republic*, Bk. II, 377: d) Homer's epic poems, *Iliad* and *Odyssey*, first circulated in an oral tradition lasting perhaps as long as three centuries. The poems were written down and assumed a canonical status during the time of Peisistratos in the second half of the 6th century. Athenians and all other Greeks of the classical era found in Homer the stories through which they interpreted their own aspirations to heroism and a connection to the luminous realm of the divine. Given the elemental human need for meaning, it is not surprising that my narrative, focused on reconstructing the subjective lived experience of 5th century Athenians, abounds with references to Homer's poetry.

LACEDAIMONIUS: Ch. 5, (Thucydides. *History of the Peloponnesian War*, Bk. I: 45), son of Cimon - Cimon named his son in honor of the Lacedaemonians, another name for the Spartans. Like some other aristocrats in mid 5th century Athens, Cimon admired the Spartan regime of military life and virtues.

LEONIDAS: Ch. 1, (Herodotus. *The Histories*, Bk. VII: 205-233), Spartan king who leads 'the Three Hundred' at Thermopylae in attempt to stop the Persian invasion of 480 from further advance toward Attica and the Peloponnese.

LYSIAS: Ch. 7, (Plato. *Phaedrus*, 227c- 234c), poet described by Plato as the 'best writer of the day', a contemporary of Socrates.

MEGACLES (mid 6th century B.C.): Ch. 14, (Herodotus. *The Histories*, Bk. VI: 127-131), contemporary of Peisistratos, an Alcmaeonid who first helps Peisistratos assume power in Athens and then later attempts to remove him from power.

MEGACLES (mid 5th century B.C.): Ch. 1-3, 5, 7-14, 17-19 & 23, (Aristotle. *Constitution of Athens*, chapter 22:5), Alcmaeonid grandfather of Alcibiades on his mother's side.

MILTIADES: Ch. 5, 8, 11, 25, (Herodotus, The Histories, Bk. VI: 132-134), Athenian commander at Marathon, 490 B.C., and father of Cimon.

MIMNERMUS of Colophon: Ch. 9, (Mimnermus. *fragment* 2: 1-8), 7th century B. C. lyric poet who composed for the symposiums (men's dinner parties) of aristocrats.

MYRONIDES: Ch. 12, (Thucydides. *History of the Peloponnesian War*, Bk. I: 106-108), Athenian general who led expeditions into Boeotia in 458 B. C. to establish Athenian friendly democracies.

NICIAS: Ch. 3, 14, 16, 17, 19, 23 & 24, (Thucydides. *History of the Peloponnesian War*, Bk. V: 16), after the death of Pericles, Nicias became the leader of Athens.

ONOMACRITUS: Ch. 10, (Herodotus. *The Histories*, Bk. VII: 6), a scribe during the time of Peisistratids in Athens, who scholars regard as the likely compiler of the 'oracles of Musaeus' concerning Orpheus.

PARALUS: Ch. 25, (Plutarch. *Life of Pericles*, 36), son of Pericles who died in the plague that afflicted Athens during the summers of 430 through 426 - Pericles named his second son after the state trireme, 'Paralus', whose officers were all men from the common people. This ship of state, thus, was especially understood to honor and represent the democracy of Athens.

PARMENIDES: Ch. 7, (Plato. *Parmenides*, 126c) Parmenides is believed to have visited Athens about 450 during the PanAthenaic Festival. Plato's dialogue, *Parmenides*, proposes that Socrates as a young man visited with the philosopher during his stay in Athens.

PAUSANIAS: Ch. 19, (Thucydides, *History of the Peloponnesian War*, Bk. I: 94-95), Spartan general recalled by Sparta and removed from command of allied Greek forces still fighting Persians in Ionia (coastal territory on the northeastern shores of the Aegean) - This event marked the beginning of Athenian control of allied Greek efforts to rid Persian threat to any of the Greek city states. It is as leader of this anti-Persian alliance, what the Athenians called the 'Delian League', that Athens gradually transformed the alliance to its commercial empire.

PEGASOS: Ch. 22, (*Pausanias I*, 2:5), missionary believed to have brought the cult of Dionysos to Athens.

PERDICCAS: Ch. 18 & 20, (Thucydides. *History of the Peloponnesian War*, Bk. II: 99-100), king of tribes in lower Macedonia in 429 B.C.

PERICLES: Ch. 5 & 7-25, (Thucydides. *History of the Peloponnesian War*, Bk. II: 56-65) Pericles held power in Athens as its 'first citizen' for three decades. Thucydides describes his role in Athens as first citizen thus, "So, in what was nominally a democracy, power was really in the hands of the first citizen."

PERICLES: Ch. 25, (Plutarch, *Life of Pericles*, 37:2), illegitimate son of Pericles and Aspasia.

PHAENARETE: Ch. 5, (Plato. *Theatetus*, 149: a), mother of Socrates.

PHIDIAS: Ch. 15, (Plutarch. *Life of Pericles*, 13: 2), Pericles' general overseer and manager for construction of the Parthenon and other public buildings.

PINDAR: Ch. 17, 19 & 22-24, (Plato. *Republic*, Bk. III: 408b), the Theban 5th century poet most famous for his odes celebrating the victories of champions at the Olympian, Nemean, Pythian, and Isthmian Games.

PEISISTRATOS: Ch. 8, 14 & 16, (Herodotus. *The Histories*, Bk. I: 59-62), 6th century tyrant in Athens whose family held power from 560-556 B. C. and then 546 through 510 B. C. when Hippias the son of Peisistratos was expelled.

POLYGNOTUS: Ch. 11, 15 & 22, (Plato. *Ion*, 533a), painter whose work decorated the interiors of the new public buildings constructed in Athens during the mid-5th century B. C.

PROTAGORAS: Ch. 3, 8, 10, 15-18 & 20-24, (Plato. *Protagoras*, 309: a-d), Protagoras, the philosopher from Abdera in the remote northeast of Greece, served as an adviser to Pericles during his long stay in Athens.

PROTEAS: Ch. 19, (Thucydides. *History of the Peloponnesian War*, Bk. I: 45), one of the commanders of the Athenian fleet of triremes sent to Corcyra in 433 B.C.

PYRILAMPES: Ch. 15, (Plutarch. *Life of Pericles*, 13:5), a dealer in rare birds who according to Pericles' critics helped procure mistresses for Pericles by giving these women peacocks.

PYTHAGORAS: Ch. 24, (Plato. *Republic*, 600: a-b), the late 6th century B.C. Ionian philosopher who taught in Greek colonies in southern Italy. Pythagoras founded a school of followers who passed on his famous teachings of the reincarnation of the soul and a cosmology which proposed that the world-order is based on a kind of harmony which can be expressed by numbers and especially the relations of ratio discernible in the harmonic scale of the music of the lyre.

PYTHODORUS: Ch 20-22, (Aristotle. *Constitution of Athens*, chapter 27:2), the *Archon Eponymus* in 432/431 B.C., the beginning of the Peloponnesian War. The *Archon Eponymus* gave his name to the year and was otherwise described as the *Archon* without other qualification. All together there were nine *Archons*, each one chosen by lot for one year from each of the ten tribes in turn. The other *archons* charged with specific functions were: the King *Archon* (charged with specific religious functions), the War Lord (*polemarchos*), and six "Lawgivers" (*thesmothetai*). These *archons* were among the most important of the officials of the Athenian democracy, charged with administering the institutions and laws of the democratic state.

SADOCUS: Ch. 20-23, (Thucydides, *History of the Peloponnesian War*, Bk. II: 29), the son of Sitalces, King of the Odrysian tribes in Thrace and an ally of the Athenians in the Peloponnesian War.

SIMONIDES: Ch. 20, (Plato. *Protagoras*, 339a-347a), Simonides of Ceos, a small island in the Aegean about 15 miles southeast of Athens, moved to Athens as a young man to pursue literary opportunities in the service of the Peisistratid family who ruled Athens for most of the second half of the 6th century B.C. Considered one of ancient Greece's notable lyric poets, extant excerpts from his work include a fragment of a commemorative poem celebrating the heroism of Leonidas and his band of 300 at Thermopylae.

SITALCES: Ch. 20, (Thucydides, *History of the Peloponnesian War*, Bk. II: 67), King of Thrace allied with Athens during the Peloponnesian War.

SOCRATES: Ch. 5-7 & 9-25, (Plato. *Apology*), Athens' native 5th century B.C. philosopher.

SOCRATES, son of Antigenes: Ch. 19, (Thucydides. *History of the Peloponnesian War*, Bk. II: 23), one of the Athenian commanders of the fleet sent to attack Spartan controlled coastal areas of the Peloponnese in 431 B.C.

SOLON: Ch. 6-8, 11, 14, 16, 17, 21 & 24, (Aristotle. *Constitution of Athens*, chapter. 2), mid 6th century Athenian reformer who cancels enslavement of native born men of Attica which resulted from debt to powerful and wealthy aristocratic landlords - Solon's cancellation of the debt which had led to slavery of native born small landowners in Attica was called the '*seisachtheia*'- 'the shaking off of burdens'. Solon is later regarded as one of the seven "Wise Men" of Greece and celebrated for his poems which praise the life of virtue based on moderation and political justice.

SOPHOCLES: Ch. 10, 11, 17, 20 & 23-25, (Plato. *Phaedrus*, 268d), Sophocles joins Aeschylus and Euripides as the three great tragic poets of 5th century Athens. Like so many other Athenians of this era, he was a man of many-sided accomplishment, having also served with distinction as a hoplite warrior and the Treasurer of the Delian League, a confederation of Greek states led by Athens to defend against the Persian threat that persisted after Xerxes' defeat in 480/79 at Salamis and Plataea.

SOPHRONISCUS: Ch. 1-14 & 19, (Plato. *Laches*, 180e), father of Socrates the philosopher.

THALES: Ch. 7, (Herodotus. *The Histories*, Bk. 1: 170), the first of the 'philosophers' whose cosmological speculation focused on explaining how order and stability emerged to grant stability and law-like regularity to Nature - Thales, a citizen of Miletus in the first half of the 6th century B.C., initiated a pathway of inquiry that comes to be associated with the theoretical inquiry that in our era culminates with modern natural science. Thales was considered one of the seven sages of the ancient world and was famous for his prediction of a solar eclipse in 585 B.C.

THEAGENES: Ch. 14 & 19, (Thucydides. *History of the Peloponnesian War*, Bk. I: 126), tyrant of Megara and father-in-law of Cylon.

THEMISTOCLES: Ch. 1-4, 8, 10, 14, 18 & 24-25, (Herodotus. *The Histories*, Bk.VIII: 56-62), the Athenian General who leads Athenian naval forces against the Persian fleet at Artemision and Salamis in 480 B.C.

THESEUS: Ch. 5, 8, 14, 16 & 22-23, (Thucydides, *History of the Peloponnesian War*, Bk. II: 15), the legendary king of Athens who was believed to have unified the villages of Attica under a single government in Athens - This unification was still celebrated in historical times during the festival of Synoecia ('the bringing all the houses together) held just before the Panathenaea, one of the largest of Athens' state festivals.

THESPIS: Ch. 22 & 23, (*Diogenes Laertius*. Book III, Plato, section 34), Diogenes Laertius writes, "Anciently, in tragedy, it was only the chorus who did the whole work of the play, but subsequently, Thespis introduced one actor for the sake of giving the chorus some rest, and Aeschylus added a Second, and Sophocles a Third, and so they made tragedy complete." Thespis was a contemporary of Peisistratos (mid 6th century B.C) and it was probably Peisistratos who established the City Dionysia Festival with the theatric productions in which Thespis' innovation first appeared.

THRASYMACHUS: Ch. 17, (Plato. *Republic*, Bk. I: 336b-354b), a Sophist, who is a contemporary of Socrates - Thrasymachus is famous for his dictum – "might makes right".

THUCYDIDES, son of Melesias: Ch. 14, 15 & 22, (Aristotle. *Constitution of Athens*, chapter 28), leader of the aristocratic party and Pericles' rival in the middle of decades of the 5th Century B.C.

THUCYDIDES, son of Olorus: Ch. 15, 19 & 24-25, (Thucydides. *History of the Peloponnesian War*, Book I: 1), the Athenian General and author of *History of the Peloponnesian War*.

TOLMIDES: Tolmides: Ch. 12-13, (Thucydides. *History of the Peloponnesian War*, Bk. I: 113), Athenian General at battle of Coronea (447 B.C) in which Alcibiades' father, Clinias, is killed.

TYRTAEUS: Ch. 10 & 18, (Plato. *Laws*, Bk. I: 629a), Tyrtaeus composed martial poetry during the second half of the 7th century B.C. in Sparta, glorifying the soldier willing to die in battle for his state.

XANTHIPPUS: Ch. 10, (Aristotle. *Constitution of Athens*, chapter 28), father of Pericles.

XANTHIPPUS: Ch. 24 & 25, (Plutarch, *Life of Pericles*, 36), son of Pericles.

XERXES: Ch. 1, 4, 8, 10, 13, 14 & 17-18, (Herodotus, *The Histories*, Bk. VII: 4 – Bk. IX), the King of Persia during the Persian expedition against Greek city states in 480 B. C.

ZENO: Ch. 15, (Plato, *Parmenides*, 127b), a philosopher contemporary to Socrates – Zeno was the author of philosophical paradoxes designed to corroborate Parmenides' claim that change, motion, and time are somehow merely illusory appearances.

ZOPYRUS: Ch. 14 & 15, (Plutarch. *Life of Alcibiades*, 1), Alcibiades' pedagogue.

PROLOGUE

The poet's function is to describe, not the thing that has happened, but a kind of thing that might happen, i.e. what is possible as being probable or necessary. The distinction between historian and poet is not in the one writing prose and the other verse – you might put the work of Herodotus into verse, and it would still be a species of history; it consists really in this, that one describes the thing that has been, and the other a kind of thing that might be. Hence poetry is something more philosophic and of graver import than history, since its statements are of the nature rather of universals, whereas those of history are singulars. By a universal statement I mean one as to what such or such a kind of man will probably or necessarily say or do – which is the aim of poetry, though if affixes proper names to the characters; by a singular statement, one as to what, say, Alcibiades did or had done to him.

Aristotle. Poetics (circa 330 B.C.)

No people have elevated talk and debate into a way of life as did the ancient Greeks. They talked all the time, in public and private, and they talked with enthusiasm and persuasiveness. Their literature was filled with talk, from the long speeches of the *Iliad* and *Odyssey* through the monologues of the tragedians to the equally long speeches and debates in Herodotus….What does human behavior consist of, after all, but talk and action?"

M. I. Finley, Introduction to Thucydides, History of the Peloponnesian War (1970)

"It is human nature, man as a whole, in his concrete reality, that is sometimes helped by outward means to achieve an inner light."
Carl Kerenyi, *Eleusis, Archetypal Image of Mother and Daughter* (1962)

A NOTE TO THE READER

The episodes depicted in each chapter of my two volume story, *The Goat Song*, aim to reconstruct the lived experience of Athenians during the years of 480 B.C. through 399 B.C. In this first volume, there are twenty-five episodes, extending from the climax of the Persian invasion in 480 through the third year of the Peloponnesian War and the death of Pericles in 429. Each episode is a portal through which the reader may step into the many-sided world of 5th century B.C. Athenians: politics, religion art, war, slavery, family life, love, eroticism, work, commerce, play, and the extraordinary passion for competition in sport, music, dance, and theater are all interwoven in the story lines of Athenian lives.

There are really two interconnected narratives unfolding throughout this two volume account of life in ancient Athens. The simpler story revolves around the life-long relationship between Socrates and Alcibiades, two of the most controversial Athenian men of this time, both of whom were regarded as guilty of capital crimes against their city. This story begins with the lives of their fathers and ends with the death of Socrates, whose execution comes five years after the violent death of his beloved Alcibiades. The larger story of fifth century Athens is polymorphous and carries the reader to and fro through episodes which reflect the dissonance within Athenian culture and politics that led Athens' own fifth and fourth century poets, philosophers, and historians to diverse and sometimes contradictory interpretations of the city's history, even though for the most part they were all men of the aristocratic class.

Every attempt has been made to follow the chronology and events recorded and agreed upon by the ancient historians of the era, especially Herodotus (*The Histories*), Thucydides (*History of the Peloponnesian War*), Xenophon (*Hellenika*), Aristotle (*Constitution of Athens*) and Plutarch (*Lives*). But not every character in this story of Athens, which I retell through the lens of particular human subjects, can be found in the extant literature of ancient fifth century Athenians or their later historians. Slaves, temple prostitutes, *hetaerai*, children, *thetes* (hired laborers without property), artisans, and rowers in the Athenian navy of triremes - all are invisible to the historical record as individuals. But these persons also appear as flesh and blood subjects in my stories of Athenian lives. What are the sources of materials from which we might reconstruct their inner lives?

The artwork displayed on thousands of 5th century vases, drinking cups, storage amphorae, and funeral urns portrays a wide array of scenes: the erotic congress of male citizens with other men of their own status and with women of every status, participation in various religious rites and festivals, the brutality of war, the drudgery of the work of women and slaves, epiphanies of the gods, and feats of heroes. This treasure trove of artistic representation of both everyday life and the exalted realm of gods and heroes can teach us much about the lives of non citizens in ancient Athens. Also, a careful reading of Aristophanes' comedies and Euripides' tragedies, theatrical productions which aimed to entertain the common people of Athens as well as the men of aristocratic lineage, provide us with a picture of ordinary lives. Quite often we can find in the works of these poets emotions and perspectives of a slave, a wife, a thete, each negotiating the challenges of their everyday life in Athens, or a 'put-upon' commoner reacting to the ways of the rich and powerful men of the city.

In our own era we are accustomed to the notion that historical accounts are 'contested' by those who see themselves marginalized within a society and oppressed by those who wield the instruments of power and wealth. A striking example of this way of criticizing ancient historical narratives may be found in Eva C. Keuls' first paragraph of the Introduction to her 1985 book, *The Reign of the Phallus*. *"In the case of a society dominated by men who sequester their wives and daughters, denigrate the female role in reproduction, erect monuments to the male genitalia, have sex with the sons of their peers, sponsor public whorehouses, create a mythology of rape, and engage in rampant saber-rattling, it is not inappropriate to refer to a reign of the phallus. Classical Athens was such a society."*

Any sophisticated reader may ask how I can avoid my own era's predilection for deconstructing twenty-five hundred year old historical and literary narratives through a 'corrective' lens which makes apparent the sexism, racism, class bias, or ethno-centrism of the ancient Greek authors. Of course one should ask if the contemporary deconstructionist is merely substituting their own particular value commitments in their reappraisal of the cultural self-understanding of a past era. I think becoming entangled in this question can be avoided by making a self-conscious attempt to set aside my own biases and contemporary political and moral commitments. This requires being conscientious about treating extant historical sources as **phenomena** of a special kind, higher order manifestations of a by-gone form of human consciousness. Just as the modern natural scientist must study the operations of Nature methodically and dispassionately if he is to develop a conjecture untainted by his own moral and emotional commitments, so too a modern author who studies the extant expressions of consciousness from a past era or culture may disclose the fundamental cast of this subjective experience, but only if the author, as an historian, begins by setting aside, as much as possible, his own fundamental moral and cultural convictions.

No doubt, such a disciplined historical understanding remains an interpretation. Nevertheless, there are interpretive approaches that are more likely than others to succeed in reproducing the subjectivity of ancient Athenians on their own terms. What would some far distant future cultural anthropologist have to say about the sexuality of men in 21st century United States if his study was restricted only to examining extant audio-visual playbacks of Viagra advertisements? How can we appraise the meaning of painted representations of the *phallophoriai* (men carrying large phalluses in a procession of the City Dionysia) represented on fifth century B.C. Athenian vases unless we reconstruct as far as possible the life-world which informs the context of this sexual representation?

To arrive at such a manifold picture of ancient Athenian life is a scholarly work that can never be finished, but the more comprehensive the manifold, the more likely there is an appropriate context to inform our understanding of each individual outer expression of the inner lives of 5th century Athenians.

Since Athenians' daily familiarity with the works of their poets, potters, painters, architects, and sculptors was as much a formative feature of their world-view as television, movies, and the internet all shape and reflect our 21st century consciousness; the reader should not be surprised to find scenes depicting 5th century Athenians citing their own historians, poets, and philosophers, repeating the wisdom of words inscribed in stone on their monuments and temple walls, and contemplating images painted on their pottery which depicted both their own activities as well as the stories of heroes and gods..

We can make considerable headway in recovering the lived-experience of human beings from a by-gone era if we understand the master-narratives in terms of which they themselves understood their lives. Albert Camus in our own time describes human beings as "meaning demanding creatures". Suffering without purpose, struggle without heroism, dying without the hope of some connection to a transcendent order or value makes one's life seem empty and pointless. We all hunger for a storied life and indeed it seems the communities of every historical era answer this need through the stories treasured and passed on from generation to generation in their religion, art, and literature. If we are to understand the inner life of ancient Athenians, then we too must see the world and the trajectory of human lives through the religious stories which represented to them the possible meanings of their aspirations and struggles.

G. W. F. Hegel, the modern German historian and philosopher, notes that such an approach can be advanced by paying special attention to the major religious festivals of the Athenian year. *"Anyone who did not know the history of the city, the culture and the laws of Athens could have almost have learned them from the festivals if he had lived a year within its gates."* Hegel realized that in ancient Athens there was no tidy demarcation between the sacred and the profane or secular spheres of life. Thus, if we are to follow the drama and development of our characters' life stories as they are part of the wider political history of Athens, we cannot ignore the part the religious festivals and narratives played in their lives. If the reader stays the course, we, like Socrates, Alcibiades, and their circle of families, friends, and adversaries in Athens, will have taken part in the seven major festivals which year after year marked the seasons and cycles of their lives. Perhaps we can then understand more clearly Socrates' complicated statement concerning his own divine commission from the Oracle of Delphi, one of the most prestigious centers of religious authority honored by Athens and all other Hellene city states. After we have joined Athenians celebrating the City Dionysia, we may begin to understand the creative genius of Euripides whose tragedies parse the tension between the ecstatic and instinctual life of the Dionysian, and the calm and deliberative Reason that best serves the law courts and the Athenian Assembly – the Logos embraced by Socrates. When we too take part in the Athenian rite of Thargelia, driving out of our city the designated scapegoat who is the *pharmakos* so that Athens might be purged of the sin and uncleanness that brings pollution and unruly disorder to the body politic; then we will more clearly understand the fates of Alcibiades and Socrates as well as the unusual 5th century Athenian political institution of ostracism.

Both the famous and the forgotten persons in the legacy of ancient Athens wove the stories of the gods, great heroes, and their venerable ancestors into the events of their city and their own lives. But as with every culture, the traditional stories themselves must ferment and mutate if they are to remain relevant to changing circumstances. Clearly in fifth century Athens philosophers like Protagoras and Socrates, politicians like Pericles, and poets such as Aeschylus, Sophocles, Euripides, and Aristophanes find new wine in the old bottles, and in so doing, these articulate men of words often unsettle their fellow Athenians. It may be that these intellectuals apprehended that the virtues requisite for the deliberative Assembly of the new Athenian democratic constitution of mid-fifth century Athens did not readily accord with the virtues celebrated in the tents of Homer's Agamemnon and Achilles. Would Athenian citizen jurors be better served by asking how they might please the gods or by considering every case in the light of laws and principles fashioned by deliberative assemblies committed to nurturing and preserving the new equality before the law which is fundamental to the ethos of democratic Athens? It is a question like this that unfolds in the drama of Socrates' fate. Socrates claims that his practice of philosophy provides a great service to Athens by searching out how both he and others might realize that kind of political virtue which is essential and peculiar to human excellence. But there are many in Athens who find his influence, especially upon the young men of Athens, corrupting, impious, and anti-democratic.

I have tested my readers' patience, I am sure. So it is time to leave behind my introductory remarks – all of which aim to convince readers that should they read *The Goat Song* they will enter into an order of experience both excitingly different and yet familiar. While I, like any fallible human, may have made mistakes, I have done my best to tell a story of Athenian lives guided by an array of evidentiary phenomena, the extant products of the minds of 5th century Hellenes, most of them Athenians. It is in this way a story which aspires to be historically 'true', or at least possible, in the sense that is offers an interpolative and more intimate 'poetic' version of the historical narratives of Herodotus, Thucydides, and Xenophon.

PART ONE
Heroic Fathers
480 B.C.

CHAPTER ONE
IN THE WATERS OF EURIPIS
(480 B.C.)

And teeming Asia's headstrong lord has shepherded his flocks godspeed against the world on two fronts land and sea...And not one has proved he can stand up to men in a ceaseless stream nor ever build a sure seawall to stay the unstoppable waves resistless, Persia's armed flood and the war-joy that crests in her sons.

(Aeschylus, *Persians*: 100-120)

The soldier lay naked, chest and loins pressed against the smooth, hard boulder. Surely, he thought, this couch-like rock, surrounded by translucent turquoise water, had served as the resting place of some lovely siren long ago. The cool water still glistened on his sculptured bronze torso in the hot mid-day late summer sun. With his chin propped by thick-knuckled hands, he gazed down into the sea from which he had just emerged. From his vantage point he could see through the clear shallow water for some ten or fifteen yards. Between the sandy bottom and the air, shafts of sunlight gave dimension to this watery space. In this realm, light and water mingled kaleidoscopically revealing to him from his god-like perspective a serene world below.

At that moment a school of small, silvery fish made its entrance into the shallow waters. Like a fleet of warships on patrol, they foraged the territory, moving in rhythmic unison. Sparkling in the sunlit water and gliding effortlessly in formation, these sleek and delicate creatures gave the impression of an existence at once busy and serene. It was as though each individual combined with the others in the simple geometry of a single ever-moving body displaying both spontaneity and order. They moved as if unaware of the absolute boundaries imposed by the glistening ceiling of the sea and its sandy floor. For the moment, life and its watery domicile gave the impression of being all of one piece, a self-contained and ever animated element. Or so, at least, it seemed to the sun-bather who looked down from above. Suddenly the charm of the spectacle was shattered by shrill cries from above. The soldier looked up and saw a sky-borne gull pull his wings in tight against his body and dive down straight toward the fish-filled shallows. In an instant, the diver had broken the plane of the water, found his prey, snatched it within his beak, and reappeared winging his way with a life rigid and then limp in the clutch of his vice-like mouth.

A tingling ache in the elbows pressing against the boulder as he propped up his chin brought the soldier back to his own body. Shifting his weight, he felt a pleasing hardness growing from beneath his belly and pressing into the dark moss-filled crevice traversing the top flat surface of the sea boulder. It had been more than two weeks since he had been with his wife and he had not availed himself of either the male or female slaves who always accompanied a military expedition. Up the beach, less than a mile from where he rested, he could see a fleet of long ships, two hundred and seventy one by count, some moored just off shore and some pulled up on shore on their sturdy oak keels. With them some 48,000 men stood ready to do battle with an enemy fleet which by all reports far outnumbered them. There would be great danger, and a man who would win honor as well as survive must concentrate all his powers. To this end he had tightly drawn the bowstring of his body, realigning the forces of Eros, until the desire for warm life could be called upon to keep cold death at bay.

It was time to return. The beach camp was now suddenly bustling with activity. The soldier stepped down into the water, waded ashore, and having girded himself with his loin cloth and arranged his cloak, he hurried towards the beached trireme around which his commander and crew had gathered.

The whole camp was in a panic. Upon their arrival at Artemisium in early morning, Eurybiades, the Spartan general who held the supreme command of the allied Greek naval force, had sent scouts across the ten mile wide straits separating their camp on the northern tip of Euboea from the mainland peninsula of Magnesia. These scouts had now returned with bad news. The Persian army had met little resistance as town after town in nearby Thessaly had gone over to the Persian side. Those few towns that had put up a fight were quickly crushed by the overwhelming power of Xerxes' large army. All that now stood between the Persian forces and the Greek heartland was Leonidas' small band of three hundred Spartan warriors at the mountain pass of Thermopylae. The countryside north of Thermopylae and directly across from the Artemisium base of the Greek fleet was completely overrun by barbarians, looting and raping every town and village in their path. Worst of all, the scouts confirmed what had been rumored. Indeed, the Greek ships faced an enemy fleet that vastly outnumbered them. The scouts had counted over twelve hundred war ships which had arrived early that afternoon off the coast of Magnesia. These ships were more heavily armed, of larger construction, and faster in the water than their own triremes. The Greeks were outnumbered almost six to one. How could Leonidas' small force possibly check the advance of the largest army ever assembled, which seemed to grow in numbers as it moved down the Greek mainland, and how could the pitifully out manned Greek navy stop the Persian fleet from gaining control of Attica's costal waters? The Persians' vast advantage in numbers would simply overwhelm the Greeks, whatever place the Greeks chose to make their stand. This, at least, is how the scouts' report was received by the generals. To make matters worse, details of the scouts' account of the enemy's fleet had already spread throughout the camp. The men, now gathered around their respective ships, were clamoring for retreat.

"Sophroniscus how is it that you can appear so serene while all the rest of us behave like stallions in a burning barn, beside ourselves with fear? Perhaps it is you, my friend, and not I who should command our trireme. Who was the god your parents called upon to vouchsafe the promise of your name, 'one of self-control'? Let us all sacrifice to this god now that we may be brought safely through this danger and live another day so as to present him with our own sons."

"It is because you lead us, Clinias, that I am confident of our safety," replied Sophroniscus as he took his place among the crew which awaited instructions from their captain.

Clinias nodded in appreciation. He knew he could count on Sophroniscus for the right words. His crew, shamed by Sophroniscus` self-possessed calm, was now ready, like a seasoned sailor facing a storm, to follow a trusted captain. Clinias stepped up upon the cargo box that had been placed in front of and beneath the bow of his beached trireme. The crew had marshaled themselves in a semicircle around Clinias` impromptu platform. Although there were 218 men who moments ago were a flurry of confusion, every one of them now stood with upturned eyes fixed on the magnificent youth of the house of Ajax. Dressed in full battle-costume, Clinias radiated an aura of indomitable courage. Bright beams of sunlight slanting down from the late noon sun cast the shadow of his plumed bronze helmet and corseted torso upon the ship's prow and keel. As the soft sea breeze set in motion the scarlet plume on top of Clinias` sparkling helmet, the huge blue eye painted just beneath the ship's prow alternately appeared and disappeared in the plume's flickering shadow. The eye of the ship, now blinking from the dark brown oak bow, appeared alive and communicated an eerie and super-human presence to the crew awaiting their captain's instructions.

Clinias began to speak very slowly and with a voice more determined than loud. "Most of you have heard the reports of the approach of the large Persian fleet and are now greatly distressed. The Corinthian and Spartan crews are clamoring for a retreat to their homes. Some of our Peloponnesian allies believe that the Great King`s lust for empire will be fulfilled once he humbles our Athens. I am not surprised when I hear such talk coming from our Peloponnesian allies. But what I cannot understand is how the men of Attica, some of you who fought so valiantly at Marathon, can now council retreat and surrender. Athenians and Plataeans, what will you tell your sons and wives when they ask why it is that the warriors who left the docks brimming with courage, lustily chanting a paean to the beat of drums, now return in panic and with shiny swords and shields untested in battle with the enemy who now quickly approaches their homes? Will you explain to your wife that lovely women have nothing to fear from the Persian conqueror? Will you console your women by recounting how the Ionian well-born women of Samos, Chios, and Lesbos, taken captive by barbarians, now in Babylon, Susa, and Ecbatana recline in the sumptuous chambers reserved for the harems of Persian princes? How will you console your sons of fair complexion and well-formed

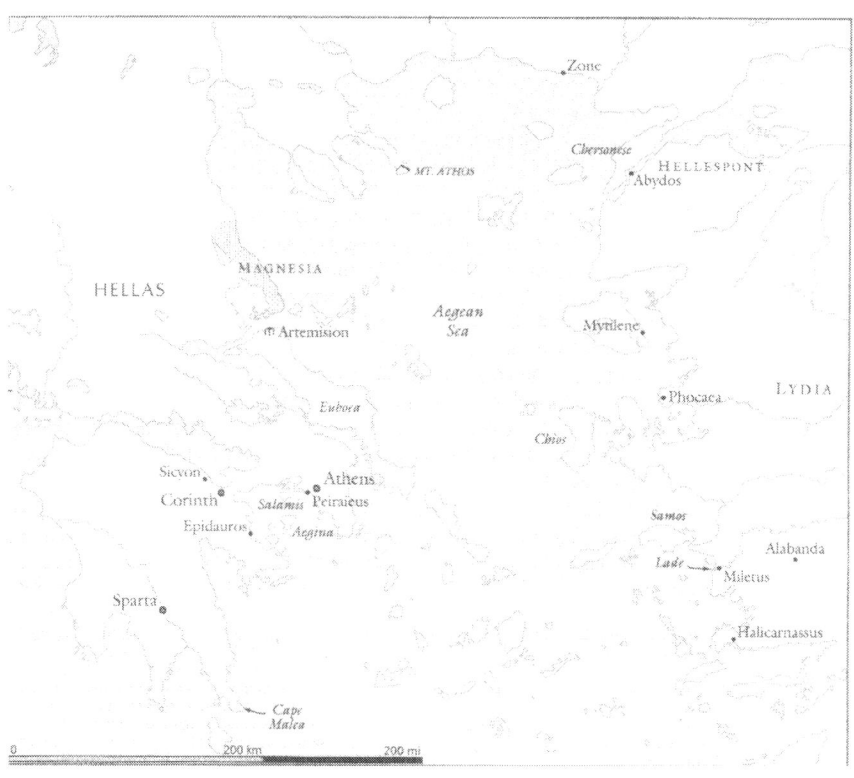

Artemision, Euboea – base of allied Hellene naval fleet as Persian fleet approaches Hellas in support of Xerxes land invasion

bodies when the long knives of Xerxes' Saracens unman them and doom them to a eunuch's life? Will you, like a groveling slave, surrender and beg for your lives at the knees of the Persian tyrant? If so, will not the spirits of our fathers, like the vengeful Furies, rise up against us and plague the hearths which have become the abode of cowardly slaves? We must not betray those who fell at Marathon and preserved our freedom."

Clinias paused and turned toward the great eye of the ship, his back to the men. He waited until the force of his words had worked their effect upon his crew. Clinias felt their eyes on his shoulders and when the silence turned to a tense attention, he knew they were again soldiers resolved to defend their homeland and ready for his commands.

"We sail for Chalcis where we can deal with the enemy fleet in waters most favorable to our skills and numbers. In the narrows of the Euripus, the numerical superiority of the Persian fleet will be neutralized. Themistocles has convinced Adeimantus that his Corinthian ships must not detach themselves from our fleet and Eurybiades has already prepared a plan of formation and tactics for battle in these waters. Gather your gear and prepare to embark. We will, with twenty other Athenian triremes, serve as the rear guard as we move to the south. Since the Persian crews have rowed all through the night and well past sunrise, it is not likely that they will follow us this afternoon. With the wind behind us and with the help of the moon's pale light, we should arrive at Chalcis by the time of the second guard this evening."

When Clinias stepped down from the cargo box, his officers set the crew to work. Before the trireme would be rolled back into the sea on the logs under its oaken keel, a light coat of melted wax had to be brushed over the outer planking from stern to bow. Although Clinias had spared no expense in building and equipping his ship of war, it had not been possible, given the rush to have her ready for the Persians, to obtain properly aged fir for the hull. Thus, it was necessary to constantly calk and seal the still porous planks of the Gyges. Wax melted over a fire and mixed with a blue pigment was used for this purpose. With ten well-supervised men the entire exterior of the trireme would be coated within an half an hour. While the war ship was coated from bow to stern, drinking water was barreled and loaded aboard, buckets were filled with pebbles and carried below deck for ballast, and anchor ropes and other gear were refitted, each in its proper place, on Clinias' 200 oared trireme. When she was rolled into the water, her freshly waxed body a shimmering blue, and her long oars all raised in unison ready to propel her through the sea, the Gyges looked more like a gigantic graceful blue bird poised for flight than the many armed monster after which she was named.

Once under way, Clinias asked Sophroniscus and his other two officers, Procleus and Hermistius, to join him in the wicker deck house. The three men, all friends of Clinias, seemed to have little in common. Sophroniscus was a farmer who had fallen upon hard times and had turned to stone-masonry in order to supplement the shrinking income produced by his small land-holdings. He appeared ill at ease to be sitting in the commander's cool deck-house while men who were both his neighbors and fellow citizens were down below suffering, pulling on the oars with calloused hands. Yes, he had accepted the responsibility of an officer and this was fitting since of all the men serving from his own township, he was the only veteran of more than one military campaign. Although he knew better than most the tactics and stratagems of battle, Sophroniscus was the type of man who neither sought nor savored power over other men. He had consciously resisted enjoying the privileges that were his as one of Clinias' officers. While Clinias, Procleus, and Hermistius sat on soft cushions, in animated conversation, Sophroniscus stood quietly listening to the master oarsman's muted drumbeat resonating from down below.

Procleus, even when half reclining with cloak and *chiton* lying about him in disarray, always gave the impression of a man who was born to dominate. Like Clinias, he had inherited from his father a prosperous and large estate, and from the time he could first walk, had been tutored in the noble martial arts. While so many of the townsmen, who rowed below deck, felt the war to be a monstrous event that interrupted their normal wage earnings and the comfort and security of their daily lives, Procleus felt quite differently. Like a dedicated and superbly trained athlete who strides into the PanAthenaic or Olympic arena confident of glorious victory, he treated the call to war as the natural and fitting stage upon which to act out the struggle for honor which defined his life. It was difficult for Procleus to cloak his disdain for the rowers, those sons of merchants and tradesmen who could not even afford to provide themselves with armor. As far as he was concerned, slaves would do just as well, if all they had to do was pull on oars. It was the company of eighteen armed men under his command who would do the real fighting. Indeed, Procleus could not comprehend this new kind of citizen, who for one day's wage of a *drachma*, was willing to forgo the glories of manly hand to hand combat in order to labor anonymously below decks. As far as he was concerned, if a man did not own equipment and maintain his own skills with shield, sword, and spear, it would be better for him if he served as an attendant or arms bearer. Men, like himself, could be counted on to be courageous and return with their shields. They would never dishonor their family by casting aside in cowardly retreat a shield bearing the same emblem engraved on the shields carried into battle by their fathers and grandfathers. Indeed, Procleus found it hard to understand how his friend Clinias could put much confidence in the commoners who manned the oars, or for that matter, how Clinias could possibly believe that a battle fought from ships was worthy of men of courage. It was this question, more like a complaint, Procleus addressed to his fellow officers.

"I don't care how large the Persian army is. We would be better off meeting the enemy with firm ground under our feet. I just don't understand why forty eight thousand free men should be hauled around in ships, risking their lives trying to stay afloat with every sudden thunder squall, waiting to bang into Persian ships that are manned with slaves. Give me two days and I could teach even our merchants and tradesmen enough about the shield, short sword, and the spear that they could serve well in the back ranks of a sturdy phalanx. With the number of men we have here, our shields locked together, we could make a wall of sharp iron stretching almost three miles, eight men thick all up and down the line. Has everybody already forgotten what the Athenian warriors, with we Plataeans at their side, accomplished on the fields of Marathon?"

"Procleus, I think you've been hit over your helmeted head too many times." Hermistius could not resist goading the now slightly paunchy Marathon veteran. "I realize you are a veritable Achilles, but even if we had a thousand hoplites as ferocious as you, it would still be suicide to take the field against Xerxes' army. I know for a fact that Xerxes' army is not twice or even ten times our number, but at least a hundred times our number. It was my own nephew Agisthius, well known to both Clinias and Sophroniscus, who witnessed Xerxes' crossing of the Hellespont from the deck of one of my fleet of transport ships. This is what he told me."

Procleus braced himself for one of Hermistius' long winded stories.

"My nephew's ship had just passed through the Hellespont and into the open sea off the coast by Signeum when he sighted the Persian fleet. He was on his way back to Athens with the hold of his ship filled with grain from the fertile fields surrounding the shores of the Propontis. Confident that he could make it safely to open sea if necessary, Agisthius lowered his main sail and maintained a position from which he could observe the large Persian fleet of galleys and triremes making their way to the straits. He counted 674 ships in all, and on them he saw the flags of Crete, Phoenicia, Egypt, and various Ionian cities, as well as the purple flag of supreme command on a Persian royal galley."

Procleus interrupted. "Can't you get to the point a little quicker? I'd like to hear the end of this story before we arrive at Chalcis, and that's only three or so hours from now. I suppose that you expect me to believe all of what you are going to tell me about Agisthius' sight seeing at the Hellespont. I can smell the bull dung already. I find it hard to believe that any merchant would care about anything but getting his goods to market as fast as he could."

"Merchants can be patriots too, Procleus. And if you will let me finish maybe you'll be able to reign in that inordinate lust for the battle field."

"Get on with it then!"

"What my nephew was about to witness had never been done before. Under the direction of the Persian flag ship, three hundred and sixty of the vessels made their way north into the Hellespont and positioned themselves just off shore of Abydus. But they did not disembark at Abydus. Another three hundred and thirteen ships proceeded towards Sestus directly opposite from Abydus on the northern side of the Hellespont. They too did not pull their vessels on to shore. The Persian royal galley positioned itself in the middle of the strait, with its stern facing toward the Aegean and its bow toward the Propontis Sea. Anchor lines were dropped from both the bow and the stern, so that the ship remained relatively stationary despite the current and winds. Then one by one from both sides of the Hellespont the vessels aligned themselves in a similar fashion, so that when all the ships were in place, the Hellespont was crossed with two lines of ships. After the ships were lashed together, wood planks were fitted crosswise over the decks of the ships, making a road over the Strait. On each side of the wooden causeway, brush wood and dirt were piled up so that the horses and other animals would not panic at sight of the shifting waves that buffeted and swayed their walkway."

"Your nephew could see all this from his ship?"

"He did, and he filed a report with all these details. My nephew is not a very pious man, but when he arrived in Piraeus yesterday morning, he told me before we set sail that the Great King who bridged the Hellespont could not have done so unless some divine power was his ally. For seven days and nights Xerxes' army crossed the bridge. Agisthius counted over a million soldiers, and when he turned his ship, loaded to capacity with grain, to open sea, he saw to the south another huge fleet of warships, flying the Persian flag, making their way up the coast toward the Hellespont. Fearing for our city and her fleet, my nephew emptied the hold, and with the twenty oars of his merchanter slicing through the water in triple time, he raced to open sea. My associates and I lost the entire shipment. Three of our rowers died of exhaustion as Agisthius continued under oar power for six hours at full speed. At least Boreas was not in league with Xerxes. If my nephew had not alerted us as soon as he did, the Persian fleet could have bottled us up and forced us to do what you want us to do, march out on land to stand like a grove of trees to be consumed by millions of voracious locusts."

Procleus bit his lip. He dared not point out to Hermistius that everyone in Athens, including Hermistius himself, did not need to wait for his nephew's report to know of the Persian expedition. Spies had been at work for months in the Ionian cities. The generals had known weeks ago of the exact date of the Great King's expedition against Hellas, and they knew that Athens was the final target. Ambassadors had scurried between Sparta, Corinth, Athens, and other Greek cities as far north as the Thracian coast. The politics of an alliance, founded not on friendship but on the necessity of combating a common threat, had been hammered out well before Xerxes reached the Hellespont. While Themistocles, the Athenian naval commander, was by far the superior of any Spartan at sea, the Spartan, Eurybiades, had been named supreme admiral of the combined Corinthian, Spartan, and Athenian fleet. The allied fleet, moored at Piraeus for the last week, certainly did not wait upon the news from a slow moving transport ship to receive its sailing orders.

Procleus whispered to Sophroniscus, "Have the bankers covered the insurance on the cargo? Three or four more such patriotic acts this month and the grain prices will go through the roof!"

Sophroniscus shifted his weight uncomfortably. The setting sun, still hot, had found its way under the awning of the wicker deck house and now bore down on his already sun-burned neck. The late afternoon breeze had shifted and now brought from the mainland biting green headed flies. While Procleus reclined in Sophroniscus` shadow, no more than a swords-length away, Procleus` whisper was all too audible. Sophroniscus slapped the fly that was on his forearm, rubbed his ear, and changed the subject. "Clinias, does not your father Alcibiades own an estate in Euboea near Chalcis? It would be good if oxen could be found. A sacrifice for Poseidon, the Winds, and in celebration of Kronia now underway in Athens will fortify us all."

Actually, Sophroniscus, the estate you are thinking about belongs to my father's new partner in his commercial maritime shipping enterprise, Megacles the Alkmeonid. And I am sure he is on the island now, although I don't know how enthusiastic he will be to do anything helpful to General Themistocles. While our Council persuaded the Assembly to enact an amnesty to all those ostracized, except the Pisisitratid Hipparchus, Megacles has told me that he will find it very difficult to put aside his enmity for Themistocles, since it was he who orchestrated his ostracism. Let us hope that Megacles hates the Persians more than Themistocles. Since Megacles has been involved in the efforts to foment rebellion against the Great King in Ionia, I think it is a safe bet that he will do anything to prevent falling into the hands of Xerxes. He assured the Council when he returned to Athens that he would, without reservation, join the fight to save our city and the rest of Hellas from Persian conquest. He was sent to Euboea to persuade others in Eretria and the rest of Euboea to do their utmost to provide our navy with support and supplies if needed."

Sophroniscus wanted to reassure the other officers that there would be no betrayal of their mission by Megacles. "I know Megacles well. He is a neighbor of mine in Alopeke, and I can assure you he is a man of honor. I am certain he will offer us every kind of assistance he can."

Clinias nodded his head in agreement. "We think together, my friend. Our crew will have need of all the courage that can be mustered. The heat, the cursed flies, and the fatigue of a mid-day shift at the oars - they have already forgotten my speech! When we land, take my two personal slaves, who know where the farm is, and make all the arrangements with Megacles to help feed the men and make arrangements for our sacrifice to Poseidon. I will speak to Themistocles and ask that he preside over the sacrifice. Indeed, he is probably already wondering whether he should offer Megacles money for the oxen, or simply presume on his love of the gods and patriotism. Now, if we can stop my officers from goading one another, I would like one more rapid maneuver drill before we land at Chalcis."

CHAPTER TWO

THE SEVRANTS' ERRAND THROUGH THE HAUNTED WOOODS

The black bolt from below comes from the slain
Of kin who cry for vengeance, and from them
Madness and empty terror in the night
Comes haunting, troubling.

> (Aeschylus. *The Libation Bearers,* line 285)

Sophroniscus was sure that he could find Megacles' farm on his own, but Clinias insisted that he take Lycon and Lysias, Clinias` own body-servants, as his guides. These youths, just now showing signs of early manhood with new grown beards, had spent their early childhood on the farm and thus were very familiar with the terrain. And so Sophroniscus followed the slave boys' lead as the three made their way down a thickly wooded hill until they came to a small stream. But his patience was being tested. Lycon, the older of the two youths, in his enthusiasm as guide had completely forgotten the manners of his station and was now foisting his own childish and servile superstitions on Sophroniscus.

"Sophroniscus, hurry! This way, before the moon goes behind that cloud! Stop, don`t go through there now! It`s too dark! Look out, Lysias, that`s a burial mound! Stay off of it! This brook is haunted. We can only cross it if we get down on all fours. Look how Lysias does it!"

Lysias was already down on his hands and knees and gingerly testing the flowing water with the palms of his hands.

"Wash, wash! Clean your hands and feet in this still pool before you cross the stream! The ghosts drink here and if you foul the water you will be a marked man, unclean! Last year a maid-servant crossed here and dipped a berry stained hand in that running water over there. Now her hand is withered and shakes. Lysias, show Sophroniscus how to put his hands on the bottom so that he does not stir up the mud."

Lycon now had also dropped to his hands and knees. Looking like a pair of hounds, the two incognito human beings were about to brave the passage across the stream. Sophroniscus raised his *chiton* and cloak so that he could wade in and give the nearest superstitious slave a swift boot in the ass.

Something moved in the bushes just on the other side of the stream. Lycon and Lysias, looking like cornered animals frozen with fear, eyed the bush from which they were sure something terrible was about to spring upon them. Under the bright moon, Sophroniscus could see the tense muscles on the back of their arched necks, and even he now felt a tinge of fear. It lasted only a second or two. Out of the bush sauntered a large raccoon. Sophroniscus watched the animal sniff the air and stare at them. What does the creature see, he wondered: two four legged hairless water animals and a featherless bipod with two huge floppy wings?

Sophroniscus waded in with his garments still held aloft and spoke sharply to the youths. "It is just a raccoon, boys. If that's a ghost in there, it has decided it doesn't want your blood. Look, the creature is retreating back into the woods. Come on, boys, enough foolishness! Let's get a move on or you will be beaten when we get back to camp!"

What had been slightly amusing to Sophroniscus now began to irritate him. Up to now it had been pleasant to follow behind the glistening moon-lit bodies of the two youths clad only in their tightly drawn britches. Lycon and Lysias were the only two slaves rowing in Clinias' crew and, in addition to possessing the usual prettiness found in personal male slaves, these two, because of the rigors of rowing, had the torsos of Heracles. Sophroniscus ironically inclined sense of humor had been tickled by their boyish banter. Although he could not remember any gymnasium joke or any of the ever popular anti-Spartan or anti-Mede barbs that had actually made him laugh, Sophroniscus found the present circumstances of role reversal amusing. But, much more than half an hour had passed and Megacles' farm still was not in sight. Clinias had made a point of assuring Sophroniscus that Megacles' farm was no more than a half hour walk from the campsite.

"Not much further now, Master. Believe me; we are going as fast as safely possible. Lysias, is not the farm just on the other side of that next hill?"

Lysias, his britches still dripping from the scramble across the stream, had regained his composure. "Yes, if we run the rest of the way, we will be at Megacles' door in fifteen minutes."

This second hill was gentle and free of underbrush and there were no more burial mounds to avoid. They reached the crest of the hill, and there they could see stretching out below them the moon-lit outline of row after row of olive trees with their squat trunks disappearing into what looked in the dim light like a soft brown carpet. On the far side of this field, just beyond the last stand of trees, the farmhouse, with lanterns glowing from its windows, could be seen. Sophroniscus led the way down the hill. Having reached level ground, he sent the servants on ahead to announce his arrival. Euboean farmers, everyone knew, always allowed their most ferocious dogs the run of the farm from sunset to morning. As long as anyone could remember, there had been cut-throats and other riffraff whose brand of piracy consisted of using the cover of night to plunder and loot the property of Euboean costal farms. However, recently these estates had little to fear from such raids thanks to Themistocles and the new Athenian navy. Athenian war ships had swept the coastal waters clean of such outlaws. But perhaps Megacles, thought Sophroniscus, is fond of his dogs and still gives then the run of his estate at night. Why should I risk a dog bite? For this reason, Sophroniscus had decided it was the better course to stay put and let the servants deal with the dogs should they be out and about.

So, while he waited for the boys to deactivate any canine security patrol, Sophroniscus sat down and stretched out his legs into the tall grass. He was seated on an old discarded wineskin with his back leaning against a solid stone Hermes that marked one of the corner boundary lines of the farm. As soon as the boys had begun to move through the grove, there was indeed a commotion of yelping dogs and shouting. Half an hour passed before the barking stopped, and Sophroniscus could see approaching from the farmhouse three figures silhouetted by the bright lantern one of them carried.

The boys no doubt, he thought, had subdued the dogs and were now returning to him with someone from the estate. The boys may never be warriors or citizens, he mused, but they had shown virtue in mastering the dogs. Human nature is a constant source of perplexity. The same youths who were terrified at the burial mounds, who believed a stream to be haunted, and who would not pass the Hermes without a short prayer to the god, proved to be braver than most when it came to dealing with the very real canine menace that awaited any trespasser on a Euboean farm. Maybe they knew the dogs, though it had been some years since either of the boys had been to the farm. As for Sophroniscus, he found the sharp teeth of a half-wild attacking dog, something he had seen many times, more frightening than the ghosts and spirits which he had never seen. How is it that I cannot believe in such invisible things, he wondered. It isn't that I lack imagination. Only moments ago he had fantasized, if but just for an instant, of lying naked between the two ardent youths on the bed of the shallow stream under the moon light. How erotic it would be to hear only the gurgling sounds of the brook and their sighs in his ears. How lovely it would be to feel the irresistible force from within drawn outward to mingle with the bubbling waters flowing around him. Of course he would never do such a thing. It would be indecent to make use of another man's slaves. Moreover, it would be wrong to take this from these two slaves, even if they were his own, since it would not be possible to give in return to them what any mature gentleman owes to a youthful lover - the lessons in virtue and nobility that prepare a youth for preeminence in the life of the city. He had not seriously been tempted by the passing fantasy. The boys were erotic, but like most youths who excited Sophroniscus' fantasies, their attractiveness seemed to disappear as soon as he listened to their conversation or watched too closely and saw their teeth being picked, or worse, their nose. In this case, for Sophroniscus, Pan had fled the scene at the brook even before Lysias and Lycon had finished their fastidious, ritual hand-washing.

Sophroniscus' reflections were cut short by a loud barking coming from the stand of olive trees off to his right. Looking into the shadows cast by the stubby trunks and gnarled branches, he could now make out the faces of the two youths and an older man who, with lanterns in hand, now made their way through the trees. Sophroniscus called out, "Lysias, Lycon, stay there! I`m coming. Hold the dogs!" Although the barking ceased as he approached them, Sophroniscus thought it best not to presume on the limited intelligence of Lycon and Lysias to hold the dogs unless they were explicitly ordered to do so. It would be humiliating to return home wounded by an overzealous canine. Officer Sophroniscus wounded in action in the great Persian War. How? Done in by a farmer's dog!

When they all met in a small clearing, Sophroniscus was glad to see that the two very large and growling dogs were on a leash in the hands of the older man. This man was not Megacles, since his clothing was that of a laborer. Yet he exuded the air of a man who was accustomed to conversing with aristocrats on equal terms. Having hushed his dogs, he addressed Sophroniscus in a spirit of amicable hospitality. "Have no fear, Lord Sophroniscus. These dogs have already eaten tonight. I am Jacob, Megacles' steward. Lycon and Lysias have explained to me your needs. We have already sent oxen on ahead to the camp. As soon as Megacles learned of the landing of the Hellene navy, he, along with a delegation of other prominent Eritreans, went directly to the campsite. We have been somewhat concerned here. Let me rephrase that. We have been devastated by the news we have heard. Is it true that Eurybiades wishes to withdraw the fleet and leave the Euripus and our island to the Persians? My Master and his neighbors have gone to persuade the admirals to make their fight in the Euripus. Thirty oxen, more provisions, and a large cash contribution to help defray the costs of the fleet are right now being given to Themistocles in hopes that such support from us, I mean the Lords of Euboea, will persuade the joint command not to abandon us to the barbarians. I lost my eldest son to those turbaned devils the last time they landed at Eretria, and though it has been almost ten years, most of the farms around here have not yet fully recovered from their burning and plundering. I cannot bear the thought of losing our olive trees now. They are the only ones that came through the last invasion."

Jacob went on to explain how indeed agents of the Persians had made the rounds among those prominent men in Euboea who they thought might wish to revenge themselves on some of the current leaders in the Athenian assembly. "Sir, I assure you, that when they called on Megacles, they were sent packing with the dogs snapping at their backsides. Heaven knows if there is anyone who has a right to be angry with Themistocles and his associates, it is Megacles. As everyone knows, it was Themistocles who just five years ago forced the vote of ostracism against my master. But in spite of everything, my master loves Athens and would never betray her."

"So, there is nothing for us to do but go back to camp quickly." Sophroniscus gently interrupted the steward who seemed to be very concerned with attesting to his Master's patriotism.

Sophroniscus already knew, as did most Athenians, about the strange circumstances concerning the treatment of the Alkmeonid estate by the Persians when they had invaded the island ten years ago. All of the surrounding estates had been plundered, their groves and their buildings burnt to the ground, but Alkmeonid property was untouched. Two years after the Persians had been defeated at Marathon, Megacles himself was charged with treason, even though many of his own family had fought bravely at Marathon. The case brought against him included the accusation that in exchange for providing Persian agents with information about Attica's costal fortifications, his estate's safety was guaranteed along with assurances that he would share power with Hippias in Athens should the Persians succeed in their attempt to subdue democratic Athens and restore the Peisistratid tyranny in Athens as a subject state of Susa.

Megacles defended himself successfully at the trial, but in the following year, the Athenian Assembly voted to ostracize Megacles rather than undergo another round of fierce partisan struggle between the Alkmeonids and their rivals. Sophroniscus had himself not inscribed Megacles' name on the *ostrakon*, but he knew for a fact that many of his fellow Assemblymen did so, still believing that Megacles' ambition knew no bounds and had included double dealing with the Persians. Such a charge made no sense at all to Sophroniscus, since it had been Megacles' uncle, Cleisthenes who had reformed the council of the 500 and broke up the affiliations of all the old political centers of power by redistricting all of Attica into townships. It was this restructuring of the *demes* and the extension of more political power to the growing number of those who were of a middle position, neither very wealthy nor desperately poor, that had made it impossible for Hippias or any of the other Peisistratids to restore their tyranny. No longer in Athens could a tyrant ride to power as the champion of the many against the landed aristocrats.

Yes, Sophroniscus, repeated to himself, it seemed highly unlikely that Megacles, himself now a prosperous man of the city's new commercial life, could ever be interested in undoing the work of Cleisthenes' reforms. But he could not help wondering whether this steward had ever been questioned by agents of the Athenian courts or the Assembly when Megacles' adversaries impeached him. He, himself, could see that such a one as Jacob, so zealous in speaking on his Master's behalf could arouse suspicions in those already predisposed to question Megacles' loyalty to the Athenian Assembly which, after all, had voted for his ostracism.

Jacob, though a slave, fascinated Sophroniscus. Although he was obviously well-educated, spoke perfect Ionian, and regarded non-Hellenes as barbarians; he could not be a Greek with a name like Jacob. Since the cities of Hellas never employed other Hellenes as slaves, the steward or his parents must have been captured on the high seas or perhaps in some battle in the Ionian cities. More than likely he was a Phoenician or possibly of some other Semitic background. No doubt, given Jacob's obvious intelligence, Megacles probably entrusted most of the administration of the estate to this slave. Yet, thought Sophroniscus, is not it striking how this man, this slave, has been so thoroughly domesticated as to now regard the landing of those who very well could be his compatriots as an invasion of barbarians? Would Jacob, if captured and enslaved by a Phoenician Lord, soon regard the Greeks as the alien enemy? Was it because the slavish nature prefers life at any expense to honorable death in war that this kind of inferior being is led, like a dog pliant and ever aiming to please the hand which feeds him, to mimic his Master's ways?

Jacob saw that the soldier sent by his Master's city was growing impatient, and while his military bearing seemed attentive, nevertheless at the same time the Athenian gave the contrary impression of being distracted by his own thoughts. And so Jacob without any further courtesies gave Sophroniscus directions back to the Hellene campsite.

"If you go on a straight line due south towards that large outcropping of rock at the far end of our fields, you'll find there a path that leads to the promontory. The campsite, I believe, is near the edge. What a view! Even by moonlight you can see across to Boeotia and several miles each way up and down the Euripus. It should not take you more than twenty minutes to reach the campsite if you follow that path. The boys know the path well."

Sophroniscus glared at Lycon and Lysias. "It seems that they forgot about it. It took over forty minutes for us to come here from the camp. Jacob, what would you do with servants under your authority who do much less than was bid of them?"

Sophroniscus himself had never beaten any of the servants who worked his farm, but he did not like being made a fool of by the two youths. While some of his neighbors, including Clinias, did not hesitate to punish the lazy or headstrong slave with a birch rod, he found that slaves would respond to gentle persuasion skillfully mixed with firm admonition.

"Don't be too hard on them, Sir. The youths, as you have already seen, I'm sure, believe this entire area is haunted by the spirits of angry and revengeful kinfolk. Ten years ago their parents as well as many freemen died along that wooded path. They were ambushed by Saracen archers who had somehow been informed of the approach of our scouting party from Chalcis. Many of us are sure that there had to be someone from among our notable leading men who betrayed their neighbors and perhaps even their own kinfolk. Strange! It was almost exactly ten years ago to the day that the Persians camped at the same promontory where your camp is today. At any rate, our strong-backed and weak-minded youths have heard all the gossip and are terrified of the vengeful spirits they believe haunt that path. While they were only very young boys when all this happened, Lycon and Lysias imagine that, as servants of one of the households rumored to be guilty of betrayal, they too must guard against the angry spirits of their betrayed dead neighbors. Look at them now. They are trembling like a pair of cornered rabbits. Unless, Sir, you intend a punishment more frightening than that evil, nameless though it is, which they fear, you will not correct their paths. If you would take the fastest path with these youths, then it is their imaginations upon which you must make your impressions and not those well-muscled and already oft-flogged insensitive backsides."

Sophroniscus` irritation with the boys was gone. "What a fine steward you must be, Jacob. Let's go boys. You are in my service tonight and surely whatever Greek spirits haunt the path will rejoice to see us making haste to rejoin Hellenes resolved to war with the Medes."

The boys led Sophroniscus at a run through the wooded path. Indeed, he could hardly keep up with them and was about to slow them down. But there just beyond where the trees thinned out and gave way to a rock strewn meadow, he could see the rows of camp fires. "Faster, boys, if you want your supper tonight."

"Halt! Who goes there?" The sentry`s loud and threatening voice made his Dorian dialect sound even more harsh than usual.

"I am Sophroniscus, second officer to Clinias, a captain of an Athenian trireme. Put your spear down! These are Clinias` servants and we are returning from a foray for provisions. Our trireme is moored on the other side of the promontory. We've come back a different way. My crew must be on the other side of the camp." Sophroniscus realized that this had to be the Spartan contingent and that they had entered the south side of the encampment rather than the north side where the Athenians were mustered.

"How do I know you are not a spy? Your speech could be that of a Lydian, or one of those Medizing Ionians from Miletus or Halicarnassus. Or for that matter, we have been warned that there are even some Euboeans who would betray the Hellene cause." While the sentry's spear was still raised, Sophroniscus could see that he had relaxed his arm.

"If you wish, come with me to Clinias, or better yet take me to Themistocles himself, and he will vouch for me."

The sentry mumbled something about Ionians and their damned seafaring, money grubbing merchants and not being able to trust any of them. But he lowered his spear and let Sophroniscus pass. As an afterthought, the sentry barked out from behind Sophroniscus, "*Deme* and tribe?"

Spartan education never ceased to amaze Sophroniscus. No doubt, this Spartan knew the names of all ten of the tribes of Attica, and many of its demes also. "I am from Alopeke. My tribe is Antichis. And I am a landlord, by the way, not a merchant."

"That will do, go on."

Since Clinias' trireme was one of those serving as a rear guard in the passage down the Euripis to Chalcis, and the various contingents of the allied fleet had arrayed themselves at the mile long promontory camp site along a north-south axis so that each crew's camp position corresponded to the order in which the triremes had been beached; Sophroniscus realized he still had to walk the entire length of the camp before he could rejoin Clinias. It would be best, he thought, to work my way directly over to the Euripus side of the camp and then proceed north, first through the Spartan contingent, then the Corinthians, and finally the Athenians, who by far made up the largest number of triremes and men.

As he hurried through the camp, Sophroniscus was struck with the way men shape and make order. Even in war where chaos seems supreme, form rules over difference. Here, assembled as though citizens of one city, were men from thirty one states, many of whom just a few years previously had been at war with one another. Indeed, he himself bore a scar on his right forearm that might very well have been inflicted by that hoplite of Aegina who was now nodding at him as Sophroniscus made his way through the encampments of the Lacedaemonians and their allies of the Peloponnesian League. Sophroniscus counted thirteen different insignias of cities from the Peloponnese and all in a space of what was not much larger than the market-place in Athens. As he worked his way north and now walked as though through a neighborhood of Athens, passing through the men of Corinth and her colonies, Potidaea, Leucas, Anactorium, and Ambracia; he experienced a feeling not unlike that which had so strongly moved him at his first visit to an Olympiad. How strange, he thought, that those who I have counted as enemies and who seemed so alien to life in Athens, now up close and in common endeavor seem in so many respects like many of my neighbors in Attica.

"Sophroniscus, over here!"

It was Clinias and he looked genuinely relieved to see Sophroniscus and the two boys back safely. "I have much to tell you. Megacles arrived here at the camp shortly after you had left for his farm and is now conferring with our Generals. The young man beside me is Megacles nephew, Leobotes. He tells me that his uncle is more than willing to do his part to help provide for the fleets' provisions while the ships are moored here on the island. And, as a token of Themistocles assurance to Megacles that all the animosity of partisan politics in the City has been put aside, Themistocles has just appointed Leobotes as an officer on his own trireme. We are on our way to the altars. All has been made ready for the sacrifice to Poseidon. We will talk at the meal afterwards."

CHAPTER THREE
SACRIFICE TO POSEIDON

When they had scattered barley grain and thus their prayer had made
The bull's head backward drew they, and slew him, and they flayed
His body and cut slices from the thighs, and these in fat
They wrapped and made a double fold, and gobbets raw thereat
They laid and these they burnt straightway with leafless billets dry
And held the spitted vitals Hephaistos' flame anigh—
The thighs they burnt; the spitted vitals next they taste, anon
The rest they slice and heedfully they roast till all is done—
When they had rested from their task and all the banquet dight,
They feasted, in their hearts no stint of feasting and delight.

(Homer. *Iliad*, II: 421)

Throughout the campsite, Dorians, Aeolians and Ionians made their way towards the promontory cliff above the waters of the Euripus. The flickering light from hundreds of camp fires made the soft moon light seem iridescent as thousands of men and their shadows moved toward the sacrificial altar. Officers had positioned their city and company standards, which were hung on poles and hammered into the rocky soil, so that the order of flags traced out a large crescent. As the throngs of citizen-soldiers took up their positions behind their standards, the campsite metamorphosed into what looked like a sprawling amphitheater. Sophroniscus and his crew stood very near the cliff's edge at the most northern end of the semicircular array. From his vantage point he had an unobstructed view of the entire length of multicolored flags and the hastily constructed altar, which stood facing the assembly. The altar had been built no more than a man's length from the edge of the cliff and had been elevated on a mound some three or four feet high. The altar itself was huge. Its hearth was at least six feet across and had been built up from the base of the stone altar so that the flat slabs upon which the burnt offering would be strewn were five feet above the top of the mound. Poseidon's sacrifice would be clearly visible to the thousands of celebrants, even to those who stood far behind the front row spectators. Surely, thought Sophroniscus, King Poseidon, the fosterer of dolphins and Lord of the earthquake, would be pleased by this offering-place. God's altar was eye level to his own awesome stature and broad enough to rest his piercing trident upon.

The sacrifice was about to begin. Three men had emerged from the assembly and took their place next to the altar facing this huge congregation. The garlands of deep orange tiger lilies crowning each of their heads declared to the assembly that these three, and not one man only, would perform the priestly tasks of the sacrifice. Sophroniscus could just barely make out the features of the three priests.

One of them was certainly Themistocles. Even at a great distance, Themistocles' bearing was recognizable to almost every Athenian. While his home was in the deme of Phrearrhi well to the south of the city; for the past decade he had been one of Athens' most visible public figures. Almost singlehandedly he had persuaded the Athenians to set aside for the use of the state the proceeds from the new found silver deposits in Laurium. Following Themistocles'

Figure 1
*Poseidon: inside bottom of late 6th century red-figured wine cup –
Poseidon would have appeared running through a sea of wine as the
drinker emptied the cup.*

plan, the Assembly voted to use the funds earned from the silver mines to construct a fleet of triremes dedicated to the military defense of Athenian mercantile commerce. Then, having demonstrated his superb seamanship and tactical skill in naval warfare, this man of humble origins had won the appointment of Commander of the Athenian fleet. Themistocles was living proof of the opportunities open to all free men in the Athenian Democracy, for neither of his parents hailed from wealthy or notable families. He was shorter than most, prematurely balding from the temples back to the crown of his head, and afflicted with unusually crooked teeth. But despite being less than physically attractive, he had cultivated a demeanor disarmingly amicable and impossible to ignore. Unlike so many of the politicians who were well-born of the oldest and most noteworthy of city families, Themistocles gave every appearance of one who genuinely took an interest in the concerns of even the humblest citizens from the outlying rural townships of Attica incorporated in the Athenian state. Indeed, as a consequence of his own contact with Themistocles, Sophroniscus believed it quite likely that Themistocles knew the name and face of every Athenian citizen.

It was just this cultivation of the favor of the commons by Themistocles that caused suspicion among the *Eupatrids*. Although Sophroniscus family could not be counted among the oldest families of the landed aristocracy, he understood that these powerful aristocratic families feared the politician who marshaled and unified the commoners. This, after all, was the usual path taken by the tyrant. But surely thought Sophroniscus, given the threat of the destruction of Athens by the Persians, all Athenians must put aside such suspicions and rally to support the commander of her ships of war- the people's last and best line of defense.

The young Alkmeonid aristocrat, Leobotes, poked Sophroniscus in his ribs and whispered in his ear. "Look at that purple sash draped over his chiton. Who does Themistocles think he is - the Great King of Persia himself?"

"Shhh! That`s your captain and our commander and if it wasn't necessary for the Alliance to pay service to Spartan pride, Themistocles, the most skillful naval commander of all the Hellenes by far, would be the supreme commander of the entire allied fleet. Besides, next to those other two, Themistocles looks like one of our solid and modestly attired hoplites. The one with his braided hair sporting a purple ribbon interlaced with the garland must be our Supreme Commander, the Spartan Eurybiades. And only a Corinthian could be so ostentatious as to bedeck himself with gold bracelets and such a heavy gold necklace, all topped off by a gold-plated belt around his chiton. If ever there was an oligarch, it's Adeimantus the Corinthian commander.

But enough, it is time to set aside all that would divide us and turn our wills and thoughts to this divine service."

Leobotes frowned and Sophroniscus pretended not to notice.

The sounding of the silver horns signaled the entrance of the consecrated ox. The noise of thousands of muted conversations gave way before the last clarion trill of the company of trumpeters. Each worshiper was called to silence. Now, for a brief moment, the only sounds heard were the voices of Poseidon's realm – the sea borne wind that rustled through the trees on the Promontory and the lapping of the inlet's gentle waves against the rocks down below. Every seaman waited on Lord Poseidon, hoping their reverence would assure their safety as they must soon venture out into the wind-tossed sea. In this sacred silence, when Ionian, Dorian, Corinthian, Spartan, Athenian, rich men and poor men all listened as one for the presence of the divine, each man was receptive to the holy communion that transformed mere mortals into the favored of the immortal Olympians. Every eye followed the procession of the massive black ox as it was led by two fair-haired youths in flowing white robes. Even from where Sophroniscus stood, he could see the yellow reflection of the ox`s gilded horns illuminated by the fire of the altar that would soon consume the animal.

The ox, though it appeared to be somewhat confused and dazed by the bright fire toward which it was being led, plodded forward coaxed by firm but not violent tugs on the rope around his muscular black neck. Then, fifteen yards from the altar, this animal, which had for many Springs faithfully strained before the plow, planted his feet, lowered his head, and would go no further. The youths, aware that in this space before the altar every movement of the victim must be directed by the mysterious forces whose portends can only be read by practiced seers, slackened the ropes that encircled the ox's neck. The ox, it appeared, was willing to play its sacred part. The massive animal shook its head and then on its own accord moved again toward the large silver basin of water that had been placed on the ground off to the side of the altar. The youths allowed the thirsty animal to drink from this basin while they tethered its feet. When the ox had satisfied its thirst, the two youths lifted the still very heavy half full basin and placed it on a tripod before the altar.

In silence and very slowly, so that every eye could take in each liturgical movement, Adeimantus, one of the priests, lit a dried laurel bough from the altar fire. Turning from the altar so that he faced the assembly again, he held the brightly burning torch high above his head which now, with every worshiper, was tilted toward the heavens. He prayed and every Hellene could hear because it was a prayer inscribed in every mind, recited at every family hearth, and the first prayer memorized by every child.

"O, Hecate, only daughter of honored Asteria, Hecate whom Zeus has exalted above all with honors, we call upon you to bless our offering and our enterprises. Receive from our hands your due and may your favor bring to us the kindness of the immortal gods."

In the manner prescribed from ancient times, Adeimantus then dowsed the torch in the silver basin, thus sanctifying the water. Themistocles and Eurybiades joined Adeimantus at the basin and one at a time each washed their hands in the holy water. The youths dried the hands of the priests with fine linen cloths. With pure hands, the priests now motioned for the youths to lift the sacred urn, which was decorated with scenes from the clash of the Titans and the Olympians, so that they might draw barley meal from it. Like the ancient rite practiced during the springtime sowing of seeds, the three priests scattered the barley meal upon the perplexed ox and on the ground around the animal. As the immortal Olympians had subjugated the Titans and imprisoned them deep within the Bowels of Mother Earth in order to found Zeus' new order, so this broad-shouldered strong animal must be plowed under in death so as to secure Poseidon's blessing for the Hellene navy in its struggle against the Titanic Persian forces.

Who would offer the principal prayer of praise and petition to Poseidon? Since Eurybiades was the allied supreme commander, it seemed fitting to Sophroniscus that he assume the most prominent role in the sacrifice. But it was Themistocles who now stepped forward with the palms of his hands outstretched above his head towards heaven. Even the Spartan commander, mused Sophroniscus, deferred to the oratorical eloquence of Themistocles. Among the Athenians who prided themselves upon the ability of any well-educated citizen to speak fluently before the assembly or in the courts, Themistocles was admired not only for the persuasiveness of his speech but also for a remarkable facility in speaking very loudly without giving the impression of yelling so that even those at the very back of the largest and most boisterous city assemblies could hear him. It was in this powerful, but now solemn, voice that he prayed to the Lord of the Sea on behalf of his fellow seafaring warriors

"Hail King Poseidon, lord of the golden trident and fosterer of dolphins, thou who loves the swift triremes with their dark blue bows riding upon the crests of thy wind-driven waves, and the contest of youths who strain for glory and suffer hardship in the chariot race, thou god of mighty steeds and lord of the earthquake, hear our prayer and receive our sacrifice. Grant us thy aid. For your glory, may the wind tossed sea strengthen the onrush of our triremes and confound the barbarians' ships. Strengthen our arms so that our rowers and warriors may fill your temples with trophies of Persian booty, silver and bronze armor, golden cups, and the precious stones that are set in the bracelets and necklaces of Persian slaves.. Accept now this burnt offering and may the shed blood of this broad-shouldered animal consumed by the fire not be mingled with the shed blood of all these who now call upon you."

The climax of the sacrifice was left to Eurybiades. As soon as Themistocles had lowered his arms, Eurybiades drew a gleaming long silver dagger from an ornate gilded case that lay along side a large gold cup on the tripod. Silently and quickly, so as to not alarm the somewhat wary animal, he moved around behind the ox and cut a tuft of hair from near the ox's left flank. Having placed the hair in the burning altar, he motioned to one of the youths who already had raised a large wooden handled stone club behind and above the thick necked black ox.

Although Sophroniscus stood at the far end of the assembly, quite removed from the altar, in the holy silence he could distinctly hear the sound of the blunt heavy stone crashing down upon the great animal's skull and see the once powerful front legs caving in while the massive body of the ox collapsed. Although Sophroniscus had witnessed this scene many times before, it always made him tremble inside. It was as though he felt some kind of ineffable kinship with the stunned animal. The powerful animal had become a victim to forces it could not resist or even foresee. How pathetic that this creature's life would be drained away into a golden cup and there was nothing whatsoever that it could do to stop it. Nothing in its day to day existence, either in the fields behind the plow, or in its barn where it contentedly filled its belly with fodder, could even remotely hint this fate to the dumb animal. It was at this moment most of all that Sophroniscus sensed his own human mortality in the presence of the immortal gods.

While the two youths grasped the gilded horns of the ox and held its head towards heaven, Eurybiades slit the throat of the dazed animal. Dark red blood streamed from the deep gash and was caught in the sacred gold cup held in Eurybiades' left hand. Black, yellow, red, and white images filled Sophroniscus' eyes, but his mind's eye fixed on the red.

Sophroniscus could not help but think of the scene reported by the lookouts just this morning. Leon, a captain of a scouting Athenian trireme, had been captured by a Persian boat. The Persian captain stripped Leon and tied him to the central mast. In clear view of the Greek lookouts posted on the Euboean hilltops, the Persian captain had slowly drawn his sword across his captive's torso, opening up deep wounds from which blood spurted. Because Leon's entreaties could not be heard by the lookouts, the Persian captain derisively shouted out each of Leon's words as his first Athenian victim bled to death. As Sophroniscus watched Eurybiades pour the blood from the golden cup onto the fire of Poseidon's altar, he tried, without succeeding, not to see the stream of Leon's blood trickling from his wounds down his torso, across the ship's deck, and into the sea. Sophroniscus closed his eyes and held back the perplexed and watery melancholy that pressed outward from his soul and up against his closed eyelids.

"Sophroniscus, are you falling asleep? I'm so hungry I could eat your share of meat, spit and all. They're taking so long that Poseidon himself will faint with hunger waiting for his share. Look at these flies. If they don't go any faster, the flies will get the best." Leobotes spoke to Sophroniscus as if they had been intimate friends for years.

How irritating this man is, Sophroniscus thought. Leobotes had now placed a hand on his shoulder and was shaking him as if to awaken a child who had dozed off during a too lengthy religious service. Sophroniscus roughly brushed the hand off his shoulder.

Clinias intervened, "Leobotes, did it ever occur to you that there are some whose reverence surpasses even your appetite? Leave him be! By Zeus, I believe you would have Prometheus stretched on the rack for leaving the fatty portions to the gods. They are almost done now. A little delay can sharpen the delights of the palate. Everyone will get his due and there is an abundance of roast pig. Just one more moment!"

The youths, under the direction of the priests, had now completed skinning and butchering the sacrificial ox in the prescribed manner. The entrails and liver of the victim lay open to inspection and Theophilus, the Athenian seer, came forward from Themistocles' contingent and with great care read the divine portends. The ox's thigh bones, its fatty tissues, and some of the less tasty joints were wrapped in a piece of sail taken from Eurybiades' trireme and with one final accompanying flourish of the trumpets cast into the sea below. Representatives from each of the crews in the fleet now came forward to the altar. All received from the hearth their portion of the communal meal. The sacrifice completed, the assembled Hellenes now returned to their own camp fires for the evening meal.

It was now quite late. Sophroniscus was tired from a hot day on the trireme and his evening trek to the Alkmeonid farm. He wished to slip away after supper to his tent. When Clinias bid good night to Megacles, Sophroniscus turned towards his tent without a courteous good night to Leobotes. But before he could slip away, Clinias called him back. Clinias wanted his officers to hear Leobotes' report of the results of the conference between the Allied Commanders and the Euboean nobles that had occurred earlier that evening in Themistocles' tent. Sophroniscus had had more than enough of this self-impressed young man, but it would be rude and inappropriate for an officer to ask for leave to retire while his captain and fellow officers were willing to stave off sleep in order to hear news from Admiral Themistocles' tent. So, Sophroniscus joined Clinias, Procleus, and Hermistius near the crates of Clinias' personal provisions that had been hauled ashore.

"Let us enjoy one more cup of this Euboean wine...Don't let that lad mix the wine this time. He wants us all to go to sleep so he can cavort with Hermistius' pretty attendant. Two parts water, one part wine this time, Procleus, if you would be so kind to do the honors! Leobotes will explain the Supreme Commanders' thinking on where to engage the Persian barbarians. Sophroniscus pass the figs around one more time and give Hermistius a nudge! He has fallen prey already to Bacchos' spell. Be brief, Leobotes!" Clinias, also, was very tired.

"Clinias, do you really want me to tell your officers about this night's deliberations in Themistocles' tent? Is patriotism well-served by a too intimate knowledge of the disputes within the allied Command? Am I to report on Themistocles' consultation with the Euboean nobles? Or is it best just to report on the instructions the Allied Command has issued tonight?" Leobotes did not wait for Clinias' reply.

"In a word, we will stay put for at least a few days here. But we are to be prepared to disembark at a moments notice." Leobotes paused and although he was at least five years Clinias' junior, he fully expected Clinias to read his furrowed brow and defer to his judgment in omitting much of what he had privately reported to Clinias.

The condescension in Leobotes' tone irritated even Hermistius, who a moment ago had appeared to be nodding off to sleep. And before Clinias, who himself seemed both irritated and embarrassed by Leobotes' presumptuous paternalism, could instruct the young Alkmeonid, Hermistius interjected. "Leobotes, while we have not been so fortunate as to have been personally instructed by such a great teacher of wisdom as Protagoras, still we may be less naive in affairs of state and human nature than you imagine. Why, even our comrade Procleus, who would be the first to acknowledge that his patriotism far outstrips his philosophizing, can read between the lines as to the real reasons for us staying put. What do you think, Procleus?"

"Bickering, indecision and fear - what do you expect from boat loads of Spartan helots, wide-assed Corinthians, and too many mouthy Athenian merchants who cannot see beyond their own noses or the next dollar?"

"Such a way with words!" Hermistius would not let Procleus' remark about Athenian merchants deter him from answering his own question. "Let me explain what Procleus, in his very concise and undiplomatic way, means to say. Eurybiades continues to insist that the fleet should retire to Salamis where it can aid in the defense of the isthmus and thus block the Persian advance into the Peloponnese. Adeimantus is sympathetic to the Spartan proposal, but would prefer a combined land and sea operation against the Persians somewhere in Attica. Both of them, of course, want to save their own forces, hoping that after the Persians have assaulted Attica and have grown either sated with victory or weary of the campaign will not deem it necessary to carry their attack against either Corinth or Sparta. Also, I suspect that there are many in both Corinth and Sparta who would not mind seeing our city's strength humbled. On the other hand, our Themistocles, who, after all, commands most of the ships in the allied navy, threatens to withdraw the large Athenian squadron from the alliance, if the Persians are not engaged somewhere in the vicinity of Euboea far from his own property in Athens and Attica. Then, how about the interests of the Euboeans? More than likely, the wealthy gentlemen from Chalcis and Eritrea have parted with more than what was required by the gods tonight, and their request to make a stand north of Euboea off of Artemisium probably is being reconsidered as strategically attractive. And finally, Leobotes, we stay put not because the plan now is to engage the Persian fleet in the narrow strait here at Chalcis, but simply because this safe distance from the Persians allows us Hellenes to do what we do best. Anyone who attends our Assembly knows what that is. Each one comes to the Assembly Grounds with his own profit in mind, and seeks to persuade all others that his interest is indeed the interest of the entire community. Since we Athenians are especially fond of such disputation and practice it even more than other Hellenes, I am confident that Themistocles' plan will prevail."

"But what is that plan?" The sarcasm in Leobotes' voice made clear his disdain for Themistocles. Whatever others might think about me, I at least, he thought, speak my mind. He could not keep to himself what he had witnessed at Themistocles' tent earlier that evening.

"I wish I could be as confident as you all seem to be about Themistocles looking out for Athens. Bags of silver and gold were brought to his tent by the Euboean nobles before Eurybiades and Adeimantus came to confer. Themistocles shooed everyone, except me his lieutenant, out of the tent while the money was counted. It is not good, he said, for soldiers to know the extent of the resources for provisions since this may dull their valorous appetite for booty. Later, of course, both the Spartan and Corinthian commanders left the conference with their shares supposedly earmarked for provisions for their soldiers. Of course, Themistocles persuaded each of the confederate commanders that these financial arrangements were best kept secret from all others. I could not help but notice that while ten very full leather bags entered Themistocles' tent, only four bags tied with much slack at the tops left the tent with the Spartan and the Corinthian, both of whom appeared to be quite pleased with what they believed to be their fair share of the campaign's finances. Of course there are more Athenian ships, but many of them like yours, Clinias, have been outfitted and provisioned by their captains. Perhaps Themistocles will reimburse all those like you who have from their own property outfitted their ships."

Seeing that this talk about bags of silver and gold had especially aroused Hermistius' interest, Leobotes continued, "I'm sure Themistocles, eloquent as he is, will explain all this after the Persians have been sent back to Susa. And no doubt, the trireme now leaving for Argos captained by Themistocles' brother-in-law carries four very full bags of gold and silver to requisition Argive reinforcements. After all, Themistocles is very good at handling such money matters. Consider how fast he has made a fortune! Just a few years ago no one had heard of Themistocles. No one then would ever have guessed that a man born of a foreign mother in one of our more remote townships near Sunium now resides in one of the city's most luxurious homes among Athens' most prestigious and oldest families. Only four years ago, this man's family eked out a carpenter's livelihood crafting the hulls of our commercial ships. But now much of the silver of Laurium has found its way into the pockets of this family of shipwrights. How tireless and patriotic were Themistocles' efforts to persuade the good citizens of Athens' to use the riches of Laurium for the state to commission the construction of hundreds of expensive war ships. Yes, where much money is to be had I am confident that Themistocles will be on the look out for what is most advantageous. When most Athenians were green with envy over the good fortune of those prospectors who discovered and laid claim to those silver veins which today, three years later, appear to be richer than any hitherto found in Attica, Themistocles gave himself to unswerving service to the state. Under his leadership in the Assembly one twenty fourth of Laurium's deposits has been claimed by the state treasury. Yet, our treasury is almost empty today. Themistocles' family is very wealthy, and under his leadership our city is advised to contract with his family and friends for our state's security. May the gods preserve our Admiral who so selflessly serves Athens!"

The sarcasm in Leobotes' tone left no doubt that he thought the worst of Themistocles. And when Leobotes' insinuations registered on the faces of even Hermistius' and Procleus' personal slaves, Clinias' patience with Leobotes gave way to anger. With clenched fists as though he was disciplining a wayward child, Clinias lashed out in reprimand.

"Leobotes, you can be such a jackass! You really don't know anything do you? Is Nicias a bad citizen because of the fortune he earned leasing slaves for the state mining operations at Laurium? Is Hermistius a bad citizen because he and his fellow merchants joined to persuade the Assembly to use the state's triremes to clear the Aegean of those pirates that robbed him and his colleagues of their trade goods? Is your own family, which has doubled its own wealth in the last five years by shipping grain from the Black Sea regions, seditious because they persuaded the Assembly to offer protection from Persian ships to Athenian round-bottoms as they make their way through the Hellespont filled with grain for our market place? Is Procleus a bad citizen because he dreams of Persian booty? What are you saying? That anyone who serves the city must forfeit every interest of his own? You cannot be that stupid. Or is it that your own envy has blinded you to what makes for greatness in our city's leading citizens. It is precisely those who can pursue their own interests in such a way that it improves the lives of many citizens who also best and most devotedly serve the city. If you do not agree with these leading citizens, then it is to the Assembly and the Courts that you must take your complaints. Do not trouble our citizen soldiers with such matters when they must stand shoulder to shoulder in common defense of our city. In the future you will keep such petty and small-minded opinions to yourself if you wish to serve the city well as a soldier and officer. Now it is late and you should return to your own crew."

Leobotes, hurt and disappointed by Clinias' scolding, realized that it was pointless to argue further. Meekly, he gathered his cloak around his shoulders, politely bid good night, and with wounded pride made off to his own campsite.

Twilight had given way to a very dark night as both stars and the moon had disappeared behind thick clouds. The rumble of thunder and forks of lightening over the hilltops of Euboea and a cool wind from the northeast all signaled an imminent thunder storm

"It is good that our fleet is in the straits. It looks like a Hellespontian blowing in. No trireme is a match for Lord Boreas in the open sea. Let us pray that Persian ships meet with the might of Boreas. Our crew and officers are not responsible tonight for sentry duty. I don't know about you, but I am ready to bed down for the night."

Sophroniscus, who shared a large tent with Clinias, answered for the three officers. ""Yes, Clinias, we are all tired. Let us hope Boreas this night is our friend. I will secure the tent against the wind. If you would unroll the mattresses, we don't need to awaken your servants." Sophroniscus and Clinias disappeared into their tent as Procleus and Hermistius with their young slaves made their way to separate tents.

CHAPTER FOUR
GYGES' FIRST FIGHT

And again, three other sons were born of Earth and Heaven, great and doughty beyond telling, Cottus and Briareus and Gyges, presumptuous children. From their shoulders sprang an hundred arms, not to be approached, and each had fifty heads upon his shoulders on their strong limbs, and irresistible was the stubborn strength that was in their great forms. For of all the children that were born of Earth and Heaven, these were the most terrible, and they were hated by their own father from the first.

(Hesiod. *Theogony*, II: 147-163)

Surely, the gods had heard their petitions. For two nights and two days, a Northeaster battered the Persian fleet, which had moored off the cape of Sepias. Although the ships close to the beach had been pulled ashore; the sheer size of the Persian fleet required that many of the boats be anchored at a considerable distance from the shore line, and these were caught by the suddenness of the storm's arrival. Lookouts on the Euboean hilltops reported that many Persian ships had been driven by the high winds and heavy sea onto the rocks and had smashed to pieces. While no one could be sure of the extent of the Persian losses, the scouts estimated that approximately four hundred war ships had been destroyed along with an even larger number of merchant vessels and other smaller boats.

The indecision and fear that had kept the Allied Fleet far from the Persian fleet now disappeared along with the dark storm clouds. Led by the large Athenian contingent, the entire Allied Fleet rowed north through the Euripus until it reached Artemisium again. It was mid-afternoon by the time Clinias' trireme laid anchor a few hundred yards off shore with its bow facing out to sea. Believing the Persian fleet to be greatly diminished and exhausted, the Allied Fleet would seek to engage the enemy this day before sunset.

Since battle now seemed imminent, Clinias had cleared the deck for action and was now instructing his crew once again on the crucial tactical elements of naval engagement. Some of his fighting men, like Procleus the Plataean, had never before served on a trireme deck. It was necessary, thought Clinias, to make sure that these soldiers understood how to coordinate their actions with the rowers' maneuvers. Clinias mounted the turret from which he would captain the ship during battle. This narrow elevated platform traversed the width of the deck and stood just in front of the position manned by the tiller men who handled the two large steering oars at the stern. The turret was completely portable since its supporting poles could be removed from their sockets on the deck floor. From this platform, some six feet above the deck, the captain could not only direct the tiller men, but also communicate directly with the officer stationed on the hold ladder so that he might convey the captain's orders to the rowers. In the din of battle, the captain could not make himself heard all the way up to the bow, but from this turret he could survey every operation of the men. It was to this commanding position that, in time of confusion, the officers throughout the trireme looked for direction. Each of the three deck officers would also be stationed on elevated turrets, two on each side at mid-ship and one at the bow. All eyes now were turned upward as Clinias began with instructions to the eighteen soldiers.

"Men, today some of you will be fighting for the very first time from a trireme deck. It is absolutely essential if we are to be victorious that each of you keep to your station and do exactly as you have been trained to do in the last few weeks. There is no room on a trireme for a frenzied warrior, no matter how brave, who roams the deck of an engaged ship, cutting a bloody path of slain enemies before him. It is even more urgent here than among the ranks of a *hoplite* formation that we fight as a unit and do not abandon our assigned tasks. Soldiers, you are the hands, the rowers are the feet, and I must be the head. If our Athenian trireme is superior to all others, it is because we free men work together in the spirit of a disciplined equality guided by intelligence. You can be sure that our Athenian triremes will be marked out by the Persians and will bear the brunt of the battle since they believe we are the best in the fleet. Let us not disappoint the enemy. If we remain firm and steadfast in our resolve to act as one, our enemy will indeed be disordered and fall prey to chaotic defeat. I cannot foresee every circumstance that might arise, but each of you above board must deal with every danger while doing your utmost to stay at your station. All of our ability to steer out of harm's way depends upon a well-balanced boat. We cannot change direction quickly if you are all on one side. Now, men, you know we are going to be trying to ram other ships. Don't panic if an enemy should approach us from the stern. It is the job of our four archers to ward them off and shield our tiller men. It is your job to assault our enemy. You have javelins, slings, rocks, and heated coals at your disposal. Use them only on command! There will be a chaos of ships in close quarters. We may have to either push an enemy away or draw closer, depending on who has the advantage. Wait for the command to use the boat-hooks."

Sophroniscus listened attentively as Clinias reviewed tactical procedures for the fighting men. He was by now very familiar with all this and found this very familiarity a comfort. Sophroniscus manned the starboard side turret mid-ship and coordinated ten of the infantrymen from this station. Procleus would be stationed at the turret near the bow with three other infantry men and Hermistius would man the turret on the port side mid-ship

It pleased Sophroniscus that Clinias entrusted him with what on Clinias' trireme was both the most clever and most crucial of all tactical uses of infantrymen. Clinias had arranged his rowers so that the strongest men were deployed toward the stern on the starboard side. This deployment had been so carefully apportioned by Clinias, that he was able to achieve a surprisingly superior capability with respect to the average trireme. In an instant, Clinias could swing his one hundred and fifty feet long trireme into a ninety degree turn to the starboard side. The speed with which he could execute this maneuver was so extraordinary that it would be unlikely that any oncoming boat could be prepared for such a tactic. Accordingly, one of Clinias' favorite ploys consisted of appearing rather sluggish as an enemy ship would approach. Allowing his boat to be temporarily outmaneuvered, Clinias' trireme appeared to be temptingly vulnerable to ramming on its starboard side. This tactic had been so thoroughly developed by Clinias that it included a scurrying about of the crew, as if they were reacting to an imminent ramming. Like one of Aeschylus' well rehearsed choruses, Sophroniscus and his midshipmen presented to the enemy captain the spectacle of a panicked crew. Should the enemy captain take the bait, Clinias would wait until the last possible moment and then turn sharply about on the overconfident onrushing attacker. With Clinias' own bow now turned towards the long outstretched oars of the surprised and confused enemy ship, his antagonist now faced the prospect of either withdrawing his own starboard oars or having them shorn off by the bow of Clinias suddenly charging trireme. In either case, the enemy's maneuverability would be severely limited, rendering him a vulnerable target for Clinias' firepower. Of course, thought Sophroniscus, this tactic could only be used in the kind of engagement in which individual triremes squared off against one another, like the great heroes who fought beneath Troy's walls. The most difficult kind of maneuvering was required when large numbers of triremes operated in close quarters against the enemy. Rowers needed to be able to ignore the din all around them and continue to respond to every command with precision.

Having finished his instructions to the soldiers, Clinias descended from his turret and made his way to the hold ladder. He went down the ladder until he was entirely visible to the rowers. Since almost all of the rowers were Athenian citizens, it was not possible to hear in his tone as he addressed them any hint of condescension or imperiousness. "Each of you, I'm sure, understands that all of our success depends upon every rower's complete dedication to excellence.

Your shield and sword are these oars. Should you drop them or fail to pull shoulder to shoulder as one mighty company, we all will..." The sentence was unfinished. It was drowned out by the clamor that arose from the triremes further down the line.

Clinias hurried on deck and scanned the horizon to the southeast. Immediately he saw the cause of the commotion. He called out to Sophroniscus, who from his mid-ship turret was counting the now clearly visible boats approaching from the southeast. "I see only fifteen triremes and they are not any of ours. They must be part of the Persian fleet. Is it a trick of some kind? Surely they can see our fleet now, but they keep coming toward us."

No matter how Sophroniscus squinted through the glare of the sea, there was not even the tiniest speck to be seen in the open sea beyond the formation of triremes now continuing to edge closer to the Allied Fleet. "Yes, there are just fifteen. There is nothing coming behind them. Are you sure they are not reinforcements?" The approaching triremes seemed identical to the Athenian warships. Even the flags looked the same to Sophroniscus.

Clinias mounted Sophroniscus' turret in order to get a better look. "Sophroniscus, we will know in a few moments. I can already almost make out the emblem on the flags. I know that Persian officers are aboard every one of their warships. Look for those felt caps and trousers those dandies love to strut. Half of their damn fleet are probably from the islands and are manned by Ionians who sail under compulsion." The thought occurred to Clinias, even as he spoke these words, that perhaps these fifteen ships were deserters and the Persian officers had been dumped overboard.

Themistocles and Eurybiades had already passed the signal for thirty ships to form up in a semicircle and intercept the fifteen ships, whoever they were. Clinias' trireme was one of the twenty Athenian and ten Corinthian ships that now made their way towards the yet unidentified ships. How difficult it is, thought Clinias, to fire my men's courage and to hold it at that high temperature needful for victory when everything is always so uncertain. Are we about to welcome brothers in arms or send enemies to a watery grave, he wondered.

"They're signaling us, Clinias, but it's not with any of our codes." Sophroniscus was now able to see the crew on the deck of the lead ship. This ship had suddenly turned sharply starboard and was now leading the other fourteen ships to open sea away from the fleet that had not responded to its signal. "They are wearing Greek armor and I see an Apollo mounted at the stern. They must be Aeolians or Ionians. Look - there, at mid-decks! They are definitely Persian officers, but the crew is Greek."

"Yes, Sophroniscus, they are lost and just now realize that we are not their own fleet. No doubt Hermistius, at some time or another, has done business with somebody on those boats. But they'll fight us now. Xerxes, you can be sure, has their wives and children in his power. Since they have already been at sea some time and the current runs against them, we can certainly overtake them

While Clinias returned to the stern turret, Sophroniscus watched the distance close between the enemy ships and his own. With pursuit underway, the men above and below deck joined in a *paean* to Athena but then became solemnly silent. Hermistius had not said a word since the ships had been sighted. Sophroniscus could see that while he appeared to be busy adjusting the wrist strap on his shield, he was trembling and beads of sweat covered the forehead beneath his helmet. Sophroniscus could not help but feel sorry for this merchant whose unproven martial manhood was being painfully displayed upon the turret. He will be alright once the action starts, thought Sophroniscus. Down near the bow, Procleus had put on his battle demeanor and, with a scowl every bit as intimidating as Ares the boar, was flexing his arm sword in hand.

Sophroniscus would not let fear enter his consciousness. From his mid-ship turret, which extended slightly out over and above the side of the trireme, he could watch the action of the oars that now drove the Gyges forward at pursuit speed. He focused his mind on this power. The long oars rising and falling, cutting powerfully through the turquoise water, always in unison, looked like the arms of a living creature. Looking down along the side of the ship towards the stern, Sophroniscus could see the leather bags that encased each oar as it protruded from the innards of the boat. If one did not know of the human bodies that strained and sweated in the cramped quarters of the rowers' benches, these rounded pulsing skin-like things seemed like the sinewy shoulders of some many-armed monster. From deep within the Gyges' chest and belly came the sound of straining life, the muted measured beat of the drum followed closely by the softer pulsing of labored breath–the life force that drove her now through the sea in chase of prey. Sophroniscus eyed his own sword and the javelins near at hand. The Gyges' teeth, he thought, and they must rip and tear the life from the invading enemy. Like the iron that must shortly cleave and push through living tissue, he must be hard and without compassion.

Only one hundred yards now separated the lead Athenian trireme from the fleeing enemy warships, which were now strung out in a horizontal line. It appeared that in their haste to escape, the enemy had abandoned any formation that would aid mutual defense. With already tired rowers and the lack of a concerted defense, thought Sophroniscus, these ships would be very vulnerable. The semicircular array of Athenian and Corinthian triremes moved in on their prey, half encircling the entire line of the enemy. Already the Athenian triremes on the right wing were pushing the enemy boats inward at the northern end of the line. The ten Corinthian triremes were in position to exert the same pressure on the other end of the enemy's line. When the outnumbered enemy ships were fully contained within the closing circle, they would find it next to impossible to escape.

"There will be close-in fighting," shouted Clinias. "There is only one Phoenician boat and I see very few archers or spear throwers. We will try to ram. Be prepared to board, but we will go only if it is clear that we have the advantage. Now, helmsmen, make for that ship flying the Paphos banner! Quick, while she is still facing the attacker off her prow! Rowers, ramming speed! Archers, aim for her helmsmen!"

The Gyges hurled herself through the water, bearing down with her massive prowl aimed squarely at the enemy ship's mid-section. Sophroniscus could see the beleaguered captain trying to direct evasive action and maintain discipline among a crew that was close to panic. There was no sign of any willingness to surrender, so the enemy ship must be sunk or taken in tow. There was no escape for her. With one attacker just twenty yards off her bow and the Gyges even closer off her port side, the Paphian captain had withdrawn the port side oars and in desperation ordered blunt poles to be used to ward off the ramming prow. Beside the captain stood a white-robed and unarmed man, a priest no doubt, who seemed to be making some kind of petition and offering to the statue of the god that was mounted on the Paphian ship's stern. It is probably Adonis, thought Sophroniscus, since Paphos was famous for its spectacular temple dedicated to this god.

Sophroniscus braced himself. Like the powerful jaws of a praying-mantis snapping off the hopelessly thin wavering legs of a spindly legged spider, the Gyges' ram splintered and snapped off the long boat hooks that pitifully reached out to ward her off. The snapping boat hooks did nothing to soften the impact of blood-thirsty Ares the boar. The massive bronze cast boar's snout mounted on the Gyges' reinforced oak prow smashed through the mid-section of the Paphian boat just below its deck. Sophroniscus' arm jerked taut while the rest of his body seemed to hurl itself forward away from the hand that with white knuckles clenched the turret railing. As though it were some cruelly driven spear blade, the Gyges' pointed bronze ram seemed to twist and tear sideways in the split second before its deep thrust ended. Sophroniscus' thigh, just above the knee where his tunic ended, burned as his body lurched sideways and scraped against the railing pole in his turret.

"Procleus, keep them off! Back row! Harder! The rest of you, back towards the stern! Hermistius, Sophroniscus, move your men quickly and keep those shields over your heads!" Although he shouted at the top of his lungs to make sure that his orders could be heard all the way up and down his trireme, Clinias remained completely composed.

Despite the back rowing, the Gyges was still coupled with her enemy. Clinias had to get a closer look at the hole in the enemy ship and the condition of his own prow. How are we hung up, he wondered? Am I into her up to my keel? He descended quickly from his stern command turret and ordered his body servant to cover his back while he, shield in hand, moved toward the bow. A javelin ricocheted off his shield and a flurry of arrows pounded into the walkway just a few feet behind him. Peering around his shield and out from under his helmet, Clinias made his way carefully past Hermistius' and Sophroniscus' men until he was only some twenty feet from the bow.

"Sophroniscus, take three of your men and assist Procleus!"

Clinias could see that Procleus needed help. One of his three soldiers lay on his back in a pool of blood writhing in pain trying to withdraw the shaft of an arrow that had struck him in the groin. Procleus, with blood streaming down his left shoulder, stood facing two enemy swordsmen. These men were attempting to force their way on board the Gyges by way of a plank that had been laid over the splintered debris. The remaining two of Procleus' hoplites were completely occupied with covering Procleus' sides from an onslaught of javelins and arrows.

The difference between victory and defeat, Clinias realized, depended on keeping the enemy off his own ship. His orders were passed up and down the entire length of the ship. "Make sure that no ropes are attached! Keep their planks off! They must not board while their numbers remain high! We must get free of them! Take the boat hooks! We'll have to leverage our prow off while we back row!"

Clinias, still careful to shield himself, moved to the very edge of his deck and leaned way out over the railing, so that his upper body was horizontal to the water below. With blood flowing under his feet, and the clashing of swords mixed with the groans and curses of men bent on slaughter, he calmly appraised the extent of the gaping hole that his ram had opened up in the enemy ship. Apparently the ram had hit into the hull low and then thrust upwards. For although the ram was still in the enemy's hull just below the decking, Clinias could see that the actual hole was a good five feet in diameter and at least a foot of it was below the water line. Just beneath the place where the Gyges' ram jutted into the splintered hull, Clinias could see into the entrails of the mortally wounded Paphian trireme. Water was pouring into the hull so fast that the rowers stationed at the lowest array of benches were already submerged up to their waists. While Clinias could only see the three rows of benches that were exposed by the tear in the hull, what he saw there told him that this ship was his. A fallen beam had pinned three men so that they were unable to work their oars since they were on their backs beside the benches for the second tier of oars. Broken bones protruded out of a grisly pile of splintered wood and contorted bodies. Those rowers who were not injured had abandoned all efforts to bale or do anything else that might save their ship. Slaves, crazed by fear, each frantically sought to free themselves of those chains that would drag them to the bottom with their master's sinking ship. At most, thought Clinias, the Paphian trireme would be above water another fifteen minutes or so. He only needed to free the Gyges from her to make sure his crew would suffer no further harm.

He stretched his body out over the side even further, straining to see the precise point at which the bronze boar's head ram on his prow was stuck in the wooden hull of the Paphian trireme. He could now clearly see what was snagged. A still attached part of the oak ribbing in the hull of the Paphian ship had broken and twisted in such a way that it lay cradled in the top-side curvature of the Gyges ram. "Damn," he muttered to himself. "What a mess! It better not be wedged in tight."

Clinias pulled himself in and quickly mounted the mid-ship turret so as to oversee what could be a very difficult and dangerous operation–disengaging the prow of the Gyges from the innards of a frenzied and mortally wounded warship. First, he looked around to make sure that no other boats were coming to the aid of his prey. There was no remaining threat from any quarter. The only enemy ships still moving about were racing for open sea to the northeast. Clinias was free to concentrate on detaching the Gyges. Victory could turn to disaster if he could not withdraw his ram from the dying carcass of this sinking ship.

Clinias called to the officer at the hatch. "Move all the ballast to the bow! We must lower the bow if we're to get clear! Once the ballast lowers the bow, back row, but only with the thirty rowers closest to the bow!"

Still the Gyges would not come free.

Clinias could not see the ram, but he could hear bronze grinding against wood. "Just a little more and we will be off! Move the stern rowers towards the bow, while the others work their oars!"

"We are away!" shouted Procleus.

The Gyges indeed was free of her victim.

"Quickly, everyone back to their station! Let's not capsize ourselves!" Clinias sighed with relief.

Sophroniscus wiped the sweat from his eyes and whispered a prayer of thanksgiving to Athena for their good fortune. He had heard far too many stories of interlocked triremes perishing together. While he and his comrades were now safe, it still required considerable discipline not to be unnerved by the screams of the rowers that came across the water from inside the water-filled hull of the vanquished trireme.

"Sophroniscus, run me through with your sword, if I ever scream like those cowards." Procleus was really speaking to his wounded hoplite. As soon as the Gyges was clear, Procleus had rushed to treat the young man who had taken an arrow in the groin. "Only slaves can cry and moan and groan like that. Here, my young hero, bite on this silver obol while I take this arrow out of you. You'll be fucking before you know it. Everything is all right. No womanly archer is going to do you in. Don't bite that coin in half! It has made it through many of my own wounds. It's out. Bring bandages and salt and get him out of the sun!"

Sophroniscus marveled at Procleus' efficient treatment. Although his language was rough, his hands were tender and solicitous as he treated the young man's wound.

"Would middle-aged, homely me get that treatment from you if I were wounded there?" Hermistius had regained his composure and had joined his fellow officers on the deck. His jocularity aimed to dispel any doubt about his battle worthiness.

"Hermistius, for you I would borrow a penny and insist you get it up so I could be sure I could see where the little thing is. I would not want to cut it off by mistake."

Clinias cut the playful bantering short. "Men, keep your eye on that captain. He might be worth a king's ransom! If he does not hail us in the next few moments, he's going to go down with his ship. As badly damaged as she is, there is no way we can take her in tow or board her and find booty. We will stand off her only a few more moments, then we must move on and assist where we can with other enemy ships."

Suddenly there were no more cries coming from below deck in the Paphian ship. The Paphian trireme had already become a watery grave for the several hundred rowers who were chained to the benches below deck. Without honor or memorial of any kind, the miserable existence of slaves, those who had perhaps forfeited their manhood somewhere else in order to escape death, would end in soulless anonymity. The stern of the ship was now fully submerged and only the Adonis mounted on the bow and a small section of the decking where the bow turret still stood were yet above water. The soldiers had jumped overboard and all that remained alive on board were the captain and two of his officers. They stood precariously perched on what was left of the deck near the bow. They were frantically untying the small skiff that was leashed to the bow railing at the feet of Adonis. When the captain saw his officers begin to lower the skiff, he quickly mounted the turret and with all the dignity he could summon up called out to the Athenian captain.

"Sir, I am Penthylus, prince of Paphos and supreme commander of the Cypriot triremes. My father Demonous rules Paphos the sacred city of our beloved Astarte, the same Aphrodite whom you revere. I request permission to come aboard your ship with my two officers and the chest you see at my feet. Spare our lives and it will profit you greatly."

Clinias had already lowered two rope ladders down the side of Gyges and instructed his men to offer rescue to those enemy soldiers who were yet floundering about in the water. Since these men did not understand any of the Greek dialects, but spoke a Semitic tongue, many of them swam away from Clinias' ship, sure that a more horrible death than that of drowning awaited them if picked up by the Athenian trireme. The Paphian captain had made his appeal in the Ionian Greek spoken in Athens and had done so without even the trace of a foreign accent. Although with his bright red turban and purple britches, this captain Penthylus was dressed in the Phoenician manner, Clinias was not surprised by his Greek speech. Athenian merchants had been doing business in Paphos' port for years. Indeed, while Phoenicians now controlled all of Cyprus, it was common knowledge that a sizable number of Paphians were descended from settlers who came from Salamis and Attica a little over a century ago.

Hearing Penthylus' flawless Ionian made it difficult for Clinias to regard this vanquished enemy as a barbarian seeking the destruction of the mother city of all the Ionians, Athens. Nevertheless, no decent officer would be so cavalier with the safety of his own crew.

"You may come aboard, but it will be my crew who sees you disregarding the lives of your own crew that will decide what is to be done with your life. You will toss your swords and knives up on our deck before you climb the rope ladder. We will haul your chest up before you board. I am Clinias, son of Alcibiades, citizen of Athens."

While Clinias and his officers watched the stern of the Paphian trireme disappear into the sea, they could see that not one ship of the enemy squadron had escaped. All were either sinking or were now being disarmed so as to be towed back to the Allied base on the beaches of Artemisium. As Clinias waited for his captive, the Paphian captain, to come aboard, he knew that future engagements with the enemy would not be so easy. While there was nothing to criticize in his crew's performance, he could not let them fall prey to overconfidence. Yet, he was thankful that this first engagement with a contingent of the Persian fleet, even if it was only fifteen ships that had lost their way, had been completely successful.

"Captain Clinias hear me out before you and your men decide my fate." The Paphian captain had begun to speak even before he stepped from the rope ladder over the railing onto the Gyges' deck.

"I know you believe me to be a coward and worthy of slavery or a dishonorable death, but consider this. I had no desire to fight against my mother's people. Her family came to Paphos from Sunium in Attica. Like so many in Xerxes' service, my father was required to provide ships or himself face the wrath of the Great King. How would my dying so as to make other free men the servants of a despot I have no love for make me feel honorable? I am young, only twenty-five years old, and yet hungry for life. What good is such empty honor if I'm dead? Yes, the chest is full of gold coins. My father does not wish me to perish. The coins are only a tenth of the ransom he will send you if I am delivered safely back to Paphos. I led ten ships all of which now lie at the bottom of the sea. I lost five brothers and many comrades because of the stupidity of a Persian admiral who disregarded the advice of Ionian sailors. They saw the signs of the coming northeaster and pleaded with the Persian command to move the fleet around the cape of Sepias and to safety. By the time the Persians realized the soundness of this advice, it was too late. The storm drove many of our ships, including nine of my squadron, into the rocks and now I am the only surviving son of my father. Twice, the stupidity of others has threatened me with a pointless death. Just now, Sandoces, Xerxes' Aeolian lackey, did not have the good judgment to hug the cape and stay in sight of the main fleet. So he led us into the hands of the enemy fleet, mistaking them for his own. If wealth cannot be used to reverse the consequences of such bad luck, then the gods are indeed pitiless of all men. Clinias, spare me that I may entertain you some day in Paphian splendor."

While Penthylus made his plea, Clinias searched out this young captain's face. He knew almost instantly that this handsome youth would not be slain by him. While the youth's face was tanned a deep brown, his skin appeared to be very soft and although he was clearly a young man, there was no sign of a beard. He had high cheek bones, piercing bright blue eyes, and coal-black curly hair, which now had come loose from his red turban and lay in thick curls on his forehead. He, thought Clinias, is far too beautiful to kill.

His words were not that eloquent, but apparently Penthylus had affected Clinias' officers in the same way. Even Procleus, who was in love, no doubt, with his young hoplite protégée, appeared anxious to rid the young man of his fears and assure him of his safety. Perhaps it was not just his beauty, but the sadness in his young eyes as he spoke of his desire for life and the ill fortune that now could send him into darkness. Who would not wish to save Adonis from blood-thirsty Ares for lovely Aphrodite, if he could?

"And what about your two officers? Clinias tried to sound harsh, but he found himself almost embarrassed before his men as he labored to hide the softness that the young man's charm had touched.

"These men are my father's most trusted aids. They are responsible for my safekeeping. My father, Demonous, will be very grateful if his son returns with his two most loyal palace officers."

Clinias turned to Hermistius who was trying to get his attention. All the while Penthylus had been making his plea, Hermistius could not take his eyes off the chest. Hermistius spoke softly, but just loud enough for Procleus and Sophroniscus to hear. "Clinias, there is probably at least a talent of gold coins here. This man's safety may indeed be worth ten such chests of gold to the Athenian treasury. I have been to Paphos and have been entertained by this prisoner's father. He is a very wealthy governor. If this Penthylus is who he claims to be, he very well may bring even more ransom then ten talents. I know you are offended by this young prince's apparent disregard for his fellows who have perished. Moreover it would be sweet to avenge Leon's cruel death in like fashion. But I would be in favor of sparing his life so that his ransom might be used by Athens to vanquish all her enemies."

Clinias acknowledged Hermistius' advice with a nod.

"Procleus, take Penthylus and his officers to the hold! When we have arrived at camp, we will interrogate them further and decide what is to be done. Now I see the signal to return to Artemisium. We will go slowly. We must conserve the strength of our rowers in case the enemy should challenge us before sunset."

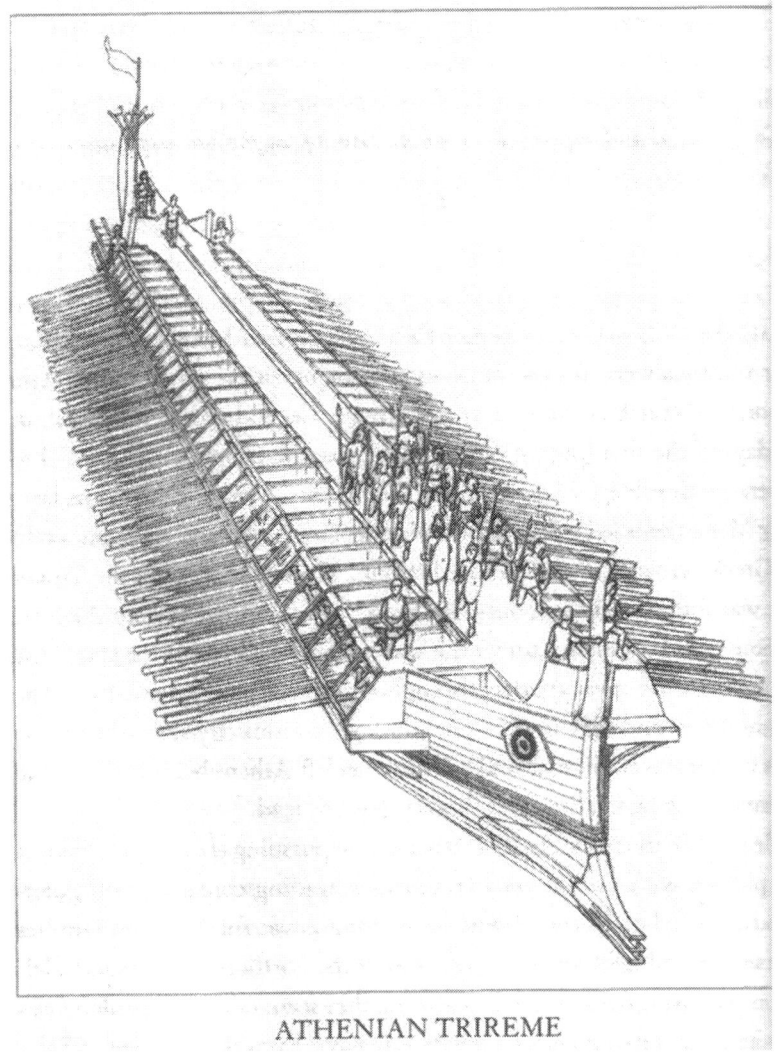

ATHENIAN TRIREME

Figure 2
Athenian Trireme

PART TWO
Scenes of City Life in Democratic Athens
Religion, Civic Virtue, and Politics
461 B.C.

CHAPTER FIVE
ANTHESTERIA: FESTIVAL OF GHOSTS AND EVER RENEWING LIFE
(Spring of 461 B.C.)

And so hail to you, Dionysos, god of abundant clusters.

Grant that we may come again rejoicing to this season,

and from that season onwards for many a year.

    (*Homeric Hymns*. XXVI *To Dionysos* 11. 10-13)

Wherefore, my lord and master, receive this deity, whoe'er he be, within the city; for, great as he is in all else, I have likewise heard men say, 'twas he that gave the vine to man, sorrow's antidote.' Take wine away and Cypris flies, and every other human joy is dead.

    (Euripides. *The Bacchantes*)

The young boy was awakened by the sound of the buzzing insect that had alighted on the end of his nose. As he opened his eyes the blurred outline of this bug, just an inch or so from his eyes, loomed large like some monstrous creature sent by angry gods to terrorize a sinner. The first rays of the morning sun had arrived through the window of his small room. Soft yellow light shone through the transparent, outstretched wings of what, he now realized, was a honey bee.

The boy fought back the sudden urge to smack his nose. Since his school mates already teased him about his unusually short, broad, and stubby nose; it would be more than he could bear to have them see it stung and swollen during the processions of today's holiday. So he remained perfectly still, hoping that the bee would soon get on with his business, which certainly could have nothing to do with walking on his nose. Sure enough, the bee took to wing and buzzed out the window.

It was a good omen, the boy thought, for spring was surely here. The warmer south winds of the last few days seemed to have broken the hold of winter. The first buds on the sycamore trees had already begun to open, the crocuses were now in full bloom, and now a bee in his room. And this day, the 12th of Anthesterion, he had been looking forward to for over a month. His father had let it slip that today he would give him a very special present, not the usual miniature painted wine-jar of which he now possessed five. Since he was eight, his father had explained, it was time for a different kind of gift.

Still lying on his cot, he listened for sounds of others up and about. His father had not been well of late. The bad left knee had gotten worse and for the last year or so he needed the assistance of a servant to move about. The knee had never recovered from a wound suffered six years ago during his last military tour in the Persian wars. One of the boy's earliest memories - he had to have been no more than 2 years old - was the combination of curiosity and horror he felt as he watched his mother change the dressing on his father's battered knee. The mutilated knee cap had never healed properly and still required attention. His father never complained though and, just in the last year, had explained to his son that he regarded his mangled knee as a fair price to pay in order to have served with Cimon at Eurymedon - where Athenians in one day defeated Saracen warriors on both sea and land.

The bad knee, he understood. What alarmed the boy was the strange bump on the back of his father's neck. It was just below where the skull bone begins. The bump had become visible just over a year ago and had slowly but steadily grown larger since then. Just in the last month or so, his dad found that he could no longer use the cane, which he had carried in his right hand in order to take weight off his knee. His entire right arm had lost all feeling and it now hung limp at his side completely useless. And so his father, not yet sixty, had become an invalid who required the assistance of others to rise from his bed or to climb onto the family's cart. It seemed to the boy that there was some connection between the odd swelling on the back of his father's neck and his recent loss of the use of his arm. But he was too frightened to say this to anyone. Besides, there seemed to be nothing that could be done, since his father had already made it clear that he would never allow a physician or surgeon near him. Too many of his comrades, he said, had died of miserable infections and gangrene after the surgeon had cut them and taken their money.

"Socrates! Socrates!" It was his father calling him. "Come to my room, I will need your help to get me up and to the table for breakfast. Your mother has gone to the fields to find fresh flowers for your sister's hair, so you are going to have to help me."

"I'll be right there. I am getting dressed. Where are Hasdrubal and Hamilcar?"

"Don't you remember?" There was irritation in his father's voice. "They took off yesterday for the city and probably are rousting about there. They won't be back to their work until dusk tomorrow. Our slaves probably have more holidays than their free compatriot tradesmen in Tyre."

Socrates hurried from his small room through the common room to his father's quarters on the west side of their sturdy stone cottage. He entered his father's room and took his father's chiton and cloak off the peg where they had been hung the night before. While smoothing out the cloak, which he had draped over his own elbow, he looked about for his father's sandals and cheerfully saluted his father with the holiday greeting. "May the fruit of our vines and fields always be health-giving. May Bacchos always fill our table and cups with the good things of the earth. God bless us on this his holy day." Socrates beamed with pride. He was no longer a child, but a youth now able to take his part in the ancient family rite of Anthesteria along with the other men.

Seeing his father's smile as he handed him his clothes, Socrates saw no harm in reminding his father of the plans for the day. "Dad, don't you remember. Hamilcar offered to give up his holidays so as to help you go in to the city for the festivities. You told him to go ahead and stay in the city all of the first day of Anthesteria after he had offered our portion of new wine at Dionysos' Sanctuary in the Marshes. I can help you move about. I'll be your chief steward while he's gone.

"Yes, yes, son, I remember. It's my limbs that are failing me, not my mind. I didn't want him driving that old cart home after dark, and especially after drinking most of the jar. Our Hamilcar is such a careful steward, and he would have given no more than the one cup that is Dionysos' due. It is bad luck to bring any of the first opened wine home from the ceremony and you saw for yourself last Anthesteria how much that Phoenician loves the new wine. So he was to take the cart somewhere nearby to the Sanctuary, perhaps in the Market place, and sleep it off, rather than end up with broken bones in some ditch. Wouldn't you agree son that prudence is best served by so serving our drunken steward?"

Socrates nodded and moved to the side of the bed where his father was now sitting, ready to get to his feet. He stood tall and braced himself as his father clasped his shoulder with his left hand and pulled himself up, balancing himself between his good leg and his sturdy son.

"And you said that this year I could ride with you in our new wagon during the procession to the sanctuary this afternoon, if I promised not to lose my temper when others insult our family or friends as the procession makes its way through the city."

"Where are my sandals? Help me to the chair, there. Look under my bed. They must be there. I'm such a nuisance of late!"

"Dad, if Hamilcar is going to take me back home early in the evening from the Anthesteria dinner at Judge Clinias' home, how will you get back? Won't you need someone to help you hitch up the cart again, and...."

"Don't worry about me, Socrates. You know I never drink so much that I lose my senses. So long as someone will help me on our cart, I will be able to get myself and the horse home before daybreak. I have asked Hamilcar to sleep by the barn so that I can wake him when I arrive."

"Sophroniscus, why do you insist on wearing that old worn out cloak day after day?" Socrates' mother was standing in the door way, with a basket full of fresh-cut laurel and delicate purple wild flowers. "Your friends will think your wife a good for nothing when they see you in that cloak on Anthesteria! Put the new one on! Aren't these flowers beautiful? The purple and green will contrast so beautifully with little Kalia's blond locks. Socrates, do you remember your crown of flowers. You were so cute at three! I wanted you to wear the crown all three days on your third Anthesteria, but you made such a fuss about it and wouldn't keep it on even till lunchtime on the first day."

"Mother, I can still remember sneezing my head off because of that flower hat."

His mother knew that her son would soon be leaving her world for good. It was over a year ago that she had sent her little boy off to Athens to begin his training at the palaestra. Now, busy with the other two teachers, one in letters and the other in musical instruction, her son seemed to come home, apart from the feast days, only to sleep and have his clothes mended. The palaestra, the gymnasium, military training at the *epheboi* barracks, male only dinner parties: all these would turn her dear child into a man who must never again find in her arms tender refuge. She was still youthful - she had not yet reached her twenty-fifth birthday - but already there was that sadness in her eyes which seemed to appear in so many of the wives and mother's of Athenian men. Her son brushed by her at the doorway, darting away from her kiss.

Sophroniscus steadied himself on the chair and had started towards the common room using the chair as his walking support. He paused, before shuffling towards his wife, who had the new cloak in her hands now. "Aren't you glad that this year we are not hosting an Anthesteria dinner? It really is getting to be too much. Will you and Kalia be going to the public meal this evening?"

Phaenarete was no great beauty, but Sophroniscus loved her. She was the daughter of a hard-working farmer like himself. Sophroniscus admired her good sense and the way she had helped her father, who had no sons. By the time she was fourteen, she had already become expert in animal husbandry and was known throughout the rural districts for her skill in assisting injured or sick animals in giving birth. And now as Sophroniscus' wife, her skills had taken a new turn. Called to a neighboring farm to help with a sick animal, the farmer's pregnant wife suddenly began to bleed profusely and Phaenarete was asked to help. She not only stopped the bleeding, but then oversaw a difficult successful delivery of the mother's first child. Word spread quickly, and soon it was Phaenarete, the midwife, whose services were requested by those who could afford professional help. She, sensitive to her man's pride, made it clear to her husband that she did this work because she had dreamed that Eileithyia, the goddess of birth, had commanded her to do so. It was not a question then of her providing for the family. Sophroniscus' love for her was sealed when she herself gave birth to a quick-witted sturdy son.

He was already fifty-one when he married her. She had just turned sixteen years old a few weeks prior to the wedding. It seemed like only yesterday that he had first spoke to Callicrates, her father, of his loneliness. At that time both his father and mother had recently died and left him alone to run the family farm. It was her father, Callicrates, who introduced his still unmarried daughter, Phaenarete, to Sophroniscus. It happened when Sophroniscus brought his bull to their farm for stud service to Callicrates' small herd of cows. Although Sophroniscus never let his wife in on the secret, her father had proposed the marriage to Sophroniscus as a way of repaying his kindness for sharing the bull. Now, this women standing with her hands on her hips in his bedroom's doorway seemed like someone who had been ordained for him from time immemorial...

"Yes, Phaenarete replied, "I'll be there with my sisters and their small children. They will bring me home before nightfall. Now, come and have breakfast!"

"I am not hungry, but I do want to sit down with my son and daughter this morning and give thanks for our blessings. And tomorrow, you and I must have a long talk." He kissed her forehead as she took his arm and helped him to the breakfast table.

It was late that morning before the family had finished preparing their wagon for the day's festivities.

After breakfast, with all the servants on holiday, Socrates was sent to the stand of trees by the north boundary of their land to fetch more laurel and wild flowers. When he returned with two large baskets filled to the brim with wild flowers in one basket and laurel in the other, he and his mother quickly wove the greens and flowers into long garlands and a robe for the holy one.

The garlands were attached to the top of an eight foot pole which had been mounted in the center of the wagon and then draped across to the railings on both sides of the wagon. The dark green laurel garlands, iridescent with the sparkle of purple, white, and pink petals made a canopy spacious enough to accommodate the wagon's passengers while seated on their benches. Before hitching the bay mare to the wagon, Socrates, standing on the milking stool, slipped a shorter garland over the horse's head. The horse snorted and tossed her head trying to shake the garland free as Socrates led her to the wagon. The wagon had already been loaded with a large wine jar of last fall's new wine that his father would take to the men's feast that evening. Finally, as Socrates hitched the horse, his mother carefully secured the family's small carved wooden statue of Dionysos to the raised box that was temporarily nailed to the floor at the center of the cart next to the center pole supporting the flowering canopy.

Kalia, wearing her own crown of Spring's first flowers, was lifted into the wagon. It was her duty to clothe Dionysos. Her mother handed her the god's regalia. Little Kalia, with all the pomp and ceremony that a three year old could muster, frocked Dionysos in his own robe of laurel. Then, standing on her tip toes so as to make herself as tall as possible, she crowned the god with a purple garland and in the child's voice of first words intoned, "All hail the king of the Vine!"

Kalia sat down in the cart and waited for approval from her father.

"Kalia, you did that so well. I almost forgot that you are my daughter. If you were just a little taller, I would think you were one of the reverend mothers who serve at the temple in the Swamp honoring Dionysos'."

Sophroniscus, for just a moment, was filled with a sense of well-being that made him forget his burdensome body. The King of Spring seemed life-like as the now high morning sun reflected off the god's lacquered smiling face. The green and purple color from his robe and crown gave his painted dark reddish brown eyes an eerie appearance of depth - as though the mysterious life of the divine did indeed inhabit this token of his presence. The vibrant colors of new growth, the strong smell of freshly plowed earth, the warm Spring sun on his forehead, and the innocence and promise of his growing children made this, his sixtieth Anthesteria a clearer revelation of the mysterious unfolding of new life from the husks of old and spent life. The feeling was one he wished to hold onto throughout the final two days of Anthesteria. He would need to be so fortified if he was to see everything through.

"Do we have everything? We really must go. What about the food for tonight's meals? Is it loaded? We must hurry, if we are to reach the procession starting grounds on time. Don't forget, we have to pick up my nephew and his family on our way." Sophroniscus was looking at their somewhat crude stone sundial's shortening shadow as he spoke to his wife.

Phaenarete hurried into the cottage and was back to the wagon in less than a moment with two large baskets filled with bread, cheeses, dried figs, salted meat, and various edible field greens. "Socrates and I will help you to the driver's seat. We should make it in plenty of time. They never get started until late afternoon. Let's go!"

Sophroniscus' farm, on the very northeastern edge of the *deme* of Alopeke, was about three miles from the city's Marathon road gate. On a clear day, from the farm's highest hill, Sophroniscus could look to the north and see the Acropolis. There, he still saw the remains of the temple to Athena burnt by the Persians almost two decades ago. If he turned to his right and looked out towards the northeast he could see the peak of Mt. Pentelicum. Most of his land, in fact, lay in the hills that stretched out to the northeast towards Mount Pentelicum, the largest mountain in Attica. From that same high hill in the center of his farm, on a clear day he could see the road to Marathon leaving the city and winding its way north toward the plain where he had first fought the Persians.

Today, as he made his way with his family on the road to the City, he could hardly comprehend how his life had passed so quickly. It seems, he thought, only a short while ago that he had marched on the road to Marathon with his two brothers and other men of his *deme* in a regiment led by Megacles of Alopeke. He had just completed his military training when they had marched to Marathon to defend their city and farms against the Persians and the traitor and tyrant Hippias. How courageously his regiment had fought that day, withstanding the brunt of the Persian cavalry attack at the center of the line. Although he lost both of his brothers on that day, Sophroniscus could never forget the glorious reception his regiment received as they marched back into Athens on the Marathon road. A crowd of joyous people lined the route from the battle field to Athens, so that the entire twenty-six mile course of the road was like one big parade ground. Today, once again, this road to Athens, especially as they approached the city gates and made their way through the city to Dionysos' sanctuary in the Marshes, would be lined with festive people. It was hard to believe almost 30 years had passed since the battle at Marathon. That was a long time past, 10 military tours of duty ago, and yet it seems as though I have scarcely had enough time to get to the center of things and make my mark. It is amazing I'm still here at all, he thought.

After almost an half of an hour drive, having made their way down from the hills and onto the plain, they pulled the cart off the main road and followed a rutted dirt path to Sophroniscus' nephew's small farm. Sosothenes, Sophroniscus' deceased older brother's only son, had acquired his small, but very fertile plot of land, from Megacles of Alopeke. Sosothenes had become a loyal client of the Alkmeonid family. This meant that Megacles could count on such a client to vote with him in the Assembly. Even more importantly, a prominent and rich patron like Megacles, who cultivated many such clients among his own tribe, would find it easier to marshal the needed support for securing the yearly appointment as one of Athens' ten generals. Thus, when Megacles sold off parts of his own estate to smaller farmers for ridiculously low prices, everyone understood that the many friends he made by such transactions would prove to be very helpful in the rough and tumble politics of the Athenian Assembly.

Sosothenes, his three young children and his wife, Melchia, were waiting under the shade of a large oak tree that was standing next to their farm house. Their wine-jars covered in burlap, baskets of food, and other provisions were quickly loaded onto the wagon. Melchia and her children joined Phaenarete and Kalia on the benches under the flowered canopy. Sosothenes climbed in front with Sophroniscus and young Socrates, sharing the permanent oaken bench from which the cart was driven.

It would take another hour for their procession to arrive at the god's sanctuary in the Marsh, another half hour on the road before reaching the city wall, and then an additional half hour once inside the city to make their way around the west side of the Acropolis, and then make their way south to Dionysos' Sanctuary near the banks of the River Ilissus. There would be plenty of time for the little children and women to chatter and enjoy a snack of honey cakes. The men would catch up with each other's news on the latest happenings at the Pynx and in their *deme*. Conversation would only become difficult when they reached the crowded and noisy city streets where the Dionysian chicanery and revelry of Anthesteria celebrants would engage everyone's attention.

By the time their wagon was back on the main road to the city, the sun had become quite warm. Sophroniscus' wife, ever mindful of his comfort, had brought his broad-brimmed straw hat along, and he asked her to hand it to him. He felt somewhat embarrassed to be seen in the city wearing the hat of a field laborer, but in the last few years he noticed that the hot sun on his head inevitably led to a throbbing pain across his forehead. Besides, his nephew wore such a hat regularly even when attending the Assembly. It had become fashionable in an Athens increasingly dominated by the common people to identify oneself as a working farmer, a man of the Middle; the sort who made up the ranks of the rugged hoplites.

"Uncle, you look great in that hat. Put it on! Be thankful it's not a day of showing the military colors. You'd cook your brains in an iron helmet today! And with all the dents in your Helmet, it can't be comfortable anymore even on a cool day. You need a little color in your straw hat, like the red band on mine, and then the hat, however worn and dirty, makes a statement of pride." Sosothenes admired and loved his uncle even though he thought him a little old fashioned.

Socrates, sitting between his father and Sosothenes, held the reins while his father adjusted his hat. Sophroniscus turned the conversation toward politics.

"Did you go to Piraeus yesterday for the parade? Were Cimon and his family there? I could not abide hearing in public the kinds of insults and rumors he is now suffering. For the past six months, every time I have gone to the marketplace, I have heard, whether I wanted to or not, the most scandalous jokes and rumors about Cimon. Tell me, have the people of Athens really forgotten all that Cimon has done for them?"

Sophroniscus himself did not understand how the holiday practice of giving license to public backbiting and exchanges of insults could be holy. But he, like everyone else in Athens, knew that the insults being bandied about in the streets of Athens during the first two days of Anthesteria , whether based on facts or not, often later surfaced as indictments in the courts or the now yearly ostracism proceedings in the Assembly. He was sure that his nephew would not have missed a thing shouted by the crowds who followed the procession of the god's ship chariot.

"Yes, I spent the entire day following the god. And I did make a point of staying close to Cimon's entourage so that I could hear the banter that some of our people served up to their leader. It was all very awkward and sometimes verged on profaning our ancestral rites. Do you mind talking about such matters with our young Socrates all ears?"

"Sosothenes, my son hears it all from his school-mates. Now days it seems our eight year old sons, who spend much of their free time in hanging about the gymnasium porches and the marketplace, know more about the intrigues and personal contests for glory and positions of power than their fathers, who busy themselves still with the work of their farms. I don't begrudge my son's time away from the farm. I can see that in the new Athens, it is this kind of education that is necessary if he is to make his way in pubic life. Besides, I want him to hear our views on these subjects so he can weigh them against the scuttlebutt he hears from others. Now what's this about it going too far? Do you indeed think that anyone else really thought the bantering profaned the rites?"

"In just a moment, Uncle, I'll.......Melchia, could you pass me the flask. I don't think the cobwebs will clear until last night's leftover wine is washed away with today's. Thank you, and would you feed the baby or something, I don't think I can abide anymore of her crying. These holidays with women and children around all day and servants off playing....the gods ask so much of us! Socrates, think long and hard before you decide to marry as I did in my thirties. It is much better to do as your father did – wait until your forties or fifties! You are eight now, right?"

Socrates nodded.

"Wait another forty years, at least. Enjoy the tools of your manhood as long as possible before plowing the fields of which you yourself must tend to the harvest."

Sosothenes drained the small flask his wife had passed to him, and shifted his weight so as to more directly face his uncle. "Now, where were we? Oh, yes.....yesterday. Well, you wouldn't believe the abuse Cimon and his family endured during the god's procession yesterday. It started at the dock area, right where the dock workers and other sailors from the cargo ships were lined up to celebrate the disembarking of the god on Attica's shore. When the Archon Basileus, masked and robed as Dionysos, was escorted to his ship chariot by Cimon and the other generals; the insults, jeers, and laughter, all at Cimon's expense, were so loud and continuous that the flutists could not be heard."

"Sosothenes, you probably were too young at the time. But both Cimon's father, Miltiades, and your neighbor, Megacles, received similar treatment on Anthesteria when they were generals and leaders of the Assembly. I was at the time shocked that these heroes of Marathon could receive such rough treatment, just a few years after their glorious military victory. It seems that the people take special pleasure on Anthesteria in humbling their leaders, even if they must invent faults and vices for them. But what were the hecklers saying about Cimon?" Sophroniscus knew that more than likely Cimon's rivals for control of the Assembly had orchestrated at least some of the heckling. He wondered whether the street hecklers' insults made plain the work of their sponsors.

"It was very crude stuff. Socrates probably shouldn't hear such talk."

"But if he had gone to the procession, yesterday, he would have heard it directly. You better keep your son on the farm all the time, if you don't want him to be thus corrupted. When he is six and ready to start school, bring his tutors to the farm and whatever you do keep him out of the palaestra and away from the gymnasium!" Sophroniscus felt slightly annoyed by his nephew's misguided effort to guard Sophroniscus' own son from the raw and rough edges of life in the city.

Sophroniscus waved his hand over his son's head, as if signaling his nephew that the path ahead was clear. "Go on, it is when the words are hurled as the weapons of cowardly gossip, that they are unmanly. In themselves as words, mere sounds made up of our vowels and consonants, they have no sinister power. Socrates, I am sure, knows how to avoid the cowardly use of such words."

"Here, Socrates, take the reins and keep the horse well to the right. It looks like some of our metic merchants are coming our way. I wonder why they are leaving the city. Give them room to pass! I hope there is no trouble in the city between the partisans of Cimon and those of Ephialtes and Pericles. There has been bad blood ever since the scandal last Spring when Cimon's nephew was accused of bribing the theatric judges during the City Dionysia."

Sophroniscus leaned back against the upper railing that served as the back to the driver's bench. He lifted his bad leg with his good hand and moved it so he could fully extend the aching leg and rest his ankle on the broad beam that had been especially fitted to the front bottom section of the wagon for this purpose. "Now, my son is occupied and I've braced myself against those bumps in the road coming up. I do want to know what the people are saying about Cimon. Don't dress it up or tone it down, tell me exactly what those dock workers and sailors were saying."

"Alright, Uncle. The first cruel remarks started when some of the dock workers spotted Cimon's little boy, Lacedaimonius, standing by the side of other family members. Some particularly crude sailor shouted from the crowd that had lined up in the street by the god's ship chariot, "Cimon, you wide-assed Spartan lover, how did your lover, get you with that Lacedaemonian child? What a stud he must be, his seed could grow even in your ass!"

Cimon must have heard, although he appeared completely impassive as he escorted the Archon Basileus between the people who lined the street where the god's ship chariot stood. The fellow, whoever he was I could not see, was not content to let it go at that. He repeated the same insult even more loudly, so much so, that for a moment the chatter of the crowd turned to a kind of nervous hush. Then, it went from bad to worse. Another man, I think he was a dock worker also, shouted from the back of the crowd, 'No, you've got it all wrong, none of the Spartan men will have Cimon. He only sleeps with their women.' They were just warming up. A third man who was standing almost next to Cimon's Alkmeonid wife's family shouted, "So the Alkmeonid princess is not good enough for your

Philiad Lacedaemonian loving cock!" Perhaps the coarsest asperity of all came when Cimon's unmarried sister appeared along with Cimon's other brothers. Not to be outdone by the other hecklers in bravado, a grizzled old *thete* with immensely calloused hands pointed to Elpinice, Cimon's unmarried sister, and pretending to be a possessed poet chanted.

'The Philiad Aristocrat is of a mind that none may be his mate for siring, but one that is kin and of his own kind. And so he plows Elpinice - of her never tiring.'

You would think this would be too much for even disciplined Cimon to bear. But Cimon did not even look into the crowd. Once the Archon Basileus had taken his place in the ship chariot, Cimon took his place with the other generals and joined the procession on the road to Athens."

"Father, can I ask Sosothenes something?" Socrates could not check his curiosity.

"Of course, son."

"Why did Cimon not halt the ceremony and call for order, or at least face his hecklers right there and demand reparation for their insults? Surely they had gone beyond the bounds of civility, even for Anthesteria?"

Sosothenes thought for a moment and then answered, "I suppose he thought that to acknowledge his hecklers in any way would only more widely publicize their exchange. What could he do? Stop the ceremony, arrest the commoners, clear the streets of all hecklers—then, he would face the charge of acting like a tyrant. No, I think his self-control and dignified reserve served him well."

Sophroniscus nodded his head in agreement. "Was that all, or did the insults continue as the procession made its way into Athens."

"As far as Cimon was concerned, the hecklers seemed to pick on others as the procession moved along the Piraeus road back to Athens. But as soon as the god's escort passed through the city walls gate and made its way through the south of the city past the Pynx and the Acropolis, the hecklers appeared again. All the same insults were repeated and some new ones were added. Here it was even worse for

Cimon, since the crowds were larger and the hecklers seemed not only more numerous but louder and more persistent. As the procession passed within sight of the Areopagus, it seemed as though a whole band of craftsmen, metal workers and potters filed by Cimon to publicly and profusely thank him for the gold pieces they let spill from their pockets. They chanted,

'No need for General Cimon to open the books.
We don't care how the Thasos expenses looks.
Extra oboes and gold piece for the battle afar
Cimon brought home for every voter's cookie jar.'

As the procession passed the Archon Basileus' Boukolerion before leaving the city again to make its way to the Sanctuary in the Marsh, another band of mockers appeared. They were older men who looked to be of the sort who spend most of their time serving on the juries. These men poked fun even at the Archon Basileus himself at the expense of Cimon

'Dionysos, Dionysos to your purple robe hold fast!
With the other hand grip your hat, the kingly crown!
A mighty aristocrat would make Athens bow at last
to the son of royal stock, the Philiad clan renown.'"

"May the gods spare us," muttered Sophroniscus, "from the mob and their bad poetry! Were any other prominent men treated like this?"

"I don't think so, Sophroniscus, but it is possible that some of the leaders of the *thetes* might have been given similar treatment by the many friends of Cimon. At any rate, the men who called themselves "friends of the common people" were nowhere to be seen at the head of the procession. I did not see Ephialtes during the entire day, which was surprising, since he is the only man in the Assembly who has been able from time to time, with the strong support of the city's workmen and less prosperous merchants, successfully to contest proposals put forward by Cimon. And so, if any of them, including Ephialtes were the brunt of an occasional Anthesteria jest or insult, it would have gone unnoticed by the larger crowds of people. I will say this, in all the years I have followed the Anthesteria procession, I have never seen such mean-spirited and malicious behavior from the people. I felt ashamed as a citizen and wondered whether the holidays might not be profaned by violence when today the heavy drinking will loosen men's tongues even more."

"I don't think there is cause for worry on that score, Sosothenes. Tonight's parties and their drinking contests will keep the hotheads mellow." As he spoke, Sophroniscus remembered that Clinias made a point of inviting the most outspoken and often contentious leading citizens to his Anthesteria feast. More than likely, tonight at Clinias' home, in the midst of good manners, the festive ritual of shared new wine, and the traditional drinking contest, cultivated and polite conversation would reveal more serious contests that engaged the energies of Clinias and the other politicians. I hope, thought Sophroniscus, that Clinias, with all the preparations for tonight's party, has not forgotten to take care of Socrates' Anthesteria gift.

Sophroniscus pulled his bad leg back up under the driver's bench and held his good hand out to receive the reins from his son. They had now reached the Marathon road gate, and now inside the city walls the road would be filled with other carts and crowds of people making their way to the god's sanctuary to the south on the other side of the city. Socrates was glad to be relieved of the reins, since he wanted to see everything going on in the crowded streets and not worry about navigating the cart through the traffic.

"Now remember Socrates, should somebody have some fun at our expense, keep our own jests light and aimed at nobody in particular. The gods gave us this part of Anthesteria to keep us humble. It would offend Dionysos' father if those who would make us appear ignoble lead us to act basely."

"Oh, Uncle, let the boy have some fun. Do you think anyone will take an Anthesteria jest by an eight year old seriously? Besides with all the noise our wives and the small ones make with their wind wands and cymbals, nobody can hear anything." As he spoke, Sosothenes pulled a box out from under the front bench, lifted it to his lap, and turned facing the rear of the wagon so the little ones and the women could pick their holiday music makers from the box.

As they made their way further into the city and approached the market place, more and more decorated carts filled with waving music-making small children and their mothers joined in the city-wide procession to the god's sanctuary in the Marsh. Street venders selling sausage and cheese, scores of half drunk servants singing bawdy songs, youths too old to be seen with their parents and too young to purposefully proceed like well-trained celebrants in a public procession, and scores of town laborers all milled about in the streets enjoying the license of the holiday. It was difficult to even carry on any further conversation, let alone hear anything distinct coming from the hubbub on the streets.

Socrates hoped that some of his school mates would see him riding up front with the men, and that his first Anthesteria ride as a public celebrant would include a baptism by the barbs of a Dionysian reveler. He, unlike his father, worried that if no one at all bothered to jest with the men of his family then they too were completely common, barred from the special prominence reserved for those who stood out from the ordinary stock of the people.

He was not disappointed. Sure enough as they pulled the cart to the side next to a stand of newly planted sycamore trees, which provided some shade from the hot open spaces of the market place, it happened. While they were munching on dried figs and waiting for their women, who had to make use of the public toilet, a young scruffy laborer approached their cart, intent on mocking them. The reveler was red-faced and quite drunk already, even though the serious drinking did not begin to after the god's wedding ceremony at dusk. The young man's tan and well-worn chiton was stained with dark red wine and out of the corners of his mouth dribbled the remains of his last cup full. He raised his hand and pointed at them as he sputtered invective in the direction of Socrates, his father, and his uncle. "Look, what we have here. Megacles' scum! Alkmeonid shit! How comes the great ones didn't hitch you jackasses to their cart?"

Although the words were certainly insulting, Socrates could not quite understand why these particular insults were directed towards his family. And while his ears burned at being likened to a jackass, or worse, its droppings, he thought it best to follow the lead of his elders in responding to this drunken *thete*.

His uncle apparently recognized the youth and, using his name, sent him away with a clever taunt applauding his early start on service to the god. "Oinomegas, you drunken sop, get off the street before someone runs you over. The god needs such as you, if all of this evening's offering of Bacchanalian juices are to flow through his devotees' veins."

After his uncle had spewed the remains of the wine still in his flask in the direction of the man, Socrates joined in the mockery. "Drink up, drink up, Oinomegas! Today's new wine turned old and rancid on your breath and clothes tomorrow will keep the ghosts from your hovel."

"Well done, Socrates. Our tormentor sees he is overmatched. He's retreating. Where are the women?" Sophroniscus labored to keep his holiday spirits up and make the day a good one for his son. But his leg was beginning to throb and he could feel a headache coming on. Even though the cart stood under the shade, the heat of midday was beginning to sap his earlier enthusiasm for attending all of today's Anthesteria ceremonies. The irritation in his voice was evident when the women finally appeared. "Ah, there you are ladies. Hurry, Hurry, we are going to miss the Queen's wedding party, if we don't get a move on."

After they had made their way past the market place district and swung south on the west side of the Acropolis, the crowds thinned out somewhat as apparently many had decided not to make the trek all the way to the god's sanctuary. Socrates had begged his father to do the entire route of today's ceremony. And so, with now tired and cranky little ones restlessly whining in the back of the wagon, Sophroniscus kept their cart moving at a brisk pace on the road leading past the Boukolerion, the Archon Basileus' official residence, through the south gate out towards the River Ilissus and Dionysos' Sanctuary in the Marsh.

It was almost sun-set by the time Sophroniscus' cart following the wedding procession of the Queen had returned to the Boukolerion in the city. Here in the square of open space in front of the Archon Basileus' palace, just after sun-set, the celebrants would mark the beginning of the third and final day of Anthesteria by partaking of a wedding feast. It was a feast that the women of Athens seemed especially fond of and they came in great throngs to stand before the porch of the Boukolerion.

Sophroniscus sat alone in his wagon on the other side of the square, waiting for Socrates and Sosothenes. His son and nephew were helping the women and small children find a spot closer to the porch where they could see Queen Ariadne's final wedding preparations for the arrival of the god later that evening. Phaenarete, Melchia, and the children along with a host of other women and servants would feast on the remains of the sacrificial victims to be offered that evening in the square. There would be plenty to eat since additional meat would be provided by the Archon Basileus. During the meal, young boys, dressed as satyrs, would entertain the wedding party with bawdy skits portraying the ecstatic and irrepressibly impulsive appetites of Dionysos. Sometime after the feasting was over, the god would come to his bride and the mystery of the marriage would be consummated in secret within the bridal chamber of the Boukolerion. Then the tired, but happy, women celebrants would make their way back to their carts and with their sleeping children bedded down in the back of the wagons, return to their homes. They would go to bed and wait for the return of their drunken husbands, wishing that they too could be a queen or a daughter of King Minos, the consort of a great hero like Theseus of old.

Socrates and Sosothenes made their way back through the crowded square to their wagon. The last rays of the setting sun were reflected off the surfaces of the portico of the Boukolerion. There Socrates, when he glanced backwards, could see long shadows of what appeared to be other worldly figures flickering mysteriously on the white marble of the porch's columns and the palace's front wall. They must be the reverend mothers in their hooded robes preparing for the sacrifice and the Queens nuptial rites, thought Socrates.

Figure 3
*Scene on a child's Anthesteria pitcher,
children enacting the Basilinna's marriage procession*

Their progress was slow, for the square had now come to life with the sights and sounds of the festival. The little children, crowned with their flowered wreathes of ivy and laurel, were now out and about, milling around their mothers and hoisting their gaily colored miniature wine jars high above their heads, pleading for refills of their sweetened and diluted new wine. Pubescent boys, wearing their satyr tails and beards, jostled one another as their merry jaunts through the crowd led them to their school mates. The fading light of the sun, with its orange and red hues, made the brightly painted miniature wine jars held aloft by tiny hands shimmer and sparkle, matching in their iridescence the joyful faces of young children on Anthesteria Party Night. Socrates was not so old that he did not still feel the excitement that made Present Day on Anthesteria the favorite holiday of children. He almost wished he could stay right here in the square for the entire evening, but then he would have to wait even longer for the special present that was to be given him by his father at Judge Clinias' home this evening.

"Come on, Socrates, we had better hurry back. Your father wants to arrive early for Judge Clinias' party." Sosothenes pulled on his young cousin's arm to hurry him along.

CHAPTER SIX
A FATHER'S SATYROLOGY

Oh! happy that votary, when from the hurrying revel-rout he sinks to earth, in his holy robe of fawnskin, chasing the goat to drink its blood, a banquet sweet of flesh uncooked, as he hastes to Phrygia's or to Libya's hills; while in the van the Bromian god exults with cries of Evoe. With milk and wine and streams of luscious honey flows the earth, and Syrian incense smokes. While the Bacchante holding in his hand a blazing torch of pine uplifted on his wand waves it, as he speeds along, rousing wandering votaries, and as he waves it cries aloud with wanton tresses tossing in the breeze; and thus to crown the revelry, he raises loud his voice, "On, on, ye Bacchanals, pride of Tmolus with its rills of gold ! to the sound of the booming drum, chanting in joyous strains the praises of your joyous god with Phrygian accents lifted high, what time the holy lute with sweet complaining note invites you to your hallowed sport, according well with feet that hurry wildly to the hills; like a colt that gambols at its mother's side in the pasture, with gladsome heart each Bacchante bounds along."

(Euripides, *Bacchantes*)

Young Socrates and his older cousin Sosothenes reached the wagon just as the city servants were lighting the torches which would illumine the streets that night for the many that would be making their way to the men's private Anthesteria parties. The day's heat and long trek had taken its toll on their wagon's festive garb. The canopy of laurel and flowers, too long in the sun, was dried up and droopy. What had been the living and vibrant tissue of the wagon's bright garb now appeared to be on the verge of falling away from its pole support, exhausted and worn down by the day's long journey.

Stretched out and leaning against the broad board that made the back of the driver's bench, Socrates' father had fallen asleep. His grey bearded chin rest on a small cushion which he had propped between his shoulder and the good left arm which was folded across his chest. As Socrates looked at his father sitting half slumped over, with his body in disarray and the life-force in his eyes hidden behind his closed eye-lids, he was saddened by the realization that this holiday of new life had become too much for his father. Maybe, thought his son, this exhaustion which now so frequently made his father's body slouch and bend into a troubled sleep had something to do with the strange pomegranate size growth that had appeared on the back of his father's neck.

Sosothenes quietly took his place on the driver's bench beside his Uncle and untied the reigns which had been carefully hitched to the decorative knob attached to one of the middle legs of the driver's bench. Taking the reigns into his hands, Sosothenes would not let his regard for his father's brother, a Marathon hero, ever admit concession to weakness or the pathos of dependence - even if such vestments are the inevitable accompaniment of aging and mortality. And so Sosothenes, wishing to deny what the young boy felt, smiled as he noted the special powers of their hero. "I don't know how he can fall asleep with all this commotion around him. We'll have to wake him. I'm not sure I know exactly the best way to go to Clinias' house."

Socrates climbed aboard from the back of the wagon. Brushing aside a part of the canopy that had become unattached to the center pole, he made his way to the front of the wagon right behind his father so as to wake him. He gently clasped his father's shoulder and squeezed it as he spoke, "Dad, we are back. Which way to Clinias' home?

Sophroniscus rubbed his eyes as he sat up straight. "I must have dozed off. I see the sun has set. We must arrive early at Clinias' home if we are to have time to see to your special Anthesteria surprise, Socrates. Hamilcar will be there to meet us and bring you back to join your mother."

"It's still early evening, Dad. You told me that Judge Clinias' symposium doesn't begin before at least one and a half hours after sunset. How far is it to his home?"

"If Sosothenes will move our horse briskly, it is about a quarter of an hour, provided that most of the holiday revelers are off the streets now. His house is just west of the market place on the road which leads to the Academy District."

Sosothenes was ready to go.. "I know a short-cut to that road. We'll be there on time for sure. Why don't you climb into the back where you can stretch out your legs and make yourself more comfortable."

"Yes, I'd like to get in the back if I can swing this bad leg over the front railing. Socrates, help me!"

Socrates helped his father to one of the benches that ran along the side railing of the cart. He then moved the small crate which held the holiday noise makers to where his father could use it as a foot rest. Since some of the city streets would be bumpy, the two large amphorae that before had been steadied by the legs of the women and children would have to be repositioned. Otherwise they would tip over at the first bad bump in the road. So before Socrates sat down, his father asked him to remove the burlap covering from Sosothenes' amphora and move it and his father's amphora where they could be strapped to the center pole just in front and to the right of where Socrates would sit. After he had wrapped a cord around the great wine jars' necks, through their handles, and around the center pole, Socrates took his seat on the bench directly across from his father. Everything ready, Sosothenes flicked his reigns and their mare, still garlanded with Dionysos' laurel, pulled their cart away from the broad plaza by the Boukolerion onto a torch-lit street filled with the traffic of holiday revelers celebrating the marriage of the Queen with Lord Dionysos.

They now reentered the city through the south wall and the flickering light of the street torches illumined the painted figures on the curved amphorae. Socrates was staring intently at the wine jars, suddenly transfixed by the black figured scenes drawn around their curved surfaces. He had seen their family wine jars many times and had never given much thought to the scenes which showed satyrs in pursuit of women costumed as Maenads.

Figure 4
Raving maenads

Since the time he had been old enough to accompany his mother to watch the religious processions of the Anthesteria and the City Dionysia, this was a scene he had seen many times playfully reenacted by costumed men and women who were part of the parades. But Sosothenes' amphora depicted a scene he had not seen before. Sure enough, there were the satyrs again, silhouetted in their black glaze against the red clay of which the jar had been cast. But in this scene there were no maenads. There were only a group of six goat-like creatures, some of them seated, some lying down and others standing upright on two legs, but all of them with man-like faces, trailing behind them tails which appeared to be like those of the black bulls on his father's farm, and protruding where there goat-like legs joined their stomach were their grossly huge and erect phalli. They seemed to be playing some strange game that involved each of the creatures pointing its phallus towards another of their kind. What could be the point of this game? He could see a satyr bent over and right behind him was another of these creatures pointing his phallus so that it was almost touching the buttocks of the other. Next to these two was another standing satyr which seemed to be pointing his phallus very close to the mouth of a seated satyr. The remaining pair of satyrs seemed to be doing some kind of strange wrestling position. One stood upright, but another upside down satyr, partly standing on his head but balanced on his shoulders, was being assisted by the upright satyr. The upraised legs of the upside down satyr were draped over the shoulder of the standing one. But there again, the upright mans phallus was pointing just below the drooping tail of the one he held in this rather strange wrestling hold. Socrates wondered what else could be on the side of the jar he could not see.

Figure 5
Ritual dance of satyrs and women

The cart lurched to the right suddenly, spinning the vases as they turned within the cord that bound them to the center post. The wheels on that side had apparently run over something in the road. Both Socrates and Sophroniscus reached for the center pole above the tops of the amphorae in order to steady themselves.

"Sorry, Uncle, some drunken street vendor must have left his merchandise crate on the road. Are you both alright?"

"We're both alright. And more importantly, the god's nectar is still safe and sound, although the jars got a good shaking. My son thanks you for rolling the scroll on your amphora. Now he can finish his education in satyrology. Could you drive a little closer to the torch posts so he doesn't go bug eyed staring at the scintillating details of satyr sexuality."

Sosothenes chuckled and with a backward glance that included a wink, he complied with a flourish. "I'll slow down under the torches and make haste in the dark stretches between posts."

Socrates felt his face grow red with embarrassment. He thought his father had been dozing; else he would not have taken this occasion for a close inspection of an amphora which usually was reserved for the privacy of the men's quarters, away from the prying eyes of wives and small children.

Sophroniscus tried to remember what it was like before the seemingly ever-present vital drive had awakened in his body as a young man. He knew his son's embarrassment had nothing to do with prudishness, but with the awareness that try as he might on this his first public excursion with men, there was still much in his boy's body and barely schooled mind which would not let him cross over into the reality and rites of manhood. Nevertheless, Sophroniscus had decided that since his remaining time with his son would be cut short by his malady, he must try his best to prepare his son for the difficulties which lie ahead for any citizen's boy who would come through gymnasium and military training in Athens unscathed by either giving or receiving improper affection in the concourse between youths and older men.

"Socrates, should I live for another handful of years, there will come a time when you will not be interested in much that I have to say. Your teachers, and other gentlemen, much younger than I, will command all your attention. You, no doubt, will find, like most youths an accomplished and worthy man who will take a special interest in you and offer to be your mentor. But now, while you can still feel the force of my eyes and think me somewhat worthy of your imitation, I thought it might be good to for me to talk with you about those satyrs you find so curious. It would be good, wouldn't it, if you knew you had to make a long and difficult journey over roads another traveler has already passed over to learn from such a traveler who might map for you where the road is especially dangerous and what, if any, dead-end turns and monster-infested byways should be avoided. Well, that is why the satyrs are on our jars."

"Father, I thought the satyrs are for fun! Why, you helped dressed me in such a costume last year for my part in the Anthesteria skit on the Boukolerion porch. I, I just can't understand why satyrs would have fun in such a way as....."

Figure 6
Satyrs at play

Sophroniscus interrupted his son, "Yes, Socrates, playing the part of a satyr during Anthesteria or the City Dionysia is even more fun for men than it is for boys of your age. But, of course, it would not be good if the men of Athens gave themselves over to being such creatures throughout the days of their lives."

"Father, I can't imagine why anyone would want to do that – to play the strange game I see on the amphora."

"Perhaps, Uncle, I can be of some help in explaining the fantastic picture of what is to your boy a strange game." Though Sosothenes was Socrates' cousin, he was twenty-two years older and now a husband and father. So talking like an older mentor, he tried to assist his Uncle. "When you become about six years older you will find that part of your body which is depicted as so large when it is a satyr's, will change and become a source of strong and pleasurable sensations. You will know it is this part of you which will draw you to a woman with whom you may then father a child. But here is what is surprising Socrates! Believe it or not, and you will soon see this is true, the most noble and intelligent sharing of the pleasures granted by our sexual organ, can rarely be enjoyed with a woman. When you become an ephebe capable of brave combat, educated enough to converse with wit and intelligence about matters of the city, and ready for the joys of sporting competition with worthy gentlemen opponents; you will find it almost impossible to find companionship with either your mother or other decent women. They are empty heads, called to spinning, weaving, and bearing children, and while nature beckons us to impregnate them, our minds seek to mingle the pleasures of desire with a companionship which can nurture the intellect and honor of our manhood. And so, in Athens and elsewhere among us Hellenes, it is a proof of our civilized natures, that the highest love a youth can experience is that of a noble man."

Socrates looked at his father and so, as not to offend his older cousin whose eyes were on the road in front of him, he shook his head side to side to indicate that Sosothenes remark only left him more confused.

Sophroniscus thought it best to start with something Socrates had observed back at home. "All this, just as your cousin says, will become less difficult for you to understand in just a few years. But for now, think about what you have observed on our farm as you have watched both our animal stock and the wild birds and other game. Have you noticed how for most of these animals, there are only a few times a year that the males seem driven to copulate with their females. When these times come, it appears that the creatures are completely possessed by a divine force which will not let them rest until male and female conjugate in a fiery embrace. I have heard that some wise man has proposed that such a force, he calls it Desire, is the primal principle which underlies the origin and preservation of the World. I don't know about that, but it is clear that it is this Power and its boundless strength which irresistibly draws male and female together for procreation. I cannot know for sure what these creatures feel, but it appears that the divine plan has arranged matters so that the most intense and body-filled pleasure is linked with the action and fulfillment of this drive. I believe that even in the crop seeds we plant, something like this happens between the moist element of Father Sky and the dark soil of mother earth so as to bring forth growing life. I don't understand how it all happens. This is a mystery and it is sacred, because year after year, generation after generation, this Power bequeaths new life. Are you following me, son?"

"Yes, father, but what does all this have to do with the satyrs on the amphora being - how did you put it - like a map for a traveler?"

I'm getting to that. Sosothenes are you still listening to this? Is it just the case that I am way ahead of what can be understood by my son - too far out of season with all of this?

"Yes, I always listen to my uncle and especially when he shares his traveling tips. Keep going, Uncle. I think you might be making some headway. Remember though, he is only eight years old and so don't expect him to understand everything you want to say to him now about his passage into manhood. But help me here for a moment! I need some guidance now also if we are to arrive on time for our dinner party. Can I turn here to pick up the Road to the Academy District?"

"I don't think this road goes the right direction. It curves east just south of the market-place. We need to go on a little further to pick up a road that intersects with Academy Road." Sophroniscus leaned towards the side of the wagon to get a better view up the road. "It is at least two stades further along before we turn.

"As for my son, you might be right that at eight years old he may not be ready to grasp everything I want to say to him about satyrs and men. But my son is very curious about everything and I might not have another such opportunity for such instruction. I am aware that I am stretching Socrates powers of understanding, but this is something he enjoys and so he is now used to me doing this intentionally. Now, where was I? Yes, the satyrs and men's ways - the gods wished to forge in men something akin to themselves. So our bodies were fashioned in a way different from the other creatures. Our covering of skin is so much more sensitive to both pains and pleasures. Mind, both a blessing and a curse, leads us through foreknowledge and memory to suffer pain and experience pleasure even more intensely than all other animals. The gods wished to test us by such an arrangement. Can men master their own natures so as to conduct themselves freely, not bending to the capricious tyranny of the ever-present procession of pains and pleasures which march through human bodies? Nowhere is the test of our divinity and freedom more daunting than with respect to the special organ of our manhood. Unlike most other creatures, our maker made humankind, and especially men, so that the desire to procreate is always in season. And so, once a boy turns into a youth who is fully equipped, he must for the rest of his life, barring some injury, either direct or be directed by this most powerful of forces. Don't misunderstand me, son! The pleasures of our sex are good and holy. However, as our sage Solon has said, 'Nothing too much!'. You will come of age and, I hope, learn too control your nature - both its pains and pleasures. For many men, since pain seems so frequent and unavoidable, there is an almost irresistible temptation to pursue and lose oneself in the strongest possible pleasures. This is what you see in the Satyr nature. Men who have become possessed with an unlimited and unruly appetite, always bleary eyed with swollen penises seeking an endless fare of pleasure in every way that can be imagined. It is as though in the throes of copulation satyr-like men could return to that lower animal life which has no premonition of death and suffering. If men are to do honorable works and lead lives of god-like freedom and mastery, then they must temper their natures through moderation and self-control. This is the great test through which the gods sort men out, the noble from the ignoble, the free man from the slave, the man worthy of governing others from those who must be ruled by their superiors. Are you following this, Socrates?"

Sosothenes turned back and interrupted briefly, "I don't know about Socrates, but I wish I could write down what you just said. Uncle, why have you not sought high office in our city? It seems to me that you are one of those few who indeed have learned to first govern well the contentious clamor of the many needs and appetites of your own human nature."

"You are kind, dear nephew, but I am of humble origins and do not possess that handsome and noble bearing which our citizens seem to crave in their leaders. Besides, I have spent too much time on my farm and know too little of the affairs of our merchants, tradesman, and craftsmen to be of help in serving the common good. Socrates, what do you think about all this?"

"Father, I do understand what you are saying about self-control. My Music teacher has been teaching me this lesson over and over again as I learn to recite Homer's tales of Odysseus' clever and masterful ways. And he never tires of calling me son of Sophroniscus, rolling your name slowly off his lips so as to remind me of the special call to self-control which is in your name. He says over and over, "if you would as your name promises rule others well, Socrates, then first lay claim to the meaning of your father's name - one of self-control."

"That is why I pay him, son. Your teacher certainly knows how to please his sponsors!"

"This must be the street, uncle. I can see the market place just ahead. How much further?", asked Sosothenes.

"After we pass the market place, Clinias' house is just on the west side past the stand of sycamore trees. We'll be there in a few moments."

When they pulled up to Judge Clinias' home, Socrates wondered how his father could pick out his friend's home from the others that were on both sides of it. There was nothing to distinguish Clinias' home from the others as looked at from the street. The wall facing the street was featureless except for the one door which opened to the street. The middle part of the wall was about 10 feet high and for the last 15 feet on each side of the middle the wall rose another six feet or so, making part of the exterior wall of second level rooms. Since there were no windows facing the street, there was nothing that could be seen which in any way would reveal the identity of the occupants. Indeed, one would never guess from the appearance of this house, that anyone wealthy or prominent in the affairs of the city lived within. But this was not unusual. When Socrates had asked his tutor who had come from Crete about the royal palaces there, his letters teacher told him that in the cities of Crete only a few men governed the lives of the many and did so without assemblies and law courts. Such royalty then heaped up for themselves treasures which were both protected and displayed in luxurious but fort-like palaces. Here in Athens because free men govern themselves, he said, and spend so much of their time in public places, the market-place, the courts, the Pynx, and the Gymnasium, and because Athenian's have chased from their midst those who would aspire to royal ways; the leading men of Athens think it unseemly to expend their personal wealth for such private dwellings.

"Yes, this is Clinias' home. Sosothenes please knock on the door, while Socrates helps me down and unloads the amphorae and food baskets. I hope we are early enough to spend a few moments with Clinias before most of his guests arrive."

CHAPTER SEVEN
COMMUNION

The father lifts up his own son changed in form and slaughters him with a prayer, blind fool, as he shrieks piteously, beseeching as he sacrifices. But he, deaf to his cries, slaughters him and makes ready in his halls an evil feast. In the same way son seizes father and children their mother, and tearing out the life they eat the flesh of those they love.

(Empedocles. *Purifications*, 415)

Sosothenes had only knocked once before the study oak door swung open. A middle-aged servant, wearing a necklace of garlic cloves and a laurel wreath on his head, greeted them.

"Welcome! Oh! It is the good Master Sophroniscus, with his young son. How shall I announce your other companion? Clinias has been asking for you. Please come in! I'll have my boy servants unload your cart and bring your jars and baskets inside. Follow me!"

Sophroniscus, with help from his son, led his party through the door and into a dimly lit vestibule as he chatted with Lycon. "Thank you Lycon. My companion is my nephew, Sosothenes. Both of us are envious of your Master's good fortune in his choice of servants like you. Lycon, you make such a handsome and polite house man. You still look stout and energetic, not prematurely old and tired like so many servants. Indeed, the years hardly show on you, whereas I am limping about looking old and worn like an old farmer with too few servants to save me from the rigors of field work. "

Lycon knew why Master Sophroniscus limped. "Sir, you are a hoplite and if you limp it is because you carry in your body the mark of your courage – a wound of a warrior who never has abandoned his shield. As for your age, you have reached the age of wisdom and are many years ahead of me. If you don't mind me saying so, Sir, if I still had a father I would want him to be like you."

Sophroniscus smiled and patted Lycon on his shoulder. The men and their guide had moved on from the vestibule and stopped in a narrow hallway just outside of the dinning hall in the men's quarters. "What a charmer, you are! Can you believe, Lycon that almost twenty years have passed since that day on Euboea, at the beginning of the Great War with Persia, when I heard your Master Clinias threaten you with a demotion to field labor on his country estate? I always have known that there would be no field work for you. But I see by your necklace of garlic cloves that you are still troubled by angry ghosts of your Euboean kinsmen. It is really quite impressive that these ghosts can follow you all the way here to Athens, flying across the water of Euripis each Anthesteria Day of the Jars. Do you really think then that such powerful ghosts will be whisked away by a few garlic cloves? No matter, Master Clinias is a man who admires your endowment of energy and good looks more than he dislikes what he takes to be childish superstition."

Lycon bowed his head as though he were about to petition his Master for overlooking a less than satisfactory service. "Yes, some of my ways still irritate Master Clinias. I should take my necklace off today before my Master loses patience with me."

"You know, I am sure, by now the limits of your Master's patience. Surely, Lycon, even you know that on this the second day of Anthesteria, the Day of Cups, the new wine of the god you honor with your laurel wreathe has placated the angriest of ghosts. Soon all the men – even the lowliest servants – will partake of Dionysos' powerful *pharmakos* of the vine. Do you really want the smell of the garlic cloves around your neck to interfere with the intoxicating divine forgetfulness Dionysos' gift brings? Well, you better get us seated in the dinning hall. It takes me a little longer to drag this bad leg around tables and their stone benches. Will there still be time before all the guests arrive for my son Socrates to spend a few moments with Master Clinias?"

"Plenty of time! And young master Socrates, I believe, will be introduced to Clinias' special guest who has come from Clazomenae. Only Clinias, his business partner, Megacles, and our special Ionian guest are here now. They are enjoying the night air in the courtyard. I have been instructed to inform Master Clinias immediately after I have escorted you to your dinning couches. I will let you know when your servant has arrived to take Socrates back to the public feast. Please, go on in." Lycon parted the thick curtains which served to separate the hallway from the men's quarters and then escorted the two men and the boy to the seats assigned to Sophroniscus and his nephew, Sosothenes.

Sophroniscus was glad that Clinias and the two early guests were not yet in the dinning room. He found it humiliating that even to walk across a room he required assistance. When, with the help of his son, he was comfortably seated, Sophroniscus asked Socrates to remain standing near his couch. The three kinsmen were alone in the room. The servant had left the room through another door which led to the inside courtyard.

"Uncle, what a beautiful room! Your friend has done well for himself. I have often wished that I could have become a seafaring merchant - if only I didn't get so damn seasick."

The room was indeed elegant. Although it was now well past dusk the room was as bright as a sun-lit mid-day. Chandeliers made of carved ivory hung from the dark cedar rafters which traversed the width of the room and helped support a pitched roof. The chandeliers, ten of them, each held six bright red colored oil lamps. The array of chandeliers was so evenly spaced throughout this large room that every nook and cranny was brightly illuminated. Yellow light tinged with a reddish hue and the sweet smell of specially scented burning olive oil announced to all the men who entered this quarters that they had left behind the smells and sights of everyday life for the sacred space of festive play. The room's furnishings were especially decorated for the Anthesteria meal. Specially embroidered cushions lay on each of the raised plaster podiums which served both as couches and dinning chairs. Each of the fifteen embroidered couch cushions, in colors of purple, yellow, and white, depicted different episodes of Dionysos' flight from the Titans; so as the eye followed the semi-circle of cushioned couches, Dionysos' entire menagerie of animal disguises appeared. The tile floor, with its simple but elegant geometric blue and white geometric pattern, was strewn with delicate fresh cuttings of laurel and pale yellow wild flowers. A large glistening golden shallow bowl, filled with incense, was mounted on a tripod which stood just off to one end of the semi-circle of couches. On the far side of the room, opposite the semicircle of couches, the evening meal's meat, roast pig, was cooking on a large spit which took up most of the length of the hearth. Although the dinning tables were set-up with drinking cups and various utensils for serving food, there was no food except for a very large bowl of field greens and five large loaves of corn bread. On Anthesteria, the guests were expected to bring their own wine and side-dishes.

Sophroniscus had begun to point out to his nephew and son some of the more exotic urns and statuary which Clinias had collected from the various ports of call his trading ships had visited. "Do you see that golden Aphrodite? It is from Paphos, and must be worth....." Sophroniscus did not complete the sentence. The host, Clinias, escorting his two other early guests into the dinning quarters, politely interrupted his guests' conversation.

"Greetings, Sophroniscus, Sosothenes, and I believe this is young Socrates. I am so happy that you have come to celebrate the Jars at my home this evening. It should be an interesting evening. Let me introduce my other guests. I believe you both already know Megacles my business partner, a cherished friend, like you Sophroniscus. And our other guest, I am sure you have heard him exhibit his great learning in the speakers' stalls in the marketplace. Although he hails from Clazomenae, he sold everything he owned there to come and take residence here in our city. Now, I am told, he is the private tutor of some of our most prominent citizens. Please greet Anaxagoras! He is the most learned man I have ever met. I am hoping that before the wine flows too heavily or my guests become too enchanted with our flute girls, Anaxagoras will grace our conversation with the fruits of his learning."

Sophroniscus raised himself up from his couch as Clinias escorted his guests to the seating area. Clinias, ever considerate of his old comrade's aversion to limping like a cripple before other men, led his guests directly to Sophroniscus' couch, first. There, Clinias warmly embraced Sophroniscus. "This man," he said, "has been my mentor, comrade in arms, and one of the most honorable men I have ever known. Anaxagoras, I believe, you will find in him a worthy partner in conversation since he is a thinking man." Clinias watched as all the guests extended to one another the embrace of friendship.

Socrates didn't quite know was expected of him as the men greeted one another. It would be inappropriate, he knew, for him to speak, unless first spoken to. It would be even more unseemly for him, being a boy of eight, to extend his arms in greeting to men outside his own family. And so he stood quietly, just behind his father's couch, looking without staring at Clinias and his guests.

Socrates could scarcely believe that right in front of him was the man, Anaxagoras, who had published the writing which his letters tutor had just a few weeks ago, with considerable excitement, brought to show his students. Indeed, since Socrates had passed so quickly from the elementary reading lessons to the most advanced within less than two years, his tutor had assigned him the task of reading out loud passages from the brand new scroll titled, *ON NATURE*. "Homer and Hesiod are far too easy for you since you have heard so much of it recited," Philemon his tutor had said. "Let's see what you can do with something you have never heard." And so for the last month he had been reading the writings of this very man who now stood before him, Anaxagoras! His tutor was right. This text was very unlike Homer, Hesiod, or any other of the poets the most advanced students had been reading. Indeed, there was scarcely a mention of heroes or the gods. As far as Socrates could tell, the writing was not intended as a record of great deeds or the gods' works. Nor was it any kind of gymnastic Manuel or text for instruction in any of the trades. While the writing did mention other men, it appeared that they were of interest only in so far as they too had treated the same topics Anaxagoras did in his essay. There was a Thales, an Anaximander, and an Anaximenes, then much mention of Parmenides; and all of these, it seemed, were also men who not only used words in new and obscure ways, but occasionally seemed to invent new ones. This all made for very difficult reading of whatever it was that they were trying to explain. Socrates was not sure he could see in their account of the nature of things, the world he observed. He had copied out some of the more perplexing passages and taken them home to ponder over. He had shown this to his father and when his father proposed various interpretations, Socrates took particular relish in pointing out how his father's conclusions seemed to contradict other passages which, of course, his father had not himself read. His father would throw up his hands then and say, "Copy out those other passages and bring them home if you are going to convince me that I can't understand what I read. Why are you reading stuff like this anyway? How is this going to help you raise livestock, be a merchant, or take part in the affairs of the City?" Even though Sophroniscus protested thus, each time Socrates came home after a session with this strange text his father asked, "Anything new we can chew on tonight?"

This Anaxagoras, thought Socrates, is indeed a strange one. He is a Hellene, but he certainly does not look like an Athenian. No Athenian would dare wear a purple robe to a dinner party. Such a robe would be worn only by kings and princes, and even the most conservative of the aristocrats took pride in their city because its constitution forbade the tyranny of kings. Maybe it is because he is a professional learned man and this is his only good robe, the robe he uses for public lectures. And even in this loosely fitting robe, Socrates could see that Anaxagoras apparently spent little or no time in the gymnasium. While, he appeared to be at least two decades years younger than his father, the frame of his body suggested that it had been many years since he had engaged in any kind of strenuous physical activity. Anaxagoras was wide of girth, very pale skinned, had very soft fleshly looking hands, and a rather unkempt thick grey beard. The Anthesteria laurel wreathe he had placed around the crown of his head made him appear slightly comic. He looks like the make believe king we dress up on Independence Day and chase off our streets. I wish I could stay and hear why this man - not at all in his bearing like his hosts - is honored by Judge Clinias and regarded as a lover of wisdom.

The other men, Judge Clinias and Megacles who was at least in his seventies, were familiar to Socrates. This was the first time Socrates had ever been in the same room with Megacles, the man who had both been the leader of the people and then ostracized by them. He still appeared to be athletic and vigorous even though he was at least 10 years older than Socrates' father. Although he had been forced to leave Athens by political opponents and live in exile for a decade; since returning, Megacles had once again made the Alkmeonid family prominent in Athenian affairs. When he reached out and patted Socrates on the shoulder he seemed like a kindly grandfather. Clinias, his father's comrade, still looked the part of the captain of the trireme which had won glorious engagements at Artemisium and then Salamis. He was tall, well-muscled, and unusually handsome. Socrates wondered why such a man as he had not himself become a general or first man of the state, given his noble bearing, wealth, and glorious military service. So this is the man, thought, Socrates, who single-handedly withstood the assault of five Persian swordsmen while defending my father who had fallen wounded on the banks of the river Eurymedon. In the past year or so his father had told him this story many times, hoping thereby to inspire his son towards greater efforts in his swordsmanship instruction.

What next wondered Socrates? The men were all seated and he stood peering over his seated father's shoulder, not sure what was expected of him.

For what seemed like a very long time to Socrates, the seated guests all seemed to be staring at him wondering why the standing boy was still there delaying the festivities of the men's symposium. Then he saw Clinias nod his head and wink at his father. The man in the purple robe, Anaxagoras, stood up and reaching inside the folds of his robe pulled forth a scroll of fine parchment which was wrapped around a cylinder of dark stained oak wood. The man from Clazomenae was walking right towards Socrates, holding out the scroll.

"Young man, your father and Judge Clinias tell me that you have been copying many portions of my writings and criticizing them. Is it true that you arrive earlier than the other students so that you might have an extra reading lesson first thing in the morning before you join the rest of your mates in the Palestra for your gymnastic training?" Anaxagoras did not pause to give the boy time to answer the question.

"Your letters teacher, I know him, said that you find my writing curious and have asked him many times if you might borrow his copy of my essay. When I asked him how a boy of eight could possibly read, let alone understand, my writing; he told me that even though you have been his student for only two years, you are far advanced beyond your peers. You were the first student of seven he has ever taught who came to him already knowing not only all the letters, but syllables and words also. You must, he thinks, have a well-educated servant at home. Your schoolmaster, it seems, wishes to employ your pedagogue as his assistant. What is his name?" Here, the loquacious learned man did pause, like the school master, as his look searched out the boy's eyes for signs of intelligence and understanding.

Socrates was flabbergasted that the stranger was actually addressing him. His father jabbed his elbow with his good arm.

"Have you lost your voice, Son? Go ahead, you may speak for yourself."

Socrates, eyes fixed on the scroll in Anaxagoras' outstretched hand, recovered his composure. "His name is Hamilcar, Sir. He taught me how to sing all the letters when I was only four."

Anaxagoras smiled and continued, "I suppose he also taught you your syllables, words, and how to read and write - all before he began escorting you to school?"

Charmed by the kindly and familial tone of the learned man, Socrates forgot his manners and looked directly into the face of the distinguished older man as he answered again. "Yes, he plays games with me where I call him Melanthios and he makes me play the part of Odysseus. Hamilcar loves to recite episodes from Homer's epics, especially the ones that show the loyal and hard-working character of the great ones' serving men."

"Well, there might be something to that - such a servant reflects well not only on himself but on the prudence and kindness of his Master. So there's a good servant behind every great one, or is it the other way around? Well that's beside the point...Where were we, now? So how did these games include learning how to read and write before you went to school?"

"He would grow tired of reciting the stories to me, so I made him make me a writing board and insisted that he teach me how to make my letters speak of these stories. He would copy out parts of his stories and I learned to sound them out when he was busy with his work elsewhere."

"Well, you're a hard-driving task-master, young Socrates and your 'Melanthios' is no mere goatherd! Your father is to be commended for owning such a versatile servant, both steward and pedagogue extraordinary. As for you, I am honored that one as young as you finds my essay of interest when you could be reading the wondrous tales of heroes and gods. Your father has persuaded me that my book will indeed receive the careful reading I wish for it, if you are one of its readers. And so, your father and Judge Clinias have made special arrangements for my own best student, Archelaus, to prepare this complete copy of *ON NATURE* for you. Happy Anthesteria! I wish you and your family well. Come and talk to me or Archelaus, should you wish to point out difficulties in my reasoning about those principles which govern the make-up of the World and its order. Your uncluttered, but obviously capable, mind may be just the soil the seeds of my thought require if they are to take root somewhere besides between my ears.

Socrates was at a loss for words. Was this portly man in the purple robe having fun at his expense? Would he really allow himself, a learned man of international reputation to be seen carrying on a serious conversation with a young boy? No matter, he certainly was handing him the scroll and this was his father's Anthesteria gift to him. He could not think of a more special gift than this. His own scroll, very thick and made from fine papyrus - he would guard it with his very life! Now he could read whenever he wanted and learn matters strange and new from this man Athenians called a 'philosopher'.

"Go ahead, Socrates, untie the strings and unroll to the first section. You will see that I have added a note in my own hand for your copy."

Socrates fumbled with the string that tied the scroll aware that all eyes were upon him. "Thank you, Sir. Thank you, Father and Judge Clinias. It's the best Anthesteria ever! I will cherish this book the rest of my life, I am sure."

His father smiled at Anaxagoras and thanked him for his generosity. Then he turned to his son and asked him to bid farewell to the guests. He told Socrates to check the shelf in the Vestibule and there he would find a case in which to carry the scroll. As young Socrates turned to leave, Lycon appeared. The servant escorted young Socrates to the street. There, as planned, Hamilcar was waiting in the family cart, ready to drive Socrates back to the Boukolerion Square where they would pick up Socrates' mother and sister for the trip home.

After the boy left the room, the men's talk turned to the day's events, especially the rough treatment Cimon had received.

It was Anaxagoras who initiated this conversation..."You Athenians puzzle me. I cannot understand why it is that Cimon was so insulted and abused by the people today. Here is a man, who perhaps more than anyone else in Athens, has contributed to the prosperity of the common people, and yet it is these same people who today tried to publically humiliate him. Isn't this the man who just six years ago made Athens and all Hellenes safe from Persian imperialism? How can they forget Eurymedon where in one day this great general defeated crack Persian forces both at sea and on land, ending all possibility of Persian incursions not only here on the mainland, but throughout the Aegean and Ionia. This is the man who has secured for Athenian merchants safe and free access to markets along all the shores of the Aegean and as far away as Egypt. The fleets and expeditions of Athens under his leadership have employed thousands of rowers, dockworkers and other craftsmen. Whatever wealth his leadership has secured through conquest or diplomacy has been shared with the people of Athens. Never has the treasury of Athens been so rich. Everywhere I walk in Athens I can see evidence of Cimon's public-spiritedness. Has he not personally paid for the construction of the new south wall, the groves of freshly planted trees in the market place and the Academy district, and the maintenance and outfitting of the most powerful navy in the world? Is not Cimon like a father who has given without reserve his wealth and energies to all the sons of Athens? What more could the people want from this man? Or am I mistaken in thinking that it is the common people and their leaders who are behind today's attack on Cimon? If you think it not impolite at this festive gathering, before the rest of the guests arrives, I would like to learn from men of great experience like yourselves what this is all about."

When Anaxagoras was done speaking, the men seemed somewhat ill at ease. Clinias glanced nervously at the expression on the face of his senior business partner and the once powerful first citizen of Athens, Megacles. He wondered whether such a conversation might not be painful to Megacles since Cimon was married to Megacles' granddaughter, Isodike, and Megacles own experience with the people's Assembly was still a source of bitterness for him. It was Megacles himself, to the relief of the others, who answered Anaxagoras.

"I see that my friends are reticent to answer your question, Anaxagoras, thinking that they might offend me in some way in discussing my granddaughter's husband, Cimon, or that they might touch a nerve with regard to the People's decision to ostracize me - even though that happened more than twenty years ago...It seems like another life-time. But there should be no such tiptoeing around among genuine friends, and we are all indeed friends here. Sophroniscus and Sosothenes are my neighbors in Alopeke and have been faithful friends of my family for many years. Clinias, I am very proud to announce, soon will be not only my business partner, but also my son-in-law. He has asked for the hand of my youngest daughter, Dionomache, and they will marry next month, right after the City Dionysia. Besides all this, one of the wonderful advantages, and there are not many, of being seventy-five years old is that, frankly, you just don't give a damn what people think about you. As for my family, the Alkmeonids, they are all self-reliant and resourceful, and they prosper most when they wrestle with worthy adversaries. So we need not worry about giving offence. Now if my friends will indulge an old man, I will, Anaxagoras, give my view on the nature of Cimon's apparent troubles with the people."

Before Megacles could continue, there was a loud knocking on the outer door.

Clinias stood up and looked out into the vestibule, where Lycon was already opening the door. He called to Lycon, "If that is the three *hetaerai* I have hired for tonight, show them to the pantry which they can use for a changing room. Let them help themselves also to the pastry we set out for the servants this evening."

Lycon answered, "It is the three *hetaerai*, Master, and they are all looking very beautiful this evening."

The guests all craned their heads towards the vestibule. Lycon appeared at the doorway of the dining room with the three young women trailing behind him. They had to pass through the men's quarters in order to go to the kitchen and pantry room. It was an opportunity for the dinner guests to preview the evening's female entertainers and companions. The girls - they could not have been much older than twenty or so - were dressed in very delicate, almost transparent, cotton gauze ankle length gowns. The gowns were dyed a pale red, almost pink, and their only decoration was an embroidered pattern of purple flower petals which circled the hemline. Each of the girls wore the traditional Anthesteria bull's tail as a belt, gathering the gown in to accentuate the bloom of their female forms, now in the season of the first unspoiled fruits of late spring. With every step the girls took as they crossed the room now thick with male desire, the dark brown end of the frayed bull's tail seemed to caress the thighs of these beautiful creatures as their gowns rustled and brushed against their swaying hips. Each girl carried her own double-flute in one hand and a small cloth bag which contained a costume change in the other hand. They made their way across the room slowly, even executing a few dance steps and twirls, so as to encourage the pleasure of anticipatory desire. By the time the hetaerai had reached the door to the kitchen area on the far side of the room, each of the men at the table, even the lame one and the septuagenarian, had been graced with a coy glance from one of this trinity of powerful Aphrodite's minions. Male eyes meeting such a glance widened as the young women's flirtatious smiles seemed to say - 'It is you and you alone to whom I am drawn like Kirke to Odysseus on the isle of love; all others are as swine to me.' When the women finally turned their backs to the men and filed through the door to the kitchen, gathering their gowns tightly around their lower body and making a show of their alluring swaying hips, the four citizen-warriors and metic-philosopher had all entered the land of lotus-eaters, forgetful of the responsibilities of hearth and city and released from their aging and mortal bodies.

It was Sophroniscus who broke the spell and brought the men back to their conversation. "Clinias, where do you find such beautiful nymphs? If their flute-playing and singing are as enthralling as their bodies and smiles, I would wager that there will be little interest this evening in passing the myrtle branch among ourselves."

Anaxagoras nodded in agreement, "Yes, my friend, it will be almost too much to bear if these beauties can touch our souls with Apollo's divine music as well as they tantalize our bodies. Are these girls from the house of the Mistress who just recently arrived from Miletus? Aspasia, I think, is her name."

Figure 7
Hetaerai, symposium entertainment in the men's quarters

"Yes, she is their manager. She herself is a great beauty and rather young to be the proprietor of such a thriving enterprise. Her girls are the best in the city. I hope you will find them a fitting accompaniment to our Anthesteria celebration. You might find it entertaining to converse with them during the dinner. I am told that they have been highly educated on the isle of Lesbos and can converse about many topics. When the drinking begins after dinner, they will perform for us and provide less conversational companionship for those of our company who cannot mix their wine with the more refined joys of philosophical discourse. I expect, of course, that neither you, Anaxagoras, nor my good friend Sophroniscus will be in that group. So I have asked our girls of Lesbos to shower their attention on you two early in the evening. Anaxagoras, maybe an examination of their inner natures will reveal a trace of mind and virtue. But I plan to keep your wine cup full." Clinias was smiling impishly – "I hope your enterprise finds only Eros at play in these daughters of Aphrodite. It's hard enough to keep you out of trouble with our holy men here in Athens when you rob

Apollo of his chariot. Heaven help us, if Anaxagoras' sober inquiry claimed to find both the beautiful and Reason in female nature."

"Clinias, I yield to your judgment. I don't know about your friend Sophroniscus, but as for me, I follow Solon's maxim, 'Nothing too much!' in all things. Too much sobriety, too much abstinence from the joys of the erotica, too much science - it would be too much of any of these should a guest forgo the pleasures of Dionysos on this his holy night. I am sure."

"Well spoken, my friend. But have you forgotten all about your question to Megacles? I see that Megacles, unlike us youngsters, is already well clear of their wiles and would like a few minutes of serious conversation before reasoned discourse and calm reflection give way to the festive spirits of wine and Eros. Let us listen to his account of our city's fickle ways with the beautiful and good men."

Megacles sighed and stretched his legs out over the length of his couch so that he might recline on his side. Propping his chin up under his fist, he asked Clinias, "May I ask your servant to fetch my food basket. I would like to nibble on some of the special barley cakes my women packed for me, while we talk."

"Yes, yes, of course! I don't know where our others are. I was planning to wait until all my guests had arrived before serving our meal. But it is getting late. Let us eat now."

Just as Clinias rose to call the steward so that the drinking cups might be filled, the sound of revelry could be heard right outside of Clinias' house. Even with the closed door and the vestibule between them and the street, a chorus of singing men accompanied by flute and cymbals announced the arrival of the rest of Clinias' dinner party.

"Ah, here they are. They must have gotten an early start on the evening's new jars. Lycon let our guests in. If they are of a mind to, let them bring their singing and dance with them. Once they are seated, see that our meal is served."

The other guests, there were four of them, were not drunk, after all. What had sounded like a drunken revelry was just the cacophony of their less than praiseworthy singing. Out of consideration for their host and the other guests, the late arrivals decided that it was best to leave their flutes and cymbals in the vestibule. The four men, escorted by Lycon, made their way into the room and gave their apologies for being tardy.

After Clinias greeted each of them by name, he introduced Anaxagoras to the new guests. There was no need to introduce Megacles, Sophroniscus, or Sosothenes, since all of the guests already knew each other.

"Men, if you have not already met him or heard him lecture by the porch of Apollo's temple in the marketplace, it is my pleasure to introduce you to Anaxagoras of Clazomenae. He has been my house-guest for the past few months and will be taking up his own residence in Athens. As you can see, I have asked him to sit in the middle of our line of couches so that we can more readily gang up on him should he get too school masterly with us."

Anaxagoras, I have asked this handsome man who insists on always wearing his plumed soldier's helmet to be your dinner partner on your left. He tells me that since he has given himself to politics and his head is not as hard as some, his helmet is necessary if he is to avoid a painful knock on the head from some unexpected quarter. Let me introduce Pericles, nephew of Megacles, and already well-regarded in Athens for his eloquence in the Courts and the Assembly. Next to Pericles, sits Procleus, the son of Hermistius. Since the death of his father, he has tripled the worth of his family's shipping enterprises. He has become as dear to me as were both his deceased father and the departed Plataean comrade in arms after whom he has been named. You would do well, Anaxagoras, to visit his import shops when you wish to decorate your Athenian lodgings. On your other side is young Lysias. He is determined to outshine his mentor, Aeschylus, who now has agreed to take him on as his assistant in overseeing the production of his upcoming trilogy of plays late next month. Lysias has promised me that he won't speak in iambic pentameter all evening. It is to keep his rhapsodizing in check that I sit him next to me, not because he is so irresistibly handsome. Finally, but not least, down next to Sophroniscus, at the end to your right, is Apodorus, grandson of Aristides and one of Athens' youngest generals. This is the man, who next to Cimon most distinguished himself in the naval and land battles at Eurymedon. He is a man of few words, but when the wine loosens his tongue he can grace the myrtle branch with the most gorgeous recitations of our poets."

"Gentlemen, I am honored that you have all come to my home. It is a source of great joy for me to celebrate Anthesteria with men of such distinction. I am indeed fortunate that on this evening of the new jars, I may enjoy the nectar of friendship drawn from well-seasoned jars - forgive my metaphor Megacles and Sophroniscus - as well as those of youthful vintage. Now, enough with similes, let's get on with quenching our thirst and filling our stomachs. You must all be hungry by now."

After Lycon had set out nine of Clinias' best drinking cups, brought each of the guests food baskets and new wine jars, and filled three serving plates with simmering slices of pork; the men stood with their wine cups raised while Clinias offered the Anthesteria Libation at the hearth.

Two of the hetaerai joined Clinias at the hearth. The hetaerai had donned ivy wreathes and carried wooden wands in their right hands. Clinias' own wine jar stood just to the side of the hearth, just a few feet from the crackling fire. On the other side of the fire, leaning against the stone work that made up one side of the hearth, stood a long poled and broad winnowing fan, one not unlike that believed to have been baby Dionysos' cradle. The women, now priestesses of Dionysos, bent to their knees by the wine jar and holding Clinias' double-handed cup between them, gently tilted the wine jar so as to fill the wine cup. Rising to their feet, they presented the cup filled to the brim with dark red wine to Clinias. As Clinias faced the fire, Dionysos' ministrants stood one on each side of Clinias. As he raised the cup to offer his prayer of libation, the women laid the ends of the pine cone tipped wands on his shoulders. Clinias raised his eyes to the cup he held above his head.

"O Holy One of the Black Goatskin, bless our gathering as we partake of the blood of your veins and the flesh of your broken body. We pray, O Goodly Husbandman that you will receive our drink offering and bless our vines, trees, and fields. We thank you,

Zagreus, Lord of the Vine, for the fruits of the harvest and pray that you will again rise from our fields, teeming and bursting with your Father's immortal life. To you, O Goodly Bull, I now offer this drink in thanksgiving and celebration of your guardianship of hearth and field. Intercede on our behalf with those who lie beneath your dark-furrowed earth, so that both the living and the dead in friendly communion may celebrate the mystery of your ever renewing life."

Clinias then knelt on the edge of the raised fieldstone floor which marked off the hearth area from the rest of the room and slowly poured half of the cup's red wine into an earthen opening in the stone floor just off to the side of the hearth. Moving back to the center of the hearth directly in front of the fire, he poured the last of the wine into the hearth itself, making sure that the wine did not actually touch the flames. The god's libation hissed as it gently splashed on the hearth's red hot stones. Then, instantaneously and spirit-like it rose in new form, a purple and pungent haze which wafted up above the flames into the chimney and out into the room.

The libation completed, Clinias returned to join his guests at the table. The altar-girls slipped away into the kitchen and quickly reappeared; now ready to play the part of serving girls. Taking direction from the steward, they moved among the couches and along the tables refilling the guests' wine cups and passing trays of breads and field-greens from couch to couch. There was so much food that the guests' own food baskets seemed superfluous. But each of the guests, as in the Anthesteria feast of old served to the Theban visitor at Colonus, made sure at least to begin their meal with food from their own baskets. Even the man of science from Clazomenae, so contemptuous of other men's superstition, would not tempt those dark spirits of the underworld who on the morrow, the final day of Anthesteria, would come to terrorize those polluted by blood guilt.

Figure 8
*Pithoigia – Hermes evoking
souls of the dead from their large pithos
on the first day of Anthesteria, Day of the Jars*

CHAPTER EIGHT
SYMPOSIUM

These are the lessons which my heart bids me teach the Athenians, how that lawlessness brings innumerable ills to the state, but obedience to the law shows forth all things in order and harmony and at the same time sets shackles on the unjust. It smoothes what is rough, checks greed, dims arrogance, withers the opening blooms of ruinous folly, make straight the crooked judgment, tames the deeds of insolence, puts a stop to the works of civil dissension, and ends the wrath of bitter strife. Under its rule all things among mankind are sane and wise.

(Solon, Fragment 2)

When everyone's cups were full, and their plates stacked with meat, bread, greens, and corn cakes, Megacles steered the friendly banter back to the contest for leadership which now swirled around his son-in-law, Cimon. It was to his nephew Pericles that he turned, unsure whether or not his Alkmeonid kinsman who had befriended Ephialtes, the most radical advocate for the commons, would speak in defense of Cimon's detractors. The oldest and most prominent man of the Alkmeonid clan could not quite decide whether this son of his sister, Agariste, could be trusted to remain true to the Alkmeonid legacy – a fierce hatred of tyranny and the protection of the liberty of well-born men.

At the very beginning of Pericles' public career, just when Megacles had returned to Athens after a ten year exile,; his nephew had been the City Dionysia *choregus* for Aeschylus' tragedy, *The Persians*, in which Athens' most renowned dramatist glorified

General Themistocles for his heroic role in saving Athens and most of the mainland from Persian conquest. That his own nephew should thus have lent financial support to winning popular favor for Themistocles, the rival whom Megacles knew for certain had secretly conspired to bring about Megacles ostracism, unsettled Megacles' confidence in Pericles loyalty to the Alkmeonid family. However, Megacles was willing to withhold final judgment concerning Pericles' political loyalties, since he understood that a young man of wealth and from a family like his own was expected to assume such a sponsorship of the performances at the City Dionysia. It was not as though Pericles had anything to do with the actual content of Aeschylus' clever tragedy. And it was to young Pericles' credit that he had taken on sponsorship of a performance which, given its theme, had a good chance of winning the prize as best performance. How could a play which glorified the Athenians as the instrument of God's wrath against the overbearing pride of the Persian King Xerxes fail to be popular?

But more recent actions of Pericles were a real embarrassment to the Alkmeonid clan. Just a year ago, Pericles at the bequest of the leadership of the commons in the Assembly, had assumed the office of the Assembly's prosecutor. The Assembly, while Cimon was away from Athens, then voted to carry out an investigation of various allegations about Cimon's mismanagement of the Athenian treasury. The allegations were all nonsense and surely, thought Megacles, his nephew knew this. But when this matter ended up in a trial, it was Pericles who had to serve as the actual prosecutor in the court. Cimon was exonerated, some say, because Pericles had not prosecuted with much enthusiasm. Still, it was almost too much to bear to see an Alkmeonid in the courtroom pitted against Cimon, the husband of his eldest daughter, and a man whose life-long service to Athens had once and for all rid the possibility of any return to power by the demagogue Hippias or any of the Pisisitratid clan.

Whatever Pericles was up to; it was clear, thought Megacles, he was extremely adept at currying the support of an ever broader constituency without irretrievably alienating those he appeared to side against temporarily. Should Pericles ever become the undisputed first man of Athens, could he be trusted to remain faithful to the Alkmeonid opposition to anyone, like Cylon or Peisistratos, who would in order to gain absolute power pose as friends of the basest elements of the city? Now was an opportunity to engage his nephew and perhaps help steer him straight.

"Pericles, it is good to see you again. It has been months since you have visited my home. People will think you are ashamed of your Uncle."

"Yes, Uncle, it has been too long. I think it has been almost six months since we have shared a meal together. Matters on the Hill have been so pressing that I have scarcely had a chance to enjoy the company of friends or family. I hardly know what goes on in my own household, let alone the rest of my kinfolk's families. All this month, I have spent most of my time in the council rooms of the Bouleuterion. I have been asked by a rather large contingent of the Assembly to draft new legislation. As you know, such work requires endless discussions."

"Well, we will get caught up on family matters some other time. But now help me explain to our metic friend, Anaxagoras, why it is that today Cimon was the target for such scandalous and harsh insults from the people in the streets during the Anthesteria procession. Just before you arrived, he had asked this, noting that he found it rather curious since it seemed obvious to him and indeed to almost everybody else from his own native region of Ionia that Cimon's leadership had proven to be of great benefit to all the people of Athens, and most of all to the less wealthy tradesmen and craftsmen who own little land of their own."

Pericles, who had been reclining as he ate, sat upright on his couch and shifted his position so that he could more easily observe the reaction of all the dinner guests to this turn in the conversation. Something in his uncle's tone of voice had alerted Pericles to be guarded in his response. And so he turned to his host, looking for a gracious way to deflect his Uncle's question, a question which Pericles had decided should not be answered by him, at least not directly.

"Clinias, my mother has told me that you will soon be marrying my cousin, Dinomache, and so being almost a relative already, I ask for your help as my future Alkmeonid in-law. We Alkmeonids have a boundless passion for politics, and left to ourselves in a dinner party with such prominent citizens we might forget our manners and spoil others' fun by talking endlessly about the affairs of state. And so I propose, with your permission, that each of us take a turn answering the question about our current first man of the state, with the provision that our speech about Cimon be no longer than a few minutes and that it treat the people's treatment of this great man as illustrative of both the benefits and risks which come to any man who attains preeminence in the governance of our city."

When Pericles paused, the host Clinias looked about to see if any of his guests were dismayed or discomfited by such a theme for their dinner conversation. They all appeared to be comfortable with Pericles' proposal. "Just the way you framed it, Pericles," said Clinias, "would be a fine topic for our conversation. And let us pass the myrtle and the lyre, so that each speech should, at least, in part aspire beyond the trivial gossip of today to themes worthy of song and poetry. Then, when the topic and our inspiration has run dry and each guest has done his part to entertain, we must not shirk our duty to do right by the second *krater* of new wine I will set in our midst. Then we shall allow our female consorts of Dionysos do their part to complete our evening's entertainment. Pericles, why don't you begin? I will have Lycon bring you a lyre and the myrtle branch."

"Clinias, at the moment, I find myself uninspired and my lyre playing is so atrocious. I fear that I will chase the muses away. Save me for near the end, when the meal's wine will have had more chance to dull the senses of our band. I see that Lysias is eager to show off his poetic genius. Let him begin."

Clinias nodded in agreement and directed his steward to bring Lysias a lyre and the myrtle branch.

Lysias indeed began, without a moment's hesitation, and though he was the youngest of the guest, proved to be masterly in the gentleman's art of composing clever verse on the spur of the moment about an unanticipated topic......

"Cimon when you were a young Philiad partying day and night
Just a citizen among others, although richer than most,
Your vices were many and in everyone's plain sight.
Indeed, among the sons of the well-born, it was your boast
That no one could drink, carouse, or brawl more than you
Unless they could do all this and bloody your nose too.

Then, no one seemed to look too close.
You were still young among the beautiful and good.
Why you later chose the way of virtue, no one knows.
Aristides, it is said, loved you like a father should.
And when his virtues became your own in word and deed
Up to high office, leadership, and power you did accede.

Today you stand in high public places, no shade so all is light.
Virtues grown too familiar seen for too long and up close
Appear to the less powerful and glorious as not quite right.
With fame, fortune, and power, resentment always goes.
Democrat, aristocrat, tyrant, it makes no difference at all,
For mortals what goes up must come down - it's the gods' law."

When Lysias had strummed the final chord on his lyre, punctuating the end of his verse, he laid the lyre to the side and passed the myrtle branch to Clinias who sat immediately to his left.

"Well done, Lysias!" Clinias grasped his young friend's shoulder in congratulations as he in turn picked up the lyre. "You have set an impossibly high standard. I hope the gods exempt poets from their law so that for many years we might all be charmed by Lysias' verse."

"Thank you, Clinias, but it is to our military men I look for help in understanding how it could be that Cimon, who has always been victorious in every Athenian military campaign, is in our time of peace ridiculed and mocked as an incompetent 'Laconophile'. Perhaps we can persuade Apodorus to take the lyre next. I know my neologisms cannot match the wisdom of our blind bard, whom Apodorus so reveres. Apodorus, I am sure will bring to our topic truly inspired wisdom - bending the verse of old to illumine the fate of our own men of might and fame."

Apodorus was ready. As Clinias passed the myrtle and lyre down to his right, asking Sophroniscus to hand it on to Apodorus, Apodorus with a kindly smile, accepted the call.

"Why, Lysias, you have already guessed my song. It is because I have spent so much time training with the sword and spear that I cannot call on my own words. If our company will indulge my rather limited repertoire, I will stand aside and bring to our symposium a voice more eloquent and a vision more insightful than anything which could come from my uninspired speech."

Apodorus turned his eyes upward until only the white of his eyes appeared visible and appearing to be in a trance called for the blind prophet of Thebes, Tireisias.

Figure 9
Odysseus evoking the ghost of Teiresias from the underworld as described in Book XI of Homer's Odyssey

"O venerable seer of seven-gated Thebes, Tireisias of old,
On this Anthesteria eve, arise from thy earthen bed,
That through your matchless inner sight Cimon's fate may be told.
Our drink offering has assuaged the nations of the dead.
So come in friendship, hold back the hoards of thirsty ghosts,
And speak through my lips prophecies true and kind for our host.

I have come, Apodorus. Put away your sword.
Let me but taste of blood, of Athens and Cimon then I shall dream.
Son of Miltiades and Philiad fathers, favorite of Olympus' lord,
Cimon, master of land ways and sea ways, why leave thy chariot or trireme,
To muck about in city politics where dark intrigues disguise the foe?
It is not yours to command the motley companies of men of commerce, O man of woe.

Yet, great Cimon, your mighty victories have prepared the way
So many in peace and plenty may flourish and live to a good old age.
Yours is the work of early morning. The bright light of mid-day
Apollo reserves for another – then Alkmeonid-born gloriously will blaze.
Men of Anthesteria, forget not the deeds of your fathers dead.
For there is no other sustenance for us no matter how much blood is shed."

With the final words of his verse, Apodorus shuddered and his chin fell upon his chest as though the spirit which had animated his verse, now in taking leave, left him torn and spent. Indeed, Apodorus was spent. It was no easy matter for a young general to lead his verse safely through three stanzas in such uncertain terrain as that which stretched between his friend Pericles and those like Megacles who harbored animosity towards those who now led the party of the commons.

Since Apodorus sat motionless with the lyre on his lap and his head still bowed upon his chest, and no one else around the table had called for the myrtle, Clinias, ever the vigilant host, called upon those practiced in the art of festivity to help move the party along. He beckoned to Hyacinthia, one of the most beautiful of the hetaerai. The three hetaerai were seated on cushions which had been laid out on the floor inside the space bounded by the semicircle of couches. "Hyacinthia, our young general has been drained dry by a too close encounter with a denizen of Erebus. Refill his wine cup and call back his soul from the edge of the dark land. Restore with your caress the sweet body of desire and revive the life-force of our poet-general. Perhaps your assistants, Melissa and Ishtaria, would perform like service for any of my guests who also felt the shade of Erebus pass too close."

Before any of the *hetaerai* could make their way to his end of the semicircle of couches across from Apodorus, Megacles lifted his own *lekythos* and refilled his cup for himself. As he poured his wine he looked down the line of couches to the center of the semicircle where the purple robed Anaxagoras sat, then to the far end across the semicircle where Sophroniscus sat next to Apodorus. Then Megacles called for the myrtle and asked his host to postpone the female entertainment.

"Clinias, bid these fair women to withhold yet the irresistible allure of their sex. I am sure our younger men, and especially Apodorus splendid soldier that he is, can forgo a little longer the loosening of the limbs and mind that these sirens call us to. We older men, Sophroniscus, Anaxagoras and I, are even more drawn to the divine forgetfulness of Aphrodite's fountains - even though our equipment often won't allow us to drink as deeply as younger men. But, if I read the faces of these other men of years correctly, they like me are very mindful of the need to brace our soft and dolorous female intercourse with the firm and bracing discourse of men."

Clinias had worried that the mixing of the older and conservative men with the new breed of younger men would make it hard to keep everyone entertained and convivial. "Yes, yes of course, let us continue our conversation. But let these beautiful creatures move among our couches so that we may enjoy the delight of Eros and logos both in play. Look, our friend Apodorus is again refreshed. Hyacinthia has restored him with a mere caress on the back of his neck. I don't know about the rest of you, but I will need some such bucking up if I am to even attempt a composition after hearing such impressive rhapsodizing as that of Lysias and Apodorus."

Sophroniscus, sitting between Clinias and Apodorus, had wondered how he could gracefully excuse himself from the myrtle and the lyre. He could not possibly play the stringed instrument with his one bad arm. But now listening to Megacles exhortation for more serious conversation and Clinias' gentlemanly allowance for festive play, he had a sudden inspiration.

"Megacles, if you don't mind, since the myrtle is next to me, let me answer its call. But I must ask our host and all of you for an exemption from its full duty. My lyre playing, I am sure, could not but jar even the least sophisticated musical ear. My meter and rhyme are so clumsy that every trace of intelligibility flees from my thoughts as I try to fit them into the pleasing form of the rhapsodist. And, as Clinias has noted, all of these deficiencies will be uglier when our mind's ear still vibrates with the harmony and perfect pitch of my predecessors verses. So, if I might take some liberty with good form, allow me to share my thoughts on our theme unaccompanied by my own lyre playing. However, lest my prose is too prosaic, I would like to draft a flutist, the most accomplished one from among our *hetaerai*. Standing beside my couch, she will not only provide welcome relief for your eyes from my tired old body, but - if she is clever with the flute - her musical replies will add charm and color to my otherwise plain speech."

Figure 10
Flute girl and hetaerai in komos with men

"A good plan, my friend, but can you really keep your hands off Melissa when she stands so close, swaying and vibrating with the sounds she lovingly draws from the instrument so close to her mouth. Or perhaps this is the only way you can think of to lure Melissa from young Lysias' couch." Clinias exchanged a lascivious smile with his old friend Sophroniscus as he acknowledged his request.

"You are on to me, Clinias. But assure Lysias that it is enough for me merely to be close to such a vision of beauty. I would not spoil the enchantment by grasping for such a delicate bloom."

Clinias beckoned to Melissa as he graciously asked young Lysias to surrender her. "Lysias, release our flute player to our most temperate of guests. He has need of her. You have heard the service he requests. She will soon return to you even more alluring. Melissa will positively glow by virtue of having a close encounter with such a supernatural satyr - one whose desire is surfeited through action at a distance!"

Melissa had taken a seat on the end of Lysias' couch where he was stretched out the full length of the couch, reclining on his side with his head resting on her knees and his arm encircling her legs. Lysias, so young and unsure of proper decorum throughout the various courses of the evening's dinning and drinking party, sheepishly withdrew his arm from around Melissa's legs. Although Melissa was probably not more than 18 years of age, at least seven years younger than her consort; the young black-haired *hetaera* moved with the worldliness and assurance of a seasoned manager of male drives and foibles. She gently lifted his head from upon her knees and rose from her seat on the edge of the couch on which Lysias lay. As she rearranged her gown and bent to retrieve her double flute by the base of Lysias' couch, she whispered in the ear of the blushing young man, "I'll be back."

After Melissa, with double flute in hand, had stationed herself standing beside Sophroniscus' couch, Sophroniscus smiled warmly at the young woman and addressing both her and the entire symposium prepared his audience for their joint performance.

"Dear girl, what a pleasure to share a performance with you. You, I believe, may be the finest flutist I have ever heard. I confess that before I heard your playing I did not find the music of the flute to my liking. The sounds all seem to blur and run into one another, not like the lyre with its precise and bounded sounds which each have a beginning and an end. And when some one less beautiful than you purses their lips and blows upon the flute, too often all I could remember of their performance was their flushed and puffy cheeks. But you somehow have mastered the playing so it seems effortless. I hear no huffing and puffing, but only the most fluent and endlessly various tones carrying me along as if in a fast moving stream. It does not matter if I recognize the tune. Indeed, and I would not have thought I could ever enjoy such spontaneous music, I find myself reveling in a rapid succession of feelings as the sounds of your flute make their way to my soul. I hope you will be willing to grace my speech with such musical fantasy.

The young woman was completely flustered by such remarks. How could he possibly have been that attentive to her flute-playing? The old man's respectful tone of voice and his words which suggested that his soul could be touched by the playing of a flute girl, a mere slave owned by a metic woman.....this was too much! Was he mocking her? Flirting and lewd advances, obeying imperious commands, and being treated like a small child - this she could deal with. Her mistress, Aspasia, had taught her the art of remaining impassive and untouched in her inner nature even while simulating the appearance of a woman thrilled by the male lust for domination. Noting that none of the other men seemed to be giggling at her expense, she regained her composure and answered the old man.

"Master, thank you for your kind remarks. How exactly is it that you would wish me to accompany your speech? Am I to play softly while you speak, or only immediately before and after? Whatever it is you wish, I will do my best. Please do not become angry with me or think ill of my manager, Aspasia, if my playing should not meet your requirements."

"Melissa let your imagination lead your playing. As I speak on our topic, I will make use of talk of animals and other very familiar things which you are well acquainted with. When I pause, I would like you to play whatever tune or made-up melody you feel is best suited to conjure up feelings which many associate with such animals or things. Wouldn't that be fun for you and entertaining for all of us?"

Melissa looked puzzled and turned first for guidance to the older of her two co-workers, Hyacinthia. Hyacinthia, still seated besides Apodorus, merely shrugged her shoulders, indicating with the gesture that Melissa was on her own. Afraid that she might offend Clinias and his guests by failing miserably to so entertain this request, she turned with downcast eyes to the Lord of the Party, hoping that he might intervene so as to save his party from being subjected to the unrehearsed performance of a flute girl.

Clinias did intervene, but only to make matters worse as far as Melissa was concerned. He was nodding his head in approval.

"Go ahead, Melissa. I, too, have heard you play before. I am confident that you can so compose as Sophroniscus has requested. Indeed, my friend Sophroniscus is very wise, for he knows that even if his speech slips into mediocrity, your music will rescue him and he will yet have a chance at winning the contest and take home for himself the god's portion of new wine. Now, before you begin Sophroniscus, allow Marsyas my youngest, and I might add, prettiest male servant to mix the second *krater* of wine."

Clinias called for Marsyas who then appeared from out of the kitchen. He was dressed only in a brief loin cloth and his body glistened with oil. As he hoisted the next amphora of new wine over the large *krater* which stood on a sturdy tripod in the middle of the room, Marsyas made a show of flexing his biceps and tensing the calves of his lower legs. The middle aged men, Apodorus and Procleus, whistled and winked at one another.

"Three to one, Marsyas, and be careful to get most of it in the krater."

When the wine had been mixed with the jars of water and Clinias' serving girls had refilled the men's cups, Sophroniscus and Melissa then were given due attention by all the guests.

"Our topic is Cimon and how his treatment at the hands of the people today might be illustrative of both the benefits and risks that come to any man who achieves preeminence in the governance of Athens. Even though I myself have never either sought or been appointed to any high position in our city, I have lived long enough to see very clearly the risks any man assumes who would assume an archonship or the status of "first citizen" of the state. I am sure that Megacles, the most famous of those who hail from my deme of Alopeke, even knows better than I the inevitable fall from the people's favor which even the city's greatest benefactors have suffered. He himself is counted among this number. The great heroes of Marathon, Salamis, and now Eurymedon, all hailed as saviors of their city, were then subsequently brought low by forces much more powerful than the armies of a foreign power. What then is at work here in our city?"....Sophroniscus paused and turned to his flutist.

Perhaps, Melissa, you could blend a brief section of our Marathon warriors' paean to Athena with the dirge of Agamemnon's funeral. I see that already some eyes are growing heavy."

When Melissa had completed her medley of the Marathon hymn to Athena which almost imperceptibly transformed into the somber funeral dirge of Agamemnon, Sophroniscus resumed.

"You may think me simple-minded and dulled by too much time spent on my farm, but I think the birds have something to teach us about this pattern. I rise very early most mornings, just after sunrise, and while I eat my own breakfast I watch as various birds come to roost on the feeding station my dear wife has built for them. She loves all animals and I could not deny her this childish desire on her part to feed the birds which, I am sure, would do just fine without her help. At any rate, I have noticed that the various kinds of birds approach the feeding station in distinctive ways. There is a very small kind of bird which comes most often to the feeder. My wife calls it a purple sparrow. It is not a sparrow at all, because it sings much more beautifully and with more variety than any sparrow. I have observed that this bird never approaches the feeder, which is mounted on a tall pole, in a straight line of flight. Instead, this little bird always zigzags; darting back and forth in short sharp turns even as it also dips up and down. Then when it lands, this very agile flier never stays still on the feeder. Constantly moving as it reaches for the seed with its tiny hard beak, its eyes are ever vigilant scanning the sky above and every direction on all sides. The character of its chirping even seems to change as often as it restlessly moves about while on the feeder. It never actually stays on the platform more than the time it takes me to pick up and swallow a bite of my breakfast bread. Never lingering over the few seeds it hastily feeds on, it is up and away and always leaves the roost in just the same way it arrived- randomly darting, swerving, and dipping as though it intended that any one watching it could not possibly anticipate its next move....... Music, my sweet little bird!"

Melissa played an especially lively version of the music she had heard played in accompaniment to Psophia's popular love poem, "Ode to the Hummingbird who drinks sweet nectar from my love's garden". After she had piped the final trill of notes, she lowered her double flute from her lips and turned for approval to Sophroniscus.

"That was charming, Melissa. I guess lovers, anxious to hold the affection of their beloved, are also always wary and agitated. It is this edginess that I wish our audience to note. At any rate, you have all these men now light and airy even though they are heavy with wine and talk of politics."

"But there are other kinds of birds I must speak of. The raven, dark and much bigger than the little purple tinted song bird, comes to the feeder in a much different way. It flies straight in, seems to scare all the littler birds away, and then, perching comfortably eats its fill without hardly stirring from the spot it first landed on. It comes always with others of its kind who also take their roost on other sides of the little platform and together as birds of the same feather they seem to stand guard for one another. Indeed, the ravens seem confident that no other creature can disturb its roost; for it is the biggest of those birds which visit the feeding station and it appears invincible amidst its comrades. Yet, there always is some bigger and more powerful predator. The small darting and ever moving birds survive longer the dangers of the exposed feeding station. But the raven is easy prey for the large hawks that come occasionally from the fields to the garden beside our farm house. He sits too still and flies too straight to avoid the talons and powerful bill of the hawk. What would you play, Erotica, to call to mind such birds as these?"

After the flutist had finished her music for the raven and the hawk- and it was a stretch for anyone to find a connection here between her melody and Sophroniscus' image of the assured big bird at the feeder - Sophroniscus moved directly to the meaning of his simile.

"There is something we Athenian men hunger for with a yearning that is much more persistent than that we feel with regard to the pleasures of food and sex. It is glory and the unmistakable affirmation of one's excellence that we crave most. I believe that everyone of us here this evening, whether we be a merchant, farmer, soldier, or a poet, would be willing to renounce feasting and love-making if he were told that it was only by this means he could earn immortal glory. Fortunately, no such course is required, unless perhaps you wish to win Olympic glory in the pankration. In our city, the feeding station for glory open to all men is the state. However, to feed in such an open public place high up, one must learn from the birds if you are to stay at the feeder. Since so many crave glory and since we Athenian's think it is only through the contests of competition that manly excellence is best exhibited, there will be no way a famous and glorious leader can ever fly straight and roost still and motionless on the pedestal of our public institutions. No, when our first men of the state, whether it be Cimon, Aristides, or Themistocles seem most solidly in place and seem least in need of devious courses to work their will in fusing the many interests of the citizens into common cause; it is just then when hawks will be approaching, out of sight, but riding the updrafts of some unsatisfied interests which can carry them to glory. It is best then, if you would wish to take a place on such a pedestal and stay there for any length of time, to zigzag on your approach and then when you have mounted the pedestal of high office move about first to this side and then to the other so that no hungry hawk, circling out of sight in the updraft of parties not quite satisfied by the policies of compromise and consensus, can take aim on you. What I am saying then, my friends, is that while the politician will indeed bask in the glory should he stay his course long enough to survive as "first citizen of the state", it seems clear to me that to do so he must oft appear to be what he is not, and not be what he appears to be. Only the gods, I suppose, know whether such a contest as this permits a man to win honorable glory."

Sophroniscus ended his discourse here, although he would have liked to illustrate his theme more fully by depicting a man whose frustrated political career was testament to his uncompromising sense of honesty and honor. However, he took the laurel from his brow and passed it on towards Clinias, thinking it best not to embarrass this honorable man, his life-long beloved, who also happened to be this evening's host. Besides, the head ache that seemed to come upon him ever more frequently was now making it very difficult to concentrate on the development of his theme.

Clinias took the laurel, but only to pass it on down to Megacles. "Megacles, I would indeed be rude and inconsiderate to all of my guests if I did not defer to you in order of our office as poet laureate. I see by your sober demeanor that you have yet a serious and thoughtful speech you would contribute to our topic. Please, take the laurel and since your words will be rich with the wisdom of your long experience, we will, if you wish, excuse you from plucking the strings of the lyre."

Megacles, although silver-haired and no longer the agile and quick handed athlete who had won glorious victories as charioteer in the Delian games, was not about to concede the competition of rhapsodists to the younger set. "Thank you, Clinias. I would like to speak now, but only on the condition that my nephew, Pericles, and our philosopher, Anaxagoras, follow me. I see that many of our younger gentlemen appear to be losing interest in our conversation and will soon press you to change the venue of our festivities. Lest I ramble on too long, I will take up the lyre and fit my thoughts to rhapsody. Since my old fingers soon grow weary, my poetry will be indeed brief.

> What men ask is the best way for the city to be ruled well?
> We Athenians, in Palestra, Gymnasium, and in all manly tasks
> Have from age to age believed competition does truly tell
> What man is best. This one should rule and in glory bask.
> Our forefathers made the games fair, no king or those they sire,
> May win the game by royal decree, birthright, or by bodyguards for hire.

> Cylon the wrestler and Pisistradids promised bread for all.
> Tyrants are often raised aloft by those who prefer comfort to freedom's chores.
> But Philiad and Alkmeonids have always answered duty's call.
> These noble clans join hands when demagogues would buy the people like whores.
> Be not deceived, all will rise higher if people elect a champion, a man who is best.
> What noble contest has he fairly won? For our rulers let this be the test.

> Should the untested man, of the common and low,
> Join the rank of archons and the Council of Ares' rock?

Surely to trust the state to such a blind throw
Would make our Athens a foolish city for others to mock.
Ephialtes, bested by Cimon in all since his days of school
Would bring all of Athens low rather than let his betters rule."

Megacles had made clever use of the lyre. Each couplet in his first two stanzas was framed by a pleasing progression of harmonic chords in which each successive chord was not only higher in its tonal quality, but also stronger in its volume. When he intoned, 'all will rise higher', the most complex chord dominated by a gorgeously accented high note blended perfectly with his chant. But when he turned in the third stanza to the corruption of the aristocratic conduct of free men's' common enterprises, then the strings of his lyre produced a series of cacophonous and ever more muted blending of sounds.

Megacles had touched on sensitive matters. Every one of the men around the table was made uneasy by the unnerving way in which Megacles had fixed his eyes on his nephew's face, never breaking eye contact with Pericles throughout his entire performance.

The younger Alkmeonid and chief associate of Ephialtes in the Assembly seemed least perturbed of all the guests. Pericles, like an attentive student heeding a tutor, looked steadily at his uncle with eyes that registered only dispassionate but steady interest. When Megacles had laid the lyre aside and taken the laurel from his brow, it was Pericles who first raised his cup and applauded the patriarch of his own mother's family.

"Uncle, you put us younger men to shame. Your mastery of rhapsodizing weaves sound and word seamlessly. Would that I had such powers to have my arguments gain admission through both the pleasing balances of harmony and the persuasive ratio of logic. If I did not know better, I might almost think you have become a Pythagorean - so masterful is your attunement of matters of the mind with music."

Clinias was about to second Pericles' compliment when Anaxagoras whose couch was immediately to Pericles' right suddenly sat up from his reclining position and interjected.

"Yes, yes Pericles you are right. Megacles mastery of the form is complete and it cheers me much to know that silver-haired men of more than three score years can still manage nimbly such fingering."

Megacles, genuinely fond of this portly and always comedic man of learning from Clazomenae, smiled at Anaxagoras as he replied in kind.

"Clearly, Anaxagoras, you are a man yourself with considerable powers. I would have thought my verses made little headway with you. Out of the corner of my eye, I could not but help noting that the most buxom of our hetaerai was rosy cheek to plump jowl with our philosopher. Indeed, although I did not look directly your way, it seemed that your ever inquisitive eyes, with the assistance of your hands, were bent on exploring the height and breadth of your consort's unusually endowed female nature."

"Uncle, I think you misjudge our philosopher's consultations with this young woman. Ishtaria is not exactly just that luscious tart she appears to be. She, like her mistress, is also from Miletus and I have heard that Aspasia herself instructs her girls on the "Way Up and The Way Down". You know what that is all about. I believe it was the Miletian theorist Anaximander who explained the underlying principle of all Reality as the equilibrium between opposites as they rise and fall in conflict with one another. So while it may appear that Anaxagoras' interest in Ishtaria's expertise with matters of up and down may be restricted to her hands on approach to male tumescence, I'm sure that our philosopher, always on the look out for new applications of theory, is teasing out with his new found assistant the operations of the 'Unbounded'".

Anaxagoras turned to Pericles. "I am impressed that you can so accurately characterize my current work. Only, I would not have Megacles or my honorable host thinking that I have not been following our discourse. You see, it requires very little of my intellect to continue the kind of studies presented by such an opportunity as provided by my current consort. And so while my body's organs may appear busy, my mind may absent itself from their work to attend to other discourse. I have not missed a word of either Megacles or any of the others. It was I, after all, who first asked that our symposium conversation take up the topic of the people of Athens treatment of Cimon. And now, I am most anxious to hear what you Pericles would have to add on this matter. I am sure I will not be disappointed. All jesting aside, I am impressed that a man as busy as you are with the responsibilities of public life yet finds time to follow the disputations of such as the Miletian theoreticians. I have heard that you are often seen with that most learned of all men in Athens, Protagoras, and have even as an older man assumed the role of his student. So, please take up the laurel. It is evident by your prominence in the Assembly and the benefits of your associations with men such as Protagoras that you must speak well."

When Anaxagoras had finished speaking, Clinias rose from his couch. He was happy that the gracious response of Pericles to Megacles and the banter with Anaxagoras had defused what could have been an unpleasant exchange between the older more conservative men closely associated with Megacles and the younger more radical associates of Pericles. It was time, thought Clinias, to draw the formal conversation to a close. There was still the traditional Anthesteria drinking contest and the *hetaerai* had also prepared an entertaining performance of exotic dancing. Given that it was already late in the evening, it would be just a few hours before sunrise by the time the final jar had been emptied and the night's contracted entertainment ended.

"Men, I see by the short length of our hearth candles that there are but 4 hours or so before daybreak. And so, unless any of you object, I am going to propose that we conclude our round of speeches and rhapsodizing with Pericles, and then, Anaxagoras. We will ask Anaxagoras to sum up the lessons of our dialogue and give them a philosophic cast. Pericles, the laurel is yours."

"Thank you, Clinias. I am honored to take my turn following my illustrious uncle. I hope that even as he has served Athens and done his part to preserve that Constitution of our city which in part was established by his uncle, Cleisthenes, so too I might build on this Constitution thereby doing honor to him as well as all the hard-working, brave, and free men of Attica. If my friends will not think me too old fashioned, I would like to rhapsodize on our topic, paraphrasing the inspired poetry of the friend of all free men, whether rich or poor, Solon. It is said that Solon only began and ended his verses with very simple chords from his lyre. You who have heard me play the lyre, I am sure, are thankful that I am content to go no further than Solon in this respect. Whether the ideas of my verse foolishly go further and thus deviate from the political wisdom of such as Solon and Cleisthenes, this I leave up to you and the rest of the free citizens of our city.

> Let me first speak of Athens' beginnings, of the lineage you know
> Of Theseus, begotten of Poseidon, who to unite the clans kingly powers did forgo:
>
> Our ancestors, it is said, Theseus long ago from tribute freed.
> Warring families and villages of Attica he united in common plans,
> So as to rescue Attica's children from King and Minotaur of Crete.
> It was this son of Aegeus who first taught Attica's clans
> That common service to Athena and law would vouchsafe liberty for all.
> Ancient enmities were set aside as men of Attica, now Athenians, answered Theseus' call.
>
> Let me speak next of Athens' days of boyish quarrels and strife
> Of Solon and when division of rich and poor would to tyranny give life:
>
> Our city lay under siege, our farms ruined by Megara's forces.
> Rich and poor, factions of Plain, Hill and Shore grew.
> Our weakness was not for lack of soldiers, arms or horses.
> But our state lay low by overbearing greed, crushing debt, and the rule by too few.

To Solon, herald and son of Nead kings, the people turned.
When things are even, there is no strife, from him they learned.

Last, let me speak of our day, to the Athens you and I belong,
Where the Assembly's accord and our courts make citizens strong:

He who would bind the titans best makes use of many stranded cords.
Impetuous violence, unbridled passions, excesses are the beasts
That must be restrained by Assembly's laws, the bonds of the Pynx's many lords.
He, who would lead, leads best when all the People are served, both high born and least.
This, I believe, is the test for all who seek Athens' thanks.
Such will be first among Athens' long remembered heroic ranks."

When Pericles had finished, Clinias was the first to raise his cup in acknowledging the merit of his poetry. Clinias praised the consonance of the song's theme with the public spiritedness of Pericles' Alkmeonid family tradition.

"Pericles, your poetry does you justice. It reminds us that whatever the motives of those who would lead our city, it is only outstanding service to the common good which wins deserved glory. While the hunger for glory and competition between often envious men may drive many to the arena of public life, what finally separates the truly noble from the merely ambitious is the capacity of the noble leader, if need be, to sacrifice himself for the best interests of the city. I believe you are of such a stock. Like your Alkmeonid ancestors, you have already demonstrated a willingness in public liturgy and military service to risk your life and give of your wealth for Athens."

"Thank you, Clinias. I am flattered that you think so. You are a far better example of such a principle than I. I must tell you I am very pleased that your marriage will link our families. Indeed, it is the secret of Alkmeonid longevity as a prosperous and noteworthy clan that our women always lift our stock higher, joining issue in each generation with illustrious men of other families such as you. I am especially impressed that my uncle who has associated with you for many years in your jointly owned shipping enterprise and has seen you up close and in action where many men prove themselves less than decent - the making of money - both trusts you completely and is honored that you will be the father of his grandsons."

Megacles was still pondering Pericles' speech and it annoyed him that his nephew already had drawn him away from that to another matter. As he turned to Clinias and with a nod seconded Pericles' assessment of his own regard for his soon to be son-in-law, he could not completely conceal his irritation with Pericles. "Yes, Pericles, I am hopeful that Clinias' union with my daughter will produce a man who remains true to the high calling of our family, a man who will serve our city well and protect our liberty from the demagoguery of those who pander to the worst impulses of the commons."

No one at the table could miss the hard edge in Megacles voice as his words, "remain true to the high calling of our family", seemed to carry a cautionary warning to his nephew. The old Alkmeonid Marathon warrior found it disconcerting that his nephew was so adept with speeches which seemed to make it impossible to tell where finally Pericles loyalties really lie. He had hoped that Pericles' speech would give him a clear read on where he would stand in the coming clash that must surely occur between Cimon and Ephialtes. As far as Megacles was concerned, everyone should know that Cimon is the last best hope for checking the demagoguery of rule by the unlettered mob. It was Cimon who had so far blocked Ephialtes persistent efforts to discredit and dismantle the Areopagite Council, the body made of former *archons* all of whom hailed from the oldest and finest families of Attica. The Council for the past thirty years, during the times of Athens' greatest crisis in the Great War with Persia, had provided the steadying hand and guidance which had steered the People and its Assembly safely through. Now, Ephialtes and his associates strove to open the highest offices of Athens to men of every class, even dockworkers and the most common laborers. Surely, thought Megacles, Pericles is intelligent enough to know that over time this would before long turn the venerable Areopagite Council into just a least numerous, and thereby powerless, reflection of the people's Assembly - a body which with the growth of Athens' town population now was filled with a majority of unlettered and often dishonorable men. Megacles would have liked to press this issue with Pericles, but he could see that the other guests were tiring of their conversation. And anyway, he thought, it seems that my nephew has mastered the art of seeming to be all things to all people. So Megacles settled for a sigh, begrudgingly acknowledging to himself that Pericles would go very far in Athens' public life.

When Pericles had divested himself of the laurel and handed the lyre back to one of the serving girls, Clinias called upon his distinguished guest from Clazomenae, Anaxagoras, to bring their poetic contest to a fitting end.

"Anaxagoras, has our conversation illumined for you the case of Cimon? Perhaps, philosopher that you are, you could make plainer in what ways our Muses have transfigured the particulars of our talk of Cimon onto a higher plane? Have we met our goal? Before Dionysos alone presides over our party, would you, with Apollo's help, share with us your interpretation of our songs? What lessons, might calm Reason find shining through our treatment of Cimon as his case may illustrate general patterns of the always perilous relationship between a leader and the people in freedom-loving Athens? You too, may win our prize if wine and our hetaera, Ishtaria, have not by now dulled that sharp intelligence the gods have given you."

Anaxagoras had already dismissed Ishtaria from his couch before Clinias finished calling upon him. He had looked forward all evening to this opportunity to exhibit his learning to this prestigious gathering of some of Athens' wealthiest and most influential men. And despite appearances to the contrary, he had been listening very carefully and pondering how to frame his own original contribution while yet demonstrating to each of the gentlemen that he had found something of worth in each of their views. After all, it would not do to unnecessarily alienate a potential sponsor because the impression was given that Anaxagoras thought him ignorant.

"Thank you, Clinias. I am both honored and yet somewhat intimidated by the task you assign me. Can the musings of a metic, unschooled in the subtleties of the ways of Athens, possibly compose a symphony which indeed blends and gathers up the music of so many gifted poets? Perhaps if I call upon the Queen of Heaven, lovely Aphrodite, she will both assist my song now and later vouchsafe a reunion with her lovely servant who has left my couch for another's. Let me begin my invocation and song, not with the lyre, but with a flute tune our maidens play at the Clazomenae holy day for Aphrodite."

Anaxagoras' flute playing was enchanting. The delicate and yet arresting melody captured the attention of all the guests as the unmistakably oriental tune carried them all out of Athens across the sea far to the east and far back in time to another people who worshiped the Queen of Heaven under the name of Ishtar. After a short prayer to the foam-born Cypriot, Anaxagoras began,

> "Let me sing a tale I have heard from a merchant of far away Babylon,
> A city very ancient, far overland beyond Phrygia where first rises Lord Sun.
> It may be that this tale of a far away people and time
> Will indeed in its elements bear seeds of all within its story.
> And so our tale, with Athens and her fruitful strife, may rhyme,
> Teaching, if we are attuned, politics' all-coursing patterns by allegory.
>
> The tale told by a merchant-scribe is that of Gilgamesh, ancient Uruk's king.
> It is he, husband of divine Ishtar, who visited the dead and saw the abyss.
> At first, this king, wore his people out. To his strength was opposed no man or thing.

Day and night he oppressed the weak, no equals stood to oppose a ruler like this.
The people's lament cried out for relief, and the sky god
Brought Enkidu, a Man of equal strength, to square off with Gilgamesh
So that Uruk's men and women might no more suffer from the king's unmatched rod.

The tale makes clear that soon Gilgamesh turned to build the city.
Where before unchecked power knew no bounds,
As his Divine consort in secret bid him plunder without pity,
Now strong man checking strong man gave birth to counsel and agreement sound.
Tyranny is checked by such arrangements, but it always lurks within every human breast.
Gilgamesh, we are told, learned that nothing is permanent and death will not relent,
When he visited the Abyss, more he was tasked than a lost friend to protest.
Build city walls of law and live within such artifice or chaotic destruction will be sent.

Athens, so many strong men, now may Gilgamesh's lesson be your wisdom and compact.
Law and good counsel should set the course for your power.
If your city would endure, then follow this tack -
Let no mob or unchecked ruler ever rule, even for one hour."

Anaxagoras paused. The expressions of both the younger and the older men seemed to indicate that his verses were too obtuse and perhaps had failed to please. And so he, anxious to please, ended his verses with a self-deprecating ditty which poked fun at all those purple-robed metic 'lovers of wisdom' like himself who speculated about things above the heavens and beneath the earth. His final couplet noted that freedom loving Athens had once and for all foreclosed the possibility of the return of the purple-robed kings, since now they only permitted such a wardrobe to freemen like him who were content for a fee to continue the work of humble pedagogues for the sons of Athens' wealthy families. Anaxagoras knew all was well when he saw the smiles of well-pleased gentlemen amused by his final verse. No one, he was sure, would feel either angry or resentful since he ended by himself playing the flute and as he raised the double flute to his mouth all could see under his right arm a hole in his worn out purple robe. No matter how learned, who could think that a man with a frayed robe would aspire to be a philosopher-king?

CHAPTER NINE
A FINAL FAREWELL FOR OLD FRIENDS

Socrates: Is life worth living with a body which is worn out and ruined in health? What about the part of us which is mutilated by wrong actions and benefitted by right ones? Is life worth living with this part ruined? ...the really important thing is not to live, but to live well.

(Plato. *Crito*, 48: a-b)

The night was giving way to the first light of the third and final day of Anthesteria when Clinias' guests, tired and yet happy, filed out of the men's quarters of Clinias' home. While they all had drunk heartily, their host and his servant had so mixed juice of the grape and the pure water of the house's own spring fed cistern, that the loosened tongues and warm glow bequeathed by Dionysos carried the guests to inspired revelry without ending in drunken stupor or the slavish excessive behavior of unbridled appetites. And indeed when each guest took leave, everyone did so in full possession of their wits and the evening's meal. The same could not be said for his hired entertainers. One of the very young *hetaerai* became so drunk that she had to be dismissed before the party ended. She had apparently come to his party already wine-filled hoping to become so drunk that she would be excused from the late-night ministry of Aphrodite.

When all had taken leave except Sophroniscus, Clinias called for Lycon.

"Lycon, give my friend, Sophroniscus, a hand and escort him to the garden portico. Then bring us a pitcher of cold water, fresh bread, and a kettle of porridge so that I might enjoy again the simple fare of a soldier's breakfast with this my life-long comrade. And, Lycon, please take that garlic necklace off....I can't bear it anymore!"

Lycon had been with Clinias for some twenty-five years now and still he did not understand his lord's cavalier approach to the powerful spirits of the deceased. "But sir, it is the day of visitation and even here there may be angry spirits about. Remember last Anthesteria when Procleus' steward forgot to post the garlic wreathes. The steward fell gravely ill and the water from Procleus' cistern flowed blood red. At least let me wear the necklace under my shirt."

"Can you believe it Sophroniscus? Here is a man almost forty years old living in a house filled with learned conversation. He has been taught to read, and he has traveled with me widely, seeing for himself the diverse and often contradictory religious practices of many peoples; and yet he still holds to the superstitions of his childhood. It doesn't even occur to him that the steward may have fallen ill because he overindulged in feasting or that the cistern water turned red because the steward himself had failed to clean the lichen from the inflow pipe. No, he is absolutely convinced that some grouchy ghost, waiting for his chance on Anthesteria, has made it his business to get even with Procleus - perhaps because Procleus overcharged him for a piece of sausage when he was among the living. Lycon, yes, tuck the necklace under you shirt, but I insist that you remove all those damn disgusting wreathes of rotten flesh and garlic from the garden portico. How can we possibly enjoy our porridge with that stink in our noses?"

Sophroniscus smiled as Lycon helped him to his feet. "Give me a moment or two, Lycon, to steady my legs. They seem to have both fallen asleep and we must wait until their numbness goes away. While we wait for my feet to wake up, Clinias, let me say a word on behalf of that part of our Anthesteria tradition which preserves the chthonic rites of aversion. Perhaps, I can persuade you then to be less impatient with your servant's rustic piety."

"We are in no hurry, Sophroniscus. I am always interested in hearing about your understanding of what true piety requires. And

I must remember that you can find even in our humblest servants, something worthy of our interest, if not respect."

"You must realize that not many men, either freemen or slave, arrive at your age, my noble friend, and remain clear of the ghosts of those they have cruelly made use of or ill-treated. Surely, you have noticed, Clinias that many of our most powerful and prosperous men leave behind them a trail of those they have pushed aside, trampled upon, and often destroyed in order that they might make their way. I suspect that for many of our ordinary citizens, such episodes fill the pages of even their family stories - let alone their dealings with their neighbors or business associates. I sometimes wonder how it could be otherwise. We see that the wild animals must devour one another if they are to survive and master their domain. It does not surprise me that we find our most illustrious citizens to be prowling predators, out and about stalking one another, seeking to advance themselves through endless conspiracies and struggles with one another. I understand fully how even the most educated, illustrious, and prosperous citizen can be haunted by the spirits of vengeance and will one day a year, at least, acknowledge the unseemly soil out of which many of the fruits of his own vine has issued. Although such a man might have taken every precaution to protect himself from what he can see as threatening; it is what he can't anticipate or see that worries him and so like any superstitious slave he thinks it best to take magical measures to ward off the rebound of life that was injured by his own hand. I also have come to understand why it is that our most powerful and sagacious politicians constantly seek to fan the fire of war with other cities. It is one of the most effective ways to deflect all the demons of the body politic aimed at their own life towards an alien people assumed to be unsympathetic and downright antagonistic."

Clinias nodded his head in agreement. "Yes, my friend, I see your point. I suppose that in this life justice always is imperfect and cannot keep pace with ambition, greed, and violence."

The feeling in Sophroniscus' lower body had now made its way to his feet.

"I am ready now, Lycon. Now that I have interceded on your behalf, I trust you will be my able helper. I will do my part to ward off the ghosts. I am sure you have had much less opportunity than our free compatriots to earn the visitation of a whole phalanx of angry spirits. Old and infirm as I am, I think together we can still shoo away the few that come calling on you. Perhaps they are the same ones that have plagued you since some unfortunate episode during your childhood in Euboea. I remember how frightened you were of ghosts on that day long ago on Euboea when you were one of my guides leading the way to Megacles' island farm. Many an Euboean family perished at the hands of pirate invaders. Even if some of these victims of pirate attacks were part of your childhood Master's family why should they be angry at you? You could not have been more than a small child when they perished and you escaped. It is time to send your familiar spirits to their final rest."

Lycon did not want to contradict his Master's guest. But no matter what Sophroniscus said, it seemed to Lycon that his Master of long ago could never forgive him for failing to sound the alarm when he ran away from the band of pirates he was the first to see. Who ever heard of a living Master forgiving anything of a slave? How could a dead Master be any different? So, like every slave who wants to remain a household servant and avoid the drudgery of field labor, or worse, the mines of Laurium; Lycon pretended to be confused by Sophroniscus and with downcast eyes acknowledged the only relation possible between a slave and his masters. "Sir, here we are. Can I help you with anything else?"

After Lycon had seated Sophroniscus at the garden bench, Clinias sent Lycon off to the kitchen. Clinias sat down beside his friend and gently placed his hand on his shoulder. He spoke quietly, choosing his words with care lest they in any way could be mistaken for pity.

"Sophroniscus, dear friend, it pains me to see you so wounded. It is a wound you do not deserve, whatever it is that grows unwanted upon your neck and saps the strength from your limbs. You must tell me what if anything I can do to help you."

Sophroniscus remained silent for a moment as he allowed the hand of Clinias to remain on his shoulder. Throughout there long and close friendship, Sophroniscus, the older man, had never acted upon the erotic attraction he felt for Clinias. This physical attraction, almost irresistible in the early years, had transformed into a mutually strong bond of solicitude and loyalty of such a quality that each one knew he could count on the other's unconditional disposition to understand and assist him- no matter what the circumstances. It was clear to Sophroniscus, from the very start, that Clinias had never felt the same physical attraction towards him. But the younger man was completely won over by Sophroniscus' intelligence and imperturbable inner serenity. It was only now, probably the last time he would be so close to Clinias, that he allowed his friend's touch to linger on his flesh, warming his shoulder with the incarnate love of a caress.

Clinias withdrew his hand and began to serve the porridge from the large cooking pot which Lycon had just brought from the kitchen. He wanted to show Sophroniscus with this simple gesture his gratitude for their long friendship. The spell not yet broken, Sophroniscus allowed himself to lean the weight of his body against the yet powerful upper body of Clinias. Clinias, leaning over the small table by their bench to dish the porridge, seemed to take no notice of the weight of his friend's upper body against his back.

When Sophroniscus felt Clinias' body straighten, he righted himself and moved the heavy and dull side of his body away. Gathering himself, he had decided that it was now over porridge and just with this human being, if anyone, that he could make himself intelligible and enjoy one last communion before he took leave of life.

"Clinias, you have already been of great help. I cannot tell you how much I appreciate the trouble you undertook to consult with the physicians at Cos on my behalf. The pharmaceutical you brought back a year ago from Cos, with the detailed prescriptions for its administration, has helped to ease the pain in my head which recently has become more severe and unrelenting. I am especially grateful for the even more powerful pharmaceutical mixture you have arranged for me to take home with me today. I believe it is some kind of medicine made of crushed hemlock weed and I am quite certain this taken in sufficient dosage will purge my soul of this painful ailment."

"You must be very careful with the tincture of hemlock, Sophroniscus. The physician who sold this to me explained that the medicine can be therapeutic when taken in very small amounts provided the body is well irrigated. So you need to drink much water before and after swallowing the prescribed portion. However, should too much be swallowed, the hemlock can act as a fatal poison paralyzing the body's vital functions. Like everything else, it all depends on the right proportions. If taken in just the right amount, it will eliminate the pain by inducing a numbness; but should too much be taken this same medicine becomes a poison which renders the entire body lifeless. Also, you must be careful not to eat anything before using this. When there is food in the stomach, this potion causes severe vomiting and convulsions."

"Yes, I understand, Clinias. I will use it properly. Perhaps if I describe my condition very carefully, we together can calibrate just how much of this pharmaceutical will provide the therapy I require. You will bear with me, I hope, as I make plain to you the effects of what you call my wound. Please, go on and eat while I talk. I have no appetite this morning and will settle for just a taste of the porridge."

"Sophroniscus, I know you well. You have been thinking long and deeply about what you are about to say to me. Please do not rush through your thoughts, worrying that I need to go to sleep after our all night party. I feel, I don't know exactly why, alert and refreshed. Do you really mean to allow me to play the physician and prescribe for you?"

"Absolutely, my dear friend! But we must both agree, as you have already noted, that the pharmaceutical dose is appropriate and fitting as a therapy for my affliction. Would you also agree that the best way to arrive at an accurate diagnosis of my wound and a remedy for its cure is first to describe the well-being of my life which it impairs?"

"What do you mean, Sophroniscus, by this 'well-being'? Surely if you wish to minimize pain and preserve pleasures as much as possible, then it should not be too difficult to calibrate the medicine to this end."

"Clinias, I wish it were that simple....a matter of arranging my body so that it could register more pleasures than pain, or at least if not enjoying pleasure be numb to pain. But you, more than most men, must understand that such a state of merely undergoing pleasures and pains is not human well-being and certainly not a kind of condition I have ever settled for in my life."

"Of course, you are right, Sophroniscus. But unremitting pain should not be accepted since it siphons off so much of a man's power in warding off the unseemly spectacle of becoming a whimpering wife."

"After watching my own wife give birth, I am not as sure as I used to be that a woman's labor makes her soft and cowardly. They often do not choose the travail of having their bodies stretched and strained to the limit so that the unusually large head of our species can breach the narrow gateway of their often still girlish bodies. Soon, when you bring that beautiful seventeen year-old Alkmeonid princess to your house, infected, no doubt, as she is with that Alkmeonid aura of superiority and love of mastery, you may have to moderate your own views on wifely nature. I have heard that Dinomache is aptly named, a spirited battler. She will not take kindly to a rider who digs the spur and is heavy with the reigns. She, my friend, I am sure will bring forth radiant new life from your loins. But I get your point, Clinias. I am very grateful that my medicine controls the pain, although it appears to have no effect on halting the gradual paralysis of my limbs or the unnatural growth on the back of my neck."

"You are probably right about Dinomache, Sophroniscus. I must learn the art of diplomacy and due attention to Dinomache if I am to command without offending Megacles. But we are wandering from our task. My marriage is not what you have waited until now to speak with me about."

"But, Clinias, I am indeed happy for you. Your life of courage and labor has won you prosperity, a bride from one of Athens' most illustrious families, and the gratitude of fellow citizens for your heroic seamanship at Artemisium, Salamis, and Eurymedon. Now, you are in a position to provide for your own sons every opportunity to flourish and serve the city with honor and glory. Look at those unfortunate accursed women of Hades damned to carry water endlessly in their sieves which your clever sculptor has engraved around the base of your own cistern. Most men could not bear such a picture of futility in the very courtyard of their homes. But for you, a man of great accomplishment, it is a beautifully crafted piece of art and its theme does not disturb your soul. It restores my faith in the gods and their justice to know you have a happiness and reward in this life well fitted to virtue.

Now, as for the question of the right prescription of the *pharmakos*, let me explain my own view by calling to mind one of Homer's stories. A few years ago, when I still regularly made my way down to the marketplace and would stop to listen to the exhibitions of the visiting professional tutors, men like Anaxagoras, I listened at some length to a Sophist intent on exhibiting his own learning by expounding on the meaning of a passage from Homer. I can't remember the Sophist's name although I am sure he was from the island of Paros. The theme of the Sophist's lecture was to praise the genius of Homer by interpreting to his audience the allegorical meaning of Homer's tale of Paris' judgment at the beauty contest of the goddesses. I don't know whether he was right about Homer's genius, but I found his retelling of the tale a stimulus to the examination of my own destiny. You remember the story, I'm sure."

Figure 11
The Judgment of Paris
Priam and Hermes lead Hera, Athena and Aphrodite before Paris

"I do, Sophroniscus, but what did the Parian make of the story? I know you are especially charmed by all things thoughtful and that is probably why you paid a coin or two for a second listening to the Sophist's recitation on this topic. So how does the story illumine the matter at hand?"

"Well, the symbolic point of the story according to the Parian is to show the different kinds of lives which men can choose to pursue. The story begins, if you remember, with the wedding of Thetis, daughter of Nereus the Old Man of the Sea, and the mortal, Peleus. Zeus, unknown to Thetis and Peleus, had arranged their marriage so as to assure that Thetis would not conceive a child by another god. It had been prophesied that should Thetis bear a son by a divine husband, this god would one day rule Olympus. The wedding was a joyous occasion attended by all the important gods and men. However, although this joining of mortal and immortal was intended to avert the kind of strife among the gods which occurred when Zeus seized the throne of heaven from his own father, the inspired poet teaches that wherever there is desire and the zeal for power, strife will soon follow whether invited or not. So the story relates that the goddess Eris was gravely offended since she was not invited to the wedding. Out of her anger at being so slighted, she set in motion a plan for revenge which would have long-lasting and grievous consequences for mankind. She crafted a wondrously appealing golden apple and inscribed upon it the words, "For the most beautiful". As Hera, Athena, and Aphrodite were together making their way home to Olympus from the wedding, Eris cast the golden apple at their feet. The immortal goddesses all claimed the trophy and began to quarrel bitterly and would have exchanged blows if Zeus had not intervened. He who rules through clever counsel proposed that the quarrel be resolved through a beauty contest in which Paris of Troy, the most handsome of all men, would choose which of the three immortal ones was the most beautiful and thereby entitled to the golden apple as her trophy.

It is at this point of the story, Clinias, that the Parian takes considerable liberty with the traditional story in order to make apparent what he calls its hidden meaning. Departing all together from the story as authoritatively compiled by our own Athenian editor of sacred tradition, Onomakritos, he describes in detail how each of the three goddesses appears before Paris to make their case for being judged the most beautiful. According to the Parian's account, Hera came first bedecked with all the implements and tokens of power belonging to her as the consort of the Supreme Ruler. She offered mastery of multitudes, the ability to inspire fear and obedience, and the prerogatives of royalty. Athena, born from wise Zeus' forehead, appeared next to Paris. She wore, according to the sophist, a finely wrought embroidered gown which depicted the ingenious works of all the crafts. On her head, she wore the crown honoring her secret mother, Metis. Wisdom is hers and will be the gift bestowed on those who love her. Aphrodite, last to appear, came to Paris and, with her irresistible allure, filled his body with erotic desire and its thirst for pleasure. She promised him the passion which makes men abandon all - their families, their cities, even their honor. She showed him Helen, the most beautiful of all women and the very mortal incarnation of Aphrodite. Paris intoxicated with the charms of Aphrodite, spurned Athena and Hera in favor of Aphrodite's pleasure."

"I think I understand the Parian's allegory, Sophroniscus. I suppose the Sophist is proposing that men can choose between three very different ends to which they can devote their energies and resources. If one were to envision their life principally as a contest with others where the prize is always to increase ones own power, then such a man would judge Hera to be the most beautiful. Those, like Paris, who judge Aphrodite to be most beautiful, are pleasure seekers. I must confess, Sophroniscus, that when I was still young enough to play the games of Eros I found myself hard pressed by Aphrodite. As a young man my creed was the one expressed by the poet of Colophon, Mimnermus.

'What life is there, what pleasure, without golden Aphrodite? May I die straightway, when her charms no longer hold me!

Stolen meetings, lovers' gifts and lovers' union– these are the only flowers worth plucking for men and women in their prime.'"

"I think that most men in their youth would find this creed irresistible, Clinias. But what do you think the Sophist believed to be the point of his story?"

" I would guess, Sophroniscus, that our Parian professional tutor, a man devoted to learning and also a shrewd business man, wished to honor our own Athena and her attributes as best. Although, Aphrodite wins the contest on that day of Paris' judgment, we know that no good comes to Paris and his city. And even his prize, Helen, is taken from him while he is yet in his prime. If one wishes to live a life of good measure, then one must avoid the pitfalls of both power unguided by intelligence and the excesses of youthful passions by subordinating the will and passions to the search for wisdom and the rule of reason. Indeed, the sophist probably concludes his recitation with a invocation to Zeus' divine brow, likening Athena's miraculous birth to the pains of those noble youths whose heads throb with his own course in philosophy."

"Clinias, you always have been quick to see the point of a story. But don't you think our Sophist has made matters too simple? Can these ends be so neatly separated out from one another? Or, as your guest Anaxagoras might urge, is it not the case that these three types of pursuit are always mixed up with one another, the seeds of everything in everything? Don't we find in any man's life course a jumble of passion, resolve, and the wisdom which comes from reflection on his own experience? As for my own case, I have come to think that all three of the above mentioned ends are not unlike a fruit of another kind. They seem to me to be most like the fruit of Tantalus, just out of reach and always receding. I would then add a very different kind of beauty to those that can be chosen. It is a kind of beauty you, Clinias, have exhibited all your life, and it is that kind of good which alone seems attainable to us mortals."

"What is that beauty, Sophroniscus?"

"I am not quite sure what to call it. But I can describe something of where it may be found....I have seen it in many guises and in diverse places, but it always seems to involve a kind of service to something higher than what is usually defined as one's own safety, comfort, and prosperity. This service is not that of a slave, one which is rendered out of abject fear of punishment or entered into out of compulsion. No, I am thinking of that kind of service in which a free man cherishes a standard of excellence, and holding before the steady gaze of his own mind's eye a picture of this perfection, aspires to meet the calling of this demand, even if he alone is witness to his course of conduct. The sculptor who tries again and again to capture just the peculiar disposition of the champion discus thrower in the instant before the discus is released; the hoplite warrior who trains and trains until he approximates that coordination of shield, sword, and spear which will maximize the effectiveness of his brotherhood's fighting unit, the craftsman who will cast and recast his mold until the artifact is as perfect as humanly possible; the athlete who searches out ever more accomplished competitors, not so that he can rub the other's nose in the mud, but so that he and his worthy opponents can drive one another to ever closer approximations of perfection in their mastery of a peculiar configuration of physical prowess; the husbandman who strives endlessly with the elements so as to optimize his garden's bounty without compromising its permanent fertility; the juror who with all his intelligence seeks to ascertain truth and render judgment in accord with the laws as fairly as possible no matter what the consequences to himself: these are all manifestations of that beauty which I aspire after.

What shall we call this, Clinias? No doubt, it requires intelligence to discern rightly such ideals for our work, our play, and our life course. But this aspiration to serve such standards is more than intelligence. I believe it is formed from some lovely combination of our passions, the will, and our judgment. When we see this combination, this disposition of character in anyone working its way in everything such a man sets his hand and heart to, then we have before us, I believe, a noble and beautiful man, even if in his striving he falls short of his aspirations."

"Sophroniscus, I would call this honor, and I would add to what you say that a life which serves this discipline is most free. Surely, this is a kind of beauty that is overlooked in the story of Paris' judgment. Indeed, often those who are truly honorable in the way you describe go unnoticed because they care little about being honored by others."

"I think you are right about that, Clinias. And to make matters sometimes even more difficult for such a man who aspires after this kind of beauty, there may be circumstances where service to such standards may even make one unpopular. This is why truly honorable men scarcely ever can succeed in politics, and should they attain political preeminence they cannot long maintain it.

Clinias, you remember that I was trying to get clear with you about my current condition and what prescription of the pharmaceutical is best suited for a therapy which will preserve for me a modicum of the good and beautiful life. Now if we are agreed that for men like you and I, it is activity aiming for excellence which confers worth and beauty to our life, perhaps we can now settle on my treatment and the calibration of the *pharmakos*."

"I am not quite sure what you have in mind, Sophroniscus. What is the connection between preserving your honor and medicating your condition?"

"It is really quite simple, Clinias, and the sadness in your eyes tells me that you do understand. Whatever grows on the back of my neck is now taking more of me, piece by piece, at a rate that soon will leave me, if not dead, totally useless to others and myself. This past year I have had to withdraw from my brotherhood's activities, my *deme* meetings, and even the tribe's veteran's militia processions. The growing paralysis of my body will soon make it impossible for me to move about at all. There are days when my speech slurs, and I believe it is only a matter of time before I cannot speak. The pain is not the issue as much as the steady and now rapid degenerative loss of my faculties. Soon, the range of my activities and their connection to the enrichment of either my own or anyone else's life will shrink almost to the vanishing point. There can be no honorable way to live in this condition of total dependence and passivity. I am ready for a therapy which will release me from such a fate. And it is my hope that with your assistance I can honorably take leave in such a way that I have met my responsibilities to my family, the city, and my friends, leaving all in good order. I plan to explain to my good wife and young Socrates the necessity for me to entrust my estate to their management under the auspices of your oversight. Will you take on this for me, Clinias? My son, I am sure, will repay you with his loyalty and life-long solicitude for your progeny."

Clinias had turned his back again. He did not want Sophroniscus to see the tears that now he could not control. "Of course, I will do this and anything else you ask."

Sophroniscus had now finally sealed his resolution. He knew that once he had declared his intention to Clinias, he would not turn back from his plan..."My son, I believe, will be able to assist in the final ministration of the requisite pharmaceutical, and I will make sure that my good cheer will exorcize from his mind any fear of an angry or vengeful paternal spirit. Clinias, will you look to his welfare? It is odd, isn't it, how so few of us ever get to know our own sons. We often are already old men when they come into the world and think it unseemly to be directly involved in their education. But due to my condition I have for the last two years spent considerable time with Socrates. We have had many long talks. He is already mature beyond his years, unusually inquisitive with a mind that seems inexhaustibly restless, and has already displayed a strong character. But, because of his lack of good looks, he is not likely to be taken on, as most young men who make their way are, by an honorable older friend. I believe that my son will accomplish great things if his education and advancement in the next ten years or so is promoted. My nephew, Sosothenes, is a good and responsible man and he will be young Socrates' legal guardian. I am only asking that you watch out for my son and should something go awry, would you keep him from harm until he reaches his manhood."

Clinias had regained his composure. "Sophroniscus, perhaps you are mistaken about the course of your affliction. Would it not be possible for the growth of this thing inside your neck to stop or even go away? If you can continue to think as clearly as you do now, would it not be best, even if your body is mostly unresponsive to your will, to continue as you have in the recent past. And why won't you let a surgeon at least remove what protrudes from the natural line of your neck? I cannot bear to think that I may be assisting you in taking your own life when the man that you are still glows brightly. But if you are determined to soon treat your affliction by yourself denying it any further degradation of your powers, I understand. You can be assured that I will always honor our friendship by looking out for young Socrates' welfare."

Sophroniscus nodded his head in thanks. "I am sure that the best prescription for saving my honor and dignity is that one which does not rob my family's estate to subsidize a surgeon's experiment on this old man's misshapen neck...I think I hear someone knocking on your outer door. It is probably my servant Hamilcar come to take me home."

Lycon appeared from the other side of the courtyard fountain, escorting a slightly drunk and disheveled looking Phoenician. It was Hamilcar. Clinias had helped Sophroniscus to his feet and slipped under his good arm a small silken pouch. The pouch contained a sealed narrow vase and a sheet of parchment on which were inscribed the directions for administering the small container's powerful pharmaceutical. Sophroniscus with his good elbow close to his side so as to hold the vial in place raised the same forearm in a final salute to this companion whom he had loved for so long. It was the last time Clinias would meet the gaze of those eyes which had so often in his life assured him of his own worth.

PART THREE
Troubled Freedom
Scenes from the Golden Age of the Athenian Empire
450 to 432 B.C.

CHAPTER TEN
CHILDREN OF STRIFE
(450 B.C.)

Baneful Night bore Nemesis too, a woe for mortals,
and after her Deception and the Passion of lovers
and destructive Old Age and capricious Strife.
Then loathsome Strife bore Ponos, the bringer of pains,
Oblivion and Famine and the tearful Sorrows,
the Clashes and the Battles and the Manslaughters,
the Quarrels and the Lies and Argument and Counter-Argument,
Lawlessness and Ruin whose ways are all alike,
and Oath, who, more than any other, brings pains on mortals
who of their own accord swear false oaths.

(Hesiod. *Theogony*, lines 223 – 233)

Clinias left his home very early to make his way to the small Magistrates' Club House which was on the west side of the Agora beside the Bouleuterion where the Council of Five Hundred conducted its affairs. The morning was grey and heavy with a chilly wind-driven mist. When he turned the corner from his own street onto the broad Panathenaic Way which ran southeast to the Agora, the drizzle turned to a steady downpour. Why is it, he wondered, that when he was at sea in the midst of a howling northeaster he never got cold or fretted about the wind-tossed watery chaos all around him? But here in the city, surrounded by buildings, streets, and all kinds of readily available shelter, his wet cloak and the squeaking of his water logged leather sandals made him miserable and irritated. It was one thing, he surmised, to face the storm at sea as a captain of the ship responsible for the safety of his crew and cargo, and quite another thing to make your way down an everyday street where all that was at stake was a dry cloak and toga. High adventure and supreme responsibility elicited heroism and determined good spirits. Whereas a sleepless night, a mild hang-over, a jittery stomach, and the prospect of sitting in a damp toga on a hard bench for most of the day at Council made Clinias feel very low and dispirited. As he drew his cloak up around his head to keep the rain from pelting his face he wondered whether he had made a wrong turn somewhere in his life.....Maybe I should be at sea all the time, a pirate perhaps. Yes, that would be better! I wouldn't have to deal with either a house full of nitpicking women and gossiping slaves or city councils where the conference tables are like rowing benches with incompetent rowers who's pushing and pulling at the oars are at cross purposes and only disturb the water without moving the ship.

"Clinias, Clinias, is that you?"

It was Callias calling him from across the street. There was no mistaking him for anyone else. He was now the richest man in Athens and everywhere he went it was like a little parade announcing his commercial success. Today, looking like a Pharaoh, he was sitting on his portable Egyptian style royal chair carried by two of his two strong-armed body slaves. His regal conveyance was outfitted with a water resistant and beautifully purple dyed cow-hide canopy. The porters and their regal passenger had stopped on the other side of the road by the cart of a vendor who sold cakes and other breakfast fare. While water poured from the ends of the canopy down over the slaves heads, Callias sat high and dry, nibbling on a sesame cake. "Clinias, it is you. Do you mind if we make our way together to the Magistrate's Club House? You know, I have been asked to join you and the others, even though I am now neither a magistrate nor a Councilor."

Clinias would have preferred to complete his journey by himself, but it would be impolite and bad for his own business to slight this man who seemed to have his finger in almost every kind of enterprise where money was to be made. Besides, maybe Callias could provide more information about today's session of the Council. Clinias wondered why he and others had been summoned by General Pericles to the Magistrate's Club House for a meeting prior to the start of the Councilors Session. "Yes, of course, Callias. But stay there, I will cross to your side of the street."

Clinias crossed the street and joined the parade, walking now beside and under the canopy enough so that the pelting rain no longer reached him. He rearranged his wet cloak, pulling it off his head and gathering it around his shoulders. His long hair would make it clear to those citizens who passed by that he was not another slave walking besides the rich man's porters as they all made their way from the vendor's cart back into the traffic toward the Bouleuterion.

"By Zeus, Clinias, I almost thought you a ghost, shrouded like you are and with nothing but dark eyes peering out into the mist. Why do you subject yourself to such a dismal walk when you can surely afford the kind of comfort you see me enjoying?"

"As for my current travel arrangements, Callias, they are both natural to me and required by the circumstances of my married state."

"Oh, you mean that even an Alkmeonid in-law would excite suspicion and undue envy from our democratic citizens should they see you publically enjoying the trappings of kingly wealth?"

"Yes, something like that, Callias. But, you know, I admire your clear and single-minded determination to enjoy life. I take this to be the reason why you have made it very clear to everyone in Athens that you have no desire ever to enter politics. It appears that our citizens are completely convinced that you regard the prospect of holding any kind of public office as loathsome. I sometimes envy you and your family for reasons no one would expect. Your family makes no pretensions of being among the "good and beautiful" set, having come by your wealth as might any hard-working merchant or tradesman who has not inherited the land and prestige of Athens' founding families. Thus, no one seems to begrudge your success or think that you must be brought low because you are an aristocrat who believes it is his destiny to lord it over common folk. So you can very well go about the business of amassing a great fortune and making use of it to make life as enjoyable as possible for both yourself and your friends.

"Clinias, after all these years in partnership with Megacles, five years of marriage with his daughter, a true Alkmeonid princess, and your own blue-blooded lineage from the house of Ajax; you appear like a city divided against itself when you so think of Callias' blessings. In your soul there is perhaps in one part an aristocrat plagued with a bad conscience about inequality and in some other part there is a democrat plagued with resentment and insecurity in the face of superiority. As for me, yes it is true I never will seek high elected political office. But have you forgotten - how could you - that I am now married to Cimon's sister, Elpinice. And so I too despite my new money am by marriage now rubbing shoulders with the families of Athens' good fathers."

Clinias chuckled. "Callias, I see that you have been spending much time again with our resident Sophist, Protagoras. I have heard that same disputation which likens our human nature to the constitution of a city. Be careful, or that man from Abderas will exact more than his fees from you. You may fall under the spell of philosophy and in your stupor forget the art of making money!"

"There is no danger in that, Clinias. I am already too far in love with the pleasures of the palate and the body - and they are expensive - to abandon wealth for the uncertain and far too Spartan regimen of service to a Reason bent on searching out the abstract, eternal, and invisible. Besides, Clinias, when you listen very carefully to what Protagoras teaches, you come to realize that he really offers a very practical course in curing those afflictions of the self-divided soul which rob of us the all too short and fragile portion of enjoyment allotted to us mortals."

"I don't know about that Callias. But before we arrive at the government buildings, let me ask you if you know anything as to why Pericles has summoned us to meet with him before the Councilors

Session begins? Neither you nor I now serve on the Council. The same is true for some of the others which he has summoned. What is going on?"

Callias demeanor changed suddenly. His face grew tense, and he would not meet Clinias' eyes. "We will be rounding the corner into the west end of the *Agora* just up beyond that last stand of sycamore trees. There is no time, Clinias, for me to sort out with you what the leader of the people has in mind. Pericles, as you know, is a very subtle and skilled politician. I have some hunch what it might be all about, but I think it best that Pericles himself explain the purpose of his meeting."

"Yes, of course. I can only hope that there is no new intrigue being planned which would entangle me. I am tired of political squabbles and wish to live the remainder of my life unencumbered by the strife of political factions." Clinias thought it best to change the subject. "The farmers, I am sure, are pleased with this weather. The newly planted winter cereal crops are getting a good soaking."

"A couple more rainfalls like this, Clinias, and I will have to reconsider my bids on the contracts for transporting grain from the Black Sea granaries. The price of foreign grain will fall if the winter crops of Attica are plentiful. You see, my friend, what Protagoras is getting at.....the farmers pray for rain and I for drought and the gods come out smelling like sweet ambrosia no matter what happens!"

When Callias' small parade made its way along the west side of the *Agora* past the Royal *Stoa*, down past the *Metroon* which housed all the official archives of Athens, and pulled up in front of the small circular building in which Magistrates informally gathered; there were already some twenty men or so gathered around Pericles who was holding court in the covered Portico which joined the Magistrate's Club House to the Bouleuterion.

Clinias recognized most of the men gathered around Pericles. Most of them were serving on the Council of 500 this year. So it was clear that Pericles intended to hold some kind of caucus before the entire Council convened to prepare the agenda and resolutions for next week's planned Assembly. It was not obvious, thought Clinias, from the composition of the group what Pericles was seeking to accomplish with their help. While all 113 demes were represented on the Council proportionate to their head count of citizens, it was certain, given the small size of the caucus, that Councilors from most of the demes were not present. What was evident though was that Pericles had brought together leading men from all the major constituencies and various political clubs in Athens.

There, standing just to the right of the helmeted Pericles was Cleisthenes, Megacles oldest son and now one of the most prominent members of the Alkmeonid clan. Cleisthenes was in deep conversation with Archaeolus, a nephew of Cimon's. And there behind these two, leaning gracefully against one of the columns that lined the covered walkway between the Magistrate's Club House and the Bouleuterion, was Cimon himself. Although it was difficult for this man, who was perhaps Athens' greatest living General and a former first man of the people, to withdraw from the politics of public life; ever since the Assembly had voted to waive the last two years of Cimon's ten year ostracism and allow him to return, he was always careful to give way to those who now held power in Athens.

Cimon no longer needed to worry about representing the interests of the aristocracy, since men like Archaeolus and Cleisthenes had assumed this role. They were men who knew that the democratic reforms of the past three or generations or so, including the most recent ones undertaken by Ephialtes and Pericles, were probably irreversible. In their hearts, they yet believed that even Pericles, whose rise to power had been accomplished through his alliance with Ephialtes and the more radical elements of the demes, would, when it really mattered, find a way to preserve within the government a sturdy citadel for the aristocratic interests of his own family.

But there were in this caucus just as many men who favored policies and institutions which would vest governing power principally in the hands of the merchants, *thetes*, and craftsmen of the city *demes*. Isocrates stood just to the left of Pericles, and he had become quite noteworthy not only for his outspoken advocacy for the military mission to the western Corinthian gulf three years past, but also for his recent campaign to provide pay for commoners who served on the juries. He was especially popular with the potters and other ceramicists whose shops lined the Ceramikos District which he represented this year on Council. They would long remember his eloquent and passionate speech which, many believed, had finally swayed the Assembly to approve funds and support for the Athenian navy's clearing pirates from the westward Corinthian gulf so as to make it safe for export of their wares to the lucrative Sicilian and Italian markets.

Hermisteus stood directly in front of Pericles. Hermisteus was engaged in conversation with a small coterie of workmen wearing leather aprons. These men worked in the iron-working shops nearby and their shins and arms were often blistered and red from the searing heat of the forges they tended. Although crude and unpolished in speech, ready always with a profane or lewd joke, and quick to lose his temper; Hermisteus was a force to be reckoned with at the Pynx when he brought along with him the laborers and dock hands that did most of the hard manual labor which greased the commerce of prosperous Athens. Although these *thetes* were the least prosperous of Athens' citizens, they were a proud and fiercely independent lot convinced that their recently acquired citizenship would allow them one day to leave behind the kind of wage earning toil that differed little from the work slaves performed for the very rich.

Councilors such as Isocrates and Hermisteus normally did not readily associate with men like Archaeolus, Cleisthenes, and especially Cimon. Indeed, only eight years ago both Isocrates and Hermisteus had taken a leading role in mustering the Assembly vote for Cimon's ostracism. Moreover, stories still circulated on the docks, in the warehouses and the work-rooms of the shops that somehow it was associates of Cimon or their ilk that had arranged for the assassination of their beloved Ephialtes nine years ago, less than a year after Cimon had been ostracized. While Pericles himself had never even hinted that Ephialtes' murder had resulted from such a conspiracy, he had supported at the time a Commission to investigate the assassination. Yes, everyone knew that it was Aristodicus of Tanagra who had killed Ephialtes and that this Aristodicus was certainly himself an aristocrat who had contacts with leading aristocratic families in Athens – but this did not necessarily mean that the assassin was an agent of Athenian aristocrats. The Commission found no hard evidence for such a conspiracy, but there were enough unfinished lines of investigation and plausible sets of circumstances surrounding what was known about the murder to fuel speculation for years - especially for those who were convinced that the well connected aristocratic families with their unlimited money could influence the work of even the most determined and fair-minded investigators.

The rest of the group included other prominent merchants like himself and Callias, some Councilors who hailed from a few of the more remote rural demes of Attica, Hamilcarus the Phoenician Metic who was often employed by Athenian shippers to deal with contractual arrangements for trade at the ports of Egypt, Crete, and Syria, and at least a half-dozen of men whose families held hereditary priesthoods to some of the city Sanctuaries and who were now also serving one of their two permitted annual appointments to the Council of 500.

Isn't it testimony to the mastery of Pericles savvy, thought Clinias, that he, and probably only he, can bring such a group together on common ground and that they are open under his guidance to the possibility of a compromise which will allow the Assembly to resolve important matters. This, thought Clinias, must be Pericles' purpose today.

When Clinias and Callias had exchanged greetings with Pericles and others, Pericles gathered everyone together and asked them to follow him to a small tree-covered plaza just behind the covered walkway and to the side of the Bouleuterion. There was now a break in the clouds and the rain had halted, so that the Plaza could comfortably accommodate Pericles' caucus. Protocol would not permit him to take the group into either the Magistrate's Club House or the Bouleuterion since not all those present held public office. And so Pericles had made arrangements for the public servants of the

Magistrate's Club House to set up a double semicircle of benches, with his own modest unadorned wooden chair at the front of the array.

The workmen who had buzzed around Hermisteus were unsure whether they should stay or go since they had not themselves been invited by Pericles. They ended up standing at the back of the benches, right behind their patron, Hermisteus. When the rest of the men were all seated, Pericles rose from his chair, and, as he was always careful not to offend the commoners who now for nine straight years had helped repeatedly to reelect him General in the demes of his tribe and lift him to the supreme command of Athens' military forces, the people's General now ordered the Club House attendants to round up another bench for the workmen. As the servants scurried back down the stoa towards the Club House's storage shed to look for another bench, Pericles began the meeting with a warm welcome for the workingmen. Like Themistocles whom Pericles as a young boy had admired, Pericles the Alkmeonid man of the people seemed to know almost every citizen by name.

Paphlageus, Charmenides, Kalisthenes, Plutoxus, and Apodorus please stay. I'm glad you are here. We will have no secrets from the people here. Take a seat and please feel free to join in our discussion or ask questions. I am very impressed that all of you are here so early on the first day after Thesmophoria. I know that our shops and businesses are now backed up with work, and even more backed up is our manly business with young wives with ready-fields primed by their three day service to Demeter. But here you are, good citizens, and I will not keep you long as the Council session will be underway shortly."

Before Pericles could continue, a suddenly ruffled and angry Archaeolus rose from his bench and began berating Athens' first man. "Pericles, must you always curry the favor of the ruffians that hang about Hermisteus' apron strings? I've heard the rumors and know why their brood will be thronging the porch of the Bouleuterion, whispering into every Councilor's ear their latest unholy demand laced with threats of direct action in the courts if they don't get their way." Archaeolus turned and glared at Hermisteus who sat behind and to the left of him at the other side of the semicircle of benches.

Hermisteus had already risen from his seat and, to the amusement of his clients, had produced an apron which he held aloft and waved in Archaeolus' direction as if to shoo him away. Before Archaeolus could say anymore, Hermisteus turned to his friends and in his Pynx voice seemed to be addressing everyone at once when he aimed his bawdy rhetorical question, like a javelin, at Archaeolus, the young champion of the "good and beautiful" aristocrats who dared challenge him in single combat.

"Pericles, it is indeed kind of you to be mindful of our other responsibilities. But why do you worry about Archaeolus and his kin? Since they are of the Laconophile clan, they have little use for their wives. I'm quite certain, in fact, that their plows, as you might say, are quite worn out from plowing the rocky and narrow backside fields of their Ganymede boys. Indeed, I have heard that the venerable father of their brood, Cimon, is planning a love feast, an honorable peace treaty I think he calls it, with his Spartan clients so that his kin can set their plows to new fields, yea in fair Laconia itself. And why do you worry that our morning caucas calls them away from an honest day's work? Do you really think, Pericles, that Cimon's brotherhood, champions of those who ride the lashed backs of helots, will begrudge the few hours at the Bouleuterion stolen from their many hours in gentlemanly horseplay at the gymnasium and the race-tracks?"

Hermisteus and Archaeolus belligerence fanned and agitated the whole group so that the meeting was quickly degenerating into a bellicose and chaotic shouting match. Fortunately, the presence of General Pericles would probably be enough to prevent the angry clusters of red-faced men from coming to blows.

Pericles himself looked more disconcerted and alarmed than angry. This was just what he did not want to happen - another confrontation between the aristocrats and the commons with all the old wounds between the city's factions being reopened. He had thought that if he could gather together a small group of relatively level-headed leaders from the various factions, he would be able to make headway in working out a compromise agenda for next month's Assembly. Surely it would be easier to move a score or so of men to agreement than the full 500 member session of the Council. A united cohort of the leading lights in the Council, then, could put forward this agenda and it would not be seen as just Pericles' agenda. He was sure that if he could get his plan through the Council, the Assembly would follow the Council's lead. Pericles calculated that in the next Assembly session it was more than likely that just the bare minimum, the 6000 for a quorum, would attend. It would be the first month of winter, wet and cold, and despite his compatriots considerable political passions, most citizens would not come to the open-air Pynx to listen to long speeches and complicated resolutions, and in so doing risk chilled and wet back-sides. This was the kind of session in which a well-organized effort could marshal the requisite majority in the Assembly for controversial initiatives. But now it looked like he might be stopped cold before he could even get under way.... Could the commoners be made to see the merit of making use of Cimon's considerable diplomatic skills so as to provide a breathing spell for Athens - a time to consolidate her recently won empire? Was he in danger of irretrievably alienating the venerable aristocratic families such as those of his own Alkmeonid clan or that of Cimon's if he indeed further strengthened the commoners hold on public life? Yes, Pericles thought, it is the case that the proposal to provide compensation to anyone serving on one of Athens' many juries would make it more likely that commoners would in increasing numbers take a more active part in the political life of the city. But why can't men like Megacles and other of the leading aristocratic men see that our city grows in strength when we increase the number of its stakeholders. It is far easier to ask thetes, shop assistants, and the rural villagers of Attica to row our triremes and serve in our infantry when they too have a voice in the conduct of our state. It is, Pericles thought, endlessly exhausting and strenuous to hold a working center together. It was in moments like these that the first man of Athens' government understood the lure of monarchy. Sometimes none of them, he told himself, could see beyond the reach of their own noses. What was he to do now?

Help came from an unexpected quarter.

Cimon, the man whom he had out maneuvered for the leadership of Athens, emerged from the shadows at the back of the plaza and made his way to the front to stand beside Pericles. The man, though now over 60 years old, was still an imposing figure. Taller than most Athenians, the top of Pericles plumed helmet only reached to Cimon's chin as the two stood side by side before the now raucous caucus. Although Cimon's hair had turned completely silver, it was still full and he wore it long, almost shoulder length. Clothed in a simple short sleeved military toga which was drawn in to his body by a purple sash around his waist, the man at 60-something still had the flat stomach, massive calve muscles and upper arm and shoulder development of an Olympian pankratiast. Even his enemies had to admit that this man had an aura of invincibility, a presence which still after all these years and after his own humiliating ostracism required one's respect.

When Cimon had bent down and whispered into Pericles' ear, requesting a moment so that he might bring the men back to civility, Pericles recognized instantly that his old adversary had indeed made his peace with him. He knew the old general who so often had fought the great enemy, Persia, was in good faith with him when he whispered, "Pericles, son of my colleague Xanthippus, hero of Mycale, let me bring them back to you so that we may get on with our great city's destiny - to lead all Hellenes to liberty, safe forever from the despotism of Persia."

"Yes, please, Cimon, stand with me now."

Cimon pulled himself up ramrod straight in a military posture before the crowd which had already become quiet. Many of them were perplexed by the unexpected sight of the two old adversaries whispering to one another. Then, with everyone's eyes fixed on the scourge of Persia, Cimon took the sash from his toga and with a dignity that could only be matched by the grace exercised by Athens' holy maidens when they lifted the robe from Athena for the rite of cleansing during Thargelia, the hero of Euymedon disrobed. With his back and chest bared, Cimon traced with his index finger and his words, the imprint of the many deep lines of scar tissue which marked his torso, his thighs, and even his neck. "You see, my fellow hoplites and sailors, how many blows this body has borne for our city and holy Attica during the sixteen seasons I have led our city's campaigns by sea and land. You will not find one such mark on the back of my body. Could I show you my soul you would see that I bear without bitterness the Assembly's judgment that exiled me as *Pharmakos* for the good of the city. What I have always done and always will do, I do for the love and honor of our fatherland."

Cimon paused and stooped down to pick up his toga which he had dropped at his feet. The men were now all seated and transfixed by Cimon's disrobing of body and soul. When Cimon had covered up again, and after he had glanced at Pericles for permission to continue he spoke again. "You must forgive the strong feeling of my young nephew Archaeolus. You see, he lost his father, his two older brothers, and his two other uncles, my brothers, at Tanagra fighting the Spartans. Although this was six years ago, I, like him, cannot rid my eyes, waking or asleep, of the men of my tribe and family fighting to the death around the stanchion on which my own armor was posted. It is not easy, you see, for either him or myself to make our peace with the ghosts of our kin who fell at Tanagra, not ourselves having been part of that fight, him by virtue of his age and me because some of you believe I, having been exiled from Athens, could not be trusted to fight against Spartans. And so I, like a coward, watched from a hill-top the slaughter of my kin at Spartan hands. I do not say this because I hate any of you, but so that you might understand our consternation when it is suggested that any of us would place any other city's interest (and especially Sparta's) before that of Athens.

Today, I enjoin you to work with Pericles to find the common interest so that Athens may mount ever higher among the cities of glory as the stronghold of liberty and best hope for all the sons of Hellen. It is more than time today to put our enmity towards one another behind us. I ask you to remember the words of our poet warrior of Marathon, Aeschylus. Is it really four years since he has left us? How I miss him......

> 'Let her who hungereth still for wrong
> Faction, in Athens neer again
> Lift on the air her ravening song;
> Let not the dust of Pallas' Plain
> Drink the dark blood of any son
> By fury of revenge fordone
> Rage not to smite the smiter, lest
> By rage the City's heart be torn:
> Bless him that blesseth: in each breast
> So shall a single love be born
> And gainst Her foes a single hate
> This also maketh firm a state.'

My Furies have all been rendered into goodly spirits. I pray, my fellow citizens, that you too will allow the wisdom of Athena full play and permit our deliberations a civil course safeguarded and guided by our elected officers, among whom General Pericles is chief."

Cimon stepped away from the rostrum and quietly returned to a seat at the right end of the back row of benches. When Pericles stepped to the rostrum, there was complete silence. Even Cimon's most hostile critic, Hermisteus, had taken his seat and had no retort to Cimon's demonstration of patriotism exhibited so dramatically in the unveiling of the many wounds he had suffered during his long years of military leadership of Athens' fleet and hoplite forces.

"Thank you, Cimon, for reminding us all of our calling as citizens and officers of our great city. I have convened this meeting because there are urgent matters which must be sorted out by all of those represented by you Councilors and officers, if we are to preserve and expand the prosperity our city has enjoyed for the past decade. You are probably all aware that we face a renewed threat from Persia. Reports are coming in with every merchanter pulling into Piraeus that Persian agents are fomenting more trouble for our allies in Ionia. Again, there seems to be stepped up Persian-sponsored Phoenician warship construction on the eastern end of Cyprus. Worst of all, Persian diplomats have been seen scurrying about between the tribes who border our fortifications along the Hellespont. It appears that an attempt is being made once again to deny Athens its rightful free trade zone in Asia Minor and the grain growing regions on the shores of the Propontis and the Pontus. It seems as if the Persians are like a many-headed hydra. We cut off many of its heads and new ones keep sprouting. We will have to prepare our city for yet another struggle with the over-reaching ambitions of this Oriental colossus. It will mean, on our part, building and manning many more triremes and readying ourselves for another large campaign."

"But Pericles, how can you possibly expect our citizens to support such a program when our hands have been full with almost yearly expeditions against the Spartans and their confederates here on the mainland? And, besides, I thought Xerxes still had his hands full in Egypt." It was Hermisteus. Great man or not, Hermisteus' suspicions were aroused when he saw two blue-bloods, even if one was Pericles, whispering to one another.

"Of course, you are right, Hermisteus, it would be foolhardy to throw the Spartans and the Persians together against us. But there are options we need to explore so as to avert that outcome." Pericles was now preparing to broach the most sensitive and possibly divisive element of his agenda. He took a deep breath, grasped the sides of his portable rostrum with both hands, and pushed on.

"Men, you might wonder why I have chosen such a public place for this meeting. As you can see, I have not really taken any steps to prevent any of our citizens who happen to be passing by our plaza from overhearing our business. I am convinced that nothing can be kept secret anyway and that is not so bad since we pride ourselves on holding all our officials publically accountable. It is gossip about what is done in secret that often hatches the greatest resentment, and this in turn often gives fuel to those who make speeches about dark conspiracies, playing upon our baser natures and appealing to our fears and unthinking prejudices. Well, let us like honorable men, in the clearing of this plaza, come to terms with yet another case of what purports to be new evidence implicating some of our citizens in the murder of Ephialtes. Even though eye witnesses confirmed that it was Aristodicus, the Tanagran, who fatally stabbed Ephialtes, there are still those in Athens who believe he had confederates here in Athens who arranged this assassination and then made sure that Aristodicus himself was slain minutes after he had killed Ephialtes so as to prevent any interrogation of Aristodicus. Of course we are not holding court today, and I by no means wish to circumvent any kind of legal proceedings, should this purported evidence concerning a conspiracy justify prosecutions. But I think it would be to all of our best interests if we discuss this matter openly and sort out what is at stake if we allow this to fester and needlessly divide our city when we once again face grave threats from abroad.

The alleged new evidence was first brought to Isocrates' attention. For this reason, I have asked Isocrates to present a summary of this new evidence as though it were a deposition. I have also asked some citizens who are named in this informal deposition to join us. They will, no doubt, be offended and angry at me for springing this on them, and that pains me since I consider both of them as men of impeccable honor. However, I want to assure these men that every opportunity will be given to answer any suspicions directed towards them, and, if need be, to provide another opportunity at another time to marshal counter-evidences of their innocence. I, myself don't think that will be necessary since it is my judgment that the evidence does not in any way overturn the findings of the Commission or provide anything but the slimmest of circumstantial coincidences towards incriminating any man here today. Unless anyone has any serious objections, Isocrates will summarize the new evidence report he has received and the circumstances of how it came into his hands."

The small congregation which just a short while ago had been loud and unruly was now completely still. When Isocrates rose from the bench, made his way to the front, and began to unfold a large document he had pulled from inside his cloak it was possible to hear the rustling of the parchment. Isocrates, a stocky man in his early forties who had delivered many a speech at the Pynx where he literally had to outshout unruly hecklers, was unsure how to proceed. This was not a time for the kind of impassioned fiery partisan speech he was so well known for, since he had privately come to an understanding with Pericles wherein both agreed that the report should be treated so as not to incite the commoners to any direct action. On the other hand, his presentation should not in any way lead his patrons in the city *demes*, men of the middling class, to believe that he had somehow betrayed their long-standing determination to bring the murderers of Ephialtes to justice. So it was that he opted to proceed in a measured even-toned voice whereby he would simply outline the major points of the potentially incendiary report.

"First, let me explain how the information I am going to give you came into my hands. One week ago today, just before mid-day, I was summoned to my friend Isagoras' shop in the Kerameikos District. When I arrived at the shop, Isagoras ushered me very quickly into his studio. As soon as I entered, he dismissed with a gesture his two apprentice potters who had been busy kneading red clay on a broad table. Sitting in the corner, just to the side of Isagoras' large kiln, was a large muscular man dressed in the Phoenician style with pants, a shirt, and a dark red turban. After Isagoras had closed the wooden door leading from the studio to his shop's front display room and made sure that no inquisitive worker was listening at the door, he introduced me to the foreigner. His name was Paradonis and he, explained Isagoras, had recently become a freedman after serving for the past nine years as the steward in the home of a prosperous man, Xanthicles. This Xanthicles lived in Xanthus of Lycia and, according to his former steward Paradonis, Xanthicles had always claimed in public that his huge estate and considerable holdings of gold had been bequeathed to him by Darius himself in gratitude for extraordinary services rendered when he served the Great King as one of his Saracen noblemen. At any rate, now his former chief steward was here far from Xanthus in Isagoras' shop and had quite a story to tell. It was a story that the ex-steward was sure would be of interest to an Athenian like Isagoras and that is why he had come first to his shop with his story.

It seems, I should add, that this man had learned from some Judean merchant he met in Rhodes that the Athenian government had put up a considerable reward for anyone from any quarter who could come forward with credible information regarding the untimely death of Ephialtes. I immediately informed him that authorization for such a reward had been withdrawn by the Assembly over eighteen months ago, and that the metic merchant he had spoken to in Rhodes must have been away from Athens a long time if he was unaware of this. When Isagoras and I asked him if he would nevertheless be willing to share his story with others without any reward and with possible danger to his own life; he assured us that he would share his information whether or not provisions would be made for his personal hardship and risks in making the journey to Athens. I also made clear to him that if he engaged in perjury or in any way attempted to deceive us, that I would personally see to it as a Counselor that he would be punished severely."

"Well, after both Isagoras and myself had satisfied ourselves that this Paradonis fellow was not merely a scoundrel hoping to loot the Athenian treasury and after he had indeed produced what appears to be a unimpeachable piece of physical evidence corroborating his story, we proceeded to interrogate him and recorded on the document you now see the salient points of his story. This is what he had to say. I am going to read to you Paradonis' statement, verbatim.

'My Master had permitted me to purchase my freedom just over a year ago. He had become somewhat dissolute and enamored with imitating what he took to be the 'high life' of Athenian noblemen. It seems that my Master had fallen in love with a young male attendant of one of his wealthy neighbors and had decided that he would purchase him to serve as his new steward and personal household attendant. None of this bothered me. I could care less who he wanted to fuck, and frankly, I was very happy that his new-found 'Ganymede' might help me become my own man. Sure enough, since my service was no longer required, he offered me the opportunity to take my leave of him as a freeman, provided I could compensate him for at least the amount he had first paid for my purchase. It was just after we had come to an agreement on this matter, but before I was actually discharged from his service, that I was to overhear and witness a strange turn of events and heated conversation between my Master, Xanthicles, and one of his guests late one evening at one of those Athenian style dinning parties he had taken to hosting.

The guest, I never did catch his name, was the professional soldier type. He was definitely a Hellene even though he was speaking my Master's native tongue. Earlier in the evening I had heard this guest recite one of your poets and I remember he did so in a dialect, certainly not Attic, which I was not familiar with. Although the swarthy soldier was already half-crocked, he sang ten verses and at the end raised his cup to somebody called Tyrtaeus. Since there was no one by that name at the party, I suppose that was the name of the poet.

At any rate, this fellow stayed very late. Indeed all the Master's other guests had taken leave and both of them were stewed by this time. While I was mixing yet another portion of wine just a short distance from the couches on which they reclined, they began to quarrel bitterly. It seems that this man of Ares had made a pass at my Master's new found love and about to be steward. Xanthicles had invited his neighbor to the party and had requested that he bring his young stud servant along, so that he could take one final look at his soon-to-be playmate and personal slave. Well, you know the type–the lascivious gone-to-pot wine-soaked man of direct action– grabbed the young boy by the rump and forcibly sat him down on this thigh. What a commotion! My Master's wealthy neighbor bolted from his couch, dragged his steward from the lap of this lout, and without a word to his host, left the party with the young 'Ganymede' in tow. The other guests too, found reasons to take leave shortly after this incident. Now, left to themselves and only the Master's not so attractive steward and a few other servants, Xanthicles verbally lit into this comrade from his past who appeared to have succeeded in shipwrecking his love plans and alienating his neighbors. The lout gave as much as he got and all that stopped them from coming to blows was their drunken stupor.

It was in the course of this loud and profane exchange that I could not but help to overhear a matter which my Master apparently had kept secret for many years. After my Master had called him a long-haired buggerer whose tool had grown as useless and dull as his mind, and after the impolite guest had called him a barbarian Saracen sissy not even stout enough to get it in a soft wide-assed and willing harlot, my Master drew a knife he always carried concealed in a sheath laced to this thigh beneath his outer garment. Then, to my surprise, this other lout draws from beneath his toga a knife which is absolutely identical to my Masters. The fact that they both drew knives is not as surprising that these knives were absolutely identical and that yet they were knives like I have never seen before. Both had the same eight inch serrated and curved blades made from some kind of polished iron and both had fine ivory handles which were inlaid with a curious design which wrapped around some kind of finely wrought calligraphy. The knives, glinting in the upraised but flaccidly wavering arms of the two drunks, were clearly part of a matching set. I was about to disarm the guest before any harm came to either of them when both of them began to laugh at the spectacle each of them presented to the other.

When they had laughed until their eyes filled with tears, Xanthicles with what sounded like real compassion for an old comrade in arms said, "So that is all you have left from that work of ten years ago almost to the day, today...You poor old sop, my friend, how did it all slip through your fingers? It was so much, enough for a life-time and I know that your pay-off, like mine, continued to be sent to the Tyrian banker until just two years ago. I thought we would both be fixed for life when we agreed to take on the job that phony Paphian shipper offered us when we met him in Paphos. I had never known any one man could be that rich - he had to be an Athenian", my Master blubbered as he reminisced now with his pacified old-time drinking partner, "because nobody but an Athenian could have that kind of money after the damn Athenians finished collecting their Delian dues from all those damn islanders still frightened more by Persian Masters than by Athenian ones. And didn't the fellow claim to be a close friend with Alcibiades the Athenian shipper? If I remember correctly, the younger man accompanying the shipper looked as though he might have been the son of Alcibiades. I remember hearing the shipper speaking Ionian – thinking I could not understand him – and calling his young associate by the name of Clinias."

The lout screwed up his eyes in an effort to clear the mists of Dionysius from his mind's eye and then answered his partner. "Yes, it's all gone.....too many horse races, too many friends with can't miss investment opportunities, a real hatred of farming and staying put, and an endless appetite for expensive good times.....nothing left but a little stone cottage in the hinterlands of Thrace, the clothes on my back and this knife... But we were damn good at what we did back then, Xanthicles. If there was killing to be done and done discreetly and without screw-ups, we were the best money could buy. Sometimes I think that all that money we got for that job at Piraeus is what ruined me. It is odd, isn't it? To this day, I don't even know for sure who it is we killed. We were instructed only to be at the docks that day and be sure to make fast work of killing the man who we were told would murder an Athenian official at noontime by the Athenian's trophy commemorating their victories over the Persians at Artemisium and Salamis. That bastard at Paphos, he probably never leveled with us. What a commotion when we knifed that poor slob on the dock as he tried to disappear into the crowd after he had just himself killed the official. He himself was probably a hired assassin. He never knew what hit him. I think he must have thought we were someone else.....maybe agents of the rich Athenian in Paphos who had told him that men dressed as we were would help him in his escape. Who knows? What a world we live in! Probably the poor slob we killed knew too much and so those who hired him hired us to make sure he could not live to incriminate them." The lout began to laugh again. "That bastard died in seconds after we slit him open, you from the back and me from the front. When the harbor guards came running and found the assassin there on the ground in a pool of blood, we had already slipped away and disappeared into the crowd. That poor assassin! That was probably the only time he had ever worn those britches and then he dies in them!

"Yeh, we were good, but you know what I have never understood is why our contractor insisted on all the secrecy. Why did the fellow at Paphos set it up so that for seven years - provided we completely dropped off the map - those huge cash payments would come our way through the banker at Tyre? This fellow is not only astoundingly rich, but he set up a murder where even his operatives, even if they wanted to betray him, couldn't finger him. I know whoever he was, he was well-connected. Remember, he did tell us that his associate who was also there in Paphos knew the Paphian crown prince himself, Penthylus, and it was Penthylus who had recommended us to his associate if some rough work had to be taken care of. Yeh, those fellows were both up to something. I'd wager my farm that both of them were Athenian politicians."

The lout sat up straight and somehow seemed to gain control of his slurring speech and thinking us servants of no concern, offered Xanthicles an opportunity to revisit their money source and perhaps score one more very profitable piece of business. Drunk as they both were, they did move closer and talked in hushed tones to one another. The only thing I could overhear was some kind of talk about going to Tyre together and tracking down the banker and strong-arming his cooperation in one last big payout. I did hear them say right before this drunken guest staggered out the door, that anyone who had gone to this much trouble to cover his trail would make a pretty target for blackmail.

I left Xanthicles' household the next week. He was able to patch things up with his neighbor and complete his purchase of his new young man. I left with the few possessions I had and while I had been an honest steward throughout my entire service with Xanthicles, I did pilfer one thing of value which I was sure he would never miss. During the confusion of the party the night before, his old comrade had dropped his knife by the end of his couch. He was so drunk that he never picked it up and did not notice it lying on the floor since it was partially concealed by the shadows of the protruding handles of the large drinking vase standing by the end of his couch. And so when I later cleaned up, I found the finely-wrought ivory handled knife and slipped it into my rubbish basket, carried the basket to the back of the courtyard out of everyone's sight, and then hid the knife where I could retrieve it later. Strictly speaking, this was not even my Master's, and so with a little prayer to your Hermes the Thief, I packed this with my things, thinking I could later sell it since I was now without money, all of it having been spent to buy my freedom. It was when I had some months later heard of my former Master's death that I finally decided it was safe to sell the knife. I had learned from some traveler from Xanthus while I was on Rhodes that Xanthicles had never returned from Tyre and word had been sent to his estate that he had died of what was believed to be a severe bout of food poisoning after eating some kind of exotic shell fish. It was when I was about to sell the knife in the shop of some Judean dealer in rare artifacts that I first learned that it was indeed Ephialtes who had been murdered by an assassin from Tanagra and that the government of Athens had posted a reward for information regarding any co-conspirators. When I showed the dealer the knife and insisted on a pretty price for it, he pulled out a bundle of old notices and documents, mumbling to himself that he was sure he had seen a drawing of knives just like this one before, and he was not going to pay the sum I was asking if it was nothing but a counterfeit souvenir from a tourist ship elsewhere. It was then, with me looking over his shoulder, that he found the notice which the Athenian Commission had so widely circulated. And so, with my last few coins, I ended up buying the document from him and decided that I should come directly to Athens. Now, it is up to you to ascertain, if indeed, this knife is in fact a absolute match to the one you recovered 10 years ago, assumed to be the knife dropped by either the Tanagran or other conspirators party to Ephialtes' assassination. Does this knife match the one you found beneath the prow of your trireme Memorial - I believe, you call it the Gyges-the Spirit of Artemisium?'

Isagoras looked up from the document. He had read through the statement quickly and had not once paused. He now rolled it up and handed it to Pericles, who had risen from his chair to stand beside Isagoras.

Pericles was holding in his hand a leather pouch. The pouch was about the length of his forearm and was tied securely at the top with a short cord. When Isagoras took his seat, Pericles opened the pouch and withdrew a serrated iron curved knife with an ivory handle. Holding the knife up in his upraised right hand by its ivory handle so that the blade and the inset engraving on one side of the handle faced his audience, Pericles then beckoned to the junior officer who served as his military secretary to join him up front. As the officer made his way to the front, Pericles moved even closer to the first row of benches so that all of the men could see the knife.

"Citizens, I want to thank Isagoras for his responsible and open treatment of this matter. You see in my hand, the actual knife we have impounded as state's evidence for the past ten years. Apollonius, a secretary to the Board of Generals, will now show you the knife which Paradonis has brought to Isagoras. If you look carefully, you can see that they are indeed a perfect match, right down to the peculiar engraving on the ivory handle. Both knives, though crafted in the Saracen way, bear a Greek inscription on their handle – 'For Liberty'. What, then, are we to make of this man's story? Are we to assume that even if this knife is an exact replica of the one we found at the scene of the crime ten years ago that it was the knife held by a co-conspirator? Should we turn our city upside-down and inside out following leads in Pardonis' story which may incriminate, at least circumstantially, some of our leading citizens as conspirators in the murder of Ephialtes? Shall we again let every mystagogue tell us what Homer has to say about our case? Oh yes, it was the stepmother of the Aloadai, Otos and Ephialtes, who came to the aid of Ares and stopped the young giants from putting an end to Ares. How we love secret codes! Our conspiracy hunters and mystagoges will say the killers in this case were men who wanted to save Ares again from a second Ephialtes – one who would bind up and emasculate the

Court of the Areopagus. Maybe, but then again any clever enemy of Ephialtes could throw such mythical sand in our eyes so as to send us down the wrong trail."

Pericles paused as there was now indeed a disturbance. The workmen had begun pushing their way through the rows of benches from their place at the back, insisting that they have the right immediately to place the informant under their surveillance. The workmen were demanding that they be told where this informant was now being held.

Pericles raised his voice and with all of the force and authority he could muster as a general he halted their advance as if they were mutinous soldiers, "You must return to your seats. I assure you that no one will be permitted to either injure or take this man away. If you insist on taking him and anything should happen to him while he is in your custody, then each of you would be held accountable. Surely, it would be better if the Council of five hundred and its pyrtanes be held responsible."

It was a rare occasion when Pericles let any anger or some hint of a threat sound in any of his public speech. But such was certainly present as his still upraised hand now clenched the knife and his other hand pointed the men back to their seats. Even Hermisteus' toughs thought it best not to push Athens' most powerful man too far, even if he was on most occasions a friend of their patron. Mumbling amongst themselves, they returned to their seats.

With that brush fire extinguished, Pericles directed his attention to where even more serious trouble might be expected, although it would not consist of a public display of unruliness. Would Callias stay, or had he already gotten up and walked out in protest of this highly irregular introduction of evidence which could be purported to implicate him in the murder of Ephialtes. And then there was his cousin's husband, Clinias, the son of Alcibiades the shipper. Surely he would be deeply hurt and angered by Pericles decision not to inform him ahead of time of all this. Pericles was almost afraid to check their seats which were to his far right. But when he glanced in their direction, his gaze was met by both men's eyes, and both of them showed nothing in their faces but what appeared to be cold indifference. Pericles realized though that there would be a price to pay for all this with these men. It would not be easy to go forward without their support since they had been a moderating force, assisting him in checking the opposition among the wealthy and well-born families of Athens. He knew that these two would never again trust him as fully as they had until this day. But, he thought, I must push on. Pericles resumed speaking.

"What are we to make of this purported new evidence? Can we believe that this Phoenician freeman, Paradonis, is telling us the truth about his former Master? I have no doubt that he is indeed the former servant of the man he names, Xanthicles. Pardonis must know that it would be easy enough for us to make inquiries in Xanthus. But as for the manner in which he came to possess the knife, that would be difficult to confirm. Perhaps he himself just purchased it from some obscure dealer somewhere in Lycia who had in fact bought it from someone else. Since Pardonis has said his former Master is dead, we have no way of independently confirming his alleged part in preventing the interrogation of Aristodicus. I suppose we could try to apprehend the other servants who Paradonis says were present at his Master's dinner party, but I would wager that they have all disappeared without a trace."

"But Pericles shouldn't we follow every possible lead as far as we can possibly take it, if we are to see that justice is done?" It was Hermisteus who interrupted, but in a very civil manner.

"Hermisteus, even if we suppose that everything this Paradonis has stated is true, and we take up every strand indicated by his account; what new ground could we possibly break in what has already been explored over the past 10 years? Should we take up the mention of the alleged hire of Xanthicles and his other anonymous confederate in Paphos, linking it to the diplomatic mission of Callias and Clinias of that period; and then proceed to indict these men on the strength of this circumstantial alignment? Yes, Clinias knows the king of Paphos. We all know that Clinias was involved in the arrangement for the ransom and return of the King's son whom he had captured during the naval engagement at Artemisium. Yes, of course, our Naval Memorial is his Gyges, and what a nice touch to the story to have the alleged conspirators set up a meeting between strangers and Ephialtes by this monument here in Piraeus. But, there must be at least one hundred other Athenians who know the Paphian crown prince. After all, before he was returned to his island for ransom, he was actually entertained by many in Athens, even while he was under house arrest for some five years after Artemisium. Yes, Callias is very rich, but we know for a fact that he got so sea sick on that trip to Cyprus, that he never made it that far. As a matter of fact both he and Clinias disembarked at Rhodes and there were able to convene a meeting with Persian diplomats. As you know, nothing came of that mission because at that time the Spartans had already persuaded the Great King to covertly support Spartan interests against Athens. So it would be very difficult to establish that either Clinias or Callias would have ever made such arrangements in Paphos at that time. And if we were to try to follow such particulars as these, wouldn't we also have to revisit the old allegations that crop up again here about Ephialtes' involvement in strong-arming our Athenian shipping interests at the docks. Again, we would have those coming out of the woodwork anxious to show that Ephialtes, as was rumored of his mentor Themistocles, had his pockets filled with bribes and black-market money. Then the alleged conspiracy would have to target not men from Cimon's circles, but men from the city demes and the shipping district. What a tangled web! Over the past ten years I have even heard it whispered that somehow I had some connection to a conspiracy to eliminate my senior associate and mentor. After all, it was I who emerged as leader of the people after his death! Our latest story - doesn't everyone know that my father had long ago spent some time in Tyre, and wouldn't it have been possible for him to have a banker friend there....And so it would go. Churning, churning, and agitating, until every festering partisan sore would again be rubbed raw. Will we ever be done with this?"

Time was growing short. The meeting of the Council was scheduled to begin very shortly and Pericles had not yet moved the caucus to his planned destination. When he realized that all of the men present who were leaders of the two largest political factions - men who had been bitterly divided over his own policies - were still listening and seemed at least receptive to his plea for putting the mutual finger-pointing and acrimony concerning alleged complicity in Ephialtes' murder behind them; he decided to go for broke. And so as on cue, both Cleisthenes and Isocrates stood at the same time to speak, Cleisthenes the most respected leader of the conservative aristocratic faction and Isocrates the leader of the most radical democratic faction.

Cleisthenes, a man now in his mid-fifties and known for his consistent championing of negotiating peace with Sparta so as to protect Athenian vineyards and olive groves of the large estates from the destruction they all too often suffered when Athens fought her battles on land with this her only serious rival on the mainland, spoke first. "What would you have us do, Pericles? I, for one, agree with you. We need to move on. As Cimon put it so eloquently, let us not again let loose the Harpies that 'hungereth still for wrong faction'. There is so much to do for our Athens and it is true that mighty Persia once again threatens to rob us all of our liberty and prosperity. It is time for us to marshal our considerable united strength and set aside anything that saps this. And so, I would urge my colleagues in the Council to resolve the matter at hand by granting our latest informant a small stipend, post the report on the public wall in the Agora, with a transcript of your remarks today, and reaffirm that the case is closed and the work of the Commission stands. Then, if the Council can be so persuaded, we could turn the attention of the Assembly to dealing with the renewed Persian threat."

Pericles nodded his head in approval and then called upon Isocrates, who had remained standing and attentive while Cleisthenes spoke. "And what, Isocrates, do you and your colleagues believe should be our course?"

Isocrates had been prepared for this moment since three days ago when he had first conferred with Pericles just hours after he had been called to Isagoras' shop to assist in the questioning of the Phoenician stranger. Since it was Isocrates who had served as the chairman of the Commission charged with the investigation of Ephialtes' murder, Pericles had insisted that they privately discuss whether or not the Phoenician's testimony should be used to reopen the case. Both Pericles and Isocrates realized when they first saw the knife which the stranger produced to support his story that this man's testimony could plausibly incriminate some of the wealthy and aristocratic Athenians who had dealings in Crete's Paphos and the ports of Phoenicia.

"Would it not be wise,' Pericles had said, 'to make use of our Phoenician informer as a kind of political capital with which we can barter? I would think Isocrates that the aristocratic party would be less likely to oppose us in the Assembly if we let them know that we will not reopen this case and possibly encourage the prosecution of aristocratic enemies of Ephialtes."

Isocrates was persuaded by Pericles that this muted response to the Phoenician informer would provide a kind of additional leverage against men like Cleisthenes and Archaeolus who still had considerable hold and influence over 'the good and the beautiful' as well as the new men, like Callias, whose wealth as merchants now outstripped Athens' aristocratic land owners. If the proposed legislation, which included granting pay for jury duty, was to gain a majority in the Assembly, then it could not but help the cause to assure the aristocrats that their cooperation would buy them an end to any further prosecutions in the Ephialtes case. Besides, arrangements could be made to send Pardonis away, but keep him on the shelf, so to speak, should his story be of use again. So today, Isocrates could take his place as a man devoted to the nonpartisan common good – a man of virtue like Cimon whose good will towards all would be apparent.

Isocrates spoke facing the semicircle arrangement of benches, even though he addressed Pericles by name. "Pericles, as you know, I have given considerable thought to this matter. We all know that Ephialtes' unflinching advocacy for Athens' tradesmen, her small farmers, and the free workmen and other craftsmen of the city demes who so often have rowed and fought on our triremes, made him a target of considerable animosity from those who wished to preserve their government of the few. Those of us who knew him and worked with him to make Athens the most democratic city in the world could never rest peacefully if we left undone anything which might lead to the apprehension of any who took part in his murder, whoever they might be. My careful interrogation of this stranger and a careful weighing of how the particulars of his story relate to every dead end the long investigative work of our Commission encountered have confirmed in my mind the futility of reopening the case. I too will recommend to my colleagues in the Council that no new impeachment proceedings be brought against any current official of Athens or any citizens such as Callias or Clinias. I agree with you that there is not enough of substance to formulate a credible deposition, unless one's only interest is to stir the fires of partisan rancor. It is my hope rather that all of us here today can agree to get beyond this kind of thing and work together to build an even stronger and more prosperous Athens. To this end, I am asking Cleisthenes and all the friends of Cimon to join us in sealing our resolve to move forward by agreeing to a kind of unifying legislative agenda."

Pericles nodded his head and encouraged Isocrates to move on, "And what exactly then would you ask the Council to bring to the Assembly?"

Isocrates, speaking with the confidence inspired by having the support of Pericles, described the plan for putting behind them the bitter partisan struggles that had led to Cimon's ostracism and the current suspicions which pointed to a political assassination of Ephialtes. "First, the agenda of reconciliation calls for a resolution which will formally and officially report that all evidence gathered by the Commission, including the recent addendum summing up the Phoenician's deposition, supports no other conclusion than this: *the murderers of Ephialtes acted on their own and at most may have been agents of some foreigner who had a long and private feud with Ephialtes' family*. Secondly, to ratify our full confidence and gratitude for the many sacrifices the people have made for the defense of our city and our liberty, the Assembly will be presented with a bill which stipulates compensation roughly equivalent to a free workman's day wages for all citizens serving on a jury. Thirdly, and out of deference to concerns for protecting our own citizen's franchise and the resources of our treasury, I am urging that the Council present a new citizenship law, which requires every citizen to demonstrate that both their parents were born in Athens as Athenian citizens. Otherwise, freeloading pretenders to Athenian citizenship will flock to our city from all over our empire to make a living as jurists without caring a whit about our fatherland. And finally, at the urging of Cleisthenes and Cimon, we friends of the people will support a bill authorizing construction of a new fleet to deal with the renewed Persian threat. And, while we are convinced that Athens can never finally be a friend to a city like Sparta who enslaves most of the inhabitants of her environs, we do see the wisdom of seeking at least a temporary treaty of peace with Sparta so that Athens may concentrate her energies on the Persian hydra. We are therefore willing to authorize the appointment of Cimon as ambassador to Sparta, commissioned to negotiate a cessation of hostilities. If all this seems agreeable, I am confident that the Assembly will be excited by the prospects of such a course for our city and will be more than willing to ratify the standing final report of the Commission concerning Ephialtes murder."

When Isocrates finished speaking, it was clear that a deal had already been cut and that the purpose of the caucas was to bring its likely aristocratic opponents around to the merits of the agenda which this day would be drawn up by the Council and then passed on to the Assembly at it's mid-winter Session. While there was some debate about the amount of compensation proposed for the jurists and heated discussion about the specifics of how one's progeny would be certified as native Athenian citizens, it was clear that the master politician, Pericles, had again crafted a wide consensus which brought the leadership of both the aristocratic families and the commoners together.

Clinias could not help but admire this man, even though he now felt considerable irritation and anger at the way his reputation had been assaulted in Pericles' compromise. The caucas had taken no more than an hour and a half, but its work as orchestrated by Pericles would probably impact the lives of all Athenians for many years to come. As the meeting broke up, and the Councilors present began to make their way into the Bouleuterion, their day's work now all mapped out; Clinias rose from his bench and with out a word to anyone turned to leave the Plaza and head home.

The skies had cleared and the morning sun, now high in the sky, made the pools of water that filled the streets' potholes sparkle. But Clinias walked home feeling as depressed and grey as the sky had been at daybreak. Another lesson, he thought, in why I could never win an election to the generalship for my tribe. I cannot play these kinds of games. I am not subtle enough and cannot play as fast and loose with other men's honor as these men do. Why, do you suppose, he wondered, that Pericles took the trouble to invite him to this meeting. Probably because I am married to Cleisthenes' sister and they thought it best for me to hear and see firsthand how little would come of the mention of my name in conjunction with the cowardly murder of Ephialtes. For all he knew, it was possible that 10 years ago he had been similarly used by men more subtle then him as an unknowing accomplice in procuring Ephialtes' assassins. For what nobody had mentioned was that while he and Callias had gotten no further than Rhodes on that diplomatic mission to the Persian satrap at Paphos eleven years ago, his old Artemisium prisoner of war, now the titular King-Priest of Paphos, had traveled to meet him in Rhodes then. As a favor to Clinias and at Callias' request, King Penthylus of Paphos provided Callias with letters of introduction to men skilled with the use of the knife and the sword who might work for Callias in ports now under the suzerainty of Persia. Clinias was told at the time that Callias' friendship with Darius, then embroiled in palace intrigues for control of the Persian throne, endangered Callias' life since there then were some men in Tyre and Paphos sworn to eliminate Darius and all those who were his confidants. This is why he needed absolutely trustworthy men who could move well within these foreign circles, and, if need be, play rough with anyone who threatened Callias' safety.

I wonder, Clinias now thought, did I in fact help procure Ephialtes' murderers. There was no use asking Callias or anybody else about this. Part of the art of getting unsavory things done and staying yourself untouched by the dirt was to arrange circumstances in such a way so that you could always plausibly deny any knowledge or responsibility for such deeds. Another political skill, I have never mastered!

"Hail, Captain Clinias, why are you looking so downcast when the skies have cleared?" It was young Socrates on his way to his *epheboi* parade ground. Clinias had turned the corner out of the Agora on to Academy Way when the stout young man hailed him. Ever since Socrates had begun his *epheboi* training, he had taken to calling Clinias, "Captain", delighting in his new found common ground with this man whom his own father had served with in many campaigns.

Clinias smiled. The sight of his old departed friend's somewhat bull-legged but stout and sturdy son carrying his father's shield and dressed in the hoplite armor brought back happier times. Ever since Sophroniscus' death, Clinias had regularly checked up on young Socrates, making sure that provision was made for his education and that no older men took advantage of him or misdirected him. "Socrates, I see you are well along in your training. I hear that you have become quite competent with the short sword and shield."

Socrates was walking beside him now, with the sheaved shin armor squeaking as he tried to slow down his stride to match that of his father's old friend, without making himself look ridiculous as he struggled to move his legs without pinching his knees in the sheaves that didn't quite fit. "Well, I am no Achilles, but at least I might survive my first battle. I am good at hacking away while keeping covered up."

Clinias chuckled. "That's all we can ask of a good hoplite infantry man, Socrates. Your father would be proud. But what are you doing walking about in the city in your armor. Have Spartans made their way to the Citadel? Since when do *epheboi* leave their barracks?"

"I was given a half-day leave and I decided it would be a good time to find you so that I might ask for your advice. There seems to be no other older man I would speak to about my situation. My kinsman, Sosothenes, has left with the colonists who will be settling the new site on the River Strymon just north of Amphipolis. And so I am just now coming from your house. Your steward told me that if I walked this way I might meet you returning from the Bouleuterion. As for my equipment, I decided to wear it rather than carry it. My mother has insisted that I visit Creon's shop to see if he can refurbish and refit my shin and breast armor."

"What is it, Socrates? Is that old letch Pansipius bothering you again?" It was hard for Clinias to imagine that anyone would have a love interest in young Socrates. He was by no means an attractive youth with his pugnacious looking face and that very flat and broad snub nose. While he was muscular enough, his body lacked that youthful grace which comes from the proportion and harmony of an evenly developed physique. No, somehow his shoulders seemed too broad for his short torso, while his stout thighs and calf muscles all seemed to run together giving his legs the appearance of thick rough hewn fence posts. But there were after all, Clinias reminded himself, old men hanging about the *epheboi* training grounds and the gymnasiums whose lechery knew no bounds and who, unable to attract the more desirable catches, would prey on the lonely or otherwise neglected youth.

"No, it's nothing like that, Captain. It seems my kind of beauty goes unappreciated even by one such as that old rooster, Pansipius. I have been told by my mates that my sharp and barbed tongue, combined with my ugly face, make a potent prophylactic to any Silenus."

Clinias could see that the young man wanted the kind of help a father or only an older and more experienced friend could offer. Clinias was not ready to go home and deal with his wife who would have just returned from her three day Thesmophoria excursion. Lately, Dionomache had become very religious and her enthusiasm for the latest batch of mystery mongers was too much for Clinias to bear. He was sure that she would come home from this three day women's festival filled with more nonsense since the festival would have stimulated her fascination with Onomacritus' tales of Orpheus in the underworld. He much preferred spending some time with his deceased friend Sophroniscus' son, then dealing with the tiresome babbling of his superstitious wife.

"Let's sit down there under those sycamores. Best thing Cimon ever did for beautifying Athens! I love these trees. You can cool down. Isn't it something that even on a cool day that gear will get you soaked in sweat? It makes you wonder why our generals have always insisted on campaigning only during the summer months, doesn't it, Socrates? Now, what is it that is on your mind?"

After Clinias and Socrates had settled themselves on the stone bench between the two shady sycamores, Socrates, feeling awkward and uncertain of himself, stared off towards the Acropolis as he began to explain his quandary to the man his father, just before he had died, had told him to turn to when he required assistance. "Clinias, I am really confused. I don't know what to do, what is the most honorable thing to do, or what I even want most for myself. Yesterday I learned that my mother plans to remarry and her intended new husband is unrelated to anyone in my father's family. This is not surprising since there are almost no men left apart from Sosothenes in our family. My comrades tell me that unless I make special provisions, it is possible that my father's farm will be further sub-divided or possibly even pass into my mother's new husband's hands. My mother tells me that she is desperately lonely and that she really needs to remarry and that she is quite fond of this suitor who has proposed to her. It seems that he has found a way, without alienating her, to make it clear that their happiness together requires that her dowry include a transfer of title of our farm to his lands, which border our farm on the northeast side. I don't know what to do. Frankly, I'm not much for managing the farm. But I also know I don't want to spend my life sweating in a city shop or chasing customers in the marketplace. Perhaps I am lazy.....but I don't think so." Socrates turned his eyes towards Clinias who seemed puzzled by what this young man was trying to ask.

"Well, Socrates, what is it that you see yourself doing with your life after your military training is over? You realize, I am sure, that you can only make your way into prominence if you build on a solid military record. And in order to easily maintain your appropriateness for officer status, you must continue to own property. I suppose, now days, it might be possible to make your way without an illustrious record as a military officer, if one were to excel as a prosecutor or an advocate in the courts. I notice that more and more of the men elected to the Council are of this sort. Perhaps it is this kind of path that interests you - becoming an accomplished advocate, a polished orator who can shape other's opinions in such a way as to advance his own power as a politician."

"I just don't know, Captain. I am ready to do my part as a soldier to defend our city - but a life devoted to the sword and military campaigns does not really excite me the way it does some of my comrades whose heads are filled with Homer's tales of the heroes. Nor can I say I really admire that crew of new men who make their way by hanging about the courts and who seem to prosper through others' troubles. There must be some way I can make my way other than these pathways. And what am I to do about my mother and the farm?"

"Socrates, you've been reading too much! There are too many possible lives swirling before your mind's eye. When your Father and I were young it never even occurred to us that one could do other than was required by our families' station. It was simply a matter of course. Let's see. You've said you don't want to be a military man, you find no satisfaction out of managing the farm, you can't see yourself locked away in a city shop or chasing customers in the *Agora*, and you don't respect the sharpies that make their way through endless litigation in the courts and assemblies. I don't think there is anything left, do you? Well, maybe it will come to you in the next few years."

Socrates shrugged his shoulders and with a mischievous smile mumbled, "Maybe I should consult an Oracle, Captain Clinias."

Realizing that young Socrates was egging him on - everyone in Athens knew that Clinias put less stock than most in the proposition that the gods would take the trouble to mind the affairs of mere mortals - Clinias played along, "Sure, and maybe the priest would convince you to give all that you have to the Oracle's temple and come join their brotherhood in service to the god. Would you like something like that Socrates? It would be a strange brotherhood of priests which would allow you to make use of that sharp wit and lively intelligence in interpreting the ways of the gods. No, I don't think that is for you either. You would drive all the supplicants away. Instead of comforting them with some blabber, your interpretive conversation would entangle them even more in the enigmas of the Divine."

"I'm sure that's so. I can't be an orthodox anything! I've developed this insatiable need to keep my mind free to think in the interrogative."

Clinias did not want this conversation to end without making clear to young Socrates what he really thought was absolutely crucial in order to secure a decent future for his old friend's son. And so he decided that it was time for a more direct approach.

"Socrates, whatever you do, do not sign anything or in any way agree to any nuptial arrangement for your mother which forfeits your sole ownership of the farm! You know how your father loved his land. Remember as he did that this land is your patrimony! I know you would do nothing to dishonor your father's legacy. Remember that he received the land from his father and I am sure that you could trace your family's title to this land back well beyond your grandfather all the way to Attica's earliest settlement by our forefathers. And you do realize, I hope, that this estate will always assure that you do not have to go begging from others. That is the first and most important thing I have to say to you right now. Don't allow tender feelings for your mother lead you to give away your birthright so as to provide a dowry for her. You, after all, are not her father. The whole thing is preposterous! This suitor should be ashamed of himself.

The second thing I would say to you Socrates has to do with the immediate future. You must be hard on yourself and push to become a respected and skilled officer in your regiment, at least a field lieutenant. If you look about, you will notice that not many of us make it to my age. I'll be fifty-two in a few months. And I'll tell you this. Unless I had reached a position of command so that I could be making some of those decisions upon which my safety and that of my men depended, I would have been dead long ago. We march out to war somewhere almost every summer, and if you want to survive many summers then you must not put yourself in that position where time after time you are entirely subordinate to a chain of command in which there is bound sooner or later to be some foolhardy blockhead of an officer, who either through stupidity or a craven willingness to needlessly sacrifice others for his own glory, will get you killed. So train hard and do not shun promotion through the ranks. You know, of course, that whatever you decide to do; as long as you are able-bodied and a citizen of Athens you will be asked to go into combat. Then too, consider this! Look at me! I'm in my fifties and yet I will still be expected to march out and fight. I assure you that if I had to take up a position on the front line of a hoplite charge at this age, I wouldn't last very long against a twenty-five year old at the height of his physical powers. No, if I am to survive with honor and still make a contribution, then I must command others and to do so effectively. Do you see my point, Socrates?"

Socrates listened intently and did understand that the advice of this tried and true friend of his father, simple and direct, did indeed make clearer what was fundamentally important for him to attend to if he was to make his way without a father or an older man that loved him. Listening to Clinias speak with such serious solicitude for him made him feel less alone and more confident, knowing he must navigate the rigors of young manhood in service to a city that often sacrificed her young men to bloody Ares.

"Thank you, Captain. I do understand what you are saying. I will attend to these matters as you suggest. Will you come to my investiture ceremony and the swearing of the soldier's oath on Marathon Day. I would consider it an honor if my father's comrade in arms accepted my salute on that day."

Clinias got up from the stone bench, lifted the shield of Sophroniscus from where it leaned against the tree, and struggling to keep his eyes clear, handed young Socrates the well-worn and frayed shield. "Of course, I will be there. Now, I must return home and you, since it is almost noon, must take care of that armor and get back to your camp.

CHAPTER ELEVEN
DEMETER'S WORK
(450 B. C.)

When we are young, in our father's house, I think we live the sweetest life of all; for ignorance ever brings us up delightfully. But when we have reached a mature age and know more, we are driven out of doors and sold away from the gods of our fathers and our parents, some to foreigners, some to barbarians, some to strange houses, others to such as deserve reproach. And in such a lot, after a single night has united us, we have to acquiesce and think that it is well.

> (Sophocles: *Tereus*, fragment 524)

Are there any men to whom you entrust less matters of importance, or with whom you have less conversation, than with your wife?

> (Xenophon. *Oeconomicus,* iii:12 - Socrates in conversation with Critobolus concerning the role of the wife)

For all these things—shining sun and earth and air and sea—
In Strife they are all separate and have their own forms,
But they come together in Love and yearn for one another.
But enemies are those which are furthest separated

from one another,
In birth and mixture and molded forms,
Through their birth in Strife, because it brought about their birth.
Alas! Wretched race of mortals! Unfortunate!
Out of such Quarreling and groaning were you born.

(Empedocles. *On Nature*)

Although it was still mid-morning and she had been up and about for just a few hours after sleeping longer than usual, Dinomache was feeling somewhat lightheaded and unsteady on her feet. She had returned to her husband's house just after sunset last evening, having spent three days away on the Acropolis celebrating Thesmophoria. The rain and dark clouds that had hid the morning sun were now clearing and she hoped her fatigue and headache would soon lift away also. It is a wonder, she thought, that the older women can come home fit and ready to step back into their household work after three days of Thesmophoria!

Just the first day of the women's festival required a Herculean set of tasks. On the first day of Thesmophoria, 'The Way Up', every celebrant had to load their own gear in the cart for the haul up the Acropolis: the sleeping gear, cooking implements, the sacramental masks, the baskets filled with the god's gifts, and a squealing pig. The pig was particularly burdensome for Dinomache since she only brought it so as not to offend her sponsor. She had no intention of eating its flesh and did not approve of the animal's sacrifice. Then, after the steep climb to the holy precinct on the Acropolis, everything had to be unloaded and set up without the help of servants. The confusion of organizing thousands of woman, many of whom were celebrating their first Thesmophoria, so that each ended up in their assigned tribal camping place ready to put up their crude huts before the sun had set, was always an ordeal. No matter how carefully the two women charged with governing the festival had planned, it was always chaotic. Why was it that so many could not remember that it was their father's tribe, not their husband's, which determined their assigned spot at the camp? Then when everyone was settled in, always somehow or other by midnight, the festival's magistrates called the entire camp to the sacred cavern for Demeter's holy ceremonies. When those ceremonies were complete, it was almost impossible to get any sleep that first night. All night long women enjoyed the dizzying freedom of no male supervision. Neither father nor husband, nor for that matter any male, were allowed anywhere near Demeter's sacred precinct during Thesmophoria. So the first night was always one long party of happy reunions of women who were renewing acquaintances of childhood friends and others they rarely could mix with in their everyday lives. The heady excitement of being outdoors not far from the Pynx, free of the normal constraints of their cloistered domestic lives, and ordering their own affairs - even if it was according to ancient usage - carried even the oldest matrons through the first day impervious to the normal requirements for sleep.

Nor was there any respite on the next day of Thesmophoria. Even the younger celebrants would lie about outside their crude huts on the hard ground well into mid-morning, exhausted from the festivities and rites of the first night. Faithful service to the goddess for the first two days of Thesmophoria required fasting and forgoing any of the comforts of civilized life. Both devout and casual celebrants grew short of patience and were quick to flare. The customary playful bantering and obscenities between the women which commenced with the official start of the second day at sunset often took on a hard edge. And this year had been especially difficult for Dinomache since her decision to celebrate the holy days in accord with her new understanding of the mysteries made her a target of some of the more hurtful joking. Indeed, when she refused to dance with those who played the part of *Kore*; there were two women who had tried to have at her with their upraised phalli, as if they would show her first-hand what *Kore* had suffered under the lust of Almighty Zeus. How could they believe so literally in such a tale? It was lucky that Elpinice was there nearby and that she took my part, she thought, or I might not have made it through! She alone seemed both curious and respectful when I tried to explain to my hut-mates the true meaning of the story, the mystery of the thrice-born. I almost broke down because of all that abuse added on top of the fasting, no sleep, the rocky ground, the cold night air of approaching winter, and no chair to sit on.

Usually the third day of Demeter's festival, the day of the 'Beautiful Birth', reenergized the celebrants. But for her this year, even this normally happy day was cause for distress...If only they knew how sinful it is to take any kind of animal life. It was not easy for her to stand off to the side, munching on her greens and barley cakes, while the rest of the women broke their fast and gorged themselves on roasted goat and pig. By the time the feasting had ended late afternoon and the cart had to be loaded up again for the return to home, Dinomache could barely keep her eyes open, let alone deal with another round of insults from commoners. If that tower of strength Elpinice had not made it her concern to stay close by, she was sure that she would have either in anger struck out at her tormentors, or worse, broken down into a sobbing mess. Elpinice, probably the best known woman in Athens, had come to her defense again, making sure that her tormentors did not so distract Dinomache that distressed and angry she might leave behind half of her gear. Then just before the women's carts began the descent down from the Acropolis, to Dionomache's surprise, Elpinice appeared again at her side and asked if she might visit her the very next morning. Who would believe that the sister of Athens' most famous general, Cimon, wanted to come visit her? Elpinice had told her that she wanted to learn more about those sacred books and this mystery of being thrice-born which Dionomache had foolishly, she now realized, tried to profess to the uninitiated.

Awake now and feeling better, Dinomache had gone down stairs, through the hallway to the house's enclosed courtyard. A woman like Elpinice, she had decided, should be entertained here in the household courtyard – not in my cramped women's quarters. So she had brought her books down to the little table in the courtyard and instructed the woman kitchen servant to prepare a modest breakfast.

Perhaps, she thought as she waited for the arrival of Elpinice, I will look back at this year's Thesmophoria not as an unhappy one, but as my very best one. For she believed that this woman would be one of the very few who would understand and perhaps even embrace the truth of her recent conversion to the 'Way of Release' and the 'Mystery of the Thrice-born'. What a gift from the god, should he send me such a friend!

But, what if Clinias comes home while she is still here?

Why shouldn't I be in the open air for one more morning since I am still in his house away from the lascivious eyes of his race! Clinias is not here and I don't plan to send a servant to ask his permission! Why should it be such a big deal? Anyways, she will have come and gone before he returns. From what he told me last night, he will be gone at least till mid-afternoon attending a meeting with Athens' leaders. And if he should come home early, well, he would have to understand! After all, it is another woman!

Thanks be to Demeter that the weather was grey, cool, and breezy. All of the day's work would have to be crammed into the afternoon after her guest left. Even on sunny days during the early winter months, the women's quarters could become almost unbearably warm. Her own quarters, although she was married to one of the richer men in Athens, were not much different from any other in Athens.

The four rooms she, the women slaves, and her two daughters occupied were on the second floor on the far side of the small interior courtyard. Once married, the wife was expected to spend most of her life sequestered out of sight from the one first-floor street entrance to her husband's house and her husband's downstairs rooms. The flat roof above her quarters meant that by noon on almost any sunny day the women's rooms became sweat boxes. While there were small windows upstairs on the courtyard side, this did not really give any relief from the heat. For when this one open area did allow a breeze to reach the women's few windows, it could only be from the south, a direction from which the wind hardly ever blew and when it did it was always a warm one. No, she thought, is it not bad enough that men lock their wives in, scarcely permitting them to go out at all? But then, to expect their wife to work at the loom, see to the children's needs, and manage the domestic servants, doing all this almost always half drenched in sweat – it seems our 'proper' gentleman treats his household slaves better than his wife! 'Today,' she said to herself again with resolution mixed with a feeling of forbidden pleasure, 'since my husband is gone and has told me he will not return until mid-day I will stay on holiday and extend the glorious liberty of Thesmophoria. But where is lady Elpinice?' It was getting late and she did not want the visit cut short by an irritated husband shooing her into her quarters and humiliating her in front of her new found friend

"Mistress, Mistress, can the girls go down and play the courtyard. They will not sit on the loom for another minute, and I can't make them stop vomiting." It was Amycla, Dinomache's newest female servant. She was a big-boned buxom twenty year old young woman, about five years younger than her new mistress. Amycla had been purchased by her husband to assist with the care of the children. Still, two years after taking her into the household, this servant was almost more trouble than doing without a nursemaid. She was almost like another child. She seemed to know little about how to handle children and even less about spinning or weaving.

"No, No, Amycla, and when are you going to learn the language?" Usually the big girl's fractured Attic was cause for amusement, but not this morning. "The girls may not play in, play in - do you hear Amycla, the courtyard. I will not have a ruckus interfere with my visit with Lady Elpinice. And Melissa and Eurydicia, I am sure are not sitting on the loom. It's at, at, at the loom! Vomiting, my dear Doric hayseed, is with a long 'a' sound. I hope you mean you can't stop them from 'squabbling'. The words are different! Can't you hear it's a short 'a' sound in 'squabbling'? You're worse than the children. Keep them busy until lunch or it will be to the fields to you. I don't care if Master Clinias likes you or not. When he put you in my quarters he made it clear that you are not here for his amusement but to work. Now, get back upstairs with the children!"

Whatever possessed her husband, she wondered, to purchase this Spartan woman. Dionomache wondered whether her indifference and uncooperative conduct during his infrequent conjugal visits to her bed over the past few years somehow had something to do with bringing the Spartan slave into the house. By Baubo, Amycla was earthy to be sure, but not pretty. Perhaps he thought she really would be good with the children. I must find out her story. How does a Spartan woman end up a slave? Probably she was exposed as a baby and picked up by some enterprising Corinthian slaver. But then why would she still be speaking that damnable Spartan Doric?

The big-boned nursemaid sighed and curtseyed before backing up to the courtyard inner door and in her husky, but servile, voice begged her mistress's pardon. "Yes, of course, I'll do butter, ma'am! But there is someone pecking at the street door. Should I......."

"Get up stairs, now. I won't have you greeting the sister of Athens' greatest General with your nonsense, *butter pecking*! You silly twit! Someone else will answer the door."

It was Lycon who appeared leading a tall robed figure into the courtyard *stoa* from the entry hall. Lycon had not accompanied his Master to the Bouleuterion. Clinias had said that he could sleep late this morning and so it was with some irritation that he had answered the door. He was still rubbing the sleep out of his eyes, before he realized that the robed and hooded guest was a woman, and a very prominent one at that! Because the guest's long robe and hood made it impossible to tell what form lie beneath the garments, Lycon had first thought that it was some man looking for the Master of the House. Respectable women, unless they were hetaerae or slaves, were always veiled in public. Indeed, now that Thesmophoria was over, what would a woman as richly dressed as this guest be out and about for? But when the guest replied in an unmistakably female voice, and when the hood was pulled back to reveal the distinctive bearing of an aristocratic female face and the just barely visible cleavage of a bosom; Lycon stuttered a surprised greeting, "My lady Elpinice! Why, what brings you to my Master's home? My lord, I mean Master Clinias, he is not here today and....."

Before the bare-foot man servant could finish his sentence, the lady had already stepped through the door and with the voice of one accustomed to such greetings by confused males, she gently upbraided the confused steward as she explained that it was the Lady of the House, Dinomache, she had come to visit. "Dear fellow, half of the morning is gone. Can that still be fair Sleep I see in your eyes? I must not allow my servants to fraternize with you! I would soon be regarded as the most demanding of task-masters - making those who serve in our household rise with the sun! It is Mistress Dinomache expecting me. If you're not sleep-walking, perhaps you could take me to her."

Dinomache had risen from the courtyard bench and made her way down the *stoa* towards the entry way to greet her guest. Lycon, with a hint of irritation in his voice directed at both of the ladies, did not announce the guest as he and Elpinice approached Lady Dinomache, but asked, "Will the Mistress and her guest require anything upstairs?"

Both women heard the implicit directive in the steward's question. "Lycon, mind your manners! I don't believe you have offered to take Lady Elpinice's robe. It will need to be dried. Surely, you noticed her robe is damp from the rain this morning. Did I miss something? Did you properly announce my guest? I suppose my husband - he is far too easy with you - told you that you could sleep half the morning. No, we will not need anything to be brought upstairs! Lady Elpinice! I am sure, would much prefer to visit in our courtyard at the little table, now that there is a little sun."

"Yes, of course, Mistress, but what if......."

"Oh don't be such a busy-body, Lycon! You're worse than any of those nosy old girls out in the kitchen. Don't you remember that my husband even permitted me to spend an afternoon here with the priest and his scrolls just a year ago?" Dinomache frowned at Lycon and shooed him away with a flutter of her hand.

Elpinice had handed Lycon her robe and smiling at Dionomache joined in reminding the man - he was a slave, after all, male or not - that it was not his place to so 'take care' of them. "Dinomache, I bet that Clinias let you be unsupervised with that holy man and even though he was probably without balls, he still had more down there than me. So, if you don't mind - of course he is your servant - why don't we send him back to his cot rather than keep the dear old boy up. Slave or not, the man in him is showing – he wants to keep us with the children."

When Lycon had left them, Dinomache escorted her guest to the courtyard table. They sat down opposite one another on the stone benches which were permanently attached to the two long sides of the small rectangular table. Just a few feet from one end of the table, there stood a small potted tree which still, even though it was the beginning of winter, carried on its higher branches worn and brown leaves still stubbornly clinging to their dry twigs. Wisps of early winter breezes descended into the courtyard from above and worked to shake the leaves free from their hold.

Dinomache sat quiet for just a moment, letting her eyes take in as much as she could of Elpinice's appearance, never letting them rest fixed on her body or face lest she appear rude. It was Elpinice who broke the momentary awkward silence.

"My dear, you look at me like you have never seen a woman my age that still has her teeth, her hair color, and a figure! Believe me, it is not as good as it appears. When you are as old as I am and you still wish to please a man, you must become a master of illusion. You must not tell anyone, but I must be twenty years or so older than you. My brother assures me that I am forty-five, since he remembers that he was fifteen when I was born."

Dinomache blushed. "Please, have some fruit and bread. We can draw cold water from the cistern, if you like. There is also some cheese under the cloth. Let me cut you some."

"Thank you, my dear, I am rather hungry. The walk here has given me quite an appetite." Elpinice saw that the younger woman was ill at ease. "Please, don't be put off by my direct manner. We, women have so few occasions to talk seriously with one another, and so I usually skip right over the small talk and posturing, hoping that my companion and I can discover something of substance to feed our starved souls. And you fascinate me. Anyone who would risk derision and hostility in order to remain true to their convictions, and at a public festival like Thesmophoria, this is not the usual meek and well domesticated wife! So let us agree, this morning, to ask anything of one another and hold back nothing. Wouldn't that be exciting?"

Elpinice's warm smile and the way she had reached across the little table with both of her hands, one to take the plate filled with freshly cut cheese and dried figs which Dinomache offered her and the other to take Dinomache's hand and gently squeeze it as though they were sisters - this made the younger woman feel a warmth and affection she had not experienced for many years now with any other adult. How can this be, Dinomache wondered. I have spent less than a few hours with this woman and already I feel closer to her than my own husband!

"Lady Elpinice, may I....."

"Please, Dinomache, just call me 'Elpinice'. The 'Lady' bit is far too formal. You know, despite the rumors, I don't really fancy myself a princess. And while I am much older than you, I do fancy knocking down such barriers if they serve no serious purpose. Before we talk about you and those sacred writings you wish to show me, tell me what you have heard about me and what you think about my reputation. And I insist that you ask me whatever comes to mind. After all, you know, we are because of my brother's marriage kind of related and there should be no secrets between kinfolk."

Dinomache furrowed her brow and then giggled. "Elpinice, I think you must be my niece. Let's see. Your brother Cimon married my father's granddaughter, Isodike. I never knew of course my father's first wife and her children. After she died in childbirth, father, I am told, made arrangements for the daughters to be taken care of by his deceased wife's family. One of these girls is the mother of your sister-in-law Isodike. My mother married Megacles when he was fifty-five, just after his granddaughter Isodike married Cimon. Actually, my mother was his third wife. Would I be your great aunt, then?"

"It could be, Dinomache. I suppose if all the men were done in, we were the last survivors of the Philiad and Alkmeonid lines, and I was childless and your daughter was about to marry; then I am sure some clever fellow would be able to persuade the inheritance court that should any citizen outside of our families marry your daughter, then all of the remaining unencumbered Philiad and Alkmeonid estates should come to his household because his mother-in-law and her great niece-in-law have no other men to take care of their family's inheritance. Yes, for sure, it's a man's world!"

They both laughed. It was a stretch, this in-law genealogy, but it tickled both of them to think that the twenty-five year old wife and a young mother could be great aunt to Callias' new bride, a forty-five year old woman of the world unmarred by giving birth and still girlish in figure.

"You know, auntie, we have many such tangled briar-patches for family connections in our city. It all comes from our men. They can't keep it in their *chitons*, and, you know they feel obligated to keep proving their manhood. It's not enough for them to pleasure themselves with the servants, temple prostitutes, and their party girls. No, should a wife die in childbirth, or even two wives, they always have to get another baby-maker. The ones who marry young, in their thirties, and live on through many soldiering seasons; they will spawn all by themselves a hornets' nest of intergenerational kinship confusion. Yes, there's enough comedy and tragedy in all that mess to keep our playwrights busy for a long time!"

Dinomache had not heard talk like this before. No women she knew talked so freely of such matters. "But they do protect us, don't they? What would happen if they did not keep us safe?"

"I don't know. Maybe I am too hard on their race. They do seem to fight all the time. It must be awful to march off every summer, knowing this might be the time you'll get an arm hacked off, or a spear in the groin, or a gash that turns gangrene and kills you. Maybe I would want to lose myself in drink and between the legs of a soft pleasure-giver as often as I could if I had to face year after year such contests where pain, mutilation, and death awaited even the most skilled soldier. How difficult it must be for our fifty-year old men to strap on their armor - if they make it that far - knowing that with all their powers diminished they may lock in mortal combat with a young powerful lion of a warrior now ready to dispatch them as so much fodder for the vultures. It really is quite something that any of our men make it as far along as your father, Megacles, or for that matter, my husband, Callias. Well, enough with the men, let's talk about ourselves, Dinomache."

Their conversation was interrupted by a loud knocking coming from the street entrance. Apparently Lycon had fallen asleep again in his small first-floor room just beyond Clinias' quarters, as no one was answering the door. Dinomache rose from her bench, "Pardon me, Elpinice, but Lycon must be indisposed. I had better see who is at the door."

"Do you mind if I stretch my legs and join you. Besides, if your caller is a male, you wouldn't want a passer by to see you opening the door alone to a man other than your husband or a kinsman."

When the two women had reached the door, they found Lycon had after all opened the door. Dinomache, still unable to see past Lycon's back, reprimanded her slow doorman. "What in Tartarus took you so long? I hope you have apologized to our visitor."

"I came as soon as I could, my Lady. I was all the way in the back. It seems as though I had a bad batch of beans last night and with my chamber pot under me reverberating, I didn't hear the knocking at first."

The visitor standing behind Lycon chimed in, "Mistress Dinomache,

> Forbear and forgive this flatulent fellow,
> For farting fanfare I did hear bellow.
> Yea, I thought it was Polyphemus himself thundering,
> To stay or flee I stood before this door wondering.
> Stout as Odysseus, I resolved to wait the sounding storm's end,
> To see who within, with belly and backside winds could such cacophony blend."

Lycon moved aside and Dinomache, like a satyr choral leader half turned towards the audience while addressing the lead actor, greeted the visitor, "Oh, Elpinice, it is my husband's young protégé, Socrates. And as you hear, he is sharp of wit and much taken with our satyr-poets."

Elpinice knew the young man, for her husband had taken a liking to this rather odd fellow and had even invited him and his tutor escort to their home for a lunch. "It sounds as if Clinias must give him more attention," she said mischievously. "He seems to be spending too much time around the versifying theater crowd. But perhaps I misjudge. Look Dionomache, he comes garbed as a soldier in training!"

The young man drew himself up in his best military bearing, chased the grin from his broad face, and with all the propriety he could muster stated his business. "I hope I have not disturbed you Lady Dinomache. I see that you are entertaining Lady Elpinice. My apologies! I had hoped I might find Captain Clinias at home. I have need of his advice and wished to speak with him this morning."

Dionomache stepped just outside the door to peer up the street as she answered, "He left the house early this morning and has gone to Solon's agora. I think you can find him there somewhere near the Bouleuterion. If he is not there, he will probably have gone on to the Gymnasium on Academy Way. I am sure he will be glad to talk with you if you can find him."

Dionomache was anxious to resume her visit with Elpinice and did not want to invite the young man in to wait for the return of Clinias. Anyways, there was no telling when he would be back, whether mid-afternoon or as late as sunset. And so, standing outside her door, she waved good-bye to young Socrates.

As Socrates ambled away down the street towards the Agora, Dionomache dismissed Lycon again, instructing him to make sure that she and her guest were not disturbed again - unless, of course, the master of the house returned.

When the women had made themselves comfortable again at the courtyard table, Dinomache did indeed throw caution to the wind and accepted the older woman's invitation to 'throw down the barriers', as she had put it, and let her curiosity lead where it may in conversation with this bold and irresistibly attractive and different woman. Indeed, for the moment, Dinomache had all but forgotten about the bundle of scrolls which ostensibly were the reason for Elpinice's visit.

"Elpinice, ever since I was a small child I have heard women gossip about you. Most of it was vicious and accused you of every kind of perversion. But as I became older, I began to realize that most of the scandalous talk about you - and it didn't just occur among the zeugites and the thetes but also among the high-born 'good' families- arose from some strange mix of envy and resentment. You know, of course, that you have led and continue to lead a life so unlike the other proper women of Athens?"

Elpinice smiled and nodded her head. "Do you mean that I remained unmarried so long? Indeed, I thought I might never marry. And I suppose the fact that I have no children and now have married Callias' with the agreement between us that there are to be no children is offensive to many of Athens' proper ladies."

"That's only a part of it. It's much more than that. You seem," Dionomache searched for the right words, you seem so serenely singular, so at ease with being eccentric, so unconcerned about pleasing either other women, or, for that matter, in spite of your beauty, men."

Elpinice sighed, "It hasn't always been like that for me. Indeed, when I was not taken or given in marriage by age twenty, I thought my life was over. I thought that I would end up a shriveled old maid consigned to a life of nursing my older kinfolk, or worse, sent packing to fend for myself as a vegetable or fruit peddler in the marketplace. If there wasn't marriage with a family of note, then there could be nothing but debasement, I thought. It wasn't that I was not pretty. But all through my teenage years, our household lived under a dark cloud which frightened all respectable suitors away."

Dinomache tried to imagine what Elpinice would have looked like at seventeen or eighteen years of age. She must have excited even the envy of Aphrodite, she thought. For even now at the age when most women are all worn out - if they have survived the rigors of giving birth many times - her shoulder-length blond hair (there was not a trace of grey to be found) framed a face where every feature seemed perfect in its proportion. Her strikingly bright blue spirited eyes, high cheek-bones, slightly flaring, but petite nose, and her thin lips all together still gave the impression that no man would ever be able to break the spell of her gaze. Dinomache wondered if her tall stature at age eighteen, surely somewhat more slender than today, would have intimidated even older men then. While her figure was not voluptuous, Dinomache could not help but envy the way this women almost twice her age, could still wear a well-fitted gown, gathered in at the waist with a broad sash, which displayed athletic legs, slender hips, and firm, still upturned breasts. She is still every inch, Dinomache thought, the image of her mother, the Thracian Princess her father had taken as his Queen when he ruled like a Persian king in his Dardanelles stronghold. It must have indeed been a very dark cloud, to have eclipsed her beauty.

Dinomache knew the family histories of all the best families in Athens and it was sad to think that the enmity between the Philiad and Alkmeonid families of thirty years ago had so affected this woman. She felt personally pained that it may have even been her kin that before her birth had helped foment the stigma that came to rest on the young Elpinice.

"I have never understood," Dinomache spoke with compassion, "how we Athenians could treat your father, Miltiades, so badly after his heroism at Marathon. How could anyone really believe that he would conspire with the Persians to bring back the Peisistratids after Marathon? And I don't understand why he was accused of embezzlement in the Paros affair. I have always admired the way your brother took care of your family. But it must have been very hard on you to be so shunned just at that time when every woman has been prepared to assume her place in society as a bride of one of the high-born."

"At that time it was very hard on me, Dinomache. But I bear no ill will towards anyone. I believe now that it was all for the best. I see it all differently today, but I wouldn't expect many to understand what you call my, how did you put it, my singular serenity, my eccentricity. Were you there for Sophocles' productions at the Greater Dionysia three years ago? His trilogy won no first prize, and that is not surprising given that so many in the audience cannot see as far or deeply as he does. I believe the name of the first play was *Tereus*. In that production, the playwright gave voice to a thought that over the years had taken shape for me but which I could never say out loud either to myself or others. Of course, since it is a woman who utters these lines and since she is a murderous mother, the words of Procne would soon be forgotten by everyone. But I often repeat them to myself.....

> '....often I pondered the status of women: we are nothing. As small girls in our father's house, we live the most delightful life, because ignorance keeps children happy. But when we come to the age of maturity and awareness, we are thrust out and bartered away, far from the gods of our forefathers and parents, some to alien men, some to barbarians, some to good homes and some to abusive ones. And after one single joyful night of love, we are compelled to praise this arrangement and consider ourselves lucky'."

"I could not attend any of the festival's events that year Elpinice. I was still recovering from the still-birth of what would have been my third child. I thought I was going to die at the time from loss of blood and exhaustion. It was especially hard on me also, because it would have finally given Clinias the son he so desperately wants."

"Yes, I had heard about that. You poor girl! It must have been terrible. But you are still young and can try again, can't you?"

Dinomache's body stiffened as she looked right past her guest towards the ornamental depiction of the underworld which decorated the cistern's base. "I will never go through anything like that again because." Dinomache stopped in mid-sentence. She was not quite ready to reveal the specifics of this most intimate resolve. She could not be sure that even this very sympathetic woman could possibly understand her recent adoption into the Circle of the "Perfected". And so she turned the conversation back towards Elpinice's story.

"But, Elpinice if you really feel as Sophocles' Procne does, than why after many years did you decide to marry Callias?"

"Well, my brother had convinced me that I should not be alone in my older years. Cimon has been wonderful. Maybe it is because he has spent some time in Sparta and there observed the more independent lives of well-born Spartan women. He has also traveled in Egypt and Scythia, where woman seem to play a more prominent role in governing their tribes. So perhaps because of these experiences, he never pushed me into marriage so as to promote his own climb to prestige and preeminence in the city. Indeed, I was almost thirty when I married Callias. Although my brother was opposed to it, Callias insisted on paying off the last of the family fine which had been levied against my father. Cimon has, of course, long since repaid Callias. But at the time, he swallowed his pride, and acting in my father's place, agreed that I should become his friend's bride. It was hard on Cimon. He could not even offer a dowry. But after those years I had spent living with him, free to come and go as I pleased, and no man's handmaiden; he worried that unless I had the protection of some wealthy man who would tolerate my ways, I would not be able to maintain the very independence I had come to prize. Curious, isn't it - my brother, urging me to marry, so that I could preserve my independence? Well, at first I thought this was utterly absurd. But then my brother introduced me formally to Callias who had just lost his wife and already had two sons and a daughter. To make a long story short, this man who already had everything fell in love with me, I mean head over heels in love, and he assured me that he would require nothing of me but companionship. Indeed, he insisted that I should continue to live pretty much as I had been, with the only proviso being that I take on no new lovers and bid good-bye to any current ones. In exchange for this, Callias promised that he would provide me with all the resources I would ever need to live comfortably and travel as widely and often as I wished. At first, I could not even consider the proposal seriously without feeling that I would simply be prostituting myself, no better than a high-priced hetaera. But Cimon and Callias were the best of friends and it seemed that he was always around. Cimon always included me in their conversations around a shared meal. Slowly I came to like, yes, perhaps even love, this utterly charming and very sophisticated cosmopolitan man. This forty-old, it seems, had had his fill of fifteen year old girls and actually was fascinated with a woman with whom he could intellectually converse and who was old enough to be a friend, rather than just a pet or another child to be cared for. As for myself, I found myself enchanted by his vast knowledge of far away places, Philosophy, and stories of the past. So, when after repeated rebuffs, Callias proposed to me yet another time, let's see - it was during my brother's serious illness just before Aristides took Cimon along in his campaign to secure our Delian League frontiers; I threw caution to the wind and accepted. He has kept all his promises and I am indeed a very fortunate woman, enjoying the benefits of his substance without undergoing the "arrangement" of our Procne's complaint!"

"Elpinice, do you mean that you will never have children?" Dinomache could scarcely comprehend how this could be chosen by any women. It seemed to her inconceivable that any woman could render such mastery over the use of her own body. And then, even if she could, how could any woman reared by Athens' noble families, abide the shame of a barren womb?

Elpinice smiled. "Dionomache, should I try to deliver a child at my age, more than likely I wouldn't be up to it. Callias has assured me that he has more than enough sons. And surely you do know that a woman who wishes to enjoy the pleasures of love may do so without risking conception. Why should our husband's hetaerae be the only ones who know the secrets of the *alabastron*? While I have never practiced their profession, I certainly did not remain a virgin all these years prior to my marriage." Elpinice shifted her position on the bench and with a twinkle in her eye struck the pose of a seated flutist. "How else could I have so inspired Athens' greatest painter to place me among the heroes of Troy, and such a flattering picture! Ah, my dear Dinomache, this was the truly difficult sacrifice my marriage required....no more moon-lit trysts with wild-eyed Polygnotus!"

Dionomache's eyes widened. "Did he tell you ahead of time that you would be up there on the colonnade wall for everyone to see as his Laodice?"

"No, that was a surprise. And, I'll tell you, that did not go over very well with big brother. But, dear Callias, he had just started to court me when the picture was finished; it didn't seem to bother him at all. I suppose part of his attraction to me was that I was naughty. But no more modeling days for me!"

Dinomache felt a twinge of envy. "But you are still so beautiful, Elpinice. Look at me, I am 20 years younger than you, and already I have lost my shape and now it has been over three years since anything like desire or the fire of passion has quickened my body. Indeed, I think all that is behind me now, forever."

Elpinice did not know what to say about that. But she sensed that this woman had set a new course, and that she would not simply dry up and go peaceably into the long and unrelieved tedium of the proper matron's fate - sequestered for service to small children and the loom. So, it was time to talk about that unusual conduct at Thesmophoria which must be part of that new life that was emerging in this obviously troubled wife.

"Now, Dinomache, we have talked enough about me. What about these sacred writings you wanted to show me? I am so curious about this business of being thrice-born you spoke of during the first night initiation rites at Thesmophoria."

Dionomache nodded, and looking very pleased, bent over and reached for the dark blue urn which she had put under the table before her guest had arrived. The urn, squat with a rather wide opening at the top, made for a safe and secure container for what over the past year had become her most precious possession, a small collection of scrolls which Clinias had purchased for her from an itinerate priest. The scrolls' parchment were not of the highest quality and she had decided to keep them in the urn which she could then place well above the ground on a wall shelf in her quarters, assuring that the scrolls could not become wet or soiled. It was from this urn that she now withdrew the bundle of six scrolls which were neatly tied together at both ends with a thin leather cord. When she had nudged the empty urn back under the table with her foot and straightened up again to face her guest, she was positively beaming with pride.

"Elpinice, I can't tell you how much it means to me that I can share with you how these writings have enlightened me. Clinias has permitted me to continue with my reading, provided the materials which come into the household do not unduly disturb me or introduce notions which might, as he puts it, infect our household with unhappiness. Just over a year and a half ago, thinking a special act of kindness might help me get over the brooding and melancholy which I could not rid myself of after the still-birth of our son, Clinias brought to the house an itinerate priest who was selling manuscripts billed as very old editions of sacred stories. After my husband saw that I was indeed excited by the scrolls which the priest displayed to us, right here on this table, he purchased them. Clinias didn't even bother to read them that day. He was sure, I suppose, that religious stories, like those of Homer or Hesiod, were safe fare and would be just what was required to indulge his wife's interest in reading without taxing his 'little woman's' moral compass or dutiful submission to her husband.

It wasn't until some months later, when I began to behave strangely as he puts it, that he took the time to read some of these scrolls. Well, when he did read them and saw where I was getting what he calls "very strange and irrational notions", he wanted to take them away. I begged and pleaded and wept uncontrollably until finally, exasperated, he said I could keep them, but only on the condition that I never discuss these texts either with him or our daughters. And so I have kept everything to myself. I feel like I'm about ready to burst. Please, don't laugh at me if I seem so excited. I have discovered that there are others in Athens who know these writings and who regularly meet together for the purpose of sharing their understanding with novices. And when my husband has been away on military campaigns or overseas in his commercial dealings, I have attended the meetings of one such religious club. I borrow one of my female servant's old cloaks, cover my head, and veil my face. No one ever would guess that it is the Alkmeonid wife of Clinias who is out and about to attend a meeting which includes other men. But no one should worry about my virtue on this score. Of course, I have not told my husband about this. He would not approve. Indeed, I am only one of a very few married women who attend these meetings. There are a few widows, a number of hetaerae and some metic women who work the stalls in the Agora, along with a rather unusual assortment of older men - all of whom have taken an oath of celibacy. None of the men come from the circles of the well-born. I don't know what Clinias would do if he found out that I leave the house without his permission. I suppose he will find out sooner or later. I don't know what I will do then. But I have found a happiness and peace I did not think possible and I would rather die than give up my new convictions and these new friends who share them with me." Dionomache paused, somewhat breathless because she had spoken so quickly. She looked into Elpinice's eyes to make sure that there would be no ridicule or scorn if she shared her new-found religious enlightenment with this worldly woman.

Elpinice now was wildly curious. Dinomache's trembling hands and the excited, but almost conspiratorial tone of her voice reminded the older woman of her first meetings with illicit lovers. "Your secret excursions are safe with me. But please explain to me what you have been reading. And don't leave out how it relates to your unorthodox conduct at Thesmophoria. How can it be that your husband, the champion of Artemisium who has captained rough-hewn thetes through stormy seas and blood-soaked combat, cannot find the courage to converse openly with you about these texts? What does he say is so terrible about their contents? And for the life of me, I can't understand why Athenian men are so intent on being their wife's jailers!"

There was only curiosity and encouragement in Elpinice's words, so Dinomache decided she would continue and explain to her guest what she regarded as her new birth. For it might be a long time, before another opportunity came along for her to discover whether or not the truths she had found would find any resonance with another woman who moved among the circles of the well-born.

Dinomache hurriedly moved the plates of fruit and cheese off to the edge of the stone table. She then carefully unrolled one of the scrolls to the beginning of its first section so that it faced Elpinice. Leaning over the table, so that her face was now quite close to her guest's, she gently ran her girlish small fingers over the parchment so as to smooth and straighten what appeared to be almost permanent creases in the parchment. Then, using both hands, she held the scroll open so her guest could inspect the scroll's title page for herself. The closeness of this beautiful woman who was giving all her attention to Dinomache in a way that she had not experienced since she was a child in her mother's quarters, the scent of the essence of jasmine perfume, and the soft-spoken promise of keeping trust made her lose track. There were uninvited feelings stirring in this wife which both unsettled and elated her. She drew back her face which was almost touching Elpinice's, and instinctively withdrew to safer ground.

"I..., I don't know quite where to begin. My husband insists that the manuscripts are fakes and not at all what they claim to be. Look at the title page of this first scroll!"

Elpinice shifted her position and bent her upper body even closer to better inspect the text. She sensed that the young woman she had just really come to know in the past few days was desperately lonely and vulnerable. It was as though, she thought, that Dinomache has not been caressed or touched with genuine affection for a very long time. For just an instant, a vague memory of her stay on Lesbos and it's brief season of tender love hovered somewhere between her and the fragile, still lovely young woman whose head and hands, so near, with a mysterious text between them awaited her response. Scholarship, she inwardly smiled to herself, is so much more exciting and illumining when it is suffused with the warmth of *eros*.

"Dinomache, the text really is almost illegible here in this section." Elpinice could just barely make out a title by filling in what must have been the obvious missing letters. It read in large capital letters, "ORPHEUS, ON HIS POEMS, DEEDS, AND THE MANNER OF HIS DEATH". At the bottom of what was apparently the title page, there seemed to be the author's name after the phrase "As witnessed by". But the only letters visible in this space were a 'M' and two 'S's, obviously just a few of the letters from the author's entire name.

Elpinice looked up from the scroll. "Its stories concerning Orpheus, I see. And I would guess that the author is Musaeus, Orpheus' pupil. So these manuscripts are either themselves very old or exact replicas of old texts."

Dinomache sat up straight, stretching her back as she spoke. "I believe so, but for me it is not all that important who wrote the text or how old it really is. The only time my husband spoke to me concerning these scrolls - when he was insisting that they be thrown out or given away - he said, let me see if I can remember his exact words, .'all of them are forgeries and the priest is a mystery-monger preying on gullible weak-minded fools who can not let go of their deceased kinfolk. At best', he opined with scorn, 'these texts were originally copied from the work of Onomakritus, that Persian-loving friend of the Pisisitratid tyrants. No freedom loving Athenian,' and this he yelled in my face, 'should ever pay homage in any way to that manufacturer of fables for the education of tyrant-lovers.'
How he saw those politics in these Orphic writings is beyond me. But he says, I'm just a stupid child when it comes to the ways of those who would rule cities by first controlling men's minds. I think it is really he who is quite blind. He seems incapable of discerning the hidden meanings of allegory and symbols."

Elpinice had herself heard of these kinds of writings and had even listened to a poet recite by memory something from what he called '*Orpheus' Rhapsodies*', but she had never actually seen the actual texts. When she had asked Callias, her husband, about these writings, he knew little about them except that they had been brought to Athens by men who claimed to be Pythagoreans from the western colonies in Sicily and Italy. She had wanted to see for herself what they were all about, and now here they were spread on the table before her. "What are the titles of the other ones, Dinomache?"

"Let me make room here to show you the others." Dinomache cleared the remaining fruit and cheese plates from the table. "We must be careful not to stain or spill anything on these. As you can see, none of them are in very good shape." She unrolled each of the remaining five scrolls so just the first section of each was visible.

"You can't tell, Elpinice, by just glancing at these first sections of each, but it appears that the rest of these scrolls only contain parts of some larger manuscripts. One is titled the *Rhapsodies*, this one with the much frayed papyrus appears to be a kind of account of the origin of the gods and all of creation, and the smallest scroll, the one with the delicate red and purple flowers drawn on the outer side, is my favorite one. It tells the story in great detail of Orpheus' journey to the underworld to recover his wife after she had been mortally wounded by a large snake while fleeing from a rapist. I have not yet been able to determine whether the other two scrolls which describe certain rites of purification are also part of the Orphic teachings."

"This is an amazing collection, Dionomache. But tell me, since I must be on my way before long, what these writings have to do with Thesmophoria and how they led you to that 'Way of Release' you spoke of to your Hut mates who ridiculed you! I think you said that we could not properly go down and then up again with Demeter's Persephone unless we were initiated into the 'Mystery of the Thrice-born'. Are the stories in these texts the ones which illumine this mystery you speak of?"

Dionomache picked up the scroll which treated the birth of Dionysius, his horrible mutilation by the Titans, and his miraculous resurrection through the intervention of his father, Zeus. She unrolled it, looking for that section which also explained how the first human beings were made by Zeus. Finding this passage, she thought it might be possible to use it as a guide to explaining her own still somewhat confused, but personally poignant, relation to the Mystery of the thrice-born taught in all of these writings. "See here, the poet reveals to us that after Zeus had avenged the murder of his son by killing and dismembering the Titans who had slain him, the world order in which man appears began when Zeus gathered up the remnants of the unruly and evil Titans and from this material created the first of our kind. What does this mean for us? It has taken me much study and many conversations with those others who are more perfect than I to begin to find the hidden meanings of the Mysteries we and our ancestors have revered. So you must bear with me if I seem to ramble or jumble together many things which seem at first so unlike one another."

"I suppose," said Elpinice, "even the most far-seeing enlightenment regarding the Divine must always retain something mysterious and so I would not expect these things you have learned to be simple or clear to an uninitiated one like myself."

Dinomache nodded and then continued. "Well, let me begin with the preparations for Thesmophoria that we women must undergo in order to commune with Holy Mother Demeter and her Virgin Maiden Persephone. I am not talking about the packing and the planning for the set-up of the camp, of course. This holiday bustle may only obscure for us the spiritual meaning of the Works of the Mother and the Maiden. Thesmophoria is exclusively for us women because no man can directly participate in the divine suffering of the Twain. And thus, while virgin maidens are barred from Demeter's service at Thesmophoria, we in whose earth the phallus has made its pass must be left fallow as a virgin from the beginning of the month till the Thesmophorian's Work is done. In this way, we are consecrated with the divine maiden and walk with her in the sun lit world of her sweet Mother. Like her, we who are so consecrated return to the days of the first-birth when all was one, and neither strife nor violence had yet given rise to giants, fierce predators, nor those who would tear and render apart others' bodies.

Oh, Elpinice, how sweet our childhood and maiden years are, carefree and happy indeed! We did not even know of mother's labor when brothers and sisters came after. If we did see this labor and stood by our mothers in this their work visited on them by their destiny and the husbandmen, then our sun-lit romps would have not been so light and airy!"

Dinomache's face constricted. Tears began to run down her cheeks. Her own words had touched something very painful inside her.

Elpinice rose from the table and moved to sit beside the grieving young woman. She gently put her hand on Dinomache's shoulder. "Dear, if this is too difficult, I mean, if it calls to mind what is best forgotten; then do not feel you must continue. I can see that whatever you have discovered is at the heart of things for you and it can't be easy to admit a stranger like me into that inner sanctum."

"Bear with me, Elpinice. I will be alright. I must say it the way I feel it. It is the only way I am able to testify to the new life I have found in the Mysteries. This part of my preparation for Thesmophoria was easy for me. Ever since I lost my son, I have been cold and unreceptive to my husband. He does not understand what that did to me. So much did I endure to come to that day, and then to writhe in pain for fourteen hours even though I had already borne two healthy daughters. He would not even come into the birthing room as he listened to my groans and screams. The frantic mid-wife could not find the baby's head. Then in that last bloody hour when only the feet had breached the womb and when the pain was so severe that I knew he had been lost - everything went black and my last thought before I lost consciousness was that I should die and join my unborn son. It had all come to this. I had left my father's home, just a girl trembling on the marriage cart. That first night, with his mother guarding the door - I'll never forget. This man twice my size, almost as old as my father would soon take my maidenhead. I knew nothing and even though he found me trembling, there was no time for tender kisses or reassuring words. As though it was some prescribed rite, my new husband lifted my wedding robe and covered my face. With my eyes closed tight and my heart pounding in fear as he mounted me, it was as though the tenseness of my body would never let go of my childhood. It seemed an eternity of fumbling and battering until that large straightened snake of his found its way into my bleeding inners. As I lay there after he had left - he did not even wait until daybreak - I wept quietly wondering why it was that the paintings I had seen on my father's vases had depicted love-making with naked women accompanied by the music of the lyre and flute. The first night behind, I endured. But never has there been music or from him the gift of pleasure to me. Two daughters later and much brow-beating about his exclusion from high office because he, **He**, mind you, bore no sons – how, he said, could a man without heirs be expected to make good decisions for the commonwealth - I yet suffered his infrequent visits in hopes of bearing him a son and securing my worth in his and my father's eyes. Mind you, my husband is not a bad man, but he even complained that he was stuck with me whether or not I produced a son. My father, he said, would not want me to return to his house since it would mean once again sending out that sizable dowry if I were to marry again. All this, and then the mid-wife telling me after I had recovered consciousness that I would not be able to give birth again, I even forgot my dear daughters and wanted to close my eyes and never open them again."

Elpinice sighed. "Dionomache, I have a confession to make. My late marriage and decision not to have children resulted not only from my desire to maintain my independence. I, unlike most of us, was one of those girls who did see my mother in labor. It was like the one you have undergone, except both she and the child died when her hemorrhaging could not be stopped. I will never forget that scene: my father away soldiering, my older brother frantic with worry in the next room, myself only a girl of nine holding my mother's sweaty hand while the midwife tried to calm her convulsive labor and then all that blood and her never waking up after she had fainted away. I was terrified and when it was over thought that if all my father's wealth and my mother's royal lineage could not avert such a bloody end for the woman who offers her body up to the goddess of birthing; then I would never so bring my body to this fickle goddess so cruelly named, she of "Beautiful Birth". And so I can understand at least a part of the feelings your unhappy and fruitless labor brought. Which one of us does not go to Thesmophoria filled with melancholy as we wistfully, like young maidens who are all sisters to the Virgin Persephone, make our camp on the high sun-lit hill unencumbered by that race of men who like Father Zeus take us from our mothers and send us below to the dark regions where life and death comingle? But what does this preparation of abstinence have to do with what you call the mystery of the thrice-born?"

"It will become clearer, Elpinice. But first, I must finish with the other part of my Thesmophoria preparations, you know, concerning the sacred 'things laid down'. Since I have married, it's been ten years, I have never missed a Thesmophoria. That year I lost my child, it happened just a month prior to Stenia, I was to be both a bearer of the sacred basket on the night of Stenia and then a Bailer, five nights later, on the final night of Thesmophoria. My mid-wife and Clinias' tribe's soothsayer had both insisted that it would be propitious for the birth of the expected child, if I offered this service to the Twain. Well, when I lost the child, strangled I later learned by the umbilical cord, I at first refused in my grief and despair to fulfill my promised service. Clinias was furious. He insisted I go since my absence would be an embarrassment to him. After all, he said, it is the duty of noble families to preserve the ways of our forefathers and he would not be that kind of husband who suffered his wife to make a public display of shirking duty.

It was my newly acquired nursemaid, Amycla, who found the words to persuade me to attend. She had, unknown to me, kept the bloody remnants of the umbilical cord after the dead baby had been disposed of - I don't know where. She had wrapped this in a small piece of scarlet linen so that the stain of bloody tissue preserved therein only darkened the color of this bundle of linen. Then, when I refused on the morning of Stenia, to join those that night who would go to the hill and down into the Sacred Cavern with their baskets of Sacred things, she told me that the spirit of my unborn son would not find rest until I laid down a token of his broken body in the dark place of grieving where even the Holy Mother must go to find her broken and stolen maiden. I don't remember now all she said or why it was that I was listening to her, a Spartan slave-girl. But something in her stammering about the spirits which must be placated, the kindness of the Good Mother, and expiating the Curse somehow began to make sense to me. With many tears she cajoled and pleaded, until weeping I joined her in filling my basket with the tokens of Demeter, the sacred playthings of her own child and her child to be, the dough images of the snake-phalli, and this time, a small linen wrapped remnant of that now dead stem which had nourished the fruit of my womb. When, on that evening of Stenia, I joined with the other Bearers by torchlight to make our way down into the sacred cavern, all of us daubed with white clay ghost-like so as to be hidden from those who seek to harm tender Persephone or baby Dionysos, I like never before berated and ridiculed the other matrons calling them whore-bitches, more venting my grief and anger than thinking of distracting the holy mother from her grief over the loss of Persephone. When I reached the dark cavern floor and laid down the holy things, I felt as if I also laid down the last remnants of my wounded and angry inners and with this my very life."

Elpinice, despite being one of the most prominent women in Athens, had never served as either a Bearer or a Bailer during Thesmophoria. Perhaps because she was regarded by so many as of dubious virtue, it was always arranged that her name was never put forward for the drawing of the lots which determined the festival's officials and special ministrants. Besides, she had never really wanted to take this kind of part in the ceremonies since she did not regard herself as one who could lend the proper appearance of seriousness and solemnity to what she regarded as only the quaint trappings of otherwise festive holidays. As she listened, however, to this bereaved mother troubled by her loss of happiness, she began to understand the power of the ceremonies. "Dinomache, you were grieving with Demeter for her lost child."

Dionomache nodded, "In a way I suppose. But it is more than that. In these texts of Orpheus and Musaios, the maiden Persephone is forsaken and indeed violated by her own Father, Zeus. It is her rape by Zeus that sends her away from her Holy Mother and brings her down to dark Tartarus to be kept by Zeus's brother, Hades. It is Zeus Melichios that rapes his own daughter. It is Zeus-Phanes that is her father, the consort of Demeter. And if you read carefully through all the Rhapsodies, you learn that the poet Orpheus, more ancient than even Homer and Hesiod, and himself the off-spring of luminous Apollo, teaches that it is Persephone, and not Semele, who conceives by irresistible Zeus-Melichios and gives birth to Dionysos. This is why we carry the sacred images of the snake-phalli below- to appease the implacable forces of vengeful Zeus who brooks no resistance to his inscrutable lusty will."

Elpinice furrowed her brow. "Now you have lost me, Dionomache. Do you mean to say that these sacred writings teach that Zeus is both father and husband to the mother of Dionysos? But then how would we make sense of our holy reverence to Demeter and Dionysos at Eleusis?"

Dionomache turned to look directly into Elpinice's eyes. The younger woman's face took on a beatific serenity as she dreamily described the beauty of Orpheus' revelation. "Unless we become born again, shedding this titan-like cavern of our bodily senses and sinful nature; we cannot see the pathway to blessed immortality which leads away from judgment, the realm of Strife of Zeus-Melichios-Hades. It is only when we are resurrected with Zagreus-Dionysos, that we can know our release from the toils of this world's lives. Each one of us carries the legacy of sins of those whose lives went before and from whom and in whom our soul is ensnared. If I am to be set free from the curse of ancestral sins - and I am convinced that my sufferings come from such a curse, daughter that I am of the accursed clan which defiled the Acropolis altar and statue of Zeus Melichios - I must purify myself and once again with Zeus thrice-born subdue and vanquish that horde of unruly Titans which would grind my soul into the pit of Tartarus."

"But Dinomache," Elpinice interrupted, "how can it be that Orpheus has anything to offer women? I had heard that he spurned all women and would not include them among his Initiated."

"There are those among us who would pervert his true teaching, Elpinice. They cannot grasp the spiritual, nor receive what eye has not seen and ear has not heard. They are far too literal and for them the mystery of the thrice born is all about magical charms and incantations which somehow will assure the sprouting of new crops from the dead things our rite of Thesmophoria buries in the earth. But Elpinice here in the story contained in the scroll with the delicate flowers around its title page, told by his own son and pupil Musaios, is the true Orpheus. Orpheus, who charms both men and beast by the music of his Lyre, descends into Tartarus to retrieve his wife who has perished by the bite of a large Snake. You see, he loved her dearly and yearned for her companionship. And note, Elpinice, Orpheus has charmed his own wife with the beauty of his lyre; for the verse tell us, I think it is right here in this section, their love is so strong that even the dark forgetfulness of Tartarus is not strong enough to make her forget her husband's melodies of love. How can anyone really think this inspired prophet and poet would not bring his beloved to the blessed isles of eternal life? What do you think, Elpinice? Is there not a higher truth in our stories of Demeter, Persephone, Dionysos and Zeus revealed in these sacred writings?"

Elpinice could not decide whether this young woman had lost her senses or indeed was part of some new and wonderful flowering of poetic vision that tapped into the mysterious and divine dimension. After all, she thought, our playwrights have often been led me to see Homer's stories in an entirely different light. But why, she wondered, did this interpretation of the writings lead to such curious practices as Dionomache's refusal to eat the roast pork when the Fast was ended on Thesmophoria's final day?

"I'm not sure I can follow all the subtleties of what you allude to, Dinomache. These notions of our Titan-like bodies in which a sin-laden soul struggles for salvation, the triple nature of Zeus, the linking of the descent of Persephone into Hades and the horrible mutilation of Dionysos: are these all symbolic for our 'redemption'- is that the word you used? I think you described this salvation as being released or set free from the curse of death and blood guilt. This is all a complicated story and I can see that you have come to it only after much study and contemplation of these writings. But what does this all have to do with your abstaining from the meat the rest of us partook of on the Day of the Beautiful Birth?"

Before Dinomache could answer, Clinias appeared striding down the colonnade, looking extremely irritated. He scowled at both the women, rolled his eyes upward in disgust when he saw his wife's scrolls spread out on the table, and then with uncharacteristic rudeness ignored the presence of Elpinice as he chided his wife. "Dinomache, have you not enough rooms of your own? Isn't it enough that I spend a minor fortune so that you, and even your nursemaid, can go trooping off for three days of unsupervised cavorting at Thesmophoria? Here, I come home in the middle of the day, mind you, and you sit here in the courtyard, unveiled, and in direct line with the front door where any passerby can see you should the door be opened. And what are you doing, after everything has been let go for three days, mucking up that superstitious mind of yours with all that nonsense in front of you. Go to your quarters!"

Dinomache bowed her head in obedience and quickly gathered up her scrolls. Scooping them up in her arms, she then turned to face her husband and in a very flat and emotionless voice begged his pardon. "Sir, I, I only came down here so as to accommodate your wish that these scrolls be kept out of sight of our daughters. Lady Elpinice, we met at Thesmophoria, wanted to see them and I invited her here today, knowing you would not be home. Would you please see that Lycon brings the Lady her rain-cloak and escorts her to the door. I would not stay here another instant if it offends you and I certainly would not embarrass you before strangers who might peer through our open front door. Lady Elpinice, I bid you good day and be assured that I am very pleased that you visited - even if it displeases the Lord of the House!" Dionomache pulled her own robe up around her face and bowing before Clinias as if she were the lowliest of the household servants, she hurried away to her own upstairs quarters.

Dionomache's bitter and false tone of servility exacerbated Clinias' foul mood. It had not been a good day. Pericles special meeting beside the Bouleuterion may have worked well for the politicians. However it was insufferable to Clinias that there could be any story floating about the streets suggesting that he would ever take part in such a dishonorable and cowardly action as conspiring to murder someone by using a hired assassin. For the rest of his life, he thought, there will be some who will believe that my many military tours of duty were not so glorious after all. They will have concluded that I was only competent at ordering others into battle while I found a way to stay out of harm's way. How unfair that Pericles, my wife's cousin, would allow such an uncorroborated and tenuous story to surface before so many of Athens' notable citizens. I should have known that marriage and a business partnership with the old man of the family itself would mean nothing to Pericles. Why didn't he come to me first?

Clinias couldn't get all this off his mind. Neither his short conversation with young Socrates nor a stop at the Gymnasium on the way home had helped. The day's session at the Gym only confirmed that his powers were in decline. His usual fencing partner, a portly man even older than himself, had roughed him up today. Clinias, the hero of Artemisium, left the gym as an aching fifty-two year old man, limping home with a badly pulled calf muscle. And so by the time he had reached his front door, black thoughts had frayed his usual even-tempered discipline. How, he was thinking as he opened the door, will I ever make it through my next campaign when I can't even get through an hour of fencing exercise without falling apart. And so when he saw his Alkmeonid wife sitting with the wife of that man who may in fact have made use of him and entangled him in a dishonorable act of cowardliness - it was just too much! And so while he watched the back of his estranged wife retiring from the courtyard, struggling to control his anger he finally acknowledged his wife's visitor by sending her packing also.

"Mistress Elpinice, I trust you have had time to satisfy your curiosity with regard to our library. Men like your Callias and me, I suppose, are favored by having such modern and literate women in their households. Indeed, there is scarcely time for such as you to grow calluses on either your hands or your backsides since the call of scholarship leaves no time for either the loom or the marriage bed. Such a pristine and intellectual prettiness more than compensates for a barren womb, my philosophically inclined friends might say. Only now, if you don't mind, I must bid you good-bye since connubial duty and the Works of Demeter require my attention. I will ask my steward to fetch your cloak and see you to the door."

This was not the first time Elpinice had been privy to a scene like this one. Many of her visits to the households of other women had ended in just the same way. Much practiced in extricating herself from such circumstances, she merely respectfully nodded in agreement with Clinias' sarcastic dismissal of her. This husband's tightly drawn face and stiff military bearing, she surmised, suggested that any further challenge to his authority would lead to an explosion of anger on his part. Thus, before Clinias had even completed his last sentence, she nodded her acquiescence to his wish and slipped by him towards the front entry hall so as to make her escape from another ruffled husband venting his rage with the world by stamping out sedition in his own little realm.

Clinias stood now alone, facing the cistern. For some unexplained reason, the memory of his last conversation with that person who had loved him longest and best, Sophroniscus, surfaced. Maybe it was because I feel so absolutely alone today, he thought. It had been some years since he had distinguished himself in any way in public life or on military tour. Indeed, it had been a disappointment to him that his neighbors and comrades had never promoted his election to a generalship. And now that he was tainted by allegations, no matter how unsubstantiated, which suggested that he was complicit in the dishonorable assassination of Ephialtes; it was clear that he could never win, this year or any time in the foreseeable future, a place among the ten annually elected generals. It seemed to him that all of his soldiering, all of his life-long struggle to win and secure his place of preeminence in the life of the city, all this often risky and exhausting service for Athens had come to naught when considered from the point of view of this juncture in his life. What had he to show? At fifty-two, he had never risen higher than that of a district judge. It was true that he was much richer today than he was even ten years ago. But what good was this if it could not be passed on to a son?

After ten years of marriage, only two daughters and a wife perhaps now unable to give him a son, what did he have to show? In his better moments, he could even see that on the whole life in Athens was more comfortable and luxurious for more people than ever before and this was due in part to the sacrifices made on the battlefield by men like him. Yet, others of his generation had successfully parlayed their military victories into appointments and elections to the highest offices. Had he been mistaken in devoting so much energy and time to commercial enterprises? Why could he not, like Callias, be content with this kind of success? It galled him that he still felt himself in need of others approbation. But there was no denying it. He counted his wealth as nothing if his honor could be questioned so readily. What good was this affluence? Indeed, he thought, soft living breeds soft men and perhaps my merchant's life has already unstrung the warrior in me. Would my departed friend Sophroniscus, if he was here today, still love me? Am I now worn out and is it the judgment of those around me that I, too, am now consigned to carry water in leaking buckets? Money to be made, dowries to be paid out; money to be made, houses to be endlessly renovated; money to be made, endlessly new appetites for exotic luxuries to be served; money to be made for what? "Enough," he muttered to himself out loud. "I will not abandon the fight for higher ground, even if I don't see it in front of me." And with that resolution, he turned and made his way to the stairs leading to the women's quarters.

As he made his way up the stairs, he wondered when it was that he had last felt even a twinge of desire for his wife. He remembered the very first time he had formulated in his own mind the possibility of taking the daughter of Megacles for his betrothed. He had seen her as a thirteen year old girl during the PanAthenaic Procession. She had been chosen as one of the maidens who would help carry Athena's newly woven garment through the streets of Athens to her Acropolis Temple. On that day, her long auburn hair was gathered up in two thick braids which circled the crown of her head and were pinned in place with a wreath of dark yellow flowers. Her refined and delicate face was glowing with pride as she had been chosen to carry the very trailing end of Athena's new sacred robe. Still pubescent, her girlish body looked like that of a fair boy. Dressed in a white linen robe gathered in at the waist with a purple sash, young Dinomache looked every bit the part of a daughter of one of the first families of Athens' aristocracy. He was standing near the procession that day and as she passed him it was then that he decided that he should ask her father for his daughter in marriage. He remembered thinking at the time that while respectable men found their sexual pleasure with women other than their wives, it would not be burdensome to father sons with this soon to be ripened but still nubile maiden of the good and the beautiful. Yes, he thought as he opened the second floor door to Dionomache's quarters, if I can hold that image before my eyes I will be able to continue the works of Demeter whether or not the field is fallow

It had been more than two months since he had made his way to his wife's quarters. How strange, he thought, that I feel like I am entering strange territory whenever I come up here. If only I had a son there would be more reason for me to take an interest in the children. But still, it was his responsibility to see that his daughters were being properly prepared for the day when they would leave the house. And so when he entered the room without knocking, it was with the eye of a somewhat distant guardian that he quickly scanned the room so as to assure that all was in order.

The room was the largest of the four upstairs rooms set aside for Dinomache, the children, and her female attendants. Clinias had himself overseen the construction of his house and he had designed this room to be a little larger than what was usually the case for the women's work room. Although he had long since abandoned the idea once he had married, he had originally contemplated having this room serve as a workroom for three or four garment makers, thus supplementing his commercial operations with a home-based textile manufacture. It was his idea that whoever his wife would be, she would both work as a spinner and weaver as well as oversee the work of the slaves. He had even bought an extra large loom and permanently mounted it on built in sockets carved into the floor. But when he first showed this room of his then new house to his prospective father-in-law, Megacles joked that all of Athens would think that he could not provide an adequate dowry for his daughter since she had to be put to work spinning garments for other people. And so Clinias, wishing not to offend Megacles, never did proceed with this plan. But the large loom was still there, and, at least, he thought with satisfaction, Dinomache has become quite skilled in its use.

In addition to the large loom and one rather long cushioned bench, the room was furnished with shelves which were mounted on two of its walls, using all available space from floor to ceiling height. Work baskets, carding combs, water jugs of various sizes, and recently washed bundles of wool filled most of the shelves. Dinomache's growing collection of scrolls were carefully stored on one section of these shelves, out of reach of the children but where Dionomache could reach them without needing to stand on a stool. The shelved walls were windowless and faced to the north and east. On the wall facing the courtyard, two small windows let the afternoon sun in, making the room very bright. On this wall and on both sides of the two windows, there were a number of pegs used for hanging various objects which could be tied there with small attached leather straps. Two small oil flasks which were Dinomache's now seldom used alabastrons, a set of leather protective knee covers which Dinomache and Amycla used while carding the wool fibers, an old and obviously only decorative distaff - it had been used by Dinomache's grandmother, a matching set of hand-held mirrors which looked very much like her grandmother's spinning stick, some rumpled aprons, and two beat-up wooden tops which her girls no longer played with: these things of his wife's life filled all the available pegs. Indeed, apart from the few shelves filled with Dinomache's collection of scrolls, the room's furnishings reassured Clinias that his daughters were indeed being prepared for their works as proper women - spinning, water-carrying, and the sexual responsibility of conception and child-bearing

Dinomache heard the door open but did not look up from her work. She was seated on a low backless stool in the middle of the women's work room, busy spinning on her distaff, and drawing already carded wool from a work basket which sat beside her feet. Amycla, the Spartan nursemaid, was nearby, seated on a higher stool and working on the loom. The two girls, Melissa and Eurydicia, were sitting on the floor by Amycla and were both giggling as Amycla in her fractured Attic was relating her favorite tale, the labors of Hercules.

It was Eurydicia who first greeted the lord of the house. Still very much a little girl - she had just turned six - she bounded to her feet and skipped her way across the room to her father's side. With an impish smile and a lisping voice, she asked, "Father, Amycla says, that of all Heracles ten labors, that of cleaning the Aegean stables was the most difficult. But mother says his slaying of the Hydra was the most difficult. Do you know why?"

Clinias softened and the day's scowl, for a moment at least, turned to a smile. "Why, Eurydicia?"

The little girl looked over towards her mother as if expecting her help, "It is because the many headed beast to this day still lives at the watering places. No matter how many times Heracles cut the many-headed serpent's heads off, always a new one will grow and he must begin his labor all over. Mama says it is like my work with the water jugs - it can never be finished."

Melissa, the older girl, was now also at her father's side and she was giggling. "But father, Amycla, makes a good point. She says that the work of Heracles of the chamber pots, his mucking about in the Augean stables, is not only endless but shittier!"

"Girls, leave your father be! How seldom he comes to see us here and you trouble him with our idle talk about Heracles. Your father, I am sure, does not see such labors as Heracles' noblest and most glorious." Dionomache did not want the girls to go on, since her own allegorizing views would be parroted by them. She did not want to give any occasion for Clinias to rant and rave about her scrolls. "Now, go to the back room and play with the draughts until your father has finished his business with me!"

"But mother, can't we stay here and show father how well we do with our letters?" Melissa wanted so much to impress her father with the alphabet she had just traced out this morning on her wax tablet.

Clinias' scowl returned. "Melissa, you would do better to spend more time working with the loom. No man wants a wife whose hands are unskilled at the loom and whose head is filled with letters."

Melissa's shoulders drooped as she took her little sister by the hand. It seemed impossible, she thought, to please her father with anything special. "Let's go, Eurydicia."

Clinias wanted the children out of the house. "Yes, Melissa, take your sister with you, but not to the back rooms. Here, I want you, Eurydicia, and Amycla to take these coins and go to the candlestick makers in the marketplace. Bring home a dozen of the long table candles like the ones now standing on the little table in the entry hall. At least, the counting you have learned can be put to good use. Don't let the merchant cheat you. Offer him only these three coins for the dozen candles and not a deinara more. Now go right away! Amycla, do you understand?"

After Amycla had taken the children from the room, Clinias walked slowly across the room to the couch, passing close by Dinomache's stool before he sat down facing her and with his back leaning against the wall behind the couch. The scowl had returned to his face. Dinomache had sensed what was coming and now had turned her back to him and with stooped shoulders had become even more intent on spinning the carded fibers onto the distaff which now seemed to command all of her attention. He would not leave this room, he said to himself, until his household was once again set right!

"Dinomache put your distaff down and face me! I will have your full attention, now. And take those ugly knee pads off. I want to see the curve of your unadorned knee so that I might remember that you are yet a handmaiden of the works of Demeter - if not exactly a ministrant of Aphrodite."

Dinomache turned towards her husband and in that same flat monotone voice she had used downstairs now undertook, as she had for some time now, to deflate and deflect her husband's unwanted advance. "But my lord am I not most pleasing to you when industriously employed with distaff and loom? Can we not talk while I catch up with my work baskets? You yourself have often said that since I have been relieved of many trips to the public wells with our own cistern, this should enable me to become even more proficient and productive with my remaining tasks."

"Yes, my Alkmeonid Princess, there is far too little for you to do in this house! I think it is because I have not asked you to carry water or otherwise exercise your limbs that you have become effete, a woman of strange books and an over-excited imagination frittered away on some cuckoo land on the other side of the grave. Indeed, this is probably why you were not robust enough to bear me a son. As for the state of your body, I believe any more rest will only lead to irreversible atrophy of that god-given power to nurture my seed. Then what will become of you, my spinster!"

Dinomache threw her distaff to the floor and with tears in our eyes ripped off her knee pads. She stood up and kicked the stool away from her and in a gesture of angry compliance lifted her dress so that its hem just brushed against the top of her knees. She spoke, both sobbing and angry, "Clinias why must you be so cruel and unfeeling? It is hard enough that you show so little consideration for me the few times a month you grace me with your company. But to humiliate me in front of my guest, and one such as the sister of Cimon, do you not have ample slaves or other women for such abuse?" Dinomache's face turned hard and cold again and she fixed her eyes on his. "Don't you feel quite silly trying to work yourself up looking at your old spent wife's flabbily ankles, when you are really dreaming of some boy down at the Gymnasium?"

Clinias did not move from his couch. Appearing to ignore his wife's outburst, he slouched even more onto the couch. When she finished speaking and stood before him lifting her dress as if she wished her body, as well as her words, would send him away, he idly stretched and repeatedly snapped between his hands a leather strap he had taken from the wall peg just above the couch. With the strap snapping between every phrase, Captain Clinias reigned in his wayward wife. "Dinomache, you must get hold of yourself! How well you have it! Is it because I have never taken the strap to you, as most husbands do to insubordinate wives, that I am subjected to such insubordinate talk? You are pushing me too far. I know about your secret outings when I am away. And all this nonsense about no meat - I suppose your hair-brained mystagoges have persuaded you that fucking is impure also! This all has to stop right now, right here! Come to this couch and bring the alabastron vial!"

"But Clinias, I have dreams which warn of a curse which will rest on any further fruit of my womb. I dream I will give birth to a most beautiful peacock that then turns into a mighty eagle, but ends as a hideous vulture feeding on the corpses of his own kind. The vulture then dies horribly when he gobbles up a fiery coal in a frenzy of feeding. My dream ends with the blood curdling screams of this bird whose innards burst into flame. Have you not heard of the curse of the Alkmeonids? I don't know exactly what the dream means, but it is sent from heaven as a warning. Remarry, if you must, or take yourself a concubine, but don't plant seed in this ground!"

Dionomache ended her plea on her knees before her seated husband, embracing his knees as if she were a fallen warrior begging mercy from his blood-thirsty victorious enemy.

Clinias reached down to the pair of hands which were interlocked behind his knees, firmly pulled them apart, and then stroking them, placed them on his thighs. Treating his now quivering wife as though she was a green recruit, for the first time in the past two years he spoke compassionately to her. "My dear child, who has filled your head with so many hobgoblins and such nonsense? You must go the course and be not afraid to do the good works of Holy Demeter. If it helps you, remember that I am not an Alkmeonid and it is my seed which carries all of the essence of your womb's offspring. You are only the container, borrowed to incubate the offshoot of my life-line. Clearly, your dream is only the result of too much reading about the horrors of Tartarus. If you must have a sign that bodes well for my husbanding, then I tell you that today I heard a voice from a long departed friend which promised that my off-spring, a son, I am sure, would rise to the heights of fame."

Dinomache saw that there was no point in further resistance. And so with no feeling and open but vacant eyes, she surrendered her hands to the work he proscribed. Still seated, but with his legs stretched out and his back now reclining partly on the couch and partly against the wall behind, Clinias waited upon the rising force of life that his maiden's hands, slippery with the alabastron's oil, called up. When all was ready, she crouched above him, like a woman on a birthing stool, and with her teeth biting into her shirt gathered up around her neck, she lowered herself onto him and prayed that her immortal soul would withdraw safe from the taint of that seed in which some impure soul may even now be cast into the punishing wheel of life.

CHAPTER TWELVE
ARES' WORK, LUST AND STRIFE
(447 B. C.)

Ares...Shed down a kindly ray from above my life, and strength of war, that I may be able to drive away bitter cowardice from my head and crush down the deceitful impulses of my soul.

(*Homeric Hymns – To Ares*)

It had been exactly three years and ten days since that day Clinias had attended the impromptu meeting convened by Pericles in the colonnade between the Bouleuterion and the Magistrates' Club House. He knew this because he remembered this meeting was the day after the holy days of Thesmophoria ended Today ten days after the women's Thesmophoria, as he had done for every year he could remember since he was a boy of twelve forty-four years ago, he was loading his gear into the cart for the short trip to his Apaturia ancestral reunion grounds just to the north of the city walls. Yes, Clinias thought, it is the first day of Apaturia and I should be happy on this day. But he felt today as he had for almost every day during the past three years. He could not block out even on the happiest of men's holidays the anger and pain which had rankled his wounded sense of honor ever since that day of Pericles' caucus. And what made it almost unbearable was that he could come to no clear plan or resolve as to how he might recover that which he felt was lost. It was as though he was a voyager tied to the mast of a forlorn ship mucking about in a thick fog without any bearings and devoid of any wind in her sails.

 The past three years had produced much that most men would regard as grounds for happiness and compensation for the blow to his reputation. His wife had borne him a son and now that she was pregnant again there might be a second son. His business enterprises had prospered making him even wealthier, and he had been honored by Pericles himself with a prestigious appointment to high office. Why then could he not be content and leave behind the sense of impairment which haunted him ever since that day in the courtyard of the Bouleuterion? After all, he thought, wouldn't this day - if any - be one for leaving behind that paralysis of wounded pride. The festival of Apaturia had always made him happy; for even as a child it bathed him in the assurance that his life was worthy and heroic. Zeus, father of all fathers, he had been taught as a child, only required during the three days of Apaturia a communion of drinking and feasting devoted to the remembrance of the heroic deeds of the clan's founding fathers. Would any one remember him in this way?

As for the birth of his first son, even that long hoped for event which seemed to him miraculous - and he was rarely given to seeing divine intervention in human affairs - did not lift the depression into which he had fallen. It was a complete surprise to both of them when she had become pregnant after their bitter intercourse on that day three years ago just after her return from the Thesmophoria encampment. They had not lain together but on that one occasion for the entire period stretching back to her miscarriage. Thus, it must have been destiny, he thought, that this bitter day had produced a healthy and uncommonly fine-featured male child. Given how determined Dinomache was to be miserable and apprehensive during all of her pregnancy, he had half-expected another miscarriage or, worse yet, the birth of a deformed creature. And yes, how proud he was for those few moments two years ago when he had introduced his three month old son to his brotherhood on the Day of Youths during Apaturia. If only that hopeful and proud feeling during the ceremonial blessing of Zeus Phratrios and Athena Phratria could have covered and closed his own wound for good, granting his own heart-felt prayer for new beginnings!

But the joy occasioned by the birth of his first son was mixed with rancor from the start and what should have been his undiluted joy of fatherhood quickly turned sour. Even before the boy had been officially presented to Clinias' own kin, there had been a bitter quarrel between Dinomache and himself concerning what to name their newborn son. She had insisted that the boy be called Meilichios, ranting and raving that only such a name could appease the Divine Power that would otherwise find a way to make her son bear the stain of the curse of the Alkmeonids. It was bad enough that his wife was half crazed with her superstitious fascination with the latest concoction to come from the mystery mongers. But what was insufferable, thought Clinias, is that she would have the temerity to try to foist this nonsense on him or his son. And even if there was something to this so-called curse, couldn't the woman see the illogic of believing that a son conceived by Clinias was an Alkmeonid. Or was there some egomania that infected even the Alkmeonid women so that they believed that children conceived in their womb by men from other clans somehow yet would be Alkmeonid? Fortunately, even Dinomache's own father, Megacles, would not take her side when she pleaded with him to intercede so as to persuade Clinias that the boy should be named 'Meilichios'. "After all," he reminded his tearful daughter, "it is just not done! Surely the gods would be offended if the boy is not named by the father in honor of his own forbearers." And so it was that over his wife's bitter and tearful objections that he formally registered and introduced to his Apaturia brotherhood his new son, 'Alcibiades' - so named after his own father.

If it had ended there it would have been something he could have put behind him. But as soon as the baby boy was brought back from the Apaturia ceremony, he was his mother's and Clinias had not once in the three years since he had held the boy before the brotherhood heard either his mother or his nurse call him by his right name. When his toddling son was brought down to the courtyard or when he would pay a visit to the woman's quarters to look in on his son, this offspring of Ajax's clan answered only to female voices cooing their soft, effeminate, and ridiculous babblings of blandishment for his attention – "Sweetums, come here!...Honeyboat, come to your loving sugar-tit mommy......Rosebudmouth, don't spit your food....Snugamuffins, let your sister cuddle you to sleep!". Even the boy's Spartan wet-nurse seemed to be in on denying the man-child his rightful cognomen. And who could have expected that a Spartan woman would be slow to wean the child. It infuriated Clinias that his three year old son was still scooped up whenever he cried - to be cradled inside the enervating soft mounds which made his son's eyes glaze over as he sucked away. Thank goodness that they only have him for six years! I must be sure, he thought, to find him a stern pedagogue if I am to undo the girlish nature of his sojourn in this far too soft mother-country.

Today, three years after his son's official registration with the glorious clan of Ajax, Clinias was sitting in the cart, staring blankly at the front of his own house and brooding over his son's inauspicious beginnings and his own disappointing failure to attain the generalship. Eyes open but seeing little, he waited for his servant Lycon to load on the last of the gear needed for his stay at his clan's Apaturia grounds. The wary and wily captain of years gone by was unstrung. He did not even notice the approach of the tall, powerfully built man who had come beside his cart and now hailed him.

"Clinias, hero of Artemisium, what are you brooding about today? You look so unhappy!"

It was Myronides. He was among Athens' most decorated soldiers and over the past eight years had been elected six times as general of his tribal regiment. Myronides was a second cousin to Clinias and just two years younger than him. Of late, Clinias found it difficult to be in his company - even though they had been close boyhood friends. His mere presence exacerbated Clinias' own growing bitterness over his failure to achieve Athens' highest office. It was as though the honor and responsibility the people of his tribe bestowed on his cousin by choosing him repeatedly as their general was also each year a verdict declaring him unsuitable for this office.

"Myronides, you must pardon my lack of courtesy. It is not like me to ignore the approach of my General. But you know how it is with us men of business - there is always some worry to occupy those of us who scurry about trying to increase our profits. Let me get down off this wagon and give you a proper salute." Clinias' tone of voice was cold.

Myronides held up his hand and with genuine affection for his boyhood companion, tried to deflect Clinias' bitter and self-deprecating homage. "Clinias, at ease, Captain! We are not on campaign are we? This is not Sparta!"

Clinias couldn't help himself. The affable and apparently open smile of Myronides, a man still unquestionably clothed in honor, is duplicitous, he thought. Since Myronides, or for that matter anyone else, had never even nominated him for the generalship; more than likely all of them regarded him as morally unfit for such an office. In their eyes, thought Clinias, I am a money-grubbing sham whose manly courage on the field of battle consists of paying others to stand in the killing zone.

"Myronides, you and I know that my service at Artemisium counts for nothing. It is only the hoplite officer who closes with the enemy in the front rank who proves his valor and deservedly is honored by his fellow citizens. But let us not talk about that. I would offer you a ride on my cart, if you are going to our tribe's Apaturia grounds, but there will not be room up here after I have loaded on all of my supplies. You know that a man like me, unaccustomed now to the simple life of the soldier, can't go camping without bringing along much furniture and other comforts."

The sun had now appeared from behind Clinias' house and was shining directly in Myronides eyes as he surveyed Clinias and all the gear loaded on his wagon. Squinting through the bright sun light, Myronides knew that his company was not welcome. "I am not going to the grounds just now. I am on my way to the Bouleuterion. The Council has been in session all morning and my presence is now required if they are to complete this day's deliberations. And so there is no need for you to feel so put out. Really, Clinias, I don't understand what it is that has put the burr in your ass. Ever since our military campaigns to the West have opened up the ceramics trade with Greater Greece on the Italian peninsula and Sicily, you and your partner have become among the wealthiest of all Athenian merchants. Do you suffer from some kind of too much money malaise?

Or, are you still brooding about Pericles' handling of that report from the run away Lycian slave? That must be over three years ago. Hasn't Pericles made it up to you? I would think you would be quite pleased after he arranged for your appointment as Treasurer to the Delian League. That must have greased the wheels of commerce for you and Megacles! Despite what you might think, Clinias, I am really quite happy for you and only wished that I had the good sense you have shown in capitalizing on Athens' military acquisition of empire." Myronides spoke forcibly, yet without any bitterness on his part.

"You are right, of course, Myronides. I should be grateful for my lot and for men like you who have borne the brunt of the dirty work of extending our frontiers and making our world safe for Athenian liberty and commerce. But......"

"Myronides, Myronides, There you are!" Clinias was interrupted in mid-sentence by the shouts of a young man who was running towards them as they stood on the side of the street. It was Callimarchus, the young man Myronides was rumored to be in love with. Myronides had chosen him to serve as his official assistant in discharging the various responsibilities he exercised as a member of the Board of Generals. Today, Callimarchus had been charged with monitoring the morning proceedings of the Council.

"What is it, Callimarchus?" Myronides was half expecting some kind of message from the Council and so was not that surprised to see the young runner coming his way. The young man was completely out of breath and was leaning now against the side of Clinias' wagon, trying to compose himself.

"May I speak freely, sir?" The young man was not sure whether or not everything he had to say should be communicated in the presence of others.

"Callimarchus, Go on! We have nothing to hide from such a patriot as Clinias. In fact, I believe it is very important that Clinias hear everything since the matters under deliberation will certainly directly concern his affairs."

Clinias had already begun to climb down from his wagon so as to go back inside his home and gather together some of the food supplies Lycon had not yet brought out. But Myronides had made it clear that his presence was wanted. So when he had dismounted from the wagon, instead of reentering his house he stood by the side of his wagon and began idly to rearrange the gear which was piled right up to the top of the wagon's sides.

The young man glanced at Clinias and then fixed his eyes on Myronides as he began to speak. "It is just as you anticipated, General. The ambassadors from Boetia representing the democratic leaders have only further enflamed the passions of our Councilors. But the truth is that at this moment the democratic leaders no longer govern. Our own man in Chaeronea has confirmed that the local oligarchs, with help from the Medizers of Thebes, have forcibly regained control of these two Boeotian towns."

Myronides frowned, "Does nothing remain firm? To think of the lives lost, the stupendous risks undertaken, and then the apparent total victory I thought our army had achieved at Oinophyta just 10 years ago when we chased all the oligarchic faction from these Boeotian cities - I cannot believe it was all for naught. How can those Boeotians not prefer rule by the many, rather than the few? How could they let a few pampered rich landlords take their city from them? And why can't those folks up there, leave our merchants alone when they go overland to the Corinthian gulf? If they could only respect our right of way to the ports there, I and most other Athenians, wouldn't give a damn if those cow-faced Boeotian peasants want to choose to become fodder for their own "high and mighty" who want to play king.

You see Clinias, everything I do counts for naught also. I was acclaimed as a great general when I with old men and youths liberated the common folk of these cities and made them right for democracy and Athens. But now in less than a decade, it's all undone."

This did not make Clinias feel any better, but he nodded his head, as if to ratify the General's assessment of the impermanence of all human accomplishments.

"What else, Callimarchus?"

"Sir, the oligarchs have sent ambassadors also, registering grievous complaints against the local democratic leaders. Of course, the Council does not acknowledge the oligarch's ambassadors right to represent the people they wish to tyrannize, but they did allow them to speak. These spokesmen for the oligarchs have lodged a very serious and scandalous charge against Chrysippus, our own official resident advisor to the Democratic leaders in Chaeronea."

"Callimarchus, it is a good thing you are so handsome. Otherwise I would be looking for an aid practiced in getting to the point. Did the Council draft a resolution favoring military action against the Boeotian oligarchs?"

"No Sir, not yet; even though after both the democrats and oligarchs spoke to the Council, there was a considerable number of Councilors who urged that Athens must send an army to once again liberate these cities from the despotism of the few rich families who have unlawfully seized power. General Pericles, however, urged that Athens should seek further diplomatic means to restore democratic government in these cities. He argued that Athens would be ill-advised to commit a hoplite force at this time so deep in hostile territory, a good three days march from Athens. After hearing Pericles speak, almost half of the Councilors were persuaded by him. Given the division within the Council though, the Council decided that the Assembly should be convened so that the citizens themselves might decide what is to be done. So, the Assembly will be convened by mid-afternoon, charged with the task of deciding between one of the two courses of actions debated by the Council."

General Myronides knew what would come next. The Assembly would want the Board of Generals, not just General Pericles, to weigh in on the best course of action. Certainly then he especially would be the one, given his past experience in Boeotia, called upon to give advice and to calculate the prospects for a successful military intervention.

"Tell me Callimarchus what exactly was the complaint brought against our official in Chaeronea? I need to know whether our man has in fact antagonized many of our Boeotian democrats, as well as inciting the expected enmity of the oligarchs. Are the Boeotians willing to suffer the return of the oligarchs, putting up little resistance, because our man has been overweening in his comportment and has fanned the flames of anti-Athenian feelings? I need to know all the specifics if I am to know how to advise the Assembly on this matter."

"I understand, Sir. It is a scandalous story and I doubt it is true. But our enemies claim that Chrysippus and his cronies had to be removed from office. They say that Chrysippus behaved precisely in the same way one of our last tyrants behaved - Hipparchus; and didn't we see that he was punished and eventually chase his family and associates from Athens!" Here the young man paused, not sure that he should go on

"Ah, you see, Clinias, it must be about lust again. How tedious, it's always the same story. I guess I am not surprised. Our friend Chrysippus has always been known as a man of strong passions and a special weakness for the charms of youthful beauty. I would guess that our man in Chaeronea has played Zeus to some Boeotian Ganymede and the natives don't appreciate an Athenian impersonating such lusty god-like behavior. So what do they say Chrysippus did?"

As soon as Clinias heard Chrysippus' name mentioned, Clinias, as Myronides had anticipated, looked up from the gear he was fiddling with and listened intently. Chrysippus over the past decade had served as an agent for his own commercial interests in the Boeotian cities which were located just to the northeast of the Northern shore of the Corinthian Gulf. It would be a serious hit to his own ceramics enterprises, if Chrysippus had somehow bollixed it all. And so Clinias now moved away from the wagon so he could squarely face the young man and not miss a word of his report. For the moment, anyways, his melancholy receded as he realized that this young man's report might alert him to a threat to that one remaining testament to impressive accomplishment - his wide-reaching and prosperous commercial enterprise.

Jarred from his own myopic melancholy, as Clinias now actually looked with interest at Callimarchus, he could not help but notice that the young man was extremely uneasy and his face had become very flushed. Had this young man himself had a brush with Chrysippus, or was it that he was afraid his talk of love affairs might somehow embarrassingly reveal his own uncertain feelings about older men's advances? Clinias didn't really care about any of that, but he wondered how reliable Callimarchus' report would be if it was delivered by a messenger in such a state of agitation.

Myronides was not going to worry about such sensitivities in his junior aid. "Oh, come on Callimarchus! Clinias is not a school boy, and heaven knows, you are no stranger to the ways of lecherous older men!" Myronides had a twinkle in his eye as he smiled at both Clinias and his young aid. "So get on with the story. You won't be trampling anyone's innocence under foot in this crowd."

Callimarchus returned Myronides smile with a shy and modest shrug of his shoulders. Looking down at his own feet, not daring to meet the eyes of either of the older men, he related what he had heard.

"The Chaeronean spokesman for the oligarchs told the following story. Chrysippus had become the wealthiest man in their city by persuading the Democratic leaders that they ought to pass a law forbidding trade in any ceramics except those which originated either in Athens or had been transported to their city by Athenian merchants. The law also prescribed that Chrysippus himself was to be granted the only authorized wholesale concession for dealing in these ceramics. This commercial monopoly guaranteed by the support of Athenian officials had enabled Chrysippus to amass such considerable wealth that he could assume the role of a very generous benefactor to any of Chaeronea's young men who appeared to have promise. So if Chrysippus favored a local young man, he would arrange for him to be sent to Athens for schooling with the best of tutors. When the youth returned, provided he vowed to defend the democracy, Chrysippus would give the youth a panoply of the best armor. Wishing to solidify his own hold on the city, he would then sign over to the youth's family additional lands from his own vast holdings - land which he personally had come into possession of as a result of the exile of landholders opposed to the democracy. Well, according to the oligarch's story, although no one could prove it at first, Chrysippus had in this way made whores out of almost every available attractive young man in Chaeronea. There were occasions when Chrysippus' love affairs led to complaints being officially filed with the local democratic leaders. But since everybody involved was in fact much the wealthier for the experience; citizens chalked up their son's trysts with the Athenian as youthful misadventures and winked at their benefactor's voracious appetite as an eccentricity."

"So what happened, Callimarchus, to change the people's tolerance of Chrsippus' behavior?"

"General, this all changed when Chrysippus took a fancy to a certain young man called Kallistus. Kallistus steadfastly rejected Chrysippus' every advance and would not accept any gifts from him. This Kallistus had been left behind by his exiled father to be superintended by the father's cousin, a man who was on good terms with the new Democratic leaders. It seems that one day Chrysippus persuaded Kallistus' guardian to allow the young man to accompany Chrysippus and a few other young men to a chariot-race Chrysippus was sponsoring. The race, Chrysippus said, was to take place around a field on his estate. Well, according to Chrysippus' accusers, Chrysippus escorted the young men through a wooded path on his estate to the edge of a large meadow. He then instructed all of the company, except Kallistus, to go fetch some ropes, bridles, and marker stones which he said would be found just on the other side of the meadow.

While the other men were gone, Chrysippus importuned young Kallistus, pleading with him that he could not sleep, eat, or even enjoy wine until Kallistus would agree to be his beloved. Kallistus, harboring a strong dislike for Chrysippus, was absolutely cold and indifferent to all of Chrysippus' desperate professions of longing. Indeed, he responded to Chrysippus' proposal by making it plain that nothing in this entire world could induce him to suffer any intimacy with such a one as Chrysippus. Well then at this juncture, and this I find hard to believe, supposedly Chrysippus gave a signal and the other young men appeared with ropes, marker stones and other gear - but not for a chariot race. Chrysippus, eyes glazed over and half crazed with lust, his accusers say, ordered the others to strip Kallistus, rope his hands and feet together in such a way so that he would be forced to crawl on all fours, and then tie a bridle strap around his neck as though he were to be a beast of burden to be ridden. What happened next seems ludicrous, but they say Chrysippus, uttering profanities and addressing the terrified young man as his Boeotian heifer, mounted him. The young man's knees and hands were bleeding from his frantic effort to break away as he bucked and reared up like a wild stallion trying to throw an unwanted rider. With the other young men laughing, Chrysippus pulled on the make-shift reins that went around his mount's neck and with his face flushed with passion called upon Almighty Zeus to assist in his conquest of this unruly beast. This supposedly continued for some time, until Chrysippus had sated himself. As a final indignity, Chrysippus then forced the young man, who by this time was sobbing uncontrollably, to roll over on his back. Chrysippus then, one at a time, took off his own sandals which were fouled with horse manure and slapped their soles on the youth's belly and genitals until the youth's flesh, red and inflamed, showed through the mottled dark manure that now soiled his still hairless phallus and belly. The youth, utterly spent by his struggle and still hog-tied, could do nothing but shudder under this final humiliation. When Chrysippus had returned to his senses, he instructed the other young men to untie Kallistus and escort him to a nearby brook where he could wash. As they untied him, Chrysippus, they say, in a kindly voice reminded the youth he had just raped that if he ever made any accusation against him, then he would see that the youth was severely punished. Kallistus' guardian would have what land still belonged to his family taken from them, and the other youths would testify that it was Kallistus who was a whore and had tried to compromise Chrysippus by blackmailing him after he Kallistus had offered himself for Chrysippus' pleasure and was refused."

Callimarchus paused and was, in fact, himself disconcerted by the horror of the story he himself had just related to the older men. Both Clinias and Myronides appeared to be nonplussed by the story.

"I suppose what happened next is that the young man did in fact, despite his terrible humiliation, relate the entire incident to his guardian and anyone else who would listen. And that it was only a short time before there were many outraged citizens demanding that the officials investigate and bring Chrysippus to trial. When the archons, personal friends of our man in Chaeronea refused, the outraged citizens conspired and fetching formerly exiled citizens armed themselves and forcibly ousted these officials." Myronides sighed. "I know the script all too well."

Callimarchus nodded. "Yes, it happened quickly, and Chrysippus was fortunate to have escaped with his life. He of course in his report to our own officials categorically denies the story. He does assert that the young man, Kallistus, had a reputation as a loose and profligate spoiled brat. This Kallistus, he says, the second eldest son of one of the richest landowners who had been exiled by the democrats, had in fact been left behind by his father to foment discontent with the new government. When further questioned about the fact that the boy would have been only seven or so when left behind and how could his father depend on him to so oppose the policies and practices of the only government he would really ever have experienced; Chrysippus presented evidence to the effect that letters had been intercepted between the exiled father and his son which urged the boy to work for the return of the "good and the beautiful" men who would vouchsafe Chaeronea's independence from the long reach of Athenian imperialism.

The Boeotian oligarchs concluded their complaint against Chrysippus by vowing to seek both Theban and Spartan assistance if Athens should decide to intervene once again in the internal affairs of either Chaeronea or Orchomenus. And it is because this whole episode, whatever happened, could precipitate renewed hostilities with Sparta on land that Pericles has urged the Council to go carefully and defer at this time any Athenian expedition to the North." Callimarchus paused. "Is there anything else, Sir, you need to know?"

"Thank you, Callimarchus. You have been very thorough."

Myronides turned to Clinias. "Do you think our enemies' story is true?"

"Part of it, anyways, but what difference does it make? Even a corrupt democratic regime is better than any Boeotian oligarchy. As for myself, I would welcome the chance to fight on behalf of those who have stood shoulder to shoulder with us in our enmity to Medizing lovers of kings and rule by the few. I am sick and tired of all the conspiratorial crap. Let's have it out on the battle-field! There are many of us Athenians, I believe, who are willing to die defending the liberty of the many, especially when its suppression elsewhere may threaten, like a spreading contagion, the survival of our own liberty-loving city and its vital life-lines of commerce."

Clinias eyes flashed as he spoke and he himself was aware that he had not spoken with such fire in his voice for a long time. Something, it seems, had crystallized in his mind as he listened to young Callimarchus. He felt himself drawn, like a moth to light, to that zone where all of one's confused and unfocused bitterness, all the ambiguous resentment of others and their success, could be ventilated and discharged in hatred of an enemy. How wonderful, he thought, it would be to march out armed with spear and sword and to engage in mortal combat, demonstrating once again his manhood and his right to the same kind of honor which men such as Myronides and Pericles had earned through their military valor.

Myronides understood. He smiled at Clinias and with genuine solicitude in his voice, invited him to accompany him now to the Pynx where the Assembly would be convened within the hour. "Clinias, listening to you, I would think you were a young man of twenty eight who, not content with victories in the Palestra, yearns to turn his prowess to the glorious service of his city. I have no doubt you would insist on taking up a position in the front ranks with our best warriors, each one of them men of good repute. No pushing from the rear for you and Zeus help the officer - who out of concern for your advancing years - would put you in the middle ranks. But now, we need your good head and experience at the Pynx. Come with me now and let us see what our citizens will decide. Our Apaturia fellows, I am sure, will all be postponing their celebration."

The Assembly's deliberations lasted throughout most of the afternoon. It was almost dark by the time Clinias found his way to this tribe's muster station in the Agora. He had hurried down from the Pynx into the Marketplace, feeling exhilarated at the prospect of silencing once and for all those unfair slanderous whispers about his courage and his patriotism. Like every Athenian man, Clinias lived in two orders: partly in the stories of super-human military heroism, and partly in the mundane everyday order of making drachmas and managing his domestic economy. For the past three years he had been exiled from the first order and had been reduced to an every-man laboring anonymously for the mere right to survive and serve the glorious ones. Today, brash General Tolmides call to glory somehow had once again made him believe he could leap the chasm and rejoin the order of the immortals. He felt this evening just as he had over thirty years ago - was it really that long ago, he thought -when he took up the commission as a trireme captain to do battle with the Persian fleet at Artemisium.

After the Assembly had been informed of the oligarchic take-over of Chaeronea and Orchomenus, listened to Chrysippus' story of how a devious son of a rich oligarch had with a manufactured tale incited undeserved hostility towards him, and were presented with the mangled corpse of Chrysippus' young Athenian body-guard who had been killed and unceremoniously tossed over the courtyard wall at Chrysippus' town-house in Chaeronea; the Assembly had dissolved into an angry mob demanding vengeance. Only the repeated appeals of both Pericles and Myronides had brought the Assembly back to some semblance of order. Both of these men, when finally they could be heard, urged that a more circumspect response be adopted. Pericles pointed out that Athens was now stretched somewhat thin with its available manpower, since the founding of the various settlements under direct Athenian rule in Euboea, the island of Naxos, and in the Chalcidice had required the presence of military garrisons. Also, he noted, with the impending end of the official five years truce with the Lacedaemonians just a few months away, wouldn't it be better to do nothing to drive the Spartans into bed with Thebes and the other Boeotian oligarchs? After Myronides seconded Pericles' advice, there seemed to be an even division between those who favored an immediate large military punitive expedition against the oligarchs in Boetia, and those who counseled waiting for a more opportune time to deal with this renewed threat to Athens' northern interests on the mainland.

It was the newest darling of Athens' commons who had ended the impasse in the Assembly. Tolmides, one of the youngest men ever to attain the post of General, strode to the raised rock that served as a kind of natural podium for the outdoor Assembly meeting ground and, with the brash confidence and patriotism of unconquerable youth, proposed that with merely a thousand volunteers from among Athens' ablest hoplites he could teach the Boeotian oligarchs a lesson they would never forget. There was no need, Tolmides said, for the Athenian Assembly to issue a general muster since just a well-commanded small force of crack Athenian hoplites would have no difficulty in defeating even a much larger infantry force comprised of Boeotian bumpkins. At first, Tolmides' proposal met with little enthusiasm from those Assemblymen present who could actually serve as hoplites, men with enough means to own the full panoply of equipment required for the armored infantryman. But when Tolmides had ended his call for volunteers with a vivid account of the beating and mutilation the Chaeronean oligarchs had inflicted on Chrysippus' young Athenian attendant - a young thete, who it turns out, happened to be Tolmides own half brother - there was such a wild outcry from the sizable number of thetes who were in attendance, that not even the richest or most prestigious men of the Athenian leading families could resist the call to defend the cause of the rule of the many against oligarchs. And so when Tolmides posted his summons for volunteers on Clinias' tribe's Ajax obelisk in the Marketplace that very afternoon as soon as the Assembly session ended, Clinias was among the first to inscribe his name on the parchment notice. It was here, as he turned towards his own home so as to set his affairs in order before marching off with Tolmides that he saw young Socrates, the son of his Artemisium shipmate and now deceased comrade Sophroniscus. In the twilight, the young man almost looked like his father had thirty-three years ago on the eve prior to that day Sophroniscus had sailed away on the Gyes with Clinias to war with the Persian fleet. Although the young man was some fifteen yards away, waiting his turn with a few others of his clan to enlist in Tolmides' campaign, Clinias had an unobstructed view of him.

Socrates, noted Clinias, was not quite as tall as his father. Indeed, the young man was at least the length of a spear head shorter than himself. But with his broad chest and massively big thighs and lower legs, Socrates gave the overall impression of a man who would make a formidable pankratiast. Indeed with his wide flaring nostrils and bulging eyes, he had the look of someone whose face had already been rearranged by blows, and in a way that certainly would not make him a favorite among those searching for beauty. But his strong compact body, and especially those thickly muscled legs, would serve him well in the push and shoving of the hoplite ranks in close quarters with the enemy line. Clinias the soldier noted, as young Socrates approached, that it would not be easy to have those legs pushing a shield into your back. If the enemy didn't spear you, stout Socrates might push the edge of his shield clean through your shoulder blades.

"Captain Clinias, what brings you to the Agora so late in the day? Are you also enlisting in Tolmides expedition against the Boeotian Medizers? I did not think such a campaign would even permit men above the 30th year to sign on. My tribe's officers have asked for volunteers only from among the ranks of those in their seventh year of call up or younger."

Clinias waited until Socrates was beside him and then warmly embraced him. "Would this not be your first campaign, Socrates? And did I not promise your father that I would look after you? Although, I see by the looks of your physique that it is you who must look after me. Yes, I have signed on and hope that Tolmides will give me a company of men to command or, at least, allow me to take my place near the first rank."

Socrates looked intently into the eyes of this man who he now regarded as his surrogate father and with a concern of one well beyond his twenty-two years, he ever so gently and respectfully proposed that Clinias reconsider. "Clinias, you know that I still spend some time with my mother out on the farm and there I see plainly lessons we should all take to heart. You know that the young bulls must fight and risk themselves to earn the right to father new calves. The bulls which lose in the annual duels for supremacy either are butchered for meat or dedicated to a holocaust. This way the young bulls which survive are clearly the strongest and it is they who live to procreate and assure that the herd they father will be as strong as possible."

Clinias interrupted. "Socrates, you remind me of your father. Now what possibly could this talk of bulls and breeding have to do with me and you enlisting to liberate our Boeotian bumpkins from oligarchic tyranny? What are you getting at, Socrates?"

Socrates shrugged his shoulders and looked down at his own feet. "Well, Clinias, it occurs to me that the gods have decreed that it is young men who must prove themselves in war, and that it is contrary to God's will that those who have been tested many times before and have already demonstrated their worthiness to sire strong human stock for their city, should after all this march out to run a course God has set aside for studs whose loins have not yet been certified for Nature's holy work. No, I believe it is God's will that the bulls who have had their season of bellowing and locking horns and have lived to sire, should now keep to siring and the care of their herd. I know I would not allow my bull, proven already in many a contest, to risk injury against young unproven animals."

Clinias laughed. "But Socrates, I am not a bull and Athens is not a herd of cattle. If I am ever to be worthy of my fellow citizens highest respect and be honored as an elected general, I must show again and again my valor and prowess as a warrior. You do understand that there is no other path for a man in Athens to prove his worth and earn the lasting respect of his comrades and the citizens of Athens."

"But Clinias, as far as anyone whose opinion is truly worth anything, you have already more than earned such respect and honor. Why would you want to go out on a field and throw your body, now made less strong by Nature's course, against twenty-something year old studs driven by a life-force still on the blind upsurge of brute strength and a devil-may-care recklessness of youth, a wild mix of elemental forces straining to procreate even as they are bent on death and destruction?"

"Socrates, Socrates, too much reading will unstring even that massive body of yours. Why, I would have thought you took your place in the mustering line before your tribe's hero pillar because the fire of patriotism burned brightly in your chest. Do you really think of your young manhood in terms of 'studmanship'? I would think that you, maybe so more than most men of your age, would want to fight to assure the survival of Athens' distinctive constitution, our way of governing ourselves through laws and institutions which we ourselves in freedom fashion. This kind of freedom must not be defended only here but wherever free men have chosen to govern themselves through their own assemblies." Clinias was beaming with a broad smile as he called his young charge to his patriotic duty and the defense of liberty. It was a smile of unadulterated joy, as for the first time in many years he felt himself once again in touch with that divine order of the higher calling.

Socrates nodded his head and gave up any attempt to change his surrogate father's course. "You are right, of course, Sir. Although I do not really see clearly what I am doing, I know that my city has been like a father to me and now I must out of love for that father be willing to serve him to the utmost, even if it means giving up my life. I do love Athens. But it is not clear to me how the quarrels among Boeotian townsmen are a threat to our freedom. Maybe if I knew as much as Tolmides, I too would clearly see that should we not answer the threat to freedom in our neighbor's cities, soon we shall be encircled by the enemies of our way of live, and our city will then be in the desperate plight of fighting too numerous and near forces of tyranny."

"For one who is ignorant of such matters, you put it quite well, Socrates! Now enough with the bull-shit! I will see you tomorrow at the northwestern parade grounds with the rest of our thousand and Tolmides. Your father would be proud of you, Socrates."

CHAPTER THIRTEEN
ARES' WORK, THE KILLING ZONE
(447 B. C.)

You are mistaken, my friend, if you think that a man who is worth anything ought to spend his time weighing up the prospects of life and death. He has only one thing to consider in performing any action – that is, whether he is acting rightly or wrongly, like a good man or a bad one.... Where a man has once taken up his stand, either because it seems best to him or in obedience to his orders, there I believe he is bound to remain and face the danger, taking no account of death or anything else before dishonor.

(Plato. *Apology*, 28.b-e, Socrates defending his honor at his Trial)

Yes, Death Demons war-grim and fierce,
glutlusty and dripping, crimson with blood,
fought over the fallen corpses,
driven by thirst for dark blood.
And they would dig their great claws
Into the flesh of the first warrior
they snatched,
either as he lay dead,
or as he collapsed, wounded
by a freshly dealt blow;
and the souls of such men
would plummet into the chill of Tartaros.

(Hesiod. *Shield*, lines 249-255)

A thousand volunteers had answered General Tolmides' patriotic call to duty and early the next morning assembled in the city's military parade grounds, prepared to fight for Athens' democratic allies in Boeotia. After the sunrise sacrifice had been offered and the innards of the slain bull had been read favorably, General Tolmides ordered the tribal company captains to form up their men for the march. When all was ready, the hoplite warriors and their supply train of carts, the trumpet sounded and the army moved out of Athens' parade grounds onto the Panathenaic Way towards the Kerameikos Gate and the road leading northwest to the Boeotian frontier. The hoplites, many on their first campaign, sang a *paean* as if they were about to charge the far away enemy forces of Boeotian tyrants this very moment. Friends and families lined the Panathenaic Way and cheered their warriors like Olympic heroes More than a thousand slaves, some riding on the supply carts and others walking along side them, followed their masters quietly and without fanfare - minding their station as their lords marched out to defend the cause of Athenian liberty.

By the middle of the afternoon of the first day's march, the expedition had come to the northwestern border of Attica. Here, before crossing over into Boeotia, once again the gods' blessing must be sought. Again animals were slain, and before eaten as part of the mid-day meal, their innards were again consecrated and divined. All signs were favorable, according to the young General's seer. After a rousing speech in which Tolmides reminded his hoplite army of the Boeotian oligarchs' cowardly defection to the Persian invaders who had burned the Athens of their fathers' generation to the ground, the troops resumed their march to the north. After a contingent of men from Plataea joined their force, even the older men whose enthusiasm was much more muted than their young comrades gave themselves over to the brash confidence of their young General Tolmides. During the remainder of the afternoon General Tolmides pushed deep into Boeotian territory towards Thebes on a path following a long line of hills which afforded the protection of high ground for his forces should the enemy attempt to halt his march.

The second day of the march, like the first day, met with no resistance. Once Thebes was bypassed and to the south, Tolmides turned northwest and followed the shoreline of Lake Copais towards Chaeronea. Without ever having to form up for battle, the Athenian hoplites made it all the way to Chaeronea. The older soldiers, like Clinias, had become apprehensive as the approach to Chaeronea through a long stretch of enemy territory had been far too easy. Why, they wondered, would General Tolmides position the force so close to the lake, thus making it easier for an enemy force of large numbers to pin the Athenians against such a large inland body of water where not even the Athenian navy could rescue them? But when General Tolmides led the Athenians through the weakly defended gates of Chaeronea's fortified outer wall and routed the few hundred armed defenders, it did seem as if the Athenians were once again the irresistible champions of democracy, favored by the gods and the unwillingness of the commoners of other cities to fight against their Athenian liberators. So sure was Tolmides of this invincibility that after he had made arrangements to sell into slavery the surviving oligarchic defenders of the city; he further reduced his own army's numbers by leaving a garrison of 100 men to remain in Chaeronea as he marched on further north towards Orchomenus.

Matters did not go quite so well at Orchomenus. While the number of defenders inside the city was again rather small, Tolmides found that he could not storm the city. The city was located on a steep hillside with its walled citadel on the ridge. For two weeks, the Athenians taunted and challenged the defenders to do battle at the foot of the hill, but the Boeotians, well supplied with provisions and water, refused to be drawn out from their secure position. Finally, with winter fast approaching and his own provisions running short, Tolmides, frustrated and angry, ordered his men to burn all the fields and farmhouses in the surrounding territory. He then decamped and with considerable boldness decided that his force could simply make its way back to Attica as though on a triumphant parade.

It was after Tolmides indiscriminately burnt both the large and small farms and fields around Orchomenus that the first signs of a loss of morale and fighting spirit appeared among the force of volunteers. Indeed, even among the youngest and up to then the most enthusiastic men who came from Tolmides' own *deme*, there was some grumbling about the rectitude of an army that was fighting on behalf of the common people now itself destroying the small farmsteads and cottages of people who well might have opposed the oligarchy.

Among the veterans there was a growing sense that brash Tolmides was leading them to disaster. Their apprehension turned to fear when Tolmides would not heed the advice of those who counseled keeping to high ground and narrow confines so as to avert any attack in the open by a large enemy force of hoplites. Such a force could by sheer length of their lines outflank them and cut them to pieces.

The march back to Athens, it seemed to Clinias, was not quite as glorious as Tolmides would have it. While Clinias had proven his metal in the storming of Chaeronea, he was now bone weary and apprehensive. Yes, he, though one of the oldest men who had volunteered, had already been decorated by Tolmides for his valorous charge at the very forefront through the gates of the enemy city. Surely this demonstration of his courage on behalf of Athens' defense of freedom would once and for all clear his name and put to rest the scandalous accusation that he was a coward who had conspired against Athens' own duly elected democratic leaders. But the last two days of marching south back over hilly terrain while listening to his comrades' doubts about their own general's regard for the commoners of Orchomenus led him to question whether his part in this campaign would dispel all the old rumors about his alleged role in the assassination of Ephialtes. Now, Tolmides sudden decision to abandon all caution and make for Attica in a straight line across through the Boeotian costal plain just 20 miles west of Thebes, a long stretch where there would be no defensible ground for his relatively small force, made Clinias fearful that he might perish without ever clearing his name. Surely, Clinias thought as he looked behind him at the cloud of dust raised by the expedition's baggage train, every Boeotian oligarch - and especially those of powerful Thebes - knows exactly where we are. Ought we not to proceed with more caution, he whispered under his breath to no one in particular.

The morning sun had now climbed higher in the sky as the Athenian's made their way down from the hills into the valley near Coronea. While it was just a few weeks before winter weather would set in, the rays of the autumn sun seemed unusually warm as a dry south wind blew the chaff of now mostly brown and stubby field grasses about in swirls. Word had been passed along the line of men who had been marching in triple file to halt so that their servants could arrange to move the wagons, which carried each of the company's armor and weapons, to a position in the procession more ready at hand should the need arise.

The redeployment of carts and men to a more prepared state reassured Clinias somewhat. Tolmides, he thought, has not thrown all caution to the wind. But why go this dangerous route at all?

The changed deployment of the ranks had brought the company of men from the deme of Alopeke up next to Clinias' company. Most of the men in this company were very young and still gave the appearance of *epheboi* in training. Clinias was scanning the faces of the Alopeke Company when a young man who had wrapped his cloak around most of his face stepped out from his cohorts towards Clinias.

"Captain Clinias, Excuse me.....Ha-choo! Ha-choo! This damn blowing chaff! What a headache it gives me! I would wager there is no hay fever to plague a sailor. I don't know what I am going to do if I'm sneezing my fool head off under that Corinthian torture box we call a helmet during a battle." It was young Socrates and as usual there was something both comical and impressive about his demeanor. "Captain, veteran that you are, would you have with you something to stop my sneezing?"

"Socrates, when you put the helmet on, you'll sweat rivers and the eye and mouth slits will gum up and before you know it, no more sneezing. Then you'll just have to worry about seeing the killing end of a spear aimed at your face and shoulders - a much more pleasant prospect than that damnable sneezing, right?" Clinias smiled as he reached out to clasp the young man's shoulder in friendship. It always pleased Clinias to see the son of Sophroniscus.

"Captain Clinias, my company captain has put me in the very last rank, so I have not yet had to worry about close encounters with Scythian iron. I suppose I am not yet judged worthy of the front ranks, and so I am a pusher who needs only to find the back of my comrade in front of me. And our company is deployed on the left wing, so I only have to lean to the right to keep in line. Indeed, when I think of the part I must play, I don't really have to see much at all as long as I can hunker down inside my shield and keep my legs pushing forward."

Clinias took his hand from Socrates shoulder and looked down into the young man's eyes. The top of Socrates head only came to Clinias' chin. Though there was nothing in Clinias' manner that suggested an air of superiority or condescension, anyone else looking on at the two would have thought that the young squat barrel-chested man who seemed to look out of the side of his overly big eyes from behind a well-worn cloak was a body servant taking instructions from his master. But Clinias knew that the thick-lipped broad-nosed youth already was, like his father, a man who better than most possessed the mettle of a good citizen-soldier. And so he spoke to him as if he were his well-pleased father.

"Socrates, surely you know that all our generals, and young Tolmides is no exception, always direct their officers to deploy the very best men in both the front and at the most back ranks. This way, the ablest and most courageous men will both meet the enemy first and as the battle wears on keep the entire army in fighting order by always pushing the ranks forward. The men in the middle ranks will be both pulled and pushed into the battle by the force of those honorable and brave men before them and at their backs. So you see, your company commander has paid you a high honor and recognizes in your character and strength a man well-suited for the responsibility of providing the steady and relentless force of the phalanx's forward charge. Already in your very first campaign you are assigned a station among the beautiful and good."

Socrates shrugged his shoulders and tilted his head sideward, so as to avoid the south wind that was pushing chaff into his red-rimmed itching eyes. "Sir, it is always encouraging to see things more clearly through a set of eyes wiser and more experienced than my own. I thought perhaps it was mainly because I was untested and rather short of stature that my captain put me in the back. Here, there would be no occasion for my overhand spear thrust to be spent ineffectually bouncing off fully shielded enemy bodies. I sometimes think too much as we trudge along and rather than clearing my vision, it only further blurs what should be simple and well-focused."

Clinias nodded his head, "Yes, Socrates, a good hoplite doesn't need to think very much. Once, the battle trumpet sounds, everything depends upon each man fixing his sight so as to concentrate all of his attention on the few yards that lie directly in front of him."

"Yes, you are right, of course. Our drill sergeant at the Piraeus always reminded us that the hoplite warrior's helmet visor is designed to protect its wearer in two ways - both just as important. First and most obvious, since the slits for the eyes are so narrow, neither a missile like an arrow or stone nor a spear thrust can find their way into the eyes. Thus our eyes, most precious for directing our steps and hand-held shields and spears, are practically invulnerable. Second, and this I find both most instructive and perplexing at the same time, the sergeant never tired of reminding every *ephebe* that the good hoplite's eyes need never to see anything behind, or off to the sides, but only directly in front and just a few yards in front, at that! Just let the helmet lead you, he would say. When its sides pinch your neck, you're out of line! The last thing the phalanx needs is a soldier with a broad view of the battle-field! I try to remember that whenever my thinking meanders too far afield, wondering why or how it comes about that we are trudging along far from Alopeke,

Athens, and Attica, so as to send other Hellenes on their way to Hades."

"Socrates, although it's more than thirty years ago, I can still remember the same training. My drill sergeant, we called him old helmet head, had a dramatic flair for teaching us the virtues of the helmet. During a charge exercise, when any of us would swivel our heads or turn about to look for the cause of a loud noise he had arranged to be sounded, he would stop everything, pull the offender out of line and with his face two inches from the trembling trainee shout, 'You idiot, do you want to get your cousin, or maybe your brother, killed. The spear point which kills can only come from the front when you stay in line. Feet will follow eyes, and if eyes wander about, your shield will follow leaving your brother, your cousin naked on his side!' Then 'old helmet-head' would rap the poor trainee's helmet with the flat side of his sword and order him then and there to look about all around, all the while smacking his body black and blue from every direction, all the time shouting in his ear – 'Did you see that coming my all-seeing Cyclops? Why did you not duck or ward that off my mighty Polyphemus?' When you had become black and blue from Sergeant Makellos's blows, you never forgot that your helmeted head had a line of vision peripherally blind. Old helmet-head always ended such a lesson by asking the now chastened *ephebe,* 'Would you see well if you took your helmet off during the battle?' Without waiting ever for an answer, old helmet-head, standing by one of the poles topped with a large over-ripe pomegranate, would bring the rock he held clenched in his hand down on the red orb, sending its blood red pulp and seeds spraying into the face of all those nearby."

Socrates smiled. "Old helmet-head is still rapping *epheboi* heads and smashing parade ground pomegranates. Maybe I should keep my helmet on all the time and I would do better at walking the line of that hoplite virtue of narrow vision and its single-minded obedience to those who lead. Then, Clinias, I wouldn't now be wondering why General Tolmides is taking us right through this broad valley where our small numbers - if we were engaged by a large force - could find no favorable position to prevent our line from being swept up on the two wings. Shouldn't we take a more protected route? Why aren't we staying to the hills like we did on the way north to Chaeronea?"

Clinias squinted his eyes and furrowed his brow as if to signal his young friend that it would be better not to continue the conversation within the hearing of so many. But a man close by had already overheard. It was Archeolus, one of the few volunteers from among the wealthy families whose estates were on the fertile plain northwest of Athens. He was inspecting the cart carrying his gear just a few yards from where Clinias and Socrates stood. He now joined, uninvited, the conversation.

"Captain Clinias, I see your elbow is still splinted. I am amazed that you can handle the strain the shield puts on that arm. It must hurt like Procreates' Bed when you have to strap splint and all into the shield grip. Do you think the elbow can take another round of combat?"

Clinias knew Archeolus well, since he was one of his father-in-law's nephews who moved in the same social circles as Clinias. This was an Alkmeonid he found curiously refreshing, since this man, unlike the rest of his clan, seemed completely uninterested in politics. "Archeolus, yes the elbow is very weak, but Lycon, my body servant, has become a first class binder of limbs. This splint makes the arm serviceable, should the need arise again."

Archeolus looked down towards the valley and then at young Socrates who was now busy untying cords that had become tangled along the side railing of one of his company's equipment carts. Drawing closer to Clinias and now appearing quite agitated, he gave voice to the fear that young Socrates' unanswered question aroused. "Clinias, up to now General Tolmides has been very careful to keep to a kind of terrain on which our relatively small force could prevail provided we employ sound tactics with aggressive fighting in close formation. We've marched from the very southern borders of Boeotia to its northern most towns without ever moving through a patch of territory where a large force could successfully out flank our own two-hundred men line. Look at that valley! It's less than a half day's march from Thebes. Why, once we are down there a mile or two from these hills and still many miles from Attica and any other natural barriers which would hamper a five or ten thousand enemy force, how could we possibly avoid either surrender or being slaughtered? I don't know about you, but I'm not ready to die in a puddle of dust and blood because of our young General's foolhardy overconfidence. No doubt, Tolmides thinks any hoplites he commands invincible, but this valley exposes more than our heel - .it is like running naked into a den of hungry lions!"

By the time Archeolus had finished speaking, Clinias knew that he must confer with General Tolmides. It was clear that men all up and down the line of march were losing confidence in the General, and now, on the way home, all could be lost if the army fell apart. Surely, he thought, Tolmides must have his reasons for this route and once he was apprised of the men's sinking morale, he would make the merits of these reasons clear to his army.

It was not necessary for Clinias to find Tolmides. His second in command, Callimarchus, appeared on horseback and called the three companies at hand to attention. "Men, as you can see we are going straight down the valley below and then along the costal plain to Leuctra where we will cut across the high ground to Plataea and Attica. This will get us home a full day sooner than if we retraced the path we first took in our march north. I have been instructed by Tolmides to inform you that our safe passage-way through the valley and along the coast has been secured. We have been assured both by our agents in Thebes and by the oligarchic leaders there that, provided we make no hostile moves towards the city of Thebes or any of the other southern Boeotian towns, no one will impede our return to Attica. We have been notified that provided we march in a straight line towards Leuctra and the nearest border crossing into Attica, send out no scouting forays, and abstain from any further destruction of property, our expedition will be granted safe passage. Indeed, the Theban oligarchs have sent us five of their young men from the finest families to serve as hostages guaranteeing the sanctity

Attica and Boeotia

of this agreement. So as soon as I have informed the rest of the companies, we will be on our way. Are there any questions?"

Archeolus stepped forward from his company. "Sir, if you don't mind, I would like to know more of our thinking on this matter. My question is this. Given that we just sacked an oligarchic governed town, sold all the well-born there into slavery, and then went to the neighboring town and burned their farmsteads, wouldn't you think that the enemy's honor and manhood require that they take revenge. Do you not suspect trickery? What possibly could deter our enemies from engaging us in battle if they could do so on clearly favorable terms with a large force? I find it hard to believe that the oligarchs of Thebes would so readily stand aside."

Callimarchus listened attentively to the question even though his horse kept turning about and he had all he could do to keep the horse facing the men. Sitting very upright and almost standing in his stirrups, he responded tersely. "It is not at all surprising that the Theban oligarchs, men who did not have the courage to face Xerxes' Persian expedition, would not want to join combat with men of Plataea and Athens who twice have defeated huge Persian forces which far out numbered them. Also, Boeotians have been warned that our force will be joined, in short order if necessary, by reinforcements from Attica. These over-fed soft-living plutocrats want only to save their property and be left at ease to indulge their luxurious and decadent appetites. Moreover, they are not anxious to face any size force which is led by our young Tolmides. They have heard of his exploits on the islands and in Chalcidice and how, even with men unaccustomed to arms, he was able to defend Athens' new cleruchies there against numerous enemies......Are there any more questions?"

The second in command turned his frisky horse loose, and he cantered up the line, stopping at each cluster of companies to repeat his message from the General to his men. When the trumpet sounded about one half hour later, the companies of men, with battle gear close at hand, formed up and continued marching deeper into the wide and flat valley.

Less than two hours later, around mid-day, the Athenians were well into the valley's fields about five miles from the hills they had left behind to the northeast. The men were again in good spirits and were doing their best to pick up the pace and speed their passage through the frontier between Boeotia and Athenian territory. There was even some good natured banter between some of the Athenian offices and the Theban young men who had been sent to Tolmides in order to assure him of safe passage through Theban territory in southern Boeotia.

Suddenly, everything changed. Tolmides and the officers who led the column ordered a halt to the march. There, less than a mile in front of them, they could now see a peculiar feature in the terrain which had not been visible from where they had entered the valley. Running east to west directly in their path was what at first appeared to be a freshly plowed furrow, but which grew more formidable as the men advanced. It now looked to be ten to fifteen feet high. But this was not the work of any farmer. No farmer ever turned the soil over this time of year. No, if this was not some kind of peculiar natural feature, it looked most like something that men had thrown up as recently as a week ago or so. The officers who had fought alongside Tolmides on the peninsula that lay to the south of Chalcidice had themselves often built such earthworks on the neck of the peninsula. Yes, it had to be – it was an artificial high ground built up to give advantage to a hoplite line. No scouting party was necessary – everyone in the front of the Athenian column gasped as the entire length of the ridge had changed from brown earth to bright glistening bronze. Theban treachery! There had to be a least a rank of enemy hoplites five-hundred men wide and even if there were only five or six ranks behind that first line, the Athenian force would be overmatched. If battle was joined, the chances of Athenian victory were small.

It was Socrates Alopeke Company, near the rear of the Athenian column, that at about the same moment the Athenians had halted saw a force of some five-hundred or so armed horsemen appear from out of a stand of woods on the far side of the wide stream that they had forded less than half an hour ago. The trap had been set, the bait taken, and now there was no escape. Tolmides and every other veteran understood the supreme danger of their predicament. No retreat was possible! A well-disciplined hoplite formation, even with a small line of 200 men, could with their wall of shields advancing in a compact charge easily break through a 500 men cavalry force if this is all they had to confront. But, a force of mounted horsemen defending a stream against a retreating hoplite force besieged from the rear by an enemy which outflanked it on both wings was more than enough to choke off any tactical redeployment. They were trapped with no route of tactical retreat. Even brash Tolmides realized that the prospect of his force being able to prevail or fight even to a stand-off was hopeless.

With panic spreading through his forces, Tolmides had the trumpet sounded to signal the call to arms. The young General, without any discussion with his fellow officers, called for a horse and with as much dignity as he could muster rode out under a herald's flag across the field to negotiate with the enemy commander. As he rode out, he ordered the two Boeotian men, who had joined the Athenians when they had first entered Boeotian territory, to follow close behind him, driving a cart which carried a chest filled with silver and gold that had been confiscated after the sacking of Chaeronea. The Theban hostages might be another bargaining chip. But this seemed unlikely to Tolmides since the Thebans more than likely had already considered their deaths an acceptable price for a total defeat of an Athenian expedition into their territory, thus perhaps putting an end to Athens' imperial claims in Boeotia. Everyone knew that invincible Tolmides would now be humiliated. The stronger take everything from the weaker and only accept a bargain when they face an enemy equally strong. And so as their young General made his way to the enemy line, Athenian soldiers already knew their young General's schooling in this hard lesson could cost both his own life and the lives of many other Athenians.

Clinias had already resigned himself to a fight to the death. The men in his company would be on the left wing of the line and would face an enemy determined to outflank and overrun them. And so the preparation for battle took on the air of a grim ritual. Clinias bodyservant, Lycon, was by his Master's side, having been summoned to bring the greaves.

"Lycon, why do you always hand me the corselet first? How many times have we done this? What are you thinking about? The greaves, boy, and see that there is no slack behind the knees or ankles when you knot the cords. I don't want to be rubbed raw before I even engage the enemy."

"Lord, this is the thirteenth time! An unlucky time! My lord, I know you think of me as foolish and childish as when your father first gave me to you thirty-three years ago to go to sea with you at Artemisium." Lycon began to sob as he lay the corselet aside and reached for the greaves that he had already laid out on the ground. "But last night I had a dream and I believe our Lady, the Virgin mighty in crafts and war, means to warn you and save you from a cruel death. The dream was so compelling that even now its images cloud my vision with tears and cause my hands to fumble, as though the goddess would prevent me from sheathing your body into an armor marked for death."

"Lycon, Hush! I swear by Hermes that if I hadn't seen that tool between your legs, I would think you are a woman. Don't presume that your bad bowel of beans last night allows you to speak for the gods. As our poet warns, a frightened woman like you is a '....*danger to house and to city. At this moment, with your storming sea-noise and your skittering about, you would drain our souls and paralyze our citizens, assisting the tides that threaten our shield-walls: thus we are being sacked from within.*' Now pay attention to what you are doing. Don't make me whack you with flat of my sword to get you on course!"

Lycon winced. It had been many years since his Lord had struck him. Indeed, Lycon just five years younger than his Master had come to regard Clinias as his feared but beloved father and protector. "But Lord, I think, if I am not mistaken it is Eteokles you cite, and did he not come to a pitiful end when he ignored the gods' warnings, a warning they put in the lamentations of lowly women. What will become of us, of your infant son, if you do not hearken to the gods' messenger. The gods you know always speak in disguise, in lowly form, in a cipher. Let me tell you my dream, I implore you."

"Lycon, there is nothing more the gods can do to torment me. Already they have strapped to my back a woman in my house who reads too much and whose overheated imagination sends her into a cuckoo-land of childish fears and wishes. Now the corselet! Get the top tighter this time and leave the bottom cords a little looser so I can bend at the waist without impaling myself on the bottom edge of the breast plates. It's as though you are doing this for the first time. I swear, if I survive this battle, its out in the fields for you and I'll find somebody who can do this right!"

Lycon pulled the back straps of the corselet tight as Clinias filled his lungs with air. It would not do to have the corselet so tight that it hindered the breathing of a man sweating profusely as he in full run labored to bring his seventy pound panoply to bear on the enemy. Safely behind his Master, Lycon screwed up his courage and persisted in delivering what he thought to be his commission from beyond. "Master, I can do it right while letting my dream speak. I must speak, for it is too strange that the words you upbraid me with were words that fit with those of my dream."

Clinias sighed in exasperation. "Go on! With my arm the way it is, I can't use it up to correct your womanly back and exorcise those slavish phantasms. But keep moving! With you as my body-servant, the battle will be joined and I'll still be in my underwear."

"Lord, it was a short dream. You and only twelve other oarsmen are on your ship, Gyges, navigating a bay. All of these men are your kinsmen. Thirteen shields decorated with the emblem of mighty Ajax hang from the port side of the ship. I don't know where the bay is, but it is very shallow and seven separate channels must be traversed to find open water. You and your crew are being stalked by an enemy ship. You all row with all your might, but you can not escape. I see the thick prow of a dark ship with a battering ram carved in the image of a sphinx smash through the wall of Gyges' 13 shields. Next, as the Gyges mortally wounded in her side flounders and begins to sink in the dark seething waters, seven furious warriors carrying huge iron and oak shields swing their shields like seven gates to the side and leap from the dark ship onto the Gyges. In unison they chant,

'Men of Ajax and Athens, this city's wealth,
this heavy freight of men, this swollen horde
must, from the stern, now be cast overboard....'"

"Enough! You go too far! You, with your slavish mind, take the words of our Marathon warrior and turn them to purposes he would abhor. You are so transparent! Yes, yes, I get it. Seven channels, seven warriors with oak and iron shields swinging – it's seven gated Thebes that attacks. Only in Athens are there such half-literate slaves who can torment their masters with bad half baked poetic fare. If you must cover your cowardliness with verse and pretence of dream, then remember,

'It is for you to remain silent and to stay indoors.'

No more, of your silly divination! The gods will certainly punish you if you usurp their ancient rites.

'At the moment of enemy attack
it is for men to slaughter
the sacrificial beast
and to perform divination.'

Now help me strap my sword around my waist, and one more word about your dream, and I swear by your seven-gated orifices, the big point of this sword will be battering its way deep through every one of your seven gates!"

Lycon quickly girded his Master's waist with the sword belt and it's sheathe. With downcast eyes and in taciturn silence, he wondered which would be worse, to have his Master act upon his threat or to be at the mercy of the enemy should the Thebans kill Clinias and capture him. Next, Lycon helped Clinias with his helmet, checking to make sure that the rounded metal ridges on the upper side of the iron helmet were resting squarely on the crown of his Lord's head. After the helmet was secured, Clinias stretched out his left arm and Lycon slid the leather bracelets attached to the middle concave inside surface of the round shield over Clinias' bandaged and partially splinted elbow.

"Make sure, Lycon that the splint is pushed down far enough that I can still bend the elbow enough to carry my shield with my arm bent in against my body. I will need to rest the lip of the shield against my shoulder as much as possible before actual contact with those men of your dreams. With this elbow, there is no way I can support the full weight of this shield - its almost as heavy, I'll bet, as your thick head."

Lycon tied the forearm, splint and the ringlet bracelets all together, but did not pull the knots completely tight. After he had looped the cord attached to the shield's outer hand-held grip around his Lord's left wrist, he then lowered his shoulder and as though he were an enemy combatant pushed himself as hard as he could against the outstretched big blue evil eye that covered all but the helmeted head and lower legs of his now ferocious and inhuman Protector.

"It's good, Lycon. Tighten everything up and fill my right hand!"

Lycon reached for the long ash wood shafted spear which he had planted in the ground by the side of the equipment cart. "I have sharpened both ends, again, Master. Both thrusting point and the spike are sharper than Kadmus' teeth."

Captain Clinias, fully armed now, stretched his body to its full height and with his right arm lifted with his elbow cocked above his shoulder, he turned quickly, faced the equipment cart that stood a few feet away, and with a downward motion thrust with force enough to test the strength of his good arm. He drove the spear's killing point into the wide pine plank that rimmed the top of the cart's side. The iron point easily pierced the wood, and just as easily was withdrawn by the hoplite's skilled arm. "Yes," Lycon, "heavy, sharp and fraught with the death of heroes."

Lycon watched his Master crouch and spring, making trial of his panoply to assure that he would enter the killing zone with his armor at the beck and call of the free play of his body's limbs. Clinias rehearsed the choreography of the hoplite first taught to him forty years ago in *epheboi* training: 'bend both legs as though straining mightily to hold in place a boulder which could roll over him, next push forward into a run, just before contact with the enemy line cover my torso with the hollow of my concave shield, then thrust the shield out as if to push from my chest and shoulders a sharp fanged monstrous harpy affixed to my shield and intent on ripping open my throat with his gaping jaws, and then with the monster off my shield thrust my spear forward to kill' – this was the death-dealing dance of the hoplite warrior.

Lycon looked up and down the line of companies that were forming, with other slaves' masters also now fully equipped and like his lord, moving about in this strange pantomime. If one did not know of the deadly serious contest for which these men prepared, faces hidden away under iron masks, the scene would strike one as quite comical. Lycon, witness to a dozen of these scenes, knew all to well that the naked ones like himself - men without armor - would be part of the spoils if their Lords were defeated in battle. And so, it was always with utter terror and fear that he backed away from the armed killers who were both his protectors and conquerors, taking his place within the circle of carts and animals that was drawn off out of the way of the sacred ground where Ares would do his work.

By the time, the Athenians and the few Plataeans who had joined their expedition were fully armed and formed up, two-hundred in a line with both wings curving sharply back to form a crescent, and behind this first crescent line four more arrayed ranks in the same formation; Tolmides had returned to his army. His expression was grim. The cart, still laden with the chest of silver and gold, came back now driven by Tolmides' own aide. Hoping for some kind of change of mind on part of the Thebans, Tolmides had left the two Boeotian prisoners with the Theban officers.

The General dismounted from his horse, spoke a few words to the officers who stood nearest, and then in a loud voice called forward two young men who had not yet shed human blood. They were instructed to go to the circle of animals and slaves and fetch twelve of the largest and most unblemished goats they could find. The goats, one for each tribe of Athens and two for the allied men of Plataea, would be offered as a blood sacrifice to seek the favor of the gods.

While the assembled hoplites awaited the procession of consecrated victims, Tolmides began the work of Ares. With anger in his voice and not a hint of fear, the young General with his head half turned towards the Theban-led battle line, recited to his own soldiers the insults and threats which he had just suffered in the meeting with the Theban general. "Athenians and friends of Athens, we have been deceived by double-dealing. The force you see arrayed against us is led by men who vow to humiliate all those who fight for Athens. The Theban general has informed me that there can be no obligation to honor agreements made with potters, carpenters, tradesmen, thetes, and those Athenian nobles who rub shoulders with such low-life. Indeed, this Theban oligarch has vowed, and he made a point of repeating the vow in my hearing before other of his officers, that this day he would see that every Athenian democrat would either die or be dragged away in chains to serve his betters. He gives us one hour to decide which it will be. He calls us blood-sucking leeches and has promised his men that this day they will fill our mouths with the blood drenched flesh of our own comrades if we do not bow our knee to him in unconditional surrender. Should we not surrender and accept slavery, he says his army will give no quarter until every last one of us suffers the indignities to our bodies which young Kallistus of Chaeronea underwent at the hands of Chrysippus, the appointed servant of the Athenian mob." Tolmides paused, his own body visibly tensing with hatred, "And that Theban boot-licking Persian-loving friend of tyrants called after me as I, unable to suffer any more of his insults, rode away, 'This time next year the unruly riff raff of Athens would be once again restored to order under its rightful rulers, the sons of Hippias.'

Men, this day we must once again teach our enemies that our city of liberty is peopled with men who will never bow their knee to tyrants or friends of tyrants. If need be, we will fight foes as numerous as Xerxes' hoards to defend our holy city of citizens whose only Master is the Laws of their own Assemblies. Let the Theban conscripts who fight as slaves to their rich Masters see in our unbreakable battle-line the adamantine strength of the fraternity of free citizens, men who only do homage to the Divine Justice of Zeus of Right-Counsel. Now let us seek the divine favor of our Protector and

Champion, Pallas Athena, and call upon the blessing of her almighty father."

Tolmides raised his hands to heaven and held aloft the sacred goat-skin even as the trumpet sounded once more signaling the beginning of the blood sacrifice. The loud short invocatory call of the trumpet mixed with the panicky bleating of the twelve goats which now appeared. The victims were all roped together and being pulled along in front of the arrayed hoplites by two young slaves. More than half of the animals appeared to be unwilling participants in the procession and were literally being dragged along. The necks of the more unruly ones were already bleeding from the rope that cut into their hides as they strained to break away. It was this spectacle of living creatures moving relentlessly towards their consecrated sacrifice for the shedding of blood that tested and steeled the resolve of men seeking both the permission to kill and the assurance that it would be the other whose blood drenched the dusty earth.

It was young Socrates first communion in this sacrament of warriors. Even the men in the fifth rank where he stood had a clear line of vision to the front and center area where Tolmides was presiding. Beginning with the second rank and all the way back through three remaining ranks, each man moved enough to his right so that his line of vision, unobstructed by the men who stood in the ranked line before him, lay clear all the way through. Indeed, Socrates who was on the left wing and all the way at the back of the array, could even make out in the distance there up on the knoll the enemy forces arrayed in like-manner, also in almost identical fashion seeking Divine favor through the sacrificial shedding of their own innocents' blood. He wondered which of the armies the immortal gods would favor. Trembling as he watched the red-necked goats dragged to their killing posts, Socrates turned his eyes away and inward, repeating to himself the words, 'know that you are not a god'. I cannot understand, he thought, all the forces which operate beyond my power to bring all mortals to the killing posts, to kill or be killed - in either case all are victims. It was the God of Afar, Apollo, whose words to Poseidon circled around and around, in his mind as he gazed past his sacrificial host to the other host on the far side of the field, *'Shaker of the earth, you could not say I was sound of mind if I were to go to war with you for the sake of pitiful mortals who now like leaves break forth full of fire, feeding on the fruits of the earth, and then waste away, heartless'.*

When all had been made ready for the ritual, Tolmides carefully lowered the sacred goat skin and handed it to his attendant. The attendant, having carefully folded the Virgin Queen's insignia, laid it upon the stone altar which had been hastily constructed for the ceremony. Tolmides drew his sword from the sheath which hung from his waist belt and turned to the killing post next to the altar. Eleven other officers in like manner approached the other killing posts. Tolmides, with his eyes lifted to heaven, led the eleven other slayer-priests in the prayer of consecration and supplication.

"O, holy ones who with Zeus the Father loose and bind the dark wrath of the Furies; we bring to you the unblemished she-goats, givers of milk to our own blood and tissue. We pray that this blood of our own sustenance poured out before you on dark earth will be well-pleasing. We pray that you may draw near and bless our service to holy Athena's city. O, Pallas Athena, we especially beseech your graceful presence. Make the pathways for our charge smooth and sure, let no glint of Apollo's burning orb blind our eyes, keep far from our ears the confusing din of Panic, and fill us with unfailing strength that in league with you we may set our own hands to work. Commend us O dread rouser of battle strife, mistress of the war cry, to thy Father, to that divine Brow of thy birth. May he who is far-sighted, the mighty Zeus who makes irresistible those he favors, show us his good sign as we give body, blood, and entrails, with no portion for ourselves, to be comingled with all those who Almighty Zeus has ordained for dark earth's dominion."

With the last words of the prayer, Tolmides as high priest turned to face the goat, an animal now greedily gorging itself on the meshed sack of greens which had been set beside it. All along the liturgical line of stakes, heads bent down and only the back of necks visible, the animals gave no sign that they were unacceptable to the holy ones. Each tethered animal, accompanied by its attendant priest, stood brimming with life. Tolmides and his co-celebrants raised their swords and with practiced and deft swift movements grasped the cord yet wrapped around each goat's neck, jerked the surprised victim's head up, and almost simultaneously thrust and slashed the sword's double-edged pointed blade deep through the now terrified animal's upraised throat. Gaping throats filled with throbbing torrents of bright red blood - that is all that in this moment filled every human eye. No sound from the animals, an eerie and uncanny silence honored by every human witness, no movement from priests or soldiers until each animal, legs buckling and body convulsing in death throes, lay still in its own dusty pool of blood, a blood now dark and slowly finding its way into the nether regions of Earth.

When every victim lay still and dead, General Tolmides and his eleven co-celebrants in solemn procession moved quietly to the killing post at the very south end of the line. All of the sacrificed animals had been carried here for inspection by the seer. Melancharchus would examine the entrails of every animal, searching for that sure sign which promised success for the coming battle. Melancharchus, dressed in flowing purple robes, was careful to face directly North, making sure that Hyperborean Apollo's holy breathe would inspire his prophecy. The seer appeared confident that the signs would be good. In a loud and ceremonial voice, he addressed Tolmides as they together prepared to butcher the first animal so as to extract its entrails.

"General, did you see that every animal was facing toward the west, without any coercion by our hands, when their blood first flowed?"

Tolmides was never quite sure, even though seers had accompanied his every military campaign, what exactly he was supposed to say in response to such observations by the wise man. And so as had become his custom of late, he answered with appropriate solemnity and in the humility of the man willing to defer to one of Apollo's ministrants, "Yes, it must have been as you saw, but what does it mean?"

Melancharchus furrowed his brow and speaking slowly and loud enough for many to hear, he prophesied with promising enigma:

"To my left there are children of Kadmus.
To my right there are children of Erectheus.
The gods have turned the blood black that fell left.
The gods take no pleasure in spilling red blood right."

The General nodded his head, but not with much conviction. It would be utter folly to go into battle against such odds, if there was any uncertainty about the omens. Surely the gods would not require an Athenian army to suffer the indignities of the Theban terms of surrender. It is we, after all, he said to himself, who have restored the temples and gods' cult statutes in Thessaly, Euboea, the islands, and even Delphi itself after the desecrations of the Persians. Surely the gods will take our part....But he needed more assurance, and certainly, he realized, his men required unequivocal guidance from above if they are to fight well in such a seemingly impossible situation. And so as the holy man, hands red with blood, now was carefully inspecting the liver which he had cut away from the gutted goat's carcas, Tolmides whispered in the seer's ear his doubt.
"But Melancharchus, might not such a sign have also been given to the Thebans. Should their every victim face our way, each animal busy with a feed bag laid on our side of the Theban line of altars, could not your words be turned about so that Lord Apollo makes sport of us?

'The gods have turned the blood black that fell right.
The gods take no pleasure in spilling red blood left.'"

Melancharchus paid him no mind, partly because in his seventieth year he had become hard of hearing and partly because his many years of interpreting the ways of the gods to men had taught him that only a series of signs, each later one linked to the cryptic meaning of the former in ways only the seer could decipher, would disclose to their interpreter the decision at hand. He was hard at work down on his knees, carefully measuring the lobes of the liver which he had just removed from the carcas of this the first victim. Something was amiss! He had never seen a goat's liver with such a pattern of faint lines, almost like very thin purplish stripes, running diagonally across the liver's top lobe so that the stripes would have pointed neither directly to heaven or earth when the animal was yet on all fours and alive. Sometimes the signs would be so ambiguous even to the practiced receptivity of the seer that hours and indeed, perhaps, a few days might pass before the omens were favorable for battle. Young men unaccustomed to this anxious waiting upon the gods as they stood armed, their nostrils filled with the deathly odor of blood soaked victims, often grew faint both from the strain of sustaining the weight of their battle ready armaments and the seemingly interminably slow procedures of the seer's necromancy. But the seer could not be rushed! After all, it was not up to him. He was only an extension of the medium whether it is the disposition of entrails, the flight of birds, or the sudden change of weather. It just happens and what comes from beyond makes itself manifest only when mortals surrender themselves, listening and seeing, attuned to everything at hand - but not grasping or forcing anything lest one's human all too human hand occlude the divine signs. Generals, in a hurry to take advantage of what they thought to be some momentary tactical advantage, had often in their impatience pressed him to shorten his procedures or to restate his reading in language less 'inspired'. But he had not lasted this long, almost thirty years, by so being pushed by a man of action to some precipitate interpretation of too few and too veiled signs, a reading that might please for the moment but would not stand the test of the gods' own irresistible fated course.

And so the old man stood up from beside the first victim and with a part of the animal's inners in his upheld right hand, he again spoke so many could hear, although this time with a tremor in his voice.

"Bacchus oft runs to and fro disguised even from his own devotees.

Neither heavenly gods above or earthly titans below are shown, whither and to what field dismembered goat-snake-Bacchus shall ply.

Even Apollo his brother cannot say, he too must wait on Zeus most high."

After he had exercised great care to return the dismembered organ to its donor in its natural and original disposition since it might be important to return to this reading, Melancharchus moved on to the next victim.

The young General did not bother to ask his seer to explain. It was clear enough. There it was. Not even Apollo was ready to say just now whether we are to take the field of battle. We must wait for a clearer sign. So Tolmides dutifully followed the old man down the line to the next victim. Realizing that the seer would not be rushed, he motioned to his officers that the men should remove their helmets, rest their shields on their shoulder, and post their spears spike-end into the ground where they stood. There was no danger of sudden attack, since neither army of Hellenes would dare anger the gods while one of their seers yet made supplication beside the sacrifice of blood.

Some three hours passed while the seer continued his divination. The General and the seer were no more than 30 feet or so from the position Clinias and his company occupied in the very center of the line. Everything Clinias could observe in the proceedings suggested that there might be no battle this day. The seer's formulaic readings had continued to be obscure and did not encourage resolute action. The uncertain readings were taking their toll on the men who waited. Apprehension added to the weariness that always came from being required to stand for long periods of time with greaves and breast plates making one's body ache. It would be better, thought Clinias, if we do not take the field this late in the day.

"Clinias, what is he doing now? He is not moving to the next victim. Why is the old man hobbling out into the field towards the enemy?" It was Archeolus, lined up just behind him in the second rank, whispering in his ear.

Clinias looked out towards the enemy line and tried to follow with his own eyes the way in which their own seer appeared to be looking. "It must be something from the birds. He's watching the sky and I can make out some large birds circling above. They look like some kind of hawks or maybe owls. We'll all know shortly. See, Melancharchus has already turned around and is making his way back to our The wild look in his eyes, I'm sure, means that heaven has spoken."

Sure enough, the minister of Apollo made his way to General Tolmides who had remained at the seventh altar waiting for the seer to resume inspection of the victims. When the seer had taken his place beside Tolmides, he raised his palms to the skies, and prophesied again in a loud voice.

"Two noble birds of prey did circle and downward swoop
between the Theban prince's and the Athenian led troop.
One warrior of the sky, young and of regal bearing,
within his sharp claws his helpless victim a dove,
swerved as if to lose the larger bird just above.

The larger bird, big headed, big-eyed, and helmeted with golden crest, looking like Athena's own mighty owl would give the other no rest.
Then, in air-born confusion with shrill calls of disputed claim, the helmeted and higher bird darted towards the other as if to maim.

Then the smaller bird of prey as victim fell,
bloodied and torn, to our seventh alter to tell,
that should seven-gated children of Thebes engage this day,
then the lesser will give way to Athena's brightest ray."

Clinias sighed. "It seems that the gods wish to test our courage and endurance, Archeolus. Morning marching, standing to in battle-readiness most of the afternoon, and no proper meal for two days: I suppose it amuses the gods to even up the fight. Those pansy Persian-loving Theban fat-boys now will need only five for every one of us, instead of ten."

Archeolus wanted to be as brave as Clinias, but he could not set aside his growing apprehension. He was wondering why he had agreed to his Uncle Megacles' offer of being the Alkmeonid family's volunteer on this expedition in exchange for the transfer of his Uncle's prize vineyards to his estate. "Clinias, if the prophecy is favorable, why is our general hesitating? Does he wonder, like me, if it is he who is the smaller bird, rather than the Thebans? Only Tolmides rivals Pericles for preeminence in Athens today. Could it be, Clinias, that our wise prophet has hedged his counsel and whether we die in defeat with Tolmides or march home victorious, Athena's favorite will win the day."

The same thought had occurred to Clinias. But he had quickly pushed it aside. There was no point in tying oneself up in knots over divine signs that seemed to point two ways at once. No mortal can force the gods' will. And so Clinias, like the good captain who always must make his men as battle-ready as possible, chided Archeolus. "We are soldiers, Archeolus, not prophets. Athena helps those who help themselves! Hush! Give the General a few minutes! We will, I am sure, be called to vow with him in offering up gifts for our impending victory."

Clinias was right. The General already was calling the assembly of hoplites to attention. "Men of Attica and our allied friends of liberty, the hour is here for us once again to join battle with those in league with despots and kings. Join me, as I offer up to our mighty warrior-goddess, Athena, our solemn tithe.

Athena, come fight in our midst, confuse our enemy, make powerful our weapons so that we might this day win glorious trophies for you. Fill our hearts with that holy wrath against those who sided with the Persian invader who burned your holy temple. Grant us the victory and we shall fill your new sanctuary with glittering arrays of the richly-appointed armor of our vanquished enemies."

When the General's vows had been sealed by the prophet's sprinkling of blood on each of the tribal officers' foreheads, the order was given to sound the trumpet signaling the command to ready the ranks for advance. Then, Tolmides took his place among the very first rank where the center of the line met the companies that made up the right wing. He would, like every other hoplite, be one among many locked in a wall of advancing shields. Looking down the line, the General surveyed what would be the first wave of the killing zone in his army. Spears held firmly in an underhand grip, peered out thigh-high from behind the unbroken line of round shields in the first rank. Behind the first rank, each man held his spear upright and stood so close to the hoplite immediately in front of him that his concave shield's outer rim appeared to be some monstrous tumor growing right out of the front-ranker's back. Looking back through the ranks, the General could see no uncertain shields anywhere. These are indeed Athens' best, he thought. Not one of these will shrink if they must step in to fill the place of a comrade in the rank in front of them.

It was time to attack! Officers had been instructed on how to deal with the much longer enemy line. The left wing would align itself with the enemy's right wing and the Athenian right wing would curve backward and to the left so as to prevent the Thebans from sweeping around the Athenian line. Tolmides had made clear to every company leader that success depended upon a determined compact thrust through the Theban center which would then produce panic throughout the numerically superior enemy ranks. He had also instructed officers to be careful to keep the line of attack on flat ground. "Under no circumstances, should our line," he reminded them, "close with the enemy line until they are well off that ridge they now occupy. Everything will depend on our first push, and we must be sure we are not running up-hill! And if they break, and I think they will, do not pursue and thereby thin our line. We must move through them and stay impenetrable until we reach a place where their longer line can be tactically negated."

General Tolmides commanded the trumpeter to signal the attack. The Athenian trumpet call was answered by the trumpet of the enemy.

And, as if the impending mayhem was indeed moved along by some unseen director, across the field the front ranks of the Theban phalanx began to advance slowly, careful to maintain their advantage of higher ground. The sound of Theban war cries, however, could not be heard by the Athenians. For every Athenian warrior, with voices pitched somewhere between a chant and a scream, had given themselves over to their ancient war-song, a song of no intelligible words but in unison sounds which seemed to lift each warrior out of himself into the one soul of an onrushing and implacable superhuman beast. It was said when men were safe from the terrors of battle, that this war-cry was a hymn to Apollo, God of Light and well-ordered Reason. But every Athenian hoplite warrior, though trained to keep to his station and never give way to uncontrolled fury of battle outside formation, chanted and shouted to unnerve not only the enemy but to dull his own sense of vulnerability and lose himself in the immortal frenzy of Ares.

Clinias own throat was filled with this hymn of frenzied chant and, like many others preparing for the killing zone, Clinias' war-song drew upon reservoirs of inchoate hate. While he did not know any Thebans personally, apart from a few brief encounters at the Olympic and Delphic festivals, he now did hate them with a force venting up from the deepest recesses of all that had excluded him from attaining the heroic heights which he had aspired to ever since he was a child. Here, he could strike out with all of his fury at that 'other' which had conspired to frustrate his most ardent desire to take his place with the kind of men made immortal by the poets. And so he found that it was Athenian faces flitting before his eyes now glazed with Ares' frenzy; but when the battle hymn faded and warriors' ears would be filled with the clashing of shields and spears, then this animosity born of resentment would vent its fury on the faceless enemy today wearing Theban armor. This is how Ares in the killing zone moved Clinias and rendered him a killer.

Four ranks behind Captain Clinias, young Socrates peered out from his ill-fitting helmet as he strained to see through the formation of hoplites in front of him. For him, the sounds of his own war cry seemed to distract his need to fix on something solid, something which would anchor all his energies to meet the terrifying unknown violence which might now claim him as victim. He was here because he had been told over and over again that there was no other route to honor than this - to show one's manhood in arms. But when Tolmides had sent out men to loot and burn farms when they could not take the city of Orchomenus; it struck Socrates with considerable weight that an honorable man may find himself ensnared by forces and designs not of his own making and yet be obliged by his station in the community to obey superiors and spend his honor on stupid or even dishonorable enterprises. What I need to know, he reminded himself, is that the comrade on either side of me requires that I stand firm and shield his side while he shields mine. This is my whole duty now and in this sacred space of my responsibility, I must not abdicate. Perhaps, some day, I may take my part in assisting our citizens in choosing wisely as to when young men's courage in arms is to be honorably expended.

Suddenly the pace had quickened. Socrates was now almost at a full run. Then through the dust and flashing shields now reflecting the low late afternoon sun, he could see right up in front of him, no more than fifteen yards from their own front line, the onrushing enemy. Their shields almost blinded him, for they were catching head-on the rays of the sun and redirecting them, it seemed, right into his eyes! And so, Socrates thought, the enemy, their bodies and weapons rendered disjointed as flashes of light intermittently blurred their oncoming advance, are favored by Apollo. Perhaps it is because I am short that I see such unhelpful light.

"Close the ranks! Close the ranks! Push with all your strength!" The shout came from officers of every company. The crisis of battle was upon them. The first rankers had closed with the enemy in the killing zone. There Ares was already at work: the clash of shields, straining legs and arms, thrusting spears from above probing for soft and uncovered flesh, men joined in a shoving match of death pushed on in front by the enemy weight of all those who would crush you beneath their feet and from behind by the weight of those comrades who would drive you like a battering ram to smash and obliterate walls of enemy metal encased flesh.

Before they closed, Clinias could see that behind his adversary were at least nine other ranks in the enemy formation. With the first clash of shields, he knew that at least five men directly in front of him would have to be dispatched if he were to survive this day. There would be no enemy retreat unless they could cut that deeply into the center of the Theban phalanx. Charging at a full run, he threw himself with all his weight into the evil eye which stared out at him from the shield of his enemy. Neither he nor his enemy had risked breaking their spears in the first clash of shields. Clinias feigned a thrust aimed low and under the enemy's shield. The opponent, even taller than him, lowered his shield to cover his thinly armored thighs. In an instant, Clinias realigned his arm and drove the spear over the top rim of the lowered shield. He felt the thrust slowed just slightly by something soft and then saw that the point of his spear had found the neck of the enemy. Pulling his spear back, Clinias saw, just beyond the end of his now red-tipped spear, his victim. Somehow Clinias' spear thrust had pulled the enemy's helmet clean off his head. Whether or not it was so, there flashed before Clinias a death mask, the face of a youth distorted by muscles all gone slack, seemingly having no mouth or nose. Instead, where the mouth, chin and nose should have been, there was a grotesque gaping tear that stretched from just beneath the eyes down into the neck. What was left of the human face, convulsed and choking with blood, stared out with eyes which in that last instant were wild and wide with the desperate awareness of life's last light. Then, with no time or space allotted for the victim's death throes, the slain warrior toppled forward, pushed face first into the earth by one of his own kin who now pressed forward to fill the hole in the Theban line.

For Clinias, there was no time to see how it went on down on either side of his own line. As long as both his right and left sides were covered by men who kept their shields up and out, there was little chance of being hacked or pierced by sword or spear from the side. It would not be likely that he would meet another such inexperienced opponent. Indeed as he closed with the next man, he could not see any uncovered body parts. This man was hunkered down, with bent knees and all of his upper body pressed inside the concave belly of his own shield. Clinias realized immediately that he faced a warrior who had fought many times and had learned that the counter-thrust from a well-covered position was best.

If Clinias had been able to see down along the Athenian line on the right side where it began to curve back to protect the flank of their army, he would have known that the battle was already lost. The long and deep array of the enemy's forces had within moments of first contact broken the right wing of the Athenian line. Already, the ranks had broken not far from the Athenian center, and the thrust of the Athenian center would soon loose its momentum as men would sense impending encirclement. The men at the very center where Clinias fought now stood their ground, but could make no further advance. Whenever an enemy fell, it seemed to make no difference since the enemy's line closed, it seemed, not only from the ranks behind but also from men moving sideward.

Straining to recover the center's forward momentum, Athenians at the center urged one another on by calling out to each other the names of their tribe's ancestral heroes. Clinias, with the name of mighty Ajax resounding in his ears, stiffened his left arm, and springing forward with all the force he could muster, attempted to force the stubborn defender in front of him backwards by pushing his own shield with so much force that the defender's outstretched shield must give way. We must break through and do so now, or all will be lost, he realized. The longer we fight, the more likely it is that their superior numbers will be brought to bear with more weight.

The impact of Clinias' fierce thrust forward sent a wave of pain through his left elbow all the way up to his shoulder. It felt as though something had given way suddenly in his arm. Indeed, when he tried to pull his left elbow back into his body so as to push his entire torso up against the inside of the shield, the pain turned to a sudden numbness. He had reinjured the arm at the worst of all possible moments. How could he possibly hold his shield firm if the arm had lost all feeling? He needed to take one step backwards and find a way to position his shield so that it still covered him but its weight could somehow be supported more by something other than the arm to which it was strapped. How would he, even if he could so reposition the shield, ward off the inevitable counter-push of the enemy, a man who he could see was very strong?

Clinias quickly glanced to both sides of himself and judged that by stepping back to his left he might make some space to readjust his armor if his man to the right stepped forward to hold off the charge of the adversary now in front of him. He took a backwards step with his left foot, following quickly with his right foot so as to keep his shielded body facing forward. But when he set his right foot down, disaster struck. He could not see the helmet sized stone that jutted from the ground where his foot came down. Struggling to rebalance his shield against his torso while keeping his eyes on the adversary in front of him, his right foot landed, with the full weight of his body, unevenly on the rock. Like his left arm, now his right foot and ankle were taken from him. The ankle followed the foot as it slid off the rock, twisting so that it was the side of his foot that met the ground first. When he tried to right himself, the foot would not respond but gave way as he tried to put his weight on it to move forward. Smiling to himself, but with a hand clenched in despair, he muttered to himself, "At least, I will not die rotting in bed from old age."

Unable to push off of his right foot, he planted his left foot, rested the lip of his shield on his right shoulder and lifted his spear high above his head, inviting his enemy to close with him. There was nothing else he could do. There was no point in drawing his sword, since he did not have enough mobility to stay clear of the long spear of his adversary. The only thing he could hope for is that his comrades would see his predicament and close around him and somehow, against all odds, preserve him till the battle ended one way or another. It would not be. Theban anger after years of abuse by Athenians who never tired of proclaiming Theban cowardliness would now take its fill of Athenian blood.

Not one, but three Theban warriors closed quickly on Clinias. Slashed from the side with a spear thrust that penetrated his right shoulder, Clinias own spear fell from his hand. When he tried to draw his sword, his hand could not close on the handle. Fumbling with the sword, he weakly shifted his shield higher. The next thrust of the enemy spear penetrated his left thigh. When the spear was withdrawn, taking with it what had been a portion of his quadriceps tissue, the fifty-six year old merchant-warrior and citizen of Athens sunk wearily to the ground beneath him which was now soaked with his own blood. On his back, his life flowing away, his eyes remained open to look up through the shapes which yet contended above him. As he looked for the last time on a patch of blue, Clinias muttered words that could not be heard by anyone but his own soul. "It is enough. The buckets will be carried by others!"

It was not clear why the Theban force suddenly sounded their trumpets and ordered their companies to stop the slaughter. For within minutes after the Athenian center broke and both ends of its line had been outflanked, more than half of the thousand Athenians that had volunteered to serve with Tolmides had been either slain or grievously wounded. The Athenian youths who made up the back ranks continued to fight even though it was clearly hopeless and if they had so chosen the Theban force could have killed everyone. There was no route of escape. So when the Theban general ordered the companies to halt the carnage and signal by way of salute to those Athenians who were still standing, an end to the battle; the remaining Athenians planted their spears into the ground, and stood motionless in surrender.

Young Socrates was among the fifty or so Athenians who were all that was left of the Athenian center. They were huddled together in a tight circle with their backs to one another and facing outwards towards the enemy that now had withdrawn some fifteen yards or so while yet surrounding them. Most of these men, like Socrates, were very young and now were befuddled and terrified by their predicament. Fighting on was hopeless. It meant sure death. But surviving the battle - if you could return to Athens provided you were not sold into slavery - would you not always be suspect as a coward?

It was Thucydides, the only veteran in this coterie of survivors, who pulled his spear from the ground, raised his shield, and first stepped out of the circle of his comrades towards the Thebans who appeared to be waiting for instructions. Speaking Dorian rather than Attic, Thucydides, challenged those enemy warriors to close with him. "Come to me, my spear and sword still wish to make your acquaintance. They will not let me grovel at your feet like a slave. The holy oak of my spear, taken from Artemis' grove, will not let me bow my neck behind the plow. The iron worked in Hesphestus' hearth is seared to my hand and will not let my hand clasp your knees to beg like a slave for my life."

Thucydides stood waiting but no Theban stepped forward. He then repeated his words, but this time in the Attic of his beloved city. This time his words called others to stand with him. Young Socrates was among the first to step forward beside Thucydides. The words had made clear to Socrates that this moment required nothing less, since a survival without honor would be an unfit survival. All up and down the battle line, where only small and separated groups of Athenians stood engulfed by yet cohesive arrays of the Theban line, similar desperate dramas of hoplite manhood were being played out, appearing almost as if scripted by one playwright.

The stand-offs which - if battle were to continue - could be nothing other than a pause in the slaughter of an outnumbered and now inexperienced company of Athens' back-rankers made clear to the Theban generals that what remained of the Athenian army yet contained young men who must hail from the best of families, aristocratic families like their own. Indeed, the supreme commander had already concluded as he surveyed the surviving enemy's response to his tactical pause that these men should not be slain since they would be worth considerable ransom.

Strict orders were quickly passed along the entire length of the Theban forces that they were to offer the remaining Athenians an honorable "capture" which would permit living captives to be returned to their homes at a price matching their unsoiled aristocratic dignity. And so as the sun set, men who had given themselves to Ares and his bloody frenzy, now with oaths and vows to the gods of promises and contracts made civil what violence had won. There would be decent burials for the dead and arrangements made to send messengers who would convey terms of ransom for the return of valued sons of Athens.

CHAPTER FOURTEEN
THE SCHOOL YARD KING OF THE HILL
(Late Summer 443 B.C.)

Of Alcibiades' beauty I probably do not need to speak, except to say that it blossomed out in childhood, youth, and manhood, at every age and season of his life, making him lovable and charming... Even his lisp is said to have added distinction to his speech and made his talk winning and attractive.

(Plutarch. *Lives, Life of Alcibiades*, 1)

If only they would give me a few minutes peace. What a commotion! The boys, on mid-day recess from their wrestling exercises, were shouting, laughing, cursing at one another, pushing and shoving, and throwing one another about in their impromptu game of King of the Hill. What a sight! Like a buzzing horde of dust covered wasps, one bunch of the first-year boys had discovered a mound of dirt on their enclosed dusty playground, and now in unison they circled about and over their newly discovered home base threatening any and all interlopers with a nasty sting. Agitated by the shouts of the king of the hill, other little boys gathered together and they joined in the fight to throw the king and his guards from their acropolis. Well, let them go at it, he thought. How much damage could seven or eight year old naked and well-oiled boys with nothing but their fists inflict on one another? I'll just keep my eye on my boy to make sure none of the older boys jump him. There will be the Furies to pay if he gets a mark on him!

Zopyrus sighed as he shifted his weight and leaned back against the trunk of one of the few shade trees that had been planted in the open area of his boy's gymnasium complex. I've only been with this one for less than a month, he thought, and already I'm exhausted. Did Master Pericles really think he was doing me some kind of favor by, as he put it, 'relieving me of the tedium of serving as one of his scribe-clerks so I could take on the oversight of his ward's education, a boy surely destined to be one of Athens' most illustrious citizens'? I'm too old for this, chasing after this spoiled brat born with a silver spoon in his mouth! He can't be anything like his father Clinias, the hero of Artemisium and one of Tolmides' thousand. There was no one to complain to about his boy. So the pedagogue talked to himself, as men of letters are apt to do. "Sure, it is easy enough for guardians that don't live in his mother's house to reprimand me because I'm not toughening him up; but let them come and deal with his mother! Every day she fills his pretty head with delusions of Alkmeonid grandeur. Well, whoever says that the lot of a pedagogue is an easy one is full of horseshit!" Yes, he had the rod and had been instructed by the boy's legal guardians to use it when needed. But, if they wanted that kind of discipline they would have to take the boy completely out of his mother's house and into one of their houses.

Second cousins or not, neither Pericles nor Ariphon would actually take the boy into their own households. When the boy's father, Clinias, had been killed at Coronea four years ago and was without surviving male kin; Athenian law directed that the orphaned son's patrimony in these circumstances could be entrusted to men of the mother's family-line until the boy came of age. Megacles, the mother's Alkmeonid patriarch, had asked his sister's two sons, Pericles and Ariphon, to assume joint guardianship over the boy. They would also serve as trustees of the considerable wealth which had been acquired by Clinias until Alcibiades came of age. Megacles himself would assist in maintaining Clinias' commercial enterprises, making sure that they remained profitable until they could be passed on to Alcibiades. The old man more than likely, thought Zopyrus, was mainly interested in keeping the loot in the Alkmeonid clan, and had come to the conclusion that there could be no better way to assure this than to entrust its superintendence to his two nephews. What a clever old geezer, that Megacles is - arranging for the joint guardianship to brothers who were barely civil to one another! Pericles, Athens foremost champion of the commons, and Ariphon, a supporter of the aristocratic faction led by Thucydides, did not trust each other. They would bird-dog each other and this was the best hedge against impropriety.

Zopyrus chuckled to himself. Megacles choice of guardians would assure that Clinias' considerable holdings would remain safely in place doing what they had been doing before his death, generating ever more wealth for the Alkmeonid commercial empire. It was all so agreeable to everyone that the boy should stay in his mother's house, with his grandfather Megacles providing additional financial help for maintaining the physical needs of the household. This way neither of his legal guardians would gain undue influence over the heir or the disposition of his patrimony, but neither would the arrangement give the appearance that Megacles was simply expropriating the holdings of a deceased business partner. And neither Pericles nor Ariphon really wanted to take the boy into their own households. Both had sons of their own and did not want to assume daily responsibility for superintending another youth.

Most happy of all with this arrangement was the boy's mother, Dinomache. And it is her strange demands which make my position impossible! The very first time I corrected the boy with the rod, the little master ran to his mother and wept on her bosom while he lifted his robe to show the welts on his back. No matter that he deserved the rod - he had allowed an older boy to caress his thigh in exchange for a promise that another older boy who had teased him for his lisp would have his nose bloodied. Mistress Dinomache ranted and raved like a madwoman. She warned me that if I ever dared to lay a rod on her child again, or in any way marred his beautiful body; she would personally see that her father's strongest field slave overseer would give me a lashing that would make my back-side look like a raw and quartered uncooked rump roast. No, she screamed in my face, this boy, who she alone called Meilichios, would not be harmed by anyone as long as she had any breathe in her body - and certainly not by a slave.

Yes, Zopyrus, thought, this is a strange household and a strange boy. I have never seen coming from the face of one so young such a devious and smug smile as that of this boy as he enjoyed the scene of his tutor threatened with the rod of instruction by a woman. I wonder if I can survive this boy's schooling. 'Meilichios', his crazy mother calls him.....maybe I should go offer a special sacrifice to Zeus Meilichios and pray that he would graciously save me from Alcibiades!

Where was that flute teacher? He should have been here by now. The boys' play would soon turn nasty if left unsupervised much longer. He could tell by the shrillness of the shouts that their games were escalating into bad-tempered violence. He would give the music teacher just a few more moments before calling his boy's recess to an end. Looking off to the other end of the park-like plaza from where he sat on the ground with his back supported by the trunk of his favorite shade tree, he wondered why it was that Athenian freemen, and especially those who saw themselves as the 'the good and the beautiful', entrusted the task of fashioning their unformed sons into good citizens, fathers, soldiers, and freemen by a foreign slave like himself. After all, they think we are somehow by nature slaves and as such incapable of the manly virtues requisite for citizenship and military valor. Were there not some Athenian sons of the 'good and the beautiful' who turned into dissolute pleasure-seekers? Did not these Athenian born freemen prove themselves unfit for the responsibilities of citizenship and military duty? Do the Masters think this is 'by nature' also? What is this 'nature', they think so assigns the different destinies of men? Should we look to the trees, the animals, the patterns of change in all growing things to find the blueprint for the unfolding of men's lives?

Look what the boy drives me to – I'm becoming a philosopher! Well, it is their fault!

Zopyrus studied a pair of trees which grew near the exterior west wall of the gymnasium complex. Perhaps, he mused, the trees can teach me about this 'nature' which makes men so different from one another. One of the trees, a thick trunked sturdy sycamore tree had grown tall and straight. Its many branches spread out wide and all turned up to catch the rays of the sun. It was a beautiful well-formed tree that soaked up the full glory of the sun-light. But right next to it, there grew another sycamore. It clearly must have grown from a seed that dropped from the mature and now old but stately tree. This tree's trunk was bent sharply to one side, as though the wind had permanently distorted its upward thrust to the sun. Growing almost sideways, the contorted trunk was anything but straight. Its branches, starved for sunlight, had followed the cue of their trunk and grown in ways that made the tree even in the full light of mid day appear as some kind of phantasm, a shadow of a tree playing with weird possibilities of shape that could never be assumed by those first trees that crowd out the sun for those that spring up late. Well, the tutor thought, what does all that have to do with me and young Alcibiades, my troublesome scion of the 'good and the beautiful'?

Zopyrus shut his eyes and let his chin drop to his chest. The boys' angry voices had given way to laughter. Just a minute or two of peace and quiet, please, lord of young boys!

He could not have closed his eyes for more than the time it takes a rooster to hop a hen, when he felt an annoying ache on his legs accompanied by a warm and slightly cheesy smelling vapor which seemed to be blowing right up his nose.

"Zoppy, Zoppy, wake up, wake up! Those big boys over there say they're going to rough me up and stretch my ears so I look like a silly rabbit."

"I'm not asleep, boy! Get off my thighs! I'm not hard of hearing." The boy had snuck up on him and somehow mounted his prone upper legs so that he could stand upon him and elevate his own face and thin chest so that it was right up against his superintendent's face. "Boy, I really must teach you some manners. A gentleman does not blow his breath - especially when it is rancid with cheese - up another man's nose!" Zopyrus shook his legs and the boy slid off.

"But Zoppy, I love you. I was just looking out for my man! There was a big greenhead between your nose and lips, sucking up the crumbs from your lunch. I only blew to chase him off your face. That's why I mounted and rode your legs so I could waft the little rascal away. Would you rather that I smacked him with my little flask?"

Zopyrus looked at the boy, wondering what to make of him. What a cipher this lad is! There he stood with that long blond hair down to his shoulders glistening in the sunlight and that perfectly formed face with lips already far too sensuous for a boy of seven and those deep blue eyes that seemed to always look right through whatever they fixed upon. How could anyone ever stay angry at this uncannily beautiful face? And then that lisp, it was so childish and sweet sounding, but always the words worked his childish but unbending will no matter how ridiculous his lisp sounded. Was it an affectation or a genuine impediment? Even though he had been with him now for over four months, Zopyrus could still not answer that question. Though just a boy, this one had already displayed a capacity for duplicity which one would think required as its motivation the cynicism of a man of years many times disadvantaged and disappointed by unrequited honesty.

"Lad, it is no use to you if you jostle with me. Now, which boy was it that was going to stretch your ears? Was it that tall third year one who now is calling you back to take your place as 'king of the hill'. Isn't that the son of Nicias, the Philiad? You would do well, if jostle with older boys you must, to make this one your sparring partner. He is of noble pedigree, and a fine strong lad. Forget about the flies on your pedagogue's chin! If you must test yourself, wrestle with such a clearly superior one as Nicias' son, Hagnon. Any boy who seeks such adversaries and survives these contests will soon be a champion."

"But Zoppy, he is bigger than me!"

"Son of the hero of Artemisium and off-spring of noble Alkmeonid champions, what would you have me do? Surely you would not have it said that your pedagogue fights your fights."

The boy shrugged his shoulders and nodded his head in agreement. "Zoppy, you are right. But not today! Can we go home? I must get ready for Eleusis. You know, don't you, I am the Divine Child this year?"

"We will go. I don't know what happened to the flute-master. And yes, your mother told me that it would be good to get you home well before sunset today, since the lots and the gods have appointed her first son as the Holy Mother's Demophoon. It seems that you will be made immortal straight away. No need for the sweat of the palaestra, or the discipline of our gymnasium for you, Alcibiades! You are the darling of the twain and your name will be on the lips of every woman. Yes, we must not tarry, lest Demeter's folk rise up and haunt me for keeping their sacred Mother's favorite from her bosom."

The boy frowned. "You have never been initiated in the Mysteries, have you? My dear Zoppy, I will speak to the Divine Mommy for you. It just won't be blessed to live forever if I can't have my old Zoppy with me."

Zopyrus laughed, "Please, Alcibiades, I will need a long rest after you reach eighteen. A dreamless sleep will be blessed enough for me. So don't bother the Holy Mother about your old Zoppy. Now go clean up, gather up your tablets and the other stuff we left inside the gymnasium! We need to hurry so we can get to the tailor before he closes his shop. Your mother will send me to the fields if we don't come home with your costume for your day at Eleusis."

Since the boy was only seven, Zopyrus could allow him to walk alone back from the open air yard, by the wrestling pits which were directly in front of the main building's portico, and then through this porch into the palaestra's main undressing room. Even the most lascivious lover of youths would not flirt with a first-year boy. Besides, since this gymnasium, one of the three large ones which was in the Academy District, was the only remaining private club still especially associated with the oldest and wealthiest families in Athens; anyone looking for conversation and "friendship" out of the noon day heat and among the broad benches of the palaestra's changing room would be of the right sort here. Moreover, there were attendants on hand especially commissioned to speed young school boys along if they tallied too long either in the changing or bathing rooms. And so without stirring from his shady seat, Zopyrus called after his boy, "If you are ready to go quickly, we'll have time to stop at the honey and melon stall for a cool treat."

Alcibiades, now at the entry way to the palaestra's changing room, turned back to his slave-guardian and, making sure those inside would hear him, loudly reprimanded his family's servant. "Zoppy, get off your ass. I'll be ready long before you." The boy-master smiled and sauntered into the palaestra dressing room.

There, not far from the end of the bench where he had left his belongings and hung his robe on the wall peg, a thick shouldered young man with a very broad and snub nose was in earnest conversation with a much older and paunchy man. The older man was wrapped in a frayed purple robe that despite its loose fit did not hide his bulging belly. When Alcibiades reached his corner of the bench, the younger man turned his way and nodded his head in friendly acknowledgement. They had met just a few weeks ago, when Alcibiades first came to the gymnasium. The young man had introduced himself as Socrates and explained to Alcibiades that he was the son of Sophroniscus who had been a life-long friend of Alcibiades' father. Although there was something slightly unsettling about the young man's manner, even though Alcibiades was uninitiated in the ways of men, he knew that this person would never injure him. Zopyrus had repeatedly warned him to avoid all conversations in the undressing room with anyone but boys his own age. Alcibiades knew from the painted vases which were kept stored in the little room off the men's quarters in his house that older men wanted some kind of odd touching from those who were yet boys. It all seemed incredibly silly to him. He was certain that he would never have to do such things against his will. While he could understand that there was much he did not know; he did know that he certainly was not going to allow a mere slave to dictate who would be his friends - whatever age they were. And so it was that he was now on casual talking terms with a grown-up man much more than two decades older than him. It made him feel special that some one this much older would take note of him and talk to him.

"How are you, Alcibiades? I see you are fresh from the wrestling exercises. I was just discussing with my teacher, Anaxagoras, the art of throwing one's opponent."

Alcibiades could not suppress his laugh. It was just too much to think that this fat and pale-skinned old man could ever have stepped into a wrestling pit. The boy looked to his new found friend to rescue him. "Socrates, what kind of throw is it that you are discussing?"

The older man was not at all offended by the boy's laugh. He interjected. "Alcibiades, I see that you do not believe that a man of my girth and flimsy arms and legs could get the better of any opponent. And you are right, if the contests are only in the mud-pit or dusty wrestling ground. But hasn't your father yet taken you to the courts or to the Assembly Hill where citizens close with one another armed only with speech?"

"Anaxagoras, the boy's father, Clinias, was killed in battle four years ago at Coronea. But he will, I am sure, soon learn the art of persuasive speech since Pericles is one of his guardians. I think that Alcibiades is in a hurry. We'll talk some other time to Alcibiades about the art of this peculiar kind of throw."

Alcibiades nodded and then excused himself. He had decided he would not even scrape the excess oil from his skin. He grabbed a towel from one of the attendants, dipped it in the bucket water which had just been drawn from the palaestra's cistern, and then used the wet towel to remove the streaks of oily dirt from his body and face. When he was done, he dressed and packed his small goat skin bag with the writing tablets and stylus which he had stored on a wall shelf nearby. When he made his way back towards the yard, he could see Zopyrus had taken up a station from which he could peer into the changing room while also appear to be waiting by the gate which led to the street outside the complex. His superintendent had been watching the two men who stood near Alcibiades as he had toweled off and clothed himself.

It was late afternoon by the time Alcibiades and his pedagogue had completed their marketing and finally made their way home - but not before disaster had struck. The melon treat, rather then refreshing them, had turned into a sweaty running retreat. Just as the melon dealer was preparing their mixed melon delight, a swarm of stinging bees descended upon them and their cups of juicy fruit pulp. These yellow-jacketed stingers seemed as intent upon giving up their lives by stinging whatever moved as they did in sucking juices from the brightly colored melon pulp. And so, running it seemed for their lives, the boy and his pedagogue arrived at their own home's front door soaked in sweat and their faces, necks, lower legs, and arms aflame with the poisoned barbs of the yellow stingers. The boy, try as he might, could not fight back the tears. And when his mother opened the door, there was her Divine Child, soon to be the elect favorite of the Divine Twain, a sobbing sweaty boy with eyes almost swollen shut and red welts everywhere there was bare skin. Her beautiful golden-haired fair-skinned blue-eyed Apollo had turned into a gorgon!

Dinomache stood motionless at the door way, looking in disbelief at the disfigured face of her boy. Then anger rose up her neck turning her pale and still beautiful face crimson red. Without even looking away from her son, she clenched her hand and like a crazed cat raked her long nails across the face of her boy's pedagogue. Her anger still mounting, she turned her eyes towards her now terrified servant, and in a cold threatening voice, delivered judgment. "Zopyrus, you incompetent idiot! I will have you lashed until your back is raw meat! Could you not keep this child safe? It is unpardonable that you let this happen on this day, the eve before my son's presentation to the Divine Twain and all of her celebrants at Eleusis. Get in here! Go to your quarters! You will be dealt with as soon as the holy days are over. I will not defile our household with your moans and groans until our grieving for the divine maiden has passed. Now go and stay away from my son until he returns from Eleusis!"

Zopyrus wiped the blood from the line of thin cuts that his mistresses nails had carved across his forehead and with his head bowed begged for forgiveness even as he tried to explain that the boy's current condition was not really his fault. "But, Mistress, I could do nothing to save us from the bees. Look at my legs and cheeks. Ask the boy, he will tell you."

"Shut up, and get out of my sight!"

Zopyrus, without another word, slid past his mistress and retreated to the small room which had been converted from a pantry into his quarters. Dinomache took her boy's hand and led him through the entry hallway and out into the courtyard by the cistern. She would clean him up there and finish her preparations for the Greater Mysteries Eve commemoration which would begin just before the sun set. Her aged father, Megacles, and her cousin, Ariphon, would soon arrive and she would not have them see her son in this state!

The last two months had not been easy for Dinomache. The boy's legal guardians, she felt, had intruded far too much in the day to day care of her son. They had insisted adamantly that Alcibiades live downstairs now. What right did they have to insist that he should now be moved out of her quarters to the downstairs rooms of the man's quarters? Oh yes, she knew that he must be sent off to the gymnasium and at seven he must begin the physical training preparing him for soldiering. But really, he is still a boy, and what harm could it possibly do for him to spend another year or so upstairs with her and his older sisters? They did not know that her son was special and, unlike others, was visited nightly by unfriendly spirits. He often called out in his sleep and tossed about as though he was wrestling some hideous creature. On many nights when he was so visited, she had taken him from his little cot and brought him in to her own bed. Caressing his forehead as she allowed his little arms to encircle her neck, she would hum the same gentle melody that her own mother had murmured in her ear when she too needed comfort. To feel his small hands on the back of her neck and the warmth of his now regular and serene breathing on her bosom brought her immeasurable happiness. To love like this and to once again be joined body to body in a union untroubled by the implacable forces of erotic strife returned her to that blessed paradise of her own childhood - a time before Zeus the ravisher had come to steal, as he always must, the maiden from her mother.

What could his guardians or even her father know about all this? She often thought to herself that after the time the little boys were driven from their mothers and made hard by their years in the Gymnasium and the *epheboi* barracks, men could never again love like this. Maybe this is why so many of the men had no interest in joining the ranks of those who would be thrice born. Men, it seemed to her, did not love anyone with the tranquil but yet passionate steadfastness of body and soul entwined together in a giving that is needed, and a need for giving. This is why, she thought, that so many men could not even imagine why anyone would wish to be reunited forever with a loved one now deceased. At most, men hope they might live again so as to bathe forever in the light of some kind of glory. Well, maybe her boy would be different. She would teach him how to love and be loved - if only they would not tear him too soon from her side.

"Sit still, Meilichios!" She was dabbing him with a soft swathe of goat fleece so as to clean the streaks of oil and grime that covered his face, arms, and legs.

"Mother, why don't you call me, Alcibiades, like grandfather and my uncles do? Isn't that my real name? Zoppy tells everyone at the Gymnasium that I am Alcibiades, son of Clinias and Dinomache the Alkmeonid." The boy was squirming and rubbing the red blotches on his neck which now were growing redder, the more he scratched their itch with his fingers."

"Let me ask you a question, Meilichios. Why is it that you don't lisp when you are alone with me? I call you 'Meilichios' because you are so sweet, and the God's kind gift to me when I thought he was forever angry at me and my kin. It is not too much for a bright boy like you to answer to two names, is it? You will always be Meilichios to me, my Darling. Now, quit rubbing those red marks. You are just making them worse. We'll find some way to stop the itch and make them go away, so you can be what you must be at Eleusis, the unblemished Divine child."

"But Mommy, am I not too old for that? The big boys at the palaestra today circled around me, all sucking their thumbs and pointing to their cocks, all chanting,

'What a *pwetty wittle* baby, Alcibiades is.
Just *wigh*t for the *Hollwy Motheh* at Eleusis.
Mommy's *wittle darwing*, like a little girl,
Alcibiades would you give my bigger thumb a whirl.'"

Tears that he would not show to anyone else, not even Zoppy, were rolling down his cheeks. He had felt such a rage then, to be laughed at and to be unable to do anything about it. The boys that had circled him were too big and too many. So only now, with just his mother, could he let out the excess of feeling that he had to shut his eyes tight against when he was alone on the little mound of dirt.

"Meilichios, they know nothing. They have never been inside the holiest of sanctuaries at Eleusis. When they grow up, they will all come to you and ask for your forgiveness, envying your good fortune to be one chosen to be thrice born and witness, while so young, the Divine Mysteries; yet not so young that you could not perceive what you see and not understand what you hear. Only, you must never tell anyone about what you will see and hear inside the holy of holies at Eleusis, and certainly not such boys as these who are all thumbs! Now, what are we going to do about all those red blotches? I could kill your Zoppy. But you know I won't. You are really kind of fond of him, aren't you?"

"Mommy, tell me again what I have to do in the procession and at the sanctuary. I get so confused about what comes when."

"I will, but not right now. I hear your grandfather and uncle Ariphon in our entry way. Come, let's greet them and they will help us get ready for Eleusis."

The visitors were already making their way into the courtyard. Megacles, well into his seventies now, was being supported by his nephew, Ariphon. Ariphon, although he was steadying his elderly uncle, was himself walking rather unsteadily. Dionomache, worrying that her unsteady father might take a fall by tripping over the uneven stepping stones that were laid out in the courtyard path to the outside seating area by the cistern, sent her son to help. "Meilichios, take your grandfather's other arm and give him the seat under the shade!"

The old man sighed and shooed his grandson away. "Alcibiades, I'm fine. Girl, you've got to stop coddling all of us! It's me holding up this starving initiate! I hope there is something we can get in his stomach now or he'll never even make it through the Potters' Quarter tomorrow morning out to the Sacred Way."

"Sit down, there, Father. Ariphon will be fine. The gods give strength to those who honor their fasts. I wish I could persuade you to receive the gift of the Mysteries. I can't bear the thought of you being turned away by Hermes when you must become one of Demeter's folks."

The old man winced as holding onto the edge of the stone table he lowered himself into his bench-seat. When he was seated, he shifted his legs until he found a position where the pain shooting up and down his lower body ebbed. Sometimes the stabs of pain would be followed by numbness in his legs that made him loose his balance. And so he always walked now, either supported by someone's arm or using his hands to hold onto whatever was near. It was hard for him to go out now and dine with others, since his hands had begun to shake. His neck, bent with age, made it difficult for him to even sit up straight. He could not eat or drink without constantly dabbing the dribble of saliva that flowed from his mouth, down over his chin and dripped from the folds of loose wrinkled flesh which hung from the apple of his throat.

"Daughter, sometimes I think you have lost your wits. Look at me. The nine day fast, the all day twelve mile procession to Eleusis, all that commotion - that would surely hasten my departure to the funeral mound. Besides, my mind is still sharp, and I'll be damned if I'm going to cloud it with hunger and fermented barley groats. Let my grandson say a prayer for me to the Holy Mother," the old man's eyes were now fixed on his grandson's face, "if she'll let him close looking like this! What in Tartarus happened to his face? He looks like he's got the plague!"

"It's stingers, Sir. They really itch." Alcibiades was always happy to see his grandfather and today especially. After the teasing at the Gymnasium, he had decided that he would not be the Holy Mother's Child. His mother, he knew, would be angry and not allow his withdrawal. He sensed that perhaps his only hope of escape lie with intervention by his grandfather. For he had some months ago overheard his grandfather complaining about the ridiculous spectacle of his seven year old grandson pretending to be the Holy Mother's suckling baby. And so with fresh tears in his eyes, he sidled over beside the old man and put his hand on his grandfather's knee. Sobbing so that his trembling body registered through his hand to his grandfather's thigh, he spoke to his mother while importuning his grandfather's intercession. "I shouldn't go to Eleusis like this, should I? Everyone will laugh at me. I hurt so much that I couldn't be still. Don't make me go, Mother."

Megacles lifted the boy's hand from his thigh and held him at arm's length, looking intently at the red welts which covered his grandson's face. He knew that Alcibiades must play his part as the boy of the hearth, but he had become sentimental and easily affected by whatever seemed to him to be fragile, delicate, and beautifully young. So he would try not to disappoint the small hand he had felt pressing him for help, even if he must quickly give way to the judgment of the more robust and those less susceptible to the siren call of life unencumbered with responsibility. Without taking his eyes off the boy, he addressed both his mother and his nephew, Ariphon, one of his grandson's legal guardians. "Can't a substitute be found for Alcibiades? Wouldn't it be better for all concerned if his admission to the Great Mysteries was really his desire?"

Dionomache shrugged her shoulders and turned in dismay to her cousin, Ariphon. "What am I to do, Ariphon? All of Athens will be offended if he does not take part. People will say, there they go again; the Alkmeonid take no heed to the laws of our holiest sanctuaries! He was chosen by divine lot! You are one of his legal guardians. Help me!"

Ariphon yawned and straightened himself up. He had been slouched over the table, with his chin resting on his own hands. Taking his elbows from off the table, he raised his hands palms outwards to Dinomache and with a wave of his hands to calm her down, he took charge.

"Uncle, the boy will be fine! Let him drink the sacred beverage with me tonight and that will take care of the sting welts. A little extra in his cup and he'll sleep like a sated Silenus tonight and still be numb at the rites tomorrow night. A little limestone powder to whiten his face and nobody will see the welts. His sacramental robe will cover everything else. Besides, your daughter is right. Now is not the time to give the rabble of Athens more cause to doubt Alkmeonid piety."

Megacles sighed and shrugged his shoulders as he deferred to his nephew. "Well, you might be right. It seems as though everyone in Athens is repeating Herodotus' tale of the miracle of Eleusis. Although, the twain is worshiped in many cities that we count among our enemies, it seems as if we Athenians think their presence at Eleusis means that they favor us above all others. Do you really believe that the God of Eleusis would turn our enemy away so that her rites might always be kept by Athenians, Ariphon?"

"I do, Uncle. Something wonderful must have happened there. I have talked to Dicaeus myself, and I see no reason to doubt his testimony."

"But Ariphon was not this same Dicaeus, who was serving the Persian invaders, a traitor to Athens and as such exiled and required to forfeit all of his family's land in Attica? Would he not wish to soften our citizen's animosity towards him by telling a tale that represents his effort to deflect Xerxes from his war of extermination against the Athenians?"

Ariphon smiled at his Uncle and repeated to him the words he had often heard Megacles himself employ whenever his Uncle had been accused by others of claiming Divine Providence at work in advancing Alkmeonid fortunes. "The gods seldom ever show themselves clearly. They often work their will right through and alongside of mortals' foibles and short-sighted schemes."

Alcibiades was all ears. He could see that the men's talk greatly annoyed his mother. She was now agitated, and appeared to be biting her lip as though to hold back some great secret she alone knew would shut the mouths of these unenlightened men. Indeed, she could not stay silent. "Men, I'm going to make sure the servants have everything ready for our sacred meal. I am so glad that my son of seven and my cousin of fifty will join the ranks of those who have seen the Great Mystery by tomorrow evening. Then you will understand why the God looks after her own not only in this life, but in the next also."

Megacles mumbled, "Isn't one life more than enough? I am happy for you, daughter, that you look forward to more." Even Alcibiades could hear in his grandfather's voice the same tone often reserved for him whenever an adult wished to make allowances for his childishness.

Dinomache knew there was no point in trying to explain anything to her father. Like her husband had, he would always treat her as a child. To both of them, a woman's religion was a concoction of emotion, fantasy, and a desperate childish hunger for attention from superiors that any free man - how often had Clinias thrown this in her face to remind her of her station - had outgrown by the time he had completed his military training. And so she rose from her seat, kissed her father on his cheek, and departed for the kitchen with a motherly word for her son. "Meilichios, I am so proud that the God has chosen you to be the boy of the hearth. The Divine Mother will have you ready by tomorrow, I promise. Grandfather will be proud of you also, even though he is unacquainted with the full blessing since he is one of those few in Athens who has never entered the sacred Palace and seen."

Megacles smiled warmly at Alcibiades. "Yes, it is a wondrous moment for one so young as you to be so lifted up before such a great throng of Athenians. But, my boy, remember always the words of our wise Solon, "Count no man happy until you see his end." Megacles patted his grandson on the head as he returned to his conversation with Ariphon.

"So, Ariphon, do you really believe Dicaeus' whole story as related by Herodotus? The cloud of dust over Eleusis thirty-seven years ago was not just the wind-driven dry red clay of the Eleusinian plain; the noise was just not some distant herd of cattle bellowing? Do you really believe, then, that when almost every citizen of Athens had fled to Salamis, and there were no mortals proceeding along the sacred way, the holy ones themselves came with a great throng of spirits keeping their own sacred rites? And did the great throng of the sacred ones enveloped in the cloud of dust indeed drift towards Salamis? And all this transpired to make clear to our treasonous Dicaeus that the Divine Host would fight on the side of the Greeks since the infidel Persian Xerxes had interfered with the Athenian's service to Holy Demeter and her daughter?"

"Yes, Megacles, I believe some such thing is possible, even if through our eyes we would see only wind, dust, and braying animals. How else can we really explain the miraculous coincidence of circumstances that led to the victory of Salamis in the face of almost impossible odds?"

"I think you underestimate the considerable seamanship skills of our captains and rowers. It is to Themistocles' credit - and I hated the money-grubbing son of dock-workers - that he understood right from the start that it was only at sea and in close quarters that our ship-based force could injure Xerxes vastly superior combined forces. And, you know, I got it first-hand from Leobotes that Themistocles was able through bribes and skillful ruses to induce Xerxes to leave the mainland after the battle of Salamis, even though there was little still to prevent his army from advancing down the isthmus and crushing the other allies in the Peloponnese."

"But Uncle, you forget that Demaratos, who was also in the Persian camp, corroborates Dikaios' story. Don't you find it quite striking that a Spartan king and an Athenian like Dikaios who fancied himself a champion of the poor of Athens would agree on anything?"

Megacles shifted his weight and leaned back to lessen the weight of his body on his tail bone. "Damn, isn't there any part of me that doesn't ache? It would have been much easier to have died in battle." The old man straightened up again and answered Ariphon.

"It is not that surprising they would agree on the story since both had similar motives for putting themselves into the best light possible with their own people. And by the way, don't forget the other story Herodotus tells about the conduct of men like Dicaeus who have set themselves up as the champions of the poor. My own father had told me the same story."

"What story is that, Uncle?"

Megacles addressed his grandson. "Alcibiades, you are becoming a man now, and soon you will leave behind the childish ways of women and boys. It is time that you understand that not everything that appears as sent by the God comes from beyond. Do you know how the tyrant Peisistratos once claimed Athena as his divine ally?"

"You have never told me that story, Sir. But I have heard of Peisistratos. Was he not the chief archon who first introduced the Panathenaic festival? Mother says that despite being a tyrant, this man did much good for Athens. Was he a bad man, grandfather?"

Megacles did not hesitate. "He was a bad man, Alcibiades. I don't know what your mother is thinking. He drove our family out of Attica and took all our land. He was a tyrant! But you make up your own mind. He may have built many fine temples for Athena and initiated a great festival for her, but I can tell you that not everyone was fooled by his scheme to persuade all of Attica that service to Athena was the same as service to Peisistratos. Right from the start almost, there were those in Athens who knew the truth. Listen to this story and you too will learn to mistrust those rulers who claim to be the special consort of some god."

"When my father and Dicaeus' own father, Theokydes, were very young men, Peisistratos went about among the poorest farmers in the Hill District and among some of the heavily indebted shop keepers who lived in what was then the Shore District promising them secretly that if they would support him, he would seize control of the government from the Council once again. He had previously held almost total power, but had been chased from Athens by his rivals. Now he secretly told his patrons that once in power, he would cancel all debt and force a redistribution of land. But to do this, he told them, he would have to be given absolute power over the Council and the prerogative to appoint only his supporters to the few courts which handled all of the grievances brought by citizens against one another. Nothing much came of any of this until one day Peisistratos decided to take matters more directly into his own hands by allying himself with my grandfather, Megacles, at least temporarily. You see, I think my grandfather thought that this time Peisistratos would share power in such a way that freedom would be preserved. Peisistratos agreed to seal this alliance by taking Megacles oldest daughter as his wife. My grandfather, you see, was being hard pressed by a rival party and he saw no way to keep his family safe but by allying with Peisistratos. What happens next, I'm somewhat ashamed to say, was partly planned by my own grandfather.

This part of the story you can hear Herodotus read from the manuscripts which he is selling down in the market place. If I had not heard the same story from my own father, I would not have believed that Athenians were so gullible when it comes to alleged 'miracles'. At any rate, Peisistratos and my grandfather Megacles wanted the common people of Athens to believe that Athena herself favored Peisistratos and wished to make him chief archon in Athens. To accomplish this, they searched about in regions outside of Athens until they found a strikingly beautiful and tall young woman. When they had found her, they dressed her in a suit of armor, placed a silver crown on her head, put a gleaming gold-handled sword in her hand, and somehow or other found a brand new chariot with two large white stallions in which she would ride. Having promised to compensate her father well, if he would reveal nothing about any of this, they then sent messengers ahead through the outlying villages and into Athens itself announcing that Athena herself was bringing her favorite, Peisistratos, back to rule Athens. By the time the impressive young woman approached the Acropolis, with Peisistratos not far behind, crowds had gathered. The people were prepared to offer this Athena their prayers, and welcome with open arms the man she wished to rule Athens alongside her from the Acropolis."

"But Uncle, I don't think anyone, even the simplest illiterate dock-worker, really believed this was Athena herself. Perhaps they thought she was some kind of possessed simple person, not unlike one of their daughters, who had been chosen by the Athena as her medium." Ariphon had to interrupt. He thought it unwise to so denigrate the eyes of faith with such a literal-minded interpretation of divine presence.

Megacles ignored his nephew. "Well, believe it or not, there were very many people who believed in this arranged miracle of divine intervention in our city's politics. While it was really a well-coordinated show of force that enabled Peisistratos to seize control of the state and maintain it long enough to consolidate his power, the tyrant had assured enough of the unlettered poor that their champion's forcible redistribution of other men's property and wealth could be entered into with good conscience since Athena herself approved. This part of his plan, he had kept secret from Megacles. Peisistratos then pushed my grandfather aside and behaved more and more like a king or tyrant. You know, Alcibiades and Ariphon, it took many years and much struggle for free men like your Alkmeonid forefathers to finally undo the enchantment of the Pisisitratid tyranny. So you should understand that when Dicaeus, a friend of Peisistratos' son, Hippias, who was willing to bring the Persian to our city in order to restore his tyranny, once again talks of miraculous appearances of the God, I can't help but think how too easy it is for the friends of tyrants to make use of simple folks' credulity and claim God's presence to vouch for their own evil enterprises. And that story, with all its unflattering truth about my own grandfather, is true."

Dinomache had returned and stood quietly by while her father finished the story. She had changed her garment. The everyday short-sleeved white linen dress had been replaced by a very long flowing earthen color robe fringed with a dark yellow hem and gathered in at the waist by a similarly colored broad yellow sash. She wore in her hair a crown of laurel interwoven with tassels that had been stripped from dried ears of corn. Two kitchen slaves stood by her and awaited her instructions for serving the special meal and the sacramental drink of fermented barley groats.

"Girls, we will set everything up here at the courtyard table. Put the corn meal cakes on the table and set the sacred drinking cups before the two younger men. My father and I will have the wine you have brought. Be careful to mix the wine properly with water from the cistern in the big vase and then pour it in the plain clay cups which Master Megacles and I will use. Do not pour the sacred beverage. I will see to that after it has been properly consecrated. And when you are done with all this, see that my two daughters are taken care of upstairs with their own regular supper."

As the servants followed her instructions in setting the table, Dionomache turned her attention to her son who appeared to be quite perplexed by the story he had just heard his grandfather relate. She could not let the innuendo of her father's story about false religion stand unchallenged in her son's mind. She would have him receptive to the true meaning of the Great Mysteries. And since the men could not simply silence one wearing the garment of a priestess, she saw no impediment to so ministering to her boy of the hearth, even though it was not part of her liturgy

"Meilichios, I am sure when you have walked about in the fields just outside the city during the hottest days of the summer, you have seen shimmering off in the distance what appeared to be a pond or a lake. Then as you drew nearer, you could see that you had been deceived. It was just a mirage, and there was no pond or lake there at all. But think how foolish it would be to conclude from that experience that since you were deceived by such an appearance, no lakes or ponds existed at all. Now it may well be that men have made pretence of the God's appearance, but surely this does not mean that God does not exist or never indeed truly presents herself to those who seek with clean hands and a pure heart."

Megacles sipped from the cup of wine which had already been placed before him as his daughter spoke. Dabbing his chin with the linen that the servants had set out by each cup, he burped and then interjected, forgetting that his daughter's vestments meant she now held a sacred office. "Girl, it is not becoming for a woman to make use of such logic. No wonder that no man comes forward to court you even though your time of proper grieving is long past."

Ariphon frowned at his Uncle and reminded him of their duty, "Please, Megacles, We are in a Holy Time, now!"

Dinomache ignored her father and began the ceremonial consecration of the initiates' sacred provisions. Since she was the only one present who in fact had already been initiated into the Great Mysteries, in this circumstance it was lawful and fitting that she serve as priestess of the family hearth.

First, she consecrated the corn-meal cakes. She lifted the silver plate on which they were served and with her arms outstretched lifted the plate before her at eye-level, facing the three who remained seated at the table.

"Eyes have not seen and ears have not heard what the Divine Twain has prepared for those who partake of the holy and secret Mysteries of the thrice born. We lift this bread of life, a gift of the Holy Mother, and ask that the young one, the boy of the hearth, nourished, will pass through the fire to eat at the table of everlasting life. Take, boy of the hearth and eat this holy gift of Demeter."

Dinomache the priestess broke a piece of the corn cake, walked slowly to where her son sat, and with her own fingers placed the cake into his mouth. Returning to her place in front of the table, she lifted the plate of bread again and addressed the other initiate, Ariphon.

"May the man who grieves with the Holy Mother for her lost one, wait yet one more day for his portion, the portion of the fallen husk that bursts forth with renewed life."

She moved around the table again, held out a piece of the broken cake to Ariphon. With upraised palms facing the priestess, Ariphon gestured his refusal of the life-giving food.

The Priestess intoned, "O, Divine Guide through the dark valley of Death, this one has fasted and is worthy. We beseech you, let him see and understand by the Great Fire. Enlighten this purified one that he might be made perfect and join the thrice born."

Dinomache then lifted the corn meal cake from the plate to her own mouth, and with her eyes focusing nowhere, ate. When she had eaten a portion for three, herself and the two initiatives, she then signaled for the servants to fill the three sacrificial cups from the vase which contained the sacramental drink of fermented barley groats made sweet with honey, the *kykeon*. Lifting one of the filled cups before her and holding it aloft before the men, she consecrated the holy cup and its ancient drink.

"O, Holy Trinity, Zeus the Husbander, Demeter-Persephone the Holy twain Virgin Wife, and the Divine Child Zagreus-Iakchos - bless this cup, womb and hearth of thy Divine Spirit. May this blessed drink course through our bodies, filling us with the holy light that will make the invisible visible and the secret things revealed. Bless each cup that we bear to thy Holy Temple, and may each one who drinks on the Sacred Way never again thirst as sinners do in Tartarus."

When the filled sacred cups were placed before the two initiates, the priestess called for the communion of the sacred cup. "Let us drain the sacred cups together and give ourselves over to that divine forgetfulness, the forgetfulness of the divine babe at his Mother's breast. Come, O Holy Trinity, that we, with your holy child, also might be thrice born."

The ceremony was over and none too soon for the old man. It was hard for him to listen to his daughter's prayers. Over the past four years since her husband's death she had grown more and more sanctimonious, as far as he was concerned. She made every festival, every rite, every ancient story a vehicle for propagating the teachings of Orpheus, one greater, she said, then Homer. What particularly galled Megacles is that he suspected that all of the supposed ancient writings of Orpheus and his son were really forgeries prepared by Onomakritos, a charlatan for hire who had helped the tyrant Peisistratos drive his own forefathers and all their kin from Athens. And so it made him very irritated to have to sit quietly and listen to his own daughter spout the phrases of the Pisisitratid lackey as if these words came directly from the mouth of Zeus himself.

"Now that we are done with our rites, do you think, girl, that you could have the kitchen servants bring your father something to eat – a proper meal? The boy will have to eat something more than the cakes after being at the Gymnasium all day, if he is to walk all day tomorrow. What about you, Ariphon, wouldn't you like a good piece of pork and some greens, or do the Priests insist that you arrive at Eleusis half dead from starvation?"

Dinomache had learned serenity. She paid no heed to her father's surly tone.

"Father, they have already been told to bring you and my boy supper as soon as the ceremony is completed. As for Ariphon, he has already told me that he plans to honor his fast in every particular as prescribed. But I am sure, Ariphon, you will stay and drink some more from the sacramental cup. And you are permitted to partake of some uncooked greens. I will leave you men to yourselves now. I must see to my daughters upstairs and make sure all our gear is ready for tomorrow's procession. When you are ready to leave, send Meilichios up to fetch me and I will see you off."

His daughter's serenity only further annoyed Megacles. "Dionomache, you've got to stop calling him by that name. It's so unmanly! We will be leaving as soon as we finish the meal. There is no need for you to see us out. Alcibiades can do that. And while we are eating together, we'll talk about his gymnasium. Unless I'm mistaken, even Demophoon, the first boy of the hearth, had to leave his mother and nursemaids behind when it came time to master the manly pursuits of the palaestra."

The old man turned away from his daughter and asked his grandson to take a seat alongside him at the table. The servants had already brought a large plate of sliced roast pork and a bowl of mixed greens.

"Alcibiades, sit down here and fill my plate, would you. Just greens on Ariphon's plate! You know, of course, that you are named after your father's father, just as I am named after my father's father. Alcibiades was a noble man as was your father. Now tell me, are you able to hold your own in the wrestling matches with your first-year mates?"

Alcibiades beamed with pride. "Sir, I'm really good at wrestling. Today, I took on many at once who were trying to throw me from my hill."

Ariphon smiled. "You were King of the Hill, were you, Alcibiades? They could not trip you up or lock their arms about you from behind. That is good. Learn to defend against every throw and you will one day be first man in Athens! Only, you must never play the part of the tyrant who would destroy the freedom of others so that he alone might lord it over all."

It was not at all clear to Alcibiades what his grandfather meant. How could you be the first man, the champion, the king of the hill, and not have all others submit to your will?

"I was champion until some older boys ganged up on me. They threw me from the hill, sat on me, and rubbed my face in the dust, shouting that now my black face really looked like that of the boy of the hearth. What should I do, grandfather, to them when they are bigger and stronger than me?"

The old man was pleased. His progeny was in fact being taught the hard lessons that toughened and prepared a boy to take his proper place as a man in the struggle for preeminence in the affairs of the city: its governance, commerce, and wars. "Alcibiades, I'll tell you a story about my grandfather's grandfather, and if you listen carefully you might learn what to do about such as this. Your Uncle Ariphon can help me if I leave something out. He knows this story well, since he has heard it from me and his parents since the time he was your age."

"Grandfather, is this story about tricking the people like Peisistratos and your grandfather had done with the goddess, Athena?"

Ariphon rolled his eyes heavenward. "Now look what you've taught the boy. I hope this next story makes a little clearer the good and honorable side of our family's heritage: the way the Alkmeonid family has always stood firm against any one who would rule autocratically and take away the freedom and property of others. You won't mind, Uncle, will you if I help out in this way."

Megacles chuckled. "No, of course not, Ariphon. But I think you will find that the Alkmeonid honor is front and center in this story. My grandfather's grandfather was the first in our family to stake everything on fighting tyranny. It was a long time ago, about 190 years ago, Alcibiades. But you know, your King of the Hill tussle today with the big boys reminds me that my namesake four fathers back knew how to deal with big strong men who would rub everyone else's nose in the dirt."

"Tell me, grandfather, what he did! Did Theseus help him? That is so long ago!"

"Well, the story started when this Megacles and his younger brother were seventeen and eighteen years old. They were almost both done with their gymnasium and were now in serious training preparing to compete in the manly combat sports, wrestling, the *pankration*, and boxing. One day, the wrestling master had left the palaestra for the day and put his most promising wrestler, a youth called Cylon, in charge for the day. This Cylon was incredibly big and well-muscled. No one among the other youths had ever defeated him in either wrestling or the *pankration* since the time they had begun competing. While he was in fact a superb fighter, Cylon was not well-liked or even respected. He was a terrible bully, a braggart, and given to cruelty.

It seems that Megacles' younger brother, Aristomache, had angered this Cylon by besting him in a punning contest in front of the letters master and other classmates during the morning of that very day the Wrestling Master would be absent. Aristomache, a shy youth, had never had anything whatsoever to do with Cylon before this day. But nevertheless, this cruel bully treated the incident as though it was some last and most terrible insult among a long series that had been directed at him by the Alkmeonid youth. And so that afternoon, when there was no wrestling master present and the boys of seventeen and eighteen were at that age where no pedagogues accompanied them any longer, Cylon decided that he would "get even" with the punster who had beaten him earlier that day."

Megacles paused as he refilled his cup from the large mixing bowl.

"What happened next, grandfather?"

Ariphon interrupted. "Uncle, do you really think the boy is old enough to hear this?"

"Yes, Ariphon, it is time. Forewarned is forearmed!"

Ariphon was not so sure. "Well, at least spare some of the gruesome details, Uncle."

"I will, Ariphon. Well, Alcibiades, Cylon gathered all the youths around him that afternoon and announced that the wrestling master had left instructions that he was to lead the practice that day, and that it was to be devoted to perfecting one of the more difficult and dangerous throw tactics, the mid-air reverse shoulder throw. To demonstrate the tactic he chose Aristomache as his wrestling partner. Megacles knew then what was about to happen. He had already seen Cylon, under the guise of practice, beat up many of those practice partners which for some reason or other had displeased him. And so he was not about to let his younger brother, who was small for his age and somewhat delicate in frame, be subjected to such a beating. So Megacles stepped out from the circle which surrounded the wrestling pit and demanded that he be Cylon's practice partner. Cylon, without hesitation, agreed. He began the demonstration by pointing out that this tactic should only be attempted by a man who was both strong and agile, like himself. He instructed all of them to watch closely so they could see all the elements of his technique. Then, without providing any instruction to Megacles, he closed with him in the standing position. Cylon wrapped his massive arm over Megacles right shoulder, across his shoulder blade, and then locked his hand with a strong grip around his back and under his left arm. Then in a sudden and violent move, he pulled Megacles on top of himself while turning himself in mid-air so that when they hit the ground together it was Megacles shoulders that were pinned underneath.

"The throw was so hard that Megacles lay stunned and was unable to get up. Cylon, laughing all the while, quickly returned to his feet and addressing both Megacles and his younger brother so all the youths could hear who got the last and best verse:

'If Alkmeonid boys were not so stuck-up and stiff-necked
And could learn to bend their necks before their betters
Then to the ground they would roll with heads unwrecked.
Like Scribes and Eunuchs, these boys must keep to letters.'"

"Grandfather, what a lousy verse! Why, I could do better than that and I am only seven. Did Cylon really versify like that?"

"Yes, Alcibiades, the verse was something like that. Cylon was not especially quick witted. If matters had ended there, there would have been no harm done. But when Aristomache, like you, chuckled at Cylon's awkward verse, Cylon insisted that he still must take the part of his opponent so that he might show the throw again. With his older brother still somewhat stunned and unable to intervene, Cylon then repeated the throw with Aristomache, only this time with even more violence. Poor Aristomache was thrown by massive Cylon, not just once, but three times in rapid succession. Then, when Aristomache cursed Cylon, Cylon instructed his friends to discipline the disrespectful trainee, by holding him to the ground belly down and caning his bare back and haunches until they bled.

"Megacles could do nothing. Although by this time he was on his feet, Cylon had him held fast by others. And so he was forced to watch his brother being caned, while all of Cylon's friends laughed and joked. Worst of all, when Cylon stopped the beating with the training rod, he then instructed his own brother who was just a year younger than himself to revive the Alkmeonid boy by inserting the end of the rod in his anus. This youth was as crude as his older brother Cylon was cruel. All the while laughing and boasting of the fierceness of his own rod, he revived the dazed young Aristomache by raping him. Afterwards Cylon made each of the youths swear with an oath that they would tell no one what in fact had been done to Aristomache. He made their oath even firmer by assuring those who were not among his friends, that should any one break the oath, he would make sure that such a one would soon find himself maimed and "half dead".

"Grandfather, how could Cylon get away with such a terrible assault on the son of a citizen?"

"They were all afraid of Cylon, Alcibiades. But Megacles and Aristomache never forgot their humiliation that day and they vowed to one another that one day they would repay Cylon, his brother and their friends. And that leads to the last part of this story when these Alkmeonid brothers and their friends, some years later, indeed did repay Cylon and his associates by chasing this bully who would be king from the Acropolis."

"Uncle, let me finish the story. It's getting late and young Alcibiades needs his rest if he is to get through all of the day long precession and then the rites at Eleusis after sunset." Ariphon could hardly keep his own eyes open now. The sacramental drink had made his head light and he knew he had to see the old man safely home before he could return to his own house. And so he wanted to hurry the story along.

"Please do, Ariphon. But don't leave out why so many of the good and beautiful of Athens rejoiced when these Alkmeonid men showed no mercy in ridding Athens of those who would make Cylon King and Tyrant." Megacles wanted his grandson to understand that, while Aristomache and Megacles were, no doubt, acting in part from motives of personal revenge, they nevertheless achieved something great for Athens.

Ariphon nodded. "Alcibiades, you are old enough to understand now that we Athenian men love to compete, each one striving with others to be the best. There was nothing in and of itself wrong with this man Cylon striving to be the best in the sports of the palaestra. Indeed, he would later win both the wrestling and pankration contests, not once, but twice at Olympia. For this he was rightly admired and praised. Our love of sports and competition of all kinds makes our city strong; since by challenging one another constantly our men become formidable as defenders of our city against all enemies. We Athenians, more than men of any other city, understand that such competition can nurture what is most precious of all. It is liberty that we prize most, but not the liberty that is the mere unbridled license of common and base folk. The true champions of liberty have always been the beautiful and good families who have repeatedly demonstrated that noble freedom which aspires after excellence and enterprises of high accomplishment. Our own family's loyalty to such an association of free men has always placed every generation of Alkmeonids in the forefront of those stake-holders in our city who like your own grandfather have risked everything to keep men who would in the name of the poor, put an end to the liberty of the good and the beautiful. Do you understand what I am saying, Alcibiades?"

Alcibiades had heard this phrase many times from his mother, "the good and the beautiful"; whenever she wished to remind her son that it was her lineage, and not the boy's father, Clinias, which singled him out as among those of whom great things would be expected. But what were those 'great things' he was to accomplish? Was it to be the boy of the hearth, be thrice born, a child of the Mysteries, a favorite of the Holy Mother? Or, was it to win the prize at one of the Pan-Hellenic games or some other prize altogether? What, the boy wondered, did it mean to be an Alkmeonid and why did people, it seem, always want something special from him?

Alcibiades wanted to hear what men such as his Uncle and grandfather thought about all this. It was confusing. How could an Olympic champion ever be bad? No, he didn't quite understand and so he asked another question.

"But didn't grandfather himself win the first prize at Olympia in the chariot races. And Mother has told me that sometime after this other men in Athens chased your grandfather out of Athens for ten years. I know that you are one of the good and beautiful. So what is it that Cylon did after winning the prize at Olympia that made him the enemy of the beautiful and good?"

Cylon's story was not completely new to him. His mother had told him the story before, but it had seemed to have in her telling a sad meaning. She always ended the story by reminding her Alkmeonid son, how even their most illustrious family of the good and the beautiful, could not avoid the entanglements of sin. She would make the sign of the thrice-born and always finish the story with a short prayer of thanksgiving for her salvation from the curse of the Alkmeonids. Although he had been away from his mother only for a short time in the men's world of the gymnasium, it had already become clear to him that the men's stories never ended with anyone being sad and sorry for anything.

His uncle continued the story. "Well, Alcibiades, Cylon, it seems took it into his head to put an end to the liberty of all the rest of the beautiful and the best men. Acting like his father-in-law, Theagenes the tyrant of Megara, he and his friends went about telling the poorest people of Athens that if he alone would be given the supreme rule, then he, Cylon, would force everyone in Athens to be equal. Whether or not any of these poor people believed this, I don't know. But every intelligent man knows that equality for all cannot be had without extinguishing liberty. Indeed, our family has always understood that genuine liberty will be best preserved by a cohort of men whose excellent enterprise, accomplishments, and honor raise the stake of each in the city so that no one of them will ever submit to the tyranny of one man rule or rule by the mob. At any rate, Alcibiades, Cylon and his friends, all heavily armed, marched up the Acropolis, and having occupied the Council House declared that Cylon alone would now rule in the name of the people. It was then that Aristomache and Megacles, realizing that Cylon would level all men and extinguish liberty, acted quickly to assemble others from the Council. These, they then persuaded to assist them in their plan to throw this man, who would be king of the Acropolis, out of their Council House. Cylon fled under cover of darkness, hoping to bring more armed men to his aid, men who were soldiers of his father-in-law, Theagenes the tyrant of Megara.

The remaining associates of Cylon, in order to hold their position until Cylon could return, shamelessly defiled the sacred chamber of Athena by claiming her protection. Megacles would not allow this shameless ruse in the name of our beloved Athena, and with the blessing of her priests, routed these scoundrels out into the open. When they refused to lay down their arms, they were slain."

But, uncle, why does my mother then think that Athena is angry with our family and that we must pass through cleansing waters and be born again if we are to escape her anger."

Grandfather would have the last word.

"Alcibiades, soon you will come to understand that the gods of women, children, and slaves must be put away if you are to become a man. But for now, my boy, you must still pass through many hard days of schooling before you can take the full measure of your man's quarters. March to Eleusis, be thrice born, please your mother and mind your slave attendant. So off to bed, but if you would really become a man, do not let the ghosts and hobgoblins of unmanly dreams chase you to the women's quarters!"

CHAPTER FIFTEEN
IN THE HOUSEHOLD OF THE OLYMPIAN
(Winter 438 B.C.)

Let me say that our system of government does not copy the institutions of our neighbors. It is more the case of our being a model to others, than of our imitating anyone else. Our constitution is called a democracy because power is in the hands not of a minority but of the whole people. When it is a question of settling private disputes, everyone is equal before the law; when it is a question of putting one person before another in positions of public responsibility, what counts is not membership of a particular class, but the actual ability which the man possesses… And, just as our political life is free and open, so is our day-to-day life in our relations with each other. We do not get into a state with our next-door neighbor if he enjoys himself in his own way, nor do we give him the kind of black looks which, though they do no real harm, still do hurt people's feelings. We are free and tolerant in our private lives; but in public affairs we keep to the law. This is because it commands our deep respect.

(Thucydides. *History of the Peloponnesian War*, Book II: 37, Pericles' Funeral Oration)

Alcibiades lay awake on the couch in his new sleeping quarters. The sun had been up now for at least an hour, but it was a holiday and so there was no need to get up for the trek to the Gymnasium. He had decided that he would just stretch out and see if he could make his toes reach to the end of this very long couch as his hands, stretched above his head, touched the other end. My father must have been very tall, he thought. Although he had been moved into his father's quarters some three months ago on the occasion of his twelfth birthday this big couch and its surroundings still seemed strange. It was too quiet. He missed the upstairs life with his mother and older sisters. Things must change, he had been told by his grandfather and his legal guardians. Now that he was about to begin the very first stages of his military gymnastic he must live like an Athenian citizen, apart from the soft and enervating intimacy of the women's quarters.

Five years had passed since Alcibiades had been initiated at Eleusis into the Mysteries of the Twain. His mother had led him to believe that he would be mysteriously changed once he had joined the band of those who had been born again. But although he had indeed been bedazzled by the great fire, the thunderous clashing of the golden cymbals, and the divine revelations of which he could speak to no one but others who had been initiated; he had found that his exalted status of that evening at Eleusis seemed to count for nothing in his daily struggles with other youths at the Gymnasium. Oh, to be sure, when the eyes of thirty thousand Athenians were fixed on him as he rode in the cart escorted by the chief priest through the gates of Eleusis' sacred precinct; he felt a rush of excitement stronger than anything he had ever experienced.

But the memory of this feeling only made his anger and humiliation bitterer when he found himself bested in the wrestling pit or boxed on the ears by a stronger boy assigned to drill with him in the *pankration*. And when it was a boy his own age that was besting him, then it was as though something deep down inside him felt so endangered, so cornered and so suffocated, that fear rose up through his chest into his neck and face, turning them dark red. But fear is not manly, he had been taught, and so it had to be turned away from him. The repressed fear became a raging frenzied outburst of violence, a violence which in its mindless force and desperation seemed to give him superhuman strength.

Just yesterday this had happened in the Palestra when Polystratus, a boy just a few months younger than him, had gained the advantage with a chest lock and was lifting him off the ground so as to win the wrestling throw. With everybody looking on and the wrestling master no more than a few paces away, the image of his grandfather's young brother bested by Cylon flashed before his inner eye, and then he heard himself shouting NO! And with no thought of anything but prevailing and unable to free his own arms, he lowered his chin onto the upper arm of Polystratus and sunk his teeth deep into his enemy's flesh. Not even the blows of the wrestling master's rod on his back could make him release his bite. Only when Polystratus, yelping in pain, unlocked his grip and yanked his arms away did he feel the blows on his own back and hear the angry voice of the master shouting, "This is not the *pankration*. No biting or eye gauging! What kind of girl are you, that you bite so?"

When Zopyrus escorted him home later that day and began also to upbraid him for this conduct, he had already rid from his mind the shame others would have him feel..."Zopyrus, the reason why you are a slave and I am one of the beautiful and good is because you would let the rules of those who rule you rub your face in the dust. I was not unmanly today. I fought like a lion rather than be vanquished. So I don't want to hear anything more about it from you."

Today and for the next three days there would be no gymnasium. It was the beginning of the Thesmophoria holy days. As she had done for every year he could remember, his mother would leave home and spend three whole days at the women's Thesmophoria encampment. Arrangements had been made for him to spend the next few days in the household of his guardian, Pericles. He was excited over the prospect of being in the household of what even his schoolmates now referred to as the 'Olympian'. Even though he still had no clear idea of how or why this kinsmen, one of his surrogate fathers, had come to be likened to Zeus Almighty; Alcibiades understood that Pericles, more than anyone else in Athens, seemed to be the one towards whom every Athenians' eyes were directed. He is very high, thought Alcibiades, and I must see how it is that he stays aloft, never thrown down by anyone.

"Meilichios, have you made sure that Zopyrus has packed the food basket that you are to take along to Pericles' house." It was his mother. She was standing at the door way of his sleeping room. Ever since he had moved downstairs into his father's sleeping quarters, his mother made a point of appearing at his doorway twice a day, both to awaken him in the morning and to bring him some book when the candles were lit at night. "You must get up now. You are expected at Pericles house by mid-day."

"Alright mother, I am awake. Will you please stop calling me Meilichios! I am Alcibiades, son of Clinias of the house of mighty Ajax. You go on to your woman's festival. I can finish packing by myself. I'm not a baby, anymore, you know."

****

It was mid-day when Alcibiades and his attendant arrived at Pericles' home. Pericles had instructed his steward to take Alcibiades' belongings and put them in the small guest room which also served as a pantry for the men's quarters. So after the steward had shown Alcibiades his sleeping room, he dismissed the boy's attendant and ushered Alcibiades through the main hall and into the inner courtyard.

Pericles greeted his young ward.

"Come and join us, Alcibiades. You must be hungry. Help yourself to the lamb kabobs there on the tray. And pour yourself some of the chilled juice from the pitcher. I want you to sit over there under the shade of the portico while you eat."

Alcibiades nodded and smiled, but could not think of anything to say that would not betray his own confusion. He did not how to address his host. Yes, he is a kinsman (his mother had told him that she and Pericles were cousins) and Pericles, he knew, is one of his guardians now that his father was gone. But what should I call him? Uncle, Sir, General, Cousin - what is best? Everything was unfamiliar. The man standing before him was not the Pericles he had seen in his own house or for that matter anywhere in public. There he was, alright, but where was his helmet? The bald crown of his head, the furrowed forehead, and long narrow cheek bones - was this really the first man of Athens? He looked so old and not at all like Zeus. And who were these two very old men with him? And who was the woman whose hand was massaging his neck? She must be a courtesan Pericles has hired for his guests' entertainment, because certainly no wife would be in the men's quarters with other men present.

"Thank you, Sir. But do you want me to go and eat upstairs so that you and the courtesan might continue entertaining your friends? My mother..."

Pericles interrupted him, waving his hand and shaking his head side to side so as to cut Alcibiades off.

"Don't worry about what your mother might or might not want while you are here with me, Alcibiades. I want you to stay and listen to our conversation. It is time for your schooling to move outside of the gymnasium."

"I will listen carefully, Sir, if that is what you want of me."

Pericles turned towards his guests and introduced them, "These two men are here to advise me on matters of our city. They are my most trusted friends and even though neither of them are Athenian citizens, they have proven to me many times that they see more clearly than my fellow Athenians what is best for the common good of our citizens. I think you have probably seen both of them in the Agora engaged in learned discussions with your friend, Socrates. They both tell me that Socrates, will soon be known as Athens' native son Philosopher. On my left is Anaxagoras and on my right is Protagoras. This beautiful woman behind me is not a hired courtesan. She is Aspasia and lives now with me. She is more highly educated than most of the high born men of Athens and has far more practical wisdom about governing than most who hold office in Athens."

So, thought Alcibiades, this is Aspasia, the bad woman my mother says has made a fool of Pericles. "I hope you don't ever have such a woman in your life, Meilichios," she said. "Look, what this woman has done to Pericles." When Alcibiades had asked his mother to explain exactly what it was Aspasia had done to Pericles, she only sighed with exasperation as she muttered something about him being too young to understand. Now this same woman was greeting him even as she was applying a lavender scented lotion to the neck and shoulders of Pericles. She did not look like other Athenian women of his mother's age. Long soft shoulder-length curls, brown and red at the same time, her hair caressed her pale and yet pink cheeks. Her lips seemed to be smiling and pouting all at once, and they were even pinker than her cheeks. Although she had draped a cloak about her shoulders, her robe was drawn together by a large gold broach so as to leave uncovered the even whiter skin of her unusually large but uplifted breasts. Her eyes were hazel colored, but when she looked at him, and the sunlight of late afternoon made her eyes shine, they turned a deep green. When she spoke to him, he felt in her voice and saw in her eyes a playfulness he had never sensed in any of his household women. "Alcibiades, you are a handsome lad! I can see why it is our friend Socrates has taken such an interest in you. He finds in your eyes, intelligence, and in your face and body the first signs of a handsome manhood. I am very pleased to meet you. Please, sit here at this little table behind me so you can help yourself to some of the figs and sweets after you finish the meat. Don't sit there under the portico. It's too far from us. And you really shouldn't eat too much of that lamb. It has been sitting out all morning. Here you will be able to hear everything, as your Uncle Pericles wants, but you will not be too close to Pericles' philosophers. They look harmless enough, but they are reputed to be like poison-ivy. Their words are never abrasive, but if you let them rub against you too much they will irritate and enflame your mind with the itch of curiosity."

"Yes, sit down there, Alcibiades." As he spoke to his young guest, Pericles reached back and caressed the hands on his neck. "You can stop now. I feel much better. The stiffness is gone. Thank you, Aspasia. Sit down beside me here. You know, don't you Alcibiades, that she is only teasing Protagoras and Anaxagoras. If only all Athenians could smile like you do, Aspasia, and let our philosophers disturb us with their unsettling inquiries without exiling or killing them. Consider this up and coming politician Diopeithes. He seems to be intent on outlawing the theories of our friend, Anaxagoras. Today in the Assembly, he has introduced a decree which would make it a criminal act to engage in speculations about the cosmos which promote atheism. What do you make of this Protagoras? Am I right, Anaxagoras, in thinking that Diopeithes means to target you especially as an enemy of our religion?"

"It is not Anaxagoras that Diopeithes aims at, Pericles," Protagoras interjected. "It is you he wants to bring down. Anaxagoras and I are metics - we can never enter the contests of Athens' political life. But he means to loosen your hold on the people by showing them the atheism and immorality of your associates."

"So, Protagoras, you think that our Diopeithes is not so much zealous for orthodoxy as he is for advancing the agenda of those who wish to shove me aside? But who are these people? Cimon is dead, Thucydides has been ostracized, and the party of the aristocracy is now leaderless and dispirited. Will there ever be a moment when our state can enjoy peace and not devour ourselves in fratricidal political cannibalism? I hear the silly marketplace chatter about Pericles the Olympian, but our poets in all their fantasies never made Zeus the target of two decades of calumny, conspiracy, poisonous accusations, and threats of violence. Look at my young cousin, Alcibiades. His face is clear and yet unmarked by the struggles of public life. I am fifty-seven and I feel one hundred and fifty-seven. And without my long beard and the helmet I always wear in public, from the neck up I could compete with our friend Socrates for playing the part of the old man of the woods, Silenus.

"Pericles, it is not like you to be so self absorbed, like a sad Narcissus. Are you not feeling well, today? Let's do what we have done many times before. We must think as clearly as possible about what is going on and then act so as to take control of the forces at work and steer them so that Athens and you continue to do well. Anaxagoras, Aspasia, I, you, the common people, and a cast of many envious politicians are all churning now, mixed up in a whirl of motives and agendas. As our friend Anaxagoras might say, we must trust that Mind will prevail if only we understand how to discern the patterns of human nature and then adopt plans, policies, and goals which will so order our city so that many may flourish."

"Yes, you are right, Protagoras. But it is good for my young kinsman to see that I, the supreme commander of Athens' armed might, am a mere mortal, and not one of the immortals who never grow weary. But, Alcibiades, mortals can storm heaven when they are of one Mind and when wise counsel is prized. Aspasia, Anaxagoras, what do you see in this edict of Diopeithes?"

Anaxagoras answered first, "But this is Athens, my friends, the most enlightened city in the entire world. Here laws already on the books protect men's freedom to speak their mind. And do not most of our Senators and Assemblymen as gentleman of education regard religious matters as open to many interpretations provided that no offense occurs in the public rites and liturgies of the city festivals? I cannot think that the edict of Diopeithes is anything more than a token of the city's determination to reassure the common people that their governors will maintain the city's holy days. Since no names are cited in the decree, I think it will be consigned to the soon forgotten collection of inscriptions that clutter the dusty shelves of some little used public building. So I think the best course of action is simply to ignore Diopeithes' edict."

"So, Aspasia, what do you think?" Pericles turned towards her like a novice about to receive guidance from an expert.

Alcibiades could scarcely believe his eyes. The first man of Athens was seeking the advice of a woman! More than that! Pericles seemed to defer to her like one of his young comrades would to the fencing master as he received his first lesson in how to parry the sword thrust of an enemy bent on killing him.

Aspasia sighed and now seemed almost solemn as she answered Pericles. "I hope Anaxagoras is right, but just yesterday I heard

Anaxagoras' former student Archelaus urge Socrates to be more circumspect in his conversation in the marketplace. Archelaus was telling Socrates how two of his own students whose fathers are associates of Diopeithes let him know that formal charges are already being prepared against Anaxagoras as an Atheist and a Medizer. Archelaus was warning Socrates that if this prosecution goes forward, the students of Anaxagoras such as he and Socrates could be next."

Anaxagoras interrupted politely, "But how anyone could believe that I am an agent of the Persians is beyond my comprehension. It was more than thirty years ago now that I turned over all my property in Clazomenae to others and left there to take up residence in Athens. Since then I have devoted myself completely to the study of the heavens and have had no time for politics. Now the charge of atheism, I can understand. But, if people just read carefully what I have written in my work 'On Nature', they would understand that I, like Protagoras and all the other philosophers, do not deny the existence of the Divine. It is just that we all deny that it is possible for humans to know with any certainty the true nature of the Divine. You, Pericles, have heard me discuss this many times here in your home and in my public lectures."

Aspasia waited a moment so as to be sure Pericles had nothing to add. Then she rose from her seat beside Pericles so as to face Anaxagoras. "Let me comment on just that point, Anaxagoras. That is precisely the fact Pericles' political opponents will seize on to make headway with the people against Pericles in the courts."

"Aspasia, go ahead! Give us the details of how you think this will play out. I see that my young protégé and kinsmen is all ears - although he appears flabbergasted to see and hear a woman speak on equal terms with men about such matters. Let him learn first hand of your political savvy."

"Pericles, it is, you must remember, very far from the normal what goes on here in the privacy of your home. I'm sure young Alcibiades has heard all the gossip about you and me - and it is not my intelligence that has made me notorious, especially to the proper women of Athens' best families. So it is asking a lot of a twelve-year-old, no matter how precocious, to set aside the lurid pictures of the Aspasia of gossip which cloy his mind's eyes and ears."

Pericles smiled and looked intently at the face of Alcibiades, searching for some sign of curiosity. "I don't see in young Alcibiades' eyes the self-righteousness of a too narrow and priggish morality. You know that he spends considerable time with Socrates. Because of this association with our young Athenian philosopher, I am sure my cousin has already been opened up to the kind of talk that takes a course, as you say, very far from the normal and conventional. So go on and tell us how this decree of Diopeithes will snag both Anaxagoras and me. You don't need to mother him, my dear. He is now on the threshold of his military training and soon will be called to risk his life for our city. It is not too soon for him to learn the realities of how our men become wily and strong first in their contests with one another."

"Alright, Pericles, this is how Diopeithes' decree will probably find you as its ultimate target. You will pardon me if, in my womanish way, my concern for you makes me dwell on the risks of real harm to you and all those who are close to you."

"Go on, Aspasia!"

"Since the decree of Diopeithes does not mention any particular sanction, it can only have judicial force if it is tied to some kind of harm to the state which, like treason, threatens the common security of our people. So, something like this will happen. One of our very patriotic and highly decorated hoplite officers who are charged with the last stages of training our young men for their military service will register a formal complaint to you as the Supreme Commander of the Armed Forces. A copy of the complaint will also be sent to the Senate Council that prepares the agenda of the Assembly. The complaint will note that copies of Anaxagoras' book, *On Nature*, have been found in the barracks of our *epheboi*. The complaint will go on to document how Anaxagoras' naturalistic account of the origins of the cosmos leaves no room whatsoever for the work of Zeus. This, the complaint will note, would not be so bad if the theory admitted it was only speculation. But passages will be cited that characterize

Anaxagoras' account as laying claim to being true, while stories like those found in Homer and Hesiod about the beginnings of the cosmos are only the fantastic opinions of playful poets. Finally, and this is the important point, the complaint will bring forward and name *epheboi* who refuse to swear the oath in the name of Zeus and Athena which promises unflinching service to the defense of Athens. It will be noted that the young men refused to repeat the oath because they claimed that their own understanding of truth, what they think to be a 'more enlightened' piety, did not permit them to subscribe to any kind of profession of belief in the gods of the poets. If the officer would strike reference to such gods from the oath of loyalty to the city, then the youths claimed that they could take part in the closing ceremony of *epheboi* training. The charge will be leveled that these young men have been corrupted by the atheism of Anaxagoras. The prosecutors of the complaint will argue that if the source of this impiety is not eliminated, then such impiety among our young men will spread like a contagion, infecting and weakening the very moral fiber which inspires our soldiers to sacrifice their lives, if need be, for the defense of Athens.

Either this, or some scenario like this, will thus lead to a legal action which aims to root out the pernicious influence of Anaxagoras. The action will not take place in the courts but in the Assembly itself. There they will call for Anaxagoras' exile and the collection and destruction of all copies of his book. And it is at this juncture that you, Pericles, will be called by Anaxagoras' prosecutors to testify to your understanding of Anaxagoras' book and how it might or might not undermine the civic virtue of our soldiers. They will be confident that this cannot but be a successful gambit which will one way or another discredit you before the people. Either you will rise to the defense of your friend, Anaxagoras, and thus yourself be seen as a protector of impiety, or, if you simply stand aside, the prosecutors will have won an easy victory and shown Pericles to be ready to abandon his friends. This will embolden them to move on to additional prosecutions against your associates until you stand alone and then can be easily pushed aside."

Pericles wanted Aspasia to continue without interruption, but Anaxagoras seemed exasperated by Aspasia's characterization of his book's impact on Athenians.

"Aspasia, I see by Anaxagoras' raised eyebrows that he finds your scenario incredible. While I am very interested in hearing more about this 'gambit' and how you would advise me to escape it's harm, let us consider his doubts about the plausibility of your hypothetical future. Anaxagoras, please, speak freely and tell us what about Aspasia's scenario you find so unlikely!"

"Pericles, I think you need not worry about any further action in the Assembly or the Courts concerning Diopeithes' resolution. I know this Diopeithes and think I understand his motives. His family lays claim to the hereditary priesthood which arranges and presides over the biannual liturgies devoted to Zeus at Acharnae. He has somehow gotten into his head that these liturgies will no longer receive any state subsidies. While it is not a fortune, his family for generations has received a stipend of one talent for presiding over the ceremonies of the Diasia and Zeus Meilichios. Diopeithes' son, who has taken as his teacher my associate Archelaus, tells me that his father has gotten it into his mind that people are losing interest in coming out for the ceremonies on holy days because, as is the case with his own son, they are intrigued by these atheistic accounts of the speculative philosophers who inquire into the heavenly things above and the things beneath in the water and the earth. Diopeithes, I am sure, does believe in the gods as described by Homer and Hesiod. But it is also the case that it would be a significant loss of income for his family, should the state terminate the subsidy. And so, when Diopeithes won election to represent his deme, Acharnae, immediately at his very first session of the Assembly he persuaded a number of assembly men to sign on to this edict that bears his name. And since to many others the edict seemed harmless and somewhat vague, a majority of the Assembly was willing to vote for it and be on record as pious defenders of Athens' religious heritage. So, I think that as long as no action is taken by you or your associates in the Assembly to withdraw the part of funding provided by the state for the Acharnae liturgies, nothing more will come of Diopeithes' edict. And you, Pericles, have always been scrupulous as a politician in maintaining the public liturgies. So this will require no new action on your part."

"Protagoras, could it be that Anaxagoras is right, that we need not worry about this provided that we assure Diopeithes that there will be no changes whatsoever in state subsidies for the holy days and liturgies held at the temple in the Acharnae district? Or should we, as Aspasia proposes, be prepared for some kind of onslaught of broader and more sinister opposition which will employ this decree as its opening gambit to undo our policies and leadership?"

Protagoras was certain that once again some kind of attack on Pericles was underway. And so now, he thought, was the time to advise him as to the kind of opposition that might capitalize on Diopeithes decree. "Pericles, you need to appreciate how your political rivals see your source of power. There are some who are still bitter about the way you have diminished the political power of those whose wealth and prestige is to be traced back to the aristocratic families who from many generations ago have owned the best land in Attica. They see you as one who has purchased the political support of the common people by providing for them large stipends of various kinds from the state's treasury. Thus, they say, while Cimon was generous and opened his land up and made gifts to the poor, all the while championing aristocratic government, what you did, not being able to compete with Cimon's wealth, was to push an agenda which taxed the properties and lives of the rich so as to buy from public funds the support of the many commoners. Thus, they say, you authored legislation which would turn over our courts to commoners by providing them with payment for what should be uncompensated jury duty. Assemblymen from the demes wherein there are many commoners love the large public works programs which you and your democratic associates have persuaded the Assembly to fund. The rebuilding of the temples, the beautification of city monuments, and the construction of showy music halls employ thousands and in this way has filled the pockets of the herd with gold coins.

Your imperial policy of constantly sending out our trireme fleet, manned by paid thousands of low-life Athenians, so as to constantly intimidate our own allies in the Delian League, is more of the same pandering to the commons, according to your critics. There is no more real Persian threat, they say; and your land grants to thousands of poorer Athenians on lands taken in the islands and elsewhere as you and your greedy party of merchants have transformed the territories of the Delian League into an Athenian empire so as to feed the avarice of the many commoners: all this, they say, is the way Pericles has firm purchase on the people's government.

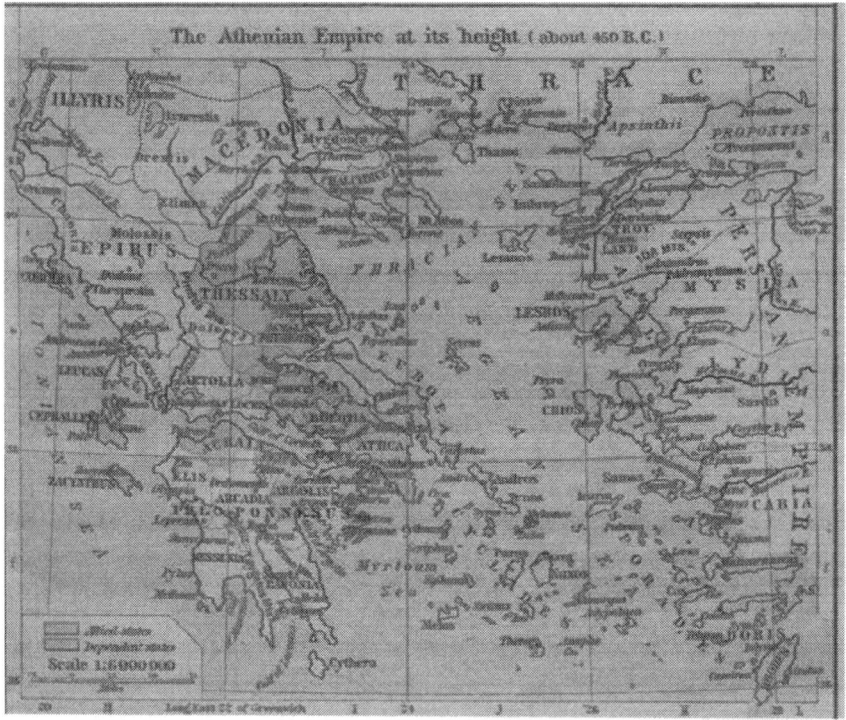

The Athenian Empire

Of course, Pericles, what they do not say is how all of this has not in any way increased your own personal wealth. Nor do they acknowledge that in every exercise of office you have held, you have encouraged the Assembly and the courts to audit your expenditures of any public funds. Envy and pride, I think, has blinded them. And so there remains - even after Cimon has died and you seem to have come out on top in the most recent ostracism of Thucydides - a reservoir of bitterness among the few and the rich. These people still view you as one who has betrayed your own aristocratic lineage. They are always plotting and working to undo those institutions that have made the common people office holders, voters, and jurors. They are instinctively conservative and delude themselves in thinking that Athens was better off when she was a market town for the surrounding farms then now when she is the capital of a prosperous commercial and cultural empire that has allowed many to flourish."

Pericles sighed. "Yes, I know there is nothing I can ever do to please these champions of the aristocratic families. To this day, there are still those among them who simultaneously describe me as the one behind the assassination of Ephialtes and the death of Cimon in Cyprus. According to these people I act only out of an endless ambition for my own glory and power. Thus, they say, it makes no difference to one like me if I have crushed beneath my march to political preeminence both a champion of the common people and the noble leader of the aristocracy."

"Yes, the aristocrats resent your accomplishments and are envious of your fame. But that is not your only opposition, Pericles. There are now a generation of commoners who have grown up with the new institutions and the prosperity of our commercial empire. They want more. They see you as too cautious. Where you counsel moderation and caution in the use of our military power, they wish to further extend the empire and look to wrestle from Sparta, Thebes and even far away Syracuse, control of commercial opportunities here on the mainland and to the West. They grow restive under your leadership and search for opportunities to loosen your hold on the government. Both these 'new men' and your older aristocratic opponents know that they cannot call into question your contribution to securing for the many a freer and more prosperous life. If there is a weakness in your standing with the commoners, it is because unlike them you are a genuine intellectual and it is just this trait that makes you somewhat alien to them. It is especially in religion that this difference becomes clear. Most of the commoners have no sympathy for what they take to be the effete idleness of Ionian speculations about Nature or the overly contentious and subtle arguments of men like me who tutor the children of the rich. They call us Sophists, but they don't really think we are wise at all. They think we are nothing but the hired hands of the ambitious sons of the rich. They say that I, Protagoras of Abdera, and other visiting metic sophists such as Zeno teach these oligarchic scoundrels how to argue both sides of any issue and how to make the true appear false, and the false appear true. Better that we honor the gods and faithfully pass on to our children the piety that helped us prevail at Marathon and Salamis. Thus, Pericles, if those who would push you aside and separate you from the people wish to make any headway, then, whether they be radical democratic imperialists or reactionary conservatives, they may forge some temporary alliance by playing upon your association with men such as I and Anaxagoras, and unconventional Aspasia and, as the commoners see it, the libertine artists who paint and sculpt themselves into a sacred history while they themselves don't believe in our traditions. You remember how tongues wagged about Polygnotus and Cimon's own sister Elpinice. I can't see it, but people say Polygnotus used Elpinice as a model for Laodice, one of the Trojan woman painted on the porch now called the Poecile. So, it was said that the painter has profaned our sacred story the *Iliad* so that he might bed Elpinice who was already betrothed to Callias at that time. Now, Pericles, the gossip is that your master painter at the Parthenon arranges affairs for you with noble women by promising to paint them into scenes on the temple frieze. The gossip doesn't stop there. It is said that Phidias finds time, even as he oversees the work of all the painters, sculptors, masons, and a host of other craftsmen involved in the construction of Athena's new temple, to serve as your pimp. Right there on site at the Acropolis in broad daylight noble wives of Athens' aristocrats have been procured for you, it is said, for the price of one of Pyrilampes' rare birds. No matter that you live with Athens' most beautiful and charming woman - Aspasia. They say your lust is insatiable, and that your circle of friends among the libertine artists is only too willing to satisfy it, provided you keep sending their way lucrative commissions for the temples and monuments to glorify Pericles."

Aspasia winked playfully at Protagoras as she pulled her gossamer shawl off of her shoulders. "Thank you for your kind compliment. But be careful or soon the gossip will paint you as the philandering philosopher whose honeyed tongue had its way with Pericles' own mistress. You are kind not to mention the gossip about me as Pericles kept woman. No matter that Pericles and his wife have divorced by mutual consent and that I have now lived here for almost ten years and that each day Pericles kisses me as he leaves the house with our front door open to the street for all to see. Then, in case anyone missed our kiss in the morning, he greets me in the same way when he returns home late in the afternoon. I am quite sure that others resent us just because we love one another and take such joy from one another's company. I have asked Pericles to save his kisses for indoors, but he insists on demonstrating to those who gossip about us that there is no shame in his love for me. You know him. He is usually so zealous to preserve his privacy here at home. Even though I tell him that this only incites envy and resentment among all those for whom marriage is kind of joyless duty, he says he will not let their unhappiness spoil his happiness."

Pericles moved closer to Aspasia on the bench they shared and reached out for her hand. "We are not like others. You are right."

"Pericles, you and I do have a happiness that has overcome so much. But the gossip continues and grows more hateful. Ask your own steward what he hears when he goes to the barber or ask your own younger lieutenants what they hear at the gymnasium. My own maid tells me what wagging tongues are now saying. 'Aspasia has turned Pericles' own home into a brothel where all of Pericles friends may come to party with her hetaerae friends.'

Yes, Protagoras, the attacks on Pericles will make headway by associating him with those whose work and lives appear to the commoners as filled with *hubris* and impiety as they invent new gods or deny their existence altogether. Envy linked with a sense of self-righteous piety is a force strong enough to blind many to the indisputable benefits Pericles' guidance and nurturing of Athens' democracy has achieved."

Protagoras nodded his head in agreement.

Pericles rose from his couch and turned towards the boy who was now leaning in his chair with his head face down resting on the small table. "Well, my friends, I see we have put young Alcibiades to sleep with our talk."

"I am not asleep, Sir. I am only trying to keep myself quiet and out of sight, for I am both perplexed and angry. I am afraid that if I do not put my head down I will blurt our something that is just stupid to you and your guests. After all, I am just a boy with much to learn."

"Tell me, Alcibiades, what is it that perplexes you?"

"Sir, are you not the most powerful man in Athens? Do you not command all the soldiers? If there are enemies that threaten you, why do you not have then arrested and either executed or exiled? I am angry because I cannot do this for you myself. I hate those who would throw our family down from our high place in the city and rub our noses in the mud."

"Protagoras, help me explain to my young Alkmeonid cousin why I cannot treat my adversaries this way. It seems that he has drawn the wrong conclusions from his grandfather's stories about how the Alkmeonid clan saved Athens from the would-be tyrant Cylon."

Protagoras nodded his head and, always glad to teach, turned towards Pericles' young kinsman. "Alcibiades, you are fortunate to live in Athens and be educated not only by your tutors, but by your guardian, Pericles. No one is more adept then Pericles at explaining how all our clans, and especially the more powerful ones, have compacted with one another to put aside personal violence, vendetta, and vigilante justice in exchange for a state of laws, courts, and civility. Indeed, I have heard him many times explain to fellow Assemblymen how we must accord to each citizen equal protection under our laws, and we must not permit any acts of violence by one citizen against another outside of the workings of the law and the courts. This is not just something he makes speeches about. It is a principle of conduct that he exhibits in even the most difficult circumstances. Just a few days ago, while Pericles spent most of the day outdoors at a table in the Agora busy working on plans for repairs and improvements on Athens' walled corridor to Piraeus, a vulgar and low born citizen stationed himself in a booth nearby and all afternoon reviled and ridiculed Pericles. Then, when Pericles got up to go home as daylight ended, this same fellow followed him all the way to his home, all the time insulting and abusing him with course and obscene names. What do you think your guardian did, Alcibiades?"

"I would have given him a good beating right then and there. But since my guardian is the supreme general of Athens, I suppose he would have this fellow arrested and publically whipped so as to set an example for all to see the consequences of disrespect towards the commander and chief of Athens' military."

"But that is not what happened, Alcibiades. Pericles, tell your young ward what you did do."

Pericles turned towards the boy and explained. "I did nothing of the sort you suggested. I called for my steward, and instructed him to take a torch and escort the man to his home down by the docks. I did this because he is a fellow citizen, though a low-born dock-worker. We are threatened by foreign enemies nearby such as Thebes, Corinth, and Sparta, and still powerful Persian forces in Asia - to all those enemies I can be ferocious. But here in Athens we are strong against all such enemies because we are a city of laws and covenants that protect each citizen equally from acts of violence. No matter how rich, no matter how high the office held, no matter how high-born, no Athenian citizen is above that law. The secret of our strength lies in this compact. This is why I would not strike or in any way assault the man. Even if his actions were illegal, it is to the courts he must be taken. I cannot claim as I beat him that I act out of self-defense when all he slung my way were words - not stones, or a spear or a sword. If words, however abusive, could justify such violence, then our Assembly would have to be shut down and let us once again submit to a tyrant. Do you understand, Alcibiades?"

Alcibiades nodded his head yes, but still he looked confused.

"What is it, Alcibiades, that you still don't understand," asked Protagoras.

Alcibiades couldn't think how to say what confused him, other than to repeat the questions he had overheard Socrates put to other young men in the Gymnasium. "I am thinking about the questions I have heard Socrates ask concerning Athenian laws and our covenants with other cities. 'Could it be that a majority in the Assembly unfairly prosecutes one of our own citizens by passing a bad law? Do we not break covenants with other cities and assault their citizens even if it is not out of self-defense? Did not Pericles order the horribly painful branding of the foreheads of the men of Samos without giving them a hearing in any kind of court? Were they not members of our Delian League and its covenants?'... I don't know how to answer them and Socrates wouldn't answer his own questions."

Protagoras smiled and nodded his head as he answered. "Yes, these are good questions. But it would take a very long discussion to sort them out and I would prefer that we enlist Socrates' assistance in searching for the truth about these matters. But for now, I think it best that you assume your place as an Athenian citizen and like your guardian Pericles never do anything to undermine the laws and institutions of Athens which are of all things the most valuable for promoting the welfare of every citizen."

"Thank you, Protagoras, for your kind words and now that we have persuaded Alcibiades that he ought not to beat up Diopeithes and my other political opponents, what should we do to derail those who would separate me from the people's support by painting me as irreligious?"

"Pericles, we must turn all this around by creating for the common people a picture of the Athens our policies have helped fashion. They must see with their own eyes a glorious representation of the power, the wealth, the beauty, and the freedom of our collective life as governed by those who saved the city from slavery to Persia and then lifted it to preeminence among all the cities of the civilized world. Since most men cannot hold before their mind's eye the long work of policies, laws, institutions, and the dedication of resources to the common good in creating a higher life for all; its leaders must repeatedly infuse them with this wisdom through religion. Man is the measure of all things, but he does best when his individual life's energies and forces are linked with something other than the narrow selfish pursuit of gratification. Refresh the people again with the spectacle of this great truth and let them see that you and all those who join in the great public works of Athens are especially devotees to the divinity which we all serve when we live through our city."

Pericles interrupted his friend. "You are talking like a philosopher, Protagoras. Aspasia and Anaxagoras, I'm sure, understand what you mean. But men of action like young Alcibiades and me need to get things moving. Aspasia, you are so clever when it comes to getting things done in the city. Give me some steps we can take to show the people we are with them in the way Protagoras advises."

Aspasia rose from the couch and stood next to the small statue of Athena which Phidias had twelve years ago given to Pericles as a model for the colossal Athena which he planned to sculpt for Athena's new temple. Looking at the statue all the while she spoke, Aspasia counseled Pericles. Remember, Pericles, next summer is time in the four year cycle for the greater Panathenaic festival. Next month, plans begin in earnest for the upcoming festival. It begins, humbly enough, with virgins from aristocratic families beginning the preparation of the new dress for Athena Polias. Of course, I can be of no help there."

"Aspasia, your mind and body remain new to me each day. No need to be so self-deprecating even in jest."

"You see, young Alcibiades, the helmsman of Athens does love me."

"This helmsman wants to hear what you have in mind in planning for the festival."

"We don't want to bore young Alcibiades with all the details. Suffice it to say that this is an opportunity to unify the people of

Athens and celebrate the glory of our city as we commemorate her divine founder, Athena Polias. The dedication of her new temple, the games, the musical contests in the new building, the parade led by the ship on wheels carrying Athena's new garment, the visiting dignitaries from throughout Athens' maritime empire, the lavish feasts prepared by the state for all the common people - all of this should be done in such a way that shows that your leadership and your policies have redounded to the glory of Athena and her city. There is no need to say this, to propagandize through speeches or manifestos. Just let the splendor of the music and games, the magnificent liberality of Athena's holiday, the beauty of her rebuilt holy sanctuary, and the obvious prosperity of the gathered celebrants do their work on the minds of all who now for over two decades elected Pericles as 'first man' for the government of Athens."

"Anaxagoras and Protagoras, do you agree that this is indeed the best way to deal with those who would charge us with a lack of piety? I, myself, think that Aspasia's advice, as always, is sound."

Both the philosophers nodded their heads in agreement.

"I can see that we are all tired, so let us enjoy one more cup of wine before we sleep. I have already made arrangements with my steward to make up beds for all of you. There is no need for philosophers to be wondering the dark allies of Athens when I have plenty of room here."

CHAPTER SIXTEEN
BECOMING A MAN
(Summer of 433 B.C.)

Well then, gentlemen, the earthly Aphrodite's Love is a very earthly Love indeed, and does his work entirely at random. It is he that governs the passions of the vulgar. For, first, they are as much attracted by women as by boys; next, whoever they may love, their desires are of the body rather than of the soul; and, finally, they make a point of courting the shallowest people they can find, looking forward to the mere act of fruition and careless whether it be worthy or unworthy consummation. And hence they take their pleasures where they find them, good and bad alike. For this is the Love of the younger Aphrodite, whose nature partakes of both male and female.

But the heavenly Love springs from a goddess whose attributes has nothing of the female, but is altogether male, and who is also the elder of the two, and innocent of hint of lewdness. And so those who are inspired by this other Love turn rather to the male, preferring the more vigorous and intellectual bent. One can always tell—even among the lover of boys—the man who is wholly governed by this elder Love, for no boy can please him until he has shown the first signs of dawning intelligence, signs which generally appear with the first growth of beard.

(Plato. Symposium, 181: b-c)

The morning sun had already made his sleeping quarters uncomfortably warm. He had not slept well. Something must have been wrong with the wine. His head was throbbing and in the back of his throat last night's wine kept threatening to come up. It must have been only a couple of hours ago that he had been brought back to his home by one of his older and more sober friends. He did not remember even how he had gotten undressed and onto his bed. What happened at the party? Did I drink so much that I had to be carried home? Why did I dream about my mother flogging me with her sandals? Maybe if I lie on my side, my head will stop throbbing and I can go back to sleep. "My Lord, Master Alcibiades, it is almost mid-morning. Last night you instructed me to make sure you were awakened no later than this." It was his body servant, Milo. He was standing in the doorway holding a basin of water and a towel.

"Can't you see, Milo, that I am sick? I must sleep more."

"But Sir, your new friend will be here in less than an hour. Remember, both of you told me that I would be severely punished if I did not have you packed and ready to join him on a trip that would take you away from Athens for six days. I don't know exactly where you will be going and so I want you to check what I've packed so as to make sure you will have everything you need for your journey."

"Yes, yes, Milo, I will get up." The headache and nausea seemed to lift as Alcibiades realized that yes indeed he had agreed he would go away with this older man. "You are speaking of the honorable Democrates whose father was a commercial partner in many of my father's enterprises. We will be traveling to Megara, Corinth, and Corcyra, and then on to Delphi so that I might learn first hand how the various enterprises left to me by my father are being managed by our agents. You will not be travelling with us. Democrates will be bringing baggage handlers and other servants for both of us. You are not to speak of this to anyone! Should my guardians, Pericles or Ariphon inquire about my absence, you will explain that I insisted on taking a trip to learn more about my father's commercial operations in other cities! And since it is less than a year to my 18th birthday when I will be assuming full responsibility for managing the commercial affairs of my patrimony, I thought it best to begin without the company of my guardians. As for the packing, make sure I have my scented ointments, my purple robe and its scarlet sash, and a warm cloak for Delphi! Don't forget to fill the small chest with enough gold and silver coins! I will need money to cover lodging and other expenses."

Milo still stood at the door as though waiting for further instructions. Was that a lewd smile that Alcibiades saw flash across his servant's usually blank face? "Milo, leave the basin and towel! I will not need any breakfast. Just bring me a slice of lemon! You don't need to hover over me like some kind of Nanny! Check everything and put it near the front door ready to go!"

"But Master, what about your mother? She is sure to ask where you have gone since she thinks you will be home from the *epheboi* barracks for the entire week of the PanAthenaic Festival."

"Damn it, Milo, just tell her I went back to the barracks since I have been chosen to undertake a special session in cavalry training! Yes, it is a lie and she will probably find me out. But that is all you will tell her! I will not have my mother any longer intruding in my affairs. She thinks that since my father is dead and my male guardians are not living in my house, she can supervise me. Remember, you are my servant, not hers! I'm a man now, and the master of this house. You answer only to me, not her. And if you can't do that, then I'll sell you to Nicias and you will spend the rest of a very short life chained underground in the mines of Laurium. Now leave the basin and towel here on the table and set out some fruit on the courtyard table for Democrates! Don't forget my lemon slice!"

Alcibiades was up on his feet as soon as Milo put the basin and towel on the little table next to his bed. He splashed the cool water on his face and then sat down by the small window that faced east so that the warm sunlight would dry his skin. Milo had brought the lemon. Thank you Daddy, for our lemon groves in Cyprus, he thought. The slice of lemon on his tongue cut through and washed away the rancid smell of what seemed to be his own fermented breathe. He would dress in a few moments, but now he wanted to gather his thoughts as he took stock in his hand held mirror of the carefully groomed beard that now covered his chin for the first time. Thank you Dad, I have your brown beard. It looks quite handsome. I'm so glad it is not as blond as the hair on my head. He looked into the eyes that stared back at him in the mirror. He wondered what others saw in these eyes when he met their gaze. It seemed to him that he could cast a spell over others in this way, but he could not yet understand to what use or purpose such a power should be employed.

"Master, your friend is here. I have escorted him to the courtyard. Will you need me for anything else?"

"If everything is packed and in the entry hall, there is nothing more for you to do. But while I am gone you will keep yourself busy. The man's quarters, the courtyard, the pantries, the entry room, and the exterior of house all are in need of a thorough cleaning and a new coat of plaster. You will see to all of this. My mother seems to have lost interest in the upkeep of our home and I will just not tolerate it looking like a hovel. Now that I have become a man, I will be entertaining guests who expect a man of my means to live elegantly and not like a pig. I expect this all to be completed when I return. You can get started immediately. Go now to the marketplace next to the potters' quarters and arrange for the materials you will need!"

Alcibiades dressed quickly. He thought it best that he make sure his mother would not interfere with his plans. So he quietly made his way to the back of the house to the stairs that led to the woman's quarters. Reaching the top of the steps, he found his mother about to come down to see who had come to see her son first thing in the morning.

"Meilichios, I mean Alcibiades, who came into the house? Is there some emergency? Since all you men were out partying almost to sunrise, I can not imagine that any of your friends would be up this early."

"Mother, there is no need for you to come down. It is one of my friends and we will be leaving the house in a few moments. I will not have you in the man's quarters when my friends are here. It is not proper, you know. Besides, we will be talking about last night's party and you don't want to know what goes on at a man's party for *epheboi*. Don't embarrass me by making me chase you back upstairs! Stay put!"

Dinomache turned away and went back into her quarters. Her shoulders sagged and she had to turn her face away from the light lest her son see the bitter tears that were welling up in her eyes. *He sounds just like his father – he does not love me anymore. I am just an embarrassment and a burden to him. I have lost him and soon he will send me away.* Of course she could not say this to him or anyone else. Real men, she thought, don't have mothers.

Alcibiades watched his mother – she seemed to him old and worn out now- walk back into the shadows of her work room. *It is hard to believe,* he thought, *that she is a year younger than the accomplished and vigorous man downstairs who now waited for him. Democrates had told him that he was the same age as Alcibiades' other older friend, Socrates – thirty-six.* His mother had the look of one with whom life was done and all that could be seen in her face was resignation and melancholy. She seemed to him to be all dried up and shrunk into a very small and sterile place inhabited only by ghosts and sacrificial victims. It was with a sense of relief mixed with excitement that he flew down the stairs to his new man's world and the open road that stretched out before him with all its dizzying freedom and possibilities.

When Alcibiades reached his inner courtyard he found his friend stretched out on the stone bench that stood by the cistern. He was lying there with his eyes closed. The shade provided by the east side of the house still protected his upper body from the intense rays of the late morning sun. *Have I kept him waiting that long? It has only been a few moments since Milo let him in. Perhaps he drank even more than I did.* "Democrates I am here. Are you awake?"

Democrates rubbed his eyes and sat up. "Pardon me, Alcibiades. I stretched out to enjoy the cool shade and the sounds of the fountain here by your cistern. The stone relief on the fountain is quite impressive. According to the Pythagoreans, we must have had virtuous forefathers. Otherwise we would have been born women and, like the water bearers carved on the fountain's base, condemned to carrying water in sieves – our lives passing slavishly consumed by endless repetitive tasks. I closed my eyes trying to visualize what kind of man you will be when you are my age. You are at the beginning of your manhood and possess advantages that lead others to expect great things from you. Your family is one of the most powerful in Athens, you have inherited from your father great wealth, the gods have blessed you with almost preternatural good looks, and you possess a first rate mind. If you can avoid being the victim of other men's envy and steer clear of self-destruction, I believe you will join the ranks of Athens' most famous men."

"What a flatterer you are, Democrates. My friend Socrates is constantly warning me to steer clear of those who would fan the fires of vanity. He says that virtue is not like a lottery. It is not granted by circumstances of birth. Even if your forefather was Solon or Theseus, they cannot do for you, he says, the hard work of becoming an excellent human being. Even Zeus himself will not make a gift of such excellence. Zeus' beloved Ganymede, after all, is for all eternity only a cup-bearer so that he might service the inexhaustible desire of the immortal Olympian. Socrates is fond of reminding me that I must be careful that I am not beguiled by lovers who would promise me that their gifts will make straight and easy the path to excellence and praiseworthy achievement."

"Come and sit down at the table with me. I feel like you are putting me in some kind of box to be sent off, standing over me like this looking down at me while I squint through the sun trying to make out whether you are being coy or serious. What are you saying Alcibiades? Do you now not want to take the trip we talked about last evening? Are you saying that I am like one of those seductive false lovers that Socrates fears will do you harm? I certainly don't want to spend a week traveling with you if I make you feel uncomfortable or in anyway ashamed."

Alcibiades joined his guest at the table, but sat so that he was as far away as possible on the other side of the rectangular table. "I drank so much last night I am having some difficulty recalling what exactly I did and said."

"There is no reason to worry about your behavior. You played your part well as a drunken reveler. And drunk as you were, you were a real stallion with the *hetaerae*. Are your sandals still in one piece? Everyone was impressed with the way you reddened the flanks of Dinoclesia. What a man you are! She has been working these kinds of parties since I was an *ephebe*, but I'm sure no one has ridden her like you."

Alcibiades was embarrassed. Everything was coming back in focus. How could I have confused that slut's name with my mother's? I can't believe I called her Dinomache. It was Democrates who had assured him in his drunken stupor that the woman beneath him was not his mother. "Now, I remember, Democrates. I hope my comrades and I proved our mettle."

"Yes, yes Alcibiades, you all showed that there is not a mama's boy in your ranks. Think of the party as a kind of initiation rite. I assure you, all of you came through your baptism into the rowdy world of hardened hoplites – ready to forgo the soft womanly world of your childhood and wield the hard and thrusting spear of the manly warrior."

"Well, that's good." But for Alcibiades it was not his behavior last night that made him anxious. "I have made all the arrangements necessary for me to be away for a week. However, I am having some second thoughts about all this."

Democrates fidgeted and looked irritated. "What is the problem? It is perfectly proper for you to make this trip and to do it without your legal guardians accompanying you at this stage of your life. Next year you will be asked to go on campaign as a citizen hoplite. You will risk your life to honor your Ephebe Oath to preserve the fatherland and vouchsafe the property of our fathers. In your case, next year you will take on full responsibility for supervision of the many commercial enterprises which have made your family so wealthy. You need to learn first-hand and on your own about your patrimony. I know about these enterprises far more than Pericles or Ariphon. It makes considerable business sense that I assist you in discovering as much as possible as quickly as possible since the time is short. You need not worry about what people may think or say concerning such a trip with me. They will say that Alcibiades is shrewd. He persuaded one of the smartest investors in all of Athens to give him an on-site tutorial in managing a complex web of commercial ventures. Besides, when I saw you looking worn out and melancholy at the party last night, I thought it would do you good to have a change of scene. By the way, what possibly could you be sad about?"

Alcibiades hesitated before answering. Democrates' features, the kindly eyes set in a round and somewhat effeminate face, made it seem unlikely that he could be manipulative or dominating. While he amused Alcibiades with his flirtatious sarcasm, the man gave every appearance of being incapable of hurting anyone. Democrates had already served in a number of military campaigns, but surely he could not have made his way through military exploits. He was rich and well connected and no doubt was good at making money. This was an older man that he could manage. But could it be that Democrates was among those democratic leaders in the Assembly which had grown restive and resentful of Pericles' leadership? Democrates had made his way to some prominence in the Assembly serving as one of Pericles' lieutenants in helping to pass legislation favored by Pericles. But this, thought Alcibiades, would not prevent Democrates from abandoning Pericles if that kindly face hides a ruthless ambition. He wondered if somehow an entanglement with Democrates could injure his kinsman, Pericles. Worse yet, could a tryst with Democrates end badly and poison his own prospects in politics. It would be best, he decided, to make clear to Democrates that he was no fool and although he was only seventeen, he would not allow Democrates to take advantage of him.

"Yes, I was not in the best of spirits when the party began. The day's opening ceremonies for the Panathenaia reminded me of what happened to Pericles right after the spectacular Panathenaia two years ago which climaxed with the procession to Athena's new temple. You remember, Democrates, that less than a few weeks later, prosecutions began against Pericles' inner circle of friends and advisors. First Anaxagoras and then Protagoras were charged with impiety. Both were forced to leave Athens and their literary works were burned. Pericles' intercession on their behalf may have saved them from heavier penalties, but it was clear that their trials were brought in order to undermine his influence with the people.

"Yes, those were hard times for Pericles. I was abroad most of the year during these prosecutions. So I don't know anything about the motives of those who initiated the prosecutions. I believe the charges had something to do with the decree of Diopeithes."

Alcibiades continued, "The prosecution which left Pericles most shaken was the case brought against Aspasia. She was accused of bribery through prostitution. I was fifteen at the time and not permitted to attend the trial. But like every Athenian, I learned of what went on there. Every word and even the gestures of its participants were repeated in the streets of Athens. What I was thinking about in conjunction with this case is how love makes us so vulnerable. The force of love, it seems to me, can undo anyone. I would never have believed that Pericles, the most powerful man in Athens could come undone in public. But he insisted on speaking on behalf of Aspasia at her trial. During his statement Pericles, Athens' commander in chief of our citizen warriors, was reduced to weeping while begging the jury at Aspasia's trial to let her return to him. Pericles said that he had sacrificed so much that most men enjoy so that he might be above reproach as a custodian of the people's common good. He challenged anyone present to show that he had ever personally profited from his many years of being the supreme general charged with Athens' defense. In fact, he noted his own family led a modest life and he was often criticized by his immediate family for the austerity of their household economy. Then, in front of all of Athens' eyes he revealed his soft spot, the place where he could be wounded mortally – his passion for Aspasia. He began by saying that, unlike other men in Athens, he throughout his long public life renounced the usual romantic affairs that others enjoyed. I was always aware, he said, of the special responsibility power brings. There should not even be the appearance of its use for personal pleasures. He said that our tradition remembers that the tyranny of Hipparchus, the son of Peisistratos, became unbearable when he employed his power to steal away a young man from Harmodius. Harmodius and his brother Aristogeiton then assassinated Hipparchus during the procession of the Panathenaia and to this day we commemorate this resistance to the tyrant as part of our city's march to freedom. And so, he said, he was careful to renounce all such involvements with the young citizens of Athens, lest he give cause for a charge like that brought against the tyrant Hipparchus. At this point, I am told, Pericles began to weep as he pointed to Aspasia. He said this was the person, a metic woman, with whom he had found a kind of love that afforded him a joy and a satisfaction that made his private life a source of renewal for the hardships of his public life. He said he did not know whether he could go on if they exiled her."

"What are you getting at, Alcibiades? I can't follow what this has to do with our trip."

"I was thinking at the party that maybe it is best never to fall in love. I mean don't let any other person occupy the very center of the soul – where to be without this person is to feel nothing but the pain of emptiness and to think that willing and desiring anything else has become pointless. I think this is the love that is a kind of madness which leads men to desperate and often foolish actions. I don't think Harmodius was thinking anything about freedom when he killed Hipparchus. He could not bear in his jealous rage to live without his beloved and so he murdered his competitor. I don't think Pericles could help himself when he wept like a woman in front of those who wished to vanquish him. It seems to me whether you love or are the beloved you are in danger of being undone by the maelstrom of this passion."

Figure 12
Zeus pursuing Ganymede

"Alcibiades, you talk like a world-weary sophisticate, already old in the ways of love. I see your beard, but I think it must be your very first one. I can't imagine you being pulled into such a storm of love. You seem to prize so highly your independence. And no one will ever be able to put anything over on you. You are so intelligent everything becomes transparent to you. It would have to be some god-like lover who could make you surrender to a will other than your own. But just maybe you have spent too much time with Sophist tutors. How else could you have come so early to such a cynical view of love? Could it be that some men could be trusted not to trample under foot the very vulnerability that you describe? Could you be loved and love in such a way that both flourish without surrendering their own daemon, their own soul?"

"Democrates, you are beginning to sound like a philosopher, and not the practical man of business who will mentor me on how to preserve and increase the wealth of my patrimony. I do like to hear the wonderful things you say in praise of me, but this is all new to me. Let's get going. By the way, aren't you supposed to bring me some kind of gift? I won't settle for a rooster, not even if you are Zeus in disguise!"

CHAPTER SEVENTEEN
ALCIBIADES AND THE
PHILOSOPHER
(Winter of 432 B.C.)

Miserable wretch, said Socrates, are you reckoning what will happen to you if you kiss a beautiful youth: instantly to be a slave instead of a free person.....?

(Xenophon, *Memorabilia* 1.3.11)

I think, I said, you're the only lover I've ever had who's been really worthy of me. Only you're too shy to talk about it. Well, this is how I look at it. I think it'd be just absurd to refuse you this as anything else you wanted that belonged to me or any of my friends.

(Plato, *Symposium* 218. D: Alcibiades' speech)

It had been almost a year since Alcibiades had returned from his adventure with Democrates. His mother had made things difficult for him. When he did not return home after a few days, she became very distraught and then went to his guardian Pericles and demanded that he find him. After questioning Alcibiades servant, Milo, Pericles understood that his ward had left town to have a fling with Democrates.

It was fortunate that Pericles was the first one Alcibiades' mother had turned to for help. Pericles sent her back home and ordered her to keep quiet about the whole affair. He had made clear to her that it would be better if others did not learn of the affair until after

Alcibiades had returned and undergone his ceremonial examination for citizenship upon completing his *epheboi* training. "There is no telling", Pericles had said to his mother, "what will happen if I set in motion any attempt to apprehend Democrates and force the couple to return home. The gossipers will turn our young Alcibiades into an effeminate soft whore whom I had procured for one of my lascivious free-thinking political associates. No, it is better if we do nothing. Say nothing about this to anyone, and wait for them to return. I will deal with both of them the very hour they first set foot in Athens."

When Alcibiades and Democrates did return after a week's absence, they did so at mid-night. Pericles appeared at Alcibiades' door at sunrise the following morning with Democrates, looking somewhat sheepish, at his side. Pericles did not berate or in any way accuse Alcibiades and Democrates of improper behavior. He unemotionally and in a detached manner asked them to describe their itinerary, the particulars of where they had lodged, and the officials, merchants, and any other public persons with whom they interacted. When Alcibiades had finished recounting all they had done in Megara, Corinth, Delphi, and Corcyra; Pericles asked Democrates if anything had been omitted by his young traveling companion. Democrates added that they had to leave Corinth in haste and cancel meetings with Clinias' commercial agents in Corinth. As it turned out, Alcibiades and Democrates had arrived in Corinth the day before the Athenian Assembly had voted to intervene militarily in Corcyra against Corinthian interests there. The next day the Corinthians became so hostile towards Athens that it was no longer safe for an Athenian to be in Corinthian territory.

After listening carefully to both of their accounts of the trip, Pericles was satisfied that each of their accounts told the same story. He then asked if they had bought anything or brought anything else back from their visits to the various cities. This was for Alcibiades an uncomfortable moment, since he had been somewhat lavish and impetuous in his expenditure for a purchase near Aphrodite's temple on the Acrocorinth. He remembered how transparent he must have been to Pericles when he tried to put the best face on what was simply an act of a rich young man's need for gratification. "Yes, Pericles, I thought it was time that I begin purchasing my own household attendants, since I will eventually marry and, making room for my wife, arrange for other living quarters for my mother and her household servants. Mother, of course, is not very happy about all this. She insists that the new maid stay out of her quarters upstairs. So I have temporarily set up a cot for her in the pantry here downstairs."

Pericles sighed as though he found the whole situation tiresome. He turned to Democrates and asked, "Was it a good purchase?"

Democrates was eager to make clear to Pericles the adult care he had exercised throughout the trip toward young Alcibiades. And so, assuming the tone of a concerned but indulgent father, he explained to Pericles his unsuccessful effort to dissuade Alcibiades from this particular purchase. "Well, Pericles, I did have my reservations about this. I took Alcibiades to see the great temple to Aphrodite so that he could appreciate the importance of maritime commerce. I hoped he would understand that Corinth, like Athens, can afford such magnificent temples and other public buildings because of sea-faring commerce. We were leaving the temple and walking through the circle of prostitute stalls which surround the temple, when Alcibiades saw a young woman about his own age being beaten by one of the managers. It was clear that she was a newly acquired prostitute and that she was not amenable to the manager's guidance on how to attract and please clients. As it turns out, I knew the manager because this franchise was financed by Alcibiades' father in partnership with my family."

Pericles cut Democrates short. "Are you going to tell me that it is this girl that Alcibiades bought? Does she have a name?"

"Her name is Deborah, Uncle." Alcibiades could still remember a year later the anger he felt rising in him as he listened to Democrates' patronizing account of his purchase. And so he explained the purchase himself rather than submit to Democrates' condescension. "Pericles, I could see that she was intelligent and that it would be a colossal waste of slave talent to have her worn out by the dock workers, sailors, and other commoners. Furthermore, I learned that she was the daughter of a woman called Rachel, a Semite, who had been sent to my father as part of the ransom for Penthylus, the Paphian prince, he had captured at Artemisium. Somehow, I thought it would be good to save something connected to my father's life - even if it is a servant girl. And besides, since she has taken on the management of my downstairs servants, she has proven that even though she is very young, she is indeed clever."

"Is she here now?" Pericles had asked.

Alcibiades now knew why Pericles wanted to see her. Pericles had grimaced when Alcibiades identified the young woman as the daughter of one of the women sent to Athens in exchange for the Cypriots captured at Artemisium by Clinias, Alcibiades' father. It wasn't because Deborah might be beautiful and would more than likely share Alcibiades' bed that Pericles was perturbed. No, it was because there was a possibility that Deborah was the lust-child of Clinias. The last thing the Alkmeonid family needed was another scandal – the son of the Alkmeonid Dionomache sleeping with his illegitimate sister!

Alcibiades called for his new maid to bring breakfast gruel and fruit to his early morning guests. When Deborah came into the courtyard, Pericles studied her as she served the three men. There was no doubt she was of Semitic stock. Her angular cheek bones, long slender nose, and dark brown eyes were framed by dark black hair which was shoulder length. Even in the humble short robe of a maid, Pericles could see that this slender but shapely young woman was somehow noble and had not yet surrendered her dignity. In her exotic features, there was an otherness which fascinated. But there was nothing in her looks that revealed an Athenian father. Pericles sighed with relief. Then with a smile of approval Pericles turned to Alcibiades and said, "What a beauty!"

Alcibiades had scarcely any contact with Democrates after that morning with Pericles. He wondered whether Pericles had said something to Democrates that had driven him away. It was just as well. He had found Democrates to be tiresome and boring by the end of the week in which he had spent every day with him. There was something petty and all too predictable about the man that made Alcibiades impatient and irritated with all of his conversation. His sarcasm wore thin when Alcibiades realized that everything other than increasing his wealth was of no interest to Democrates. This is why he can so glibly demean and devalue political ideals, the work of the artists, and the great achievements of athletes and warriors. He honestly thinks that all of this is simply of no value. Alcibiades suspected now that Democrates had shown interest in him only because he hoped thereby to actually seal the business connections between both their families. I don't think that man is capable of any deep passion for anything other than money. What good is wealth if there is no zest and appetite for the beautiful in all of its various forms? How could he have been with me all week and never really once touch me, the most beautiful youth in all of Athens? Oh, thought Alcibiades, how I yearn for the company of a many-sided man!

It did not surprise Alcibiades that his 'fling' was quickly forgotten by everyone except his mother. And she wouldn't forget because she blamed Democrates for me bringing home Deborah whom she called the 'off-scouring of a whore'. Perhaps it was Pericles' doing or maybe it was because so many people found it incredible that Democrates, the tireless banker and broker of far-flung commercial interests, could ever abandon his client-reassuring decorum enough to lose himself in erotic love. The year had gone by so fast. There had been other suitors. Indeed there was no shortage of them. But not one of these had ended so badly as to cause scandal. Recently he had even grown tired of Deborah. There was nothing left to explore with her and he found her stubborn and scrupulous adherence to her strange Semitic religion as silly as his mother's superstitious Orphic theology. In a few weeks he would take his oath of full citizenship. He looked forward to leaving behind the long course of *epheboi* training and turning all of his energies to winning the glory he had been taught was the birthright and calling of the best and beautiful.

Tonight it would be good to spend the evening with the one suitor he actually found endlessly fascinating. This man clearly was interested in him, but he nevertheless seemed so elusive and yet irresistibly charming. How could this be, he wondered, since this man, Socrates, had such a singularly unattractive face? They would talk about everything, but Alcibiades would find a way to steer the conversation towards the things of love. After all, it should not come as a surprise to Socrates. In the past month we have exercised together at the gymnasium at least twice a week. Surely he has felt something when we have closed together in our wrestling drills. How could he not notice my gaze trying to capture his eyes?

Socrates would be his only dinner guest. It would be the first time they would be entirely alone together. Like many other young men in Athens, Alcibiades had spent countless hours in conversation with Socrates in the public places he loved to frequent. Whether it be some shady unused pavilion down in the marketplace, the yard of the Gymnasium, on the steps of the King Archon's hall, or on the road to Piraeus, Socrates would engage others in his search for a wisdom that he proposed would help a man attain human excellence and the virtue which promotes the good of their city. No one knew what to make of all this, since this kind of inquiry was so different from that kind of science of Nature sought by such philosophers as Socrates' own first teacher, Anaxagoras. And, although Socrates seemed in some way to be a teacher of young men, unlike other men such as Protagoras and Gorgias who offered to teach young men the oratorical skills necessary to succeed in public life, he neither accepted nor sought any kind of fees.

Alcibiades had been asked by his own cousin, Ariphon, what Socrates was up to. It was difficult for anyone to believe that Socrates spent so much time with the young men simply as an unpaid educator. The orators of influence in the courts and the Assembly wondered when this charmer of the best and brightest among the young men would make clear his own political agenda. But Socrates had taken up this kind of public life now for the past three years and though he was now thirty-seven years old, he showed no interest at all in advocating the commercial or economic interests of any constituency in Athens. It was just this complete indifference to courting or pleasing any party of clients which led to Socrates' penchant for irritating so many of the politicians. Inevitably, when Socrates engaged a politician about whether his advocacy of a particular law was just or good, it would become apparent to all who listened that the politician could not give a reasonable account of what justice or public good the law might serve. Socrates would press the questioning, insisting that justice or the good be defined in such a way that it could serve as a general standard manifestly fair and applicable to all the citizens of Athens. Every partisan slogan or vague and sanctimonious appeal to poetic and religious tradition, the usual fare of politicians, was subjected to Socrates' unsparing critical logic and shown to be rife with contradiction. The politician, in embarrassment and exasperation, would usually abruptly end the conversation, angry that the youths, among whom might be his own son, were amused by the politician's confusion concerning his proposed law's rectitude.

Alcibiades wondered what it would be like to know such a man up close. Can it be that he indeed could assist me in achieving the highest kind of human and political excellence? Why am I so attracted to this peculiar man and his dedication to the search for what he calls a kind of 'human wisdom'?

Alcibiades knew that he too appeared peculiar to all this peers. It was not just that he had been fatherless since he was an infant. After all, there were a number of other young men who had lost their fathers to Ares. But he felt that from both inside him and from all those who knew him there was a relentless demand that he become among the most glorious of all those who had achieved greatness in Athens.

This is why as soon as he had come into his patrimony and assumed control of the considerable wealth of his father's commercial assets, he had purchased two of the very best racing chariots and four stallions from a Lydian noble whose chariots had won the last three Olympian races. He would begin his march to glory with Olympic victories of his own. The very same week he arranged for the purchase of the chariots, he also contracted with the best shipwright in Athens to build two new triremes for his own use. He planned to commission his own crew of rowers and hand-pick military men who could serve as both fighting men and officers on the trireme he would personally captain. If he were to ever become commander and chief of Athens' military, he knew he must be prepared to be an admiral of its navy, skilled in the tactics and strategy of the Athenian fleet of warships. He would delegate the day to day management of his commercial enterprises to the same managers who had maintained them since the death of his father until now. After all, they had done well, increasing the income of their enterprises some tenfold over the past fifteen years.

Freed from the day to day management of his assets, he would devote himself to training. Cool mornings would be set aside for the race course grounds just outside the Marathon Gate of Athens. Soon, he would be one of the best charioteers in all of Hellas. Hot afternoons would be devoted to short but demanding training sessions on his trireme. Yes, there would certainly be the call to military duty as a citizen hoplite. But he was sure fate would preserve him and as a mounted member of the cavalry he would prove his mettle as a young officer. And when circumstances demanded, he would soon be chosen to lead a squadron of triremes in defense of Athens maritime empire. He would miss no opportunity for glory and would use all of his resources to shove aside and outshine every other man who stood in his path to being the first man of Athens.

Yes, he was just starting and should be careful to find those peers and older men whose assistance could prove valuable in making his way to the pinnacle of power and glory. Young and inexperienced I might be, but I know from my cousin Pericles' mastery of the Athenian ship of state that the crucial asset for such a life of political accomplishment in Athens is the cultivation of an agile intelligence armed with the power of persuasive speech. Let Socrates play Pericles' Protagoras to Alcibiades. This is the gift of love I will demand of my sophist, Socrates.

It was now almost sun-set and Socrates would be arriving any moment to join Alcibiades for dinner. No doubt, Socrates would be coming directly from the marketplace or the gymnasium, wearing his usual dusty sandals and plain cloth robe. There was nothing affected about his humble garments. It was clear to everyone that he just did not pay much attention to his appearance and would consider it bothersome to spend time with a shoemaker or a tailor. Since Socrates had not yet married and his mother had died some years ago, there was no woman in his life who might temper his utter disregard for his wardrobe.

It would certainly set tongues wagging should people see – as they certainly would – lustrous young Alcibiades in his regal purple sash and richly embroidered blue robe greet outside his front door what looked to be a humble shepherd fresh from tending his flock in the hills of Attica. Alcibiades wanted everyone to know that Athens' most peculiar of its citizens and surely its first genuinely native philosopher had agreed to dine alone with the most sought after of all the young men in Athens. It amused Alcibiades that everyone would be perplexed by what possibly could be the attraction between such a pair. Alcibiades so rich, so beautifully handsome, so connected with the very best families in Athens, and so ambitious for fame – Socrates so poor, so unremarkable in appearance as to border on the ugly, a son of a middling family which has fallen on hard times, himself content to settle for a modest income from his farm while piddling away opportunity for political advancement by engaging in the life of an ascetic philosopher claiming to seek a wisdom that he himself has admitted might not be easily attained. How could any two as these ever find in one another anything to embrace?

Alcibiades was making his way to the front door when he heard Socrates talking to his servant Milo.

"Milo, I believe, you are young Alcibiades' steward. I hope preparations for this evening's dinner guest have not been troublesome. You have probably heard the gossip about the strange diets of some of those known as philosophers and mystagoges and worried about whether the menu would please me?"

Alcibiades opened the door and greeted Socrates before Milo could answer. "Socrates, I am sure Milo has no idea what you are talking about. Do you really think that servants would have any interest in the Pythagoreans or the Orphic prophets? We are having a fine cut of pork slow roasted and garnished with beans. You are always easy to please, my friend. Unless, I am mistaken you do not find meat and beans unholy – fare polluted by some unwholesome vapors of life ensnared in corrupt matter."

Socrates smiled broadly. "Alcibiades, you are such a quick study. I would not think you would remember my joke about the ten beans and the Pythagorean and Orphic doctrine of reincarnation. You are right. I do not share the superstitions of some of our misguided acquaintances. I am not a vegetarian and I do not abstain from beans. A little flatulence is good for the bowels – don't you think? But I hope you have left the onions out of the garnish. They really don't agree with me and what a nuisance. Athenians scarcely prepare any dish which is not sprinkled with shaved onions."

Alcibiades took Socrates by the arm. "You really are a lot of trouble, Socrates. But it is always amusing and interesting trouble. Come into the house, my friend. You need not worry about the onions. I remembered how you sniffled, rumbled, and broke out in hives when we shared the onion coated lamb kabob at the marketplace stall. The cook has been instructed to substitute radishes and red peppers for the onions in seasoning the meat."

"Thank you, Alcibiades. That is very considerate of you."

"I want you at your best, Socrates. Now that I have you to myself this evening, I hope you will satisfy my curiosity concerning what it is you offer a young man like me. Come, let us sit in the courtyard and enjoy a cup of wine while my servants finish preparations for our dinner. I have asked Milo to unseal a vase of Cypriot wine that is quite different from our local vintages. You will find that it is far too tasty to be mixed with water. You need not worry about our sobriety. Milo will bring us cheese and bread to keep Dionysos at bay."

Socrates sat down on the stone bench that was pulled next to the small circular wicker table which Alcibiades had set up beside the fountain. His young host sat down beside him. "You have done well in refurbishing your home. How do you manage to find such flowers that bloom here in the fountain pool?"

"They are lilies which come from an Egyptian garden. It is one of the benefits of being heir to a large commercial enterprise of maritime shipping – there are so many beautiful and rare things that I can enjoy! Here is our wine and cheese. Milo, these wine cups will not do. Please bring us the Phoenician silver goblets from the chest by the pantry door."

"Alcibiades, you know that my father and yours were very close friends. I remember coming to this house on my eighth birthday and being introduced to your father and some of the guests he had invited to his dinner party. I will never forget that evening, because it was on that night that my father had arranged for me to meet Anaxagoras and receive directly from him a copy of his treatise on Nature. I could not stay very long since the evening was devoted to entertainment fitting for men. I will never forget that Anthesteria celebration because it was one of the last happy times spent with my father. He died just a week later. Unlike so many Athenian fathers and sons, we spent much time together and he never tired of talking to me. I missed him terribly when he died. I remember seeking solace in occupying my mind with the study of the works of Anaxagoras and any of the other books of those who speculated about the origin and governing principles of the cosmos. Now, here I am twenty nine years later with the son of Clinias who is fatherless and just ten years older than I was then. I see tonight that the guest list is considerably shorter than at my first men's dinner party. I do not see the flute players or female companions that usually help with the entertainment. It is a puzzle – the question you ask. What can I alone, I have no help here, possibly offer you? You have everything that most people covet, except perhaps a caring father who might offer guidance. But then this does not seem to be a lack, since most Athenian fathers are too busy for this and leave such mentoring for their sons either to paid tutors or to other older men who might take an interest in their sons. I have no experience with these kinds of relationships since my father could not pay for a tutor other than my pedagogue and I was not the kind of young man whose appearance could attract an older man's attentive interest."

It was hard for Alcibiades to imagine that Socrates could ever have been at loose ends or in need of solace. He seemed always so self reliant and serenely cheerful. It was in a way encouraging to Alcibiades, hearing Socrates speaking of strong feelings even if they were something from long ago in his childhood. Perhaps this man is much more than a mind; his body is not chiseled out of some stone his father somehow brought to life.

"Socrates, I know you are fond of analogies, so let me picture what I ask of you in this way. Imagine a trading ship laden with costly goods which must make its way through very treacherous waters filled with reefs, submerged rocks, and ship-sinking turbulent currents. There also lurk in these waters pirates waiting for the unwary ship. The ship must negotiate all these dangers if it is to arrive at a distant port where it may realize great profit by trading its cargo. Now unless there is a skilled helmsman to steer this ship, the prospects for it reaching its destination are very slim. Wouldn't the owner of the ship be willing to give whatever he can to make sure the helmsman is taught these skills? Does this picture help you see what I might be expecting of you Socrates?"

"Alcibiades, would you mind if I pour myself a little more of the Cypriot wine. It is wonderful. It seems the long walk from the marketplace has made me very dry. I must confess I am very partial to a delicate red wine like this and I find that my mind's eye is made sharper by such a treat for my palate."

"Yes, of course, Socrates. That is why I asked Milo to leave the Cypriot vase here on the table. I will join you and perhaps we can finish it. Once the seal is broken on such a wine, it never taste quite the same later."

"Thank you, Alcibiades. Now let me ask you about this helmsman and his ship. I am a little confused about how this might, as you say, have some resemblance to what it is, as you put it, that I may offer you. Surely, you are not suggesting are you that I could be hired to be your helmsman? We Athenians all prize our freedom and I cannot imagine that you, proud and accustomed to going your own way, would now want to hand over the steering of your life course to another man. Then there is another question also. Isn't the helmsman on our ships of commerce usually himself in need of guidance?"

"What do you mean Socrates?'

"I have heard that you have already assumed some of the responsibility for the commercial shipping enterprise began by your father. Surely you would not leave it up to your helmsmen to decide the final destinations of their cruises. This is a question that only the owner and master of the ship can decide. Are you then looking for guidance on how to navigate or where it is you should arrive on your journey? Aren't they two different questions, Alcibiades?"

"Could you explain the difference more clearly as it might apply to a young man starting out on his pathway to achieve, as you say, human excellence?"

"Would you agree that most young men of good families in Athens aspire to political power and to fame? Is this not the case for you also, Alcibiades?"

"Yes Socrates I am determined to be the first man of Athens and to achieve a fame that will be remembered long after I am gone."

"But wouldn't it be foolish to devote an entire life to achieving power over others and then be utterly ignorant as to what end or purpose this power over others could serve? Would you want to be famous because you had become a tyrant whose power over others was employed simply to provide unlimited gratification of base appetites? Since one's fame is remembered by others, would such fame be celebrated or favorably memorialized by others?"

"Certainly not, Socrates!"

"Then don't you think the question about how to acquire power and the question concerning the purpose of power are clearly different questions? Is this not like noting that if a helmsman knows how to tack well with the changing wind, negotiate strong currents, nimbly avoid shoals and reefs, and in general masters the art of seamanship; but has no reason or purpose to exercise his seamanship so as to reach far away destinations – then his seamanship is frivolous and he may as well go anywhere perhaps risking the loss of his life and ship for naught?"

"Socrates, as always you make me so uncertain about what I thought I knew so clearly. Tell me straight out then. Am I foolish when I practice the art of seamanship or train with my horses and chariot so as to win Olympic glory? What are those means by which I might attain a worthy fame and the capacity for an honorable exercise of power?"

"Alcibiades, these are very difficult questions. We will need much time and patience to even make a beginning of such an inquiry. Perhaps it is best that we go in and enjoy the dinner that your servants have prepared. I think this inquiry will require that we be fortified with meat and beans so that strong bodies will sustain lively minds for the long haul."

"Yes, I'm sure the dinner is ready for us. I hope you will not be disappointed by my arrangements. There are no flute girls or harpists here this evening because I wanted more than anything to converse with you without any interruptions. I find it requires all of my attention to follow the twists and turns of your conversation. So I did not want the distraction of having to supervise any more than the few servants necessary for preparing and serving our meal."

Socrates followed Alcibiades out of the interior courtyard through the vestibule leading to the door to the street and the men's room which opened up to the vestibule and took up the entire length of the side of the house adjacent to the street. Since there were no windows on the street side, the room tended to be dark all the time except during the afternoon when sunlight illumined the interior courtyard and shone through the two small windows high on the inward facing wall. The room was now aglow with candle light, but still seemed dim and a place designed for meetings of a secret society.

Socrates had not been in this room since that time he was a boy of thirteen. But the memory of his father standing next to Clinias, Alcibiades' father, was vivid again. That is just where they stood, under the chandelier which hung suspended from the ceiling in the center of the area surrounded by the semi-circle of raised podiums with their stone dining couches. He wondered if his father had felt as he did now. These city houses of the rich, with their lack of sunlight and fresh air and their seclusion from the sounds and sights of life, always made even the large men's room seem so confining and stuffy.

Alcibiades escorted Socrates to a small table that had been set up between the two couches that curved towards one another at the far end of the semicircular array. "Please recline here, Socrates. I think you will find these cushions very comfortable. Do you like the changes I have made to the room? The floor mosaic is new and I have dressed up the walls with some Persian tapestries. I hope you do not think me too lavish. Certainly, you have seen in the PanAthenaic procession the long line of suits of armor with their banners from all the cities which give honor to Athens for her part in defending them against the Persian threat. Now that Athens is no longer a sleepy market town for Attica, we must not allow the somewhat excessive modesty of our provincial past to stifle a modern cosmopolitan and more elegant way of life."

"I must say, Alcibiades, it seems that you are indeed right in step with our city. Just yesterday I took the time to read through the final financial accounts of the costs incurred for the construction of Athena's new temple. You know, don't you, that Pericles has had these accounts inscribed on the stone wall which runs along the colonnade leading to the Treasury Building? I suppose he wants to make sure that there are no suspicions concerning these funds and so he his inviting public scrutiny of the financing of the Parthenon. Well, anyway, when I contemplate the elegance and splendor of this building project and what it costs, I would have to agree with you that Athens, as you put it, has left behind its more modest and austere ways."

"I have not yet had an opportunity to read through all that, Socrates. It is quite long, isn't it? I hear it takes up most of the wall's length. I am interested, though. Can you summarize for me the essentials? But, here, please help yourself to the roast, the beans, and the greens. There is more wine of course, not quite as tasty as the Cypriot, but good."

"Thank you, Alcibiades. Everything looks so appetizing. As for the accounts, I must say that like you, Alcibiades, the city has not denied itself anything in commemorating the grandeur of its new role in the world. Also, it is really quite wonderful how the glorification of our patron goddess, Athena, is at the same time so enriching for our own citizens."

"What do you mean, Socrates?"

"When I totaled up all the expenditures for the construction of the Parthenon, it came to approximately 700 talents. It is difficult for me to comprehend how much money that really is unless I compare it to some kind of wages which an Athenian might earn. Let's compare that sum in this way with some kind of salary you would be familiar with, Alcibiades. Now you will never have to worry about earning wages. However, since you have built and will soon commission two triremes, you have probably already calculated what it would cost to pay your rowers. Tell me, Alcibiades, what approximately would one talent cover in rower wages?"

"Yes, Socrates, I have already made this kind of calculation since I must be careful not to outspend my annual revenues. If I remember my figures correctly, one talent, which is roughly equal to 6000 drachmas, could fund the salaries of the entire 170 men rowing crew of one of my triremes for one year. On that salary they could eat well, and manage a small household. Seven hundred talents, then, could take care of my two crews of rowers for 350 years. I don't think I'll need them for that long, unless I have ten lives. That sure is a lot of money! The temple is gloriously beautiful, though, don't you think? The sixty foot high cult statue of Athena overlaid with gold and ivory itself must have cost many talents. But why do you say, Socrates, that such an expensive temple for Athena enriches our citizens? Are you being ironic? Do you think that my house and the house of Athena would have been better if they both were furnished in a much more modest way?"

Socrates held up his hands as if to slow Alcibiades down. "Whoaah! So many questions all at once! Let me finish chewing what's in my mouth now, before I fill it with other food."

"I'm sorry, Socrates, is the roast a little tough?"

"Alcibiades, you do enjoy the play of metaphor! But let me ask you a question before we investigate your questions. Where did this money come from? I mean the funds for the Parthenon. Did our government impose a large tax on all of our citizens? Or, as often has been the case in the past, did certain rich Athenians offer their wealth as a sacrifice to Athena?"

"Neither, Socrates. Pericles certainly would have been removed from power long ago if his government levied such a huge tax burden. And as rich as men like Callias or Nicias are, none could afford such largess."

"Is it a miracle, then? Has Athena herself out of her sunlit and golden radiance showered us with gold talents?"

"Socrates, I know you have difficulty believing in such stories. It is no secret where the funds have come from."

"And where is that?"

"Pericles persuaded the Assembly to draw the funds from the treasury of the Delian Alliance."

"Yes, of course, this is what happened. But I had no idea that the funds still collected from our ally's cities totals about 400 talents a year. I counted 165 suits of armor go by in the PanAthenaic Procession. It is all very impressive and must make every Athenian's chest swell with pride for their fatherland. But I wonder how some of these cities, having paid their dues to Athens, can still afford to sponsor their PanAthenaic panoply. Did you know, Alcibiades, that this sum of 400 talents is approximately the same annual amount which our Assembly, through sales taxes, licensing fees, fines, and other assessments, levies on our own citizens?"

"Do you think there is anything wrong with that, Socrates? If it were not for Athens' navy, all of these cities would be enslaved by the Persians. How else could enough ships be built and sufficient numbers of rowers and soldiers funded unless all the cities contributed to supporting this cost?"

"Well, Alcibiades, I suppose there must have been something to this, since the cities voluntarily supported the alliance at its beginning some three and a half decades ago."

"What is the something else missing, Socrates?"

"I wonder, Alcibiades, if Athens now is not unlike the ruffian Theogenes who collects funds from his neighbors out in the remotest hill country parts of Attica. He claims that there is band of cutthroat thieves who would rob and pillage the local farm houses if it were not for his vigilance and the patrol of the hills his retinue of hired men undertake. No doubt, he has professional armed men on his estate and he shows them from time to time to his neighbors. But no one has seen an armed bandit in these parts for some thirty years. But he still each year collects his protection fees from all of his neighbors and threatens them himself with force if they refuse to pay. It is hard to believe that there is any threat from any armed robber except Theogenes himself. The government of Athens does nothing about this, because Theogenes is repeatedly elected leader of the deme of this part of Attica and this seems to certify to his fellow Assemblymen that all is well. Meanwhile this man who styles himself as the offspring of God has become very wealthy and has been able to build himself a brand new city house as well as renovate all of the buildings on his farmstead."

"I don't understand what you are implying, Socrates. Did we not save our own freedom and the freedom of the other Greek cities through our leadership of the Delian Alliance?"

"No doubt our ships played a crucial role in forcing Xerxes to retreat back across the Hellespont after the destruction of his navy at Salamis. But that was almost fifty years ago, now. And we must not forget that the Spartans and other hoplite troops decimated his army at Plataea and Mycale shortly after Salamis. There has been no credible Persian threat over the past three decades. This is why our patrols of triremes often are ill received at many of their ports of call in the Aegean since every year they are employed to coerce some of our now unwilling allies to make their payment for protection. I suppose it is also true that because we so dominate our allies, we have found it easier to arrange for favorable terms of trade and to guarantee our own citizens access to both essentials like grain and luxurious goods like lilies from Egypt and tapestries from our former enemy, Persia."

Alcibiades nodded his head in agreement. "I think your account has something to it Socrates. But isn't this all quite natural? Why shouldn't the stronger impose their will on the weaker? And isn't it possible that our commercial empire has made life better not only for Athenians but for all those cities which trade with us?"

Socrates yawned. It was late and the long walk home awaited him. The conversation had taken a turn that he had heard many times from men such as Gorgias and Thrasymachus. No doubt, young Alcibiades was also familiar with the way these professional teachers could appeal to Nature or man-made law in their defense of the interest of the stronger.

"Alcibiades, I can see that much of the seven hundred talents spent on the Parthenon finds its way into the hands of the craftsmen who labor on it and that they are grateful to Pericles' on this score. It is wonderful, isn't it, that our attention to Athena brings prosperity to her devotees. I suppose something like this might be going on in other cities that are part of the web of commerce Athens dominates. Subservience to Athens surely benefits at least some of those who live in the cities of our empire. I suppose we have to consider whether the prosperity that allows more and more of our desires and appetites to be satisfied is the best way to promote that excellence and virtue which humans alone can exhibit. This, no doubt, is a difficult question which could occupy us for many days. It seems that many Athenians are convinced that the substance of the freedom they fought to preserve consists of the satisfaction of ever expanding appetites and desires. On this matter I am of another mind. But now it is quite late, and I must be on my way home."

"You must be tired, Socrates. It is not like you to talk at such length in declarative sentences."

"Yes, it has been a long day and I must confess that all the sights and festivities of the PanAthenaic celebrations of the past week have made for many long nights with little rest."

"Of course I am many years your junior and it would be presumptuous of me to tell you how to take care of yourself; but Socrates, I really think you are too hard on yourself. Here it is almost midnight and already tired, you would undertake an hour walk back to your home. Really, there is no need for you to leave. What kind of host would I be if I let you at this late hour make such a walk? Are you not worried about the out of town PanAthenaic toughs – you know the *pankratiasts* – who half-drunk still wander through our streets at night? I insist, spend the night here and go home in the morning!"

"You are very kind, Alcibiades. But what would the neighbors think if they saw me leaving your house in the morning? You know that young men like you are constantly watched by others."

"Socrates, I am surprised that you of all men are worried about the opinion of others."

"It is not I that I am worried about myself Alcibiades. Indeed, I must confess that I enjoy your company and would under other circumstances be happy to stay longer. But you have already sent the servants to their quarters, there are no other guests who might chaperone their young host, and so all this might appear to others as serious impropriety on your part."

Alcibiades smiled and shook his head. "Socrates, I can think of no other man with whom I would be safer. And if there is anyone who can help me on my way to becoming a better man, I think it is you. I can see you are made uneasy by my desire to make our bond to one another closer. But if you can teach me the virtue of reasoning well and the power of persuasive speech, then I think these gifts you can bring to me make you the only one whose love would be worthy of me.

"What are you proposing, Alcibiades? What kind of love is this that you offer in exchange for these gifts?"

"I think you are too shy to talk about this, Socrates. I will tell you, though, how I look at it. I think it would be just absurd to refuse you this as anything else you wanted that belonged to me or any of my friends."

Socrates looked intently into the eyes of Alcibiades. He could see that the young man was entirely serious in his proposal. No doubt Alcibiades was already at eighteen a youth who knew how to play the high stakes game of seduction from both sides. Fully alert now,

Socrates found it powerfully attractive to be in a role he had never experienced before – he was being seduced!

But he must be careful if he was to keep himself unstained by a dishonorable descent into slavish desire which could injure both himself and Alcibiades.

"Tell me Alcibiades, more exactly the meaning of 'this' which you now think you should not refuse me! Is it like that which Laius, the father of Oedipus, sought to enjoy with Chrysippus?"

Alcibiades furrowed his brow and wondered why Socrates asked

Figure 13
Laius' abduction of Pelops' son, Chrysippus

for clarification about what seemed straightforward and obvious. But this was just Socrates' way – and after all it was his way of unsettling what others thought they understood that made him so hypnotically fascinating. "Yes, Socrates, 'it' is like this in some way. This is the story which some Athenians believe records a royal and ancient example of the passion which an older man can feel towards a youth."

"Would you agree, Alcibiades, this story seems to imply certain troublesome consequences for such a passion? Is there not something discomfiting in the poet's description of Laius' conduct towards the youth he loves? Does not Pindar say that Laius kidnaps Chrysippus, causing great grief to the youth's father, King Pelops? Does it not seem curious to you that our own Sophocles tells us in his poetic drama of Laius and his son Oedipus, that Laius' passionate love of Chrysippus leads to a curse upon the house of Laius, a curse which leads to Laius' death at the hands of his own son? Is the 'this' you speak of in the love of an older man for a youth akin to such a passion which brings in its aftermath the curse of reckless blindness?"

"Socrates, I have no father. You certainly are not kidnapping me. Was not Chrysippus just a boy? I am already with beard. Certainly these differences matter. I do admit the obvious, that the story proposes that the desire a man can feel for a youth is strong and that care must be taken to protect the youth from coerced affection."

"Yes, Alcibiades, there are these differences you mention. But would you say the passion the older man feels for a youth is often something that can so distract the man that he may become, as it were, obsessed with his beloved?"

"I suppose so, Socrates. I guess it is like a kind of intoxication."

"Yes, for the older man this is the case. I suppose, though, for the youth, the wild-eyed look of the lover must seem quite strange. It is as though the man of years has fled from the scene and what remains behind in the young man's embrace is some kind of quivering animal."

"Socrates, I think you have looked at too many of our potters' sketches."

"Alcibiades, don't you think that perhaps our painters and poets are indeed sometimes inspired? Perhaps the painted satyr or the poet's 'Laius' depicts the truth about how Dionysos and Aphrodite may possess a human soul."

"But Socrates, is it not a taste of the divine, of immortality itself, to commune with such god-like ecstasy?"

"Alcibiades, I think you are too young to flee to the gods like this. It is an older man, who feeling his own mortality on the back of his neck, seeks solace with Aphrodite and Dionysos. As for myself, I prefer the company of Apollo. If you would have me assist you in bringing forth reason and the law of self-mastery in yourself, then I must show you this when I love you. Is this not the love you ask of me?"

"I suppose so, Socrates"

"Why is it, Alcibiades, that Solon was able to persuade the Council to pass a law forbidding men, who had ever received money or gifts for their sexual favors, to speak before the Assembly?"

"Pericles explained this to me, Socrates. It is, he said, because Solon led his fellow citizens to understand that a man who was willing to sell his own body for money or other gifts would more than likely be willing to sell out the common good of the city for a bribe."

"Well, then, do you think that either you or I should make an exchange with one another where one's body is surrendered for the sake of some kind of gifts? Would other citizens trust the state with a man, who even in his youth, so bartered with his body? Do you not aspire to be a speaker who can be trusted to lead the Assembly?"

"I had not thought of it in this way. But if this is as you say, then it would be very risky behavior for a young man to accept gifts at this price. But Socrates is there not some domain left for us where our conduct is entirely private, where what we do is no business of others and therefore should not be subject to the laws of the city?"

"Alcibiades, it seems you do have a gift for philosophy! Such a question as this would lead us on to a thicket questions which would be very difficult to resolve as we try to understand the boundaries of a citizen's freedom. But however we define the limits of an individual citizen's liberty, would you not agree that the people of Athens always hold their leaders to a standard of accountability and transparency that allows little room for a 'private' life?"

"Yes, Socrates, even Pericles, the most powerful man in Athens, is open to almost limitless scrutiny and is thus required, as it were, to live out his life always giving accounts of his conduct."

"But it is not just our generals and speakers who must deal with such accountability, is it Alcibiades? After all, you will undergo an examination this very week as you have completed the *epheboi* training and will be administered the oath of citizenship. A youth is required to demonstrate that he has become a soldier ready to die for his country before he is admitted to citizenship. Is it not the case that if someone could show that the youth has bartered away his body and become like a woman, surrendering his body to the pleasure of another; then this would be grounds for denying the youth entitlement to the manly duties and privileges of citizenship?"

"I would think in my case there can be no doubt about my readiness to fulfill the oath of citizenship. No man could ever Aphrodite me. I would do what my Alkmeonid forefather Megacles did to Cylon's men – kill him on the spot. You can be sure, Socrates, that when I have finished my part in the history of our city, I will 'hand down the fatherland not diminished but enhanced and improved'. I will lead the city to new heights of glory. Indeed, I am determined to outdo my fathers so that the Athens of my sons and grandsons will be richer, more powerful, and more secure than ever before."

"Perhaps, Alcibiades, you will succeed. As for myself, I find it a daunting challenge to master my own nature. I would hesitate to take on governing or leading the city when I have not yet finished the work of governing myself well. It may be that, young as you are, you are much further advanced than me in this work."

"We shall see, Socrates. I will call for Milo and have him extinguish the candles on the chandelier. It is very late now. So you really must sleep here. My couch is the only one fit for sleeping. Recline here with me. There is plenty of room."

After Milo had extinguished all the candles but one small one near the door to the hallway, Socrates got up from his couch, gathered his robe around him, and then sat down on the edge of Alcibiades couch. "Yes, Alcibiades, I will stay for the night. I am so very tired. If you have a cloak to spare, I will be very comfortable on this side of the couch."

After Socrates had lay down with his back to Alcibiades, Alcibiades stood up and took his sleeping cloak from the peg on the wall near the hallway door. He disrobed completely, hanging his garments on the same peg. In the dim light of the one candle, he looked with satisfaction at his own torso and the way it still glistened from the scented oil he had applied earlier. He moved quietly back to his couch, arranged his sleeping cloak so that it would cover both himself and Socrates, and then crawled under the cloak beside the philosopher. "Socrates, are you still awake?"

"Yes, Alcibiades. Thank you for covering me. My robe does not keep me warn the way it did when it was new."

Alcibiades moved closer, so that his thighs gently touched Socrates' backside. Socrates stirred, but his breathing remained even and Alcibiades knew that he would soon be asleep. So Alcibiades turned on his back and fell asleep, assured that he had won the friendship of the strange man beside him.

When they awoke in the morning, it was if Alcibiades had slept beside an older brother.

Socrates thanked Alcibiades for the bed and the supper, and while the morning sun was still very low in the sky left the house and made his way out of Athens back to his farm.

CHAPTER EIGHTEEN
DUTY CALLS - ALCIBIADES AND SOCRATES AT POTIDAEA
(Winter of 432 B.C.)

"It was after all this, you must understand, that we were both sent on to active service to Potidaea, were we messed together. Well, to begin with, he stood the hardships of the campaign far better than I did, or anyone else, for that matter."

(Plato. *Symposium*, 220-a: Alcibiades' speech)

"For no man ever proves himself a good man in war unless he can endure to face the blood and the slaughter, go close against the enemy and fight with his hands.

Here is courage, mankind's finest possession, here is the noblest prize that a young man can endeavor to win, and it is a good thing his city and all the people share with him when a man plants his feet and stands in the foremost spears relentlessly, all thought of foul flight completely forgotten, and has well trained his heart to be steadfast and to endure, and with words encourages the man who is stationed beside him.

Here is a man who proves himself to be valiant in war.

With a sudden rush he turns to flight the rugged
battalions of the enemy, and sustains the beating
waves of assault.

And he who so falls among the champions and loses
his sweet life, so blessing with honor his city, his
father, and all his people, with wounds in his chest,
where the spear that he was facing has transfixed
that massive guard of his shield, and gone through
his breastplate as well, why, such a man is lamented
alike by the young and the elders, and all his city
goes into mourning and grieves for his loss."

(Tyrtaeus. The Spartan Creed)

It had all happened so fast! Just a week after Socrates had slept at Alcibiades' side in the privacy of Alcibiades' home they were both sent on active duty to Potidaea. It was early winter on the western most peninsula of Chalcidice and already frost and ice covered the fields and ponds that surrounded their encampment which had been deployed a few miles to the north of Potidaea. Usually, Athenian generals would avoid undertaking any military action that required the use of the fleet during the winter. Frequent severe storms at sea, the empty fields making provisions more uncertain in hostile territory, and the extra hardships of cold and sickness made the odds less favorable for success. But this was an emergency. Pericles himself had persuaded the Assembly that Athens must immediately put down a rebellion of those cities in the Chalcidice which now, at the urging of Athens' enemies, were refusing to pay their assessments and accept the governance of those democratic leaders approved by Athens. Corinth had sent a force of volunteers led by their most able general, Aristeus the son of Adeimantus, to assist the rebellion. If this rebellion was allowed to succeed, soon other subject cities would join them and then Athens would be vulnerable to attack from her other enemies. And so here they were, sharing a tent together and trying to stay warm until their generals ordered them into battle against the rebels who held Potidaea and their allies from Corinth.

"Socrates what in the world have you been doing standing out there all this time?" Socrates had entered the tent as quietly as he could, but Alcibiades was wide awake. "It must be midnight or later. Are you trying to make the rest of us feel like softies? There you are out in the open, far from the warmth of a campfire, shoeless and with only your tunic and a summer cloak. You must have been in some kind of trance. How else could you not feel the cold ground under your feet and the icy wind on your uncovered head and face? I know your strange ways, but this is too much! Have a little consideration for me. How do you expect me to go to sleep worrying about whether or not we will find you half frozen to death in the morning?"

Socrates laughed. "Really, Alcibiades, you sound like a mother! I think our officer agreed to my request to mess with you so that I could look out for you."

Alcibiades sat up and pulled his thick woolen cloak around him so he could better see Socrates in the dim light that reached their tent from one of the campfires. "Zeus Meilichios! You look like a bogeyman from some icy cave. Your beard is full of ice sickles."

"Yes, my scruffy beard keeps the icy barbs at bay, as our poets might say. My big flat nose, my heavy eyelids, my squat thick legs, my callused big feet, and my barrel shaped chest also do me well. I may not win any beauty contests, but my body is really very serviceable. It keeps me warm."

"I suppose you were wrestling with one of your philosophical problems. How do you do that when you are by yourself? It is hard to imagine you making any headway unless you are interrogating some one else."

"Well, Alcibiades, if you must know, I was working through a question which led to one conundrum after another. And you are correct. I did have a partner, albeit an imaginary one."

Alcibiades stretched his legs and propped his back up against the small chest in which he carried his armor. "Well, since something I ate has my stomach full of dancing bears, would you be so kind to share your inquiry with me? Perhaps, like you, it might engage my mind so as to anesthetize my body. Only, I hope your imaginary partner was not a young man more attractive than me."

Socrates sat down and began to smooth the straw which would serve as his bed. "It is quite late Alcibiades. Shouldn't you be sleeping? You must be hale and fit should we be called to battle. Besides, I'm not sure that you would find the problem as lively as I do. You do know my imaginary interlocutor. It is your kinsman, Pericles."

"I'm fine. All we did today was loll around camp. So let me into the conversation. After all, I know Pericles very well and I will make sure your virtual Pericles is not dissembling."

"You are a clever young man, my friend. I suppose if Pericles is my imaginary similitude and this image is far off the mark, then I am only like the ventriloquists who make their puppets speak. In that case it is only a monologue going on in my mind. I much prefer a dialogue. Perhaps you do know the mind of Pericles better than I. But still, I worry that my problem and all its uncertainties may be peculiarly mine and may not be suited to a young soldier eager to do his patriotic duty with unclouded zeal."

"Socrates you are every young man's favorite just because you never patronize us. Let me decide what is suitable for me."

"Alcibiades, the question I'm pondering concerns how the care of the improvement of my own soul relates to my obligation to the authorities which govern Athens. Since Pericles, as our supreme commander, is the most powerful authority in Athens and since he is not adverse to the spirit of critical inquiry, I have called upon him to assist me. Of course it would be better if he were here, but it is part of the hardship of these campaigns that I must do without the better things and make do with whatever resources are at hand. Now since you have offered to authenticate my Pericles, I will share with you my inquiry."

"Yes, let us talk until I tire and can then go to sleep, Socrates. But first, would you make clearer to me what you mean by 'caring for the improvement of the soul'? I don't think of you as being religious in the usual way, so this talk of the soul, on your part, is confusing to me. Do you mean by the soul something like the Orphics who preach there is some immaterial being in us which is immortal and must be purified if it is to escape the tortures of Tartarus?"

"My young friend, I can see I must damp down my fervor for the search for wisdom. Philosophy, it seems, tonight must serve as a sleeping pill."

"Socrates, sometimes I think you regard everything in life, every activity, as only a platform or a means to philosophy. Would it detract from philosophy to suggest it might be a sleep aid?"

"If it is because rational inquiry concerning fundamental questions which do not provide us with ready closure is so boring that it stupefies one to sleep, then philosophy's pharmaceutical power to induce restful sleep is no better than the tedious chatter of an ignorant slave. But if it is because philosophy's search for wisdom may lead closer to the peace of mind and serenity which is conducive to untroubled sleep free from the terrors of the superstitious mind, then philosophy is a healing *pharmakos* worth more than all the treatments of Asclepius himself."

"Socrates, I think we are straying from our topic. I am ready to play Pericles' part. Now explain to me how what you call the improvement of the soul relates to a citizen's obligation to the governing authorities of our city."

"Is it not the case, my young Pericles stand-in, that we fought the Persians to preserve our freedom?"

"Yes, of course!"

"Does this freedom only apply to our city as a whole?"

"What do you mean by that Socrates?"

"It could be said that a city is free if it decides upon its own policy towards all other cities and accepts no laws except those which arise from its own constitution, whether it be a monarchy, a homegrown tyranny, or a democracy. It operates under no compulsion from a foreign power. It could be said of such a city that it is free as a whole. But if, over and above this, the city is so constituted that each of its citizens enjoys a liberty of self-determination which affords each one the latitude to make basic choices defining the course of their lives, then such a city is one that grants its own citizens freedom. Now would you say, kinsman of Pericles, our Athens fought to preserve this liberty for its individual citizens, and that it is this liberty which is far more precious then the mere independence of our city from foreign domination?"

"Yes, Socrates, it is this more precious liberty which is the true freedom our forefathers preserved at Marathon and Salamis. But tell me, what does this have to do with the improvement of the soul which you are always talking about?"

"Pericles, I know you must have thought much about what your teacher Protagoras means when he says 'Man is the measure of all things'. Tell me, then, what do you think is the quality of that 'measure' which a man may exercise with respect to all things!"

Alcibiades frowned and then smiled. "Where is my guardian when I really need him? I don't understand, Socrates, what you are asking."

"It seems to me that Protagoras, in a somewhat cryptic manner of speaking, meant to say that each human being is a kind of being which is at liberty to determine its own relation to all things. More simply stated, human beings have a natural capacity to be free or self-determining. Now tell me, what is this natural capacity for freedom? I mean what is it in the nature of being human that enables us to realize a kind of freedom in which we can assume responsibility for our own life-course?"

"Isn't it as simple as defining this freedom as doing whatever I want to do without coercion by anyone else?"

"But, Alcibiades, don't wild animals do whatever they want? I think it is alright now if we dispense with our fiction and send Pericles away. I am confident that you can help me in my inquiry. So tell me, are animals doing what they want, as you understand it?"

"I suppose so Socrates."

"But do you really think animals, say a dog or cat, are free in the way a man may be. We see animals driven by powerful appetites and instincts. Wild animals migrate, mate, fight with one another, rear their young, and perform other such actions, all driven by a law within them which is set in motion by the change of seasons, the growth of their own bodies, and circumstances in their environment. When such animals are tamed, men manipulate these appetites and instincts so as to channel the animal's behavior in a fashion useful to men. But whether an animal is wild or domesticated, wouldn't it be a mistake to describe the animal's behavior as something it is responsible for? Thus, we don't say of an animal that it is either wicked or good. It just is what it is – a creature which carries the law of its behavior inscribed by Nature in its very body, its instincts. Now it may be that human beings often act in a similar way. But when they act driven only by powerful appetites or instincts, do we not often blame them for impetuous or irresponsible conduct?"

"Socrates, I am not so sure that all our behavior isn't shaped by appetites and instincts. And this is why some people insist that however one has acted it is always correct to say that they acted just as they wanted."

"If I follow what you are proposing, then when a man falls before his enemy and begs for his life, offering himself up to slavery, it is what he wants to do. I take it this means that he wants to live as a slave more than die as, we say, a 'free' man."

"Yes, that what is I mean Socrates."

"But if another man fights to his death rather than save his life by offering himself to slavery, then you would say, I suppose, that this man did what he wants to do also. He wanted to die with honor rather than live as a slave. Yet we praise the one who dies to preserve his honor while defending his city and hold the other who will do anything, including accepting slavery to save his life, cowardly and base. Would you agree, Alcibiades?"

"Yes Socrates, our poets sing the praises of those who sacrifice their lives defending our city and heap scorn on the man who throws down his shield and flees or accepts slavery in exchange for his life."

"But why, Alcibiades, should we either praise the brave warrior or blame the cowardly warrior if their action, like that of other animals, was determined by either instincts such as that of survival or by irresistibly powerful appetites triggered by circumstances over which they have no control? Wouldn't it be the case, if this is what you mean by a man always doing what he wants, that his behavior is determined by forces that he does not freely direct? And if this is the only way his will operates, then he is no more responsible for his acts than any other animal."

"Well, Socrates, I suppose this is how it might really be. Don't we say that some men by nature are base and others noble? I have heard my grandfather Megacles explain why it is that some men end up slaves and others Masters in terms of the way Nature has sorted them out from birth into different kinds of stock."

"I have another question for you, Alcibiades. Isn't it because human beings can deliberate before they act and relate their act to some standards or principles which may trump their own immediate appetites that we say a good man may find that his duty requires doing something other than what his appetites or instincts would lead him to do. Or do you think, Alcibiades, that the only force which keeps a hoplite at his station in the line, is the fear that if he throws down his shield and flees he will more likely die or suffer terrible pain then if he stands steadfast in the line to meet the enemy's onslaught? Honor then has nothing to do with it, but only a calculus of the chances of living and dying."

"I am not sure what I think about honor, except that I know it would be unbearable for me to be regarded by others as a coward or as base." Alcibiades yawned and rubbed his eyes. "I am beginning to feel quite sleepy, Socrates, so tell me what you think this freedom is if it is more than simply following one's desires and instincts."

"I would not want you to be anything other than at your most vigorous when morning arrives. It may be that we will engage the enemy tomorrow and you must have all your strength if you are to fare well. I can state concisely how I understand human freedom and the way it is essentially related to what I mean by the improvement of the soul. What I cannot see through as clearly is how my freedom is to be reconciled with the dictates of those who govern our state and command us to take up arms against other cities and their men. Are you sure you want me to go on?"

"Yes, go on! Only, I will lie down now and let my eyes close. If you are brief, I can hear your account before sleep overtakes me."

"Alcibiades, when we Athenians call anything good, isn't because we think this thing excels in that function which especially defines the nature of the thing. So a knife which is designed to cut is a good knife if it is sharp and cuts well. If we are thinking of a good horse we first ask ourselves what function is it that a horse can uniquely perform better than any other animal. Obviously, from a human point of view, a horse's unique function is the capacity to run fast carrying a rider on its back. We say the horse is good then if when mounted it runs fast well. And isn't it the case that we think of this function as its characteristic purpose or what we call its *telos*? Are you following this Alcibiades?"

"Yes, Socrates, I am still awake."

"Well, then, what would you say is the characteristic function or *telos* of a human being? Or to put it in a different way, what kind of being or function that a human being can do is distinctively human? What way of acting is uniquely human and thus different from every other kind of animal behavior? Isn't it, Alcibiades, what Aeschylus dramatizes in his play, *Prometheus Bound*?"

"I am not so familiar with that work. After all it hasn't been staged in Athens for over thirty years. So you will have to share your interpretation with me. I suppose you have studied Aeschylus' text in great detail, just as you have the texts of your philosopher friends."

"It is true, Alcibiades, I do enjoy meditating on the various ways the poets' and playwrights' highly inventive symbols and metaphors often point to some fundamental insight about human nature and its relation to the powerful forces at work inside ourselves and the Cosmos outside us. So I think Aeschylus' story of Prometheus intends to teach us how man is lifted from mere animal life to a civilized human life. Aeschylus emphasizes in his version of the story the manner whereby Prometheus rescues man from his dream-like animal existence and his precarious subjection to the whimsical will of Zeus who is about to annihilate him. Prometheus is the personification and representation of the unique human capacity of fore-thought. Thus, Prometheus makes possible for man the power of forethought. Promethean man is able to reckon the seasons and predict various cycles and forces so as to steer them for his own benefit. This is all to say that human beings win their way to a measure of independence from Zeus, the controller of the most terrifying force of Nature, the fire-filled thunderbolt, and thereby secure themselves by a unique power of forethought. Animals run from the fire guided by instinct only. Man can think ahead and plan a course of action to deal with a terrifying state of affairs before it happens. Man can take this very power, the power of fire, and turn it into a tool to keep other animals at bay and then refine and mold other powerful tools. This is part and parcel of what it means to claim that what is unique to a human being is the capacity for behavior guided by rational thinking rather than mere instinct or powerful appetites. Of course forethought, which is literally the meaning of our mythic proto-human tragic god's name, can never comprehend or subdue the infinite power of the universe itself. Thus our Promethean project of autonomy is tragic. Promethean man must forever find himself again and again subject to the revenge of forces that will not bend readily to his purposes. Zeus will not readily release Prometheus from his dominion."

Figure 14
Prometheus and Atlas

"Zeus Almighty, Socrates, you find all that in Aeschylus! So is this freedom – to act with forethought or a plan?"

"It is and more, Alcibiades. Does not Sophocles in his play *Oedipus Rex* teach us more about our human calling? Isn't it striking that Oedipus, who in a fit of anger impulsively kills his own father and then becomes entangled in a course of consequences which lead to marriage to his own mother, is nevertheless celebrated in Sophocles trilogy of plays on this subject as a great benefactor of Athens? We follow in Sophocles' story Oedipus' determination to learn all there is to know about the man in Thebes' whose transgression, according to the seer, has led to the plague that afflicts Thebes. The blind seer leads Oedipus to recognize that he himself is the transgressor. When he understands his own actions and reflects upon their consequences, he takes responsibility for what he has done. And while he blinds himself he now sees with the eye of his understanding that actions guided by reflection and circumspection, mindful of principles of prudent conduct with both kin and strangers, offer a more human course free from the horrors of the dark and demonic furies. Oedipus at Colonus exchanges the furies for the graces, the angels of persuasion, law, and conduct guided by principles forged by rational self-examination and reflection."

Socrates paused and stared intently at Alcibiades face as it peeked out from the blanket that he had pulled up to cover everything except his eyes and the top of his head. The camp fires had grown dim and so he could not quite see whether his young man had gone to sleep. He spoke softly, "Alcibiades, are you asleep?"

There was no answer and Socrates now could hear the deep regular breathing of his beloved. I am alone, he thought to himself. He would think through for himself the puzzle that now threatened to unravel his determination to perfect his own human freedom…This is what we Athenians should care for most of all if we are called to risk our lives to preserve freedom. A good life is a course of life guided by principles forged through a reflective and rational examination of myself and others. If we have a divine spark in us, it is this process of unfolding autonomy which to me is best described as the improvement of the soul. My young friend dreams of Olympic victories, leading men into battle as their supreme general, achieving fame and glory like that of Pericles, the most powerful politician in Athens. I too will serve Athens, but not as a general, a politician in the Assembly, or as an Athenian Olympian hero. I will be Athens' helper going about trying to convince every citizen that they too should care most of all for the improvement of their souls if they are together, through reasoned reflection and deliberative discourse with one another, to forge a good state founded on wise laws and just institutions. This after all, he thought, is the way a free man may be at home in a city where he might see his own freedom mirrored in the collective life of his community. But there was no avoiding a bundle of possible contradictions that this very moment threatened to scramble this script. He could not go to sleep until he tackled them head on. Now he would have to resume his dialogue with his imaginary Pericles.

"Pericles, how can it be right for Athenians to ally themselves with the Macedonian, Perdiccas? We all have heard that he is a terrible tyrant who treats his own subjects as slaves. He has ordered executions of any of his own citizens who dare to criticize him. It is probably misleading to even call the subjects of his rule citizens. They have no rights whatsoever. They are executed without trials and are given no opportunity to defend themselves through legal recourse of any kind. We have evidence that he tortures officials who even display a hint of disloyalty. He has seized properties from his own most prominent farmers and then exiled them to far away wastelands. If our alliance with him helps him extend and secure his power over all of Macedonia, pushing aside his more moderate brother as he seizes the throne from his father Alexander, then would not we Athenians have joined forces with an enemy of freedom? Is this not wrong? Is this not a case when a good man ought not to lend his sword to such a campaign?"

"Socrates, you are sometimes simple-minded. Perdiccas' forces are needed to assure the success of our campaign against the rebels in Potidaea. Already Corinth has sent a force joined with others from the Spartan alliance. They have tried to enlist Perdiccas to join them and coordinate an attack that would trap us between enemy forces both to the north and south of us on the peninsula. Military necessity means that a commander charged with defending Athens' empire and other interests must sometimes temporize."

"But Pericles, if the rebels of Potidaea see us in league with Perdiccas would not all the people of Potidaea conclude that it is we who are the enemies of freedom and thus have right on their side as they resist Athens, the ally of a tyrant?"

"Socrates, you don't mean to argue that each individual soldier citizen of Athens has some kind of right to refuse military service if he does not approve of the state's decision to go to war. After all, Socrates, it is a vote of the Assembly which authorizes any major deployment of our navy or our hoplite forces. Imagine what would happen if individual soldiers were permitted to refuse to serve because they did not agree with the state's decision."

"There is considerable weight to your argument, Pericles. But surely if an officer commands me to kill a diplomat who comes into camp carrying the sacred emblems of an ambassador, I should not obey that order. Is that not an unlawful order?"

"But this is different than a soldier refusing to serve in a military campaign."

"Suppose the Assembly approves a military campaign that is to include acts of atrocity such as the systematic torture of every male in a city and the rape of all its women. Surely a good man could not take part in such a campaign."

"Socrates, we are Athenians, not barbarians. Our great city would never treat a vanquished enemy in this way. No true Athenian would ever speak before our Assembly and urge such an atrocity. We need not consider such a case because Athens would never make use of its strength in such a way."

"But if such a thing should come to pass, would you agree that a good man in this situation should abide by his own principles of civilized conduct rather than be party to such barbarous conduct – even if it is approved by a majority in the Assembly. There are some men in Athens who were shocked by your treatment of the men of Samos. Would you have punished one of your soldiers if he refused to take part in the branding of the foreheads of every Samian male in such a way as to burn away the scalp so that the brain itself became exposed?"

"Socrates, you go too far. My order to so punish the Samians only repeated what they had done to Athenian prisoners they had captured in an earlier battle."

"Socrates, stop mumbling and come with me to breakfast! You look like you haven't slept at all. Have you been talking with yourself all night?" Alcibiades had awakened and was surprised to see Socrates sitting up in the same position as he was when they spoke during the night.

Socrates turned and pulled the tent flaps up to let in the early morning light. He gathered up his cloak about him and followed Alcibiades out of the tent towards their company's emblem which was posted just a short walk from their tent. There they would share a breakfast meal of stale bread and some cheese.

The men had just finished their breakfast when their supreme commander, Callias, sounded the bugle calling them to arm themselves and assemble on the west side of the open field adjacent to their camp. Alcibiades could hear the bugles of the other Athenian commanders calling their troops to prepare for battle.

"We must hurry Alcibiades. I will help you with your armor. There is no need to call the slave boy. I think he has gone to the supply tent on the far side of the camp." Socrates was already standing beside their tent as he called to Alcibiades.

Alcibiades hurried into the tent and opened the armor chest. "What is going on, Socrates? I thought that with our superior force and the help of Perdiccas' Macedonian forces, there would be no way the Potidaeans would venture out to meet us in battle."

"Something has changed. I am sure our Commander will make our situation clear when he issues orders for our deployment. Here let me help you secure your breastplate. When you cover your shins, be sure the greaves do not tangle and constrict the movement of your lower leg!"

When both of them had finished arming and taken their shields, short swords, and long ash spears, they made their way with the rest of their comrades to the field.

"Where is Callias, Socrates? Won't he be leading our phalanx?"

"Apparently not, Alcibiades, look, it is Cleon who will lead us. He has already begun to address our units. I suppose Callias will be coordinating all our forces and he has entrusted command of various units to the four generals sent to assist him."

Alcibiades could not help feeling uneasy as he listened intently to the general. Was not this the very same man who could be seen among the commoners in the market place, merchants who owned their own stalls and spent most of their days there selling their wares? How did this leather dealer persuade the Assembly to appoint him a general? Although Cleon was mounted on a stallion dressed in what certainly was an impressive new set of armor and he carried the mace of a general, he did not look the part! It was hardly reassuring to see on the armor not even a scratch or a dent. Had this man ever fought before, let alone command a large force of hoplites?

Socrates could see the fear in Alcibiades eyes. He remembered his first tour when not much older than Alcibiades he was called out to march to Megara to face a combined force of Corinthians and Spartans. He had actually trembled with fear as he dressed for battle.

"Alcibiades, there is no need to worry. Our units are filled with veteran lieutenants who will see to our safety as they keep our lines in fighting order. Listen carefully to the battle orders. It is a great help, I have found, to understand clearly our particular place and objective in the deployment of our forces. When the din and rush of battle begins, you need to keep your wits about you by focusing on your immediate duty of keeping the man to your left covered by your shield and being prepared to move forward in the ranks if needed. This focus is courage. Courage is steadier if you understand how our advance is supported by our other phalanxes."

Alcibiades nodded his head, but said nothing. He was straining to hear Cleon's every word. This was not easy since this general had not yet perfected a commanding voice.

"Citizen Soldiers of Athens, we have learned from our Macedonian friends that Perdiccas has betrayed us. He is preparing to send the cavalry he has stationed just seven miles north of us in Olynthus against us. This attack from the north aims to hit us from the rear as we will be forced to confront the Corinthian forces and the Potidaeans who now are forming their battle line outside their city walls. We need not worry about Perdiccas' force. It is small and our reliable Macedonian allies will send their cavalry to turn Perdiccas back. Numbers are now on our side. You are all aware that our force of two thousand hoplites has now joined with the thousand hoplites that our Assembly had sent on ahead of us. We are well over three thousand strong, given the help of our local allies. Our hoplites will be deployed in four phalanxes, each phalanx with a line of 75 and 10 ranks deep. Our phalanx will take the right wing and our plan is to engage the enemy's left wing close to the shore-line to our west. We have been charged with cutting off any attempt by the enemy to outflank us and fold up the rest of our line. I am confident that we will be victorious. The gods are with us. All the signs are favorable. It is a good day for our youngest soldiers to prove their mettle. Our ranks are much deeper than those of the enemy and filled with battle toughened veterans. Remember our password: 'For Athena and her glory'! Should we need to signal a shift in our line during the din of close engagement, your officers will send the orders, certified by this slogan, down the line."

Alcibiades would be in the second rank with Socrates right behind him in the third rank. Socrates had already gained a reputation for his skill with the shield and his stamina and strength as a pusher. When two hoplite lines collided and both forces locked together in the clash of a wall of shields, often the outcome of the battle depended on the weight and mass of the forward momentum that back rankers could marshal. Alcibiades could not make up his mind whether it was a good or bad thing to have such a force directly behind him.

"Form up men, we will move forward on the bugle call to advance."

"Alcibiades, go ahead and pull your helmet down. You want to make sure everything is clear in the eye and mouth openings. It is a good idea to get used to the constricted line of vision. You will be able to see all you need to deal with in front of you." Socrates had already adjusted his helmet and was flexing the arm in which he held his shield. He wanted to be sure that Alcibiades remained as calm as possible.

"Is it true, Socrates, that Aristeus, the son of Adeimantus, commands the Corinthian volunteers who fight with the Potidaeans?"

"Yes, I have heard that Pericles even sent a message to him, imploring him to find a diplomatic solution to our dispute concerning Potidaea. Aristeus sent word back to Athens that if she would stop behaving like imperial Persia and let the Potidaeans have their independence, then there would be no cause for Corinth and her allies to fight for the liberation of other Hellenes just as his father Adeimantus and Themistocles the Athenian had against Xerxes. Well, here we are. So much for diplomacy! Now force, not persuasion, will sort it out."

The bugle sounded. The entire phalanx stood at attention with shields and spears raised, ready for a charge. Alcibiades could not see much more than straight out in front of him. He was in the second rank and could not yet see the enemy line. But they must be close. He felt the firm pressure of Socrates' round shield on his shoulder blades and, like all the other men in his rank, his legs now belonged to the body of the phalanx. They must move in unison with the great body armored and armed to smash and splinter another armored and armed bronzed body hurtling towards them. When the second bugle sounded, he must charge forward or be run over by the ranks behind him.

Although it was a cold winter morning, sweat already poured down Alcibiades' forehead and into his eyes. It was good that both of his hands were occupied with shield and spear. Otherwise, he might have given into the urge to rip his helmet off and wipe the sweat from his eyes. What kind of warrior can I be if I am half blinded by the sweat burning in my eyes? How can I feel tired already? The armor is so damn heavy and it is rubbing me raw and we still await the signal to charge.

It was as though the corporate body understood. In front, on both sides, and behind him the phalanx of men began to sing the sacred ancestral paean. The words did not matter. He too began to sing. There were no trumpets, no flutes, and no minstrel's harps. But as he sang with the chorus of Athenians around him, his eyes cleared, the armor became as light as his own skin, and his body filled with the spirit of Ares. Through his body and mind, there coursed the bracing and healing balm of the music of the divine that lifted the frail and vulnerable individual out of himself to feel the power of the transcendent life force of his tribe.

The second bugle sounded and like one man their phalanx charged forward. Out in front of him Alcibiades could see, just beyond the small rise in the open ground, the charging enemy. Everything was so clear. There was no dust. The ground was as hard and cold as the murderous war cries that now raced out ahead to strike fear into the enemy. I am king of the hill, thought Alcibiades. No one will throw me to the ground. I am invincible.

"We fight Corinthians, men. Let us make short work of these whore-loving..." Before the lieutenant who served beside Alcibiades could finish his sentence, the collision of the two charging walls of shields, like the crash of lightening-filled thunder so close that it crackled, announced the arrival of Ares – the killing zone.

Alcibiades pushed his shield out far from his own chest, careful still to provide cover to the right side of his comrade to the left. No enemy spear was going to reach him easily, even if it pierced his shield. His long spear now pointed high over the shoulder of the first ranker who, hunkered down in a crouch, was straining to keep his feet as he and his enemy both were locked vice-like in the grips of the opposite forces now pushing to annihilate each other. Alcibiades leaned his weight into his rigid left arm so that his shield could carry through the force behind him which aimed to propel the first ranker through the enemy line.

Socrates strained to see from his third rank position right behind Alcibiades what was happening in front of them both. The pushing was fierce and yet neither side was making any headway. Was cruel Ares playing? If there were gods looking on from high, would they be entertained by the spectacle of the two armies locked together like some ridiculous mating creatures that could not disengage from their frenzied intercourse? This is no time for such musings – I must look after my young man in front of me. Why is it that our commanders always put our youngest and untested men in the first two ranks?

Alcibiades felt no fear, only anger and determination. It is a test, he thought, and no other man is going to bloody me and trample me into the ground under his feet showing himself my better. The enemy was close at hand. Just beyond the top of the shield of his first ranker, he could see his assigned opponent. The man was a tall and burly man whose shield seemed to be pushing downward as well as forward. His helmeted head stood out above the fray. There was something odd about his helmet. Why did his eyes seem so large and fierce? Alcibiades muttered to himself. 'It is only a talisman to terrify cowards. The brute has modified his eye slits to make his eyes look more ferocious, confident that he can ward off any thrusts aimed at eye-level.'

The Athenian line broke right in front of Alcibiades. The wide-eyed opponent was the first to breach the Athenian wall of shields. He had employed a tactic that caught the Athenian first ranker off guard. The big man stepped back, as though his legs were giving out. Then, when his opponent pushed forward by Alcibiades came towards him with more momentum, the brute stepped forward again and with great force thrust his spear directly into the center of the shield held by the Athenian first ranker. The spear smashed through the shield and penetrated the breastplate of the young Athenian. Alcibiades watched as his front man fell to his knees with the shaft of the spear transfixed in his breastplate which was now drenched with bright red blood spurting from his chest.

"Move forward, Alcibiades! There is nothing we can do to save our man. You have the advantage." Socrates could see that the enemy could not withdraw his spear. Somehow the back of its point had wedged itself in the Athenian's breastplate.

Alcibiades moved forward, careful not to trip over the fallen warrior in front of him. His opponent had drawn his short sword and held it high above his shield. If Alcibiades was careful and stayed in line, there was no way the enemy could get at him with such a short sword. Holding his spear low, he bent his knees and then, thrusting with his legs and whole torso, he drove his spear into the shield that separated him and the man who now wanted to shed his blood. Alcibiades' spear point struck with great force but to no avail. All the way up and down his right arm, Alcibiades felt the shock of recoil. What now? Damn! The shield must be reinforced from the inside with some kind of bronze layer. Only a big man like this one could carry a shield with this kind of heft.

"Stay squared up with him, Alcibiades! Don't let him turn you to either side. As long as you are covered on both sides by our shields you can use your spear to keep him off you."

The din of the battle was all around Alcibiades. He could barely hear Socrates even though he was right behind him. The clash of shields, the screams of men who had been speared, the bugles signaling who knows what – all mixed together in a cacophony of chaotic confusion. There was no time to think. I must get by this brute in front of me. But there was no way to avoid him. He now was pushing hard on Alcibiades shield, having lifted his shield higher so that he might leverage his superior height and push downward again against the shorter Athenian.

Alcibiades couldn't believe his good fortune. The brute in his haste to counter Alcibiades' ineffective spear parry, had left his upper legs exposed as he repositioned his shield. Bracing himself for the impact of shields, Alcibiades aimed his second spear thrust just above the kneecap at the uncovered thigh of his enemy. What came next happened so fast that it seemed to Alcibiades a blur that mixed together his spear arm missing again, his upturned face covered by a dark shadow, a sickening thud pounding through his helmet into his forehead, and the strange sense of floating down to the ground enveloped suddenly by a painless almost beatific sense of an overwhelming sleepiness.

The phalanx was disintegrating all around Socrates. As Alcibiades fell to the ground dazed by the shield blow to his head, Socrates could see that the first two ranks in Cleon's phalanx were no longer a solid line. The enemy was pouring through the gaps where Athenians in the back ranks had either turned and fled or failed to properly realign themselves at the front. This may be the day I die, he thought, but I will not make the final act of my life one of dishonor. Before the big man could finish Alcibiades off with his sword, Socrates drove him back with his long spear. Exhorting the men beside him and behind him, he took the position at the front and called upon them to form up in a semicircle on his right and left side. Their only hope, he realized, was to move into a defensive position which would channel the charging enemy forces around them. And so Socrates and his six comrades hunkered down and repelled every attack. They would not surrender their small patch of ground which, like a small but sturdy sandbar, would not succumb to the wild rushing waters all around it. Socrates fought not only for his own survival but also for the life of his beloved young Alcibiades. If it had not been for the valor of Socrates and the six who stood their ground with him, the life of Alcibiades would have been washed away in the torrents of blood that flowed all around him.

Enemy officers urged their men forward wherever the Athenian line had been broken. It was clear to Socrates what was happening. The right wing of the Athenian formation had been defeated and now the Corinthian phalanx which made up the left wing of the enemy's forces was attempting to swing around behind the remaining three Athenian phalanges and crush them as they faced the other Potidaean forces in the center and the right wing. *This is why they overrun our positions and don't tarry to either take prisoners or kill all of us.*

Alcibiades regained consciousness just as the Corinthian phalanx had moved completely through Cleon's force and was now well beyond the original line of engagement. The Corinthians had turned their attention to engaging the Athenian center which was to their southwest. His head throbbing with pain and his vision blurred, Alcibiades was not sure who was helping him to his feet.

"Alcibiades, you are going to be alright. I don't see any serious wounds. Your Corinthian helmet saved you. I guess like repels like. I've never seen a Corinthian hoplite use his shield that way before, as though it were a sledge hammer! But apart from your black eye and the goose egg sized bump on your forehead which will soon go away, Ares has left you as handsome as ever. Now we have got to get you to safety. I am sure the battle is not over."

Alcibiades sighed with relief. It was Socrates voice calling him back to his senses. "What happened? Is the battle lost? I'm not seeing very well and I'm dizzy."

"Hold on to my shoulder! We have been overrun by the Corinthian force, but remnants of our phalanx have survived. We are all going to make our retreat south and around to the east so that we can form up again with our forces that make up the center and left wing – if they are still there."

Alcibiades was now on his feet and, though wobbly, able to walk. "Where is my spear and shield?"

"We have all your gear, Alcibiades. There will be no questions about your valor. You can barely walk and will need your hands to hold onto one of us if we need to move quickly."

They had just begun to make their way south along the seashore when an Athenian officer on horseback intercepted them. "I am Callias' lieutenant. The battle lines have shifted and I have been ordered to relieve Cleon of his command. We have heard that he has suffered a wound and is no longer able to command. Our other phalanxes have defeated the Potidaean forces in the center and their right wing. The remains of these enemy forces have fled and taken refuge back inside the walls of Potidaea. The Corinthian phalanx led by Aristeus is now isolated and will more than likely also try to return to the city by way of the seashore. Wait here! I will gather up the rest of your comrades and together with the rest of our forces we will engage Aristeus when he comes back this way. Any of your wounded men can make their way further inland and return to our base camp."

Socrates smiled at Alcibiades. "You will be a hero. You have survived hand to hand combat, been wounded, and taken part in a victorious battle for Athens' forces. I will take you to the camp."

"I'm alright now, Socrates." Alcibiades, certain he was now out of danger, felt steady enough to take back his shield and spear. He did not want to walk away from the field of battle in his first engagement until it was finished. Tongues would wag back in Athens if anyone suspected that he had shirked his duty due to just a bump on the head.

It was only a few minutes before Aristeus and his phalanx of Corinthian volunteers reappeared. They were now being pursued by a much larger force of Athenians. The Corinthians were in a disciplined retreat. They had formed up in a line that stretched from north to south right along the seashore. The first rank was in knee deep water with waves breaking right behind them. The Athenians could not get at them, since it was difficult to mount a hoplite charge in the water. Athenian archers and javelin throwers concentrated their missiles on the Corinthians, but the Corinthians made good use of their shields to provide cover as the entire force in this formation kept moving back towards Potidaea, wading knee-deep in the breaking waves. Alcibiades and Socrates, with other men of their regrouped phalanx, joined in the attack. But every attempt to break the Corinthian defensive formation made little headway. While Aristeus lost some of his hoplites in the water, most of the force was able to make its way back behind the fortifications of Potidaea.

Callias ordered a halt to any further attack on the enemy. It would require a well planned and lengthy siege to capture the city itself. A temporary truce was arranged so that both sides could gather up their dead and arrange for their burial.

Alcibiades, weary and shaken by his close encounter with death, sighed with relief when his company was ordered to return to their tents. Walking besides Socrates, Alcibiades could see that Socrates shield was so dented and battered that it was no longer serviceable. He knew now, beyond all doubt, that this strange man loved him and had saved his life. But why was Socrates looking so sad when everyone around him appeared jubilant and excited by their victory.

"Socrates, you could have with honor retreated backwards or moved to either the right or the left when our line broke. You moved forward and put yourself between me and the charging enemy. I will see that you and those who stood with you are nominated for badges of courage."

Socrates shrugged his shoulders as if it would be nothing but a bother to be vetted for such an honor. "Alcibiades, it is enough that you clasp the hand of those who stood by you and they receive your salute of respect. None of us have been wounded, and I suspect our officers would reserve such an honor for those like yourself who bear the marks on their own bodies of the enemy's weapons. Did you know our young first ranker in front of you?"

Alcibiades looked away from Socrates' eyes. Sometimes it was very difficult and discomfiting to deal with Socrates' questions. "No, I didn't really know him, Socrates. I think he trained with me, but he hardly ever spoke to anyone and not one of my friends knew anything about his family – except that they were former thetes who had just recently leased land for farming. I suspect that his armor was of a poor quality and this may have led to his death."

"I did know him. His parents work the small rented farm next to mine. They had scratched and struggled to buy him his armor so that he could be the very first in their family line to serve as a citizen soldier. He was a sensitive youth and probably said little because he was embarrassed by his humble origins. So I am not surprised that he went unnoticed among other *epheboi*. Because his family is poor and of humble descent, his death will be scarcely noticed. At best, his parents will raise a stone in his memory on the edge of their property and, like the nameless herms that serve as boundary markers, the stone will all too soon be neglected by all except those who survey the property when it is passed on to other tenants. I wonder, Alcibiades, if it is true as the poet Tyrtaeus, our Athenian admirer of all things Spartan, intones,

'And he who so falls among the champions and loses his sweet life……
He is lamented alike by the young and the eldest,
and his entire city goes into mourning and grieves for his loss.'

Tyrtaeus' patriotism knows no bounds. Does he not say that it is better for a man to die young in battle for his country than to live to be an old man and die in bed? Is it the best thing for a man to die young like this, rather than to live out the full measure of a life rich with wisdom and the flowering of human powers different and more creative than the death-dealing skills of an obedient warrior?"

"Here we are at our tent, Socrates. I am too weary to sort it all out. Is it that you really are a democrat after all and are complaining about the fate of commoners who are used up by our state so that a few may live in glory? Or are you suggesting that the loss of life in such battles as these is a tragic waste and could be avoided if men and cities honored the arts of persuasion, reasoning, and diplomacy, rather than taking recourse to coercion and violence so as to satisfy ambition and avarice? Socrates, you are always the philosopher and I love you for that. But I know how our fellow citizens deal with philosophers – they would silence them all if they could, driving them from their midst as they have Protagoras and Anaxagoras. Isn't it perfectly clear to you that in this world, no man can make his way to political greatness unless he proves himself glorious in war?"

"Alcibiades, you age so quickly – already sophisticated in matters of glory and political greatness. I can only hope that you will not overlook tending to the improvement of your own soul. I promise that should you allow me to stay in Athens I, like a faithful friend, will always honor and respect that divine intelligence within you which searches for the true good of human excellence."

"Thank you, Socrates. Now let's get this armor off and heat some water so we can wash away the sweat and grime of battle."

PART FOUR
Athenian Tragedy,
Scenes from the City Dionysia
And the Time of Plague
431 to 429 B.C.

CHAPTER NINETEEN
DEFENDING THE EMPIRE – ATHENS DECLARES WAR
(Summer of 431 B.C.)

Then it is right and proper for you to support the imperial dignity of Athens. This is something in which you all take pride, and you cannot continue to enjoy the privileges unless you also shoulder the burdens of empire. And do not imagine that what we are fighting for is simply the question of freedom or slavery: there is also involved the loss of our empire and the dangers arising from the hatred which we have incurred in administering it. Nor is it any longer possible for you to give up this empire, though there may be some people who in a mood of sudden panic and in a spirit of political apathy actually think that this would be a fine and noble thing to do. Your empire is now like a tyranny: it may have been wrong to take it; it is certainly dangerous to let it go.

(Thucydides. *History of the Peloponnesian War*, Book II: 63, 'The Policy of Pericles')

People's feelings were generally very much on the side of the Spartans, especially as they proclaimed that their aim was the liberation of Hellas. States and individuals alike were enthusiastic to support them in every possible way; both in speech and action, and everyone thought that unless he took a personal share in things the whole effort was being handicapped. So bitter was the general feeling against Athens, whether from those who wished to escape from her rule or from those who feared that they would come under it.

(Thucydides. *History of the Peloponnesian War*, Book II: 8)

The regiments of both Socrates and Alcibiades were among those recalled to Athens once the siege of Potidaea was underway. Having returned to Athens, the officers in their regimental units had recommended that Socrates be honored with a special commendation for his courage and promoted to a field officer. However, Socrates urged the officers to award both the medal and promotion to Alcibiades.
"Given this young man's promise and his family connections and wealth, it would do Athens well to encourage Alcibiades to further service to his city by awarding him the insignia of honor. If our young Alcibiades is so honored, he will be even more zealous to use his considerable means to learn all the arts of war – those of the cavalry and the trireme as well. Who knows, perhaps honoring and promoting him now will be a step along the way to Alcibiades becoming one of our Generals and a generous patron of our many public festivals. Then we will look back on the humble part we played in keeping him safe in his first battle as our company's great service to Athens."

All this was cause for some embarrassment to Alcibiades. He was acutely aware that it was Socrates who had saved his life, as well as the lives of others, by his clever and courageous tactic during the charge of Aristeus' Corinthian phalanx. It had been six weeks since he had returned from Potidaea when he heard that plans were under way for a ceremony to honor those who had shown special courage during the campaigns in Chalcidice. He rose early the next morning, skipped breakfast, and went alone to Pericles' home, determined to set the record straight. His mother had tried to intercept him at the front door. She was distraught and mumbled something about needing his help today in moving some things. But he growled at her, "That is what slaves are for!" In his haste, he almost knocked her down as he rushed out the door. He would not ever want to be the beneficiary of a bogus honor, an honor that could later diminish deserved glory. This was why he wanted to go right to the top of Athens' military leadership and make sure that no medal ceremony for him was already in the works.

Pericles greeted Alcibiades as though he were a life-long beloved friend who had returned from the dead. It was unsettling to Alcibiades to see Pericles so genuinely moved by his safe return from his first hoplite battle. But Pericles did not seem at all interested in hearing any further details about the part Alcibiades had played in the fighting. After escorting him into the courtyard, they both sat down on chairs that had been pulled up to a small table on which a bowl of figs and corn cakes had been set out for breakfast.

Pericles had anticipated the reason for Alcibiades unannounced visit. "Alcibiades, you need not worry whether you merit Athens' acknowledgement of your courage and worthiness to promotion. That is up to your commanding officers. Besides, you will soon have the opportunity to demonstrate over and over again your daring and courage. I am sure that you have heard the news. It seems that all our enemies now are determined to ally themselves with Sparta and bring us to our knees. Athens has need of you to play a vital role here in maintaining the defense of the city."

"Yes, Pericles, everyone in Athens, talks about nothing but the Spartan ambassadors' offer of peace and our Assembly's rejection of their terms."

"Well, it was not easy to persuade the Assembly. Nicias and others who were close to Cimon continue to have personal connections with prominent Spartans. These men urged that we find some way to come to terms with the Spartans. Nicias argued that it would cost us little to revoke the Megara decree. This would be enough to secure peace, he said. We would not have to abandon the siege of Potidaea or repudiate our claim to control of Aegina – either of which he said would do real damage to our territorial empire. Nicias claims that our artisans, our merchants, and our traders will always out sell Megarian merchants in foreign markets no matter how associations of Megara's money men try to subsidize their own merchants; and thus, according to Nicias, there is no need for our regents forcibly to exclude them from our foreign markets."

Alcibiades grimaced. "I can't stomach Nicias, Pericles. He has made all his money procuring slaves to work our mines here in Attica at Laurium. It is easy enough for him to overlook the sleazy collusion of the cartels in foreign cities led by men of Megara. Their merchants, subsidized as they are by Megara's tyrants, have dropped their prices so low that my family's enterprises in Italy, Thessaly, and even on some of the islands in our Delian League, are verging on total collapse. We had every right to exclude them from the markets we have made safe from pirates, the Persians, and unscrupulous traders like themselves! I am so glad, Pericles, that your counsel prevailed."

"It will not be easy to stay the course, Alcibiades. Our enemies are clever. They will try to divide us. Nicias, thank goodness, did not even acknowledge the demands of the ambassadors the Spartans sent six months ago – that Sparta would find it easy to be on friendly terms with Athens if she would 'drive out those under the curse of the goddess'"

Alcibiades shared with Pericles the conviction that this 'curse of the goddess' was no black mark against the Alkmeonid family. "That is another reason why we should never accommodate those damn tyrant-loving oligarchs of Megara. If it had not been for the virtue of our Alkmeonid forefather Megacles, Theagenes, the tyrant of Megara, and his Athenian son-in-law, Cylon, would have reduced all of Athens' best families to cravenly servitude. Surely, Athena herself did not wish to extend her protection to such as Cylon and his friends."

"That is how you and I see it, Alcibiades. But many of our citizens revere the gods in a different way. The sanctuary of a goddess is holy ground and to their way of thinking not even the defense of liberty can justify shedding blood on sacred ground. So, even though

Megacles, who killed the associates of Cylon at the sanctuary of Athena, is six generations removed from me and this happened over 100 years ago, many pious Athenians believe that somehow, like some kind of contagion carried in the blood, there is a curse that is fated to bring punishment upon me and those who would join me in any enterprise. I find it all incredible."

"I know all about it, Pericles. My Alkmeonid mother is forever reminding me of the curse. She constantly plagues me with her Orphic nonsense, pleading that I must practice the rites that will confirm my initiation at Eleusis and thus assure me of salvation from the wrath of the gods. But I am beginning to think that Critias, has got it right, Pericles. Those who govern must treat the stories of the gods as tools by which they may manipulate the passions of the people so that they indeed see their leader's governance as the will of heaven."

"I am not as cynical as Callaeschrus' son, Critias. How does one become so cynical so soon? He is not much older than you, Alcibiades. I suppose there is no harm in the comfort provided by the Orphic doctrines about life after death. After all, women and slaves often find this life a vale of tears. You should not be so hard on your mother. She is indeed very melancholy and needs comfort."

"Is it good, then, to count an illusion as true provided it gives comfort? My friend, Socrates, urges me to examine all my convictions and to test them before the tribunal of reason. Would you, Pericles, embrace what you knew to be a fiction so as to escape anguish concerning the future or past harm you have caused to others? Would you not think that unmanly?"

"As for myself, Alcibiades, I must confess that, unlike Critias, I do not know with any certainty what is true or false about those great forces beyond the human will, forces which we call Divine. Thus I am not so quick to dismiss the divine mysteries related by our poets. And while I admire and applaud Socrates' uncompromising search for truth, I often find that the necessities of political leadership require decisions which can not afford the luxury of waiting for a full disclosure of truth – a truth which may not be eternally the same but is forever in the process of becoming. This is why I do not hesitate to negotiate all this uncertainty with the assistance of the mysteries which speak to the people. And so, in this way, we were able to answer the Spartan gambit, by a counter offer – Athens would 'drive out the curse of the goddess' if Sparta would drive out the curse of Taenarus and that of the goddess of the Brazen Horse. Of course, if all the relatives of those who slaughtered the helot supplicants at the alter of Poseidon and all the relatives of Pausanias whose *hubris* had betrayed the Spartans in the struggle with Persia were driven out of Sparta, then there would be scarcely any leadership left in Sparta. This approach, Alcibiades, seemed to satisfy the Assembly. Even its most pious members, men like Diopeithes, were ready to concede that the ways of the gods are sometimes beyond all human reckoning. It seemed in this case to our literal minded believers, that the gods might be just as likely to use the Athenians and Pericles as their instrument of divine wrath against infidels in Sparta as they would the Spartans to punish religious transgressors among the Athenians."

"It seems that you have the people behind your policy"

"Nothing is certain when the suffering and heavy costs of war begin to be felt. There will always be among us those whose religion is enthralled by the titanic forces of Nature and who will see in these forces the displeasure of the gods. And so even now, some of our seers and professional prophets warn that the shaking of the earth at Delos last month is a portent of the Olympians' displeasure with Athens' imperial conduct. My opponents in the Assembly will use such episodes to challenge those of us whose counsel is to reject capitulation to any of the Spartan demands. These men should know better! Should we surrender to even the milder of the Spartan demands, our enemies will only conclude that we are weak and other more grievous demands will follow accompanied by the threat of war."

"What is it, Pericles, that you think will happen next? What is it that I can do to help?"

"When you knocked on my door, I was just about to go to the Strategeion for an emergency meeting with the Board of Generals. We need to agree on what strategy will best assure our security and eventual victory against Sparta and her allies. Come along with me and join our meeting. I have asked officers from the Council of Five Hundred, the War- Lord Archon and the Archon Eponymus also to join us. I would prefer that nothing in these discussions be kept secret from any of our citizens, so there is no reason why you should not be there. Indeed, you will hear for yourself the strategy which I will recommend if we are to prevail in the renewal of our war with Sparta and her many allies. It is my hope that the others will agree to promote you to commander of a company of cavalry and commission your force to check the Peloponnesian army from having a free hand to pillage and destroy property outside our city walls. This will be dangerous duty and everyone will see for themselves your courage and skill in the military defense of our city."

Alcibiades was flattered that Pericles would include him in such a meeting. "Pericles, I will not disappoint you. I am ready to serve Athens in whatever capacity her leaders require."

"Good! Please, take some figs and corn meal cakes. We'll eat them while we walk to the Strategeion."

Pericles rose from his chair and called for his steward. "Please bring me my helmet and military tunic. Help Alcibiades fill our small provisions bag with our fruit and cakes."

Usually the walk from Pericles' home to the southwest corner of the Agora where both the Strategeion and the Council's building, the Bouleuterion, were located would take no more than half an hour. Pericles' home was just off of the PanAthenaic Way, a broad city street which ran from the Dipylon Gate at the northwestern wall through the Agora to the Acropolis and the Parthenon on the southeast side of the city. When Alcibiades and Pericles turned the corner from the narrow street that led from Pericles' neighborhood onto the PanAthenaic Way, the thoroughfare was full of people on the move. Though it was still early morning, well before even the stalls of the Agora would be open for business, the Street and many of the side-streets were choked with horse drawn carts, large box-like vans pulled by slaves, household stewards accompanied by their masters, and even well-dressed wives of the rich supervising slaves carrying chairs, vases, gold and silver utensils, carpets, and other expensive household furnishings. It appeared to Alcibiades, that the procession of moving vans and slave porters stretched all the way to the Dipylon Gate and beyond, like the great PanAthenaic parade; but there were no happy faces, only somber and, occasionally, angry ones. Just as they approached the narrow street that led to Alcibiades' home, Alcibiades saw some of his own household servants bearing on their shoulders a make-shift canvas litter which though held high above the ground drooped with the weight of gold and silver dishes, goblets, utensils, and candle chandeliers.

"What is this, Pericles?"

Before Pericles could answer, a courier sent from the Strategeion appeared from out of the crowded Street and hailed Pericles.

"Sir, I have been instructed to give you this 'for your eyes only' communiqué from General Nicias."

Pericles took the small sealed scroll and opened it quickly. "Well, Alcibiades, it is just as I expected. The Peloponnesian army has abandoned their siege of our fortification at Oenoe on the frontier between Attica and Boeotia. The Spartan King Archidamus is advancing now towards Acharnae with hoplites from Sparta, her allies on the Peloponnese, and others from Megara, Boeotia, and Aetolia – a combined force of about ten thousand. What you see in the streets are the country manor people who waited until the very last moment to bring their personal property inside the safety of our city walls so as to escape the oncoming storm of war. They dare not panic! I gave them plenty of warning. I am sure that they moved their livestock to Euboea weeks ago."

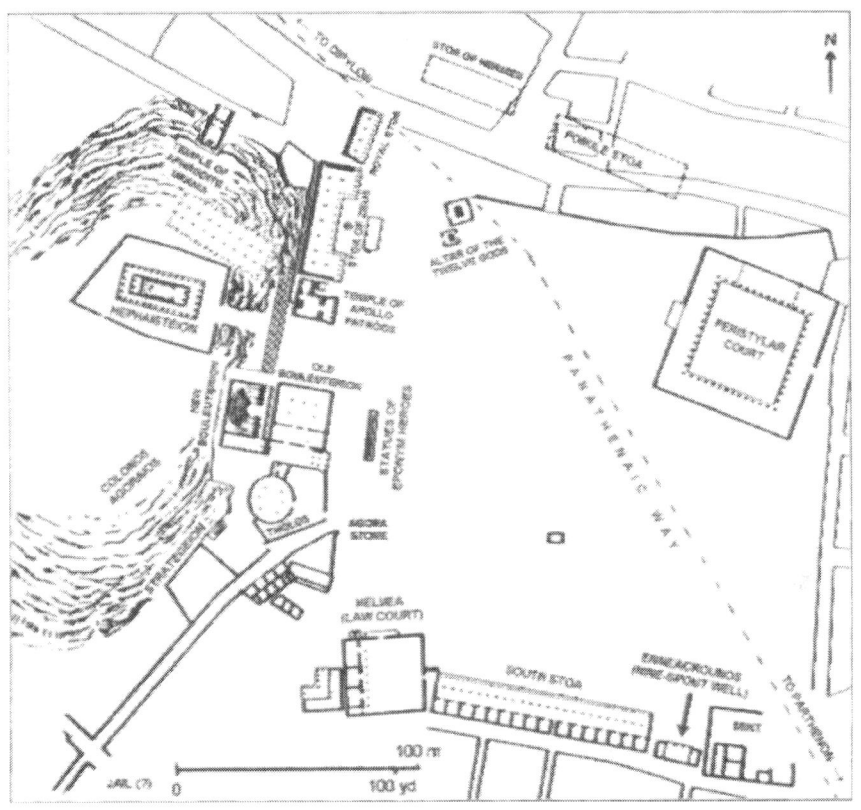

The Agora in Pericles' time

Pericles and Alcibiades walked as fast as they could, but finally had to take a longer route to the southwestern corner of the Agora so as to avoid all the congestion. Pericles, instantly recognizable in his helmet and military tunic, had to avoid the streets filled with those who were bringing their property into the city. He could not possibly answer all their questions about the emergency arrangements for storing their valuables in buildings other than those of their city relatives, or their questions concerning the living arrangements for the country folk that worked their estates. Winding their way through the narrower and emptier streets, it was more than an hour later when they arrived at the Strategeion.

Pericles led Alcibiades to a side door which opened into a small waiting room used by the Generals for debriefing officers returning from military missions. There were already nine men dressed in military tunics waiting in the room.

Pericles then put his hand firmly on Alcibiades' shoulder and spoke to his kinsman in the voice of a commanding officer. "Alcibiades, there will be a brief ceremony here today in which you and the others in this room will be honored for your service at Potidaea. You will find in the wardrobe there in the corner, the military tunic which we ask all honorees to wear. Please dress and wait here with the rest of the men until summoned for the ceremony in the assembly room."

By the time Pericles made his way into the assembly room of the Strategeion, the meeting of the ten generals, the current fifty pyrtanes of the Council of Five Hundred, and the two Archons, the Polemarchus and the Archon Eponymus, had already been called to order by Socrates the son of Sophroniscus, the acting pyrtanes chairman for this day. Well, thought Pericles, I'm sure Socrates is no happier than I that he presides. The lots have been cast and he must do his duty! The philosopher would much prefer his unfettered inquiries with handsome young men in the gymnasium or under the shade of the sycamores in Academe. I would prefer that the discussion concerning the conduct of our state at war with Sparta did not have to deal with the critical acumen of Socrates. Perhaps Socrates will behave. He looks quite different in his official robe. Maybe his five week stay at the Thalos with the other forty-nine Counselors from his tribe has imbued him with a political sense of seriousness and responsibility. He is no dummy and he must realize, charged with the executive oversight of day to day governing, that it would be grounds for impeachment of his citizenship if he made use of this position to engage in the all too easy dialectical criticism of every proposal – leaving those who seek to govern irresolute and confused. The last thing Socrates would want is to get entangled with our Heliasts! Almost any jury of five hundred of our citizens would be sure to have among its number merchants, poets, or politicians who have felt the sting of Socrates' all too public examination of their opinions.

Socrates interrupted the clerk who was reading the most recent military reconnaissance report which had just arrived from Acharnae minutes before Pericles had arrived. The report had already led to contentious and heated exchanges between the Generals whose families owned country estates in the demes in the plains north of Eleusis or along the river Cephissus just east of Acharnae and those Generals whose country estates were to the south of Athens. "Please, let us pause for a few moments until Pericles is seated with the Board of Generals. Welcome, General Pericles. We have just started our meeting with the preliminary formalities. The report we are now having read by the clerk is time urgent, so we thought it prudent to read it immediately. You will find an agenda for our meeting at your place at the Board's table. Of course, you may propose other matters for our discussion if you think them timely and crucial to the crisis at hand."

"Thank you, Counselor Chairman." Pericles had taken his seat. "I apologize for my tardiness. As you know the streets are full of our citizens on the move and I found it difficult to avoid all of the congestion and the insistent ones who would not let me pass without answering their questions about the state of emergency. Let the clerk continue with the military report. If you don't mind, let him start from the beginning so that I hear everything the rest of my colleagues have heard. I'm sure all of us will find it germane to the decisions we need to make today."

Socrates turned to the clerk. "Terias, please read the entire report again. Counselors, Generals, and other officers, please let the entire report be read before we begin our consultations. It is short and we all will have the opportunity to sort out its implications for the best course of action in marshalling our resources and citizens' support for the defense of our homeland."

The scout who had written the report was concise and unemotional in his description of the military operations the Spartan led army of hoplites and cavalry had undertaken this morning. The report described how the Spartan led invaders had discontinued their siege of the fortifications at Oenoe and moved their entire army into Acharnae which was the largest of the Attic demes and home to some of Athens' founding aristocratic families. Terias, the clerk, read from beginning to end, careful not to omit anything.

"Abandoning the siege of our fortified frontier town, Oenoe, King Archidamus has set up camp between two streams just east of the village center of Acharnae. Already, companies of cavalry and hoplites have begun to selectively burn the corn crops, olive groves, and grape vines of the larger estates which lie to the south of their camp and closer to Athens. Indeed, smoke from these fires can be seen from the northern walls of Athens. It appears the army plans to stay for a sustained campaign. A swathe of corn fields, groves, and vineyards which lies west and north of the camp has been left untouched. The army, as large as it is, will be able to harvest food enough for itself from these fields throughout the summer. It also appears that their leadership has targeted specific country houses, barns, and other permanent structures for destruction. They first burnt to the ground most of the properties that belong to the wealthy and politically powerful families that belong to the deme of Acharnae. But even as I was riding away from their pillaging parties, I could see that they had begun to systematically destroy the properties that lie in Acharnae between their camp and Athens. As far as our scouts can determine, the raiding parties have left untouched the estates that border the northwestern tributary of the Cephissus River just south of Mount Panes. This report has been prepared by........."

Before the clerk could identify the scout's tribal regiment, Pericles was on his feet and speaking. "My fellow Generals, Counselors, and Archons, I have no doubt the report is accurate. King Archidamus would like to win an easy victory by first sowing dissension among Athenians and then provoking us to throw away our strategic advantages and fight them with the largest hoplite force we can muster in the open plains of northern Attica. This is why he strikes hard at the estates of Acharnae and makes sure his actions are highly visible from the walls of Athens. He knows that Acharnae is one of the largest demes and that its estates are owned by some of Athens most illustrious families. He knows that the three thousand hoplites of Acharnae which fill the ranks of General Proteas' tribal regiment are a major factor in the military might of Athens. He thinks that this cohort of our armed citizenry will not stand by and do nothing while their ancestral homes are being destroyed. Our men of Acharnae, King Archidamus believes, will press the case that all of Athens' tribal regiments should come out and save Acharnae. He hopes that if we do not go out with all of our forces that are in Athens and face in one decisive battle his Spartan led allied hoplite army, than the Acharnaens would have little enthusiasm for risking their lives for the defense of other Athenians' property. We must not let this ploy draw us into an uncertain battle."

"General Pericles, what are you saying?" As everyone present expected, it was General Proteas, the regimental commander of the Acharnians who rose to challenge Pericles' strategic leadership. "What will the valiant hoplites we are about to honor for risking their lives for our control of far away Potidaea think if we are unwilling to risk lives for the defense of our fellow citizens' homes? If we do not stop the enemy from their brazen pillaging in Acharnae seven miles from our walls, soon they will be taunting us beside our walls with bonfires fed by Cimon's sycamores of Academe. Did not my Philiad uncle and your own father fight to make sure that never again would an enemy of Athens desecrate our ancestral homes? I fear that it is too easy for you to stay behind the walls of Athens. You do not have to watch the estate of your fathers going up in flames!"

General Proteas paused and turned away from facing Pericles so as to assess the other Generals' response to his challenge to Pericles' strategic leadership.

Before anyone else could stand in support of Proteas, Pericles, still standing and again facing his opponent, answered as he had on so many occasions over the past twelve years in which he had won election to the generalship and de facto leadership of the Athenian state. Calm, deliberate, and without rancor – he never lost his temper no matter how he might be insulted – he would explain to the Board of Generals and the acting leadership of the Council of Five Hundred the good reasons for the strategic policy that should drive the tactical military decisions at hand.

"First, let me make clear to all of you that I will ask no sacrifice of any Athenian citizens that I myself am unwilling to make. I am not surprised that King Archidamus has made a show of leaving my family's estate untouched. All of Athens knows of the act of friendship extended to me by Archidemus seven years ago when I traveled to the Pythian Games at Delphi. This was a time when we had friendly relations with the Spartans, since our cities some years earlier had signed the treaty negotiated by our now deceased General Andocides and General Proteas' Philiad cousin, the diplomat, Callias. Well, anyway, when young Archidamus, who was not yet King in Sparta, made a point of meeting me at the Stadium in Delphi and presented me with the original manuscript on which Pindar penned his *Ode to Megacles,* my Alkmeonid mother's father, commemorating his victory in the four horse chariot race at that very stadium held in the same year as the battle of Marathon; I was indeed deeply affected and felt a genuine affection and gratitude towards Archidamus. I don't know what exactly in his mind remains of these feelings of friendship today. But I am sure that, like me, his duty to his city trumps any personal feelings he may have towards a foreigner. I would think less of him as a General if he did not avail himself of the opportunity to capitalize on a tactic that could possibly undermine confidence in the integrity of the enemy's leadership. It is my duty – which I gladly assume – to make clear to my fellow citizens that the interests of the state require that its leaders should not even give the appearance of allowing personal and private interests to inform their policy proposals for the common good of the state. And so I have brought to our meeting today, my signed statement ceding ownership of my family's Cephissus River Estate to the Athenian Treasury. From this day forward, this land will belong to the people of Athens and any revenues it may generate will be theirs to expend as the Assembly sees fit. I submit this deed of transfer to our presiding chairman of the Prytanes, asking that he immediately seal and publish the transaction."

General Nicias now rose. He seldom spoke at such meetings, but never failed to acknowledge genuine acts of patriotism. General Nicias applauded his fellow general as he spoke. "I for one am sure of your love for our city, Pericles. You have my full confidence and I am sure that we all will be called to make sacrifices if we are to prevail in our struggle with Sparta. Our enemies are many and while we see ourselves as the defenders of liberty and democracy, many other cities chafe under what they perceive as an Athenian hegemony designed to provide for our luxurious freedom by taxing their resources and denying them their economic autonomy. Spartan hoplites remain the most formidable fighting force among all the Greeks. Allied with other Peloponnesian cities, Megara, Corinth, and cities of Boetia and Thessaly and claiming to be the liberators of all of Hellas, this time the Spartans pose a supreme threat to our survival. Since we all must be clear on how to best meet the threat, I ask you once again to explain the strategy you recommend."

Pericles was glad to have General Nicias support. It would be very difficult to persuade the younger generals if a veteran like Nicias also favored facing the Spartans on the plains of Attica. Now he must make the case once again to newly elected generals like Proteas that his policy was well-founded and one that would have the best prospects of defending Athens and preserving her empire.

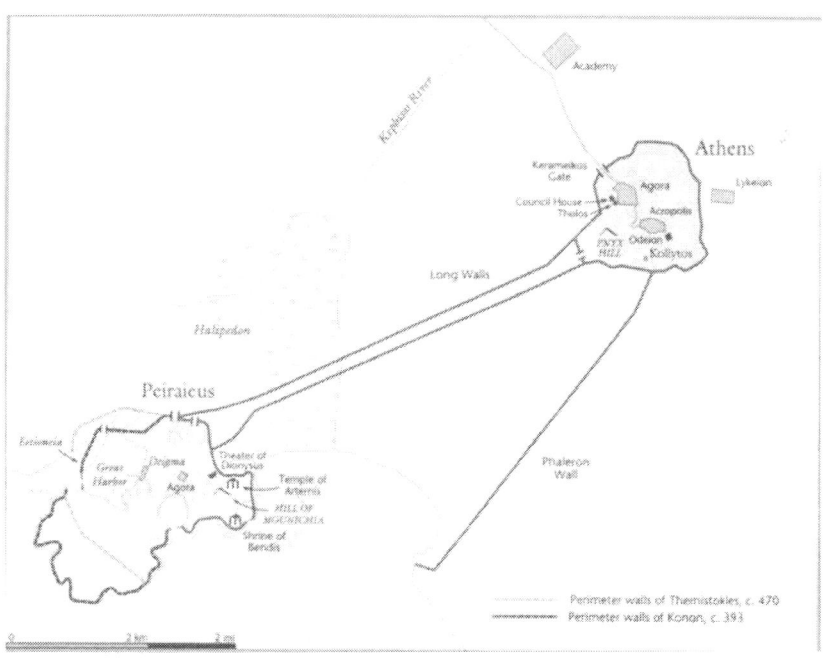

Athens' long walls to Peiraieus and the Aegean Sea

"Two weeks have passed since I urged our people who live in our countryside to pack up their valuable belongings and take shelter inside our city walls. Most took my advice and now are safe from the Spartan invasion. It is our lives of course which are most valuable. Our land will still be there, just as it was after the Persian invasion. Some of you may think it unduly timid to not confront the Spartan led confederacy so as to save our country estates from destruction. But why should we risk battle on their terms? Yes, our hoplites fight with courage and skill. We might indeed defeat the Spartans here and now if we committed all of the thirteen thousand of our men now here in the City. But waging everything on one battle is a risky business. No one can be sure that some chance circumstances might not lead to catastrophe. The Spartans themselves are formidable in any hoplite engagement and they will be matched against our youngest and oldest soldiers. Many of our seasoned hoplites are garrisoned on foreign shores protecting our sea lanes and allies. Why should we take the risk of engaging Spartan forces on such terms? It is our navy and the resources we can draw upon from our maritime empire that makes Athens strong. It is my plan to defend our city as though she is an island. Our walls around the city and the long walls protecting our access to Piraeus cannot be breached by the Spartans and so long as we can protect our sea lanes with our superior navy we will have sure access to the provisions and wealth which will bring us victory over the enemy. So as long as I hold the supreme command of our military there will be no major engagement in Attica between the hoplite forces of Athens and the Spartan forces. The Spartans will grown weary of a protracted campaign and return home with no victory. They never keep their army away too long out of fear that their enslaved helots might revolt."

Socrates, like everyone else in the Hall, wondered how anyone could disagree with such an eloquent and persuasive man! Only a moment had passed since Pericles had finished speaking, but no one else rose to take the floor. But it was his duty as acting president of the emergency meeting of the Board of Generals and the Council to be certain that any course of action undergo the examination and deliberation of the people's governing officials.

"General Pericles, as you know, my farm is in Alopeke south of the city. My farm buildings and house are not going up in flames today. But I can sympathize with those who must watch passively from our city walls the destruction of the villages and homesteads in which they played as children and which they hoped to pass on to their own children. The feeling of passivity, of standing by and doing nothing as the enemy desecrates our homes and local shrines, will quickly turn from frustration to anger towards us leaders if we do nothing but hunker down behind our walls – no matter how well fed we are. What might we militarily undertake that would dispel this frustration and utilize our superior naval power?"

Pericles again rose from his chair to answer. "The question is a good one, Socrates. I agree with you that we would all find it insufferable to stand by and watch our enemy pillage our homes while we do nothing. Soon, our own citizens in their anger would demand that either we sue for peace and meet Spartan demands or that we empty our city of all its hoplites and do battle, even at risk of suffering a catastrophic defeat. I urge the Council and the Board of Generals today to counter the invasion by approving the following plan. First, even while Archidamus is here in Attica, we should commission a sizable fleet of triremes to sail around the Peloponnese and make incursions with small and very mobile hoplite forces in the Messenian territory west of Sparta. Our aim will be to stir up the helots against Sparta and where there are allies of Sparta along the coast, there our forces will burn and pillage. We will bring to bear this kind of pressure in their own neighborhood so as to hasten their withdrawal from Attica. I would think General Proteas would be an excellent commander for this mission. He is a superb naval commander and also has considerable experience in coordinating landings for attacks on coastal villages and cities. We have more than three hundred triremes in our fleet here at Athens, so we can certainly send out at least one hundred triremes for this mission."

General Proteas nodded his head in approval as he rose to speak. "It is a commission I will undertake as soon as the men and ships can be readied. If the mission is to make a real difference in Sparta's calculation of leaving her own territory unguarded, I would think I need at least a thousand hoplites and four hundred lightly armed bowmen. We would do well to commission General Carcinus, the son of Xenotimus, and Socrates, the son of Antigenes, to share the command with me. The number of ships, soldiers and requisite supplies will require the coordination and attention of all three of us. We have all served together before and will be able to effectively and harmoniously coordinate a joint-command. Generals, are you prepared to join me?"

There was no hesitation among the generals. The Board unanimously ratified the mission and the fifty pyrtanes, on behalf of the Council, directed the War-Lord Archon to arrange all provisions for the mission so that the fleet could be underway as soon as possible.

Pericles was encouraged by the cooperation. Given the floor again, he urged that the Council and the Board of Generals also ratify the remaining two elements he hoped would solidify the citizens' support for what he knew would be a long and difficult war with Sparta and her allies.

"We must make it clear to the Spartans, and those who help them, that every cost they inflict upon us will be repaid with interest. I, too, can feel the pain of those who see their homes and fields destroyed by gleeful bands of Megarians, Boeotians, Locrians, and scoundrels from Aegina – protected by Spartan hoplites. I urge the Council and Board of Generals to commission the forced evacuation of the entire island of Aegina. Let the Spartans find new homes for them! Too long have the men of Aegina plotted against our City! The fertile lands and estates of Aegina will be incorporated into our state and all those in Acharnae who wished to be compensated for the destruction of their estates will be offered title to a comparable estate in Aegina. The island will also provide us with an ideal base for conducting raids all along the coast of the territories allied with Sparta in the Peloponnese."

"But General Pericles, are there not some men in Aegina who have been our friends? Are there not among their citizens some who have looked to us for assistance in strengthening their own democratic governance?" When Sparta claims to be the liberator of Hellas, would not such an action on our part only seem to confirm this? Could it be that should we annex Aegina, then even those members in our Delian League who are still our friends may be drawn to the Spartan side?" It was unusual for the presiding chairman of the Prytanes to respond directly to a speaker from the conferees, but Socrates felt it was his duty to raise this issue.

Pericles did not have to answer Socrates' questions. Proteas was on his feet again and spoke in favor of the annexation of Aegina. "It is imperative that we have absolute control of Aegina. We can not risk it becoming a naval base for our enemies. It would undermine our naval superiority if we were required to deal with an enemy fleet moored this close to our city. We cannot worry about the few who might be exiled unjustly when our entire population is at risk. And Pericles is right to find compensation for those of us in Acharnae who have lost their homes. We all understand that all men fight with increased zeal when they fight to preserve not only their lives, but the property which gives them a stake in the survival of their city. Finally, I should say, that it will require only a small number of our triremes to cleanse the island of all those who would resist our evacuation order."

Pericles pressed forward. "If there are no other objections to the Aegina proposal, then I would urge the Council and Board of Generals to ratify this operation and set it in motion this day. In war, it is imperative that we move quickly."

The Prytanes and the other nine Generals unanimously endorsed the proposal.

Socrates wondered if there were ever times when General Pericles did not prevail. But he remembered that long ago when Socrates had just received his commission as a hoplite, Pericles' advice was ignored and this led to a crushing defeat of an Athenian army at Coronea. Alcibiades' father Clinias was killed along with General Tolimides and half of the entire force of one thousand hoplites that had volunteered for the expedition. Socrates himself had come home alive from the military disaster, but not without his friends helping raise the ransom for his release. In the sixteen years since that disaster, Pericles strategic leadership had met with little opposition. It is best, I suppose, that I defer to the general. "General Pericles, you mentioned a third military initiative in your plan."

"Yes there is a third prong to what I think will be a constant pattern in our war with Sparta and her allies. I have no doubt that we will have to endure repeated campaigns by the Spartans in Attica should the war drag on. If we are to keep the morale of Athenian citizens steady and committed to our long term strategy of utilizing the resources of our empire to supply and defend our walled city from the sea, it will not be enough to win victories in the Peloponnese or overseas. Outlasting Sparta will require that our citizens have heroes who sally forth beyond our walls to harass the Spartans and win, if not the war, small engagements with contingents of the invading army. I am hoping that some of the men we will honor today will be commissioned as cavalry officers charged with fighting in these hit and run operations – never risking a major engagement with massed hoplite enemy formations. Let them be dashing with plumed helmets, spears festooned with the colors of their tribal regiment, and red capes which trail behind their shoulders as they gloriously race their mounts like a pride of lions in search of prey on the edges of a herd of thousands of wild cattle. Our people here behind our walls will need such heroics if they are to remain steadfast in the face of the taunts of an enemy that raids the villages of Attica."

Pericles was not done. "Before we bring the citizen hoplites out of the waiting room, I have one more request for the Council to consider. I am sure there will be times when the pillaging of our enemy will so enrage our citizens that they would throw prudence to the wind if permitted to hold a general Assembly. I am afraid a majority might vote in anger to send forth all the hoplites that could be mustered here in Athens, and then, as I have already said, who can be sure that we would win such a battle? I am asking that our seated Prytanes charged with convening the Assembly and drawing up its agenda make certain that no Assembly is convened while the Spartan forces occupy any locale in Attica. I will make the same request to any other of the 50 executive Pyrtanes which happen to be serving their tenth of the year when the Spartan forces campaign in Attica. I believe we are in for a long struggle and our victory will require that we endure many seasons of incursions into Attica overland from both the south and the north."

General Cleon, who up to this point had not risen to speak, was now on his feet. He stood with some difficulty since the bone broken in his lower leg during the campaign at Potidaea had not yet mended. Leaning on the table with his right hand, he gestured with his left hand opened palm up and waving towards Pericles. "But General Pericles, how can you expect the support of the legion of thetes and zeugites, who row our triremes and serve as adjunct troops to our hoplites, if you deny them their democratic franchise? Athens' great strength rests on the principle that when our soldiers march off to war, they do so as free men who are enacting the collective will of their own Assembly. If they demand an Assembly, are they to be denied? Will you allow the war and our enemies to take away our democracy? Would you undo the work of Ephialtes and once again reinstate a Council of Athens' elite that governs by its own edicts alone? How can I face my regiment of men, many of whom are tanners, potters, dock workers, and small farmers and expect them to risk their lives for Athens if you deny them their right to participate in state decisions that put own lives at risk? If the Assembly is only convened when the agenda pleases a few officials, are we not on the way to an Oligarchy? How can I as a speaker in the Assembly persuade my fellow citizens that our work is serious if our most important decisions never reach the Assembly?"

Cleon spoke as though he were addressing a crowd of thousands on the hill at the Pnyx. His voice was strident and loud enough to project through the Stategeion's open windows out into the nearby Agora. It was all very irritating to almost everyone, especially Nicias and the older generals. The Prytanes themselves looked perplexed. Some of them were tradesmen, not from the so-called 'good and beautiful' aristocratic families that fifty years ago always filled the nine archonships, the courts, and the Council. Did Cleon, himself a man who had made a family fortune through his tannery, mean to claim that they were oligarchs? General Pericles had turned to face Cleon and gave every appearance of listening respectfully and attentively. When Cleon sat down and was looking about to see if his speech had been well received, Pericles waited for a moment to see if others would rise in support of Cleon. But no one rose.

There was not even a hint of disdain or irritation in General Pericles voice when he responded to Cleon, the latest and most radical champion of the commoners. "General Cleon, I am appreciative of your concern to honor and preserve our institutions of democracy. I agree with you wholeheartedly that the source of our great strength lies in our democratic unity. Since I have devoted my entire life in politics to the reforms which have extended access for our citizens, whatever their relative wealth, to state offices, juries, and the Council itself, I also would be deeply alarmed if the defense of our state entailed the dismantling of our democratic institutions. If you would but consider with me now how intimately the people's will works its way through all the operations of our governance, I think you could be assured that the course now advised in no way runs roughshod over the people's will or interests."

"General Pericles, I hope you do not think it necessary to subject me and all your colleagues here to a civics lesson!"

"I want only to remind you, Cleon, that the will of the people is expressed in all our institutions of governance, not just our Assembly. I am sure you are aware that every one of us who serves in the one year appointment to the Generalship of each of the tribal regiments is elected by every single man who is free born in Attica. We must remember that long ago Cleisthenes arranged the tribal structure so that each tribe was made up of a mixture of urban and rural demes so as to assure that tribal selection of generals, or other elected officers, would not be captive to any narrow economic class such as the old aristocratic landed families. All nine Archons are chosen by lot only for one year, from each tribe in turn. Any free-born man is eligible to be so chosen by lot. And then there are our Heliasts. Each year six thousand jurists, six hundred from each tribe, are chosen from a larger pool of volunteers. Most of these jurists are not men of great wealth or sons of the *eupatridae*. It was I, you remember, that persuaded the Assembly to provide a salary of three oboes a day for jury duty so as to make sure that tradesmen, thetes, and others who lacked an inheritance of family wealth would not be discouraged from volunteering for the juries due to economic hardship. Now, as you are well aware, my friend, every exercise of office in Athens – whether it be the most prestigious and powerful like that of the Archons or the Generals or the more humble offices held at the local level of the deme – is held accountable to an audit and review at the end of the official's year. This proceeding is in the hands of the Council of Five Hundred which also is chosen by lot, fifty from each tribe. I can think of no more effective check on corruption or tyranny on the part of any official. If, per chance, citizens believe the Council has been derelict in its review of an official, a citizen is free to bring a suit to the Heliasts against any official. Now, General Cleon, do you really think that my proposal to entrust fifty officials of the Council, who by the lottery come from every kind of constituency in Athens, working in consultation with elected Generals to make emergency decisions with regard to military tactics suited to deal with an invasion of Attica without convening the Assembly – that this is a subversion of our democratic institutions. If so, you of course, are yet free to testify in the full Council's review of my Generalship three months from now or bring suit against me in our courts by filing your case with the appropriate Archon. I hope I have not bored my colleagues, but I suspect any one in position of leadership in the months ahead should remind our citizens of the warp and woof of the many threads of the democratic mantle that clothe every Athenian state enterprise."

Socrates had listened with great interest to Pericles response to Cleon. Pericles had always in the past been regarded as the great champion of democracy. Now he was being accused by Cleon, who of late had become the champion of the commoners, as being antidemocratic. It was clear to Socrates that Pericles did not want the strategy of the War entrusted to the people's Assembly. Socrates the philosopher was curious about how Pericles himself would guard the state against demagogy. This was no time, though, for the presiding chairman of the Prytanes to engage the First General in a debate about the fickleness of the Assembly or the limitations of entrusting so much of the conduct of the state to men picked through a lottery. So, as acting chairman of the Prytanes, Socrates decided it would be best to skirt the issue raised by Cleon and grant Pericles his request.

"I think I can speak for the Prytanes now serving their term. We would certainly not convene the Assembly to propose any specific military action without prior consultation with the Board of Generals. And I'm reasonably certain that any session of the Prytanes would follow this procedure."

General Pericles was grateful that Socrates formulation did nothing more to antagonize General Cleon. It appeared that Cleon was satisfied since he nodded his head in agreement. And so Socrates moved on.

"Well, we have kept the citizens who are to be honored today for their military service waiting for some time now. Are there any other matters that we should resolve today before we conduct the ceremony?"

General Nicias and Pericles both stood to speak. Pericles had already discussed with Nicias in private the need to prepare the Athenian citizenry for a long war. The first step, they both agreed, was to set up a fund which would be set aside specifically for the defense of Athens. So, knowing what Nicias was about to propose, Pericles sat down, thinking it best that Nicias lead here so that antiwar critics could not complain that the War was all Pericles doing. General Nicias was known for his caution and reluctance to undertake any military enterprise except those which were required absolutely for the defense of Athens. Clearly now Athens was under attack!

General Nicias turned and spoke to the body of fifty Prytanes who sat at the two long tables on both sides of their presiding officer, Socrates. "Councilmen, I have conferred with Pericles and all the other eight generals. We all agree that we must mobilize the resources of our state for a protracted war with the Spartan League. Accordingly, we urge you today to petition the rest of the Council to authorize our Treasury to set up a fund of one thousand talents earmarked exclusively for the defense of Athens and replenished each year the War continues. Part of these funds are to be drawn upon for the purpose of maintaining here on the coasts of our own territory a fleet of one hundred triremes manned by our best captains and crews. This fleet's mission will be to guard our shores against any possible attack of Athens from the sea. We recommend that the fund and this fleet be set up immediately."

"Generals, let me assure you that the full Council will set all this in motion before the sun sets today. We will certainly have no difficulty in securing the approval of the Assembly for these provisions in the near future."

"Thank you, Chairman Socrates. I think we Generals have concluded our agenda. We are ready for the medal ceremony. Please have your clerk summon the citizen hoplites and the buglers to the stage behind your tables."

CHAPTER TWENTY
MAGNIFICENT ALCIBIADES
(Winter, 431 B.C.)

The magnificent man is like an artist; for he can see what is fitting and spend large sums tastefully....... Magnificence is an attribute of expenditures of the kind which we call honorable, e.g. those connected with the gods—votive offerings, buildings, and sacrifices—and similarly with any form of religious worship, and all those that are proper objects of public-spirited ambition, as when people think they ought to equip a chorus or a trireme, or entertain the city, in a brilliant way.

(Aristotle. *Nichomachean Ethics*, Bk. IV, Ch. 2)

Pericles had proven to be right in dismissing Alcibiades' objections to receiving military honors for his part in the Potidaea campaign. In the weeks that followed the awards ceremony in the Strategeion there had been no questions about Alcibiades' medal of courage or his appointment as a cavalry officer. The difficulties and dangers of the Athenians' predicament left no time for gossip about the selection of medal winners from last winter's campaign in far away Potidaea. The Spartan led army stayed in Attica all summer long. They plundered and burned to the ground most of the estates in the demes of northern Attica. The war for most Athenians was an ordeal to be endured. But for Alcibiades, it provided an exhilarating opportunity for accelerating his climb to glory.

Within a week of his commission as a cavalry officer Alcibiades was assigned to lead cavalry sorties against elements of King Archidamus' army. Unlike some of the veteran cavalry officers who balked at the Supreme General's determination that new tunics of scarlet, emblazoned with the owl of Athena on their front, would help the fighting morale of cavalry units, Alcibiades found the new tunic a uniform that encouraged his natural bent for bravado and daring. Alcibiades took it upon himself to outfit the handle of his fighting spear with a strap of leather dyed a deep blue which he let fly out behind his spear as he galloped into action. Yes, he thought to himself often as he mounted his horse, I am vain, but so was Achilles.

Alcibiades led more than fifty sorties against elements of the invading army. His daring and courage were the talk of the City. While cavalry units like his own never pushed the invading army out of Attica, their harassment of the enemy did boost the morale of the Athenians and kept the enemy at some distance from the city walls. When the Spartans and their allies finally left Attica at the end of the summer, Alcibiades had established himself as a bold and competent officer – although at twenty he was younger than most of the men in his unit. Even General Pericles was impressed with his young kinsman.

It would certainly help the cause if the Alkmeonid family remained firm in their support of Pericles' War policy. And so Pericles had decided to take on Alcibiades as his protégé and do all that he could to advance the young man's political career. That was why on this cold and dreary winter morning more than two months after the Spartans had left Attica, Alcibiades had been summoned to another meeting with Pericles and other officials.

Since there was no word of any movement of enemy forces, Alcibiades wondered what the meeting could be about. He mentioned to the General that he would be in Eleuthera attending their country Dionysia the day before the meeting. Pericles had told him not to worry. "You will be pleased," he said, "when you hear our plans for your next assignments." Alcibiades had no reason to doubt Pericles. But he wondered why the meeting was to be held in the Odeion – a building many in Athens thought to be an unnecessary pet project of Pericles, undertaken so as to ingratiate himself with his poet and artist friends. Alcibiades had to hurry if he was not to keep the General waiting. The Odeion was located on the south side of the Acropolis and it was a long walk from his home. He would much rather be home and in bed. He had spent all of yesterday and well into the evening hours at the Country Dionysia. Even though he had cut short the dancing, drinking, and carousing with hetaerae which customarily followed the day of theatrical performances, he was still hung-over. Wake up, he muttered to himself. If General Pericles is to regard me as more than a brash knock-about and a courageous dandy on a horse then I must present myself as a sober, intelligent, and responsible man ready to take on the responsibilities of Athens' leaders.

Pericles was waiting in the Stoa which led from the Orchestra of Dionysos' Theater to an open alley adjacent to the Odeion. The General was not alone. As Alcibiades made his way around the side of the Odeion and along the Orchestra level stone seat reserved for the priest of Dionysos, he could see General Pericles pointing out to his companion, a young man no older than Alcibiades, the grooves which had recently been cut into the rear of the Orchestra stone floor next to the Stoa. Alcibiades did not recognize the young man and now, as he approached closer, he could see why. The red-headed young man was wearing the leather vest and the kind of britches that he had seen among the Thracian allies of the Athenians at Potidaea. Clearly he was a Thracian.

"There you are, Alcibiades. I hope the early meeting is not too inconvenient. I remember when I was twenty I loved to stay up most of the night and sleep late until mid-day. How were the performances at the Country Dionysia at Eleutherai? I was just describing to my guest, Prince Sadocus, how our temporary stage building for our City Dionysia is mounted over the rear of the Orchestra floor on wooden posts that fit into the stone grooves. I can see by the dark half circles under your eyes, that you must have enjoyed the *komos* afterwards. I'm getting too old for those late nights. That is why I wanted to introduce you to my young guest. It would be a much more enjoyable stay in Athens for him if he could be in the company of young men like you."

Alcibiades saluted General Pericles and embraced the Thracian. Smiling graciously Alcibiades spoke to both of them. "General, you have more energy than anyone in Athens. You are the only man I know who can keep moving on more enterprises at once than can be counted on both hands. You seem to the rest of us mere mortals indefatigable. Indeed, if we do not want to tire your guest, it would be best if you share him with some one who moves along at a more human pace. I would be glad to entertain him. May I ask what brings you to Athens, Prince Sadocus?"

Sadocus was somewhat unsure what to say since he was in Athens on a diplomatic mission and his instructions were to avoid any discussion of his mission with anyone other than General Pericles.

Pericles spoke on his behalf. "He is here as a diplomat for his father, King Sitalces. You have heard, haven't you Alcibiades, how Sitalces and his father unified all of the Odrysian tribes to form a kingdom which now extends over most of Thrace? The Prince tells me that his father wishes to enter into an alliance with us which will include an economic opportunity for both of our peoples for profitable trade. Indeed, our Assembly has already begun to discuss how we might offer a trading franchise at Piraeus to our Thracian friends. But no politics or business now! Prince Sadocus, there is no one in Athens more qualified than Alcibiades to show you the many and varied pleasures of Athenian life."

Alcibiades did not need General Pericles to explain why a military alliance with the Odrysian Kingdom was of supreme value to Athens. The siege of Potidaea could be brought to a successful end more quickly if King Sitalces would assist in checking the interference of King Perdiccas' Macedonian incursions into the Chalcidice. But even more important, given the Spartan assault on the farms of Attica, Athens ability to feed its people during a long war with Sparta would absolutely depend on Athens control of the coastal ports and sea lanes along the southern shores of Thrace. This was the route her ships must be able to safely sail, if Athens was to make safe her corn supply from the fertile regions on the northern shores of the Pontus Sea. Alcibiades had become familiar enough with his family's mercantile interests to know that the corn trade, subsidized in part by the Athenian Treasury, had become a driving force in Athens' strategic alliances with, or outright domination of, all the islands and coastal regions of the Northern Aegean. And so Alcibiades nodded his head indicating to his General that he understood what was at stake.

"When Prince Sadocus is done with his diplomatic chores, I would be honored if the Prince would be my house guest for as long as he wishes. All I ask in exchange is that Prince Sadocus share with me some of the secrets of the superb Thracian horsemanship which is unrivaled by any other people."

Pericles knew he could depend on Alcibiades. "You see, Prince Sadocus, how my young kinsman, like every Athenian, knows how to strike a deal. We should complete our state discussions within a few days and then, I think, you would do well to spend more time in Athens and do so in the company of Alcibiades, one of her brightest young luminaries."

The Prince looked relieved. Everything was going so smoothly and he did want to spend more time in Athens. He had begun to fall in love with this feverishly busy and cosmopolitan city which seemed to his Thracian eyes open to everything new and different. And so with genuine warmth he reached out his hand and squeezed the muscled shoulder of Alcibiades. Speaking in his recently learned language of the Athenians he accepted the invitation, "Signed, sealed, and delivered – it's a deal, Alcibiades. And please, my new Athenian friends, there is no need for a royal title – Sadocus will do."

Pericles straightened his body and readjusted the helmet he always wore in public. He pointed to the steps that led down from the porch and gestured for the two young men to follow him. "Well, now that we have settled all that, it is time for us to go into the Odeion and meet our Archon Pythodorus. I think our Archon has some service in mind for you, Alcibiades."

Now was the moment that Alcibiades would deliver the little speech he had prepared for General Pericles. He hoped it would not sound too eager to please.

"I am grateful for any opportunity to serve Athens. It is true, Sadocus, that I have some reputation for loving a good party. But now that I am a hoplite-citizen it is time for my partying to come second to my responsibilities as a citizen. I was inspired to see General Sophocles' play, *Antigone*, produced again at Eleutherai. I'm sure General Sophocles did not party all night and sleep late! I believe Sophocles was elected General of his tribal regiment, appointed Secretary of the Delean League Treasury, and found time to write and direct this first prize winning play at the City Dionysia - all in the same year! Let me see, that year I would have been eight years old - still playing in the Gymnasium yard."

Alcibiades paused to see if Pericles was listening or was he bored by his young kinsman's banter and just being polite? Pericles eyes were difficult to see as they were hidden by the shadow of his helmet in the grey morning light. Pericles, though, did seem to be nodding his head in an encouraging way. And so as Pericles led Alcibiades and Prince Sadocus down the steps of the porch, then down the alley along the side of the Odeion and around to the front of the building, Alcibiades continued, hoping to impress his sponsor and mentor with his thoughtful application of Sophocles' drama concerning Thebes to present circumstances.

"I found the theme of *Antigone* remarkably congruent somehow with what I saw still standing in Eleutherai. The Spartans left undisturbed the homes of the families of the Dionysian priests in Eleutherai and were careful to prevent any desecration of Dionysos' Sanctuary there. Anyway, it occurred to me that King Archidamus and the other generals leading the Spartans and their allies share with Sophocles' Antigone the conviction that there is a sacred law higher even than the interests of states and the authority of those who govern them. That is why the god's precinct and his priests' homes still stand, and that is why Antigone buries her rebel brother – she so honors and fears the gods and the sacred laws of honoring the dead kinsman that even the commands of the Theban King Creon and her duty to him must be set aside."

Pericles did want to encourage his protégé to appreciate the work of the dramatists. It would not hurt to show some interest in Alcibiades' remark, although it was on the level of what the gymnasium tutors teach to their twelve-year olds. "I'm glad, Alcibiades, that you took time from your revelries to attend the theater and think about the themes of Sophocles' tragedy. It shows that you are ready to take part in promoting our theatric festivals."

They had reached the main entrance in the front of the Odeion. Pericles opened the wide oak door that led directly into the large central room, an open and roughly square hall that gave the appearance of a place for large groups of people to move about freely. Even though the day was grey, light streamed into this unusual auditorium wherein there were no benches to be seen. Alcibiades looked up to see where the light was coming from. All along the four sides of the building, up high on the walls just below the ceiling of the building and beneath the slanting roof, were open windows. Then, and this was quite unusual, the very top of the roof was pitched like the top of a tent canopy and there too, at the very top, was an open window. Even in the dim morning light, Alcibiades could see the pulley which was connected to the window and hung down alongside one of the center supporting columns, the pulley machinery reaching low enough to be operated from the floor of this large room. There must be some kind of sliding cover that can open and close this window, he thought. It is probably covered with tiles to match the exterior tile roof. How ingenious!

"Have you had an opportunity, Alcibiades, to see the inside of the Odeion? I know this is Sadocus' first visit here. I am quite pleased with the building. You know that I helped draw up the plans with our architects. This main room of the Odeion is where the choruses in our tragedies, satyr plays, and comedies dress and wait until they make their entrance onto the Orchestra floor in front of the god's sanctuary. This same room is used to assemble the singers in our men's and boys' dithyramb performances so that, like the choral groups, they can make a dramatic entrance onto the Orchestra floor. From this room all these performers, once they are costumed and organized, move out the side door which opens facing the Stoa. As you know, during the City Dionysia, the Stoa is temporarily enclosed by portable wooden screens. So, although everyone knows that Oedipus the King, or the satyrs, or the crowd of Persian women are their neighbors; it is always a surprise to see for the very first time the masked and costumed players as they make their entrance onto the wooden stage above the dancing floor and present themselves to the gaze of Dionysos. All the poets and performers tell me that this procedure has made it so much easier to transport themselves and their audience into the sacred and divine suspension of everyday life in the service of the Dionysian. It is as though consorts of Dionysos come through a mysterious portal of the god's own sanctuary, pay their respects to the seated god, and then make their way down to the Orchestra as they invite the assembled celebrants to join in the mysterious play of passions which unfolds in ever renewing life."

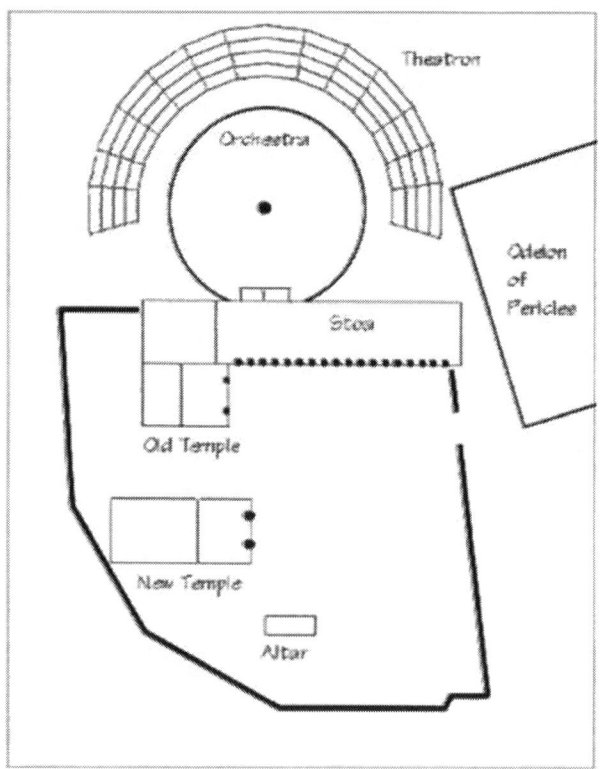

Athens' sacred theater district of Dionysos Eleuthereus

Pericles would be happy if his young kinsman understood why the conception and construction of the Odeion, like the Parthenon and the other great public works Pericles had persuaded the Athenian Assembly to fund, wasn't just the pet project of a vain leader. It was much more than that. More, even, than the theater people understood. Yes, he had lent his own eloquence and intelligence to transforming the Delian League into the Athenian empire. But did not the beauty of their sculpture, their monuments to the divine, the genius of their poets, the brilliance of their mathematicians and philosophers, and the creation of a civil society that allowed an expression of individual liberty of thought and speech found no where else – did not all this in the balance outweigh the tribute demanded from other cities, the slavery of those who worked the mines of Laurium or felled the timber in far away Thrace, and even the occasional cruelty to the enemies who would bring Athens down? The seemingly ceaseless criticism of his every public endeavor by his political rivals sometimes made him feel like an exhausted Atlas – condemned to carry a heavy world with no relief until old age or death would shift his burden to others.

"I'm getting old, Alcibiades, sixty-five this year. Sometimes I think too much and speak to no one in particular. Well here we are. Now that we are in the central assembly room, come this way, Alcibiades, where the others are waiting for us.

I think you have already met Pythodorus our current chief administrative archon. I thought you might also enjoy meeting some of the poets who will be competing to win a place in the theatrical productions of the upcoming City Dionysia. Here, looking very uncomfortable is Euripides. Beside me is my friend Sophocles. It was he who persuaded the architects to include storage rooms in the Odeion for some of the more rare and very costly gifts and trophies from our many colonies. Once a Treasurer, always a bean counter! Sophocles is always keeping an eye on his fellow thespians – to make sure that the fine gold and silver utensils are returned if they are borrowed for one of their productions. And over there, looking at the theatrical props stored in the side room, are Agathon and Simonides."

Alcibiades smiled and nodded his head in greeting. "I am honored to be in the company of Athens' most illustrious poets."

"Prince Sadocus, would you think it rude if we turn our attention to making some arrangements necessary in the preparations for our Athenian City Dionysia?

"No, not at all, General Pericles. You are kind to show me the building. I will wander about and look at its statuary and the fine detail your masons have worked on the interior columns – if that is alright."

"Please look at whatever you wish. We have no secrets to keep in this building." Pericles turned back to Alcibiades to continue where he left off.

"Let me get to the point, Alcibiades. Our poets are anxious to return to their Muses. I have asked Pythodorus to consider you as a possible *choregus* for the theatrical productions. You know, don't you, that I myself undertook this liturgy when I was starting out in public life. I think I was twenty-three at the time and didn't have anywhere near the resources you possess. But even with my somewhat limited means I was able to sponsor Aeschylus' dramatic production, *The Persians*, which won the prize that year."

"Yes, General, I have seen that performed in one of our rural Dionysia festivals. I am proud that my kinsman was its original sponsor."

"Thank you, Alcibiades. Well, as all of you here know, I am a great admirer of all the arts and think it a high honor to be a patron of works that bring beauty and insight to their audiences. It is also the duty of those of us who have some wealth to do this kind of service for the state and the gods. The people are always grateful and if the sponsorship is done with generosity they will always be ready to support such patrons should they seek elected positions of leadership. I can think of no better way other than military duty for a young man to show his love of the public good."

Alcibiades now understood. "Yes, I agree with you."

Pericles continued. "This year, it is especially important that our City Dionysia be spectacular. Rich and poor Athenians have all endured considerable hardship this past summer in our war with Sparta. I am almost certain that this summer will bring more hardship. If we are to endure and prevail, then our great festival of play and divine forgetfulness must lift our cares from our shoulders – at least for the short season of the holy days – and renew the bonds of our shared spirit as one people. You, Alcibiades, are among our richest citizens and now, I might add, one of our young heroes. I am sure it would please our citizens to find that their hero is also willing to be their benefactor by undertaking a liturgy on behalf of Dionysos and all his celebrants. We don't know yet which poets will be chosen. But you see here today likely candidates. I thought you might enjoy talking to them about the works they are about to submit to our judges who will select this year's scripts."

"I am honored to be a candidate for this liturgy, General."

"I thought you would be ready to undertake this, Alcibiades. Well, my part in the meeting is done. I must return to the Strategeion. But if the rest of you would spend a few more moments with young Alcibiades and explain to him what exactly is expected of the liturgist - that would be good. Pythodorus, we would not want to be presumptuous. Of course, after you have discussed all the particulars with Alcibiades, it is finally your call as to whether a good match is to be made between Alcibiades as *choregus* and one of our poets. Given the shortened time of our festival and the other pressing duties you must undertake during wartime, I thought this kind of meeting would be very helpful."

"No, you are never presumptuous, Pericles. This is all very helpful. I am glad I have this opportunity to talk to Alcibiades. In fact, in reviewing possible candidates for filling the ranks of the fifteen *chroegoi* required for all our musical, dance, and play performances, I had already put young Alcibiades high on my list. So go on to your other responsibilities. Our poets can give Alcibiades a summary of the responsibilities that are assumed by a *choregus*. Then he and I will decide whether he is prepared to take this on."

Pythodorus had already made his decision well before this meeting. A week ago Pericles had given him a list of twenty prominent and wealthy citizens which he was recommending be considered for *choregi*. Pericles had positioned Alcibiades at the top of his list which, it was clear, was not alphabetically arranged. After Pythodorus had examined the records of Alcibiades' tribal regiment and found that he met the minimum age requirement of twenty, he then made other inquiries to make sure that this young man did have full control of the considerable financial resources of his deceased father's commercial assets. There was no doubt, he discovered, that Alcibiades could be generous in his support for recruiting the most talented actors and making sure no expense was spared for choral costumes and other needed theatrical paraphernalia. There was nothing worse than a financially strapped and stingy *choregus*. No *Archon Eponymus* had ever been awarded a gold crown for his supervision of this Festival by the Council of Five Hundred if he had made the mistake of selecting such sponsors. As for Alcibiades' youth, Pythodorus considered that an asset. He would be more anxious to please those in authority and thus less likely to be one of those *choregi* who thought they knew better than the supervising archon or the artists how to put on a great show.

Pythodorus wanted very much to bring Alcibiades on board today. So after he had walked to the door with Pericles and assured the first man of Athens that he too was in favor of Alcibiades selection, he returned to Alcibiades' side and clasping the young man's shoulder in friendship, officially offered him one of the three appointments as choregus for the tragedies.

"Alcibiades, I see you have been talking with our poets. All of them here today have submitted their plays to our panel of judges. There will be other submissions, I am sure. I am always hesitant to interrupt such gifted authors of drama lest I earn their ire and find myself written in to their plays as a villainous scoundrel. But, like General Pericles, my many duties require that I too must go on to another meeting. I have decided today that you will be my very first appointment as a *choregus* for the tragedies. I am completely confident that you will bring honor to this service."

Alcibiades smiled like a child who had just been given a magnificent present. "Polydorus, I accept and look forward to being able to assist in this service to the god and our people. When will I know which of the poets will be assigned to me?"

"Our board of judges will be making their final selection within the next two weeks. As soon as the selection is complete, we will introduce you to the poet you will be working with. That will give your team about three months to prepare for your production in the City Dionysia. Now, I must really be on my way. Should you have any other questions about your part in the production, Euripides can answer them. He has already had twelve of his tragedies performed at the City Dionysia and is very familiar with the details of the relationship between the *choregus* and the poet."

Alcibiades spent the rest of the morning at the Odeion. Once it was clear that he was to be one of the sponsors for the tragedies, he wanted to know as much as possible about the kinds of things it would be his responsibility to finance. And so, he began by asking Euripides his questions about how exactly the *choregu*s goes about the business of procuring and pricing the materials required for the City Dionysia theatrical productions.

Euripides was very polite, but seemed anxious to be on his way. It was obvious to Alcibiades that the poet had no interest whatsoever in the costs of theatrical productions and seemed to regard all matters pertaining to the production and procurement of the costumes and other equipment as a nuisance to be relegated to theater clerks and slaves. Alcibiades wondered why Euripides even needed a sponsor, since he belonged to one of the wealthier families of Athens. Perhaps, he thought, it would be bad form for a poet to stand in the way of those ambitious men who undertook the City Dionysian liturgies as a demonstration of their beneficence to the city and the gods.

Alcibiades was not surprised when Euripides passed him off to the state employee charged with stewardship of the Odeion. "Alcibiades I want to introduce you to Barnabas. He has been associated with the Theater here even longer than I have. I think he was the steward in charge of the humble temporary theater storage rooms that were put up beside the Sanctuary during Aeschylus' time some fifty years ago. Back then, he was a state slave who had been captured during the Persian War. When I first competed in the City Dionysia twenty four years ago, he had earned his freedom for his meritorious stewardship of the growing stock of theatrical equipment and became the theater's first permanent paid official. When the Odeion was completed, there was no question as to who should be charged with its day to day management - Barnabas the Phoenician. He is an absolute genius at keeping track of things and keeping the accounts straight. He knows much more than I do about the details of arranging for the staging of a poet's drama or comedy during the City Dionysia.

"Well then, I suppose Barnabas will be my tutor. Of course it is silly for you to have to deal with matters like this. I am such a novice and you have already competed in the City Dionysia many times. If you were a brilliant sculptor, it would be a waste of time for you to concern yourself with carting the stone from the quarry or even sharpening your chisels. If I am fortunate I may be assigned as your cart bearer and chisel sharpener. Forgive my analogy, but I would prefer that you return to your sanctuary with your muses and perfect the form of your sculpture so that I might be credited with assisting the master in producing a masterpiece."

Euripides smiled and now looked with interest at the young man in front of him. "Not just a rich and empty young man following thoughtlessly every ambitious aristocrat's way to curry the favor of the people, I see. Do I hear my friend Socrates at work in your ironic and self-deprecating play with analogy? Well, Alcibiades, I will be more careful where you are concerned. But really, believe me! Barnabas will know much more than I do about the work of the *choregus*. So there is no insult intended in charging him with answering all your questions. Now, if Barnabas will make good what I lack, then our Archon's commission is satisfied and I may, as you so poetically suggested, return to what I do best – chisel away until the stuff of human behavior shows its elemental form."

Alcibiades turned to Barnabas. "What do you think, steward? Has he paid his dues? Has he shown due deference to his Archon and done his part to make straight and easy the path of the young liturgist?"

Barnabas, grey and wrinkled and a few years past his eighth decade, knew how to banter with such as Alcibiades and Euripides, both friends of a philosopher. Though still a noncitizen, his advanced age and long tenure as a valued custodian of state theatrical property had made him unafraid to talk, howbeit with ironic deference, with wit and intelligence to the aristocratic citizens who usually financed all the theatrical performances. "Yes, young master, do not make him tarry. Women, slaves, humble metic freemen like me, thetes and dock workers all are given the voice of inner life, a soul and intelligence, by this poet. There is no reason why a young man like you bursting with ambition and the energy of a wild stallion, may not be an occasion for his poetic art to bring soul and intelligence to a neophyte knight. Send him on his way and you too may see and hear yourself made a complicated and living spirit staring back at you in one of his creations on the stage."

"Well spoken, Steward Barnabas. Are you really a Phoenician? Your Greek is impeccable, but I think I hear behind it a Semitic accent like my household maid – a young woman whose people were exiled from a place she calls Judah."

Barnabas looked intently at Alcibiades as he spoke to him as though he were a long lost friend. "I see Euripides has taken his leave. It is really quite amazing. This great student of human nature who peers deeply into the human psyche has never asked me about my origins – and so he has taken me for a Phoenician. You, a young blond-haired blue-eyed stunningly handsome buck who appears to be completely self-absorbed and concerned only with making his own way, and who has just met me and talked with me for a few moments, guess my lineage and true home. You have a keen ear, Alcibiades. I am a Judean, but like the rest of my people we have been scattered among all the nations. Now without our own homeland, we stubbornly cling, usually only in our inner life and invisible to those around us, to our peculiar polity. I have met your servant in the marketplace. She was muttering something in our Hebrew tongue and I overheard. We have become close friends and meet from time to time to read together a compilation of some of our people's ancient hymns to our God.

"So, Barnabas, you are my maid's reason for tarrying so long sometimes when she goes out to the marketplace"

"I hope this has not caused her difficulties with you. I would hate to think her kindness in sharing memories of our homeland with an old compatriot has made her own life more miserable."

"I have no cause for any disappointment in my maid's work."

"I will do my best, Alcibiades, to assist you in any way I can. Are there some questions you have today that I might address?"

"Is it true, Barnabas, that the theatrical costumes and various temporary stage settings which previous sponsors have bought have all been donated to the god and stored here in the Odeion? So, is the magnificent chariot which Agamemnon is shown riding on in returning to his palace in Sophocles tragedy still kept here, for example? That chariot must have cost a small fortune."

"Yes, it is the custom for every *choregus* at the City Dionysia to endow the Sanctuary with everything which was purchased for the production of the performances. The chariot you speak of is kept in our largest storage room. Would you like to see it?"

"Maybe some other day, Barnabas. Given the cost of such things, one would think that costumes or other stage furnishings from previous productions would be made use of again at the City Dionysia."

Barnabas furrowed his brow and after thinking for a moment answered Alcibiades with a question. "Would any man from Athens' most wealthy and powerful families, who takes on the liturgy at the City Dionysia which is witnessed by almost all of the city's citizens, want to ever show that his beneficence borrows from another man's gifts to the god?"

"I see your point, Barnabas."

"But if we set aside the matter of pride, Alcibiades, your question makes perfect sense if our theatrical performances were enterprises like the commercial holdings of your family. In shipping and trading, instruments of production are considered most economic and profitable if their cost can be kept down and they remain serviceable for reuse as long as possible. But this is very different, Alcibiades. The *choregus* is undertaking a religious service. He is not supposed to make a profit – at least not in any direct way. His service entails a sacrifice to the god and the city. The more expensive it is; the more impressive is his sacrifice."

"And then there is another consideration, Alcibiades, if you and your poet are to be honored with first prize by the judges. Both the judges and the audience are pleased most by novelty. Not only do they demand that all the City Dionysia entries in the theatric festival of comedies and tragedies be new scripts, but they are always impressed by those costumes, masks and stage props which have not been seen before. Let the satyr plays and the dithyrambic choruses appear dependably the same – that is expected! But any *choregus* who dresses up his tragic or comedic actors in last years costumes risks seeing his stage production pelted with sweetmeat scraps and olive pits."

"Your advice is much appreciated, Barnabas. I will spare no expense in my Dionysian liturgy. But still, it would be good if you share with me your knowledge of those vendors and suppliers who compete with one another in providing the *choregus* with the inventory of goods and services required for the production of a first class production at our City Dionysia."

"I will be glad to give you a list of such tradesmen and craftsmen, including my notes concerning the quality of their work and their fees and prices. I think you will be pleased to see that many of the tradesman, craftsman, and merchants are in fact incorporated with your family's commercial holdings. So it would be difficult for you to spend liturgically without the return on your family's holdings increasing. We Judeans have an ancient saying about service to God in such circumstances. 'It is best to reach out with the right hand without knowing what the left hand takes back'. But I must say I have always admired how your gods move and have their being within the human circle of things. So no one really minds in Athens if the gods get only the hide and the bones in the sacrificed animal while the humans enjoy a feast of meat!"

"It is always a pleasure to deal with an intelligent man, Barnabas. Maybe I should have you take bids on what I will be requisitioning for my assigned performance. Then you, being my right hand, will sort it all out and I, the left hand, will not know the details. Then no one could say of Alcibiades that he made use of his liturgy to fill his own pockets."

"Alcibiades, I am honored that you would entrust me with such a task. But I am forbidden by a vow to the Head Priest of the Sanctuary to take any part in the purchase of liturgical objects. So you are on your own. I don't think you need to worry about such a charge of enriching yourself. Nobody wants to go down that path since every man's service to the gods and the state is often inseparable from some kind of self-interest. Besides you will spend plenty and no one can think it all comes back!"

"I can see almost everything must be bought for my poet's production. But I am curious Barnabas, about what happens with all the stuff that is accumulated. Surely all of the stagecraft, costumes, and other production materials from each year's performances would fill every storeroom, as well as every nook and cranny of the Odeion in just a few years. There are at least eight sponsors every City Dionysia just for the tragedies and the comedies. Like legendary King Midas' treasury palace, the rooms would be so filled, that there would be no room for you or anyone else to move about in the Odeion, the Sanctuary, or for that matter, the Treasury Building. As the Miletian philosopher Anaximander might have put it, 'The stuff on the way in must be countered by the stuff on the way out – or else by now there would be no balanced order of things stored and things expended, no storage rooms and open hallways, but only a chaos of a boundless dump.'"

"Alcibiades, I wonder if you, being an ambitious young man, will stay with philosophy much longer. Socrates, I have heard, is in love with you. Like so many youths your age, you talk the talk of Socrates and his philosophical companions. But I doubt he will be able to hold onto you. You seem to be a walking bundle of contradictions – but for an old man like me you are a treat. The simple answer to your question is that the family charged with the priesthood of Dionysos' Sanctuary here in Athens both rents and sells a considerable part of the theatrical endowments to the various outlying towns in Attica. You know that these towns celebrate their own Dionysia and often reproduce the prize winning plays of our City Dionysia. So there is a lot of demand for all our theatrical props, costumes and other equipment. Don't ask me about how, if at all, an accounting is made of all this, because I am forbidden to even broach that subject."

"Well, that explains the balance of things, if not the balancing of the books, Barnabas. I guess that will have to satisfy my curiosity for now. As for Socrates and me I would hope that, like Pericles and Protagoras, we will remain friends even should I become the first man of Athens."

Alcibiades did not mind the old man's speculations about what kind of man he would become. Rather than find Barnabas' characterizations of him presumptuous or offensive, Alcibiades liked it when he was at the center of others' stories. So reaching out his hand to Barnabas, he patted the old Judean's shoulder and took his leave of the Odeion.

The days and weeks following Alcibiades appointment as a *choregus* for the City Dionysia were so busy that he could barely find time for his daily physical training at the Academy District Gymnasium. Looking down his own torso, he could see loose flesh where his ribs ended just above his stomach and hips. I really must make more time for the gymnasium, he thought. It will not do for a cavalry officer to look like one of our bakers or peddlers of sweetmeats. Well, things should slow down after the City Dionysia.

It hardly seemed possible that the time had gone by so fast. Yes, there had been the endless bickering with his poet about the staging of his play. It had turned out that Polydorus' pairing of Alcibiades with the last poet to be chosen for the tragedies was not exactly a marriage made in heaven! Who would think that Euripides would balk at Alcibiades efforts to procure lavish jeweled costumes fit for royalty, masks made of a new incredibly elastic and skin like material that his own shipping agents had found in a Greek outpost along the Nile in Lower Egypt, and a iron crane that would make for a stupendous special effect at the end of the production? Alcibiades had taken the trouble to carefully read Euripides' script and then identify what to him seemed to be the most spectacular artifacts that money could buy to create an unforgettable stage production.

But Euripides urged Alcibiades to keep it simple. "I want the audience to pay attention to the dialogue and to the poetry of the chorus – not to be bedazzled by sparkling jewelry, weird novelties of masking, and some big special effect at the end of the drama that makes everyone forget the theme of my story."

None of this made any sense to Alcibiades, and it wasn't until Alcibiades threatened to seek mediation from Pythodorus and the high priest of the sanctuary that Euripides agreed to accept Alcibiades' lavish and spectacular staging. Alcibiades was sure that no one would remember Euripides rather curious tragedy about a woman who kills her own children unless in fact it had something spectacularly new to charm the audience. "Let me help you stage it this way," Alcibiades had said, "and I am sure our production of 'Medea', the centerpiece of our triadic tragic cycle, will be a prize winner."

Alcibiades and Euripides barely spoke to one another after Alcibiades got his way. In the weeks that followed, Euripides rehearsed with his actors and the chorus, never hiding his irritation of having to deal with what he took to be the distractions of the overly contrived staging purchased by his rich, young, and surprisingly obstinate *choregus*. Alcibiades, frankly, was glad that the whole thing was going to be finished in a few days. It had turned out to be a genuine nuisance that took far too much of his time. Fortunately, the other project he undertook at Pericles' request provided welcome relief from dealing with a poet who was too full of himself to know what really entertained people!

As Pericles had proposed, Sadocus, the Thracian prince, had accepted Alcibiades' invitation and moved into the guest room that adjoined the large dinning room in the men's quarters in Alcibiades' home. The two had become close friends as both young men seemed to share in an almost preternatural zeal to miss no male pleasure. Since both possessed great wealth and were among the most attractive young men in Athens, there was nothing except the opinion of others to check the satisfaction of every whim and appetite. Indeed, both men had become the subject of scandalous gossip for their conduct during the Winter Lenaia festival. After leaving the comedic performances, Alcibiades and Sadocus had danced and sung in the revelry of a *komos* which included a company of a dozen hetaerae. The drinking, dancing, and singing band roamed the streets of Athens late into the night, keeping everyone awake except those few Dionysian enthusiasts who observed Lenaia by staying awake all night so they might address a special prayer and drink offering to Dionysos at sun rise. The gossipers claimed that Alcibiades had then paid all of the twelve hetaerae to return to his house and help Sadocus and him sober up through their ministrations. There were many such nights for Alcibiades and his house guest. Even so, the gossipers made little headway in curtailing the pleasure-seeking romps of Alcibiades and his new found Thracian friend.

Alcibiades was thankful that Pericles, who usually looked unfavorably on such public behavior on the part of those who wished to govern in Athens, said nothing to Alcibiades about his Dionysian revelry with the Thracian Prince. Less than a month after the affair during Lenaia, Pericles, on behalf of the Assembly, presided at the ceremony conferring all the rights of Athenian citizenship upon Prince Sadocus. Alcibiades stood by his friend's side as he received the official documents certifying his citizenship. Immediately after the ceremony, Pericles took Alcibiades aside and thanked him for the part he had played in making Sadocus feel at home in Athens.

"You will see," Pericles had said, "the dividends our alliance with Sadocus will pay towards the ongoing security and prosperity of Athens. Like every other man given the opportunity to lead our city, I will soon pass from the scene. Either the sicknesses of old age will take me or the people will tire of me and send me away. All that matters is that Athens endures. If Athens and its accomplishments all are extinguished then there has been no purpose for the life-long ambition that drove me to become the first man of Athens. This is why, Alcibiades, I have asked you to help me make the Thracian king Sitalces and his son Sadocus a steadfast ally of Athens. This is why I want to help prepare you to take on the same stewardship for our city that has been the work of my life. You are still young and it is too early for you to give yourself to the single-minded political ambition that plays the power game, always maneuvering so as to gain control over the machinery of our state. But believe me, Alcibiades, there is satisfaction only in power that is guided by service to higher purposes. Otherwise, power becomes only the ugly tool of the uncontrolled and destructive appetites of the tyrant who devours his own city. My hope for you is that you will not be swallowed up by the hatreds, the gamesmanship, and the fleeting flush of power which accompanies the routing of a political rival so that, as your friend Socrates might say, you gain the whole world and forget about that excellence of soul which should animate those who would guide the collective life of our city."

Alcibiades found it puzzling enough whenever Socrates urged young men to care most for the improvement of their souls, but when a practical man like Pericles talked about the nurturing of one's own soul it seemed utterly incomprehensible! What more could there be to life than knowledge, pleasure, and power. And as far as Alcibiades was concerned, knowledge was worthless if it didn't promote pleasure and power. Why all this talk about this mysterious inner man – the soul. It all sounded too much like that womanish religious nonsense his mother babbled on about whenever she urged him to remember his sacred initiation at Eleusis into the ranks of the thrice born. But, grateful for Pericles assistance in promoting his entrance into public life, Alcibiades had assured Pericles that he would never betray the Athenian state and its commitment to democracy. "You and the rest of Athens will see next week during the City Dionysia that young Alcibiades, like his kinsmen Pericles, will spare nothing in his liturgy for the city and its gods. I will not disappoint you, Pericles."

On taking his leave, Pericles actually embraced Alcibiades with genuine warmth – something that his Alkmeonid older cousin had never done before. Smiling as he turned to go, Pericles gently teased his former ward. "Last month, Alcibiades the Satyr, next month, Magnificent Alcibiades, Patron of the Theater - Sing fair damsels of Athens of his many peerless ways!"

CHAPTER TWENTY-ONE
FAREWELL TO ARTEMIS
(Spring, 431 B.C.)

How could the faith in the gods have been reft from the web of human life with which it had been interwoven by a thousand threads? ...Religion, particularly an imaginative one, cannot be torn from the heart, especially from the whole life and heart of a people, by cold syllogisms constructed in the study..."

(G. W. F. Hegel. *Positivity of Christian Religion*)

"Are you ready, Alcibiades? Today, the ninth day of Elaphebolion, the City Dionysia will begin at mid-day with the ceremonial 'bringing in from the sacrificial hearth' of the ancient wooden cult statue of Dionysos Eleuthereus. You, Alcibiades, have been chosen to serve the god and the people. We have suffered through a summer of siege and the hardships of war. More than likely, the Spartans will return again once the summer season begins. So both the people as well as their leaders will bring to their celebration of the god of ecstatic forgetfulness a hunger for the god's presence. We yearn not only for relief from the everyday drudgery of the cares of life, but for a respite from the anxious uncertainties of a future filled with war."

Who was that speaking in his dream? It must have been General Pericles or maybe Alcibiades' poet, Euripides. No one his own age speaks so elegantly! He was awake now. The early morning sun had found its way into Alcibiades' bedroom and already felt warm on his face. How pleasant, he thought, to feel the arrival of spring as Apollo in his sun chariot mounting higher in the sky calls forth Persephone, Demeter, and Dionysos from the cold darkness of short winter days.

Hmm? Maybe that was me speaking in my dream. I'm such a chameleon and I have spent so much time around my poet.

He would get himself up this morning. His body servant must be asleep. Today is the ninth day of *Elaphebolion* – his dream soul was right! He, along with every other *choregus* charged with sponsoring the City Dionysia performances, would be officially presented to the public just before noon at the Odeion. As he rose from his bed, he could hear his other servants moving about in the kitchen down the hall from his bedroom. They had been instructed last night to prepare a special breakfast for him, his house guest, Sadocus, and one more guest, Socrates.

It had been some time since Alcibiades had enjoyed Socrates' provocative company and he had decided it would be interesting to discover what the philosopher thought about his part in the production of Euripides' new trilogy of tragedies and their accompanying satyr play. So he had invited Socrates to join them for breakfast this morning so that he could enjoy the festivities of the City Dionysia as the special guest of Alcibiades. After breakfast Alcibiades would lead his small but prestigious entourage to the Odeion. He would make sure he arrived early enough so that Socrates and Prince Sadocus would have front row seats when Alcibiades, as *choregus*, introduced himself, his poet Euripides, and their distinguished cast of actors.

The Archon Pythodorus insisted that each *choregus* keep his remarks short. "You don't need to tout the merits of the tragedies or comedies." he said. "Everyone trusts that the Archon and his assistants have chosen worthy scripts. Your only job is that of the herald who ahead of time announces the title of the play, the poet author, and the principal actors. If all fourteen of you feel the need to say more than that, our audience will slip away before we are done. Believe me, whether or not our little Odeion preview is well attended, two days later the seats at Dionysos' theater are always full well before Dionysos Eleuthereus' high priest intones the dedicatory invocation to Dionysos.

Alcibiades had practiced before going to bed last night what he would say. He would end his remarks with the promise of something special: "Our production of Euripides' new trilogy of tragedies, spectacular in every respect, will leave you spell bound as if you too had come too close to witchcraft." Now that the morning had arrived when he would perform his first public official act, he was not so confident that his bullying of his poet into accepting the exceptionally lavish and novel staging of his tragedies would lead to a prize-winning production. As he finished dressing, he wondered if Euripides' festering irritation with his *choregus* might have infected the actors and members of the chorus, distracting them so that a confident and spirited performance would hardly be possible. Well, he thought, there is no point in worrying about it now. Euripides has every reason to get the best out of his performers.

Where is Castor? Do I have to do everything for myself? Alcibiades could not find his sandals. His new body-servant had not yet appeared as he should the moment his master awakened. Just as he was to call for him, his newest and still untrained servant appeared at the doorway to his bedroom.

"Master, your guest Socrates has arrived. Both he and Prince Sadocus await you in the men's banquet room. I see you are already dressed. I will help you with you your sandals. They are right there by your feet, just under the bed."

"Castor, if you are to be my body servant then you must be here when I get up in the morning. That is why your sleeping mat is always in a room next to mine – so that you can be aware of my every need."

Caster turned his eyes away from his Master and knelt before him as he reached under the bed for Alcibiades' sandals. Like a small child with his eyes misting over with tears Caster looked up again at his Lord, intent on winning his protector's favor, as he carefully tied the sandals' leather straps around Alcibiades' ankles. "Master, I was about to come to you, when I heard a knock on our front door. Since no one else was answering the door, I went and opened it. I knew you were expecting your friend Socrates early this morning and I thought it would not do to keep him waiting while I looked for your steward."

"You did well, Castor. I suppose the steward and the other servants are all busy in the kitchen and didn't hear the knocking. Lay out my gold studded staff and my new purple robe and the gold sash which I will change into before leaving for the Odeion this morning. Make sure there are no wrinkles in the sash or the robe! Then go to the kitchen and tell Debra to begin serving breakfast to our guests."

Alcibiades only used his small sleeping room when he was not partying. The room faced towards the east and was on the corner of the house with two windows facing the interior courtyard. It was not often that he slept alone in this room, and so, he thought, it is to be expected that his servants find themselves at loose ends when the Master's routine changes. Thank goodness for Debra! I can count on her to keep the household accounts straight and to manage the servants when I entertain.

When he made his way down the hall, he could smell fresh baked bread and the cakes molded out of uncooked dough, honey, and sesame-seeds which were already being served to his guests. His cook, Nestor, had suggested that Socrates, being from Alopeke where some elderly country folk still celebrated Elaphebolion in honor of Artemis- the Shooter of the Deer, would appreciate the traditional serving of uncooked dough. Nestor had muttered something to the effect that they should be eaten by his masters since they hadn't done his grandfather any damn good in bringing divine blessing from the goddess.

The cook, Nestor, was an old man himself. Nestor had been brought to Alcibiades' household in Athens by Alcibiades' mother, Dinomache, before Alcibiades had been born. Dinomache's family Alkmeonid country estate had also been in Alopeke. According to his mother, Nestor's grandfather had owned a very small farm in the hills of Attica. Due to a series of crop failures this man had to borrow a considerable sum of money from the Alkmeonid family. Unable to pay when his debt came due, he was required to surrender his own person as a slave in order to repay the debt. This, his mother had explained, all happened right before the time of Solon's 'unburdening' which was supposed to have outlawed holding a person himself as a bond for his debt. Indeed, Solon's legislation had required that anyone native born in Attica who had been a freeman and had become a slave in this manner must be emancipated and, even if they were in a foreign city, returned to their land. But, somehow this man's progeny still remained slaves to this day.

Alcibiades was not going to trouble himself with looking into this. The old man was a good cook and he didn't want to lose him. More than likely, somebody had already dealt with this and discovered that Nestor's grandfather was not native born, but some kind of vile foreign peasant who through piracy or other unsavory means had come up with enough cash to buy his land.

Nestor was so old he probably celebrated *Elaphebolion* as a small child with his enslaved grandfather on the Alkmeonid estate in Alopeke. No doubt, some of Socrates' grizzled old neighbors still remembered Nestor's family and like them still offered on their household hearths, out of faithful devotion to Artemis, their little stags, shaped out of uncooked dough. Most Athenians, and especially the younger ones like Alcibiades, were scarcely aware that the month in which they now celebrated the City Dionysia was named after a festival honoring the huntress who provided venison for her country folk. Since most of the woods had been cut down to be replaced by farm fields and all the better people spent a good part of their time in the city, the festival had faded away with the disappearance of the deer from Attica. The cakes, called stags because they were the peasants' substitute for the meat offering of venison to Artemis, were actually quite tasty. Alcibiades had sampled one yesterday and had suffered no ill effects from the uncooked dough. It would be fun to share the peasants' quaint food for the god with wealthy Prince Sadocus and his own philosopher friend, Socrates. His new found Thracian friend would try anything at least once - that included eating anything put before him. But what would Socrates have to say about the sesame seed and honey soaked uncooked dough? Would he simply enjoy it as an unusual breakfast pastry or would he find some reason to set it aside in order to search out, as Socrates might say, how this thing which was sacred yet points to the divine presence in all things human?

Alcibiades, like many Athenians who actually listened to Socrates' conversation with the theologians, found Socrates himself to be an enigma. Socrates was scrupulous in his faithful adherence to the requirements of traditional piety practiced in the festivals and the ceremonial performances celebrated publically by the people of Athens. There could be no doubt that he, like every other Athenian, always looked forward to the holy days, all their ceremonies, and especially the communion of the feasts which followed the great public sacrifices of the bulls or other animals. Yet, if anyone listened to him for just a few moments when he engaged one of the local poets who fancied himself an expert in all matters concerning the gods, it became quite clear that Socrates did not for one moment believe any of the stories about the gods in the way that most Athenians held their religion. However, since most Athenians believed that the ways of the gods were mysterious and it was always possible that some new manifestations of the divine could arrive from unexpected quarters, it would not occur to anyone to think that this inquisitive and honest seeker of truth could ever by accused of hypocrisy. But still, Alcibiades wondered if Socrates could avoid the fate of his metic philosopher friend, Protagoras. Even Pericles had not been able to save Protagoras from a prosecution for impiety and a forced departure from Athens.

Alcibiades, still fastening the clasp of his robe, stood at the doorway of the men's room surveying the scene.

"Alcibiades, why so pensive? Are you ill? Is there some forgotten errand that calls you and holds you caught between its commission and breakfast here with your friends? It is not like you, young man of resolute action, to stand still lost in thought. Or is it that you have forgotten all about me? It has been months, it seems, since we have shared a throw at the gymnasium or crossed paths even in the marketplace. Perhaps you are wondering why this stranger is eating breakfast at your table? Please, come in, and eat before your guests leave their host with nothing but scraps!"

"It is good to see you again, Socrates. I hoped I might, unseen, watch you work your charms on my new and very handsome friend, Prince Sadocus. Perhaps then I can better discover your tricks and thus myself be forearmed in your company. I have warned the Prince about what a terrible flirt you can be around men half your age. Well, I see I'm here in time, since Prince Sadocus does not yet look to be entranced by the charms of your conversation."

"Alcibiades, I hope you don't think me rude – sampling the breakfast before our host comes to the table. I just could not resist taking a nibble on one of these sesame and honey confections. I think your servant called them 'stags'. Socrates, you see, has better manners than me. He passed the plate without taking one himself."

"I'm glad you've sampled the stags, Sadocus. I hope you find them tasty – you know the principle ingredient is raw corn meal dough. If any stomach can handle it, I'm sure it is yours. If you don't mind, Sadocus, I'll sit here next to Socrates so that I can make sure he doesn't wolf down all the breakfast sweet meats. Aren't you going to try one of the stags, Socrates?"

"I better not, Alcibiades. My stomach does not do so well with uncooked grain mush. Besides, even though I am not a devotee of abstinence as an act of piety, still I am somewhat squeamish about eating what had been for my forefathers an altar sacrifice to Artemis."

"Really, Socrates, I am surprised that a philosopher like you who renounces all superstition shares the same dietary scruples as my household slave Debra. When I insisted she sample one of the stags to see if they were sweet enough, she became sullen and began to tremble as if I were asking her to eat hemlock. She muttered something about the food being unclean and that she would not defile herself by having anything to do with graven images. I took the thing from her hands and bit into it myself, threatening her with a beating for being so childish and disobedient. But I could see that she would have suffered through the beating rather than eat the stag. So I let it pass, considering it part of being a master that one must overlook occasionally the silly superstitions of barbarians who are spooked by an invisible god."

"It is different, Alcibiades. I do not think Artemis will become angry with me and curse my farm with sick animals should I eat the stags. I do still have vivid memories of my grandfather who brought his stag to the family altar beside the hearth in our farmhouse in Alopeke. I live in a farmhouse that has been continuously inhabited by my family for four generations and all around me is the presence of the fruits of their hard work and the faith that sustained them through all the uncertainties of winning sustenance from the land and the nearby wooded hills. So for me, it would be disrespectful of my fathers and a hurt in my own soul should I treat emblems of their sacred experience as merely a profane breakfast cookie. I know you will not threaten me with a beating, Alcibiades. But please do not think me ungrateful or rude if my gratitude for the gifts passed onto me by my fathers is expressed by my passing on the plate of stags."

"You see, Prince Sadocus, my friend Socrates will never travel far from his beloved haunts here in Attica and Athens – unless he is commanded to don his hoplite armor and either by ship or overland march to face our enemies in foreign lands. His paths, his hands, his sustenance all still spring from the rocky soil of Attica and though he is a modern man, his intellect still vibrates with a reverential duty to serve the city that has lifted him, and others like him, to the spirit of philosophy. I am very young, I know, but I don't think I will find any other whose patriotism is so firmly rooted."

Sadocus' swallowed the mouth full of his third stag and pushed the plate of stags away to the end of the table, far from Socrates. "We are not like Socrates, Alcibiades, are we? I hardly know my own father. He is always away fighting somewhere. And you, Alcibiades, lost your father to war when you were a small child. We make our way and often, even unbeknownst to ourselves, are trampling or crashing into the 'old ways' so that it seems to others that we are terribly disrespectful or full of *hubris*. Be that as it may, there is one thing that I know I have in common with your friend Socrates – I love Athens! Maybe I love her differently than he, but I too would be content to spend the rest of my days a citizen within her walls. I only hope that one day I can repay the generosity your city and you have shown to me. Like Socrates, I too, as a citizen of Athens will gladly answer the call to defend her against her enemies."

Alcibiades nodded his head and extended a salute to Prince Sadocus. "Well said, Citizen Sadocus.!"

"Would you mind, Alcibiades, if we ask Socrates to share his understanding of the rites of the City Dionysia with us. Although we Thracians also observe rites devoted to Dionysos, I am at a loss to understand many of the rites and practices that you Athenians undertake in honor of the god. I was quite confused by how you Athenians celebrate the birthday of Dionysos at your festival of Lenaia during the coldest month of the year – although I thoroughly enjoyed the day of comedic performances and the late night revelry with fellow satyrs and maenads that lasted until the following morning. Then, a month later, during Anthesteria, you celebrate the marriage of Dionysos who is taken to wed the King Archon's Queen. But Athenians have no kings and queens and I can't understand what this has to do with avoiding the wrath of Demeter's people. I am sure that this month's City Dionysia will be just as confusing to me. Now that I have been honored as a citizen of Athens, it would be good if I could enter into her City Dionysia not as a mere visitor or some kind of official spectator, but as a celebrant in communion with his fellow citizens."

Alcibiades laughed as he threw up his hands as if to stop a run away horse that was about to run him over. "Sadocus, you don't know what you are setting loose! Ask Socrates anything and he will lead us into a thicket of questions which may well keep us so curious and perplexed that we will lose track of all time. Breakfast will never finish and I will think that nothing could be as important as joining Socrates in his search for Wisdom and true piety. I do not think our Archon Pythodorus would understand should I fail to appear at the Odeion this morning, He will not understand me if I tell him that Socrates' call to philosophy is more seductively enchanting than even the music of Orpheus' flute. Socrates will accompany you tomorrow as we celebrate the god's grand procession into the city. I am sure that there will be time between the various stages of the procession for you to search out with Socrates how we Athenians treat Dionysos' presence in our midst.

Socrates nodded his head in agreement as he seconded Alcibiades' proposal to postpone discussion of the rites of the City Dionysia. "Prince Sadocus, I think we should accept the direction of our *choregus*, Alcibiades. No doubt, our consideration of all things Dionysian here in Athens would lead us on a long and difficult inquiry. We would do well to wait upon the god's arrival tomorrow and then as witnesses of his rites and ceremonies we could together trace out how we Athenians on this day represent the divine life of Dionysos."

"But Socrates, will you not join in with those who dance and sing? Will you not don the apparel of Dionysos' company, the satyrs and sileni? Will you not leave behind your reflective mind for the ecstasy of Dionysian frenzy? I would not have you miss all this so as to be a guide to me – even if I am a Prince. And I wonder if any detached and, as you say, 'theoretical' account can ever translate to the uninitiated the mysteries of participation in the divine life of the god?"

Socrates furrowed his brow and turned to Alcibiades. "I see that your friend, like you Alcibiades, is quick-witted and knows how to make a philosopher squirm. If there is to be any dancing, singing and cavorting with satyrs and sileni – that will be your part tomorrow Alcibiades. Perhaps in your sober moments, you can share with Prince Sadocus and me how the god inhabits your ecstasy. Or would it be better for our Prince to join the god's company in ithyphallic costume? As for me, I have danced and sang now some twenty times in the City Dionysia. I am ready to step aside and let younger men play this part."

"Prince Sadocus and I both think it best that given my official responsibilities during the festival, that we leave the revelry to others this time. I would not give the theatric festival judges cause to denigrate my production of Euripides' tragedies because Prince Sadocus and I in a City Dionysia *komos* revived all the gossip concerning our exuberance during Lenaia."

"Nothing too much, as my father and Solon would say – that is the path best followed. But, I dare say, it will be very difficult for young and beautiful men like both of you to reign in that pride of manhood we Athenians especially celebrate on the day of Dionysos' grand parade to his Sanctuary beneath the Acropolis."

"We will do our best, Socrates. Now if we can finish our breakfast, it is time we make our way to the Odeion and I play my part as one of this year's City Dionysia *choregi*. Please help yourself to more of the fruit and cheese. I must leave you for a moment so I can change into the special *choregus* robe I have purchased for my public appearances as an official of Dionysos Eleuthereus. We will leave in just a few moments. We will have time later for you to tell me what you think about my role in the production of Euripides' tragedies. Your critical remarks are always so productive and will help me focus my development as a public leader."

CHAPTER TWENTY-TWO
POMP AND CIRCUMSTANCE
(The Tenth Day of Elaphebolion, Spring of 431 B.C.)

Give way, make room
For the god! For it is his will
To stride exuberantly
Erect through the middle

(Semos, poet of Delos, cited by Athenaios XIV 622 B)

If they did not order the procession in honor of the god and address the phallus song to him, this would be the most shameless behavior. But Hades is the same as Dionysos, for whom they rave and act like bacchantes

(Heracleitos of Ephesus in H. Diels, ed., *Die Fragmente der Vorsokratiker*)

Yesterday's event at the Odeion had gone well and Alcibiades could not be more pleased. The Archon Pythodorus had commended all of the *choregi* for their part in formally introducing themselves, their cast of performers, and the titles of the various tragedies, satyr plays, comedies, and dithyrambic choral productions.

This was not easy, Pythodorus noted, since the main hall of the Odeion was as crowded as he had ever seen and it required the officials to move the proceedings along quickly so that the crowd did not become restive and ill-tempered. Many in the crowd were dock workers and other thetes who had taken advantage of Pericles' subsidy of two obols per citizen for those who otherwise could not afford the price of the ticket for the theatric festival. Now these day wage earners could readily attend the festival without having to sacrifice a day's wages. Men such as these had never before attended the Odeion Preview. It appeared that these commoners' holiday celebration had set aside King Amphictyon's prescription for mixing water with wine since some of them appeared to be already drunk even though it was not yet mid-day. They were unhappy since there was no where to sit down and already the hall had become quite warm. There was jostling and shoving punctuated with loud exchanges of insults as commoners pushed their way by the upper class men of the city's venerable families of the 'good and the beautiful'. Everyone, it seemed, felt entitled to be closer to the temporary stage set up in the front of the Hall than those who had arrived earlier and already had stationed themselves up front.

Alcibiades had been very nervous about his part in the program. He was by far the youngest of this year's *choregi*. Nevertheless, Pythodorus had arranged the agenda so that Alcibiades would be the first *choregus* to take the rostrum since his poet's plays had been chosen to lead off the three day schedule of the theatric festival. But once the trumpeter had called the crowd to order and Alcibiades rose from his chair and mounted the temporary stage; it was as though he was himself a seasoned actor whose appearance on stage could captivate an otherwise unruly and impatient audience. Perhaps it was his dazzling jeweled robe and the golden scepter that he waved towards the crowd, or maybe it was the sight of the young and already famous heroic cavalryman of Alkmeonid lineage, or perhaps it was the shock of seeing just last month's most notorious, if not scandalous, Lenaia reveler now as an official calling others to order; but whatever the reason, the raucous crowd hushed and composed itself before Alcibiades even began to speak. When his first sentence spilled out all tangled up in a stutter, some burly *thete*, standing right beneath him at the foot of the stage, soaked in sweat and smelling like spoiled wine, leaned forward and in a hoarse whisper offered him stage direction – "Slow down, Sir, we all are your men here and no one is going to be rude to Captain Alcibiades and our shining Heracles of the Dionysian revel." After that, Alcibiades like a confident horseman cantered through the introduction of his poet, Euripides, the cast of actors and the chorus, and the theme of the trilogy of tragedies and the satyr play without so much as a hitch.

After the crowd had left the Odeion, Archon Pythodorus had singled out Alcibiades for special praise when he met with the *choregi* to review final plans for setting up theatric equipment on the temporary stage that now stood above the orchestra in front of Dionysos Eleuthereus' Sanctuary. "Who would guess that our twenty year old *choregus* could tame such an audience? Well done Alcibiades!"

Today will be fun, Alcibiades thought, but not so much fun as if I could play the part of a satyr reveler. But no speeches today! And the tens of thousands, who did not see me in my spectacular *choregus* regalia yesterday, will have their chance today.

"Castor, bring me my *choregus* robe! I must hurry. The Procession begins at high noon."

"Here is your robe, Master. I have pressed the wrinkles out and removed the wine stain from the right sleeve. Will you eat something before you leave?"

"There is no time for sitting down with my guests. It will take me almost an hour to make my way to the grounds of the god's sanctuary near the Gymnasium in the Academy District. I'm sure the streets will be full of people all the way to the Dipylon Gate. So, ask Debra to prepare a small bag of fruit and cheese I can take with me. Hurry! And bring me my ceremonial sprig of grape vine, and the staff wrapped with laurel."

"What about your gold scepter and the other jewelry?"

"Castor, have you not seen the City Dionysia procession over and over again? Have you not noticed that even the most important officials who walk in Dionysos' Procession adorn themselves as his companions? There is only one King in the divine procession to the Sanctuary and that is the enthroned Dionysos. It would not do to appear in the Divine Company as a scepter carrying Corinthian

King. Castor, it is good that you are a handsome youth, or I would have long ago tired of your dull-witted nature."

"Yes, Master, I have difficulty understanding the finer points of the dress code of the 'good and beautiful' freemen. I will do better next year."

Alcibiades could hear the note of seditious irony in Castor's meek voice even as the youth spoke with downcast eyes. But there was no time for quibbling with a slave. So he dressed quickly and then made his way to the men's dinning room where Socrates and Prince Sadocus were just finishing their breakfast.

"Good morning Socrates. Prince Sadocus, have you had enough to eat?"

"More than enough, Alcibiades. I understand that you must be on your way to undertake another duty as *choregus*. Socrates and I are ready to go and join the others to watch the Procession of Dionysos Eleuthereus. And we will not go hungry waiting for tonight's feast. It is so considerate of you, Alcibiades, to send Debra along, bringing a basket full of snacks. I understand your mother will also accompany us. And is it true that all of us are to meet General Pericles and Lady Aspasia to watch the Procession together?"

"Yes, the plan is for my household company to meet General Pericles and Aspasia where the PanAthenaic Way passes the northeast corner of the grounds of the Altar of the Twelve Gods. The General, I believe, is going to mix some diplomatic work for you, Prince Sadocus, with your Athenian holiday festivities. I'm sure it won't take long. Anyway, it will be a motley company, just right for Dionysos. He never goes anywhere without his women attendants nearby. And our god of wine doesn't mind rubbing shoulders with the humblest mule-riding peasant or servant. Indeed, you see my large painted *amphora* in the corner by the cupboard, I think it is the work of Polygnotus - it depicts Dionysos of Anthesteria arriving on the back of a mule at the Queen's Boukolerion. So it is fitting that our first man of Athens and his consort, though not a king and queen, stand together with my lowly servant woman Debra, my mother an Alkmeonid highborn eupatrid, a farmer-philosopher from Alpeke and a Thracian Prince - all to greet Dionysos Eleuthereus. I suppose the ecstatic wine service of our Lord Bacchus melts away all differences of station and placates even the most virulent bitterness between the poor and the rich."

Socrates stood up and waved for Alcibiades to be on his way. "Don't let us delay you, Alcibiades. You are in rare form today! As handsome as ever in your purple robe gilded not with gold and silver, but draped with laurel and sprigs of the vine - the sacred rustic emblems of the Lord of inexhaustible life. We will miss your company this afternoon. Already you have instructed Prince Sadocus on the special provenance of Dionysos in our city of *demes* where the lowly and the highborn share in the life of our common polity."

"Yes, I must really be on my way to Dionysos' Academy shrine if I am to be on time to take my assigned place in the god's company. All the choregi are expected to take part in the procession. Look for me. I will be near the end of the procession – just behind the companies of choral groups who will sing and dance the dithyramb along the way. We will all meet for the great feast tonight by the main door of the Odeion right after the 'worthy bull' has been sacrificed."

Alcibiades' house guests tarried a few more hours before leaving for the City Dionysia Parade. It was just before noon that Socrates escorted Prince Sadocus and the others along the PanAthenaic Way towards the northwest side of the Agora. They found General Pericles and Lady Aspasia without any difficulty even though thousands of others had congregated near the Altar of the Twelve Gods. This shrine was the first of the five stopping places where the Procession halted while two of the ten tribal dithyrambic choruses in the Procession performed and so this place attracted a large crowd. General Pericles and Lady Aspasia, accompanied by two of their household servants, were seated just off to the south side of the PanAthenaic Way on a raised temporary platform overhung by a canvas to provide shade from the afternoon sun. When Socrates and Prince Sadocus had made the turn towards the far northwest corner of the Agora, just a stone cast away from the Altar of the Twelve

Gods, they could see General Pericles in his plumed military helmet seated above the milling throng of standing spectators.

As Prince Sadocus led the group to Pericles' humble platform, both General Pericles and Aspasia rose from the small wooden benches which served as their portable chairs and greeted them. Pericles smiled warmly as he spoke first to Prince Sadocus and extended his hand to help his cousin, Lady Dinomache, step up onto the planks resting on the temporary stanchions. But she had retreated back behind Socrates and looked as if she was turning to return home. "There you are, Prince Sadocus. And what an interesting retinue you bring along – an Athenian philosopher, a reticent Alkmeonid Lady, and an exotic stewardess from a far away Persian province. Please, step up here and get out of the sun. There is room for all of us and we have brought our portable benches for you."

"Thank you, General. It is an honor to join you and Lady Aspasia." Prince Sadocus stepped up onto the small stage ahead of the women. He wondered how any diplomatic business could be transacted in such circumstances.

Pericles, always considerate of those around him, turned to Socrates who seemed hesitant to step up onto the viewing platform. Perhaps, thought Pericles, the philosopher worries about being seen aloft as though he had suddenly become like other ambitious men in Athens – climbing to the heights by sideling up to Athens' Supreme General.

"Socrates, I'm so glad you are here. I miss my conversations with Protagoras and his always provocative commentary about the origins of our representations of the gods and the ceremonies in which we celebrate their presence in our city. I know you have studied his treatise on the nature of the gods. Perhaps there will be time during the Procession to share your thoughts about how Protagoras and other philosophers like yourself understand our Athenian fascination with Dionysos. Think of our elevated viewing station as a humble tent shading us from the sun, or an elevated knoll underneath Cimon's sycamores in the Academy District – only before us unfolds the spectacle of Dionysos' Procession as an opening for us to be curious and to wonder what it means. You see here no trappings of office, no royal regalia, nor any pomp and circumstance around our little stand. Our fellow Athenians understand that a sixty-four year old man needs to get off his feet, stay out of the sun, avoid the jostling crowd to save his aching joints, and yet be able to see the grand parade of the god and his company. Please, step up and take a seat here with us."

"Thank you, General. What holds me up, I must confess, is how remarkably plain I am to sit next to such spell-binding beauty as Lady Aspasia. I must say the yellow-orange of her saffron robe, the purple crocuses that crown her flowing auburn hair, her cedar staff garlanded with the tender green leaves of the grape vine, and the radiance of her hazel eyes make me think that Dionysos himself would be unstrung in her presence. You can see that my threadbare garment and less than handsome face is ill-suited to be seen so close to one whose beauty can enchant a god."

Aspasia turned to Pericles and pointing to Socrates asked for Pericles' help. "You see what a flirt our philosopher is. I don't think he can help himself. He knows I love you completely. He knows I have now lived with you for many years and given birth to our son, and yet he tries to turn my fancy his way! And you know once he starts talking philosophy, he is such a charmer and his interlocutors are then powerless to resist wherever he leads them with his questions. So just to be safe, my dear Pericles, sit him there on the other side of you and let young Prince Sadocus sit between you and Socrates. Then in this arrangement, I, like Odysseus tied to the mast, will not fall prey to the siren call of his philosophical charm."

"Yes, Aspasia, that is the way to handle our philosopher. Surely Socrates, your attire will hardly be noticed sitting here farthest from the street, sheltered from the view of the crowds by my lovely Aspasia, the distraction of my plumed helmet, and the handsome Thracian Prince. I know a gentleman like you would not want Lady Aspasia to feel unsafe, so it is best if we do as she proposes."

Socrates had already taken his seat at the end, when Pericles then stepped down from the platform to embrace his cousin, Dionomache.

He knew she hated Aspasia and had never forgiven Pericles for divorcing his lawful wife and then bringing Aspasia into his home to replace her.

"You thought I have forgotten you, my dear cousin, didn't you? No need to scowl, I will myself bring you on board and sit you here right in the place of honor, the front and center of our stage so that you can best see the enthroned god and all his company, including your son, Alcibiades the *choregus*."

Dinomache had been biting her lip, scarcely able to hide her contempt for Aspasia and her anger towards both Socrates and Pericles for putting that prostitute on such a pedestal. May the thrice-born Zagreus save me from knocking her off the platform, she muttered to herself. She has some nerve dressing like a priestess of the suffering Dionysos. What a slut - all a glitter with a plastered face, dyed hair, and a bodice stuffed full with the tricks of the *hetaera*! It was fortunate that Pericles had sat her well away from that woman and then asked Alcibiades' servant Debra to make sure that Lady Dionomache's chair would be moved even further away as the afternoon sun's rays would make their way under the sheltering canopy above.

With everyone seated, Pericles took his seat again. Dealing with my cousin, he thought, is more exhausting than any of my struggles with Cimon or Thucydides. Damn it, why can't she just enjoy the day!

The crowd had grown very large by the time Alcibiades' household company had settled in on Pericles' roost. Although the crowd noise surrounded them on three sides, surprisingly, Pericles' guests were able to carry on a conversation without having to shout over the crowd. Pericles would not let Dionomache's prudish religiosity rob them all of the joys of the City Dionysia. Perhaps a little wine will loosen everyone's tongue and gladden Dinomache so she stops scowling. "Should we open the wine and sample some of the cheese and bread? The Procession should be coming through the Dipylon Gate right about now."

Sure enough, just as Pericles had passed the *lekythos* to Prince Sadocus, all the sounds of the crowd – its thousands of conversations, its laughs, the cries of restless small children, its rustle of a sea of bodies moving to and fro – all were pierced and then submerged by the shrill and loud crescendo of the Herald trumpeter who led the Procession and announced its entry into the city through the Dipylon Gate with a mighty blast of his salpinx. The sheer volume of the long horn's sounding, one would think, could wake the dead!

Figure 15
Procession led by a salpinx

Prince Sadocus' head throbbed as the sound echoed off the stone of the Altar of the Twelve Gods. "I know that sound all too well. During your Anthesteria Festival for the marriage of Dionysos with the Queen, I thought my ears would rupture when each time the blowing of the salpinx signaled a new man to try his luck at staying upright while dancing on the slick wine skin which his company of revelers had just emptied. I don't know how the Official presiding, the King Archon, could have any hearing left after ten or so blasts of that horn, unless he too is filled with wine up to his ears so that the sound drowns in there somehow without doing any harm."

Pericles laughed. "Yes it is loud – but it is the only way to command the attention of satyrs and sileni whose frenzied intoxication makes it difficult for turn to follow turn in the game. I think that horn came to our city from our Italian colonists and they found it among natives there who call themselves Etruscans. We only use that weird looking very long horn for the ceremonies that require a very loud and awakening call to attention. But I have heard an even more ear-splitting sounding of many *salpinge*s blown simultaneously in Argos. When I was a young man, I was chosen to be Athens' *theoros* to observe the Dionysian liturgy that is part of the major Dionysian festival held in Argos. You know, Prince Sadocus, that even as sophisticated as we Athenians are, just like every other Greek city, we would not want to offend a god by ignoring one of his special festivals held elsewhere. So like every other Greek city, we send a delegate with the instructions that he is not to participate in the sacred liturgy of the festival but only to observe it. Anyway, when I was the *theoros* I learned that the Argives believe that Perseus had tried to prevent the arrival of Dionysos in their City by striking him down and casting the god, in the form of a bull, into the deep lake of Lerna. However, his worshippers had hidden *salpinges* in their fillet-adorned staffs and then drew them out to call their lord back from the water. They call him 'Dionysos Bougenes', the cow's son. So it is part of their liturgy, to go out to the side of Lake Lerna and repeat the miraculous resurrection of Dionysos.

"Why the need for such an ear-splitting call to attention now? Is it to make more solemn and holy the entrance of the god into the city?" Or do you Athenians also believe that Dionysos, the bull god, must be called back from the dead?" Prince Sadocus did not need to hear the answer to his question.

Suddenly, the crowds on both sides of the PanAthenaic Way pushed and surged, like an outgoing tide in a tiny cove, away from the broad street so as to make it as wide and unimpeded as possible. Seconds later the sounds of clashing symbols and the shouts of young men accompanied by a dull ominous sound of the earth beneath vibrating as if it was being pummeled by thousands of stone hammers echoed off city walls and down the stone paved PanAthenaic Way from where the *salpinx* had sounded. A fast moving rampage of panicked black bulls appeared from around the turn that led to the Dipylon Gate. Anyone foolish enough to be on the street or too close to it risked being trampled to death. The bulls were being herded along – though it seemed more like a stampede – by *epheboi* on horseback carrying both cymbals and lances displaying their tribe's insignia. The bright multi-colored tribal banners tied to the young warriors' lances - the yellow, blue, red, orange and purple cloth streamers rising up and down as they prodded the on rushing torrent of black bulls forward - barely kept the panicked herd from spilling over its ordained course onto the courtyards and plazas filled with frightened children and the now wide-eyed celebrants who thrilled at the 'bringing in of the victims'.

Pericles stood up and saluted the company of young *epheboi* as the herd stormed by their high platform. As the thundering herd rushed by, Pericles with his voice raised to almost a shout, expressed his pride in Athens' young horsemen.

"Prince Sadocus, see how our mounted *ephebo*i can sound the cymbals, and then unsheathe their long lances to sting the leathery hide of these fierce Minotaurs and still, without their reins, keep their balance and guide their steeds so as to contain the maelstrom. There are over two-hundred bulls in the herd and our young *epheboi* are charged with escorting them the entire length of the PanAthenaic Way and then around the east side of the Acropolis on Tripod Road into a slaughtering pen by the Great Altar of Dionysos Eleuthereus' Sanctuary. In all the years I have watched the Procession, not even one of these bulls has strayed off course. Even our least religious celebrants are thankful for the skill of our escorts, since they assure that there will be enough meat for every feaster later this evening."

Pericles' voice lowered as the hammering of the hoofs and the shouts of the horsemen faded into the distance. The women on Pericles small viewing stand were all standing so as to get one last look at the magnificent young horsemen. Prince Sadocus did not have to shout to make himself heard by Pericles.

"Yes, General, if I did not know they were Athenians, I would think such skillful horsemen were Thracians. They are as one, like centaurs, the riders and their horses. But tell me, is there some reason why the Procession begins near the Academy District and thus requires such a long and dangerous drive of the bulls through the city?"

Pericles sat down again and turned to Socrates who, like the women, was still gazing in admiration at the young horsemen who were now disappearing from sight further down the PanAthenaic Way towards the southwest end of the Agora. "I think Socrates – if we can persuade him to turn away from the handsome youths he spends so much time looking after in the Gymnasium – could answer your question more fully than I. This is just the kind of question he enjoys, one that appears quite simple but turns out to lead those who ask it into almost an impenetrable thicket of ever multiplying questions."

Socrates turned his small bench towards Prince Sadocus and the others so that he could be better heard over the noise of the crowd that now awaited the Procession of the god. "It is true, Prince Sadocus, that your question leads to many more interesting questions. At its simplest, I suppose, the straightforward answer can be found in the epithet Dionysos assumes this day, 'Eleuthereus'. Athenians believe that the public cult of Dionysos was brought to Athens by a missionary-priest named Pegasos, who came from Eleutherai, a mountain village on the Boeotian border of Attica. And so, since the deme of Academe would have been the last stopping place outside of Athens on the road from Eleutherai, this has for many years now been the traditional starting point of the Procession. Indeed, ten days before the beginning of the City Dionysia, the high priest of Dionysos Eleuthereus' Sanctuary in Athens escorts on a cart the ancient wooden cult statue of Dionysos, believed to date from the days of Pegasos, to a small shrine in Academe. There sacrifices to the god are offered by priests from each of our ten tribes. And then on the day before the Grand City Dionysia Procession the wooden masked god is brought back to his temple beneath the Acropolis. This is done with little fanfare and only the priests and a few others, who are members of the more devout Dionysian clubs, join in this procession. And so, as you will see in a few moments, the cult statue which today enters our city is not the ancient wooden sacred image of the masked god. This is why my simple explanation will leave you puzzled."

Socrates looked about to see if the others had already become bored with his account. They all appeared to be interested and encouraged by Pericles nod of approval, so Socrates continued. "Have you noticed, Prince Sadocus, the statue of Pegasos that stands near the large framed clay tablet which is mounted on the retaining wall that is in the center of Kerameikos, the potters' district here in Athens? Our potters have commemorated Pegasos' as the founder of our state cult of Dionysos by placing his statue next to their clay tableau depicting the legendary third king of Athens, Amphictyon, greeting a procession of gods among which is Dionysos. The painters and potters are especially devoted to Dionysos, since the most valuable of their painted pottery are vessels for the god's gift of wine. We Athenians, following the lead of our talented potters and painters, believe that this district is named after Keramos, the son born of Dionysos and Ariadne."

"Yes, Socrates, I saw that statue of Pegasos and the clay tableau you speak of when Alcibiades guided me through the potters' quarter. He was giving me a tour of the pottery shops that are part of his family's commercial enterprises. But the Dionysos cult symbol he showed me, and which he said was dedicated by Amphictyon to Pegasos' Dionysos, is completely different from the masked wooden god."

Socrates knew the sanctuary and the Dionysos cult object which Alcibiades had shown Prince Sadocus. It was not far from the potters' quarter and tradition did teach that King Amphictyon had set up the stone emblem of Dionysos there in gratitude to the Lord of the Vine. It was said the when Dionysos introduced the art of winemaking, the god also taught the king and his people how to mix wine with water. But Socrates knew why Prince Sadocus found the tradition of such a sober Dionysos, linked as it might be with the solemn death masked wooden statue of Dionysos, confusing. "If I know my young friend Alcibiades, I am sure that he has explained to you the real meaning of the sacred inscription on the altar that names the emblem of Dionysos found in the sanctuary of the Horai."

Prince Sadocus, like Alcibiades, was not bashful about his manhood. "Yes Socrates, Alcibiades showed me the stone phallus in the sanctuary of the Horai. This, he said, as well as the inscription on the altar outside the sanctuary, makes clear why the City Dionysia is, more than any other, a festival for men celebrating their part in the powerful and joyous renewal of life – Dionysos *Orthos*, the Dionysos who stands upright."

"My son has got it wrong." Dinomache could not abide such lasciviously literal misunderstanding of the sacred stories. My Lord Dionysos is sometimes called Dionysos *Orthos* because it is he who taught us from the very beginning how to mix wine with water so that his celebrants may stand upright as they partake of his wine. The cult image you see in the Temple of the Horai was placed there many years later so men could sanctify their lustful sexual nature."

Pericles looked amused and smiled kindly at Dionomache, as though she was still a small girl. "Dionomache do you really think that the very old story handed down from the days of Pegasos is to be so easily dismissed? After all, the men of Athens at that time, according to the story, resisted accepting the wooden masked god that Pegasos brought to Athens. Pegasos and his daughters called him Dionysos *Melanaigis*, 'he of the dark goatskin'. Pegasos' daughters were the first to see Dionysos, but they saw him, the story teaches, dressed in a black goatskin. At first the daughters rejected Dionysos and for this he drove them mad. They were healed only when they agreed to worship the dark Dionysos who hailed from the realm of the spirits of the dead."

Dinomache interrupted Pericles. "That part of the story, I believe is true. We women have always been the first to receive Dionysos and our relation to him in our liturgies of the Anthesteria and Lenaia celebrate both his suffering unto death and his miraculous return to life. I believe that the dark Dionysos is the suffering one who was slain by sinners and as such moves among the dead in the Underworld with Persephone. But the rest of the story you men relate about Pegasos is scandalous and an insult to the holy one who is the first of the thrice-born."

Pericles rolled his eyes towards the sky and shook his head in exasperation. "But even Herodotus, in his careful study of this story, confirms its details. Granted, his *History* claims that it was Melampous from Pylos who probably first introduced the Dionysian cult emblem of the phallus which was later adopted by Pegasos. Why would our Athenian men make up a story which says that such a Dionysos was first rejected by Athenian men? Socrates, what do you think about all this?"

Socrates, like every Athenian *ephebe*, had heard the story related from the time he was first officially entered on the citizens' list and eligible to join the Dionysian men's clubs. But he had always found the story perplexing, if not incredible. "Pericles, the story certainly explains why our satyrs, sileni, and for that matter, all our comic actors appear ithyphallic. It is rather strange, though, that our physicians have never reported actually encountering in any of their patients a case of satyriasis. And yet the story says that when the men of Athens first resisted accepting Dionysos' cult, the god inflicted them with this condition. Of course, the god being a good god heals their condition, as the story goes, when the men promise henceforth to honor Dionysos by carrying and bearing *phalloi* in a yearly festival celebrating his arrival in Athens. No doubt such a story makes room for men in the company of Dionysos. But I have carefully read Herodotus' account also. According to him the practice of carrying phalloi in conjunction with service to Dionysos may have originally come from ancient Egypt as part of their cult of the dying and resurrected god Osiris."

Pericles wanted Socrates to continue his explanation. "Well, you see, Prince Sadocus, Athenians seem to disagree on exactly what the clay tablet means and how the likeness of the phallus in the Sanctuary of the Horai relates to the wooden cult statue Pegasos is said to have brought to Athens. Socrates, what does our friend, Protagoras, in his book *On the Nature of the Gods* have to say about such a story?"

Aspasia interrupted before Socrates could take up Pericles question. She did not want Pericles on this day to be reminded of any of the painful memories concerning the attacks on both Pericles and Protagoras that had led to Protagoras' exile and Pericles' temporary loss of his elected post as a tribal general. Talking about Protagoras' book would certainly lead in that direction.

"Look, here comes the holy Procession! Isn't the *Kanephoros* beautiful! She walks so gracefully, balancing the winnowing basket on her head as if it were the cradle of her new born baby. She can't be more than fifteen. See how her golden yellow robe, so light and almost transparent, clings to her yet boyish body. To look at her, I cannot think that such innocence could ever harm anyone or anything. It is a mystery, isn't it, that within the basket there is not a baby, but the implements to shed the blood of the 'worthy bull'. She is a girl, still more a child than a woman, but she leads the whole Procession! Our Dionysos, no doubt is our wine-god, a bull god, but also always a god of women. Who is that girl, Pericles? She has such a noble bearing and appears completely at ease as the eyes of all of Athens take her in."

"Aspasia, it is Hipparete, the daughter of Hipponicus. Archon Pythodorus, I think, did well to choose her for this great honor. She is indeed beautiful and without doubt as lovely and unspoiled as the first flowers of spring. She, I am sure, will marry well and bring to her husband the good graces of the House of Hipponicus and his son, Callias. You know, of course, that Hipponicus is one of Cimon's cousins and thus related to the Philiads. I am always moved by the way our holy days bring us all together and set aside the old enmities." But Pericles sighed as the basket-bearer moved by their stand. On her robe was stitched an insignia honoring her kinsman's heroic death in far away Cyprus. Looking at the girl, Pericles was reminded of his part many years ago in the fate of his aristocratic opponent Cimon. Although Pericles himself had not taken a public role in arranging for the vote of ostracism that led to Cimon's years of exile from Athens, it was his associates that had managed the vote so as to assure that ostracism fell on Cimon, and not Pericles. Later, when Cimon had returned to Athens, the Assembly managed to keep General Cimon far from Athens on military expeditions. Cimon had died at Kition in Cyprus, some said, because the Athenian Assembly had not voted sufficient funds to supply Cimon's effort to chase the Persians and their Phoenician allies from their last island strong hold in the eastern Mediterranean.

Only Aspasia heard and understood Pericles' quiet sigh. In the years since the exile of Protagoras, one of his closest friends and advisors, Pericles had seemed to lose that self-assurance and steadiness of purpose which for so long had allowed him to cast aside any pangs of regret concerning his victories over his Athenian political opponents. But this is not the place or time, she thought, to assuage his recently acquired tragic awareness of the cost of his long tenure as the first man of Athens.

"And who is the young man carrying the holy fire in the golden censer, Pericles? Is he chosen also by the Archon Eponymous?" Aspasia wanted Pericles to move on.

"No, he is chosen by our high priest of the sanctuary of Dionysos Eleuthereus."

Prince Sadocus, determined to learn all that he could about his new city and its ways, wondered what the role of the third person was who walked with the two youths that led the Procession. He was a man well along in years and although he walked right in front of the enthroned god's ship-cart, he was dressed in a very plain robe that gave no sign of any special connection to Dionysos' company or any of the liturgical actions performed during the day of the Procession. "What," he asked, "is the old man doing in Dionysos' company? He looks as if he just stepped out of his shop here in the Agora or perhaps just awoken in his sleeping robe."

Socrates knew the man. "I will explain, but if it is not too much trouble could I refill my wine cup?" Socrates lifted his cup and Debra, Alcibiades' servant, refilled it while he spoke. "That is Theodorus, the high priest of our sanctuary for Dionysos Eleuthereus. He is not wearing any priestly vestments because he is marching before the god disguised; since later he must wield the knife that takes the life from the holy bull. So the high priest, in reverent respect for the god, must disavow his part in the sacrifice of the worthy bull by divesting himself, at least in appearance, of the priestly office. Our mysteries teach that Lord Dionysos took on the form of a young bull as he attempted to disguise himself from the titans who sought to kill him."

Socrates paused. Alcibiades' stewardess, Debra, had laughed out loud and in her haste to hide her laugh by turning her face away, had spilled some wine from the large *lekythos* from which she refilled the cups of Pericles' and Alcibiades' guests.. Socrates knew that Debra came from a far away people who worshipped an invisible God. It would be interesting to learn what her laugh might reveal. It was always fascinating to parse the epigram of Xenophanes of Colophon concerning various peoples' beliefs about the nature of the gods:

> 'The Ethiopians say that their gods are snub-nosed and black, the Thracians that theirs have light blue eyes and red hair. But if cattle and horses or lions had hands, or were able to draw with their hands and do the works that men can do, horses would draw the forms of the gods like horses, and cattle like cattle... '

Socrates wondered whether all her people were either atheists or philosophers – after all an invisible god could not be imagined or likened to anything seen or imagined.

"General Pericles, would you think me presumptuous or rude if I asked Alcibiades' servant why she hides her laughter from us?' It would be a breach of good manners to include the non-citizen slave in their conversation without the permission of her Master's family.

"Yes, yes Socrates, let her speak her mind. Debra, tell my friend Socrates what it is that amuses you so? You may speak freely here. We Athenians are always curious about the ways of other peoples – even their estimate of our religious practices is of interest to us."

Debra blushed as she answered the General. "I am only an ignorant barbarian slave girl and if I were to displease you or my Master Alcibiades, I might end up as one of Nicias' water girls for the miners at Laurium. I apologize if my demeanor has offended you or your guests."

Pericles smiled warmly, like a kind father, "You are obviously intelligent, Debra, and I am sure that since you speak, I am told, three languages you have heard and seen the many different ways foreign peoples serve their gods. Neither I nor Socrates will ridicule you or be insulted should you share your perspective on our City Dionysia."

Debra chose her words carefully. "Well, Sir, it is difficult for me to understand you Athenians and especially since you pride yourselves on the use of your reason in drafting your laws and institutions for the conduct of your city. Your philosophers teach that something cannot both be immortal and mortal, round and square, true and false, pious and impious at the same time – and yet I see grown men today speak of the immortal Divine One dying, of a man in disguise avoiding the all-seeing presence of God, and then this same one slays the Divine One so that his devotees may feast on his flesh. Am I mistaken in my estimate of the respect which you accord to the kind of thinking and speaking which is persuasive because it does not allow contradictory or absurd claims to pass as truth? Have I overstepped my station, Lord Pericles?" Debra bowed to the General and like a good servant bent down and began to rub away with the hem of her own robe the small splash of red wine that had spilled on the platform planks.

Aspasia smiled so as to assure the servant that there was nothing to fear and with her hands, Aspasia directed Debra to stand up. "Go on, Debra, it is good for the men of Athens to discover that women too, even those from barbarian tribes who have fallen into slavery, can be well-educated and capable of intelligent conversation. Finish your thought. I am sure Socrates and General Pericles will not be offended."

Debra rose to her feet reassured that General Pericles and Socrates were indeed different than other Masters. They would not punish her for speaking her mind, especially when Lady Aspasia had encouraged it.

"I cannot fathom how Socrates, General Pericles, or any other rational Athenian can celebrate such irrationality. But I suppose that since I am a stranger to your traditions, I may be entirely mistaken in thinking that you enter into them in the spirit of religious dedication. Perhaps they are to most of you only playful and whimsical fancies which provide distraction and entertainment in the midst of your otherwise often strenuous and bloody struggle to maintain pre-eminence and power over other peoples. After all, every year since I have been brought to Athens, I see your men, both very young and older like Socrates, go marching off so as to bloody others or to be bloodied and die far from their homes. Since my people long ago were carried away into slavery by conquering peoples, it may be that the one invisible and un-namable God we Judeans worship is not of this world and does not deign to reach down into human affairs to champion any tribe, ours or anyone else's. So what does it matter if I smile? What else can one do?"

Pericles, ever careful to keep his own religious views far from public discussion, acknowledged that, like his Aspasia, this young servant woman could stand toe to toe with the philosophers. "May Zeus strike me with one of his thunderbolts if I ever thumb my nose at Euripides' articulate slave girls, insightful women, or clever peasants as complete inventions of his poetic fancy! Socrates, we will sleep uneasy in our beds should we listen too often to our women and our.... Look, I have never seen such a lavish ship-cart for our enthroned Dionysos."

Figure 16
Dionysos on a ship-cart in the procession of the City Dionysia

The fantastic ship-cart carrying Dionysos now rolled by and the attention of Pericles, in mid-sentence, moved on to the next scene of the god's *pompe*. The god himself passed directly in front of Pericles mounted station. Dionysos was riding on a replica of a small cargo ship mounted on wheels. Four strong creatures of Dionysos, ithyphallic satyrs with their goat-like ears and goat skin coats, labored at the side of each of the cart's four wheels pushing and pulling their Master's ship-cart towards his Sanctuary. Pericles stood up so that he might better see the workmanship of the carved ivory and gold tripod upon which the brightly painted and ivy draped likeness of Lord Dionysos sat. The enthroned god's face, a mask made of wood from the grape vine, appeared in its exquisite detail to be animated as the god smiled with wide eyed joy.

Aspasia joined him in standing and, unlike Debra, found beauty and joy in the arrival of the god. "He looks as life-like as the satyrs, sileni, and maenads which ride with him. Old Silenus is already intoxicated! See how the sileni sway back and forth as though the ship is being tossed on a stormy sea. And am I mistaken, or is that the deep red stain of Dionysos gift on the beards of the satyrs that lean on the ships' side rails?"

Figure 17
Silenus treading out grapes

The ship-cart on which Dionysos rode had come to a stop in front of the plaza by the Altar of the Twelve Gods. The whole Procession then came to a halt while the company on the ship-cart performed a brief pantomime of satyrs and sileni going backwards and forwards with feet hopping and stamping as though they were treading underfoot the fruit of Dionysos' vine.

The maenads danced, circling around the throne of Dionysos, as if they in their frenzied and mantic convolutions would frighten Dionysos himself to bolt from his throne.

Prince Sadocus, with his friend Alcibiades, had played the part of satyrs and sileni during the festival of Lenaia. Having downed three large cups of wine already, he had once again joined the fellowship of the god's intoxicated company. "Lady Aspasia, those satyrs and sileni are surely not men - how could they be so aroused while that drunk? How will the dancing maenads avoid such lecherous creatures?"

Lady Dinomache blushed and the servant Debra shook her head in disgust.

Figure 18
Maenad defending against advances of a satyr

Aspasia giggled and pointed to the maenad that now danced at the knees of the enthroned Dionysos. "Prince Sadocus, have no fear for our maenads. Are they not themselves fearsome and only to be approached if invited. I think our tale of Medusa and Perseus must have been inspired by our holy raving women and their secret sacred rites of Dionysos. Look, a live snake wriggles coiled within the braided long hair which falls down around the shoulders of Dionysos' dancer. Her gown is of the finest linen with a hem of delicate embroidery and yet she clutches a freshly killed rabbit in her hand as she gyrates and her hips undulate. And although her eyes are rolling about and appear to see nothing – as though she is mad or in a trance – would you, Prince Sadocus, amorously approach such a woman when in her other hand she carries the maenad's wand, her *thyrsus* - that long fennel stalk topped by a jagged pine cone? Her emblem of fruitful Dionysos has many uses!"

Prince Sadocus steadied himself holding on to one of the side poles which supported the platforms canvas canopy. He was able to speak coherently, although it took considerable effort.

"Lady Aspasia, our Thracian women also know Dionysos *Mainomenuos* (the Dionysos of divine madness). Our spring festival in honor of Dionysos takes place over three days. When the first wild flowers appear in our mountain meadows and the warm sunlit days grown longer, our people mark the beginning of Dionysos holy days on the day on which the moon will be full. The festivities begin that day at noon with the sacrifice of a goat followed by a feast of meat and much drinking. A company of unmarried young women are designated as the nursemaids to the god. They are not permitted to feast with the men but are kept apart. In their own enclosed sanctuary they drink all day the new wine from the previous harvest of our grapes. That night Dionysos' nurse maids, draped with laurel and carrying the pine-coned wands, make their way to the mountain top. Here under the full moon, they drink even more and then in a trance of intoxication begin chanting an invocation to Dionysos Mainomenuos as they dance. Their wild dance and chanting mixed with high pitched calls to Lord laurel-loving Bacchius rouses some young wild animal from its hiding place in the low-lying brush. The maenads, in their madness, treat the startled animal as prey. Capturing the terrified animal with their bare hands they tear it apart and devour it raw. Our Mystery teaches that the god has miraculously consented to be their victim in the form of the animal. Filled with the god, they then return to our valley village at dawn. After a brief rest, these consecrated ones are then taken to the newly plowed fields where they are entrusted with the sowing of the seeds for our crops. At the end of the second day as the sun sets all these consecrated women will be married in a common ceremony. As the third day begins, their grooms will reenact with their brides the sacred union of Lord Dionysos with the Queen of the Underworld. We believe that since these women are filled with the god who rises from the dead, both our fields and their wombs when plowed and seeded will bring forth new life."

Socrates listened attentively to the Prince's story of Thracian maenads. He wondered if the slightly inebriated Prince somehow was confused about his own people's sacred Dionysian rites. "Prince Sadocus, perhaps we Athenians have misunderstood the accounts given by our Athenian settlers in Amphipolis who are your neighbors. They repeat a story about Dionysos that is told by our ancient poet Homer in the *Iliad* which supposedly explains the origin of your holy rites devoted to Dionysos. In this story, your ancient king, Lykourgos discovered the women of his realm secretly offering sacrifice to the new-born Dionysos. In a rage that led to temporary madness, King Lykourgos picked up the ox club that the women used in their sacrifice and attacked these women who posed as Dionysos' nurses, killing them all in a horrible blood bath. Dionysos, then, blinded the king and assured forgiveness for this sacrilege only if the king and his people promised to institute the sacred rites celebrating Dionysos' as the god who brings the blessings of fruitful earth – the joy of the fruit of the vine and the sustenance of the earth's crops."

Prince Sadocus nodded his head. "Socrates, my father has told me that story also. But he explained to me that our tribe has never acknowledged King Lykourgos as one of our own. No one from our tribe would ever have so profanely treated the god and his company. And so we do not commemorate such a story when we celebrate Dionysos' gifts in our sacred rites."

"I suppose your father might be right, when I think about it, Prince Sadocus. It seems suspicious to me that the name Lykourgos is so close in its spelling to the wild animal enemy of the goat and his ewes – the wolf. I do know that the Argives tell a similar story concerning their ancient King Perseus. And yet it is perplexing to me that you think that it is somehow less a sacrilege that the women dispatch Dionysos – even if only mystically. Do you believe that Dionysos hands himself over to be a victim of the divine madness he himself inspires. And is this good? Does it mean somehow that the drunken passions of ecstatic intensity, whether it is the intoxication of wine or erotic attraction, carry within them the suffering of self-destruction? It is sad to think that such intensity of life, these passionate moments of uninhibited feeling, is linked to death. But it is comforting to believe that out of the husks and debris of excess and destruction, somehow new life is sown and all is forgiven."

General Pericles interceded on Prince Sadocus' behalf. He though it best to let Sadocus enjoy his Dionysian intoxication unencumbered with sober conversation. "Socrates, I would be surprised if many of our City Dionysia celebrants ever thought that deeply about the happiness afforded them by their days of drunkenness, dancing, amorous adventure, and attendance at the theater. Their City Dionysia is for them both a celebration of the joys of life and a welcome retreat from the burdens of everyday concerns. It may be that philosophers and poets remind us that all mortal joys carry within them a peculiar intensity as represented by the suffering god, Dionysos – that our joys are transient and all too often premised on the suffering of others."

Aspasia pretended to scowl and, like a pedagogue upbraiding a petulant child who is spoiling his companions' game, wagged her finger at Socrates. "Look what you have done, Socrates. This is no time for sad thoughts. Pericles looks so glum. But tell me, Socrates, have you not made the pilgrimage to the Delphic Sanctuary and seen the holy tripod upon which the Pythian Prophetess sits. Could it be any more spectacular than the one upon which our Dionysos Eleuthereus is now enthroned on his ship-cart?"

Socrates was always willing to follow Lady Aspasia's lead.

"General, did you persuade the Assembly to commission one of our craftsmen to fashion the ship-cart's tripod-throne? It appears to be a much more comfortable seat for Lord Dionysos than the large kettle-seat fitted to the tripod which the Pythian priestess must mount to undergo her divine madness."

"No, Socrates, it was sent to Athens as a gift from Miletus. After all these years the leaders of Miletus' Assembly wished to express their gratitude for Athens' assistance in settling their dispute with Samos over Priene. So they commissioned gold and ivory smiths from their city to craft a throne that could be used in our ship-cart for Dionysos. Aspasia and I were embarrassed when they wanted to place both of our names on a dedicatory plaque engraved on the bottom of the throne. You know, of course, that Aspasia is a native of Miletus and the Milesians are proud of her contributions to the good relationship between Athens and their city. But anyway, we asked that the plaque be inscribed only with the words, 'A GIFT TO DIONYSOS ELEUTHEREUS AND THE DEMES OF ATTICA, FROM THE PEOPLE OF MILETUS'. The Milesians even went to the trouble of bringing the smiths to our City Dionysia last year so they could configure their work in line with Athens' way of honoring Dionysos Eleuthereus. I'm sure that somewhere in today's crowd, the craftsmen from Miletus are here admiring their work."

"Yes, I'm sure that they are here, General. They must be very proud. The throne is magnificent. Sometimes I think, General Pericles, that on occasions like the City Dionysia, our city is indeed a city of cities. There are visitors here today from Asian cities, Egypt, Crete, Ionia, Sicily, the Peloponnese, Thrace, Macedonia, the cities north of Athens in Boeotia, Thessaly, Aetolia, and Acarnania, and all of the islands in the Aegean. When I walk among the crowds lining the PanAthenaic Way, I can hear not only the dialects of the Dorians and the Ionians, but also languages which are completely strange to me. It is indeed a holy day when cities forget their enmities and share with us the joys of Dionysos Eleuthereus."

Pericles smiled with civic pride. "Socrates, you would be surprised how many of those from non-Greek speaking cities have mastered our language. They have been doing business with our merchants for many years now and leaders of these foreign cities have found it beneficial to establish a permanent diplomatic presence in our city. Consequently, you will find that there are many Greek speaking visitors from these cities who make it a point to attend the dramatic performances of our poets which they regard as the high point of the festival. I don't know who to credit with fixing the date for our City Dionysia, but I am thankful that it coincides with the beginning of sailing season. Otherwise, it would be very difficult for overseas visitors to make it here. I suppose it makes perfect sense to many of them that Lord Dionysos arrives on a ship. Every island city has such a story of the god's arrival. And even here in Attica, our demes by the sea such as Phaleron, Ikarion, and Semachidai still practice rites celebrating Dionysos' arrival by ship on their shores."

The Procession was on the move again. The god's shipboard company had finished their rite, so the ship-car and the entire Procession again resumed its journey to Dionysos' Eleuthereus' Sanctuary. Now, the 'worthy bull' led by a priestess of Dionysos embodied another epiphany of the god. Aspasia took up her husband's theme and wanted to explain to Pericles' company how this manifestation of Dionysos would be familiar to those who lived on the islands just west of the Hellespont.

"Isn't it mysterious how Lord Dionysos rides enthroned in the ship-cart and then, right behind the cart no more than the length of the porch of his sanctuary away, the god walks before us as a spotted calf – a bull only a month old. Is this not what we signify by calling the animal, 'the worthy one'? I was prepared to understand this scene in the *pompe* in this way by my residence in the Islands. I wonder if this part of the *pompe* was brought to Athens long ago on one of those sea arrivals of Dionysos. After all, the priestess leading the 'worthy bull' must be a descendent of Semachos, the founding hero of Attica's coastal deme Semachidai." Aspasia paused because Dionomache had suddenly turned around from the bench that was in front of her and Pericles. Pericles' cousin's face was tense and filled with emotion.

Dionomache was ready to pounce on Aspasia. Here this *hetaera* was treading on territory where she could not possibly know as much as one who had studied all the books of Orpheus and Musaios concerning the Mysteries. Dinomache interrupted, not trying to hide her contempt for the woman.

"How can it be that a woman from far away Miletus can know more about our sacred rites than we who have celebrated them all our lives? I am really curious about this and ready to be instructed."

Aspasia was well aware of Dionomache's hatred for her. It was clear that no matter what account she gave of the religious meaning of the 'worthy bull', it would be anathema to the bitter Alkmeonid cousin of Pericles.

Pericles saw the trouble also, but encouraged Aspasia to continue. "Go on, Aspasia, I'm sure all of us would be interested in how our City Dionysia sacrifice of the worthy bull might trace its origins to a more ancient liturgy from a kindred Island people of the Aegean."

Aspasia smiled politely at Dionomache and continued. "When I was staying at Lesbos, having gone there to be educated by those who have continued Sappho's school, we were taken to the island of Tenedos to witness a very ancient rite devoted to Dionysos as god of the underworld. We were introduced there to a priestess who explained to us the rite we would witness. She told us that many months before a cow had been dedicated to 'Dionysos, crusher of men' and then this cow was specially fed. When the cow calved, she was treated like a woman in childbirth. The newborn calf was then fitted with hunting boots like those believed to be worn by the very young Zagreus-Dionysos. This calf while still mottled was sacrificed so as to assure the fruitfulness of the new sprouting grape vines. But then whoever struck it with the double ax was subjected to a ritual

Figure 19
Motley bull in procession

public stoning. The holy victim's executioner was permitted to escape, yet the celebrants believed the aggrieved god was placated. Does not this illumine the religious meaning of "the worthy bull" in our City Dionysia and the reticence of our high priest of Dionysos to show himself during the god's procession?"

Prince Sadocus was now completely confused. "Let me try to understand all this. First, two hundred or so bulls run ahead of the entire procession. Athenians call this 'the bringing in of the victims'. These animals will be taken to Dionysos Eleuthereus' sanctuary and be slaughtered by the *epheboi* for tonight's public feast, as I understand. But are they a sacrifice to Dionysos and not Dionysos? Do you Athenians feasting on the flesh of the bulls, like our Thracian maenads; believe that the meal is a holy sacrament since the bulls in some way stand in for the bull-god? Then, if I understand what Lady Aspasia is suggesting, the lone and very young 'worthy bull' that follows behind the ship cart is indeed the very young Dionysos who is to be slain. Appearances do suggest that you Athenians believe that the high priest himself is tainted with the guilt of a murderer and that is why he hides himself by not wearing his priestly vestments. I take it that it is this particular male calf which is actually sacrificed before the assembly of celebrants on the high altar by the god's orchestra in front of the Sanctuary. Is this sacrifice a holocaust? Or is the flesh of this animal also eaten? What really confuses me is that the most striking image of Dionysos is his appearance on the ship-cart where he is enthroned and very much alive and like a powerful king, come of age and in full possession of his powers. I can't put this together with the 'worthy bull' or the death-like wooden and fig wood masked god who awaits the arrival of the Procession at the Sanctuary."

Socrates nodded his head in agreement with the young Prince. "It seems, Prince Sadocus, it is best not to think too much about Dionysos' Procession. Perhaps, Alcibiades' stewardess, Debra, is in part right about our Dionysos – it is better if we leave behind the spirit of seriousness and calm reflection when we celebrate the god of wine. I have had many discussions with both our poets and the priests of Dionysos and to this day I cannot understand their explanations of the god. It seems that our stories about our City Dionysia make the god young and old, dead and alive, a victim and a powerful king, the sacrificed animal and the God. I wonder if Protagoras is right about all this. When it comes to the Divine, each man is the measure…"

"Socrates, you of all people should not expect the discovery of truth to be easy." Dionomache had decided that she would not sit by while supposedly clever ones like Aspasia and Socrates missed the deeper truth couched in the rites of Dionysos. "I am not a philosopher like you, Socrates; but I believe that if you could set aside your prideful skepticism and with piety study the inspired books of Orpheus and Musaios like I have, then the hidden truths behind the symbols of our City Dionysia would begin to show themselves. You would not get all tangled up in the literal and often vulgar interpretations of the many stories concerning Dionysos – whether they be the ones some of our poets often bend to their own purposes or like Aspasia's simple-minded story of Tenedos. It is a sad day when you Socrates, who are regarded by many as a teacher of our young men, defer to a barbarian servant girl concerning our religion. No wonder my son is so uncertain about his Eleusinian initiation. He spends far too much time with philosophers!"

Socrates knew there was no point in trying to challenge Dinomache's theology. There was neither time nor the likelihood that he could dispassionately discuss the nature of the divine with a mother who was convinced that he endangered the salvation of her own son from the torments of the underworld. Before Socrates could simply express his concern for Alcibiades and reassure his mother that he would never harm her son, Pericles intervened.

"Dinomache, we are interested in what Orpheus and Musaios have to say about our rites. But please, do not be irritated with us if we don't resonate with the books of Orpheus and his son the way you do. Here in Athens we don't expect all our citizens to agree on all matters concerning the divine. We only expect our citizens to honor our public rites and traditions. Making up their own minds about the meaning of our stories when they are in their private households or clubs – that is a freedom our citizens enjoy and we tolerate no tyrant or rule of priests over our private lives."

"But when the souls of those we love hang in the balance, can we really tolerate false religion?" Dinomache was not convinced that the liberty to teach error should be protected.

We must never allow the zealous followers of Orpheus and their mystery loving priests to hold power in our state, Pericles thought. The king-archon's court will be filled with heresy trials. Thank goodness Dionomache can't hold office!

Pericles eyes followed the procession of bottle carriers, bread carriers and the tray bearers that followed right behind the 'worthy bull'. There were ten wine porters and ten bread porters, representing Athens' ten tribes. Ten stately men in purple robes, metics, carried the silver trays filled with other tokens of last fall's harvest.

"Share with us, Dionomache, what the books of Orpheus teach about the symbols of our *pompe*. What about the companies of those who follow the 'worthy bull'? Are they not all bringing sacred gifts to the god to be offered along with the worthy bull on the high altar? It may be that our sacred rites mean more than a license for drunkenness and revelry, but surely you would not have gentle Orpheus or his son rob us of our joy in dance, song, wine, and the theater?"

"I would not rob any one of joy, Pericles." Dinomache was thinking of her son and the curse of the Alkmeonids. She was certain that only the Orphic teachings showed the way to the liberating joy of salvation for every soul polluted by sin. "But it is very difficult to understand Orpheus' teaching concerning Dionysos unless you first acknowledge the pain of sin and injustice. It seems to me that you men, so accustomed to making your way through power over others, often have no idea of the harm you bring to your victims."

"Dear cousin, do not our laws and institutions in Athens protect every citizen from the abuse of power? Do you think that those who are pre-eminent in our government as powerful men are nevertheless great sinners?"

"Let me finish my explanation, Pericles. I mean no disrespect to our officials. Wrong-doing and harming others are, sadly, paths all too many of us follow. I was only saying that men find it more difficult to feel the pain of others."

"Well, I suppose that is correct to a degree. But aren't many women far too sensitive, like little children ready to cry if their caretakers are not giving them uninterrupted attention? If we are to prepare our young men to defend our city, they can not be overly sensitive to the pain of their adversaries."

Dinomache would not let Pericles take her off course. "But it can not be that almighty Zeus allows the unjust to go unpunished or the just to be tormented without hope of justice in what comes after the grave. The *Rhapsodies of Orpheus* teaches that the rites and stories of Dionysos are to be interpreted as symbols for the salvation of souls if we are rightly guided through the Mysteries of Eleusis. Of course, no one is permitted to describe the secrets of this initiation. It would be a sin to expose the divine work of salvation to the poisonous attack of unbelievers. But I can say this about what we today see before us in the Procession of our City Dionysia - all the visible things of Dionysos are at best signs which point to what is invisible to our senses."

Dionomache paused, searching for a concise formulation of how the story of Dionysos, the Liberator, is at least dimly apprehended in the panorama of the City Dionysia *pompe*. Pericles had stopped listening to his cousin and looked by her to see the company of revelers that now followed close behind the company of the "worthy bull" in the order of the procession.

Socrates did not want the day to end with Alcibiades' mother angry with him. When Pericles appeared to be growing impatient with his cousin's womanly religion, he thought it wise to show his interest in her explanation of the Mysteries. So he, without any hint of sarcasm or irony, deferred to her more extensive acquaintance with the teaching of the Orphics.

Figure 20
Orpheus among the Thracians

"Dinomache, please continue. I must admit I have not been able to afford the purchase of these wonderful books, so I do not know much about them. I am very interested in your account of their teaching. I am sure that Prince Sadocus also is curious about these books concerning Orpheus. After all both our ancient poet, Homer, and one of the most honored poets of our own time, Pindar of Thebes, tell us that Orpheus was a Thracian like Prince Sadocus."

Dinomache had found the way to testify and now, like one of the 'Perfected', could help those whose minds were clouded and untutored in the Mystery of the Thrice-born Dionysos. Her bad feelings had disappeared. She would introduce sinners to Dionysos the Savior.

"Our City Dionysia parades before us the mystery of the thrice-born Dionysos. Our enthroned King on the ship-cart represents the Lord of everlasting Life who has been lifted up and assumed the Governance of the Third Age. Even as Zeus has raised up his son to rule over all things, so too those who have passed through the waters of confession and partook of the Holy Sacraments of Eleusis will be thrice born as they are raised from the realm of the dead to join Lord Dionysos in everlasting life. Those dead who are not among the Perfected must continue their dark sojourn in the underworld with all its tortures and anguish – the punishment for both their evil-doing and the sins of their forbearers. The Third Age is the end of all things, end without end where the Son of God clothes his company with blessed immortality. The ecstatic joys afforded in the forgetfulness of wine and erotic love which we see in the company of the enthroned ship-cart Dionysos is but a pale shadow of the joys which await those who shall be raised to the Third Age. As Musaios sings, 'Eye hath not seen, and ears have not heard what awaits the sons of God – the thrice born company of Zagreus-Dionysos'."

Socrates wondered if the human excellence and political virtue of a citizen who concerns himself with the good in his city would perish should Dionomache's Orphic yearning for the after-life become the religion of men. Would not true liberty be emasculated if its purpose was ripped from the life of our city and instead ensnared in the fantastic phantasms of something beyond the grave?

Dinomache was not finished. "The full context of this liberation must include the story of Dionysos' birth and his subjection to the murderous violence of the Titans in the Underworld, events which precede his resurrection and ascension to the Divine Kingship. Our City Dionysia is like a compendium of all our Dionysian Festivals. So, in today's *pompe*, the young girl who carries the threshing basket in front of the ship-cart points to the celebration of the first birth of Dionysos. Her cradle-like basket remind us of the festival of Lenaia where women preside over the opening of the new wine, and the nurturing of the new life it represents. Again, our jubilation over the birthday of the god is but a shadow of the work of Almighty Zeus unfolding the drama of redemption. We see both in the confused stories concerning a 'young bull' which is slain by sinful hands and in the confused Thracian stories of Lykourgos and the maenads that either the god or the god's attendants are murdered by a raging king, a figure of the rule of violence, sin, and *hubris*. The books of Orpheus reveal that young Dionysos comes from the First Age, an age of chaos and violence. As a child of this First Age Dionysos is conceived by the rape of Persephone and born in the underworld in the company of titanic forces of restless violence. There the Titans, who in Orpheus' book symbolize the unruly violence of sinners, learn that one day Dionysos will become the King of all. Out of jealousy the Titans fall upon him and tear him to pieces, devouring some of his flesh raw before boiling the torn body parts in a large kettle so that they may complete their monstrous meal. However, his heart is left cast aside by the Titans and this is found by Athena and then carried to Zeus in a leather sack. When Zeus learns of the Titans' crime, he strikes them down with his mighty bolts of lightening and reduces the Titans to soot. It is out of this soot that Zeus then fashions mankind. Thus, we humans carry within us not only the original taint of the Titans' evil, but a trace of the devoured Son of God." Dinomache needed to catch her breathe. She had spoken so fast. There was so much to say.

Pericles shifted in his chair and looked impatiently at Dinomache. "Is there more to the story, Dinomache? The company of the many satyrs, sileni, and maenads now approach with their riotous music of many flutes and cymbals. We will not be able to hear you."

"I am almost finished, Pericles."

"Go on, then! But don't keep Prince Sadocus from enjoying the dance and music of the *bakchoi*!"

Dionomache thought it wise to help General Pericles understand how the Orphic Mysteries had a special link to his beloved Athens. "The most ancient statue of Dionysos in Athens is the one in Dionysos' Sanctuary beneath the Acropolis. This wooden coffin like Dionysos Eleuthereus veiled with the fig-wood death mask signifies the suffering Dionysos slain by the Titans. Our tradition here in Athens on this day commemorates the second birth of Dionysos. Our story, as I said, teaches that it is our patroness Athena who brings the sack carrying Dionysos heart to Zeus. Then the heart of Dionysos is sewn into the thigh of Zeus and out of Zeus' very body

Figure 21
Dionysos second birth out of the thigh of Zeus

Dionysos is born again. The second birth of Dionysos *Eiraphiotes*, 'he who is sewn in', points to the Greater Mysteries of Eleusis. In our City Dionysia *pompe* the leather bottle-carriers and bread-spit carriers who walk behind the soon to be slain 'worthy bull' carry their red wine and bread as tokens of the flowing blood and broken body of the slain Son of God. We Orphics know the great invisible truths here signified. If we are to be raised with Dionysos, then we must pass through the Eleusinian sacred rites of cleansing, confession, and a second birth. Only a childish mind would think it necessary to eat the meat and blood of an animal so as to be worthy of communion with the resurrected son of God. Even those who have not yet been born again at Eleusis dimly perceive this. That is why the 'worthy bull' in our City Dionysia is sacrificed totally to the fire of the altar. This is also why, the *Hoisoi*, the holy men of Delphi who sacrifice the goat before every approach to the Oracle, never eat any of part of the goat. Only a carnal man whose lust of the flesh blinds the eyes of the soul would think that Lord Dionysos is pleased by acts of lust. If a mortal soul is to put on the clothes of immortality, then we must undergo the Greater Mysteries of Eleusis and do so guided by the enlightened path marked out by the holy books of Orpheus. The Perfected then can be sure that when Zeus' herald, Hermes, sounds the mighty salpinx at the last judgment and announces the ascension of Lord Dionysos to the everlasting throne, they too will join forever the company of the thrice-born. But although all are called to Eleusis, many do not answer."

Dinomache realized that, given the din being raised by the raucous band of satyrs, sileni, and maenads who now cavorted directly in front of them, no one could hear her last sentence. Her cautionary conclusion would go unheard and unheeded by Cousin Pericles and the rest of his company on the platform. Orpheus himself was ignored or even worse persecuted by the unenlightened, she thought. So she turned away from the men, wondering if anything she had said had been understood. Maybe their minds are made of dried up leather – just like the pendulant male parts of the sileni and satyrs that now drag the heavenly Dionysos back into the Titan-like muck of mortal flesh.

Pericles was relieved that the raucous company of Dionysos of the Vine had paused long enough in front of them so as to bring

Dionomache's Orphic preaching to a halt. He shouted, even though she was just a few feet from him, "It won't be long now, Dinomache, before your son the *choregus* parades in front of us. And is not his younger brother, Clinias, a member of one of the boy's dithyrambic choruses performing here in front of the Altar of the Twelve Gods? I am sure you are very proud of both of them."

Aspasia smiled at her husband and when the company of revelers had moved on so that she could speak without shouting she gently corrected him, "But Pericles, there are at least two hundred companies of *phallophoriai* lined up now almost half way back to the Dipylon Gate. Let's not leave them out! After all, don't most Athenians believe the *phallophoriai* company also signifies homage to the god in step with the secret thing carried in the basket of the *kanephoros* at the head of the procession – a part of the whole Dionysos which signifies his indestructible life? After the *phallophoriai*, then come the *choregi* and their companies of actors, choruses, and dithyrambic dancers at the very end of the Procession. It will be at least an hour before all the companies of *phallophoriai* pass by."

Pericles answered softly, wanting only Aspasia who sat beside him to hear. You are right about the *phallophoriai* on two counts. They do believe the hidden thing in the *kanephoros*' basket to be something other than a likeness of Dionysos' heart. And there are so many of our *phallophoriai* carrying their Dionysos *Orthos* and singing the phallus song that they will take some time to all pass by. But, dear, it is much more pleasant and time goes by so much more quickly when we don't have to listen to my cousin's preaching."

Figure 22
A comic scene of phallophoriai in City Dionysia procession

Dionomache bristled and moved her chair even further away from Pericles as she muttered something loud enough for all them to hear about Pericles' kept hetaera'.

Pericles had had enough of his cousin's behavior. And so now he spoke to the entire company, making no effort to hide his disdain for what he took to be the Orphic spirituality of priestly eunuchs and unhappy women like his cousin. "I prefer the repetitious renditions of male pride to the fare of the mystery mongers. And surely our men are not completely wrong about the mystery of Dionysos. After all, I know that even in the Orphic books themselves there is ambiguity about what is carried in the baby basket that Dionysos' nurse Hipta took from Zeus and carried on her head. The Orphic story tells us that this first Dionysian nurse carried *Kradiatio*s Dionysos. Orphic literalists insist that the epithet is derived from our word for heart, '*kradia*'. But the real mystery here is much too earthy for our prudish Pythagorean and Orphic religious ascetics. It is forbidden to speak directly concerning the special sacred token that lies within the winnowing basket. But suffice it to say, and this is the key to the secret, that '*kradiatios*' has two meanings. It can just as readily be derived from our word '*krade*' (fig tree) and as such it would mean 'made from a fig branch or fig wood'."

Socrates could not resist the charm of pulling away the cover from what was hidden. "Could it be then, Pericles, that our otherwise unabashed ithyphallic parade, here must hide what one of our stories from Ikarion describes as another gift from Dionysos lest we offend the sensibilities of our legions of Dionysian women?"

Aspasia poked Socrates with her elbow as she whispered to him. "We must be careful. It is forbidden to connect the winnowing basket of today's procession with the story you have in mind."

Socrates wondered why in a procession where men costumed in ithyphallic britches and where the *phallophoria*i carried explicit reproductions of the phallus signifying Dionysos' life-giving power; it was forbidden to speak of the Ikarion Dionysos who, according to their story, himself fashioned a phallus from fig wood which was to be used in the mystic spring rite to reawaken him and assure his return from the underworld. But he knew that Aspasia's prudence concerning popular religious sensibilities was well founded, given her own bitter experiences with Athens' religious zealots. So when Pericles appeared not to hear his question, Socrates did not repeat it.

The *phallophoriai*, accompanied by maenads playing merry music on their double flutes, now made their way through the Agora. The crowds of celebrants grew restless as over two hundred large wooden and sometimes carved stone models of Dionysos *Orthos* passed by. Some of these models were so large that they could not be strapped on the shoulders of the *phallophoria*i, but had to be mounted on carts and pushed along. The afternoon sun, now high in the sky, made the young men's bare chests and strong arms glisten with sweat as they carried or pushed along the token of Dionysos' strong and renewed manhood.

Socrates and Prince Sadocus joked about how difficult it would be to bear such a burden if their own bodies were cursed with such a weighty member. Although Dinomache sat facing away from them, Aspasia could see her back stiffen and her neck grow red. The servant girl, Debra, was saying something to her Master's mother and had begun packing up some things as though she was preparing to leave the group.

Holding one of the baskets now filled with empty wine flasks, Debra stood up and addressed General Pericles. "Sir, would it be alright if I return to my Master's home and make sure that everything is in order for our overnight guests. Lady Dinomache does not object and I am sure Lord Alcibiades would not want me to spend the entire day away from my household duties."

Pericles understood that Alcibiades' stewardess had no more work to be done that day. But, whatever her reasons for wanting to go, now that the food and wine was here and served, there was no reason for her to stay. "Yes, you may go."

Debra packed up some more utensils and then climbed down from the platform. I am so glad, she muttered under her breathe, that I don't have to be part of a company of women that genuflects before a parade of men who worship their own unruly members. What a crazy and profane idolatry – to hold up as an image of the divine the tumescence of a man's unclean organ and parade it through the streets. How can they believe this has anything to do with the one invisible God? Do these men really believe that the god commanded them to perform such a ceremony to heal some outbreak of what they call '*satyriasis*? It is more likely that they would wish to be permanently erect in the middle, blissfully happy in their animal trance!

While Aspasia did not find anything obscene or vulgar about either male or female bodies, she did find the procession of *phallophoriai* somewhat tiresome. There were just too many of them! Pericles had explained to her that it was wise Athenian policy to insist that all of the members of the Delian League and Athens' other tribute-paying cities celebrate the great public religious festivals of Athens. And so, all these cities were asked to bring their own company of *phallophoriai* and a Dionysos Orthos to Athens' City Dionysia *pompe*. Just as the people of Attica had become more united by including the various rites of Athens' outlying villages in Athens' state sponsored rites and festivals, so other cities of Hellenes will find our governance less foreign if they find fellowship with us and their gods here in Athens. If nothing else, Pericles said, it will make their yearly assessment less burdensome if their ambassadors and delegates can look forward to the partying and the entertainments of the City Dionysia and the PanAthenaic festivals. Aspasia knew that not every Athenian agreed with Pericles. There were critics who thought that Athens' demand for tribute from those cities she claimed to protect had become excessive and far too imperial. Even I had to chuckle, she thought, when at last year's Lenaia a comic poet portraying a Samian ship captain in one of the prize-winning comedies quipped that his ship bound for Athens' City Dionysia would sink if its cargo had to include both the tax, heavy bags of silver and gold, along with the team of *phallophoriai* and their gigantic Dionysos *Orthos*.

Watching the young porters of Athens' Dionysos *Orthos* labor in the hot sun, it occurred to Aspasia that the heavy lifting of sustaining Athens' greatness must soon pass from her aging husband to younger men. Would they have the political wisdom of either a Pericles or his now exiled advisor, Protagoras? It would be wise of Pericles to groom a successor, but this is not a monarchy. It will not be any of his sons. She wondered if young Alcibiades might some day become Athens' first man and preserve Athens' preeminence. He was already, although just a young man of twenty, a favorite of the commoners. She must ask Pericles what he thought about Alcibiades' prospects.

The crowds had now grown restless as the procession of the companies of *phallophoriai* seemed as though it would never end. It was one thing to look for your brother, son, or friend among the Athenians who marched by. But when so many strangers all dressed the same as *phallophoriai* were mixed in with the Athenians, it just was tedious to remain still and attentive. Young boys were running about and would try to cross back and forth on the PanAthenaic Way whenever there was a space between carts carrying Dionysos *Orthos*. Angry pedagogues would wait until their boy darted back across and then collar them and threaten to take them back to their homes. Adults seemed indifferent to their children's behavior as they were now involved in enjoying more wine and sweetmeats. 'Let the kids wear themselves out now', Aspasia heard one of the mothers say. 'They will have to be quiet once the *dithyrambic* performers arrive.'

Even Pericles had excused himself along with Prince Sadocus from their viewing station. "Aspasia, Prince Sadocus and I are going to take a short walk, over into the shade in the stoa behind the Altar of the Twelve Gods. I need to discuss with the Prince some diplomatic matters of importance to both his father and Athens. We will return in time to see the *dithyramb* performances and, of course, *choregus* Alcibiades leading his theatrical company."

It was late afternoon by the time the theatric companies made their way down the PanAthenaic Way and passed in front of Pericles' platform. There was considerable excitement since the crowd would now be treated to a preview of the dithyrambic performances that would be presented in the theater tomorrow. The first to appear among the theatric company *choregi* as the leader of the entire theatric contingent was Alcibiades. Dressed in his magnificent purple robe, he carried an ivory staff and wore a crown of laurel. The crowd, and especially the young women, applauded him as if he were an Olympian champion. On this day there was no one more handsome, they were sure, in this world.

When all the *choregi* with their companies had lined up just beyond the Altar of the Twelve Gods, the crowd was called to attention with the clashing of loud cymbals and the sounding of a military trumpet. One of the boys' choruses formed up into a circle in the roped-off temporary dance floor that had been set up in front of the Altar. The boys, all no older than sixteen and all dressed in the tunics of the *epheboi*, then performed their *dithyramb*. It was almost hypnotic to the crowd the way the band of boys in perfect unison seemed to be one large one-hundred legged creature, circling about and moving backwards and forwards as if they were parrying some dangerous enraged wounded animal. While dancing they sang the ancient hymn of Delphi,

"Cry out to him;
we shall sing Dionysos
on the holy days,
him who was twelve months absent.
Now the time has come, now the flowers are here."

Pericles was enthralled by the boys' performance. "Aren't they wonderful? I am so glad they have chosen this verse – it teaches that whether we are from Attica or Phocis we all are quickened by the divine life of the bull-god. Even as these dancers reenact the holy sacrifice of the bull, their song of this occasion celebrates the irrepressible new life that stirs out of sight in the womb of mother earth."

The boys' performance was followed immediately by a chorus of men. They performed a much longer dithyramb. Their song treated the heroic descent of Heracles into the underworld and his attempt to liberate Theseus from the Chair of Forgetfulness. The dance again was ever so lively, but the verse of the singers could not but make one melancholy. Even powerful Heracles, with all his strength and wiles could not free Athens' heroic Theseus from the underworld realm of Hades and his bride, Persephone.

Socrates was moved by the men's *dithyramb*. Would he too want to be rescued from the Chair of Forgetfulness if there was no return from the underworld realm of darkness and shadows? Would not the memories of the sun-lit world be all the more cause for misery if they only increased the yearning for the land of the living? Well, he thought, is not this dithyramb's tale a tragic one? His questions brought to mind again a conversation with Sophocles who had once explained to him how Thespis, the first to produce a performance with an actor and a chorus, was simply extending the reach of the *dithyramb*. Turning to Prince Sadocus, Socrates wanted to share with him Sophocles' explanation of the origins of the tragedies the poets now composed to be performed on the stage and orchestra in front of Dionysos Eleuthereus' Sanctuary.

"Prince Sadocus, when I was just a few years older than you are now, I happened to be serving as an assistant to General Sophocles here in Athens. One day as we were inspecting a military road that leads to the coastal area near Ikarios, General Sophocles stopped on a hill from which we could see the small town of Ikarios down below. Pointing to the town, he told me that this is the home town of Thespis, the man we Athenians credit with writing and performing the first staged tragedy. 'Now days,' Sophocles said, 'we call Thespis an Athenian, but in his days the Ikarions were not yet a part of the Athenian state that today encompasses all of Attica.' Anyway, according to Sophocles, it was Thespis who first introduced an actor along with the chorus of the *dithyramb*. He, according to our own tradition here in Athens, would pack up a wagon with his theatrical costume and other equipment and then bring them to Athens for a performance at our Dionysian Festivals. I think General Pericles can tell you more about the details of Thespis innovations than I can."

Pericles did know this story of the origins of the theater in Athens as well as anyone. After all, when he had helped draw up the plans for the Odeion, he had made space for a large statue of Thespis in the vestibule of the building so as to memorialize Thespis as the father of the theatrical tragedy.

"Socrates is kind to defer to me. There are few learned topics concerning which it could be said that I know more than Socrates. But yes, I have made many inquiries concerning Thespis' part in developing our theatrical production of tragedies. His particular invention was to add the part of an actor who would then engage the *dithyrambic* chorus. Since, by the time of Thespis, the poets who composed the verses of the *dithyramb* were already composing stories of increasing length and complexity that sung of heroes as well as the birth and sufferings of Dionysos; in a way it was a short step taken by Thespis. Nevertheless, there is no doubt that he was the first to introduce the key elements of what we today see in our theatric festivals whether here in Athens or at the various Country Dionysia in the smaller towns of Attica."

"I did wonder, General Pericles, what exactly the statue in the Odeion is all about. Now I understand. But I am curious as to why your theatrical productions which seem to have evolved from the *dithyramb* are then called 'tragedies' Why are they not referred to in a way that would acknowledge their connection to Dionysos as the bull-god? After all the *dithyramb* is unmistakably a story in song which originated as a sacred service in conjunction with the religious sacrifice of the bull. Is it not the case that the winners of the *dithyrambic* performances during the theatric festival are given a bull as their prize?"

Pericles laughed. "You are such a good student, Prince Sadocus. You are not satisfied until everything mysterious or unclear is made transparent. I turn you over to Socrates. If anyone can straighten out our names for things, whether they be human dispositions or cultural productions of our invention or anything else; it is Socrates who of all our Sophists most excels in the art of definitions. Only, if I were you Prince Sadocus, I would ask Socrates to abandon his usual question and answer approach and simply state the answer to your question as a conclusion. Otherwise our dialogue, even about this matter, might keep us from tonight's feast at the Sanctuary."

Socrates was not sure whether General Pericles meant to praise his practice of philosophy or to denigrate it. Perhaps, Pericles preferred the eloquence of Protagoras' story laden disputations to Socrates' more court-room like back and forth of critical dialogue. But he did have a short answer to the Prince's question.

"Tonight, as Alcibiades' guest, you will attend the ceremony of the sacrifice of a he-goat in the sacred precinct of the theater. The table on which the *tragos* is sacrificed is sometimes called the '*eleos*' and it differs from our word for pity or compassion only in a matter of accent. I don't think this identical spelling of the two terms is an accident. And it is in such a detail of the sacrifice that we have a hint of the deeper meaning of the origin of our term tragedy. Our name, *tragodia*, for the theatric dramas which follow on the next day literally means 'song on the occasion of a he goat'. We call the poet or the chorus sometimes a '*tragodos*' which is to say 'singer of a *tragodia*'."

"Well done, Socrates, that is very concise and to the point."

"Thank you General, but I am afraid the answer is rather superficial and does not do justice to the way our name '*tragodia*' conflates different strands of our stories about Dionysos in such a way that it does point to the characteristic content which distinguishes a tragedy from say a comedy or a satyr play."

"I knew that was too simple to satisfy a philosopher." General Pericles turned to Prince Sadocus. "Are you still curious? Would you like Socrates to go further?"

"If you don't mind, men, I think I can see where Socrates is going." Aspasia did not like to be excluded from any learned conversation. "Perhaps Socrates won't mind if I venture a conjecture as to why the name is not just an arbitrary coincidence with priestly ministrations on the eve of the theatric festival."

Socrates did not want to be responsible for making the group late for the festivities at the Sanctuary. He noticed that Dionomache was already showing signs of impatience and wanted Pericles to be ready to lead them to the Sanctuary once the last of Dionysos' Procession had cleared the south end of the Agora. "I am always happy when

Lady Aspasia is willing to take my part. I am sure her account of these matters will hit the mark."

"Is it alright, Prince Sadocus, if Lady Aspasia takes the baton from Socrates. If we are to finish the course in time, we must sometimes let the speedy runner shorten the course."

"Yes, Pericles, I am curious about what Socrates means to suggest about the 'deeper' meaning of '*tragodia*' and I have heard from many Athenians that Lady Aspasia's learning is second to none. I hope you do not find my curiosity about Athens' ways tedious. I think I have become a lover of all things Athenian. I think of her now as if she were my extended family. I never tire of exploring her genealogy and especially the origins of her magnificent festivals. I cannot fully express how grateful I am that your Assembly has extended to me the privilege of Athenian citizenship."

Aspasia winked at Pericles. "This young man will go far! When he expresses his love for our city and praises its ways, I cannot doubt his sincerity. He either means exactly what he says or he is a master of duplicity. In either case, he will win the hearts of many should he turn his mind to political greatness. I will be brief, Pericles, in answering his question. I see that Lady Dinomache is already anxious for us to be on our way to the People's Feast."

"Go ahead, Aspasia, we will listen as we walk. Our servants will disassemble the platform and return it home. I see that the last of the Procession has cleared the Agora. We will be able to make our way without dealing with so much of the crowd."

Aspasia walked between Socrates and Prince Sadocus as Pericles, with his cousin Dionomache at his side, led the group through the Agora towards the Acropolis. Since the crowds had dispersed, Pericles and Dinomache had no difficulty in hearing Aspasia.

"It seems to me, Socrates and Prince Sadocus, the central theme explored by all of our poets who compose tragedies depicts the suffering of some great hero who by virtue of an action undertaken with great passion trespasses against the gods and thus must become a victim punished for his excess. There is always added the element of pity for the hero because in some way he is nevertheless sympathetic to the audience and his sacrifice is beneficial to others. Would you agree, Socrates, that these are the crucial elements of the theme that typifies our poets' tragedies?"

"I think, Aspasia, that your description seems accurate. I suppose I might add only one other thematic feature. I think our poets always depict the tragic hero as one who in a certain way chooses his own fate and thus is both a victim and author of the suffering which is his lot."

"Well, I think you may be right about that, Socrates. Maybe the most compelling evidence of this is the particular tragic production which appears to be an exception to this, Sophocles' *Oedipus the King*. Even though we learn from the blind seer, Teiresias, that Oedipus is fated to kill his father and marry his mother and all kinds of measures have been taken by the characters so as to avoid this outcome, still when this comes about Oedipus insists on taking responsibility for his actions by punishing himself with his own hands. It makes no difference to him that out of ignorance linked with strong passions he killed his father and married his own mother."

"Well, since we seem to agree about the general theme of our poets' tragedies, Aspasia, we need only to explain to Prince Sadocus how the religious significance of the high priest's sacrifice of the goat in the theater precinct sets the stage, so to speak, for the audience's understanding of the characteristic theme of the tragedy."

Pericles was glad the streets had cleared. It would not do to have a crowd of people gathering around Aspasia and Socrates as they discussed matters concerning the gods. Part of Aspasia's charm for Pericles was that she had a keen intellect and like the philosophers she investigated what others simply received as authoritative truth. No doubt, there would be someone listening if there was a crowd nearby that would be even more zealous than Dinomache and could cause trouble. When Pericles turned down a side street so as to take even a more private route to Dionysos Eleuthereus' Sanctuary, Aspasia knew why. She lowered her voice and continued.

"I have often, like you Socrates, been accused by many in Athens of being irreligious. But I never fail to be moved by the way our artists and poets draw inspiration from our religious rites and the divine stories that illumine their meaning. Yes, it is true as you say that Athenians are prepared to resonate with the meaning of the poets' tragedies because both they and the poets see our human experience through the rites and stories depicting the suffering Dionysos. This is why the goat sacrifice always moves me because it is like a cipher which when deciphered by our poets leads to the beauty and power of our theater. I think the richness of this sacrament, its powerful capacity to inspire creative story-telling by our dramatists, can be attributed to the way the goat sacrifice here in Athens associates all at once different rituals and stories from various communities scattered throughout Attica and other locales where Dionysos is worshipped. It is just this compounding or conflating of diverse manifestations of the god which sometimes so frustrates the philosopher who insists our theology be logical. But I don't think symbols which inspire work that way. They are the bearers of many meanings all at once and sometimes this ambiguity of the symbols strikes those who value precision of thought as irrational. Artists, on the other hand, find in such ambiguity the play of creativity."

"I think you have made clear to me why it is my conversations with the poets always end unsatisfactorily. It is always provocative for me though, Lady Aspasia, to converse with you. You seem to be able to move back and forth between the passionate realm of the poets' images and the dispassionate general concepts of the philosopher in a way I can't. I wish we could explore what you mean by this notion of a cipher at greater length. But we must not forget about Prince Sadocus. It would be rude to take him into a thicket of questions when he wants only to understand as most Athenians do the congruence of meaning between the religious Dionysian goat sacrifice and the somber and serious productions of our theater."

Pericles wondered when Dinomache would join the conversation. She, he saw, was listening with great interest since her Orphic faith considered the story of how the Titans slay the young Dionysos who has taken the form of a young he-goat or kid as an essential element of the Greater Mysteries. Perhaps she was waiting to pounce again on Aspasia should her erudition trespass into the sacred things which must not be spoken. He thought it wise to warn Aspasia.

"We will soon be on Tripod Road and again join the crowds of celebrants. So, if you can Aspasia, just give a very short summary of the various rituals which, as you say, are somehow gathered together in our goat sacrifice in the sacred precinct of the theater. And please be careful not to share with the uninitiated among us what is forbidden by the Mysteries of Eleusis. I know you would not do this intentionally."

"Yes, Pericles, I will be careful. We have had enough trouble with those who regard you as the friend of impious artists and philosophers. I think I can make this clear to Prince Sadocus without unveiling what must remain secret. As for Socrates, you don't need to worry about him with respect to the Eleusinian mysteries. He, for some reason, has never availed himself of their promise of salvation and so he cannot reveal what he has never witnessed."

Socrates nodded in agreement. "I will be a respectful listener, Lady Aspasia. I would not want, like an ignorant drunk, to stumble into a private place I am unwanted. I take it that since you know how to guard the secret of the Eleusinian mysteries, that you must have been initiated and walked with the *mystes* at Eleusis."

"Yes Socrates, I have completed the journey through both the Lesser and Greater Mysteries of the Twain. Now let me see if I can help Prince Sadocus understand the rich significance of the high priest's sacrifice of the goat on the altar in the theater precinct. There are various Dionysian rituals and their corresponding stories coming form different communities which I believe we can see taken up in this religious ceremony. I suspect this goat sacrifice was instituted near the time of Thespis. It certainly seems likely that this ceremony somehow made its way to Athens from Thespis' Ikarios. The Ikarions, many of whom still are shepherds, each spring conduct a rite in which they dance around a he-goat and then sacrifice him. Their priests relate two stories concerning this sacrifice. It is said that the he-goat is the enemy of Dionysos because in the early spring, when there is not yet much that is green, the goat often breaks into some vineyard and eats the tender shoots on the vine. The vine, it is said, is somehow especially a gift of Dionysos and the eating of its new life is akin to killing the god. Thus the goat must be punished for his trespass so that the vine might live. Still, the goat is himself dear to the humble shepherds from whose flocks the goat has wandered. Thus it is with a mixture of pity and joy that they sacrifice the animal. You and I, Socrates, might find in this charming story a perfectly rational insight into the struggle of each living thing, namely that all living things must somehow secure their own life at the expense of other living beings. Should we take a larger view, one that treats life itself as an abstract force, the story symbolizes a process in Nature itself where all finite forms of life must perish but the vital principle is immortal and forever renewed."

"But, Lady Aspasia, I am not a philosopher like Socrates. Can you make plainer to me how the poet who composes a tragedy for Dionysos' theater is as you say singing about the '*tragos*'? It seems silly to say that Sophocles' 'Oedipus the King' of which you and Socrates just spoke and which I saw performed recently is a song about the goat."

"Prince Sadocus, I am impressed that you have found time to see Sophocles' tragedy. You have only been in Athens for a few months."

"Alcibiades made a point of taking me to see this work at the Country Dionysia in Eleutherai. I am familiar with the story of Oedipus' fate, but it seems that I don't understand exactly how Sophocles' treatment of the story is 'tragic'."

"There is another story told by the Ikarions that is related to their rite of the goat sacrifice. I think we can find in this Ikarion story, when it is combined with their simpler one concerning the goat rampaging in the vineyard, the way Dionysian religion begins to identify the suffering human victim with the suffering god. The story relates how the Ikarions first were introduced to the grape vine and its wine. A stranger came ashore to their village and not recognizing him as Dionysos, the wine god, they killed him. However, Erigone, a companion of Dionysos, and in fact the first Dionysian woman, took his body and carefully laid it out in a furrowed field. The first grape vine then grew from the wine god's body and thus the Ikarions believe that Dionysos willingly sacrificed himself so that he might give birth to the wine-making fruit. Indeed, this story comes to be linked with the goat sacrifice so that the goat is no longer the enemy of Dionysos, but his double."

Socrates found all this fascinating. He could not just listen. "Would it then be likely, Aspasia, that Dionysos Eleuthereus' surname, 'Melanaigis – 'he with the black goatskin', somehow can be traced back to the Ikarion cult? In Eleutherai, the women of Dionysos to this day reenact the arrival of Dionysos there by acting out his mystical appearance as an apparition of Dionysos dressed in a black goatskin."

"Yes, Socrates, I think it highly likely that the cult spread from the coastal area of Attica inland and north through Attica, then to the region of Thebes, and eventually all the way up to Prince Sadocus' Thracian mountains. Indeed, when I hear the stories which originate from many of the Aegean islands and the southern most coastal areas of Attica near Sunium which often make Ariadne the consort of Dionysos, then I am led to surmise that Crete may be the original home of the worship of Dionysos. But that is another story. What I am trying to make clear for Prince Sadocus is that the Ikarion goat sacrifice and its accompanying stories teach that the god suffers and that this suffering is itself somehow edifying or redemptive for those who are in his company. But if we are to understand the final Dionysian development of the theatric tragedy, we must turn to the rites and stories of Dionysos which are found in Thebes and Delphi."

Pericles knew where Aspasia was going. "I suppose, Aspasia, you are thinking of Thespis' most famous production, the *Pentheus*, where the protagonist is not the god himself, but a heroic figure who partly as a consequence of his over-reaching or an excess of passion, suffers in a manner similar to the subterranean Dionysos. How fitting that our conversation comes to this point now. Look, our walk has brought us to the intersection of Tripod Road and the sacred precinct of the theater. From this spot we can see both the holy altar of the goat sacrifice and across the way, through the open entrance of the Odeion and into the vestibule, we can see in the red light of the setting sun the statue of Thespis lit by Apollo's radiance."

"Well, you've stole my climax, Pericles. And just in time – look the crowd is lining up around the cooking pits on the far side of the sacred precinct. The feast is about to begin. But, yes, Thespis is rightly credited with originating the dramatic and tragic dialogue between a human character and the chorus of Dionysian devotees who from ancient times had chanted or sung at both the bull and goat sacrifices. And it is in his play inspired by the Theban story concerning King Pentheus that we find the characteristic juxtaposition of the suffering of Dionysos and the human hero."

Prince Sadocus was beginning to understand. "So, Lady Aspasia, if I remember the story of Pentheus correctly, he is the Theban King who opposes the introduction of maenadism as a cult of Dionysos. And when, uninvited, he follows the maenads to their mountain-side dancing ground, they in their frenzy mistake him for the animal-double of Dionysos, fall upon him and tear him apart. The story is particularly bitter because his own mother is among the maenads that kill him. Is this the version of the story Thespis takes as the subject of the drama?"

"Yes, Prince Sadocus, and even though Thespis is the only actor, his dialogue with the chorus unfolds a drama in which the death of the king is likened to the sacrificial dismemberment of Dionysos. Indeed, we find in the priestly invocation to Lord Dionysos at Delphi that the reenactment of the maenad's hunt for Pentheus, 'the man of suffering', on Mount Parnassus in the region between Delphi and Thebes is a prelude to Dionysos return to Delphi after his winter sojourn in the Underworld."

"So," Socrates added, "a common theme in our poets' tragic dramas is that the hero's own actions and passions are what lead to his own destruction. And yet the audience who watches finds the hero sympathetic. They both pity him and believe that the inevitable suffering and even death of the hero is a kind of creative destruction that brings in its wake benefit to others. In this way, could it be, Aspasia, that we who only observe this play of Dionysian passion are edified. Even if our poets' tragedies, unlike the Orphic story of Dionysos where the god's suffering unto death carries along with it the promise of new life, don't always offer deliverance for the company of the tragic hero; at least they edify those who merely observe like the *theoros* sent to observe another city's patron god's principal religious rites. The audience in their *theatron* learn the wisdom that it is best to set aside excess and be wary of strong passions."

Aspasia nodded and smiled. "Socrates, I suppose you must find our conversations far less lively than those you have with others. It is really quite striking how often we share the same understanding of even the most complicated topics. There seems to be little occasion for the thrill of an argument won or the intensity of a contest of wits. Well, here we are at Tripod Road's end, facing the theater precinct. It is fitting then that I conclude our summary of the religious-laden meaning of the 'song of the goat', the *tragodia*, with the story of Delphi's coming and going of Dionysos and Apollo and how their concourse issues in divine revelation. I can do this in one sentence. The scripts of our most talented tragic poets follow the service of Apollo's priests for the supplicants at Delphi: where there is Dionysos dark, mysterious and frenzied with the bacchanalian dance of the passions, let there be Apollo – light, understanding, and the often sober resolution of a chastened mortal, 'nothing too much'."

Socrates wanted to add something about the tripod, the Pythian Prophetess ecstatic trance and the interpretation of her mantic cries by the priests; but Pericles interrupted. "That story will have to wait for another time, Socrates and Aspasia. Here is where we are to meet young Alcibiades. There he is and look, our magnificent *choregus*, like one of Enthroned Dionysos' heralds, is signaling us with his raised and waving ivory staff to come to our communion meal with the god. I am sure that he is anxious to escort us to our special table far from the cooking pits but close to the god's own sacrificial table, the *eleos*"

CHAPTER TWENTY-THREE
MEDEA'S MAN

The Athenians on the occasion of the Dionysian plays used to walk to the theater after having broken their fast and having had a drink. Throughout the whole performance wine was poured for them and sweetmeats were handed round. As the chorus entered they filled their cups to drink and when the play was over while the chorus was leaving they filled up again.

(Philochorus writing in the third century B C, found in *Franmente der griechischen Historiker*, edited by Felix Jacoby, Berlin, 1923)

When a tragedy displeased the Athenians, they said: Ouden pros ton Dionyson – "It has nothing to do with Dionysos."

(Carl Kerenyi. *Dionysos Archetypal Image of Indestructible Life*, p. 329)

Prince Sadocus and Alcibiades as it turned out could not resist the lure of the late night *komos*. After spending a few hours feasting on spits of roasted beef, they went off to join a party of other young men who had planned a night of drunken revelry in the company of Aphrodite's women. Alcibiades, to the dismay of his drinking companions, left the *komos* well before sunrise so that he could be sober by the time the theatric festival began in the morning. Prince Sadocus, however, did not return to Alcibiades' home that evening. It seems that his *komos* had ended with a secret assignation with a very proper Athenian lady whose husband was away on military duty at the siege of Potidaea. One of the lady's servants had appeared at Alcibiades' door just after sunrise, and explained to Alcibiades' stewardess, Debra, that the Prince would meet Alcibiades at the front steps of the Odeion a half hour before the scheduled opening ceremonies of the theatric festival.

When Alcibiades arose in the morning, he did not find Socrates in his guest room. Where, he wondered, could Socrates be? He probably spent the night outdoors on some bench with just his cloak for a cover. Yes, that is what happened, he thought. It turns out that Pericles had invited Euripides to join them at their feasting table. When Alcibiades and Prince Sadocus left the group, Socrates and Aspasia were questioning the poet about his craft. Socrates and Aspasia had challenged Euripides to refute Socrates' conjecture that no poet could display genius both as a composer of tragedies and comedies. Poor Euripides! I hope he is not entirely spent by last night's contest of wits with Socrates and Aspasia. They, I am sure, kept him up far too late! Otherwise Socrates would have walked back here.

Alcibiades left the house in a hurry, fretting that he would not be able both to meet Prince Sadocus and find Socrates in time so as to arrive together for the opening ceremony of the theatric festival. But when Alcibiades arrived at the porch of the Odeion looking for the Prince, Socrates was already there waiting for him.

"There you are, Alcibiades. My, how splendid you look in your gilded purple robe. Don't you worry that some tipsy ill-mannered fellow might spill his wine-filled goblet on you?"

"We don't have to worry about that, Socrates, where we will be seated. But I see that you are wearing your usual toga and cloak. I was hoping that you would remember to wear the new robe that Castor had hung on the peg in your guest room. But I suppose you spent the evening elsewhere and so……"

"Yes, Alcibiades, I ended up sleeping here in the vestibule of the Odeion. It was very late when our feasting party finished the last of the wine. Euripides was kind enough to find the Odeion's manager, Barnabas, and have him set out a sleeping bench for me here. As for the robe, it didn't become me, Alcibiades. I asked Casper to return it to your closet yesterday. Besides, it will serve you well if the commoners see you sitting beside one dressed like me."

"I don't know about that, Socrates. If they are not close enough to see your face – anyone who comes to the Agora knows you – they would think that wealthy Alcibiades neglects his own servants. 'Look at the tattered hem of his man-servant's toga and his threadbare summer cloak!'

Well, it is the theater. I suppose the audience will enjoy the spectacle of seeing you between Prince Sadocus and me. I'm sure Prince Sadocus made arrangements to come to the theater dressed in a manner befitting his station. He should be here soon."

As Alcibiades and Socrates waited for the Prince, they could see throngs of theater goers rushing to claim the best seats. It would be at least another hour or two before the first actors and chorus would appear on the dancing floor and the stage above it.

"Will we be able to find good seats if we are not there early? I have heard that Pericles has increased the public fund to be distributed to commoners for the purchase of tickets. So even the humblest worker for whom the two obols price of a ticket is a stretch will now have his ticket. There will be a real mob, maybe up to twenty thousand cramming every available bench and all the open ground between them."

"Socrates, our seats are reserved and they are right up front on level ground just an arms length away from where the actors will perform."

"Of course, Alcibiades, how could I forget that the *choregi* and their guests are escorted to the seats of honor? Will Pericles, Aspasia and your mother join us again?"

"Pericles will meet us at our seats. The women will be somewhere else in the audience. It would be an offense even to the most radical of our democrats should Pericles allow a woman such a seat of honor. After all, it was quite a concession to allow then to attend the morning theater. No decent man would ever tolerate their presence anywhere in the theater during the afternoon comedies. But Lady Aspasia and my mother will join us in the Odeion for a mid-day meal during the break between the morning and afternoon productions. Here comes the Prince. Let's go! We can intercept him on our way to our seats."

They arrived just in time. The high priest of Dionysos Eleuthereus had just taken his place in front of Dionysos Eleuthereus' ancient wooden statue which had been brought outside and set up where the Sanctuary porch met the back of the temporary stage. Alcibiades and his party hurriedly took their seats besides Pericles and other officials. The high priest called the audience to attention and then turning to face the god, called upon him to bless all his devotees – both those who performed in service to him and those who came as observant celebrants.

The invocation ended and as the priest made his way to his elevated stone chair on the porch of the Sanctuary, two trumpeters and a company of flutists made their way onto the smooth stone floor of the orchestra. The military musicians then filled the precinct with a musical rendition of the battlefield paean that from time immemorial Athenian hoplites sang as they prepared to charge the enemy line. While the music played, a special company of *epheboi*, whose fathers had been slain in battle and were as orphans educated and trained by the state, marched from the sacred precinct of the theater across the Orchestra and up the ramp to the temporary stage that during the Festival extended the porch of Dionysos Eleuthereus' Sanctuary. There, in front of the thousands, many of whom had lost their brother, son, or father on the battlefield or at sea in military service, this company of eighteen year old new soldiers was officially commissioned.

As the newly commissioned soldiers left the stage, Socrates whispered to his young friend. "Alcibiades, it is hard to believe that just two years ago you were on that stage in this ceremony. Heroic cavalry officer and among the richest men in Athens – who would think that a ward of the state could rise so far and fast?"

"Our state is indeed generous to the families of those who lose their men in honorable military service. It makes no difference whether the family is wealthy or of modest means. Although I went to General Pericles and requested that I pay for my own armor and military education, he pointed out that this would be unacceptable since the Athenian Assembly had long ago instituted this practice as a promise to every soldier who risked his life for Athens. 'It is a great honor," he said, 'to you and your father that the city supports your military education and then during the City Dionysia applauds your family on its most illustrious stage.'"

General Pericles stood up and saluted as the company of *epheboi*, there were fifty of them, formed up into a small phalanx and made their way down the ramp to take their seats of honor near the orchestra. He was joined in standing by every Athenian citizen in the audience. The women, the slaves who attended, and foreign visitors sat quietly while the brotherhood of hoplite-citizens paid their respects to fallen comrades and their sons.

Sitting down again, General Pericles turned to Prince Sadocus and beaming with pride pointed to the long line of officials from other cities which now, even as the company of new hoplites settled into their seats, was making its way to the augmented porch-stage of the god's sanctuary. "Prince, we Athenians are very proud of our city's role in defending other Hellenes from the tyranny of the Persians. We do not think it unseemly this day to demonstrate on this stage our grand accomplishment. No doubt, our defense has led us to be the leader of a great empire; but whether we are humble rowers who come from the poorest of our citizens or mounted knights and generals who come from our wealthiest families we all believe that we have earned and deserve the prosperity and power Athens now enjoys. This day we ask all our cities to bring to this stage their due for our historic protection against the Persian threat and the safety our navy provides for their maritime commerce."

Waiting on stage to receive the 'League assessment' from the long line of foreign dignitaries stood Callicles, this year's Treasurer of what was now simply called the League. It had become some what embarrassing to continue calling it the 'Delian League' since the treasury about twenty years earlier had been moved to Athens. Everyone but the Athenian officials regarded the yearly payments from Athens' league of subject cities as tribute. Callicles had the difficult task of both personally welcoming each foreign official and then publicly announcing in a loud voice the city of each dignitary and the amount of the assessed fee he brought to the stage. It took almost two hours for all the foreign dignitaries in single file to make their way to the center of the stage and present their tribute to the Athenian Treasurer. After Callicles saluted each approaching foreign dignitary in a show of friendship, he then like a priest directed each of those who now offered their gratitude to Athens and her gods to present their tithe, the bag or bags of gold coin, by emptying them right there in the center of the stage in front of Athena's divine brother, Dionysos, and all his assembled celebrants. By the end of the ceremony the emptied bags of gold coins would grow to a shining mound taller than Callicles. Every Athenian citizen stood and watched, satisfied that on this stage they could see their many years of military service paying golden dividends – even if the gold didn't find its way into their particular purses.

Prince Sadocus was both impressed and perturbed by this spectacle. He now understood why his father had made a point of explaining to him over and over again that he must do everything he could to cement an alliance with Athens founded on genuine friendship and mutual self-interest. As the last of almost 200 officials wearily spilled their hard earned sacks of gold coin as homage to imperial Athens, the final instructions of his father, Sitalces, now took on added weight and unsettled his recently acquired love for everything Athenian. 'Remember son, I don't want you to join the line of those servile porters who each year must humiliate themselves on Athens' stage by surrendering their wealth to their imperial master. Strike no alliance with Athens which sacrifices our independence!'

Pericles could see that young Prince Sadocus was troubled by this scene. So as state slaves shoveled the gold coins into a large cart and last minute preparations were underway to prepare for the performance of the first tragedy; Pericles wanted to assure Prince Sadocus the diplomat that Athens was not a rapacious imperial predator, but rather a beneficent ally and honest broker of the common interests of the cities in league with Athens. Pericles thought it wise to address his remarks to his kinsmen and protégé, Alcibiades, hoping that they would better hit the mark if the Thracian Prince was not asked to answer to his host's point of view. Pericles did not want a confrontation that could unsettle the accord that he had with considerable effort persuaded both the Athenian Assembly and King Sitalces' diplomat to adopt. Pericles had persuaded the Assembly to grant King Sitalces' Thracians a permanent trading concession at Piraeus, free of all Athenian import taxes. In exchange for this, Prince Sadocus had signed on behalf of his father an agreement of alliance promising King Sitalces' assistance in protecting Athens' interests on the Chalcidice peninsula. Indeed, just yesterday during the City Dionysia Pompe, Pericles had already secured from King Sitalces' son in a short private meeting behind the Altar of the Twelve Gods a promise to apprehend and execute anyone from either Corinth or Sparta who would approach either Thracians or Persian agents nearby requesting a military alliance against Athens anywhere in the Chalcidice.

"Alcibiades, have you been down to Piraeus at all this week? The first week of the sailing season is always exciting for commerce. Our foreign dignitaries' ships scarcely had room to dock. I suppose many of the officials who were on our stage actually came here on board one of their merchant's transports. It is such a boon to all our trading partners that our navy has cleared the major sea lanes and ports of all the pirates. Now days you can count on having your valuable commodities get to their market whatever your point of departure in the Aegean Sea, or for that matter, most of the sea between here and Egypt to the south. I am not surprised that throughout the islands and all the cities on the coasts of Ionia that those in these cities who depend on maritime commerce are our friends. Athens may have her enemies in various cities in our League, but they are scarcely any but oligarchs who are enemies of democracy and the kind of commercial enterprise that spreads the wealth more evenly among the people. By the way, I hope you are continuing to train your trireme crew and perfect your seamanship. I'm sure that when your cavalry commission expires, Athens will need you at sea to keep the sea-lanes safe from pirates and the enemies of Athens who would shut down the commercial life of both our city and others. We are fortunate to have resources to fund such naval operations. Now days, doesn't it take a talent, a couple of sacks of gold coin, to pay the rowers of one trireme for one sailing season?"

Alcibiades nodded in agreement. "I think that is correct."

Pericles continued. "I would guess that most years we deploy fifty to one hundred triremes to keep the peace at sea and make the world safe for trade. Even now, when we are under attack by Sparta and her allies on land, our supremacy of the sea remains firm. I wonder what the profits, Alcibiades, from your shipping interests looks like for a typical week during sailing season. I wouldn't be surprised if one week's maritime commerce nets two to three talents or more. I know that your enterprises must each year remit to the Athenian Treasury fees for maintaining our own ports and providing for the safety of our shipping lanes. Is it imperial greed that we ask other cities to help fund this? Take away the theatrics, and it is a simple case of a commonwealth of cities financing necessary policing for all by remitting a small portion of profits to the one city that has proven most capable of providing this service."

There was no need or time for Alcibiades to answer Pericles. The poet, Euripides, was on stage and introducing his trilogy of tragic productions. After a few brief words about the ancient stories of Jason and Medea, an acknowledgement of the invaluable support of his *choregus*, Alcibiades, and a wave of his hand to summon on stage the chorus of the first tragedy; the audience clapped and shouted 'let the song of the goat begin'. They were ready to enter into the sacred and timeless realm where Dionysian passion drove mere mortals to some tragic fate.

It was high noon by the time the cast of Euripides' satyr play had left the stage, having provided the audience with comic relief from Euripides' tragic trilogy of plays. There would be a two hour intermission followed by the scheduled dithyrambic performances and the two comedies. Alcibiades had made arrangements for his party to take their lunch in a small room in the Odeion that had been emptied of its stage props. So now Pericles, Socrates, Prince Sadocus, Socrates, and his poet Euripides pushed their way through the throngs of theater goers now milling about as they stretched their legs and searched for the lunch cart venders. Alcibiades led the group through the first few rows of benches and then over to the walkway that led to a side door of the Odeion where they would wait for Lady Aspasia and Alcibiades' mother, Dinomache.

On their way both Euripides and Alcibiades could hear the comments of those in the audience who, ahead of the ten official judges, had already determined whether the poet's plays and the *choregus*' staging was deserving of any of this year's prizes. A burly *thete* who must have earned a seat near the front in exchange for some service to a wealthy Athenian kept repeating over and over, "How did they manage that! I was almost on top of the stage and I could not see how the actor playing Medea was able to hover above the palace appearing to fly. It had to be some kind of crane with ropes and so forth, but I couldn't see it against the background of smoke and bright torches out of which she rose. If for nothing else, the production of the second tragedy in the trilogy deserves a prize for this spectacular staging. How did they do that?"

Hearing the burly man, Alcibiades turned to Euripides and could not resist reminding Euripides of his opposition to building the crane. "And you didn't want to introduce this contrivance – I think that is what you called it!"

Alcibiades' elation was short-lived. Before they had reached the side-door of the Odeion, Critobolus, one of this year's officials charged with supervising collection of taxes at Piraeus' port and who had sat just behind them, offered a much less favorable review of the morning's tragedies. Walking just in front of Alcibiades party, Critobolus summed up in an animated and loud voice to a merchant from Samos who was his guest at the theater why Euripides' tragedies had no chance of winning any of this year's prizes. "It has nothing to do with Dionysos!" Just in case those around him had not heard him, Critobolus repeated this damning and stock dismissal of a dramatist's entry in an even louder voice.

Alcibiades wanted to shove his fist right into the man's mouth to shut him up. Euripides had heard this kind of thing many times before and so he reassured Alcibiades' that wiser heads than this man would decide the order of merit once all of the tragedies had been performed.

Before they had stepped into the Odeion and left the theater crowd outside, the *choregus* and poet heard a number of other puzzled theater-goers asking what possibly could the poet have in mind by allowing Medea, a murderer of her own children, to escape without paying for this crime and then, according to the poet's story, be given refuge in Athens by Aegeus, father of our city hero Theseus. 'Does he mean to suggest that there is no moral order, no justice for such as Medea? Isn't it a discredit to our city and Athena that this child-murderer is given sanctuary here? Ah, that Euripides is always so perplexing, but this is just too much!'

Alcibiades' mood darkened even more when the first words out of his own mother's mouth as she stepped from the crowd and joined them at the side door of the Odeion almost repeated verbatim this same doubt about the propriety of Alcibiades' poet's representation of the alliance between Medea and Athens' ancient king, Aegeus.

Young Alcibiades looked positively glum when he sat down at their lunch table. Socrates and Pericles both wanted the young man to be pleased with his liturgy for the city. So as the wine was being poured and the lamb and pickled eel were served along with corn meal bread and sweet red peppers from Crete, the General and the philosopher joined forces to cheer up the downcast *choregus*. It would not do, they both agreed, to have a young man of such promise already soured on service to the people of Athens. It was Socrates who took the lead in reassuring the young *choregus* that the judges' official verdict on his poet's dramatization of Medea's story would surely be favorable.

"Alcibiades, you really must not mistake the often unreflective and simplistic criticism of half-soused overly literal-minded men who rush to judgment even before the chorus has sung its epilogue. I remember just seven years ago almost to the day, when I heard similar boorish remarks about Euripides' play, *Alcestis*, even as the last of the chorus in this production was making its final exit from the orchestra. But five days later when the judges awarded the prizes, it was this play that they honored as one of the best. Only Sophocles bested Euripides that year, but I am sure that result was in part because of Sophocles' good fortune with the draw. Sophocles later told me that he thought Euripides' *Alcestis* was superior to his production that year."

Pericles nodded in agreement. "Yes, the verdict of the judges works in a way after the manner of the Spirits and the Gods described in the final words of Euripides' chorus in that very play:

'Spirits have many shapes,
Many strange things are performed by the Gods.
The expected does not always happen,
And God makes a way for the unexpected.
So ends this action.'"

Euripides allowed a smile to break through the tension that had made his countenance look like one of those wooden actors' masks that fix their tormented character's face into a permanent grimace. "I am flattered General that you remember these lines. I am curious what men such as you and my friend, Socrates, find in this epilogue. I have often repeated these words or something very like them in every tragedy I have composed. In my own mind, I think I am expressing both reverence and humility before the divine, acknowledging the limits of our own human understanding. But more often than not many religious people find me irreverent."

General Pericles did not want to venture into theology. It would be tiresome to deal with Dinomache concerning the topic of piety a second time during the City Dionysia. "Well, Euripides, I suppose many theologians think that they know the mind of God very well. That is why so many religious experts are irritated by those whose reverence like yours or, for that matter, Socrates' humbly acknowledges uncertainty, if not ignorance, when it comes to divine providence. But I was thinking along different lines just now."

"Go on then, General, and I will follow my own counsel and be open to the unexpected otherness of your interpretation of my oft repeated formula."

Pericles turned to Lady Aspasia as he continued. "I must confess that I was thinking along lines that Aspasia mentioned yesterday when she spoke of the aesthetic play of ambiguity made possible by the religious meaning of our Dionysian rites and stories. And then too, I was thinking of the play of chance involved in our manner of arranging a democratic and incorruptible process for awarding prizes in our theatric contests between the poets. But I don't want to bore you with my ruminations. The food is so good, the wine is spectacular, and soon our bellies will be shaking with laughter if the comic poets are in form."

Alcibiades eyes brightened. He was no longer despondent, just curious. "Please go on, General. I have so much to learn from all of you."

"You should not think, Alcibiades, that our average theater spectator is the best prognosticator of the concourse of 'Spirits' at work in the Dionysian inspiration of the poet and the Apollonian interpretation of seasoned theater critics nominated as judges. Then too, there is the immeasurable uncertainty of just which particular judges' interpretive evaluation will shape the final verdict. Our democratic procedure for designating the judges who actually will determine the awarding of the prizes not only makes bribery of the judges or any favoritism on their part unlikely, but also, I think, makes it more likely that the power of artistic genius will find a way to sway the collective judgment."

"You have completely bamboozled our Thracian Prince, Pericles." Lady Aspasia was certain that Prince Sadocus had no idea about how this procedure worked. "The machinery of our democratic ways must indeed seem strange to one who comes from the royal court of his father, King Sitalces."

Alcibiades, having eaten and refreshed himself with wine properly mixed with cold water, could now see that he had let himself be unduly discouraged by a few spectators who might be as unsophisticated as some one young like himself or a stranger to Athens, like Prince Sadocus, whose evaluation could not draw upon the Athenian tradition of tragic theater which stretched back now over 100 years, all the way back to Thespis. He would explain to the Prince the complex process that assured the integrity of the judges' decision. This would show the General that his young kinsman the *choregus* had recovered his balance.

"Prince Sadocus, some two weeks before the theatric festival of the City Dionysia began, our principle administrative archon, Polydorus, required each of the ten tribes to submit ten candidates which could serve as judges for the prizes. Usually the citizens who take the trouble to attend their tribal assemblies convened for the selection of these judges take this matter very seriously. They only nominate men of their tribe respected for their own working knowledge of the various kinds of theatric performances. Once each of these tribal assemblies has agreed upon their ten nominations the names of the ten tribes' total of one hundred candidates are inscribed on small shards. All these shards are shuffled together and placed in a large vase. Next, the Archon's assistant draws from this large vase ten shards and then seals this set of ten nominations in its own vase. He repeats this procedure nine more times until he has ten sealed vases which each contain ten nominations. The ten vases are then deposited in the treasury building of the Acropolis. At this point there is no way of knowing which vase holds any particular tribe's candidates. When the morning of the theatric festival arrives, the ten sealed vases are retrieved and then the Archon himself draws one shard from each of the ten vases. It is the ten judges whose names are on these shards who act as the official judges. When it comes time to award the prizes for the best tragedies at the end of the festival, all ten of these official judges inscribe on new shards their choice of poets for the first, second, and third prizes. These ten shards are placed in what is called the 'judgment jar', and the final determination of the order of merit, according to our more pious citizens, is left in part to the inscrutable will of Bacchos. The Archon invites Lord Dionysos to guide his hand as he blindly draws from the 'judgment jar' just five of the ten shards. It is the majority decision of these five judges which decides the awarding of the order of merit for the first, second, and third prizes."

"Now I understand why Alcibiades you are doing so well in handling your family enterprises. You have the head of an accountant! Who else could possibly give such a detailed account of our peculiarly democratic Athenian manner of awarding prizes to our poets, their actors and the tribes' various performance companies?" General Pericles was both impressed and surprised that Alcibiades would ever have taken the time to attend to such details in the governance of the City Dionysia theatric festival.

Socrates, on the other hand, wondered whether such procedures, while pandering to the appearance of democratic fairness, would in fact render the best judgment. As far as he was concerned the awarding of the prizes rarely corresponded to his own evaluation and he assumed that the judges were often men perhaps quite competent as carpenters, merchants, farmers, or soldiers, but more than likely not well prepared to evaluate the complexities of the poetic drama. Socrates was not so sure that this democratic procedure was any fairer then simply having one incorruptible expert judge award the prizes.

Socrates noticed that the Prince also was having difficulty appreciating the need for such a complex procedure. He spoke on behalf of both himself and the Prince. "The gods themselves must be hard pressed to keep track of all that – that's a lot of trouble to pick the winners."

Prince Sadocus had been trying to figure out the last part of the procedure by moving around nine pieces of three different kinds of fruit that now filled his large lunch plate. To his way of thinking, his three kinds of fruit could stand for the three tragic poets each of whom presented a trilogy of tragedies. Since he had three pieces of pomegranate, three slices of melon, and three strawberries, there ought to be a way in this fruit salad to see how five judges could come to a majority decision on which of the nine pieces of fruit would win the first, second and third prizes as most tasty. But no matter how he played with his fruit, the puzzled Prince could not see how the final random selection of the five judges' order of merit could in fact assure such a numerically certain judgment.

Exasperated with his unfruitful calculations, Prince Sadocus picked up the largest piece of fruit, a skinned pomegranate, and squeezed its juice into his mouth. Wiping the red juice from his chin, he asked the question that had popped into his mind and did not need such demanding figuring. "But wouldn't it be possible Alcibiades for six of the ten judges to all have agreed on the same poet as being worthy of the first prize, and yet the Archon's final draw from what you called the 'judgment jar' might select among the five that are drawn the other four judges who had chosen another poet for the first prize? Do you expect the gods to guide the lottery so that such a happenstance could not rob the deserving poet from his first prize?"

Alcibiades furrowed his brow and nodded his head in agreement with his Thracian friend's reservation about the fairness of the design for determining which *choregus* and poet deserved the first prize. "I asked that same question, Sadocus, when Archon Polydorus explained this procedure to me after informing me that I had been chosen as a *choregus* for one of our poet's production of the three tragedies and satyr play. I wondered why it wouldn't be better just to appoint a few of the most respected and experienced men who have spent much of their adult lives busy with theatric productions. Wouldn't their decision be more reasonable than one which opens the collective judgment up to all the vicissitudes of a popular tribal wide process capped off with two lotteries? Our Archon had to hurry away that day and so I never heard his answer."

Socrates was delighted that Alcibiades had for the moment set aside his anxiety over always currying favor and could think clearly about the nature of the contest in which he was engaged. "Such good questions! It is good Alcibiades that we have the real expert on this procedure in our midst. If I am not mistaken, I think it was General

Pericles along with Cimon who persuaded the Assembly some thirty years or so ago to codify this judicial procedure for awarding prizes at the theatrical contests held at the City Dionysia, the Lenaia, and the choral singing during Thargelia."

Lady Aspasia sighed. Wouldn't it be wonderful if our day at the theater would give dear Pericles respite from the cares of politics? She decided to answer for him, hoping to save her husband and the first man of Athens from having to revisit the difficult days of his rivalry with Cimon and the unsolved murder of Pericles' colleague, Ephialtes.

"Pericles, if you don't mind, I will explain to our company the circumstances surrounding the institution of this procedure for the state-sponsored theatrical awards. When I first came to Athens, I was immediately fascinated with the politics of the city and it seemed to me then that the episode which led to the statues governing state supervision of the religious theatric festivals would teach me a great deal about the better side of Athenian politics."

"So, what did you discover, Lady Aspasia? Were the statues so fashioned as to correctly evaluate the aesthetic merits of our poet's productions or is the legislated protocol tainted by the desire of our politicians to please as many people as possible?"

"Socrates, I was shocked to learn that the community tradition of the 'judgment jar' arose out of rather petty and mean-spirited circumstances. However, it would be a long and spirited philosophical discussion to sort out whether the value of a work of art is something other than what pleases its audience. It seems to me that your remark indicates that you think a popular judgment more than likely cannot be correct. I see that our company grows restless and the men will soon want to return to their theater seats. So let me just relate the events that led to the current protocol of the judgment jar and for now not deal with the question of what makes an aesthetic judgment sound."

"Go on, Aspasia! I will save that question for another conversation with you."

Aspasia smiled at Socrates and continued. "Some of the leading men of Athens had become embroiled in a bitter partisan dispute over the awarding of the order of merit at the City Dionysia during the last year that both Cimon and Ephialtes were still in Athens. By the following year, Cimon was exiled and Ephialtes had been assassinated. I am not suggesting that this episode was the principal cause of these men's removal from the scene. But the theater episode does play out in the context of the highly charged political contest between those who supported granting more political power to the commoners and those who favored reserving the government of Athens for the aristocratic families. This all happened just a little more than a year before I came to Athens from Miletus with my older sister and her new husband, Alcibiades II."

Aspasia paused. Dionomache was scowling at her and at the same time whispering something into her son's ear. Alcibiades, looking somewhat confused by whatever his mother had whispered into his ear, turned to Aspasia and urged her to continue.

"My mother was just telling me how my father and his brother, Alcibiades quarreled over my Uncle Alcibiades' marriage to Axiochus' daughter. For some reason, my mother never told me that you were the younger sister of my uncle's Miletian bride. I wonder how it can be that I have lived some twenty years in Athens and no one has ever taken me aside and said – 'I am surprised, Alcibiades, that you do not know that Aspasia famous throughout all of our cities and now the companion of Pericles, is almost one of your kinfolk.' I'm sure there is more to this story than my mother cares to share with me. But, please, finish your account of the dispute over the theatric awards. My family's connection to yours is a story for another day."

"I agree with your mother that it is best not to dwell on such personal matters. Suffice it to say I did not reside long in your uncle's home before I was able to find an independent means of supporting myself and taking a house of my own. Anyway, even though the dispute over the theater award took place prior to my arrival, I made it a special concern of mine to converse with the men who were directly involved in this episode, trying to learn everything I could. I was curious about how the rivalries of Athens' leading men unfolded and

I believed this City Dionysia episode, less charged with dire consequences, would be easier to investigate."

Dinomache could not remain silent. Surely everyone knew that Aspasia did all her interviews on her back! The very idea that she of all people could form a sound account concerning the origins of the sacred procedures which guided the theatric festival of Dionysos Eleuthereus was a sacrilege, an offense to everything holy in the mysteries of thrice-born Dionysos. She spoke to no one in particular, but Dinomache could not let go unchallenged the right of the harlot to speak on matters concerning Lord Dionysos. "I have always respected our current high priest of Dionysos Eleuthereus, and he has explained to me many times that this procedure for determining which of our poets' song of the goat most honors the divine spirit of Lord Dionysos was guided by the counsel of the *Hosioi* at Delphi – not by the banter of our Assemblymen!"

Pericles eyes were fixed on Dinomache as he spoke to Aspasia. His cold and threatening stare was a warning to Dinomache.

"Yes, Aspasia, I'm sure you will remember more clearly than I or anyone else the details about all this. I must confess my mind is occupied with the near future and our troubles with the Spartans."

Aspasia turned her chair away from the end of the table where Dinomache sat. She did not want to have to deal with the hostile religious zeal of this woman. Realizing that her narrative of events would stretch back some eleven years before the birth of young Alcibiades, she would not want to be distracted by Dinomache's nonverbal but vitriolic and pained expressions of disapproval. The topic was difficult enough since discussion of events of that time still often led to controversy between the democratic and aristocratic parties. Yes, Aspasia thought, Dinomache is very pious; but it seemed to Aspasia that Dinomache's brand of piety made her into one of those Alkmeonids, like her father Megacles, who had little sympathy for the democratic policies of her kinsman, Pericles.

Facing the men, she spoke with no emotion and in a manner like that of a courier charged with relating without error the details of the outcome of an important judicial procedure. "I'm sure Alcibiades you are familiar with the philosopher Anaxagoras. You were just a boy when he was exiled from Athens after having stood trial for impiety. The same year Anaxagoras first arrived in Athens, the city leaders were faced with a very nasty scandal that arose right after the end of the theatric festival of the City Dionysia. At this time, there were in fact three judges, appointed by the Archon Eponymus. These three judges decided the order of merit for the theatric performances. When all the performances were over the three judges would confer and it was required that two out of the three must come to agreement before any prize winner could be designated. Sometimes, I was told, their deliberations might take many hours. It was not always easy for even two of the judges to agree on the order of merit. But this system seemed to work well enough, that is until this particular year. On this occasion the judges came to their decision concerning all the prizes in less than two hours. This was an unusually speedy deliberation. Somehow it became known the next day, after the prizes were awarded, that one of the judges was outraged by the speed of the deliberations. This judge had not agreed with the other two on any of the order of merit for the three competing poets who had composed their trilogies of tragedies. The dissenting judge happened to be a kinsman of Ephialtes, the leader of the democratic party and the most powerful man in Athens at that time. It is still not clear who filed the charge in the King Archon's court which accused the other two judges of accepting a bribe. There is no record indicating that either Ephialtes or the theater judge who was his kinsman had brought this prosecution to the court. Anyway, the complaint brought to the King Archon's Court stated that there was evidence that two of the City Dionysia theatrical judges had accepted a bribe and that their awarding of the prizes could not stand since this would constitute a sacrilege that defiled all Athenians. If their verdict was allowed to stand, the complaint alleged, it would be a grave insult to Dionysos Eleuthereus. All of Athens was in an uproar as the day of the trial approached. But on the day before the scheduled court day, the complaint was withdrawn."

Dinomache could not keep quiet. After all, she knew the person who had filed the complaint and then who had withdrawn it. "There is no reason to see politics in any of this. It was the high priest of Dionysos who filed the complaint and then withdrew it when advised to do so by the Hosioi of Apollo at Delphi."

Lady Aspasia continued as though she had not heard Dinomache. "I learned a week later that the trial was averted through the joint intervention of Cimon and Pericles. Pericles at that time was a colleague of Ephialtes and played a prominent role in shepherding Ephialtes' democratic reforms through the Assembly. The trial would have been particularly bitter because one of the two concurring judges was a Philiad kinsman of Cimon. Cimon, at that time led the party of aristocrats who were opposed to Ephialtes' agenda of extending the political power of the commoners. To make matters even more volatile, the judges had awarded the first prize to the poet Aristias, a cousin of Cimon, for his production of *Theseus*. This play has not been produced since then, but I believe a copy of its written text can be found in the Odeion's small library. What is most striking about the lyrics of the chorus in this play are the repeated references to Theseus' heroic exploits in terms that unmistakably liken them to Cimon's victories against the Persians. Well, you can guess, Alcibiades, how all of this might have led to a very bitter and divisive trial that could have weakened Athens internally just when our city was on the verge of complete victory over the Persians and solidifying our leadership of the Delian League."

Alcibiades nodded his head in agreement. He did not want General Pericles, who was listening attentively, to think he was utterly ignorant of the developments that led to Pericles' position as first man in Athens. "Yes, Lady Aspasia, I can see that Cimon and Pericles both had little to gain by risking stoking the animosity of their respective political factions just when Athens required a unified front to deal with Persia and hold together the Delian League. So how did their intervention defuse the complaint brought against the two judges?" It appears that the tensions remained high. After all, wasn't it not long after this scandal you describe that Ephialtes was assassinated and Cimon was forced to leave Athens by the Assembly's ostracism?"

Aspasia knew that young men are prone to reduce the very complex play of political forces to a cult of personality. If Alcibiades was ever to match the political greatness of her beloved Pericles, he must learn the art of compromise and how to gage the tides of events and the currents of public opinion. So she would take the time to explain Pericles' art of legislative compromise.

"Aristias' production of *Theseus* was immensely popular with all the *thete* rowers and lightly armored infantry who served as auxiliary forces in Cimon's overseas expeditions against the Persians and their allies. General Cimon was loved by these men not only because he personally exposed himself to the same battle risks he asked of them, but also because once he returned to Athens he became their advocate in the Assembly, making sure they and their families were beneficiaries of the opportunities for title to land in the new colonies that their victories had made possible. So it would be far too simplistic to treat Cimon as simply an oligarch bent on protecting the wealth of the few against the interest of the many commoners. Indeed, since so many men in his expeditionary forces came from the poor and the commercial classes of craftsmen and free workers, these men formed a sizable cohort of Cimon's supporters. They were ready to follow his lead even though their usual interests in the state were better served by the agenda of Ephialtes. Thank goodness we had a man like Pericles with a political vision subtle and sophisticated enough to work with Cimon so that government by the many, rather than the few, did not abort itself with untimely and excessive factionalism."

Prince Sadocus was having more difficulty than Alcibiades following Aspasia's account. His father as a king would simply have issued an edict to resolve the situation. The Prince wanted her to fill in the details. "What happened next, Lady Aspasia? "

"Pericles negotiated with Cimon, agreeing that the City Dionysian theatric judges' decision of the order of merit should stand. The trial would not go forward if Cimon would agree to a new procedure for all future theatric and choral contests under the auspices of state officials. Both men agreed that the religious authorities should be consulted about changes in the procedure." Aspasia nodded her head and for a second turned towards Dinomache, acknowledging that there was some truth in her naïve recollection of this episode.

Turning back to the men, Aspasia continued her account. "The procedure Pericles proposed and Cimon accepted would make it practically impossible for anyone to bribe the judges and it would remove, in the case of the dithyrambic and other choral contests, any possibility of tribal favoritism prejudicing the evaluation of the order of merit. And indeed, Alcibiades, if you consider very analytically the mechanism of the procedure we have as a result of Pericles and Cimon's compromise, this procedure, I think, makes it most likely that the competition is evaluated without special advantage to any of our tribes or the taint of corruption due to bribery. And this is most important – any one of our citizens might be elected by his tribe and thus all are equally positioned to serve as one of the five judges who actually decide the worth of performances enjoyed by all our people, both rich and poor. Is not this a magnificent moment in the democratic life of our city which weds our love of competition which gives rise to excellence with the conviction that our city does well when free men, whether they be poor or rich, are afforded equal access to office and standing before the law? It is a wonderful service to our city, Alcibiades, that rich men like you undertake the cost of Athens' artistic and religious spectacles. But it is even more wonderful that our less wealthy and often work-weary thousands can without resentment richly award you, your poet, and his chief actor, all men usually of wealth and leisure. I do not know whether poverty and work that is like carrying water in a sieve is the consequence of a man's own chosen character or a matter of some kind of irresistible Fate ordained by the course of Nature. But this I can see with my own eyes here in Athens. Each citizen, whether he is a common laborer or one of those whose lineage has released him from the economic necessity of working with his own hands, is lifted higher in a city where the beauty of art and its recognition afford a common joy and grace guaranteed by a jurisdiction constituted by all the free men of Athens."

Aspasia could see that Alcibiades, at least, understood the politics that shaped the theatric code for determining the prize winners. But Socrates, she knew, would not be satisfied. She turned towards her philosopher friend and invited him to ask the question he always raised. "What is it, Socrates, that you would add so as to encourage our young *choregus* and his poet in their hope for a theatric victory? In my long and maybe too complex account of the procedure for awarding prizes, I have tried to show Alcibiades that he should not put much stock in the instantaneous opinions of the audience which have not have passed through the reflective, fair, and collective process of the 'judgment jar'.

Socrates wanted to talk about why Euripides' tragedy might be worthy of the prize. Aspasia had made clear the how of a fair procedure but not why the content of Euripides' '*Medea*' might merit first prize. As always, Socrates genially turned the conversation to his own persistent question about what it is that makes anyone or anything 'good'. "How unfortunate we are that Aspasia cannot speak before the Assembly! When I hear her speak in praise of democracy, I cannot help wondering what greatness she would achieve for our city if she were a citizen. She always speaks with such eloquence and intelligence. I for one am convinced, having listened to Aspasia, the judges' decision can neither be bought through bribery nor in any predictable way shaped by the judges' tribal loyalties. Our people's judges will no doubt, as far as they are capable, fairly consider the merits of Euripides' and Alcibiades' tragedy. And, I suppose, they will do this trying to satisfy the popular slogans – 'Is this really a 'tragedy'? 'What does it have to do with Dionysos?' Now we come to the essential consideration. So in this way, I would like to pretend, as if the people and the lottery had so ordained, that I am one of the five judges trying to persuade you other four judges of the reasons why Euripides' middle 'tragedy', "Medea" deserves the first prize because it best unfolds the essence of our human experience of Dionysos' epiphanies."

"Socrates, we will follow your direction and play the part of fellow judges, provided that this judgment will not keep us from this afternoon's dithyrambic and comedic performances. We must really be making our way back to our seats soon. I am looking forward to seeing how our comic poets will tweak my nose this year."

"Of course, General. We will break off our conversation when the trumpeter calls us to Dionysos' *Dithyrambos*. As for the comedy, on this day, General, you will be spared. I have heard that after today's dithyrambic performances, it is the turn of philosophers to feel the sting of poetic wit. It seems that our newest and youngest comic poet will this year have fun dressing up a philosopher or two as purple robed phallic fools. I don't want to miss that!"

Euripides was going to enjoy this. Socrates as one of his judges – what a treat and he has to be brief and to the point! "Socrates, I think young Aristophanes will spare you and have his fun with our metic philosophers. But, please tell me how I might answer those critics who say my *Medea* has nothing to do with Dionysos! Perhaps you can convince my *choregus* that he has not spent a fortune in vain – but that his name and that of his tribe will be inscribed on one of those golden tripods which will be added this year to the monuments along Tripod Road. If any one could be my advocate, I think it is you. I am always amazed that even months after the first performance of one of my tragedies, you are still able to recite almost verbatim the words of my chief actors or the rhapsodic chants of my chorus. How this is possible I don't know, since you don't, like a court hall scribe, take notes recording all the speech in my drama."

"As you know, Euripides, I seem to have little musical talent, at least in the ordinary way. I have never mastered either the flute or the lyre. To this day, and I am almost 40 years old now, any boy in his second year of musical instruction surpasses Socrates when it comes to playing either of these instruments. However, it seems that my daemon has compensated me for this incapacity with another wonderful power. Whenever a thought-filled iambic pentameter first reaches my ear, its melodic quality seems to gain some permanent hold on my mind so that long after first hearing it I can recall the voiced lyric and reflect again on the meaning of the poet's inspired words. I must say, my friend, that your mastery of the union of musical measure with a subtle and alluring language which explores the depths and heights of our human experiences affords me ample opportunity to play my peculiar instrument."

Figure 23
Chorus performance in 5th century tragedy

"Thank you for your kind praise, Socrates. In all fairness though, I should admit to the rest of our company that it is you who often partners with my Muse to inspire my poetic imagination. Why, just some few months ago, before I secluded myself in Aphrodite's rustic temple to compose today's service to Dionysos, I, along with your usual retinue of young men, was mesmerized by your dialogue with Nicias concerning whether justice is really, as so many say, 'nothing more than helping your friends and harming your enemies'. I went home mulling over your dialectical challenge to our conventional moral slogan and vowed that I would, as my daemon directs me, clothe your penetrating and critical *logos* with the garments of flesh and blood set at variance in the dramatic dance of human conflict."

Aspasia had always suspected that Euripides' work bore the marks of the poet's friendship with Socrates. She wanted to hear from Socrates himself whether he found in Euripides' drama a kind of poetic reproduction of the dialectical course of his own conversational inquiries. Clearly, from Aspasia's point of view, there was something very different about Euripides' and Socrates' sensibilities. Euripides seemed to have a resonance with the kind of religious dread of death and the departed that was completely absent in Socrates' philosophical inquiries. If they did treat similar themes, Euripides was a somber poet who darkened Socrates cheerful rationalism. "Tell us, Socrates, how your student Euripides' tragedy of Medea is in the service of Dionysos? But first let me pose the question in sharper terms so that I might elicit from you your best and most persuasive defense of Euripides' rightful claim to outstanding service to the spirit of the Dionysian."

Socrates was in his element now and quite pleased. "Yes, Lady Aspasia, I would think both Alcibiades and Prince Sadocus would be entertained if you test one of Athens' purported 'philosophers'. But remember, I must be brief, so do not make your question too difficult! It may be that they will see that I am not so good at answering the questions' of a truly learned person and therefore am not being ironic when I deny that I myself possess wisdom."

Aspasia had heard Socrates say something like this many times. It did not seem anything to her but a frank admission that he pursued questions that might not lead to a settled conclusion. He was always open to the possibility that he might have to revise his own conjectures. Otherwise, he would be nothing but a fool when he invited others to join him in testing their convictions through an examination conducted in accord with the *logos* of reason.

"Socrates, I suspect that many in the audience today might agree with the criticism of our tax collector, Critobolus. Think how many of our most popular tragedies have straightforwardly dealt with the theme of the tearing in pieces of some hero and thereby presented a kind of similitude to the murder of Dionysos by the Titans. Consider how many of our well-received tragedies, as I noted yesterday, treat the legend of Pentheus, the ancient king of Thebes who is torn to pieces by Dionysos' company of maenads. There are five 'Pentheus' tragedies that continue to be produced somewhere in Attica during the Country Dionysia season. Thespis, our first tragic poet, produced a 'Pentheus' that is performed almost every year in one of Attica's outlying villages. Aeschylus treats this theme in two of his tragedies. There are at least three other 'Pentheus' tragedies, two by Iophon, and one by Euphorion. These tragedies are clearly similar to the story of Dionysos' violent suffering at the hands of the Titans in the Underworld. Indeed, 'Pentheus' which means 'one who suffers' is sometimes an epithet of Dionysos and so it is clear to all who view the poets' tragic productions of the Pentheus story that the spectacle of his suffering is in some way akin to that of Dionysos. But surely, Socrates, Euripides' *Medea* is not at all repeating this story."

Socrates nodded his head in agreement. "Yes I agree, Lady Aspasia. I could not argue that Euripides' *Medea* is Dionysian because it retells the Pentheus story. I am sure though that it would be a narrow and stifling tradition of the tragic form if every poet had to restrict his work to some version of the Pentheus story."

"Of course, you are right about this, Socrates. I myself especially admire the work of Euripides just because his tragedies so often find ways to bring the many epiphanies of Dionysos closer to the human experiences of our own mortality and the tangled web of human conflict. Dionysos is a god of many names and all these names express some emotion of his worshipers or some encounter with the uncanny. He is *Bacchos, Baccheus, Iacchos, Bassareus, Bromios, Euios, Sabazios, Zagreus, Thyoneus, Lenaios, Eleuthereus, Dendrites, and Dithyrambos* – need I go on! I suppose many centuries from now, should our religion disappear, some historian like our Herodotus, looking at our monuments devoted to Dionysos, might think that we worshipped we knew not what – but a fleeting ever dancing phantasm that made us mad. Those in Athens who want their Dionysos simple and orthodox in spite of his diverse manifestations do not judge Euripides kindly. Let us hope, Socrates, our judges this year are open to the many powers of Dionysos and not wedded to this almost literal reenactment of the story of Dionysos' dismemberment. I think there is good reason to be optimistic."

Aspasia turned to Alcibiades and offered encouragement. Remember, Alcibiades, as Pericles noted yesterday, Thespis himself was an innovator. It was he who first answered the chorus of the dithyramb with human dialogue – thus making way for stories concerning humans and not the god. Think how Athenians today are completely at ease with a dithyramb which does not treat of the sacrifice of the bull or the birthday of Dionysos – even though these were the only themes treated by the dithyramb of old."

Socrates followed Lady Aspasia's lead. "I am sure there are many among our educated Athenians who are open to new meaning being poured into the old traditions. Thespis no longer treats the story of Dionysos in his tragedy concerning Pelias."

"But in this case, Socrates, the audience would still find in this story a striking parallel to the story the Orphics relate concerning Dionysos' suffering. Perhaps Thespis was charmed by Orpheus' *Rhapsodies*. If so, he might have found in the story of old man Pelias who instructs his own daughters to cut him up and cook him in a large pot in the hope that this would work the magic of miraculously resurrecting him as a young and vigorous man, an instructive contrast to the true mystery of Dionysos' rebirth. I think the Orphics find in King Pelias a foolish and proud man wishing to storm the gates of immortality without availing himself of the gift of this Mystery and the rites of Eleusis. One of these stories about the Titans' crime relates that after consuming some of Dionysos' raw flesh, they roasted other parts of his body in a large kettle and then consumed these also. Zeus, we are told by the writings attributed to Orpheus, sends a thunderbolt which turns to ash the evil Titans and their unholy meal. Yet, the Orphic mysteries teach that the second age of man begins when Zeus then proceeds to give new birth to youthful Zagreus-Dionysos out of his own thigh. And how did this happen? It seems, if I understand what Lady Dinomache and other Orphics believe, that the heart of the dismembered Dionysos was cast aside by the Titans and that, miraculously, Athena herself takes the heart in a sack to Father Zeus who then has sewn into his thigh this still vital part of his son. Dionysos then later is born again from the thigh of Zeus."

Dinomache could not believe her ears. The whore had actually read the *Rhapsodies*! And she actually understood what I explained yesterday about Zagreus-Dionysos. Well, she thought, the Mysteries of Dionysos Zagreus and Eleusis after all offer salvation even to the worst of sinners if they undertake the path of the *mystes*. Even Aspasia could not be turned away on Judgment Day if she has undergone the initiatory rites of purification. Oh, how sweet it would be - she could not yet cleanse herself from the fierce resentment and hatred this woman aroused in her - if she were turned away with the words, 'Not everyone who carries the wand is one of the *bakchoi*'. But my gentle and loving Orpheus teaches that even this proud and most impure of all women, whore to all the most lascivious men of Athens, may be saved from the torments of the Underworld. Mustering all her restraint, she smiled at Aspasia and, as though she was her guide to the Mysteries, reminded the acolyte of the mystery of creation.

"Remember, Lady Aspasia, if we are to give Zagreus Dionysos his due, we must acknowledge the mystery that it is from his body mingled with the ashes from the lightening struck Titans that Zeus created mankind. The sinful Titans had not only dismembered the child of God, but in their haste to hide their crime they ate some of his raw flesh. The clay and ashes from which we are fashioned then is made both from perishable Titans and the incarnate immortal one. And if we can purify our souls from the sinful nature of the titanic passions and lusts of our flesh, then the divine one within us will be liberated from the death and suffering that is the lot of our mortal and animal bodies."

General Pericles sighed, but said nothing. Here we go again, he thought. Must she always bring every conversation around to this?

Aspasia acknowledged Dinomache with the polite smile that she had learned long ago was best to show when she wanted to shoo away an unwanted client. This was a smile that she had almost forgotten since she had moved in with Pericles and had become a mother to his child. Lady Aspasia, seeing that Dinomache seemed to be pacified by her smile, resumed with the elaboration of her question for Socrates.

"And don't forget Aeschylus' homage to Orpheus in his production of the *Bassarides* which treats the murder and dismemberment of Orpheus. Again there is a literal resemblance between the violent death of Orpheus and the Titans' murderous dismemberment of Dionysos. Yet in all the tragedies treating Pentheus, Pelias, and Orpheus, the poets have extended the reach of the Dionysian story by treating the death of heroic, but mortal, humans as in some way intersecting with the story of the inextinguishable life of immortal Dionysos. Taken literally Aeschylus' or Thespis' Pentheus cannot be simply identified with Dionysos. After all, the Theban king is said in all of these tragedies to be one who opposes the Dionysian rites and is killed by Dionysos' maenads. The story of Orpheus' murder by Thracian devotees of the ancient Dionysian rites is less perplexing if we believe that it is Orpheus who taught a reformed more spiritual rite concerning the death of Dionysos. Thus Orpheus, misunderstood as a heretic, may have been killed by the Thracians of long ago so as to preserve the ancient rites involving the eating of raw flesh. I suppose that all these tragedies about Pentheus, Pelias and Orpheus could be said to heighten the audience's identification with the suffering of Dionysos while they also invite reflection on the mysterious meaning of the rites that commemorate Dionysos violent death and his miraculous rebirth."

Socrates appreciated the way Aspasia's summary of these plays sharpened the question at hand. "Yes, Aspasia, it is easy to understand why the tragedies you have mentioned are clearly in the service of Dionysos. So now we may again return to our consideration of Euripides' *Medea*. Lead on, Aspasia!"

"Would you not agree, Socrates, the three tragedies of Euripides, generously financed through the liturgy of Alcibiades, appear to have wandered far afield from the Dionysian stories commemorated in our City Dionysia and other festivals such as the Anthesteria or Lenaia?

The first of his trilogy, *Pholoctetes*, is concerned with the story of the famed archer who is left behind on a remote island during the course of the Achaean expedition against Troy. What does this have to do with Dionysos? The third tragedy, *Dictys*, at least treats an episode related to the first arrival of Dionysos in ancient Attica or elsewhere among Ionians on the Islands. But this story of the sailor Dictys' attempt to abduct Dionysos when the god mysteriously appeared among his shipboard passengers seems unconnected to any of our Dionysian rites, except perhaps Dionysos Eleuthereus' cult statue's ride on the ship-cart during the City Dionysia *Pompe*. Then when we consider the middle drama, *Medea*; the story of Jason and his foreign wife in Corinth does not even include so much as any mention of Dionysos. I think the story-line of Medea is gripping and powerful, but in this play even more than the other two in the trilogy, I can understand why the traditionalists in our audience would ask 'what does this have to do with Dionysos?'. So Socrates, taking *Medea* as Euripides most engaging story in his trilogy, how would you convince the other judges that despite its lack of any explicit reference to Dionysos, it is this play especially that should be honored with the first prize? Please, if you can, help us understand why Euripides and his *choregu*s, Alcibiades, should be awarded the golden tripod signifying the gratitude and praise of the people of Athens for this year's best rendition of tragedy in the service of Dionysos."

Socrates was sure there was no time to make his case in the way he was accustomed. "I see, my friends, that we have finished all our lunch treats and that the mixed wine flasks are now empty. We shall soon hear the trumpeter signal the start of the afternoon performances. So, if I may borrow a couplet from Pindar,

'*Long were it for me to go by the beaten track,*
For the time is nigh out,
And I know a certain short path'."

"Wait, Socrates, just a moment or two before you lead us down the 'short path'." General Pericles wanted to make sure that they had not somehow failed to hear the trumpet signaling the beginning of the afternoon performances. He rose from his bench at the lunch table so he could better see beyond their room out into the large main hall and through the open Odeion door. Standing, Pericles could see the lower section of the theater's seating area on the hillside that rose above the orchestra, the ancient natural smooth stone floor in front of Dionysos Eleuthereus' sanctuary. "Yes, go on Socrates. We still have some time before we men must return to our theater seats. I can see from here that the Theater officials have not yet summoned the audience and there is no sign of the Orchestra being prepared for the men's and boys' dithyrambic dance."

"Of course, General, I will not be offended if we must break off our discussion. Most of my conversations remain unfinished and that is not so bad since it makes me quite sociable as I am forever seeking the company of my partners in some unfinished inquiry."

Socrates hurried on, forgoing his usual procedure, by stating his conclusion first. "I want to propose that Euripides' *Medea* offers for our theatrical experience a provocative spectacle of Dionysos' actual presence in our own behavior rather than a retelling of the traditional stories about Dionysos himself."

Alcibiades was fascinated by this formulation. "Socrates, what do you mean by Dionysos' 'presence in our behavior?"

Socrates began with the most obvious ways Athenians experienced Dionysos' presence. "The passions displayed by Medea herself should be very familiar to those who would join the Dionysian company of maenads and satyrs given over to the intoxicating spirit of Dionysos. There can be no doubt that Dionysos kingdom is established through his gift of wine. While we Hellenes are usually sober in our daily lives, still many of us are especially drawn to Dionysos' holy days just because they invite us to cast aside our normal restraint and approach the divine forgetfulness his gift provides. We find in our rites of Dionysos various manifestations of self-forgetfulness which we acknowledge as a kind of temporary madness. What intense suffering and our most passionate pleasures have in common is that in both cases we feel as if something from beyond has possessed us and now our very bodies are in the service of forces that we cannot and often do not want to resist."

"But, Socrates, why do you say 'we'? No one has ever seen you drunk, even once." Alcibiades wondered if Socrates even enjoyed wine, since he seemed to have no interest in its intoxicating power.

"Alcibiades, I am as prone as any other mortal to intoxicating passions. But what concerning this call to Dionysian revelry in my own nature is presented for my contemplation in Euripides' *Medea*?" I would say, in answering my own question, that this presentation of the characters of both Medea and Jason is very provocative because I cannot help but recognize in both of them the tragic flaw inherent in our most powerful passions. Both characters appeal to Righteousness in the guise of *Themis* who, as a daughter of Zeus, is especially associated with enforcing the sacred obligation undertaken by any mortal who swears an oath – whether to an immortal god or to another mortal. Yet, when we observe the words and actions of both characters, we find that both of these great ones are driven by passions which lead them to sin against Themis. Moving outside all the constraints of sacred law, trust and love turn to distrust and enmity when Jason does unto Medea what Medea had done out of her passion for him – break the vows of kinship. This is especially clear if we follow Euripides' lead and take into our purview the back-story of the circumstances that led to the 'ill fated' marriage of Jason and Medea."

Socrates remarks were quite unsettling to the rest of the group, but especially Prince Sadocus. He politely interrupted. "Pardon me, Socrates, I am really confused by all this. How can a woman get the better of a hero like Jason, killing his children, and then escape to find a safe refuge in Athens? It is quite incredible to me that a woman, and a half-crazed one, is the protagonist who makes everything happen in this drama. And how can you think Euripides' story about such a woman, as you put it, can be suitable for meditating on 'the call to Dionysian revelry' in one's own human nature?

Lady Aspasia nodded her head as she reassured the Thracian Prince that his reaction was perfectly understandable. But she knew that Euripides often employed women, slaves, and other non-citizens as mediums through which he depicted the foibles and flaws of his fellow Athenian citizens. "Leave it to Socrates to confuse us. Wouldn't almost anyone else in the audience simply identify Medea as an evil witch, and find in Jason a heroic man seeking to make his way in the world? I can see how we women might understand Medea's jealous rage, but none of us could approve of Medea's murder of her own children. So, Socrates, help us understand what you call the back-story. I think you said that this would make clear how both Jason and Medea are swept away by passions which lead to unrighteousness."

"Socrates turned to Euripides. "I suppose, Euripides, since you are a very learned man, that you are completely familiar with all of the stories told by Pindar and the Argive poets about Jason's quest for the golden fleece?"

"Yes, Socrates, I would not dare compose a tragedy concerning Medea without drawing upon the many stories which my audience already knows. I am sure that most of my audience is also familiar with Thespis' tragedy, *Pelias*. The story told by Thespis explains why Jason and his wife Medea do not stay in Iolkos after he returns with the golden fleece. In Thespis' drama old king Pelias refuses to abdicate even though he had agreed to do this if Jason would succeed in bringing the golden fleece to Iolkos. King Pelias, now quite old, wishes to defy even the gods who have set an appointed limit to our lives. Wishing to be beyond the reach of death, Pelias believes that he can restore himself to youth if he will undergo an immersion in a cooking pot filled with a magical *pharmakos*. Jason's Medea, acting on behalf of her husband's interest, has persuaded the daughters of Pelias that if they administer this strange rite, Pelias indeed will emerge rejuvenated so he might rule Iolkos for many more years. Old Pelias is not made young again, but dies miserably in the boiling pot. Jason's suspected complicity in his uncle's death must have raised the specter of the pollution that follows the shedding of kindred blood. Thespis ends his *Pelias* with Jason and Medea hastily leaving Iolkos and seeking refuge in Corinth. The entire action of my play then is staged in front of the Corinthian home of Jason and Medea, after Medea has learned of Jason's decision to divorce her and marry the Corinthian princess. The play opens with Medea's handmaiden commiserating with the bitter grief and anger of her mistress who has just learned that Jason is casting her aside so he may marry the daughter of Corinth's King Creon.

> *'She....bemoans her father dear,*
> *her country and her home,*
> *which she gave up to come hither*
> *with the man who now holds her in dishonor.'*

Everyone in Athens knows that the homeland Medea has left behind for Jason is Kolchis. Think how thin and incredible my story of Medea's crime of passion and revenge would be if my audience was utterly ignorant of the stories concerning her part in assisting Jason at a cost of sacrificing all connection to her own family in Kolchis."

Socrates aimed to make clear that the Medea of the larger story could not be treated as irreducibly other and barbarian. "And is it not the case that in Pindar's story of the role Medea plays in Jason's acquisition of the golden fleece, Medea is characterized as King Aietas' 'great-hearted daughter' and a prophetess 'speaking with immortal passion'? She is by no means portrayed by Pindar as a purely monstrous and evil woman – a witch. I suppose, Euripides, your account of Medea's passion is meant to touch us all, precisely because along with Pindar we know her also as a heroine and lover of our man, Jason. I would think that since we Athenians honor Pindar as one of the greatest of poets, it would be difficult for an Athenian audience then to demonize Medea and treat her as utterly alien. After all, when Pindar's native city, Thebes, fined him for praising Athens as the 'bulwark of Hellas' and the city which at Artemisium 'laid the foundation of freedom'; our Assembly voted to pay the fine for him, name him our *proxenos* in Thebes, and honor him by placing a statue of him in our Theater district."

"Yes Socrates, I like every other Athenian, cherish the many odes of Pindar. I draw upon his inspired stories as spurs to my meditation on the humanity of our heroes and heroines."

"I suppose, then, Euripides, that Pindar's story of Medea's great love for Jason, a passion which overcomes her bonds to her own father and brother, should render her spirit sympathetic to any of us who have fallen under the powerful spell of Aphrodite. Does not sexual love often made us mad with desire, ready to forget everything but the object of our desire? Do not others think us love-sick and warn us not to be rash and excessive in the pursuit of the beloved? Indeed, your chorus in *Medea* sounds this cautionary note.

'When in excess and past all limits Love doth come,
he brings not glory or repute to man;
but if the Cyprian queen in moderate might approach,
no goddess is as full of charm as she.
Never, O never, lady mine, discharge at me from thy golden bow
a shaft invincible, in passion's venom dipped.'"

Aspasia saw where Socrates was heading. She answered for Euripides. "Although, we all would consider it ill fortune to be so smitten with such passion for another if the love is unrequited, still most of us would think our life missing something sacred if we had never been so in love. This same Ode of Pindar of which you both speak, the Ode Pindar dedicated to Arkesilas of Kyrana honoring his chariot race victory at the Pythian Games, so wonderfully depicts what it is to be overcome by such passion. It is though we are smitten from beyond by a force that runs roughshod over our own will to resist its charm and power. Pindar describes Medea's powerlessness to resist this passion in the presence of Jason.

'After that they came to Phasis; there they fought with dark-
faced Kolchians, even in the presence of Aietes.
And there the quest of keenest darts, the Cyprus-born, first
brought to men from Olympus the frenzied bird, the speckled

wry-neck, binding it to a four-spoked wheel without deliverance, and taught the son of Aison to be wise in prayers and charms, that he might make Medea take no thought to honor her parents, and longing for Hellas might drive her by persuasion's lash, her heart afire with love.'"

General Pericles laughed. "Aspasia, is not Pindar's fabled love charm from Aphrodite the very same one that made me forever yours? If I am not mistaken, you wore the necklace with its engraved amulet of the 'speckled wry-neck bound to the four-spoked wheel' until you gave birth to our child. There is no doubt it worked! Forgive me, Socrates! I am sure the poets are right. We do well to acknowledge that when this passion arises we are often in a thralldom best described as a kind of heaven-sent enchantment. It is true that such a passion leads men and women to sever any ties which stand in the way of union with their beloved. This then is part of what Euripides would have his audience understand in the way Medea loved Jason. And your point, Socrates, I suppose is that we should be ready to sympathize with both Medea's grief and anger if we understand what she forfeited so as to wed him.

"Yes, General, you have explained it all the much more personally than I could. I have not yet experienced this kind of passion. Perhaps this is so because Aphrodite does not want to waste her darts on one as homely as me. If I follow Euripides' allusions to Pindar's story, Medea loves Jason this way and now he betrays her. Awakened from her enchantment by Jason's plan to take a new wife, Medea grieves over the cost of her enthrallment. She has sacrificed her homeland, betrayed her own father, killed the brother who would prevent her union with Jason – and now her beloved coldly throws her over so that he might link himself to the throne of Corinth. The 'heart afire with love' now turns to a raging hatred capable of the same excess – a severing of all familial ties."

Alcibiades was not ready to grant to Socrates that Medea was worthy of any compassion or that she should be admitted into the company of those akin to Hellenes. It seemed to him that if this was essential to the meaning of the production he had sponsored, then there would be little chance that his fellow Athenians would award him and his poet the first prize for any one of the three tragedies in Euripides' trilogy. Medea was certainly the most dramatic and spectacular of the three, clearly the one that might merit a first prize. Alcibiades desperately wanted his production to be popular and it could not be, he thought, if this slayer of her own children made his audience uncomfortable by seeing themselves in Medea's behavior. "But only a barbarian would kill her own children. Perhaps Euripides means to affirm the difference between civilized Hellenes and this barbarian princess from the shores of the Black sea in Asia."

"I wonder, Alcibiades, if you are familiar with the stories about Jason's own family or the stories told about the concourse between the gods and the progeny of Hellen, the father of all we Hellenes?"

"Yes, Socrates, although I haven't thought about these stories since I was a very young boy."

Socrates pressed forward. "Jason, of course, we regard as one of our own race – not a barbarian. After all, according to our poets, he is descended directly from Hellen. Perhaps Prince Sadocus is not as familiar with the stories of our demigods and ancestral genealogy. So, let me help him understand the issue as to whether the wife of our hero Jason is really so different from us Hellenes by recounting the stories we tell our own children about our origins."

Euripides nodded his head in approval. He did want his audience to see in Medea a kindred spirit, not unlike those demigods, heroes, and ancient founders whose stories still explained to Hellenes their origins and way of life – especially if it provided insight to the sometimes dark and destructive side of a human nature that was to be found both in Hellenes and those called barbarians. "Socrates, it would be charming to hear more of your account of my back-story, as you say. If we do not interrupt, can you unfold what I only by way of a word or phrase ask my audience to recall?"

Socrates laughed. "It is impossible for us Athenians to forgo interrupting. But let me try to make my point directly: Medea, her passion and her murderous actions, are all of one piece with our own tribe's family history. Her actions in Euripides' tragedy repeat a pattern already played out a number of times in our Hellene hero Jason's own immediate family story. If this is true, we can't simply attribute her behavior to being a barbarian, someone completely alien, a foreign devil or witch."

Alcibiades was not convinced. "Refresh my memory, Socrates. When has any Hellene woman ever behaved like Medea, killing their own children?"

"Have you not heard the story of Tyro, Jason's paternal grandmother? Certainly you remember how Homer's Odysseus with the help of the ghost of Teiresias is shown the ghost of Tyro among the shades of the dead in the Underworld.

'Here was the great loveliness of ghosts! I saw
before them all, that princess of great ladies,
Tyro, Salmoneus' daughter, as she told me,
and queen to Kretheus, a son of Aiolos.'

Tyro is certainly no foreign princess, but a direct descendent of Hellen, the father of all Hellenes, whether they be Ionians, Dorians, or Aeolians. Her father, Salmoneus, the founder and king of Elis, is the son of Aiolus from whom all Aeolians today trace their descent to Hellen. Not once, but twice, according to our poets, this 'great lady' Tyro decides to kill some of her own children. While married to Kretheus, Jason's grandfather, she bears the twin boys, Pelias and Nelius conceived by a lover who is said to be Poseidon. These infant boys are abandoned on a mountain top by Tyro so that they might perish. Although they are saved by a herdsman who discovers them and later one of them, Pelias, becomes the king of Jason's home city, still this does not negate Tyro's intention to kill Pelias and his twin brother. Then later, Tyro, after Kretheus' death, marries Sisyphus, king of Corinth and has two children by him. The stories of the Aeolian poets relate that Tyro is warned by a seer that one day the children of her union with Sisyphus will as adults murder her own father, Salmoneus, and so she has these children killed so as to save her father."

Alcibiades now was thoroughly confused. "I have heard those stories. But Socrates, I have heard you many times ask others whether they really believed such stories as these were true – that such a thing as a god lying with a woman actually happened. So how can citing such stories by our poets serve to show that Medea is not a monstrous barbarian for killing her own children?"

"I do have difficulty with such stories, Alcibiades. But I suppose the point I am making is that for many of our pious fellow citizens, such stories of the behavior of our ancestral kin are taken as faithful records and so, you would think that Athenians should recognize Medea's behavior as within the range of conduct attributed to the heroes and 'great ladies' portrayed by our poets. Thus, Alcibiades, I think a more thoughtful and careful consideration of Euripides' presentation of this old story about Jason and Medea will not treat Medea's murderous rage as simply a consequence of her tribal origins or some kind of concourse with magical power that has turned her from a human being into a witch or demon.

Euripides' Medea explains her motivation for killing her children. She kills her own children not only so as to exact a bitter vengeance on her unfaithful husband Jason, but also out of a fierce pride that will not allow the enemy to hold within their hands the instruments of her children's death.

> *'Nay, by the fiends of hell's abyss, never, never will I hand my children over to their foes to mock and flout. Die they must in any case, and since 'tis so, why I, the mother who bore them, will give the fatal blow'.*"

"It is indeed impressive, Socrates, that you can recite lines from my tragedy after hearing the actors recitations only one time. But do you understand Medea's statement here as simply meaning that since she has taken the life of the new wife of Jason, daughter of the King of Corinth, she can be sure that her act of revenge will surely be followed by the execution of her own children by the Corinthians. Or, my friend, do you think that here too Medea's determination to kill her own children is also fated by her understanding of an all too common story of royal step-mothers killing the children of their husband by another mother." Euripides could not resist encouraging an appreciator of his art who could make apparent to others the subtlety of his drama.

Socrates smiled and followed Euripides cue. "Surely, Euripides, there is as you say often, 'a troublous coil to untangle' if we are to give Medea her due as a human being driven hither and thither by passions like pride, vengeance, and erotic love on the one hand, and on the other hand by her own understanding of the stories of the conduct of powerful Hellene kings and their queens. How can any thoughtful consideration of Medea's story ignore her own father's involvement in the story of a Hellene queen and step-mother who attempts to kill the children of her royal husband's first wife? If we begin to untangle as Euripides says, the 'troublous coil', Medea would never have met Jason if his uncle, King Pelias had not persuaded Jason that he might surrender his throne at Iolkos to Jason's father, provided Jason would help Pelias assuage the pollution wrought by Ino, the second wife of Pelias' brother, King Athamas of Orchomenus in Arcadia. Ino had attempted to murder Phrixos and Helle the children of Athamas by his first wife, Nephele, so as to assure that one of Ino's sons would ascend the throne of Orchomenus when Athamas died. Hermes, however, had intervened and sent a golden ram to carry the children far away to Asia. Although Helle fell off the flying golden ram into the sea near the shores of Asia (we Hellenes call her watery grave the Hellespont), Phrixos arrived safely in Kolchis. Thankful for his miraculous delivery, Phrixos persuaded King Aietas, the father of Medea, to build a shrine and dedicate the fleece of the ram to Zeus by hanging it on a tree near Zeus's shrine. It was this fleece which Jason brought back to King Pelias. This fleece once returned to Iolkos, Pelias had claimed, would atone for his aunt's attempt to murder the children of King Athmas' first wife. Medea knew that King Pelias real intent was to send Jason on a dangerous quest which could easily have led to this death. It had been with Medea's help that Jason and Medea had ended King Pelias' life. But when Jason betrays their marriage, it is the story of Ino's complicity in the death of the child by another mother which looms large in our troubled history with Jason's royal family. There is a certain desperate logic to her claim that she will not allow foreign hands to take the lives of her own children, given her knowledge of the recent conduct of Hellene royal families."

Pericles found Socrates' interpretation of Euripides' *Medea* so provocative that he could not resist perhaps extending their conversation, even though surely they must very soon return to their theater seats for the afternoon performances. "Socrates, it occurs to me that perhaps Euripides' point, in part, is that kings and powerful men and women of old, not subject to a civic law that treats all citizens as equally accountable to the law, are hardly reliable guides for just conduct. Then too, as you have argued many times in your public discussions with the poets and young men, since the poets intend to entertain us, and not necessarily edify us all the time, we should not look to the poetic stories as consistent and reasonable sources for the principles by which we should live righteous lives. Are we not better served by forging our laws and standards through the often contentious, but deliberative, discussions that take place in our Council, the Assembly, and our Courts? I know that our traditions and the stories we are told from the time we are very young children influence our ideals and drive the ambitions of many. But surely we would regard a man who cannot distinguish between the merely fantastic and entertaining aspects of these stories and the more sober and possibly edifying elements of the poets' stories as very childish and unduly credulous."

Alcibiades, sure that both Socrates and Pericles were asking too much of the audience and the judges that would award the prizes, wanted the discussion to return to Prince Sadocus' question. "Would not Athenians find it incredible and far too unsettling to see on stage a woman who somehow represents the foibles and conduct of the powerful heroes of ancient Athens? Our theater goers are not philosophers. "No man would be apt to sympathize with a mother who robs a father of his own sons."

"But Alcibiades, it is not just mothers who do away with their own children. Our Erectheus, whom we honor with the Erectheion on the Acropolis and still regard as one of our revered ancient kings, sacrificed one of his own daughters at the bidding of the Oracle of Delphi so as to assure a victory against the men of Eleusis. And then there is Agamemnon who sacrifices Iphigenia so as to honor a vow he has made to a holy man who requires a sacrifice to assure an end of a plague and bad winds that prevent the Achaeans from sailing to Troy. Does not Laius intend to kill his own son, believing that by killing him he will avert the outcome of a prophecy predicting that Laius will die by the hand of his son? The stories we tell our own children must indeed frighten them – although I suppose our theologians would find in them lessons about the pollution that follows a family guilty of shedding the blood of its own kin. In any case, the story of Jason's family, not Medea's, seems to render quite ordinary the killing of children by their own parents."

"Socrates, I grant your point. Fathers as well as mothers sometimes kill their children. Still today in Sparta, parents often take an unwanted infant and leave it in the wilderness to die. I am sure this still happens in Athens also. But still, Medea has no right on her side when she kills Jason's children."

"I am satisfied, Alcibiades. You have conceded that Medea's conduct should not be attributed simply to her alien and Asian tribe, but should be judged by whether or not she has 'right on her side'. But do you not find in Medea's case against Jason another issue which we should consider? Do you think an Athenian merchant would continue to honor a contract once its terms have been violated by the other party – especially if the breach of contract was injurious to the merchant's profits?

"No, Socrates, of course not! I would be regarded as a fool if I allowed myself to be treated that way in my commercial dealings with others."

"And I am sure General Pericles would not last long as our Supreme General if he allowed other states to break their treaties with us and in so doing injure the interests of Athens. Are not all these treaties sealed with oaths and do we not regard breach of oaths as cause for treating those cities who were our friends and allies as now our enemies?"

"Yes, that is true – although it seems to me that a more powerful city, including our own, will not hesitate to unilaterally terminate an agreement with a less powerful city if the treaty no longer serves the best interest of the stronger party."

'You may be correct about Athens' way of regarding treaties, Alcibiades, but should some one claim to be righteous when they conduct themselves in this way. Now consider Medea's plight when Jason violates his marriage oaths and agrees to marry the daughter of Creon, King of Corinth. Up to this point, all the well-known stories of Medea portray her as a powerful agent whose friendship and alliance is a boon to her friends, and especially to her husband Jason. Indeed she is the equal of an exemplary 'good' and heroic man. The woman who helped Jason tame the fire-breathing oxen of King Aietes, slay the dragon that guarded the golden fleece, dispatch those in her own family who would prevent Jason's return to his home, and then in league with Jason arranged for the death of Pelias is not boasting when she lives before us again and guided by Euripides' Muse, speaks like mighty Achilles, Heracles, or our own Theseus:

> *'Let no one deem me a poor weak woman, who sits with folded hands, but of another mould, dangerous to foes and well-disposed to friends; for they win the fairest fame who live, then, life like me.'*

Do we Athenians not find Medea's pride of power familiar? How often have our leaders promised new allies that they will find in Athens a great boon to her friends and a dangerous adversary to the enemies of her friends? Could this be why Euripides, ever our most provocative poet, brings Medea to Athens for refuge? Is Medea's line of conduct, one that simply identifies justice with helping her friends and harming her enemies, our poet's extended reference to Athens' often harsh treatment of former allies?"

"But she is a witch, Socrates. Her powers are deviously wrought and she kills by deceit." Alcibiades was not finding Socrates' identification of Medea with the imperial conduct of Athens a line of interpretation likely to win his play the golden tripod.

Socrates started to explain how Jason had no objection to any of Medea's magic when it worked for him. But there was no time now. The loud trilling call of the trumpet interrupted the philosopher in mid-sentence, and announced the imminent commencement of the afternoon *dithyrambs*.

Aspasia made her way to Socrates' side so that she might let him know that she, at least, understood something of his interpretation of the poet's revelation of Medea the maenad. "Socrates, you, I take it, see in Medea a Dionysian drunk with her own passions of wounded pride, love turned to hatred, and a mistaken and ruthless principle identifying righteousness simply with harming one's enemies and helping one's friends. I think you find in Medea reference to our ambitious and powerful men in Athens."

Euripides joined Aspasia and Socrates as they tarried in the vestibule of the Odeion. "Why is it that my most thoughtful critics speak in the shadows? Aspasia, you still worry that our friend Socrates will go the way of Protagoras – chased out of Athens by those who can play upon the people's feckless patriotism and simple-minded piety. I don't know how Socrates can stay clear minded and unperturbed in his search for reason in his dialectical appropriation of my tragedy's rendition of Medea's story when he sees the sadness in your eyes. We really must say good-bye and return to our seats. You know it would be quite an offense to the other *choregi* and poets if I skipped their productions."

"Yes, of course, I must be on my way. Otherwise tongues will wag about crazy Aspasia, who dared to tarry too long, intruding on the men's time at the theater. But I insist that both of you join me in Pericles' home for lunch next week so that we might finish this conversation. I would find it fascinating to hear how Socrates would set aright the ways of heroes, demigods, and our ancient royal families. I know Socrates does not mean to suggest that Medea's conduct is excusable or in any way right. No doubt, Euripides, your *Medea* in a way dramatically illustrates Socrates' view that excesses of passion allied with superstitious and inconsistent stories about gods and demigods offer no canon fit as a guide for justice and righteousness in a city which, at least in its ideals, rejects the often arbitrary willfulness of tyrants and the cynical maxim of 'might makes right'. Yet, Euripides, I wonder if Socrates thinks too highly of our human nature – thinking it like a ship that can be piloted by calm and deliberate reason. I have come away from many of your dramas convinced that you find in our mortal nature a darker and less exalted *daemon*, one more at home with the earthly Dionysos. I would think, Euripides, that unlike our friend Socrates, you would not have our Apollo alone, but insist that the inner sanctum of our nature, like our holy Delphi, will always be double – host to both Apollo and Dionysos."

The philosopher and the poet embraced Aspasia and promised to join her and Pericles for lunch once the City Dionysia celebrations concluded. Aspasia made her way out of the Odeion, following the large company of women who were now being escorted out of Dionysos Eleuthereus' sacred precinct. Socrates and Euripides rejoined Alcibiades and Pericles in their seats of honor just as the first company of the dithyramb made their way onto the ancient dancing floor directly in front of them.

For Alcibiades, the rest of the day and the following three remaining days of the City Dionysia seemed interminable. Have I done enough, he wondered, to be worthy of the golden tripod? He found the remaining productions, especially the tragedies, somewhat tedious. But since he and Sadocus spent each evening after the theatrical performances making the rounds at the men's drinking parties, he could not be sure that his attentive faculties were sober enough to judge artistic merit. Sober or not, Alcibiades wanted to believe that his production was by far the most spectacular entertainment and would surely be awarded the first prize.

But the City Dionysia ended with bitter disappointment for Alcibiades. He had spent a small fortune financing the production of his poet's trilogy of tragedies and his satyr play. He was sure no *choregus* had ever matched his financial contribution and yet in the end all he had to show for it was a humble third prize – a ceremonial laurel crown and a large amphora filled with wine from Delos. Hagnon, the son of Nicias, had won the golden tripod and a week later the trophy was mounted on Tripod Road. For the rest of Alcibiades' life, year after year, every time the City Dionysia Procession made its way around the Acropolis to the Sanctuary of Dionysos Eleuthereus, he would be reminded of the glory that was not his. It would have been easier to bear, Alcibiades thought, if the golden tripod had been awarded to Sophocles and his *choregus*. After all, no one would think any less of him and his poet if they took a second to Athens' most famous tragic poet. But to think that Euphorion, a poet who had never before even presented in the City Dionysia, would win for a production treating the tired old story of Theseus' slaying of the Minotaur - this was too much! And Hagnon, even though he and his father Nicias were among the richest men in Athens, had obviously done the production on the cheap. Hagnon had even borrowed props stored in the Odeion from a long past production of a Theseus story. To make matters worse, Hagnon, still a young man, had been elected his tribe's General the week before the City Dionysia. How will I ever become first man in Athens when I am already falling behind one of my peers? Answering his own question, Alcibiades promised himself that from now on he would never spend so much in service of the people and the gods unless he was more fully in control of an outcome that assured his preeminence and glory.

CHAPTER TWENTY-FOUR
ATHENIAN TARTAROS – THE PLAGUE
(Late Summer of 430 B.C.)

"One's sense of honor, is the only thing that does not grow old, and the last pleasure, when one is worn out with age, is not, as the poet said, making money, but having the respect of one's fellow men."

(Thucydides, *History of the Peloponnesian War*, Bk. II: 44, Pericles' *Funeral Oration*)

"The bodies of the dying were heaped one on top of the other. The temples in which they took up their quarters were full of the dead bodies of people who had died inside them. For the catastrophe was so overwhelming that men, not knowing what would happen next to them, became indifferent to every rule of religion or of law......Seeing how quick and abrupt were the changes of fortune which came to the rich who suddenly died and to those who had previously been penniless but now inherited their wealth, people now began openly to venture on acts of self-indulgence which before then they use to keep dark. Thus they resolved to spend their money quickly and to spend it on pleasure, since money and life alike seemed equally ephemeral. As for what is called honor, no one showed himself willing to abide by its laws, so doubtful was it whether one would survive to enjoy the name for it.....No fear of god or law of man had a restraining influence. As for the

gods, it seemed to be the same thing whether one worshipped them or not, when one saw the good and the bad dying indiscriminately."

(Thucydides. *History of the Peloponnesian War*, Book II: 52-53)

"Thus provided for, they lived at first in scattered groups; there were no cities. Consequently they were devoured by wild beasts, since they were in every respect the weaker, and their technical skill, though a sufficient aid to their nurture, did not extend to making war on the beasts, for they had not the art of politics, of which the art of war is a part. They sought therefore to save themselves by coming together and founding fortified cities, but when they gathered in communities they injured one another for want of political skill, and so scattered again and continued to be devoured. Zeus therefore, fearing the total destruction of our race, sent Hermes to impart to men the qualities of respect for others and a sense of justice, so as to bring order into our cities and create a bond of friendship and union.
Hermes asked Zeus in what manner he was to bestow these gifts on men.......
'To all,' said Zeus. 'Let all have their share. There could never be cities if only a few shared in these virtues, as in the arts. Moreover, you must lay it down as my law that if anyone is incapable of acquiring his share of these two virtues, he shall be put to death as a plague to the city.'

(A story told by Protagoras to Socrates and Alcibiades in Plato. *Protagoras*, 322)

The coldness was spreading about as far as his waist

> when Socrates uncovered his face, for he had covered it up, and said – they were his last words – Crito, I owe a cock to Asclepius. See to it and don't forget.
>
> (Plato. *Phaedo*, 118)

In the weeks that followed the City Dionysia, there was considerable unrest in the city after General Pericles had sent couriers to all the outlying demes of Attica. The Supreme General's couriers notified the farmers that no late spring planting or cultivation of crops should be undertaken until it was certain that Sparta would not again invade Attica during the summer months. The couriers were authorized to explain to the rural deme leaders the military necessity for this step. And so they read from a short communiqué co-signed by the officers of the Council and by the nine other tribal generals serving on the Board of Generals.

> 'Citizens of Attica's rural demes must again make preparations to take shelter within Athens' city walls. All late spring planting and cultivation of crops is to be halted. Plans should also be in place to transport livestock to Euboea or other offshore Athenian colonies. The invading enemy forces must be denied access to provisions in Attica. Their occupation will be shortened if there are no crops or livestock to be found in Attica. Should Attica's farms again be attacked by our enemies, our own needs will be more than adequately met through our access to grain shipped from the shores of the Pontus.'

The evacuation notification made it clear to everyone that they might once again suffer through the hot summer months with overcrowded conditions within the city walls. Worst of all for the wealthy aristocratic families, they would again be required by Pericles' military strategy to allow the Spartan King Archidamus to lead his confederacy of Megarians, Corinthians and other enemies of Athens on a rampage through Attica, burning and pillaging their country estates.

During the winter there had been some hope that further war with the Spartans could be avoided through diplomatic resolution of the various grievances. Indeed, one of the oldest and most prestigious families in Athens had taken the lead in advocating a peace treaty with the Spartans and a peaceful resolution of the conflict with Corinth over Potidaea. Callaeschrus, who could trace his family's lineage through Solon all the way back to one of the ancient Kings of Athens, had persuaded the Council of Five Hundred to send him as an ambassador to Sparta empowered to negotiate directly with Sparta's *ephors*.

But this diplomacy all came to nothing due to developments in Thrace and Chalcidice in the weeks following the City Dionysia. While Callaeschrus was still in Sparta Athens discovered that Sparta and her allies had secretly approached King Sitalces, who ruled all of the Odrysian tribes in Thrace, and offered him ten talents of gold if he were to abandon his alliance with Athens and help the Corinthians and Spartans defeat the Athenian forces besieging Potidaea. But at this same time Prince Sadocus, the son of King Sitalces, had just returned to his father's palace after his stay in Athens. Upon learning of the diplomats offer to his father, Sadocus, now himself an honorary citizen of Athens, persuaded his father to send the diplomats away. King Sitalces told the Spartan and Corinthian diplomats that he would not undermine his friendship with Athens by making war on any of her forces. However, wishing to avoid future conflict with the Spartiates, Sitalces did assure the diplomats that his forces would remain neutral in the battle for Potidaea. Learning about this attempt to turn King Sitalces against Athens, General Pericles and the rest of the nine Generals appointed for the year considered it ill-advised now to make peace with Sparta.

The animosity between Athens and both the Spartans and their ally the Corinthians became implacable when the Corinthians and Spartans learned how the Athenians later treated their diplomats. Once the Spartan and Corinthian diplomats failed to gain the alliance with King Sitalces, they requested that the King at least assist them in making their way across the Hellespont. However, Prince Sadocus, a true friend of Athens, immediately informed the Athenians who had accompanied him in his return to Thrace concerning the diplomats' plans to cross the Hellespont and seek assistance from the Persians in their war with Athens. Acting on Sadocus' knowledge of the diplomats' route, a company of Athenian cavalry apprehended the Corinthian and Spartan diplomats before they could make their way to the Hellespont. Since the Corinthian General Aristeus, the man who had caused most harm to Athenian interests in the Chalcidice and Potidaea, was among these diplomats; it seemed prudent to the Athenian officers that the captured diplomats be rushed back to Athens on a swift and fully armed Athenian trireme. On the very same day of the trireme's afternoon arrival at Piraeus, the captured diplomats were hooded like common criminals and marched to the Bouleuterion. Fearing that the eloquence of Aristeus could persuade Athenians to extend clemency, the *pyrtanes* and the Board of Generals decided to execute all of these diplomats immediately, denying them any opportunity to speak in defense of themselves before any larger body of Athenian citizens. Most Athenians did not even know of their presence in Athens until a small company of Council Guards were seen carrying the diplomats' bodies by litter to a recently excavated garbage pit just outside the Kerameikos Gate. The bodies were unceremoniously dumped into the pit and then on the same day covered over with refuse from the Agora. Some of the older Athenians who remembered that Aristeus was the son of Adeimantus, the Corinthian commander of his city's fleet which had helped the Athenian fleet defeat the Persians at Salamis, were aghast that Athens' officials should so summarily execute and then desecrate the body of the son of a man who helped save Athens and the rest of the Hellenes from Persian subjugation.

When an account of all this made its way to Corinth and Sparta, all diplomatic ties were severed. Callaeschrus was immediately sent back to Athens having accomplished nothing to advance a peace treaty. A few days later a courier from Sparta arrived with a sealed document addressed to the Council of Five Hundred. The document demanded that the following conditions be met: (1) Athenian reparations for the gold and properties taken by the Athenians and their agents from Potidaea's aristocrats, (2) withdrawal of all Athenian forces from Potidaea and the restoration of the rightful government of Potidaea and its ancestral ties to its mother city, Corinth, (3) recovery of the bodies of the diplomats and their return to their native cities, (4) the return of Aegina's land and government to its own people, and (5) the repeal of Athens' decree excluding Megara's merchants from all ports of commerce under Athenian control. The ephors of Sparta ended the document with what amounted to a renewed declaration of war – but one calculated to sow discord between the aristocrats and the common people of Athens: '…only if all these conditions are immediately met, will Athens be saved from another invasion of Attica that will bring total destruction on the ancestral estates of her leading citizens.'

Once Sparta's ultimatum had been delivered and read in the presence of a full session of the Five Hundred, some prominent members of the Council urged the Council to seek some kind of accommodation to the Spartan demands – provided this assured no further Spartan-led destruction of the landed estates in Attica or the dismantling of Athenian military power. General Nicias, one of Pericles' colleagues on the Board of Generals, and Callaeschrus, a leader along with Nicias of the Athenian aristocratic party, proposed that if peace could be had for a score of talents and revoking the Megarian decree, this would avert another summer siege of Athens. Again Pericles, this time with greater difficulty, persuaded a majority of the Council that Athens should not capitulate to any of Sparta's demands since this would only encourage both Sparta and Athens' other enemies to demand more later. He pointed out that while the Athenian League had started out as an alliance of equals led by Athens to defend against the Persian threat, there was no doubt that over time she had become an imperial power who now had made many enemies. His speech, as always was eloquent, subtle, and far reaching.

"There are many who believe the propaganda of the aristocratic Spartiates – that they are champions leading the liberation of those under the tyranny of Athenian imperialism. I say it is duplicitous rhetoric on their part because they behave no differently than other powerful or rich men. We need to look no further than their subjugation of the helots. And I am sure that should they have the means they will reach out for the hegemony of empire. But, we need to be realistic and realize that Athens is indeed an empire. And there are days in Athens when even our most zealous democrats are proud of our empire. Think of the patriotic fervor of our PanAthenaic Festival or the tribute ceremony of our City Dionysia. It is because we are a commercial empire that we have access to a wide array of material resources including a grain supply that has allowed our city to feed many more than the rocky soil of Attica allows; our considerable leisure - freed as we are by the wealth that flows into Athens from our many subject cities – is the fount of our magnificent art and other intellectual accomplishments; our ability to steer a course of relative peace between those who have little and those of great wealth by providing gainful employment for most of our commoners as they man the workshops, docks, and ships so that they might rise to a middling means of life which includes the pleasures of the theater and other respites which in former times were only for the rich: **these assets of our great and creative liberty are now all premised on our empire**. So, should we listen to those who would have us give up our empire? Even if we would willingly part from all the good things it brings us, do we really think those whom we have antagonized would let us surrender without, as they see it, revenge and requital for their unwilling service to Athens' interests. There are many men, especially aristocrats in the islands, Ionia, and the coasts approaching the Hellespont who for years have chaffed under Athens' commercial domination and refusal to grant autonomy to their local aristocratic governments. They see our support of democratic elements in their cities as a cover for installing pro-Athenian governments which will serve Athenian interests and even pay tribute – usually by unduly taxing the wealth of the aristocratic families whose efforts and genius founded the city. If we are to leave to our sons an Athens undiminished, as we have sworn in taking on our citizenship long ago in our hoplite oath, then there is only one course we can follow. We must not capitulate to the demands of those who would take from us what we with great sacrifice have won. I am confident that our best chances for success rest on a strategy which draws unashamedly on just those resources that define our empire. We must lean heavily on Athens' naval superiority, the vast resources of her maritime empire, and the ability to defend and sustain our city and its long walled fortified access to Piraeus without engaging Spartan forces on their terms – a massed hoplite battle."

Finally, having persuaded a majority of the Council to reject all Spartan demands, General Pericles urged the Council to convene the Assembly as soon as possible so that the majority Council recommendations could be ratified by the People. He warned that should the Assembly be asked to express its will later during a protracted occupation of Attica when the hardships of the Spartan led siege of Athens would weigh heavy, no one could be sure if popular decisions made under such duress would be sound. Even before the Assembly could be convened on the day following the Council meeting, word reached Athens that King Archidamus had already began the march towards Attica. And so, when the Assembly did convene, there was barely a quorum present for the vote. Many of the Assemblymen from the rural demes of Attica, assuming that the Spartan invasion was inevitable, had decided that they should oversee the transport of their families and movable household property into the City immediately. What remained of the Assembly, mostly representatives from the City demes and the demes from those regions of Attica with few farms, hastily approved the Council's war resolution.

And so again, like last summer, Athens served as a fortified refuge for all of the rural population in Attica. King Archidamus led an even larger army into Attica and this time pillaged and burned demes to the south of Athens as well as those to the north. The devastation of country estates and other properties throughout all of

Attica went on for 40 days. It was hard enough to sustain support for General Pericles strategy of avoiding a direct challenge to massed Spartan hoplites when they were so near to Athens and destroying the ancestral homes of many of Athens' founding families. But when the overcrowded City suddenly found itself in the grips of a deadly plague which dealt death to both rich and poor, young and old, free citizen and slave, the hitherto healthy and the sickly; then desperate measures, including an attempt to strip Pericles of his Office as General, were undertaken in a panic.

It was in these circumstances that Pericles had called upon some of his friends to undertake efforts for the introduction of a state sponsored festival and cultic center honoring Asclepius. So one week after the Spartan Army had left Attica, fearful that if they remained any longer their own troops would be struck with the plague, Pericles, accompanied by a priest of Asclepius from Epidaurus, made his way at mid-day to a small grove of fir trees that still grew on the rocky slope of the south side of the Acropolis, just above the theater district of Dionysos Eleuthereus' Temple. As Pericles made his way past the back of the Odeion and up along the Temple side of the hillside that served as the Theater's seating, he could see up above on a outcropping from the steep slope the small pavilion and large stone altar that had just been completed by the masons and would serve, at least temporarily, as the sanctuary of Asclepius for Athenians. For now, the outdoor pavilion, with a sculptured outdoor fountain at its center and a stone altar on its western side, was all that could be afforded, given the need to set aside most of the state's funds for the War.

Standing just beyond the stone altar, under the shade of the few fir trees, a group of ten men were waiting for Pericles. A man, heavily bearded and walking with a cane, stepped out of the shade and onto the stone platform in front of the altar. It was Pericles friend of many years, Sophocles. Sophocles looked down the narrow stone paved pathway that wound its way from the new altar for Asclepius all the way to the walkway between the Odeion and the Orchestra in front of Dionysos Eleuthereus Sanctuary, searching for the last of the two men who would join the very first congregation at the new sanctuary. When he saw his colleague, the first man of Athens, accompanied by the priest who would preside over the rites of Asclepius, he called down to them.

"Be careful General, there are still some stone steps on the pathway that have not completely settled. You have only one more turn in the trail and about fifty stone steps until you can see all of the site and the lovely fountain around which the rest of our congregation is gathered."

Pericles, a little out of breath, mounted the last steps that led to the sanctuary. When Pericles had caught his breathe again, he embraced his comrade Sophocles and introduced the priest accompanying him.

"Sophocles, you have chosen a splendid location. If old men like you and I can make our way up this path, you with a cane and me with my aching knees, then surely others with infirmities can either make the climb or be carried by their porters. Perhaps I have been helped along by the ministrations of my companion, Therakleios. I have been with him all morning and he has already shared with me some of the anodynes that the brotherhood of Asclepius prescribes for aching joints. Is everyone else here already?"

"Everyone is here that you invited, and I have brought along a few more men of considerable learning and experience whose counsel, I think, would be helpful in moving forward with the introduction of the *Asclepieia* here in Athens. Doesn't this site remind you of our poet Pindar's description of Cheiron's abode in Pelion's glens? Of course there is no cave here; but something about these crag clinging firs, the bubbling spring that here flows from the side of the acropolis, and the yet wild and secluded refuge this spot offers seems perfect for Cheiron's tutelage of the young one Apollo pulled from the funeral fire. I am always amazed at how water flows from this rocky acropolis, and nowhere is the water cleaner or cooler than that which comes from the spring that our craftsman have channeled into the fountain shaded by these ancient fir trees. The trees themselves seem preternatural. One wonders how such sturdy giants can draw upon so little of Mother Earth. They seem magically to spring from the crevices in the rock. Even our young Critias, often so skeptical about all that is divine, is moved by the elemental beauty of the grove now graced by the presence of Cheiron and his young charge, Asclepius. You see how well our sculptor has captured their likeness on the base of the stone fountain. Is this not all a theophany, a sign of the presence of the sacred, a stone upon a rock from which endlessly flows the purifying element of life? Here, at least, it seems that there can be no plague, no stench of death, but only the clear clean water, the sweet smell of fir, and the rock all around us from which all corruption has been swept clean."

"Always the poet, Sophocles! Yes this is the very best place for our new sanctuary and rites celebrating the heroic healing arts of Asclepius. I see that you have brought your house guest from Apollonia."

"Pardon me, Pericles, how can I be so rude as to overlook properly introducing you to Diogenes. I am so enchanted by this place that I have forgotten my manners."

"You are never a rude man, Sophocles, but sometimes you can be a little distracted. It was just yesterday that you introduced me to Diogenes just outside of the Odeion. You were showing him, I think, some of the props from the prize-winning productions. Diogenes, I am glad that you, with your special knowledge of the healing arts, are here today. I have read your treatise, *On Nature*, and find its section on human disorders of the mind and diseases of the body quite fascinating. I suppose you then are not only a philosopher, but a physician. It is quite remarkable that you have braved a sea voyage from far away shores of the Pontus to come to our city while it is at war with the Spartans and a death-dealing plague. We all are thankful that there are men like you that have not given up in the search for both a cure and prevention of the highly contagious disease now stalking our citizens. Many of our resident physicians have themselves fallen prey to the plague while treating others and so it requires unusual courage for anyone to care for those who show any symptoms of the plague. You, I see, have a robust constitution, like our native philosopher Socrates and perhaps, like him, will follow your curiosity wherever it leads. How wonderful that you will have the opportunity to share your knowledge with my companion, Therakleios, whose service on behalf of the brotherhood of Asclepius includes, of course, the healing arts."

Diogenes extended his arm in a salute to General Pericles and nodded his head acknowledging with respect the priest of Asclepius. "I am indeed thankful for Sophocles' hospitality and your graciousness in permitting me to be here today. I have followed the horrible course of the plague that now afflicts Athens elsewhere in other cities in hopes that I might understand its causes and find a way to treat and cure its victims. I suspect that it was carried to Piraeus from the isle of Lemnos where there has been a recent earlier outbreak of disease much like the one I see Athenians now suffering. Perhaps it has been brought to Piraeus by one of the grain ships and then made its way by contagion into your crowded city. And so when Sophocles wrote to me, inviting me to Athens, to help in combating the plague and take part in the installation of an Asclepieia here, I was both honored and considered myself fortunate that I could continue my research while possibly rendering a service to Apollonia's Ionian kin in Athens."

Pericles embraced Diogenes and then turned to the rest of the gathering. "I am sure all of us will assist you in any way we can to combat the plague, Diogenes. Of course, our determination to introduce a religious center for the healing arts of Asclepius would be wise even if there were no plague. But now our Assembly and its politicians, our poets, and even our philosophers are all cognizant of how urgent it is to offer our citizens hope. Athenians now suffer doubly from the wounds of war and the horrors of a plague against which, unlike the war, there seems to be little defense. And so when Sophocles came to me with the plan to found an Asclepieia with its own festival and rites on the Day of the Proagon of the City Dionysia, I immediately presented the proposal to the Council and they unanimously recommended to the Assembly legislation authorizing this new state sanctuary and its festival day. We are able to move forward so quickly because our Assemblymen unanimously approved the plans for the site and occasion of the Asclepieia. So, our first Athenian festival honoring Asclepius will be celebrated next spring. That is why, of course, we have arranged to bring Therakleios here from the most famous and first Asclepieia among we Hellenes – the brotherhood's Asclepieion at Epidaurus. Therakleios has agreed to oversee the institution of Asclepieia here. So, Therakleios let me introduce you to the rest of us Athenians who today have come together here to assist in Asclepius' arrival in Athens.

Here is Socrates, our own philosopher. He is very modest in appearance, but I think no one else in Athens has more influence with our young men. Indeed he has brought along today, two of his most illustrious young mentees, Alcibiades the son of Clinias and Critias the son of Callaeschrus, our ambassador to Sparta this past winter. This is Alcibiades here all covered up with his winter robe. And beside him is Critias also covered from head to foot in his thick robe. I suppose our young scholars have been discussing with Socrates some philosopher's conjectures about the natural causes of the plague and its spread among our citizens."

The two young men stepped forward to greet the priest. Critias, a few years older than Alcibiades and more unabashed in his pride of learning, gently corrected Pericles as he made it clear to the priest that both he and Alcibiades were not foolishly out of season in their dress. "Socrates rarely takes any interest in discussing with us the various treatises concerning Nature. He seems to hold the view that virtue will assure health and that we should care most of all for what he calls the improvement of our souls. Both Alcibiades and I have spent some time with the metic Gorgias who has, for a fee, taught us the way Empedocles of Acragas might explain how disease occurs in our bodies. According to Gorgias, Empedocles in his treatise *On Nature* proposes that the various elements and composites of elements may mix with our body through either the very small pores found in our skin or through enlarged portals in those openings like our mouth, nose, ears, and eyes. Although Empedocles himself does not apply his atomistic theory concerning the pores to the mechanism of disease, Gorgias argues that this is a reasonable way to account for the onset of illness. Some of the effluent composites that enter our body may be the causes of disorder and diseases. Alcibiades and I find this explanation plausible. Young as we are, virtue is a work in progress. But it is easy to put a long covering robe on and who knows – it might be a better prophylactic measure for the plague in our midst than sleeping in the temple of Epidaurus."

Therakleios did not miss the insinuation that perhaps the brotherhood of Asclepius offered only superstitious nonsense as its therapy for those wishing to ward off disease.

Pericles wished Critias could be a little less abrasive. He continued with his introduction. "It is good that Socrates is sympathetic to our plans, for he will be of great help in explaining the wisdom of Asclepius to the young men like Alcibiades and Critias who will soon be our leaders. Here, to the right of Socrates is his neighbor and friend, Crito, who is as man of considerable means and has come forward to offer as his liturgy a considerable sum of funds for the eventual construction of Asclepius" temple. Over here, besides Sophocles, is Euripides, a poet whose tragedies are, I think, the only ones on a level with those of Sophocles and venerable Aeschylus. I do believe Euripides' muses may soon honor Asclepius by dramatizing the demigod's human tragic story. Standing here beside the fountain is the young acolyte, Theophilias. He is the son of Diopeithes and takes a special interest in all things concerned with the divine. Like his father, Theophilias is zealous in his defense of piety and the service due to the gods. Finally, over here by the tallest of the firs are two of our most prominent citizens. Nicias has served as my colleague on the Board of Generals on three occasions. And just a few months ago his son, Hagnon, was elected General by the tribal district where he has set up his own residence. Congratulations, Nicias and Hagnon! It is as far as I can determine, the first time a father and son have both served on the Board of Generals at the same time. It is fitting that General Hagnon is with us today, for he has just returned from commanding an Athenian force at Potidaea which lost over a thousand of his hoplites not to the enemy, but to the Plague. In his report to the Strategeion, he expressed his conviction that his life must have been spared by the gods, perhaps Apollo the father of Asclepius, for some special purpose. He and his father have vowed in gratitude to Apollo to provide whatever further funds are required to assure that Asclepius' temple honors both Athens and Apollo *Paieon,* the physician of the gods."

"It is indeed an illustrious congregation you have convened, General Pericles." Therakleios, a learned man, realized that he must not offend any of these men, since they had been especially brought together to promote the installation of a center for the brotherhood of Asclepius. Here, he thought, are pious men, rich and powerful men, Generals, and men of great learning. I must speak in such a way that all will see in the installation of Asclepieia here in Athens a service to the state. "May I, Pericles, begin our conversation with a brief explanation of the mission of the priesthood of Asclepius?"

"Yes, that would be very helpful. Sophocles has explained something of the brotherhood's history and shared with me the rites and details concerning the festival of Asclepieia which he has observed in Epidaurus. But it would be good for all of us to hear from you, the superior at the original Asclepieion. I must warn you that we Athenians are accustomed to asking questions and are apt to interrupt, as we do in the Assembly. We mean by this nothing disrespectful or rude. It is just that we think we understand better through the give and take of a sometimes critical conversation. And since we have Socrates and Diogenes here, two philosophers, you can be sure that all of us will be emboldened to ask many questions."

"I will welcome such an exchange, General. We all revere Apollo, the father of Asclepius, and he is the patron of our courts in which the speech of luminous reason searches out Truth and Justice. Perhaps it would be wise, though, to appoint from among our number a judge or referee who will keep us on task and reign in any uncivil speech. I would think Sophocles, a man who has reached the age of wisdom, could be such a referee for our conversation – if he is willing."

Sophocles, who had been standing quietly behind Pericles in the shade of the tallest tree, came out into the sunlight and straightening himself out with the help of his cane answered. "If it is acceptable to the rest of our called assembly, I accept the appointment and will do my best to keep all rancor and mere quarrels from poisoning our new church of Asclepius."

Even Euripides, who did not like always being second to Sophocles, joined all the rest of the men nodding their heads in approval.

Sophocles then, like a director of one of his theatric productions, gave direction to the opening conversation. "Why don't you begin, Therakleios, by explaining to us what the brotherhood takes to be the special *daimon* which inhabits the Asclepieia. I think this is a good place to start our conversation. Only let us find seats out of the sun here on some of the larger stones that lie beneath these ever green fir trees. And it would be good if my body servant would fill the cups I have brought along – so everyone can enjoy the cold water that flows from the depths of our acropolis."

After everyone was seated and the cups filled with cold clear water had been passed to everyone, Therakleios began to explain what he took to be the bonding spirit of the brotherhood of Asclepius.

"Let me begin, guided by the genius of Pindar. Are you familiar with the Ode he addresses to Heiron of Syracuse. This Ode commemorates Heiron's horse race victory in the Pythian Games. Perhaps our young men, Alcibiades, Critias, and General Hagnon, have never heard this song or read a text of the Ode. Pindar composed this ode thirty-eight years ago, a year before Heiron's death. Not only does the Ode celebrate the victory, but Pindar's song seeks to encourage and console Heiron who is mortally ill. It is in this context that Pindar retells the story of Asclepius' heroic but tragic life and how he became the hero of the healing arts."

Young Critias, always striving to be first among Socrates' circle of youths, was the first to interrupt the priest from Epidaurus, hoping to impress Socrates with a show of his philosophical skepticism concerning stories of the gods and demigods.

"Sir, you are of course much wiser and learned than one as young as I could ever be. Yet, I must ask you, do you really believe all the stories Pindar spins in his efforts to praise the rich and powerful men who so often win at our various Sporting Festivals, whether it be the Olympian, Nemean, Isthmian, or Pythian Games? Could it be that Pindar's stories are mostly about pleasing his patron who will pay well to have the poet glorify him by associating his family with the gods? Or do you think that the inspiration that guides the compositions of Pindar is indeed unspoiled by the desire for money and gain? Should we grant his stories the authority of divine revelation, bearers of sacred and unassailable Truth, or should we see them as testaments to human vanity – rife with error and delusions of grandeur?"

Therakleios smiled graciously and without any impatience or condescension replied to young Critias.

"How many bards and poets, Critias, do you think have plied their art throughout our villages and cities now for at least the past five hundred years? And yet we cherish and sing over and over again the songs of so few. The best known poets who have been honored by scribes like Onomacritos, or other collectors of antiquities, and actually have their lyrics written down is even fewer. I do not myself presume to know everything that has guided this selection which has been handed down over and over again to succeeding generations – our tradition. But I must say, when I hear these select songs, when I ponder the longer epic compositions whether they be Homer's, Hesiod's or the work of forgotten bards whose genius is passed on without honor to their names; I find in these works a repository of human experience that is far wiser than my paltry limited experience. I must admit I find in this tradition what is timeless and touches the very deepest concerns of my existence. Therefore I have no difficulty in humbly acknowledging that the musical lyricism of our celebrated poets, however base their instruments, is indeed a kind of sacred medium. Poets like Pindar reflect on the limits of our human condition and contemplate the gulf between the mortal, changing, corruptible nature of our own animal bodies and the immortal, eternal, incorruptible dimension our mind or soul envisions through its contemplation of some deathless divine order. Listen to Pindar's own words!

'One race there is of men and one of gods, but from one mother draw we both our breath, yet is the strength of us diverse altogether, for the race of man is as naught, but the brazen heaven abideth, a habitation steadfast unto everlasting.'

Unlike the animals around us, we can contemplate our own death and then imagine ourselves deathless. This peculiarly human capacity for some makes death more painful and for others offers a hope that robs death of its sting. I must say, that though Pindar is just recently departed from the land of the living, I, at least, will not hesitate to be one who will humbly pass him on by retelling his stories and writing them down. I do not worry myself about how this wisdom has made its way to me, whether a god literally whispered in the ear of the poet or whether the wisdom, wedded to human genius, somehow through the tangle of human all too human base motives nevertheless shines through.

Critias, there are those in Athens, I hear, that denigrate Themistocles as a man who simply driven by greed helped save Athens and perhaps all of Hellas from the Persian conquest. They say it was just to increase his family fortune that he persuaded the Athenians to build the trireme fleet which eventually saved the freedom of Athenians. After all, they say, was not Themistocles family of shipbuilders those that would profit most from the state's decision to build a large fleet of triremes? What these people overlook is that many Athenian citizens found Themistocles counsel aligned with the general interest of the Athenian state and therefore did not listen to Themistocles detractors. Those who denigrated Themistocles' naval policy, blinded by the fires of individual avarice that always are at work in a commercial city like Athens, could not see the general interest. I suppose, Critias, you are asking whether Pindar is merely a clever fellow who has come up with a scheme to fleece rich and vain sportsmen. If you will bear with me then, Critias, let me try to show you the wisdom and images of the sacred I cherish in Pindar's story of Asclepius. Perhaps you along with most Athenians then will be convinced to embrace the spirit of Asclepius Pindar presents. I believe that this spirit will contribute to the health and well being of the Athenian state."

"Please, Therakleios, continue." Sophocles was pleased that the priest had met young Critias' skepticism head on. Sophocles had heard from others that the religious brotherhoods devoted to Asclepius were not antagonistic to philosophy and its accompanying inquiries into Nature. The sophistication of Therakleios' response to Critias made it clear that the Asclepieia, led by such a priest, would not fan the fires of religious superstition or the fanatical zeal of a narrow-minded and intolerant orthodoxy like that which had led to the prosecution and exile of Sophocles' and Pericles' friend, Protagoras.

Therakleios nodded and returned to his account of Pindar's story of Asclepius.

"If it were in his power, Pindar writes in his *Ode to Heiron*, he would persuade Cheiron, should he still be dwelling in his cavern, by the magic of *our sweet-voiced songs*, to send another son of Apollo or Asclepius himself to Syracuse along with Pindar's Ode so that such a *healer of hot plagues* might cure Heiron. Pindar's story of Asclepius teaches us that it is within our reach to help those who suffer, but we must at the same time acknowledge the limits of our therapy – we cannot finally be cured from our own mortality. In Pindar's own words our maxim must always be:

> '*It behoveth to seek from gods things meet for mortal souls, knowing the things that are in our path and to what portion we are born. Desire not thou, dear soul, a life immortal, but use the tools that are to thine hand.*'

So, even if Asclepius himself were to come to Heiron's bed of illness, there can be no guarantee that death can be sent away.

How does Pindar's story bring us to this maxim which guides the spirit of every physician who honors Asclepius? It is important in Pindar's story that we appreciate the duality of human nature. The story makes clear that Asclepius is both a mortal and yet one who bears within him the seed of divine transcendence.

Asclepius is born of a young woman who has lain with youthful Apollo, the god whose special epiphany is likened unto the power that turns what is dark and mysterious into the illumined and understandable. And so Asclepius will employ the god-given inner light of reason to search out every means possible to heal and prolong human life. But Asclepius is also one with us, born of a mortal woman prone to error and sickness unto death. In the language of his story, Asclepius' mother Koronis ...*had lain with Phoibos of the unshorn hair, and bares within her the seed of a very god.* However, while pregnant, Koronis is struck with plague along with many of her townspeople. It is said that she has been unfaithful to her immortal lover. Her dying plague wracked body is consigned to the funeral pyre. But her unborn son, Asclepius, is pulled from the fire by Apollo who could not abide that his seed come to naught. Apollo then takes the infant to the cavern of the centaur, Cheiron. Here, according to Pindar's story, the untamed Centaur teaches Asclepius the healing arts. Of course, we must remember that Apollo himself is surnamed *Paieon* because he is the physician of the gods themselves. And so Pindar's story reminds us that the tutelage of Cheiron only works upon the divine element within Asclepius. However, when Asclepius comes of age, a mortal animated by the divine gift of Reason; then, like Prometheus, Sisyphus, Tantalos, and other of our demigods and titans, Asclepius would challenge even the gods - stealing fire from heaven, chaining up death, sharing with mere mortals the nectar and ambrosia of the immortals and, if he could, storm heaven and grant immortality to we creatures of a day. Asclepius is human, all too human, and can err and offend against that immutable order of creation which consigns all human creatures to mortality. The end of Asclepius' life, according to Pindar, is tragic:

> '*Yet hath even wisdom been led captive of desire of gain. Even him did gold in his hands glittering beguile for a great reward to bring back from death a man already prisoner thereto; wherefore, the hands of the son of Kronos smote the twain of them through the midst, and bereft their breasts of breath, and bright lightning dealt them doom.*'"

Therakleios paused, offering others the opportunity to explore with him the meaning of the Asclepius story.

Diogenes of Apollonia had been listening intently to the priest's interpretation of Pindar's retelling of ancient legends concerning Asclepius. He was impressed with the priest's understanding of the religious basis for their commitment to the healing arts. "Therakleios, there is much wisdom in Pindar's tale of Asclepius. We in Apollonia have not yet read or heard this Ode of Pindar. I would be very grateful if you would allow me to copy your text, if you have one. I hope that you will have time to speak at more length about the work of the brotherhood of Asclepius. I find it surprising that your brotherhood has not expunged this story of the tragic end of Asclepius' life. It is rather unusual that the priesthood serving the divine hero of a cultic center would include such a story chronicling the demigod's transgression or flaw."

Therakleios smiled warmly, thankful that one as learned as Diogenes found his explanation, as he put it, one with 'much wisdom'. "I will be glad to copy for you this Ode. I have memorized it and will dictate it to one of my assistant scribes. As for the tragic end of Asclepius, it is a cautionary tale that keeps us humble and careful in honoring our vows to share our knowledge of the healing arts. All members of the brotherhood have vowed to accept only offerings for the maintenance of the sanctuary and modest provision for the feeding and clothing of the few brothers charged with overseeing the Athenian Asclepieion."

Diogenes was about to ask a question about how, specifically, the brotherhood participated in the actual application of the healing arts. But before he could continue, Theophilias, the young acolyte of Diopeithes, had risen to his feet so that he might pursue a question about the brotherhood's understanding of the role of human wrongdoing as a cause of such outbreaks of disease as the plague now killing so many Athenians.

Theophilias was in his mid-twenties and unlike most young men of the aristocracy showed no interest in associating with Socrates or any of the metic Sophists who visited Athens. Theophilias not only looked like his father, Diopeithes, but as his acolyte shared in his father's traditional piety. His father was the same man who had persuaded the Assembly to pass an edict forbidding the publication or teaching of any doctrines which denied the agency of the gods in directing the motions of the heavenly bodies and the affairs of men. It was this edict which had been employed to bring about the prosecution of Anaxagoras and his exile from the city. Later the threat of charges of atheism and a prosecution in terms of this same edict had also driven Protagoras out of the city. It was apparent to Pericles that Sophocles wanted somehow to win over the approval of religious leaders like Diopeithes so as to avoid trouble between the brotherhood of Asclepius, a religious community that had made its peace with philosophy and its speculations concerning Nature, and the more conservative and literal minded religious establishment of Athens.

"Therakleios, as you may be well aware, many of our citizens have found our current leadership sometimes to be too lenient, if not sympathetic, with metic professional teachers who have filled our young people's heads with atheistic and morally suspect conjectures about the role of religion in our city's life. I am sure that your brotherhood will do its part to preserve our religious traditions and especially promote reverence for Apollo of holy Delphi as well as his sister Artemis and all the other gods of Olympus. In this regard, I have a question concerning your understanding of Pindar's retelling of our sacred traditional stories of Apollo and his son, Asclepius. It is not clear to me what the brotherhood of Asclepius believes with regard to the gods' punishment of those who anger them. So let me ask you straight out. Do you believe that part of Pindar's story in which he explains that it is Apollo who causes the plague to strike his unfaithful lover, Koronis, and her neighbors? This is part of the story you seem to have skipped over. But Pindar himself in the very Ode you are citing makes clear that the gods punish those who offend them with sickness unto death. Is this not what Pindar means when the Ode relates that Apollo, angry that his consort had taken to be her husband a mortal,

> *'...sent his sister* (Artemis) *fierce with terrible wrath to go to Lakeria..., and thus a doom adverse blasted her* (Koronis') *life and smote her down: and of her neighbors many fared ill therefore and perished with her; so doth a fire that from one spark has leapt upon a mountain lay waste wide space of wood......?'*

Do you agree with Pindar, Therakleios, that there are circumstances in which the diseases that afflict us are punishment by the gods for our transgressions? And when it is clear that such is the case, it is not the physician that we should turn to, but the priest or the soothsayer who knows how to appease the anger of the gods. It may even be that wicked or misguided men in our midst have to be held accountable and purged from the city if the wrath of the gods is to be turned away. Would the brotherhood of Asclepius, and you in particular, agree that ministers of the gods must be willing to call sinners to account and urge their fellows to serve the gods and their city by excommunicating the evil doers? Think of our story concerning Oedipus the King of Thebes. Is it not clear that Apollo sends his blind prophet Teiresias warning Oedipus and all the people of Thebes that the plague will not be turned away from their city until the murderer of Laius is driven from the city? We who honor the gods must not gainsay the truth of such prophecy. All of our religion hinges on this belief that the gods know the future and from time to time reveal to our seers and holy men the fate that awaits those men who offend the gods.

Therakleios turned to the poets for help. "Theophilias, your question is straightforward enough, but I think there is no easy uncomplicated answer to your question. We have all seen Euripides production of Medea recently. I happened to be visiting Athens during your last City Dionysia, and, like the rest of the audience, I was both enchanted and perplexed by Euripides' tragic rendition of our stories concerning Medea and Jason. How could Medea, who kills her own children, escape and be taken in and protected by Athens and King Aegeus? Has Euripides deviated from our oldest and most sacred stories of Medea? No one, least of all you Theophilias, would dare to say so, since we all are familiar with this venerable story about Medea's stay in Athens. Surely, as everyone in the audience expected, a woman who commits the atrocity of slaying her own sons should be punished by the gods immediately. What does Euripides' Chorus teach us about divine ways in the last words of his production? Euripides, would you recite those closing lines? I am sure you remember them, since you wrote them and rehearsed their recitation numerous times with your singers.

Euripides was quite pleased that Therakleios had called upon him to answer the literal-minded acolyte, son of Diopeithes. Standing up and chanting as though he were a member of one of his choruses, Euripides recited,

"Many a fate doth Zeus dispense, high on his Olympian throne; oft do the gods bring things to pass beyond man's expectation; that, which we thought would be, is not fulfilled, while for the unlooked-for god finds out a way; and such hath been the issue of this matter."

"Thank you Euripides. You understand the point, Theophilias, I am sure. Even we priests and ministers of the gods' sacraments must in all humility acknowledge that the ways of the gods are often beyond human understanding. Pindar reminds us, '*From Zeus there cometh no clear sign to men*'. Therefore, we should not expect to see the hand of God immediately at work in every affair or condition of human interest. Ant then too, we must be on our guard against the words of the false seer whose vision is corrupted by love of money or deference to powerful men. Our brotherhood is open to the god's intervention should all human efforts to remedy human suffering fall short; but first the brotherhood deals with what is at hand for we humans and makes do with the Promethean gift of intelligence. We should by all means try to understand how sickness and disease overtake us, so that we might do our part to avoid unnecessary suffering. Finally, Theophilias, I see no contradiction between on the one hand philosophical and physical explanations which clarify how disease both enters and may be purged from our bodies, and, on the other hand, the claim that Divine Providence may be at work in making use of the operations of Nature." Therakleios hoped the answer would satisfy the young acolyte.

But Theophilias was not satisfied.

"Therakleios, I fear that your brotherhood's love of Pythagoras has darkened your mind to the obvious truths of our religion. I would hope that the brotherhood's rites at least include those like our Thargelia and holocaust sacrifices of Anthesteria. Given the extremities of the plague that now each day claims many victims; we must seek guidance from above and be open to the messages of our own prophets."

Sophocles answered Theophilias. "We need not worry on that score. I have witnessed the rituals of the Asclepieia in Epidaurus and can tell you that Therakleios does not neglect supplications to the gods acknowledging their power and our need to atone for those transgressions of the Laws of High Heaven. Indeed, one of the most sacred rites of the Asclepieia acknowledges that it is to the gods, and especially Apollo the Healer that we must turn to when all else fails. Next Spring we will all see, during our Athenian Asclepieia, the many priests of our temples ascending in a sacred procession to this place. They will approach the altar here, carrying laurel staffs wound in wool, so as to signify a supplication to Zeus's son, Apollo Paieon, which acknowledges the need for his divine intervention. I am sure, Theophilias, that your father will be most glad to join our procession."

The young acolyte could hear the irritation in Sophocles' voice. He realized that there was no point in further testing the piety of this priest brought to Athens by Pericles. Even Sophocles, always genial to all, could not be counted on to oppose the puffed up intellectuals who would ridicule and corrupt true piety. He could see that apart from Nicias and his son Hagnon, it was not likely that any of the others were men of genuine piety.

Pericles, usually impossible to read, had become agitated by Theophilias' last remarks about being open to the message of

Athens' prophets. In the final week of the Spartan occupation of Attica, Theophilias' father, Diopeithes, had conducted a public sacrifice near the Pynx just before the Assembly was convened to begin a review of Pericles' leadership in the War with Sparta. Diopeithes' reading of the entrails had insinuated that the gods had sent the plague to Athens as a result of the transgressions of the city's leadership. While Diopeithes did not mention the ancient blood guilt of Pericles' family, the Alkmeonids, he did ask for divine guidance in searching out whether or not gods were angry because of the desecration of the body of Aristeus, the son of the Corinthian hero Adeimantus. Pericles was sure that Diopeithes was blaming him for the plague and prophesying that the plague would not lift from Athens until Pericles be removed from power and sent packing in exile, like Oedipus the King of Thebes. It had been almost too much for Pericles to bear when the up and coming leader of the commoners, Creon, announced that he was acting on behalf of the people in leading the prosecution of Pericles in the special session of the Assembly. How, wondered Pericles, could the people have such a short memory and abandon him after all that he had done to empower the people? When the crass and vulgar Creon called on Diopeithes to offer up the invocation seeking the gods' blessing for their judicial review of Pericles generalship, Pericles left the Assembly grounds and gave instructions to the clerk of the Assembly that he was to be called when and if the Assembly drew up formal charges against him. No charges were made on that day, but just before he had set out for this meeting concerning the installation of the Asclepieia in Athens, a messenger had informed him that the Assembly would convene next week to take up his impeachment. Already, it has started, Pericles muttered under his breathe. He would not suffer standing quietly by here, even as he was undertaking his due deference to the piety of Athens, and let the young acolyte, like a puppet of Creon, paint Pericles with the stain of the *pharmakos* who must be driven from the city. And so, despite his own intention to keep this meeting free of the controversies challenging his leadership of Athens, he would not grant Diopeithes' son a pass to accuse him of impiety, a line of attack that had been taken in the courts and the Assembly in past political attacks on Pericles and his associates.

"Theophilias, our government is not that of Kings, priests, soothsayers and prophets. Why is it that a government that has helped rebuild all of the temples destroyed by the Persians, has arranged for generous stipends for the priestly families and the maintenance of their assigned rites and sanctuaries, and has been careful to maintain adherence in all our public festivals and to the traditional ceremonies and rites – having done all this has nevertheless earned the persistent hostility of your father and now yourself? I can understand the hostility of our enemies, the Spartans and their oligarchic allies. I can even understand how those of us who counsel avoiding a large hoplite engagement with the Spartan led invasion of Attica are being blamed for the overcrowding of Athens which may be contributing to the spread of the plague in our midst. But to suggest that our current leaders or I in particular are titanic sinners who have brought down the anger of the gods so that they have sent Death to stalk all those we love – this really is the height of presumption. It is a mean spirited show of piety that only sows divisiveness in our hour of great crisis when we must stand together to meet the determination of our enemies to utterly defeat Athens and strip her of all that makes her great. I am perfectly willing to be accountable to a deliberative body of our citizens who will consider some actual evidence as to whether I have corrupted my office or betrayed the general interest of Athenian citizens. But it is contrary to our institutions and laws to incriminate the accused with vague and unspecified claims that the gods have already marked the defendant as guilty. In a time like this when our citizens are already unsettled by the fear of the plague, it is throwing oil on a fire to incite others to believe it is caused by some one or few who allegedly are a religious pollution to the entire community. It will indeed be insufferable if the sickness of the plague which now threatens our capacity to resist destruction by the Spartans is exacerbated by a plague of disrespect for other citizens and a subversion of the due processes of our justice system."

Pericles stopped and with open hands asked Theophilias, "Can we not all agree to set aside our old animosities, graciously embrace the hope of the healing arts offered by the brotherhood of Asclepius, and united as one remain steadfast in our defense of Athens ?"

Before Theophilias could answer, Sophocles interrupted.

"General, young Theophilias' piety is sometimes so zealous that in his enthusiasm he mistakes our Athens for the ancient days when the gods banqueted with men, like Tantalos the father of Pelops, at Sipylos. In those long ago times, the man who offends the immortal gods, is marked out by the gods themselves and in due course one such as Tantalos is punished in Tartaros in a way fitting to his trespass. And so Tantalos, who sinned against the gods' hospitality by stealing the food of the immortals, hoping that their ambrosia and nectar might make him and his friends immortal, now must forever in Tartaros tremble with mortal anxiety beneath a monstrous boulder dangling by ever so slender a cord. What man among us today would claim such intimate dealings with the immortals of Olympus? We all want to live storied lives but we poets, prophets, diviners, and priests who call for inspiration in discerning the concourse of mortals and immortals must be very circumspect in the stories we tell about our fellows. And as you and I know, Pericles, when we are young plants circumspection has not yet flowered."

Pericles was not ready to dismiss Theophilias' call to prophetic judgment of prominent Athenians as the folly of youthful exuberance.

"If only everyone in Athens could be as wise as you, Sophocles, then religious piety like that of Theophilias and his father's would not so enflame our courts, our Assembly, and our Council with unreasoned passion and childish superstition. You are much more sanguine about those who claim to speak so unequivocally and dogmatically about the gods' judgment than I am. It is no easy thing to hear men such as Theophilias' father, Diopeithes, insinuate that it is Apollo's wrath with my sins that has unleashed Artemis' arrows of plague against my own sons, Xanthippus and Paralos, sending them down to Tartaros cursing their own father for their fate. Was it not enough that Protagoras, Anaxagoras and others who have been my friends have been chased from Athens by such misguided zeal? But I must say, Sophocles, I am very grateful that you have taken a leading role in bringing to our city a religious voice like that of Therakleios and his brotherhood - a voice of moderation and religious circumspection, both tolerant and reasonable in its reading of the divine presence in human affairs. I am sorry, I have spoken so bluntly. I suppose, like everyone else in Athens now, it is difficult to keep to an even demeanor when those so close to you waste away and you are powerless to stop it. I am curious about what others have to say about our plan to install the Asclepieia as one of our major Athenian holy days.

Our young priest seems to have his reservations because the brotherhood of Asclepius may not be zealous enough in their devotion to the miraculous intervention of the gods in human affairs. I wonder if others here today have their own reservations, despite the decision of the Council and the Assembly. Perhaps our resident philosopher, Socrates, is less than enthusiastic about adding the Asclepieia to our cycle of holy days on grounds quite different from that of Theophilias. I am thinking his silence up to now may mean he too has his doubts about Therakleios and his brotherhood. Perhaps he thinks they will only add more superstition to the irrational representations of our poets' theology, thus further confounding the already acrimonious and illogical discourse of our political debates."

Turning to Socrates, Pericles asked, "Socrates, can you in good conscience welcome Therakleios and his brotherhood of Asclepius to Athens? I do value your opinion and worry that should you be opposed, then the best of our youth will follow your view and make it very difficult for the institution of the Asclepieia to take root in Athens."

"General, I am honored that Sophocles has included me in this first congregation convened to welcome the brotherhood of Asclepius to Athens. I am not surprised that you find it worrisome that Socrates can sit quietly and listen, holding his tongue and not interrupting with endless questions. There must be something amiss if Socrates is not cross-examining anyone who proposes to explain the 'wisdom' of poets or anyone else."

Pericles nodded his head agreeably. "Yes, Socrates, this is what I am thinking."

"Well, General, this is one of those rare occasions when I am quite impressed with the subtle and thoughtful account of a priest's interpretation of our poets' stories concerning the gods and our heroes. I find much to ponder in the way Therakleios has explained the guiding spirit of the Asclepieia and the work of the brotherhood which attends to the sanctuary and ministry of Asclepius. He has given me so much to think about, I have been content to listen and sort out my own thoughts. I must say, that of all the poets, I, like Therakleios, find Pindar's stories of the divine nature most intriguing. When Sophocles mentioned the story of Tantalos just a minute ago, I was reminded of why I am so receptive to his stories. In retelling the old story of Tantalos and his son Pelops that had been passed down to him by other poets, Pindar warns his listeners of stories that are 'beyond the truth':

> *'Verily many things are wondrous, and haply tales decked out with cunning fables beyond the truth make false men's speech concerning them. For Charis, who maketh all sweet things for mortal men, by lending honor unto such maketh oft the unbelievable thing to be believed.... Meet is for a man that concerning the gods he speak honorably; for the reproach is less....'*

You all remember, I am sure, that Pindar revises the tale about the feast that Tantalos hosts for the gods. According to the older story, Tantalos, wishing to impress the gods with his willingness to withhold nothing from them, kills his own son Pelops, dismembers him, and then boils him in a pot, before serving him up as food for the gods. Pindar will have no part in telling such a dishonorable story about the divine nature – making the gods cannibals. He revises the story, explaining that Pelops' was born from his mother with an ivory shoulder and that Poseidon, taken with love for Pelops, took him off to Olympus just as his brother Zeus had done out of love for Ganymede. Thus, Pindar's poetry, at least in this instance, does not attribute to the gods an ignorance which leads to complicity in wicked conduct.

I am drawn to Therakleios' interpretation of Apollo's fathering of Asclepius and the human fate of Asclepius – striving to undo human mortality through the work of the divine principle of luminous Reason, but finally unable to cross over the separation between mortals and the immortals. I am sure there will be other occasions when I can talk in my own manner with Therakleios."

Pericles smiled. "I see, Socrates. You are ready to welcome the brotherhood of Asclepius, especially a man like Therakleios, because here is a priest whose theology intrigues you and you foresee many enjoyable hours, if not days, of discussion with him about divine matters and the true nature of piety."

"I am not completely selfish, General. One would have to be made out of stone, not flesh and blood, if the suffering of those who die from the plague, the tragedy of those who have contacted the disease while caring for those they love, and the fear of those still healthy – all would be without the palliative of any hope. It is not unreasonable to hope that the gift of the divine principle within us may make headway in healing our mortal afflictions. It is because Therakleios has made clear to me that this is part of the work of the brotherhood and the hope encoded in the story of Apollo's son, Asclepius, that I will do my part to assist their ministry."

Sophocles, even more pleased than Pericles by Socrates' endorsement of the installation of the Asclepieia in Athens, could not resist asking what kind of assistance Socrates had in mind. "Do you plan, Socrates, to march in the holy procession during the festival? You know you would have to don a priestly garment and divest yourself of that threadbare garment you call a robe. You might be asked as a supplicant then to offer a prayer in public."

Socrates pursed his lips as though about to carefully taste a new but possibly toxic mushroom. Then still facing General Pericles, but turning his eyes sideward towards Sophocles and with that unmistakable ironic voice that he saved for his attentive audience of young men, Socrates answered the question. "I am not a rich man and so I would be unable to purchase such a robe. I would not ask for a stipend from the state or the brotherhood – for then my role as a ministrant would be a burden not a service. I would not deign to inflict on any congregation of those who honor Asclepius and his divine father, Apollo Paieon, my stumbling, bungling speech offered to the god. It seems that what little fluency I possess completely leaves me when I attempt on behalf of myself and others to petition and praise the gods. I am afraid such a service would only be viewed by the gods and those who worship them as worse than Prometheus' counterfeit gift to Zeus – bones wrapped in glistening fat!"

Sophocles now was very curious. "What then, Socrates, will you offer in service to the brotherhood's work on behalf of Asclepius?"

"I will follow Therakleios' guidelines for the offerings which are most acceptable to the brotherhood. While I am not much of a farmer and now days keep very little livestock, my small holdings in Alopeke still include about a dozen hens and usually a couple of roosters. The brotherhood, I am sure, will have its hens in hand when they come to their grounds here near the sanctuary. After all, they will need to eat – and a ready supply of eggs will help with their food provisions. I would like to give a gift, as one of our clever township treasurers has quipped, which is 'the kind of gift that keeps on giving'. And so I promise this day before heaven and this first congregation called to welcome Apollo's son to Athens, that every fifth year as long as I live I will bring my finest, most randy, and irresistibly handsome rooster to service all the hens of the brotherhood. I hope this gift pleases the god and will be acceptable to Therakleios and his brotherhood."

Therakleios laughed with Pericles, Sophocles, Crito, Critias, and Alcibiades. The priest of Asclepius stood up and stepped over to Socrates side. "Let me embrace you, Socrates. Your service is perfect and I look forward to our friendship and discussions. I hope our meetings will be more frequent than the arrival of our ever randy, young, and handsome roosters."

Sophocles did not want the introduction of Therakleios to pass without an opportunity for Nicias, now the leader of the aristocratic party in Athens, to voice his support for the installation of the Asclepieia in Athens. "Nicias, I know you especially honor Apollo and have made arrangements to house one of his diviners in your own household. It is wonderful that you have offered to help finance the construction costs of the sanctuary. I trust that you are happy with this site and find Therakleios a worthy choice for leading the brotherhood of Asclepius here in Athens."

Nicias, always reticent to speak in public for fear he should unwittingly antagonize the people, seemed to be at a loss for words. The only thing Nicias feared more than the disapproval of the people was the anger of the gods. He was deeply troubled by Diopeithes' prophetic warning concerning the gods' displeasure with the way the Athenian Council and Board of Generals had profaned the bodies of Aristeus and the Spartan diplomats by denying them a decent burial. Still, General Nicias was a man of honor, and so he rose from his seat and turned towards General Pericles and at the same time addressed Theophilias, the son of Diopeithes.

"All of the ten tribes' generals concurred with the decision to treat Aristeus, the Corinthian general and Spartan diplomat the way the Spartans and Corinthians have treated our men and any of our allies' men captured at sea. Athenians, even those on merchant ships unfortunate enough to be intercepted and boarded by Corinthian or Spartan triremes, have had their throats slit and been thrown overboard at sea. Two of my own nephews have perished in this way. When Aristeus fell into our hands and when our interrogation made it clear that it was he who had urged the Spartans and the rest of her allies to carry out such executions of any of our allies or Athenians captured at sea; then the vote at the Strategeion and the Council was unanimous to likewise execute Aristeus and deny him a proper burial. Thus, if such behavior is an offense to the gods, and it may well be; then all of us, not just Pericles, must appease the god. I have sent to Delphi and asked the Oracle about all this. The priests of Apollo have interpreted the Pythian prophet's response to my petition and they have assured me that it is pleasing to the gods that the Asclepieia will now be observed in Athens. As to whether Apollo or any of the other gods are angered by both Spartan and Athenian withholding of proper burial rites from their slain enemies, the Hosoi reminded me that all the Hellenes are dear to Zeus *Meilichios* and his son, Apollo *Paieon*. I hope and pray that this service to Apollo *Paieon* and his son, Asclepius, will speed the lifting of the plague from our city. My son and I have offered further service to Apollo and will return to Delphi again next summer asking the god's guidance as to what this service might be. So knowing it is with Apollo's blessing that we bring the Asclepieia to Athens, I am honored to be of service to the god in this way. It is my prayer that Zeus and his son Apollo will accept our service and send the evil thing of corruption in our midst back to Tartaros."

General Pericles seconded Nicias' politic piety. "Nicias, all Athenians share in your prayer. I am especially grateful to you and others, like Critias father, Callaeschrus, who hold the respect of so many of the Eupatrids, that since our Council and Assembly have rejected the Spartan demands, you have accepted the will of the people and have closed ranks with your fellow citizens in the defense of our city and empire."

Pericles was relieved that neither Nicias' piety nor ambition would lead him to take part in Cleon's prosecution of Pericles. Turning towards Sophocles and then Therakleios, he thanked them for their service and asked for the priest's benediction, hoping to end the meeting before any further exchanges might undo the concordance of the two most powerful leaders in Athens. "Therakleios, it would appear that all of us have had an opportunity to welcome you and begin our religious instruction on the rites and service of the Asclepieia. Unless someone has some pressing concern to air, perhaps you can end our meeting with a prayer to Apollo *Paieon*, asking his blessing on our undertaking to embrace the healing arts and healing hope of Athens' Asclepieia."

It was late afternoon when all but Socrates, his neighbor and oldest friend Crito, and Socrates' two young friends, Alcibiades and

Critias, made their way back down the rocky path to Tripod Road and then to their city homes. Sophocles had arranged temporary accommodations for Therakleios in a sturdy stone guest house near the Bouleuterion. Therakleios', along with a few foreign dignitaries, then were granted some refuge from the plague, since their residence was in one of the few spaces near the Agora which remained free of the squalor and overcrowded conditions of the temporary ramshackle straw and mud huts which housed many of the poorer refugees of Attica. Even though the Spartan led occupation force had left Attica, most of the refugees had neither farm nor food to return to in their former outlying villages of Attica.

Socrates and Crito were in no hurry to return to the city down below, since the lingering heat of the afternoon would drive even more of the sick to the public fountains in the Agora. Those who had fled the countryside and were living in temporary huts had no cisterns or wells of their own. It was almost too much to bear to see those in the final stages of the plague, who suffered from what seemed to be an unquenchable thirst and appeared like some kind of living dead, stumbling and sometimes crawling towards the pools of filthy water that now were left unattended in the public fountains. It would be better to return to Crito's city house after sunset. His modest house was just off of the PanAthenaic Way, a five minute walk from the Altar of the Twelve Gods. By then, the walking sick would have left the public fountains near the Altar if they could, fearing that what little coin they carried in their purses, would be stolen by those even poorer and more desperate than them. Socrates had persuaded both Alcibiades and Critias to stay behind in the still shaded outcropping of the Acropolis, promising them a stimulating and philosophical conversation concerning the lessons of the Plague.

Socrates had stretched out, half reclining while leaning against one of the large boulders that somehow had come to rest on this one flat outcropping of the otherwise steep rocky south side of the acropolis. Alcibiades and Critias sat down across from him on the stone bench that had been positioned facing the fountain. Crito had decided he would sit higher up on a fallen tree trunk where the incline again began to slope steeply. Here he could listen to the conversation while enjoying a spectacular view of the city below reddened with the light of the western sun beginning its journey into Darkness. The shade of the tall firs now had disappeared, but the late afternoon sun here was yet cooled by the spray from the fountain and a breeze that here on the heights was cooler than down below.

It was Alcibiades who began their conversation. He had been unusually silent during the entire meeting with the Priest of Asclepius. Now, with no need to worry about offending the religious sensibilities of this small company of friends of Socrates, he could unburden himself with a question that had troubled him since learning from his household steward the details of the final days of his mother's fatal struggle with the plague. No doubt, Socrates would turn his question to and fro until it's searching out would lead to an inquiry concerning the improvement of the soul and virtue. But still, Alcibiades wanted to hear what the philosopher would make of his question.

"Socrates, I wanted to ask the priest if a pleasing illusion sincerely believed should be corrected if the truth which replaces the illusion is painful and robs the believer of all consolation and hope."

Socrates knew that the young man was thinking of his mother's death. Alcibiades had chosen to avoid any contact with his mother after it was certain that she had become infected with the plague. His mother had suffered with the plague over a three week period, before dying with only a slave at her side just two days after the summer's occupation of Attica had ended.

"Let me ask you, Alcibiades to give an example of what you mean by this question. Then we can examine whether or not there is some wider principle which might illumine the issues raised by your example."

"I am thinking of the circumstances of my mother's death. There are those who are angry with me because I did not go to her and directly assist in her care. But she herself had sent word to me while I was camping outside the city walls with my cavalry unit that I should not risk the contagion of the Plague which now had found its way into my city home and infected her. So I stayed outside of the city the entire course of her illness. Indeed, I had determined even before my mother Dinomache came down with the plague that I would stay away from the city as much as possible, unless my superiors ordered me to go there. I must admit that even today I would not have come to this meeting, having to make my way through the city streets filled with the stench of plague and rotting corpses, if it had not been for knowing that General Pericles had a hand in arranging it. My friends, like you Socrates, I could easily meet outside the city walls in some pleasant, clean, and open place, now that the Spartans have left Attica. Anyway, I did everything I could short of coming to our house and her sickroom. I arranged to have an Orphic priest visit her, thinking he would provide her with comfort. Whether or not their shared faith helped console her, I don't know. But I learned that within ten days, this priest himself became infected with the Plague and is now dying. Having considerable wealth, I spared no expense in procuring a physician who would treat her. He visited her twice, my household stewardess tells me, and then stopped coming after he too came down with the plague. Somehow Debra, the Judean slave you met, Socrates, at the PanAthenaic Festival two years ago, has been able to be in the house and even in her sick room without falling ill. She tells me that my mother was serene in her last hours and kept muttering as she refused the water offered to her, that now was the hour when 'my corruptible flesh will be burned away and my soul will fly free to join the other thrice-born in the heavenly fields of the Third Age.' She died then quietly and with a child-like smile on her face, even as her cheeks, neck, and the rest of her body were covered with hideous red blotches and festering open sores. I am a warrior and a man now, but I will not deny that hearing of her death, I grieved in memory of the warm and unconditional love I knew as a child in the arms of my mother. Long ago, I learned that there can be no return to that kind of love. But I honored my mother in a fashion that would please her. I have commissioned a sculptor to add to our fountain a small stone façade with her name and a scene showing her soul, like a butterfly, being led by Orpheus and his flute upward to the Third Heaven. Am I duplicitous, Socrates, by so inscribing a monument to her faith? Should I have gone to her bedside as a good son? Should I, if I loved her, found a way to console her even as in the name of truth, I disillusioned her? Is the error that consoles the childish faith in the face of inevitable death to be cast aside? What could I give her that would provide the comfort accorded by what you and I regard as illusion?"

"I was saddened when I heard of your mother's death, Alcibiades. It would be presumptuous of me or anyone else to hold you blameworthy in any way for the manner in which you treated your mother. Putting aside the question of our responsibility for other persons' convictions, I would think we best start with an easier formulation of the question."

"What would that formulation be, Socrates?"

"I should ask the question this way, 'Are my convictions better founded and apt to promote a sounder well-being and virtuous character if they are forged through a life-long search for truth – even if this truth requires the acceptance of what our poets call the tragic side of the life of mortals?' I see many of our citizens now in what appears to be the throes of a complete disregard for honor and their responsibility to the city. They complain that it makes no difference whether or not one is pious and tends to the gods since both the pious and the impious are struck down by the plague. They seem to believe that if the gods do not reward the pious with long life and happiness and the impious with suffering such as that brought by the plague, then there can be no other foundation for justice and honor. They then conclude, finding now that their religious convictions fail to comfort them, that they should give themselves over entirely to pleasure seeking and not abstain even from the kinds of actions of lust and greed that they formerly had thought wrong. It never occurs to them to ask, as you have Alcibiades, whether the convictions they formerly held, which do not sustain their honor and righteousness in the face of death, have failed them because they are not true. What do you think, Critias? Will this help us begin in a simpler way to make some headway in addressing at least part of Alcibiades' question about comforting convictions?"

Critias was not so sure that this approach would make much headway. "Socrates, this only begs the question, 'what is truth?'. It seems to me listening to Therakleios' remarks about Pindar's stories that they are open to all kinds of interpretations. Is it really possible to say any one of these interpretations is truer than others or alone true? Once we acknowledge that the poet has himself interpreted a story about the gods, why should interpretive understanding stop with the poet? I cannot help thinking of Protagoras' maxim that 'man is the measure of all things'; and, in the case of our received stories about the gods, this means that each community of believers, or, perhaps, each individual believer, is the final arbiter of the meaning of the story. You applauded Pindar for rejecting the older story about the gods eating the stew made from Pelops' body, but, Socrates, you did not seem put off by Pindar's revision – which proposes that what actually happened was that Poseidon had abducted young Pelops to be his beloved, just as Zeus had taken Ganymede to be his cupbearer. Then later, so as to punish Tantalos for his theft of the food of immortality, Pelops, his son, is sent back '....*to be once more counted with the short-lived race of men'*. How are we to interpret that part of the story? Would I be in 'error' if I held the conviction that powerful men who, like Zeus and Poseidon, are superior to others, may do as the gods and steal away the young boy they find infatuating?"

Socrates smiled at the young men and then turned to Crito, a man like him now in his fifth decade. "You see, my friend, how difficult it is to converse with young men with nimble and inquisitive minds? Critias is right. The search for truth in the company of the poets will lead us into a labyrinth from which not even Daidalos himself could escape. Since our sunlight will soon disappear, and we do not want to make our way down the stone path in the dark, we shall have to postpone our inquiry. Alcibiades, will your question wait for another day?"

"Yes, of course Socrates!"

CHAPTER TWENTY-FIVE
THE DEATH OF THE OLYMPIAN
(429 B.C.)

....Pericles, because of his position, his intelligence, and his known integrity, could hold them in check. It was he who led them, rather than they who led him, and, since he never sought power from any wrong motive, he was under no necessity of flattering them; in fact he was so highly respected that he was able to speak angrily to them and to contradict them......... So, in what was nominally a democracy, power was really in the hands of the first citizen.

(Thucydides, *History of the Peloponnesian War*, Bk. II; 65)

Socrates: It is not contentiousness that makes me to ask, but a true desire to know what you consider the right standard of public life in our city. Or when you embark upon a public career, pray will you concern yourself with anything else than how we citizens can be made as good as possible? If then the good man ought to contrive this for his own city, carry your mind back to those men of whom you spoke a little earlier, and tell me whether you still think they proved themselves good citizens — Pericles and Cimon and Miltiades and Themistocles. Are the Athenians said to be improved by means of Pericles or, quite the contrary, to have been corrupted by him? For I am told that Pericles made the Athenians idle and cowardly and talkative and covetous, *because he was the first to establish pay for service among them.*

(Plato, Gorgias: 515, c-e)

Pericles' sickness began mid-day on the sixth day of Boedromion, the day Athenians had set aside for memorializing their victory over the Persians at Marathon and the many soldiers who had died since then in Athens' wars with other Hellenes. Pericles and Aspasia had been supervising servants as they polished General Pericles hoplite armor and weapons in preparation for the Marathon parade when Pericles first felt the onset of a pounding headache and a kind of burning inside his throat and ears. Pericles first thought this might have been merely some passing discomfort caused by something they had eaten that day. He had been determined to remain cheerful and like any military man was not going to let a headache keep him from marching with his tribal regiment in tomorrow's parade. After all, despite all the grumbling in Athens about his policy of avoiding a hoplite engagement with the occupying Spartan forces in Attica, his tribe had once again reelected him as their general and thus made possible his resumption of the supreme military command. And so after they had finished with his armor he spent the remainder of the afternoon resting in the shade of his courtyard, discussing with Aspasia the speech he would deliver tomorrow at the Marathon Day ceremonies by the Altar of the Twelve Gods. But by the time the sun had set that evening, Pericles had become so ill that he could not keep his supper down. After several episodes of convulsive regurgitation, he was overtaken with a high fever and a relentless thirst which could not be quenched. Even water would not stay down and the thirst only seemed to worsen with the convulsions which wracked his stomach and throat after every attempt to take in water.

Over night the pain had moved from Pericles' head and settled in his chest so that the pain accompanied by congestion in the lungs led to a coughing that failed to clear the chest. Neither Aspasia nor Pericles slept during the night and when they saw in the first light of morning the red blotches on Pericles chest and small enflamed pustules breaking out on his shoulders and arms; both knew what the skin sores portended. Pericles had seen just these symptoms and their attendant underlying disease take the lives of both of his legitimate sons, Xanthippus and Paralus, within the last year. Indeed, near the beginning of last summer, all his efforts to arrange for the assistance of the best medical care had not saved either of his sons' lives. Then, not long after their deaths, his younger sister who had become quite dear to him also died of the plague. All three had died within three weeks once these symptoms had appeared. Their cases had been especially lethal. The disease not only took these victims more quickly than was normal, but seemed more contagious. The two physicians and all the servants who had provided the actual medical treatments contracted the disease shortly after treating Pericles' sons and sister. When the death of the Alkmeonid family physicians became known throughout Athens, it became almost impossible to find any physicians willing to take on the care of those sickened by the plague. Indeed, the plague's fatality in Pericles' household, more than the deaths of any other notables, added to the general despair which made many of those who later fell sick with the plague even less able to resist its lethal course. People said to one another, 'If Pericles' famous physicians and Alkmeonid wealth can not ward off the disease, than what hope do any of us have?'

So, knowing all that had happened to those who came into contact with members of his family who had died of the plague, Pericles had already thought through how he would manage his own sickness if overtaken by this disease. This was why his self examination of his condition this morning had made him so agitated when Aspasia insisted on applying an ointment to soothe the burning itchy rash that now was spreading over his entire body.

"Aspasia, I can bear up under this and will not allow the sickness to rob me of my dignity and gratitude for the happiness you more than anyone else have brought to me. But what I cannot bear is the possibility that I could be the occasion and cause of your death by the plague. You must stay away from me! There has not been one moment in our time together that I have not done my utmost to defend and cherish you. I will not, if I must succumb to this disease, let it defile this intent, this spirit, which up to now has animated my love for you. So please, leave this room, hang thick curtains in all the windows and doorway of my sick room, and if you want me to have peace of mind while I contend with whatever it is that Nature and the gods have in store for me – then honor our love and stay clear of my contagion. You will need now to send word to General Nicias that I will be unable to attend today's ceremonies and it is my wish that he deliver the tribute to those of our soldiers who have recently given their lives for our city."

"I have already sent a messenger to General Nicias, informing him that you have become very ill and you are now unable to join the rest of the Generals in the Procession. I am sure that he will arrange for another speaker if he himself does not wish to deliver the funeral oration for this year's fallen soldiers."

"Please, then, my love, be gone from me, before this damnable disease also infects you!"

Aspasia could not hide the tears that now streamed down her cheeks. Lest Pericles' agitation make him even weaker, she had put the ointment aside; but she still sat on the bench she had pulled up next to Pericles' bed. "Pericles, even if I knew that being at your side now would certainly lead to my death, I would never abandon you when you are in mortal danger. I have seen you stand by your friends and family even as the plague struck them down. I could not live with myself if I fled from you when you yourself now wrestle with the demon of death. Besides, the doctors have told me that those who have already been infected with the disease and then recovered, are immune to a second infection. I am quite sure that as a girl in Miletus I contacted this disease and then recovered after a month or so."

"At least you must wear a veil so that you do not inhale any of the vapors that may come from my breathing and carry the contagion of the plague. Go to the kitchen and find clean cloth that can be dipped in pine resin and then cut the cloth so as to cover your mouth and nose. Such a veil should keep you clear of any vapors carrying some kind of polluting particulate – should this be one of the ways the plague spreads from the infected to the uninfected. If you insist on staying with me, I will not have you touching me at all. If you do take these precautions, we will minimize the chances of you catching the plague from me. And no more tears! We will have much to talk about should this be my time to die."

Aspasia left the room and was gone only a few moments before she returned, veiled as Pericles had instructed. She carried with her a tray bearing a pitcher of water and a small bowel of porridge. When she entered the room, she found Pericles sitting up on his couch which he had pushed against the windowless wall of his sleeping room. He had wrapped himself in the cloak he had worn yesterday and sat up with his back supported by the wall. This position, at least temporarily, provided relief from the terrible coughing and stomach convulsions that had robbed him of all sleep during the night. When Aspasia entered the room, now dressed in a saffron dress that covered her from neck to feet and veiled with a dark red hood that covered everything but her eyes, Pericles, sick as he felt, smiled, glad that Aspasia had returned.

"Aspasia, even all that drapery cannot hide your beauty. I am reminded of the very first time I saw you – the symposium at my brother's home when he had hired you and others to provide the entertainment for his guests. That evening, let me see, must have been twenty or so years ago. Then too, you entered the room draped and veiled like some exotic courtesan from the Great King's Palace of Susa or the Pharaoh's court at Memphis. When you removed the veil that evening, I was smitten by Eros with such force that I knew I would not be able to sleep, eat, or carry on my daily responsibilities unless I could hold you close. And so I moved heaven and earth to bring you into my arms: divorcing my noble born wife, alienating my oldest son, Xanthippus, and providing my many aristocratic political opponents with endless opportunities to slander me since they could never accept you as my wife, but only as a hetaera. I tell you today that I would do it all over again. And as I look at you now, even though my sickness has made me ugly to myself, I desire to meet your gaze and feel as I always have in your presence the joy of our intimacy, a joy which when all else has failed me assures me that I am not alone in this often dark and cruel world. So yes, I am glad you will stay with me, and may the gods who cherish love protect you from the death-dealing plague that will take me from you."

"Still the charmer, after all these years, my love - but is it not possible that you may recover? Why do you say the disease 'will' take you? Should we not fight together as we always have in the face of adversity? It seems this morning, as bad as the night was for you, that you are a little better. I have brought you cold water and a corn meal porridge which should be very easy on your stomach. You must try to eat and drink so as to give your body the sustenance it needs to fortify you against the attacks of whatever it is that works to harm you." Aspasia pulled beside the bed the small table that Pericles sometimes used as a stand for the room's lantern and set the pitcher of water and bowl of porridge on the table.

"I will drink. I feel so parched and hot inside, and yet no matter how much water I drink my thirst does not diminish. It is as though all at once I must be Tantalus and one of the unfortunate souls condemned to carry water in a sieve. I would quench my thirst, but the disease seems to burn through the water so I remain parched and dry. My body seems like a sieve that spews forth whatever I take in. The porridge, I dare not take now. My stomach, I know, will not accept it and I will not spend all morning with my stomach feeling as though it is turned inside out and is straining to choke me to death by throwing its solid contents up my throat. As for recovering from my illness, I think it is unlikely. In all my sixty-six years, the last three years have sapped my strength and rendered me more vulnerable than all of the battles and crises I have survived throughout my three decades of military and political leadership in Athens. I am so worn out, so frail in spirit, that there is nothing to call upon, no resilient life force or powerful will to oppose the course of Nature's script for all mortals. Perhaps later I will be able to eat a little. For now, while I am lucid and still in full possession of my hearing and ability to speak, I need to discuss with you how best to take care of our household should I die soon. And since I will not ask any citizens who now share in the governance of Athens to risk their life by visiting me, I would hope that you now are willing to be my confidant and advisor, continuing as before in discussing how my policies and their legacy might fare in Athens after my death. We will not worry whether such a conversation between us is only a monstrous egoism on my part or, perhaps, an inquiry genuinely concerned about the common good of Athens' people and the city's reputation as a benefactor to posterity."

"Pericles, you put the philosophers to shame! There are very few men who could remain so serene, so self-possessed, and still look ahead to the future welfare of others when under assault by what might be a fatal sickness. If only those who charge you with being a cold, calculating man bent only on heaping up glory and power for yourself could know you as I do, they would cherish and love you rather than harass and prosecute you."

"Perhaps my opponents think I have grown too warm – they can not forgive me for my public display of my love for you. Indeed, when I was a young man, had a seer foretold that one day while I was general I would weep before the Council of Five Hundred as I pleaded on behalf of a woman – that she not be exiled from Athens; I would have become very angry and taken such a prophet to be a fool."

Aspasia sighed and, disregarding Pericles' instructions not to touch him, reached out and held his hand. "Athenian men will never understand our love for one another. They cannot conceive that your disposition towards me can be anything other than lust or a joyless responsibility – even though we have lived together now for twenty years and I have borne you a son."

Pericles gently withdrew his hand from Aspasia's and covered his mouth as he coughed. When he had stopped coughing and had drunk a small cup of water, he spoke with a voice already weak and faltering due to the prolonged over-night coughing spells and the burning dryness in his throat. "But everyone in Athens knows that you are now the mother of my only surviving heir. And it must occur to any moderately intelligent man that if our son is named after me, then I honor you and our marriage. You must keep young Pericles away from me. I am so grateful to the Generals for persuading the Council and the Assembly to pass legislation granting full citizenship to sons born of metic women married to citizens. Now the way is clear for young Pericles to make his way. No longer is our Pericles barred from citizenship and the offices of our government. I worry though, that should I not recover, you and our son will be vulnerable to those in Athens who would be happy if all traces of Pericles' legacy disappeared. We should talk now about how to keep you both safe."

Aspasia knew what Pericles was about to propose. "You will recover, so there is no need to make such plans."

"But, my dear, you know that if I die from this illness and our twelve year old son is fatherless, with no uncles or brothers, and is solely in the care of his mother who remains a widow and unattached to any Athenian household since she herself is a metic; there is no telling what will become of our young Pericles. Surely, you must know that it will be necessary for you to remarry as soon as possible. I would want you to marry well. Hopefully a citizen of means who can afford to promote the prospects of his adopted son. And if possible, my dear, I would think it wise to marry one who does not carry with him a long list of political adversaries who would not hesitate to harry and obstruct or otherwise make mischief against him or his adopted son. Promise me, Aspasia, that you will not wait long should I die to find such a husband so that you and Pericles might stay in Athens and our son may count upon the protection of a citizen and his household."

"I cannot think about this now. But I promise you, Pericles, by all that is holy in our love that I will so provide for our son that he may reach the full stature of citizenship and, like his father, stand for election to the highest offices of his tribe."

"It would be enough if he did well as a juror or a deme treasurer and served honorably in his military regimen, or, surviving all this, excelled as a merchant, a sculptor, a poet, or perhaps even one of our men of science – a philosopher. I have dedicated my life to serving a city that affords such many-sided possibilities to its citizens. If he is wise and wishes to live a life untroubled by constant strife and intrigue, he will avoid, like your friend Socrates, seeking the highest offices such as that of the tribal general. I hope that our young Pericles is not consumed with the political ambition for preeminence that inevitably leads to the enmities I have struggled with all of my life."

"I do believe that our son is destined to follow in his father's path. When I urge him to master the lyre or the flute so that he might have the satisfactions and charm of music-making in his life, he grimaces and tells me that his father has mastered the highest arts of governing and warfare by not wasting his time on the work of flute-girls or poets whose plucking of the lyre adorns their fantastic tales of heroes and the gods. No, already he is determined to be a General and perhaps one day, like you, the leader of the people. As for strife and contention, like most of you men, he looks forward to the contests with others so that he may demonstrate his superiority and worthiness for the prize of glory."

"Aspasia, there is another young man for whom I feel responsible and for whom I must enlist your assistance in helping him on his way."

"Could it be that at your age of sixty-six, you still have a clandestine lover – a young man you have kept secret from me and your other friends."

"No, no! Ever since I have met you, there has been no need for such a companion. Indeed, the few friends I have among the aristocrats think me rather strange that I have shown absolutely no interest in romantic trysts with youths or the revels of the *komos*. There are rumors, I have been told, that I have suffered some kind of injury which has rendered me a eunuch whose only pleasures now are of the most perverse kind. I find it surprising that my critics will not credit me with even a modicum of civic virtue. Can they not understand that I have abstained from all such erotic entanglements, not only because our love has satisfied my whole nature, but because

I would not expose my exercise of public office to the liabilities incurred by private sexual engagements – attachments which open a leader to charges of abuse of power and conflict between his private interest and the common good."

Aspasia frowned. "I know all about those malicious rumors. There are those who have been jealous of you and over all these years that you have been the leader of the people they have made little headway against you. So they come up with the most salacious tales about our private home life. They say that you invite your cronies to make love with me and that you then watch so that you might somehow resuscitate the dead force of Eros within your damaged body. What nonsense! We have always had more important work than to deal with such rumor mongers. But there have been times when I would have liked to have seen such men prosecuted for libel and punished with the lash in the yard of the city's prison. But, who is the young man you would have me assist in some way?"

"It is my ward, Alcibiades, for whom I am concerned. He is now twenty-one and I fear that I may not see him again if indeed the sickness persists and takes my life." I fear that his wealth, his almost godlike beauty, and his considerable personal charm will lead him to a dissolute life of pleasure seeking and careless adventures which will ruin his reputation. It will be difficult for anyone to discipline him if he persists too long without a household, a father, or the responsibilities of high office. Please, Aspasia, go to him soon and convince him that he must not wait until he is thirty or older, like most men of Athens do, to marry. It will anchor him to marry and have children. Tell him that I would have him start his own household with wife and children before he reaches his twenty-sixth year. Of course, you should not share with him my worry that he is unable to persist in his bachelor life without running amok. Alcibiades is a proud man and will not abide such a judgment of his character. Tell him rather that with the uncertainties of life in the time of the plague, he must not postpone marriage if he is to have heirs to whom he may pass on the commercial enterprises he now manages. Remind him also that Athenians will not consider him as a candidate for the highest offices governing the affairs of the state – especially that of the generalship – unless he himself has sons. So he had best get started on that early if he is to satisfy his ambition to become a General and a leader of the people. Tell him that most Athenians believe that a man without sons has little stake in the future of Athens and therefore such a man would be more apt to make rash decisions careless of the survival and long-term welfare of the state. Let us, Aspasia, put all this in a letter which you can deliver to him so that he does not have to come here and risk contact with the plague."

"Dear husband, today I will draft a letter to Alcibiades with your very words concerning this matter. You may sign it today, and I promise you that it will be delivered promptly should you not recover from this illness."

Pericles shifted his weight, sitting more upright, trying to ease the pain which now ran up and down his back and chest. His entire torso, from his waist to his shoulders, now was covered with bright red blotches and each one of them prickled with pain. He had taken off his robe since even the touch of its material against his skin was unbearable. "So, Aspasia, this is what it comes to – if we live long enough and do not die at the hands of another man in battle, then Nature takes us and we are not a pretty sight when our bodies slide away devoured and corrupted by aging and disease. If we hang on long enough we pass through a state of helplessness just like that of the newborn baby – we can neither feed ourselves nor evacuate our body's excrements without it all being a mess. How humiliating! The newborn baby seems not to care, but as long as the light of consciousness is not extinguished the dying man who has reached this stage must suffer the anguish of a demeaning dependence that inflicts on the ones he loves the tending of a decaying and unattractive remnant of a doomed and broken body."

Aspasia reached for his hand again and taking it between her own two hands would not let Pericles withdraw it. "But, Pericles, while neither of us believes the stories about the soul's after-life, you should not underestimate the power and bond of a love like ours. The communion of our minds long ago prepared us for sharing together our common condition as mortal creatures both blessed and cursed with self-consciousness and its yearning for an impossible endless life untroubled by failing powers and the loss of the bloom of youth. We together share the same condition and we have known its tragic truth that we are transient creatures. You can be sure the passion we have shared in each others arms, sharpened by the awareness that its ecstasy must pass away, still burns in my consciousness and while the light of our shared lucidity remains, Nature cannot undo this bond. You must know that it is my heart's deepest desire to hold you close, now more than ever, and none of the elements of Nature – however noxious – can separate us."

Pericles smiled and asked Aspasia to fill his cup again with water. After taking just a small sip from the cup, he lay down again on his side still facing towards Aspasia. "How fortunate I am to have found you. Your poetry has always been a balm for me and, if I may mix my metaphors, a tranquil port sheltering me from the stormy sea. Sappho herself could not be any more eloquent than you. And while I myself lack your poetic powers, I find that your words always seem to capture what it is my less articulate tongue would sing to you. Will you be my muse and now help me find the words that if I could, I would speak to my other great love, the only one that I have remained as faithful to as you. I think you know her just as well as I do."

Aspasia pretended to look wounded and jealous. "Yes, my dear, I know of whom you speak and it has not always been easy to share you with her. I suppose if there is a goddess, in your life, it would have to be Athena. Her epiphany is the City and no lover has been more attentive to his mistress than you have been for more than forty years. What would you say to her that you have not already said to her many times?"

"I would leave to her my last testament and will – professing my hope and aspiration that she might flourish and endure well beyond the measure of the generations of her clans, tribes, enemies, and founding families. Tell her that Pericles cares not to rise again in some nether world with Osiris, Adonis, or Dionysos as his Savior.

Tell her that like so many of her sons, Pericles wishes only that what legacy he may have lives on in the City. Tell her that it is my hope and enough for me that the work and play of my own intelligence and will, joined with that of others – sometimes in harmony and sometimes in struggle – live on after I am gone, incarnate in Athens' laws, institutions, and the architecture of the people's common life. Tell her that it is my hope that the spirit of Athena, which for me represents the best of our people's civic virtue, will always preserve a city where liberty flourishes and nurtures the higher many-sided powers of our distinctively human nature."

"Pericles, can I say it any more eloquently than these very words you are able to call upon even as your body is enflamed with pain?"

"I am sure you can do better, Aspasia. Perhaps you could take the ideas behind my words and formulate a speech that should I live could be delivered on some solemn public occasion, maybe a holiday ceremony like that of Marathon Day. Should I die during the days of the plague, you can be sure that there will be no public funeral. No one will want to risk rubbing shoulders with a crowd, fearful of the contagion. No, it would work I think, if you could deliver my last testament to Athens disguised as a funeral oration dedicated to our fallen warriors. Yes, many of my detractors already credit you with writing so many of my speeches delivered to the Council or the Assembly. There would be nothing dishonest if when I am gone you should hand such a speech to one of our orators – who might graciously agree to have Pericles speak from the grave!"

"You must be joking! Do you think the oligarchs and aristocrats of Athens, who have always strove to silence your public voice, will allow Pericles to speak even when he is dead and in the grave?"

Pericles sighed. "You are probably right. But let's have it out now, you and me, with my detractors. Perhaps if we take them on now together, I can find solace, delusional though it might be, in an adjudication of their complaints which finds in my favor. Be my Socrates, Aspasia, and play the part of those who would blame Pericles and besmirch the reputation of my legacy to Athens. Let us engage them in a critical dialogue, testing whether Pericles' legislative agenda and public leadership as a leading General have benefited the City. We should both be very competent in courtroom speechifying. Heaven knows, we have spent enough time in the courtroom defending ourselves over the past three decades."

"Well, I suppose it would be good to start with our friend Socrates himself. I have heard him discuss with many young men questions concerning a good life and how this good life may either be advanced and encouraged or stunted and ruined by the laws and institutions of their city. Socrates then asks whether any of those who govern or lead the state can be said to be worthy of praise unless they promote a kind of polity which nurtures the virtue of its citizens."

"So, tell me Aspasia, what would be the kind of complaint Socrates might bring against me with regard to his view of the good life?

"As you know, Pericles, Socrates rarely offers any straightforward thesis about virtue and the good life. But if we listen carefully to the drift of his criticisms of those who identify the good life with the enjoyment of wealth, the increase of power, and the winning of fame, it is possible to discern the outline, at least, of what Socrates means by excellence of soul and that kind of virtue which he calls 'human and political virtue'.

Pericles nodded his head in agreement. "Yes you are right about this, Aspasia, and I think Socrates, like so many of the philosophers, urges each human being to cultivate that kind of liberty wherein the faculty of reason is the guide of one's conduct. Although I cannot myself follow all of his public discussions, I am sure that he believes rational inquiry may discover those principles which should underlie all our laws and institutions so as to optimize the good life for our citizens. I have always agreed with this conviction and that is why I myself have promoted as far as possible our deliberative assemblies, such as the Council and the Assembly, as the means by which we Athenians formulate our laws and institutions governing the City. Indeed, this is what I understand to be an essential commitment of our democracy. So how could Socrates find fault with my role in advancing the democracy of our city?"

"I think, Pericles, Socrates is less sanguine than you are about the machinery of a democratic state that counts votes and allows the majority then to have the final word on the actions of the state. I have heard him often compare our use of the lottery for designating many of our officials and the votes of our Assembly for authorizing such major initiatives as declaring war to turning over the task of steersman on one of our ships to crewmen who know nothing of the science of navigation. Then too, it seems that while Socrates urges each citizen to lead an examined life and listen to the voice of reason within, he also points out to whoever will listen to him that Athenians care more for money, pleasure, and fame than they do for virtue and human excellence. I heard him gently upbraid the love of his life, young Alcibiades, for his impulsive behavior in which he is enslaved by voracious appetites. How many aristocratic young men have felt the sting of Socrates call to virtue? Why, just last week, I heard that young Critias now refuses even to speak to Socrates because he scolded him for attempting to seduce one of the youths drawn to Socrates' circle of friends. I worry about our friend Socrates. He seems to aggrieve men of both parties, the aristocrats and the democrats."

"Yes, you are right, Aspasia. It is good that Socrates lives in Athens where the law protects his freedom of speech and requires that anyone who wishes to accuse him of malicious libel must prove their case before a jury of other citizens. Without such laws as these, which by the way are the work of our democracy, by now some one of the many who have been stung by Socrates' ironic demonstration of their ignorance may well have assaulted him and ended his practice of philosophy. Surely Socrates cannot blame democratic institutions for the failings of individuals who make poor use of their liberty. After all, Socrates points out that whether a man is a commoner or an aristocrat, he may make poor use of his faculties and thus forfeit his freedom, becoming a licentious man led about like an animal by unruly appetites rather than realizing his true freedom as a virtuous human being guided by wisdom and reason."

"I am sure Socrates sees our wealthy commercial democracy as prone to encourage decadence and the irrational excesses of the tyranny of unchecked license just because it has been so successful in lifting so many of our people to a level of affluence where they now have the means to pursue their many appetites and make pleasure the measure of the good life."

Pericles sighed. "But isn't it all about the scale of opportunity afforded by providing more gainful work for all our citizens. More men than ever now can demonstrate their ability in offices before closed to them. Athenians as a people now are among the most literate of all citizens because even the poorest thete now finds a way to learn to read so that he might take part in the deliberations of the Assembly and the Courts. Now, the accident of birth is less likely to consign our men to only the most servile of lives. Many men will still live lives of little distinction and without major accomplishment, but in our democratic state the laws and institutions of our public life should not be blamed for blocking their opportunity to excel in service to the common good of the City and to cultivate their higher powers of reason and creative imagination. Indeed, when we consider that the power and wealth of our city rests on the shoulders of our thousands of citizen thetes who as free men row our large fleet of triremes; is not this a demonstration that the unity of great numbers made possible by our democracy is the secret of our superior strength in contests with other cities ruled by oligarchs and tyrants?"

Aspasia could hear Pericles' voice sounding weary and weaker. "Should we not postpone this conversation until you have rested? After all, you slept vey little during the night."

Pericles sat up again and draped the robe around his shoulders so that Aspasia would not have to look at the sores that covered his torso. "Bear with me, Aspasia! I will rest more comfortably if I know I have finished my own eulogy. Dying in the time of plague drives men to such measures."

"If this is Socrates' complaint about my role in advancing the economic prospects of such men as the thetes – that my leadership of Athens has led to a prosperity that makes possible decadence, I would acknowledge that there is some merit to his complaint. And as for Socrates' lack of confidence in counting up the votes of the people in the Assembly as a means of making decisions of state; it must gall him that I named my second son, Paralus, acknowledging and honoring our special ship of state, the 'Paralus', in which the steersman and chief officers are drawn by lot from the ranks of the thetes who row this trireme. If Socrates would charge me with undermining our city by extending participation in its governance to the commoners, then just like the most reactionary of our aristocrats he must bring the same complaint against Themistocles, the man credited with preventing our destruction by the Persians. After all, when Themistocles persuaded the Assembly to expend the newly found silver from Laurium to build a fleet of one hundred triremes, he also persuaded both the Assembly and aristocratic members of the Areopagite to use the funds to pay the salaries of seventeen thousand thetes so that they might as free men, not slaves, row our ships of war. From that day on, the poorest of our commoners were franchised in our state and became the very strong oaks of the 'wooden wall' that saved our city from the Persian threat. The cryptic Delphic counsel to trust the 'wooden walls" in those days when the very existence of our people was threatened by the Persians, we now all believe, referred to the new found strength in franchising the thetes as citizen rowers in the navy – and it was our navy that saved us from the Persian threat. Then too, Socrates, I suppose, would enter his complaint against Aristeides the Just, who after the defeat of the Persians urged the small farmers and other poor country folk to leave the countryside and take up residence in Athens so that they all might share in the governance and defense of our city. He urged the Athenians to seize the leadership of the alliance that had defeated the Persians and then levy contributions from the various cities for the common defense. These revenues were used to provide salaries for more than twenty thousand Athenian commoners who then became state employees in our navy, our army, and our dockyards. Others became jail keepers, or any of numerous other civic functionaries. If Socrates were here today, and I would not want him to risk infection, I would in good cheer ask him to consider this thesis in my defense. 'There could be no City Dionysia showcasing the genius of the tragic poets such as Aeschylus, Sophocles, and Euripides, no city tolerant enough to allow the comic genius of such as our youngest comic poet, Aristophanes, who at our City Lenaia in his satirical plays freely criticizes our most powerful leaders, no vibrant cosmopolitan discourse between our metic Sophists, and no one like you, Socrates, practicing philosophy in the Agora and gymnasiums of our city. None of these fruits of prosperous freedom would have matured in Athens unless they grew from the sustenance provided by our commercial empire and our city's democracy.' Liberty for our own citizens is expensive and until men all become as virtuous as Socrates, it will be mixed with license among our own people and Athens' oppression of other cities. Would Socrates free the foreign slaves of Laurium whose labor made possible the capital that saved our state by financing our navy, the sea power that won us our commercial empire? Some day far off, perhaps liberty will reach further. But now I am convinced that my work and that of others who have led Athens to be a powerful commercial democracy, wherein power rests with the majority of our native born men and not in the hands of a minority, will be passed on and celebrated as long as men cherish liberty and the works of human intelligence."

Pericles speech slurred as his last sentence repeated a formula he had again and again called upon in his many speeches before the Councils and Assemblies of the Athenian people. He stopped and his eyes were half shut as his whole body, lying on its side seemed visibly to droop in disarray, unable even to muster the strength to turn itself over.

"I will remember all you have said, Pericles. Somehow I will find a way to publish these words for all Athenians and cities near and far – so that they might ponder and weigh the counsel of Athens' Olympian. Now, you really must rest."

That was the last day Pericles could speak coherently. His condition deteriorated so fast that by near sunset of the next day, after being unable to eat anything, his fever returned and remained so high that he could not even sit up or converse. Overnight, wracked with convulsions and overcome by weakness, he turned face down on his bed and then became very still. When Aspasia, just before dawn, attempted to turn him over to apply a cold compress to his feverish forehead there was no response of any kind from Pericles. Without a final struggle or desperate fight for one more breath, he had passed away. Aspasia, alone with Pericles' still and dead body, wept.

It was early morning when, with the help of Pericles' body servant and one of the maids, Aspasia washed Pericles' body with water from their courtyard cistern. She then sent word to their son, Pericles, to come home for his father's funeral. He had not been home now for several weeks since he had been staying with his pedagogue in quarters near the gymnasium used by the ephebes. That afternoon Aspasia made all the arrangements for her husband's cremation inside their courtyard. It was sunset when only Aspasia and her twelve year old son, the only surviving son of Pericles, stood beside the pile of wood that had been carefully stacked near the cistern. The body of Pericles, dressed in his military tunic, now lay on the crematory. Aspasia lit the wood with a torch just before the last red rays of the setting sun reflected off the plaster wall of the second story women's quarters of their home. Moments passed as the red light of the sun disappeared and the fire burned brightly. Aspasia held her son's hand as his father's body disappeared, consumed by the fire.

Two days later Aspasia, without any fanfare, led her son, an elderly aunt of Pericles, and only one of General Pericles' longest serving military officers to a burial place just outside the City walls near the potters' quarter. There household slaves under her direction placed the large funeral urn that contained Pericles ashes into the ground so that only the very top of the sealed urn remained uncovered. She then ended the ceremony of his burial with her own eulogy, the words of which she had written on a scroll on which she had also inscribed Pericles' final words.

...So ended the life of Pericles

GLOSSARY

All italicized entries are Greek language words spelled phonetically with the English alphabet.

agora - meeting, congregation, assembly; council; speech; eloquence; market-place, market; victuals; commerce, trade.

Alkmeonids - prominent aristocratic Athenian clan famous for its part in ending the tyranny of the family of Peisistratos around 511 B.C.; Pericles and Alcibiades are both descendents of this clan on their mothers' side.

amphora - a large two handled storage jar having an oval body; used mainly for wine or oil and set on a foot, as a commemorative vase awarded the champions of contests such as those held in the Panathenaic games.

archon - leader, ruler, chief, magistrate; nine *archons*, each charged with different administrative responsibilities for the governance of the Athenian state were elected each year.

bakchoi - devotees of Dionysos who dance and chant, calling for Dionysos.

Basileus - a king; the Athenians had ended the reign of kings at least two centuries prior to the beginning of the fifth century B. C. The term, however, was retained to designate the 'religious' functions of one of the nine archons elected each year. The *Archon Basileus* administered state sponsored religious festivals and various court proceedings which treated certain kinds of irreligious behavior as a danger to public morality. The trial of Socrates, since the charges brought against him accuse him of corrupting the minds of the youth, and of believing in deities of his own invention instead of the gods recognized by the state, was held in the King Archon's Court.

Bouleuterion - the building in the agora where the Council of 500 met. The Council of 500 was charged with the day to day management of 5th century B.C. democratic Athens.

Boukolerion - the "bull's stable, a building situated on the official estate of the *Archon Basileus* (official charged with supervising public religious occasions). During the festival of Anthesteria, the ceremonial queen (wife of the *Archon Basileus*) is taken to this building so that she might wed Dionysos.

choregus (pl. choregi) - the *Archon Eponymous* (*'eponymous'* – this archon's proper surname is used to specify the year in histories written by ancient Greek historians and in the official archival records kept by the ancient Athenian state) selects from the wealthiest men of Athens the three *Choregi* who will be assigned to the three tragic poets chosen to present their tragedies during the City Dionysia. During the 5th century the *Archon Eponymous* also appointed five *Choregi* for the comic poets and also officially acknowledged the *Choregi* presented by the ten tribes of the men's choruses and the boy's choruses, and the comic choruses at the City Dionysia, and for the men's choruses and boy's choruses at the Thargelia (see Aristotle's *Constitution of Athens*, chapter 56). The *Choregi* provided the financial resources required for these various performances. Wealthy citizens were thus expected to undertake such a 'liturgy' as a public service to the city and the gods.

deme - a township in Athens or Attica which functioned as the smallest local unit of governance. Any citizen was required to be able to prove that his birth was registered at a specific *deme*. Usually any citizen was officially acknowledged by noting the deme from which he came, thus – Socrates of Alopeke.

Dionysos - the god particularly associated with ecstatic experience in all of the Hellene cities. Dionysos was credited with bringing the gift of wine. His mythology is complex and he is associated with many epiphanies and religious rites – all of which lead to an array of surnames often linked to his name (such as 'Dionysos Eleuthereus'). Some of the surnames are here listed and defined:

Bougenes - "cow's son" and "worthy bull" who was expected to come to the Dionysian women "with riotous bull's foot".

Bromios - this name anticipates the Dionysian "swarming" during the time of the Dionysian festivals of Lenaia and the city Dionysia.

Dendrites - "of the trees", the surname associates Dionysos with fruitful trees.

Dithyrambos - "of the dithyramb", the song and dance that accompanied the sacrifice of the bull.

Eleuthereus - a surname indicating the small village north of Athens through which Dionysos passed when he first arrived in Athens. The temple of Dionysos Eleuthereus at the foot of the Acropolis of Athens became the site of the theatrical productions of the City Dionysia.

Eiraphiotes - "he who is sewn in", This surname refers to one of the myths of Dionysos' miraculous resurrection after having been slain in the underworld by evil Titans. According to this story, the heart of Dionysos is recovered by Athena and then taken to Mt. Olympus where it is sewn into Father Zeus' thigh so Dionysos, the son of God, may be born again from this rather curious womb.

Euios - an epithet the Hellene wine treaders, while in the wine press, called out to evoke the work of Dionysos in changing the grapes to wine.

Lenaios - associating Dionysos with the festival celebrating his first birth, the Lenaia celebrated in the Athenian month of Gamelian (our month of January).

Mainomenuos - madness, to be caught up in ecstasy and thus out of one's mind. Since it was believed that Dionysos presence often affected his followers with ecstasy, this surname was often used during Dionysian celebrations.

Melanaigis - "he with the black goatskin"; refers to a story that described Dionysos' appearance to the daughters of Eleuther (the founder of the settlement Eleuthera) dressed in a black goatskin.

Orthos - upright or erect; an epithet that associates Dionysos with phallic potency, a potency seen in the way satyrs are always represented with large and erect phalli as they revel with Dionysos.

Sabazios - a god of ancient Asia Minor worshipped in a mystery cult which celebrated the union of this god with the "Great Goddess". Sabazios is associated with snakes and among the Hellenes becomes an aspect of the phallic power in bringing forth new life associated with Dionysos.

Thyoneus - the epithet which associates Dionysos with the raving of the maenads, women in his company who in a state of ecstasy danced wildly and called for Dionysos. The epithet is derived from the verb, *thyein* – to rave.

Zagreus - the Cretan Dionysos who is taken up in the Orphic version of the mythology of Dionysos. This mythology identifies Dionysos with the final manifestation or revelation of the supreme god, Zeus, in the form of the son of God.

dithyramb - the dance and chant that accompanied the ancient Hellene sacrifice of a bull. The performance of the *dithyramb* takes on an artistic life apart from the sacrifice and becomes part of the celebrations of major religious festivals when *dithyrambic* groups of men and boys from the ten tribes of Athens compete for prizes.

eleos - pity, mercy.

ephebe (pl. *epheboi*) - a young man of Athens in military training. After completing the training these youths take an oath of allegiance to Athens as hoplite-citizens.

ephor(s) - overseer or supervisor; in Sparta's government a board of 5 ephors. These five ephors were elected by the Assembly each year. The board of ephors was responsible for the day to day government of Sparta. The board also supervised the behavior of Sparta's kings (2 kings by birthright held the kingship simultaneously).

eupatrid - "well-born"; the social class of Athenians who could trace their lineage back to the earliest aristocratic families of Athens or from the legendary kings of Athens.

hetaera (*hetaerai*) - a female paramour or concubine in ancient Greece. Aspasia, who became Pericles' common-law wife, was one of the most famous of the *hetaerai* of 5th century B.C. Athens.

Horai - the goddesses born of Themis and Zeus; the goddesses with golden fillets, who bring the glorious fruit. There was a temple devoted to the Horai in Athens.

Hosioi **of Delphi** - holy men (priests) who presided at the temple of Delphi.

hubris - excessive pride, overstepping limits, failure to behave with proper respect and restraint in relation to other citizens in Athens or the gods.

ithyphallic - of or pertaining to the phallus carried in ancient Greek festivals devoted to Dionysos.

kanephoros - a basket carrier in a religious procession in ancient Greece.

Kerameikos - the potters' district of Athens. The district was believed to be named after Keramos, the son of Dionysos and Ariadne.

komos - festal procession, revel, merry-making; band of revelers; feast, banquet. The Athenian term, '*komedia*' (comedy) for the funny and often bawdy theatric productions performed in honor of

Dionysos during his festivals of Lenaia and the City Dionysia is derived from this more ancient word.

krater - a mixing bowel used to mix wine and water. The *krater* was set between the open arrangement of the couches upon which ancient Athenian men reclined during their symposiums.

laconophile - a term used by Athenians to describe anyone of their own citizenry who admired the Spartans and their way of life.

lekythos - an oil jar having an ellipsoidal body, narrow neck, flanged mouth, curved handles projecting vertically from the shoulder, and a narrow base terminating in a foot. The *lekythos* was used chiefly for ointments.

logos - a saying, speaking, speech, mode of speaking; eloquence, discourse; conversation, talk; word, expression; assertion; principle, maxim; proverb; oracle; promise; order, command; proposal; condition, agreement; stipulation, decision; pretext; fable, news, story, report, legend; prose-writing, history, book, essay, oration; affair, incident; thought, reason, reckoning, computation, reflection, deliberation, account, consideration, opinion; cause, end; argument, demonstration; meaning, value; proportion.

mystes - the initiates who came in ritual procession to the temple of Eleusis during the Festival of the Eleusinian Mysteries. The *mystes* at Eleusis experienced the 'vision' at which the state of 'having seen' was attained. Absolute secrecy was prescribed for all those who had been initiated during this festival.

obol - a silver coin of ancient Greece, the sixth part of a drachma.

paean - a hymn of invocation or thanksgiving to Apollo.

Peisistratid(s) - a prominent clan in Athens whose most famous member, Peisistratos, institutes a tyranny in Athens which lasts for almost three decades before ending in 511 B.C.

phallophoriai - carriers of ceremonial phalli who marched in the City Dionysia procession devoted to Dionysos.

pharmakos - poisoner, sorcerer; poisons; the scapegoat victim ceremoniously driven from Athens to purge the city of pollution during the Festival of Thargelia.

Philiad - prominent Athenian clan; Cimon, the rival of Pericles for Athens' leadership during mid-5th century B.C., is a Philiad.

pompe - a sending; an escorting, conduct, escort; a sending home; solemn procession; intervention.

proxenos - an Athenian designated by another city to represent that city's interests to Athenian commercial and political agencies.

prytanes - the title of the fifty presiding members of the Council of 500 in 5th century B.C. Athens. The 500 Councilors were chosen by lot among citizens, 50 selected from each of the ten tribes. Then, for one tenth of the year, 50 members of each tribe would jointly hold the presidency (*prytaneia*) and thus they are called '*prytanes*'.

satyriasis - abnormal, uncontrollable sexual desire in men, a term inspired by the satyr's behavior in the company of Dionysos.

seisachtheia - the "unburdening", the name given to Solon's cancellation of debt, a debt so heavy that it had forced native born Athenians and other native born men of Attica into exile or slavery.

sileni - satyrs who are associated with Silenus, the oldest of the satyrs who in some of the stories concerning Dionysos is a teacher of the young Dionysos. *Sileni* are often represented as hairy old men with the ears and legs of a horse, drunk and seated on a cask of wine or a donkey.

theoria - a looking at, beholding, viewing; curiosity, presence at a festival.

theoros - spectator, ambassador sent to a religious festival with instructions to witness or observe, but not to participate in any of the rites or ceremonies.

thetes - hired workers (no property of their own) in Athens who were granted citizenship and access to office in 5th century B.C. democratic Athens.

tragodia - "song on the occasion of a he-goat" (definition proposed by Carl Kerenyi in his book, *Dionysos, Archetypal Image of Indestructible Life*).

tragodos - a tragic poet or actor; the singer of the goat song.

tragos - he-goat.

Made in the USA
Charleston, SC
09 April 2013